A Dictionary of the

CUIRASSIER OFFICERS

of the First Empire
1804-1815

By Olivier LAPRAY
Uniform plates by André JOUINEAU
Composition by Giuseppe RAVA
Translated from the French by Alan McKAY

Histoire & Collections

I ask Lucas and Thomas, my little sons, to forgive my numerous absences, and dedicate this book to my wife Alicia for all her patience, and the support she has always given me.

Commandant
Olivier Lapray

Note about the «Légion d'Honneur»

After the Revolution in the name of equality had abolished all the former Knight's Orders, the Légion d'Honneur, instituted 29 Floréal An X (19 May 1802), set itself up from the outset as an award of rather a new kind.

Rewarding personal merit, civilian or military, without distinction of birth, it was *"the beginning of the organisation of the Nation"* to quote the very terms used by the First Consul.

The rules of the institution allowed for no insignia, no motto; a simple letter of notification from the Grand Chancellor was sent to the members. It was only two years later with the decree of 22 Messidor An XII (12 July 1804) that the illustrious decoration saw the light of day.

"The decoration of the Légion d'Honneur will consist of a star with five double points.

The centre of the star, surrounded by a crown of oak and laurel leaves, will show the head of the Emperor with the following caption: Napoléon, Emp. des français (Napoleon, Emp. of the French) on one side; and the French Eagle grasping a thunderbolt with the caption, *Honneur et Patrie (Honour and Fatherland)* on the other.

"The decoration will be white enamel.

"It will be made of gold for the Grands-Officiers, the Commandants and the Officiers, and of silver for the Légionnaires; it will be worn in one of the coat buttonholes and attached to a red-mottled ribbon."

Four days later, the Emperor himself wearing the famous star (whose design is attributed to David, the painter) proceeded to award the insignias for the first time in the Church of the Invalides then again on 16 August 1804 *"with the distribution to the brave men of the army"* during a grandiose ceremony assembling almost one hundred thousand men at the Camp at Boulogne. Ever since its creation, the shape, the motto and ribbon colour of the insignia of the Légion d'Honneur have not changed. Only the tips of the stars, at first sharp, were given a small ball-tip so that they would not snag uniforms and costumes.

On the other hand the leather loop and the centre of the star have changed with the different political regimes in France: addition of a loop crown, on the obverse side profiles and inscription of Napoleon, Emperor of the French, Henri IV King of France and Navarre, of Bonaparte the First Consul, once again of Napoleon Emperor then the face of the Republic in Ceres; on the reverse side, eagle, fleur de lys, tricolour flags, eagle and once again tricolour flags.

The model shown here dates back to the Second Republic. It is the only one which shows not the effigy of Napoleon Emperor, but that of Bonaparte First Consul with the date of the creation of the Order of the Légion d'Honneur, 19 May 1802 on the obverse side. The ribbon has a bouffette, a knot reserved for the Officiers at the origin of the famous rosette.

The campaigns of the 14 cuirassier regiments

1st Cuirassiers
Austerlitz 1805, Prussia 1806, Poland 1807, Austria 1809, Russia 1812, Germany 1813, France 1814, Belgium 1815.
Inscriptions on the 1812-model standard: Ulm, Austerlitz, Jena, Eylau, Eckmühl, Essling, Wagram.

2nd Cuirassiers
Austerlitz 1805, Prussia 1806, Poland 1807, Austria 1809, Russia 1812, Germany 1813, France 1814, Belgium 1815.
Inscriptions on the 1812-model standard: Ulm, Austerlitz, Jena, Eylau, Eckmühl, Essling, Wagram.

3rd Cuirassiers
Austerlitz 1805, Prussia 1806, Poland 1807, Austria 1809, Russia 1812, Germany 1813, France 1814, Belgium 1815.
Inscriptions on the 1812-model standard: Ulm, Austerlitz, Jena, Eylau, Eckmühl, Essling, Wagram.

4th Cuirassiers
Army of Italy 1805-1806, Poland 1807, Austria 1809, Russia 1812, Germany 1813, France 1814, Belgium 1815.
Inscriptions on the 1812-model standard: Essling, Wagram.

5th Cuirassiers
Austerlitz 1805, Prussia 1806, Poland 1807, Austria 1809, Russia 1812, Germany 1813, France 1814, Belgium 1815.
Inscriptions on the 1812-model standard: Ulm, Austerlitz, Jena, Eylau, Eckmühl, Essling, Wagram.

On the 1815-model standard: Austerlitz, Jena, Eylau, Eckmühl, Wagram, the Moskova, Montmirail.

6th Cuirassiers
Army of Italy 1805-1806, Poland 1807, Austria 1809, Russia 1812, Germany 1813, France 1814, Belgium 1815.
Inscriptions on the 1812-model standard: Essling, Wagram.

7th Cuirassiers
Army of Italy 1805-1806, Poland 1807, Austria 1809, Russia 1812, Germany 1813, France 1814, Belgium 1815.
Inscriptions on the 1812-model standard: Essling, Wagram.
Inscriptions on the 1815-model standard: Wagram, Montereau.

8th Cuirassiers
Army of Italy 1805-1806, Poland 1807, Austria 1809, Russia 1812, Germany 1813, France 1814, Belgium 1815.
Inscriptions on the 1812-model standard: Essling, Wagram.

9th Cuirassiers
Austerlitz 1805, Prussia 1806, Poland 1807, Austria 1809, Russia 1812, Germany 1813, France 1814, Belgium 1815.
Inscriptions on the 1812-model standard: Austerlitz, Jena, Eylau, Eckmühl, Essling, Wagram.

10th Cuirassiers
Austerlitz 1805, Prussia 1806, Poland 1807, Austria 1809, Russia 1812, Germany 1813, France 1814, Belgium 1815.
Inscriptions on the 1812-model standard: Ulm, Austerlitz, Jena, Eylau, Eckmühl, Essling, Wagram.

11th Cuirassiers
Austerlitz 1805, Prussia 1806, Poland 1807, Austria 1809, Russia 1812, Germany 1813, France 1814, Belgium 1815.
Inscriptions on the 1812-model standard: Ulm, Austerlitz, Jena, Eylau, Eckmühl, Essling, Wagram.

12th Cuirassiers
Austerlitz 1805, Prussia 1806, Poland 1807, Austria 1809, Russia 1812, Germany 1813, France 1814, Belgium 1815.
Inscriptions on the 1812-model standard: Ulm, Jena, Eylau, Eckmühl, Essling, Wagram.

13th Cuirassiers
Created 21 October 1808, Spain 1808-1813, France 1814 (Army of Lyon) disbanded August 1814.

14th Cuirassiers
Created 18 August 1810, Russia 1812, Germany 1813, France 1814, disbanded 13 July 1814; No inscriptions on the 1812-model Standard.
Inscriptions on the 1812-model standard: Ulm, Austerlitz, Jena, Eylau, Eckmühl, Essling, Wagram.

A Dictionary of the Cuirassier Officers of the First Empire, 1804 - 1815

*A*S THE AIM OF THIS WORK is to present a picture of Cuirassier officers of the First Empire, only French and foreign soldiers who served with officer rank (from the equivalent of sub-lieutenant to senior officers) within a French Cuirassier regiment during the Empire (between 1804 and 1815) have been included here. The officers of the provisional regiments have not been forgotten either.

The officers are shown here according to their complete patronymic, mentioning where appropriate the name that was used the most or their nickname. The reader will therefore be able to help himself by means of the cross-references in the dictionary, the use of the de being mentioned at the beginning of the article with the *titres de noblesse* (titles) if any were acquired during the Empire. Such is also the case with foreign names using a handle. The entries have also been put in alphabetical order since most of them served within several successive regiments.

In these biographical entries, only the titles, functions and military ranks which were obtained during the First Empire, the First Restoration and the Hundred Days are mentioned. As for the ranks of the Légion d'Honneur, the dates of admission are mentioned at the end of every entry, together with any *titres de noblesse* obtained only during the Empire and the date of the letters patent (l.p.) and/or the decree (d.).

Each entry includes the date of birth with, if known, the place (départements of the time - including the ones which had been occupied); the dates of promotions, successive transfers, wounds and feats of arms where known. All these facts stop at 31 December 1815 so as to indicate whether the men would be re-employed under the Second Restoration or simply put on the non-active list. As far as decorations are concerned, only promotion within the order of the Légion d'Honneur is indicated.

Finally as the aim of the present work is not to rewrite the biographies of the Marshals and the Generals of the Revolution and First Empire, they are only mentioned if they served in the cuirassier regiments before they were promoted to general, or if they commanded brigades or cuirassier divisions. In the entries, as indeed for the rest of their comrades, only their service before 1815 is shown and once they were promoted to general, only a simple summary of their successive commands is given. For more ample biographical information, the reader is invited to consult Georges Six's invaluable dictionary, and other works about Napoleon's Marshals and Generals.

The entries were compiled using the registers and the rolls of the officers of the fourteen cuirassier regiments which existed between 1804 and 1815; in each entry we have also shown how the names of the regiments changed. The regiments' various campaigns do not appear in each individual entry; instead they have been re-grouped by regiment at the end of the study.

The coats of arms which have been represented show the highest title which was awarded under the Empire with the delivery of the letters patent. Failing that the arms of the titles awarded earlier, if any.

Olivier Lapray

AARDENBURG (Pierre van, 1759-?): born in Haarlem (Zuydersee) on 2 March 1759. In the service of Holland as quartermaster in the Navy 25 April 1780, cadet 25 January 1781, appointed lieutenant 3 May 1782, dismissed at his own request 22 April 1793, replaced 28 May 1783, dismissed on his own request 25 July 1785, volunteer in a mobile column 12 May 1786, lieutenant in the Palardy-Infanterie 14 May 1787, artillery lieutenant 12 September 1787, emigrated to France 1790.

He was lieutenant in the Chasseurs à Cheval in the Légion Franche Etrangère 10 October 1792, lieutenant with the functions of aide de camp to General Blondeau and took up his post in the 13th Chasseurs à Cheval 27 August 1794, cavalry captain in the service of Holland 9 July 1795, deputy to General Daendel 29 June 1797. He returned to his regiment 9 October 1797, commissioner for War 9 June 1803, entered the 2nd Batavian Cavalry 1805, in the same regiment when it became the 2nd Dutch Cuirassiers 14 July 1806 then 14th French Cuirassiers after the annexation 18 August 1810, retired 6 December 1810.

ABBECLE called ABEL (Pierre van den, 1783 -?) born at Saint-Nicholas (Escaut) on 23 September 1783. In the 10th Chasseurs à Cheval 20 June 1802, Brigadier 15 June 1805, Maréchal des Logis 18 October 1808, Gendarme à Cheval in the 15th Squadron in Spain 27 December 1809, in the 1st Légion à Cheval "Burgos" 15 December 1810, Brigadier 1 Mars 1812, disbanded with the unit 27 February 1813 and promoted to Sous-Lieutenant in the 5th Cuirassiers 28 February 1813, dismissed and put on half-pay 23 December 1815. LH CH 28 September 1813.

ABOS de BINANVILLE (Alexandre Maximilien d', 1781-1808): born in Paris (Seine) on 22 August 1791. in the Gendarmes d'Ordonnance 31 October 1806, joined 8 November 1806, maréchal des logis 9 November 1806, confirmed 18 November 1806. He was second-lieutenant 22 November 1806, confirmed 1 December 1806, took several prisoners at Alberg 7 March 1807, first-lieutenant 16 July 1807,

lieutenant in the suite following the 3rd Cuirassiers 10 September 1807, took up his position in the 7th Cuirassiers 18 November 1807, left to join his regiment 31 December 1807, instated 7 April 1808, shot in the left thigh in front of Saragossa 23 July 1808. He died from his wounds in Pamplona hospital 18 September 1808. LH CH.

ADAM (Pierre, 1771-1810): born in Hiche (Jemmapes) on 16 October 1771. Trooper in the Royal-Pologne 2 October 1786 which became the 5th Cavalry 1 January 1791, brigadier 1 April 1793, brigadier-fourrier 18 August 1798, maréchal des logis 19 June 1799. He was maréchal des logis-chef 16 July 1799, sub-lieutenant 13 March 1800, lieutenant 1 July 1802, in the same regiment when it became the 5th Cuirassiers 23 December 1802, elected captain 23 November 1804. He retired because of haemorrhoids which turned into a ulcerous tumour from which he died in Metz 3 October 1810.

ADMANT (Jean François, 1786-?): born in Moyenvie (Meurthe) on 19 February 1786. Volunteer in the 3rd Cuirassiers 19 April 1806, fourrier 1 January 1807, maréchal des logis 14 May 1809, maréchal des logis-chef 16 March 1810, adjutant sub-lieutenant 6 July 1813, sub-lieutenant 2 December 18113, lance wound to his right thigh at Leipzig 16 October 1813, dismissed with the regiment 25 November 1815.

ADNET (Hyacinthe, 1780-?): born in Villers-Marnery (Marne) on 18 December 1780. In the 10th Cavalry 16 March 1800, brigadier 11 April 1802, in the same regiment when it became the 10th Cuirassiers 24 September 1803, fourrier 19 December 1806, maréchal des logis 1 March 1807, wounded by a Biscayan shot to his left knee at Essling 22 May 1809, sublieutenant 21 March 1812, shot in the neck at Waterloo 18 June 1815, retired when the regiment was disbanded 25 December 1815.

AIGREMONT (Antoine Pierre d', 1778-?): born in Paris (Seine) on 11 January 1778. In the 20th Cavalry 8 October 1798, in the 1st Hussars 14 March 1800,

brigadier 23 September 1800, maréchal des logis 22 March 1801, sub-lieutenant in the Guard of the Grand-Duchy of Berg 22 September 1807, lieutenant 15 February 1808, adjutant-major 8 July 1808, captain 1 February 1809, taken prisoner at Borisov while crossing the Berezina 26 November 1812, returned to France, put on subsistence pay in the 8th Cuirassiers November 1814, non-active on half-pay end of 1814, captain in the 12th Cuirassiers 14 May 1815, back on half-pay 3 August 1815.

AIGREMONT (Charles d', 1787-?): twin brother of Louis, born in Marville (Meuse) on 3 May 1787. Admitted to the Ecole Militaire at Fontainebleau 3 May 1809, corporal 16 April 1807, sub-lieutenant to the 1st Cuirassiers 16 May 1807, went with his company into the 1st Provisional Heavy Cavalry in Spain 16 November 1807 which became the 13th Cuirassiers 21 October 1808, lieutenant 29 June 1810, captain 12 June 1813, incorporated into the 9th Cuirassiers 9 August 1814, struck off the rolls 26 November 1815 - he had remained at home at the end of the Belgian Campaign with his colonel's permission.

AIGREMONT (Louis d', 1787-?): twin brother of Charles, born in Marville (Meuse) on 3 May 1787. At the Fontainebleau School 29 November 1806, corporal 16 April 1807, sub-lieutenant in the 1st Cuirassiers 16 May 1807. He went with his company into the 1st Provisional Heavy Cavalry Regiment in Spain 16 November 1807 which then became the 13th Cuirassiers 21 October 1808, lieutenant 1 February 1811, captain 27 August 1813, incorporated into the 9th Cuirassiers 9 August 1814, dismissed with the corps 25 November 1815 and put at the disposal of the Minister of War 26 November 1815.

AIME (Pierre Joseph, 1775-?): born in Senoncourt (Haute-Saône) on 18 August 1775. In the 4th Dragoons 10 February 1800, brigadier 4 August

AIGREMONT (Guillaume François d', Baron, 1770- 1827) : born in Paris (Seine) on 1 April 1770. Dragoon in the Angoulême Regiment 1 June 1788, resigned 3 March 1790, sub-lieutenant in the 2nd Battalion of the Paris Volunteers 30 July 1791, lieutenant 10 January 1792, sub-lieutenant in the 21st Cavalry 25 January 1792, lieutenant 1 April 1793.

He saved one of his comrades who was a prisoner of the Barco Hussars fighting alone against 15 of them 14 July 1793, in the same regiment when it became the 20th Cavalry 4 June 1793, captain 1794, non-active from 30 October 1797 to 8 December 1798, aide de camp to General Gobert 22 December 1799, two sabre wounds to his head at Marengo and held prisoner for two hours 14 June 1800, deputy on Dupont's staff 28 August 1800, squadron commander in the 20th Cavalry 11 October 1801.

Aigremont dismissed with the corps and went over to the suite of the 14th Cavalry 8 April 1806 which became the 23rd Dragoons 24 September 1806, took up his appointment in the 8th Cuirassiers 2 February 1804, major in the 1st Cuirassiers 26 April 1807, commanded the 1st Provisional Heavy Cavalry Regiment in Spain 6 December 1807, which then became the 13th Cuirassiers 21 October 1808, regimental colonel 13 February 1809, brigadier-general 10 April 1813, returned to France 29 September 1813, commanded the Somme Department 18 December 1813, available 3 April 1815, with the General Inspection of Cavalry 28 May 1815, in the Army of the North 3 June 1815.

He commanded the Allier Department 1 September 1815. LH CH 14 June 1804, O 18 July 1809, Chevalier of the Empire l.p. 13 February 1811, Baron l.p. 25 May 1811.

Near Lille on 5 April 1793, while a cavalry lieutenant in the 21st Cavalry, alone he infiltrated the village of Ronques guarded by 600 Hussars and shot their colonel with a pistol at the moment he was ordering them to mount up.

In July of the same year, he saved a comrade who was prisoner of the Barco Hussars having to fight alone against fifteen of them.

1802, maréchal des logis 26 March 1810, simple grenadier in the Grenadiers à Cheval of the Guard 1 October 1812, brigadier 21 January 1813, sub-lieutenant in the 1st Cuirassiers 8 February 1813, left with his squadron for Hamburg May 1813, incorporated with the regiment into the 1st Provisional Heavy Cavalry Regiment in Hamburg 11 September 1813, returned with the garrison 27 May 1814, non-active with full pay 1 October 1814.

ALBAN see **VERGNETTE d'ALBAN**

ALBIGNAC see **RIVET d'ALBIGNAC**

ALBIN see **NEYROUD SAINT-ALBIN**

ALIX (César Hector, 1790-1832): born in Marle (Aisne) on 22 July 1790. Volunteer in the 8th Cuirassiers 21 July 1808, brigadier 16 October 1808, fourrier 15 May 1810, maréchal des logis 1 December 1810, sub-lieutenant 12 August 1812, instated 15 August 1812, lieutenant quartermaster-treasurer 14 April 1813, dismissed with the corps 5 December 1815 and left, non-active at home.

ALIX (Jean Baptiste, 1768-?): born in Neuville-sur-Saône (Rhône) on 24 January 1768. In the Colonel-Général-Cavalerie 6 November 1783 which became the 1st Cavalry 1 January 1791, brigadier-fourrier 1 July 1792, maréchal des logis 1 June 1793, sub-lieutenant 16 September 1793, with ten troopers captured a canon and 200 English soldiers at Mont Castel 17 May 1794, with his detachment captured an officer and 52 Austrian infantrymen after his horse was wounded and his sword broken at Lers 22 May 1794, lieutenant 11 September 1794, captain 15 February 1799. He was named squadron commander in the 2nd Cavalry 21 January 1800, joined his unit again 2 March 1800, took a flag at Marengo 14 June 1800, commanded the regiment temporarily in 1801, in the same regiment when it became the 2nd Cuirassiers 12 October 1802, retired 1 October 1808, pensioned 11 October 1808, became Mayor of Neuville-sur-Saône. Holder of a Sabre of Honour for his conduct at Marengo 23 June 1800, LH CH by rights 24 September 1803, O 14 June 1804.

ALLARD (David, 1761-?): born in Bason (Ardennes) on 14 August 1761. Trooper in the Franche-Comté regiment 21 November 1779, incorporated into the Colonel-Général-Cavalerie 21 May 1788, in the same

regiment when it became the 1st Cavalry 1 January 1791, brigadier 14 January 1792, maréchal des logis 1 June 1793, maréchal des logis-chef 19 February 1794, sub-lieutenant 15 January 1799.

He was lieutenant by governmental choice 27 July 1799, confirmed 12 December 1800, in the same regiment when it became the 1st Cuirassiers 10 October 1801, captain 20 February 1807, retired with his pension 16 May 1809, left 1 January 1810. LH CH 1 October 1807.

AMAURY (Pierre François Xavier, 1785-?): born in Blois (Loir-et-Cher) on 29 September 1785. Boarder at the Ecole Militaire at Fontainebleau 4 July 1805, sub-lieutenant in the suite of the 3rd Cuirassiers 14 December 1806. He took up his appointment 4 April 1807, returned to the depot because he had gone mad 15 January 1811, in the suite again 11 February 1811, allowed to go home then discharged 29 March 1811.

ANDEVILLE see **LEPORCQ d'ANDEVILLE**

ANGELLOZ (Joseph, 1772-1859): born in Grand-Bornand (Mont-Blanc) on 14 August 1772. In the Volontaires Nationaux à Cheval from the Ecole Militaire 24 November 1792 which formed the 26th Cavalry 21 February 1793 which then became the 25th Cavalry 4 June 1793, brigadier 2 March 1801, brigadier-fourrier 18 September 1802. Incorporated into the 4th Cuirassiers 24 November 1802, he was maréchal des logis 22 December 1804, two sabre wounds to the head and neck at Essling 21 May 1809, sub-lieutenant 3 July 1809, lieutenant 9 February 1813, wounded in the arm at Neuss 3 December 1813, wounded and his horse killed under him at Waterloo 18 June 1815, retired 21 December 1815. LH CH 27 December 1814 confirmed 11 April 1815.

ANOULT (Jean, 1786-1813): born in Bruxelles (Dyle) on 23 August 1786. Velite in the Grenadiers à cheval 12 February 1806, sub-lieutenant in the 22nd Cuirassiers 25 March 1809, joined his unit 26 May 1809, lieutenant 12 March 1812, killed at Dresden 27 August 1813.

ANSELME (Denis Philippe d'1791-?): born in Gargas (Vaucluse) on 6 March 1791. Pupil at the Ecole Impériale de Cavalerie in Saint-Germain, sub-lieutenant in the 9th Cuirassiers 30 January 1813, wounded at Leipzig 16 October 1813, is no longer mentioned on the rolls 9 August 1814. LH CH 4 March 1814.

A NOULT (Prosper Victor Ernest, 1794 - 1862), younger brother of the above, born in Bruxelles (Dyle) on 15 February 1794.

At the Ecole Impériale de Cavalerie in Saint-Germain 8 December 1810, brigadier 12 November 1811.

He returned to France 20 May 1814, resigned November 1814, in the service of the Netherlands as a sub-lieutenant in the Carabiniers 11 November 1811, lieutenant adjutant-major wounded by a Biscayan shot to his right hip at Waterloo 18 June 1815.

LH CH 1813, O 17 March 1815.

At Leipzig on 16 October 1813, Anoult was a sub-lieutenant in the suite of the 14th Cuirassiers. At the head of his platoon, he captured an enemy battery but was captured after being wounded by a bayonet in the right thigh, by Biscayan shot in the hand, and a burst of grapeshot to his right side, he had his horse killed under him.

ANTOINE (Simon, 1756-?): born in Abbeville (Moselle) on 18 June 1756. Trooper in the Royal-Lorraine 7 December 1774, brigadier 5 September 1784, brigadier-fourrier 23 April 1785, maréchal des logis 1 May 1788, in the same regiment when it became the 16th Cavalry 1 January 1791, sub-lieutenant 10 May 1792, in the same regiment when it became the 15th Cavalry 4 June 1793, lieutenant 20 June 1793, captain 15 January 1794. Discharged 6 February 1796, appointed captain in the 10th cavalry 13 March 1797 which became the 10th Cuirassiers 24 September 1803, retired 24 September 1806, pensioned 1 December 1806. LH CH 14 March 1806.

ANTONIN (Jean Baptiste Emile Christophe, 1794-après 1823): Colonel Lefaivre's nephew, born in Belfort (Haut-Rhin) on 28 February 1794. Page to the King of Naples 12 January 1810, sub-lieutenant in the Chevau-Légers of the Royal Neapolitan Guard 2 March 1811, resigned 17 July 1813, officer in the Haut-Rhin Guard of Honour 1814. He was lieutenant in the suite of the 8th Cuirassiers 4 January 1815, commissioned 26 January 18151, rejoined his unit beginning of March 1815, dismissed with the corps 5 December 18115 and non-active 11 December 1815.

APATIN see **DABADIE APATIN**

ARBEY (Louis Pierre Alexis, 1781-?): born in Baume (Doubs) on 8 June 1781. Volunteer in the 21st Dragoons 30 September 1802, fourrier 9 October

1802, maréchal des logis-chef 11 July 1803, adjutant NCO 22 January 1804, sub-lieutenant 3 April 1807, lieutenant 8 February 1813, shot and wounded at Vittoria 21 June 1813, adjutant-major 4 August 1813, captain 25 October 1813, captain adjutant-major in the 6th Cuirassiers 4 August 1814, instated 25 August 1814, wounded and his horse killed under him and his belongings lost at Waterloo 18 June 1815, dismissed 21 November 1815. LH CH 6 January 1811.

ARBOGASTE (Jean, 1775-?): born in Niderbronn (Bas-Rhin) in 1775. In the 12th Cavalry 28 June 1793, brigadier 9 August 1803, in the same regiment when it became the 12th Cuirassiers 14 September 1803, maréchal des logis 21 April 1806, sub-lieutenant 9 August 1809, lieutenant 12 June 1813, in post 14 July 1814, dismissed with the corps 10 December 1815. LH CH 4 December 1813.

ARBORY de MAMONY (Amant, 1789-?): born in Paris (Seine) on 17 January 1789. In the school at Compiègne 2 May 1800, brigadier in the 23rd Chasseurs à Cheval 2 March 1805, maréchal des logis 12 March 1805, sub-lieutenant in the 3rd Cuirassiers 14 May 1809. Named lieutenant 25 November 1811, aide de camp to General Valence 21 August 1815, wounded at the Moskova 7 September 1812, returned to the 3rd Cuirassiers 10 September 1812, in the Escadron Sacré in Russia December 1812, captain adjutant-major 14 May 1813, cannonball wound to his left knee at Waterloo 18 June 1815, dismissed 25 November 18145. LH CH 4 December 1813.

ARENSTORFF (Goettlib Georges d', 1794-?): born in Oise (Bouches du Weser). Pupil at the Hanover Military School 9 April 1806, left 15 July 1808, sub-lieutenant in the 2nd Cuirassiers 21 April 1813, went over to the enemy 8 March 1814.

AREXY (Raymond, 1789-?): born in Mirepoix (Ariège) on 5 September 1789. In the 4th Cuirassiers 17 May 1808, fourrier 1 September 1810, maréchal des logis 16 April 1812, three lance wounds to his forehead, his right thigh and right knee and his horse killed under him at la Drissa 11 August 1812, sub-lieutenant 19 November 1812. Wounded and his horse killed under him and taken prisoner at Epinal 11 January 1814, returned and sent home on half-pay 6 August 1814, reinstated and appointed sub-lieutenant in the same regiment which had become the Angoulême Cuirassiers, had not joined his unit in May 1815.

ARGENTIN (Jean François, 1754-?): born in Royon (Pas-de-Calais) on 31 December 1754. Trooper in the Royal-Roussillon 2 June 1773, dismissed 2 June 1781, reengaged 18 August 1783, brigadier 3 July 1784, in the same regiment when it became the 11th cavalry 1 January 1791, maréchal des logis 1 September 1792, sub-lieutenant 26 August 1794, in the suite 11 March 1796, took up his appointment 19 August 1800, lieutenant 30 July

Standard belonging to the 12th Cuirassier Regiment, 1802-1804 model. (RR)

1802, in the same regiment when it became the 11th Cuirassiers 24 September 1803, retired 25 October 1804.

ARMAND (?-?): in the 5th cavalry 15 July 1801, brigadier September 1802, brigadier-fourrier November 1802, in the same regiment when it became the 5th Cuirassiers 23 December 1803, maréchal des logis 25 October 1803, maréchal des logis-chef 1804, with three comrades saved his colonel several times during Austerlitz 2 December 1805. He was named sub-lieutenant 23 February 1807, wounded at Essling 21 May 1809, lieutenant 25 May 1807, in the 6th Provisional Dragoons 13 October 1809, remained in the 5th Cuirassiers 26 December 1809, retired 15 November 1810. LH CH 14 March 1806.

ARMENGAUD (Jean Antoine, 1768-before 1852): born in l'Isle-du-Tarn (Tarn) on 22 February 1768. In the Chasseurs à Cheval of the Regiment d'Alsace 15 March 1789 which became the 1st Chasseurs à Cheval 1 January 1791, maréchal des logis-chef in the Legion of the Pyrenees 6 February 1793 which formed the 22nd Chasseurs à Cheval 22 November 1793, sub-lieutenant 6 August 1795, discharged with pay 25 February 1802, appointed sub-lieutenant in the 7th Cuirassiers 12 December 1806, joined them and instated the same day 4 February 1807, in the 6th Cuirassiers 1 April 1807, left to join them 7 August 1807. Seconded to the 3rd Provisional Heavy Cavalry 1808, lieutenant in the 17th Legion of Gendarmerie 8 October 1811, taken prisoner in Prussia 13 October 1813, returned 11 September 1814, non-active on half-pay 1 November 1814, in the 10th Legion of the Gendarmerie in the Gironde Company 18 March 1815, retired 6 April 1816, pensioned off 7 August 1816.

ARNOULD (Nicolas Joseph, 1746-?): born in Lunéville (Meurthe) on 4 February 1746. In the Artois-Cavalerie 25 January 1766, brigadier 1 September 1770, maréchal des logis 1 September 1784, maréchal des logis-chef 10 August 1789, in the same regiment when it became the 9th Cavalry 1 January 1791, sub-lieutenant 10 May 1792, lieutenant 1 July 1793, wounded 22 July 1793, captain 11 November 1793, wounded 19 June 1794, in the same regiment when it became the 9th Cuirassiers 24 September

1803, on retirement pay 1 September 1803.

ARONIO (Roland François Marie, 1785-1816): born in Lille (Nord) on 11 February 1785. Pupil at the Ecole Spéciale Militaire at Fontainebleau 3 February 1805, sub-lieutenant in the 1st Cuirassiers 19 April 1806, in the suite of the 11th Cuirassiers 29 April 1806, left to join them 9 May 1806, took up his appointment 24 November 1806, wounded by a Biscayan shot to his right shoulder 8 February 1807, in the 2nd Carabiniers 17 March 1809, captain 5 November 1811. Wounded at Waterloo 18 June 1815, on half-pay 19 November 1815. LH CH 1 October 1807.

ASBECK (Gallrieg Menno Watze van, ?-?): born in Leuwarden (Frise), page to the Emperor, lieutenant in the 14th Cuirassiers 5 February 1813, dismissed with the corps 13 July 1814.

ASINARI DE SAINT MARSAN (Charles, 1791-1841): born in Turin (Pô) in 1791. Sub-lieutenant in the 8th Cuirassiers 28 February 1812, rejoined his regiment 1 May 1812, lieutenant ordnance officer to the Emperor 3 July 1813, resigned from French service, retroactively cavalry captain 11 April 1814.

ASTRUC (Jean Louis, 1784-?): born in Geneva (Léman) on 21 November 1784. In the 5th Cavalry 20 July 1803 which became the 5th Cuirassiers 23 December 1802, brigadier 8 December 1804, brigadier-fourrier 12 January 1806, maréchal des logis 10 October 1806, wounded at Eylau 8 February 1807, sabre wound at Essling 21 May 1809, sub-lieutenant 13 August 1809, lieutenant 28 September 1813, dismissed and non-active 23 December 1815. LH CH 28 September 1813.

ATHIAUX (Claude Marie, 1781-?): born in Roanne (Loire) on 23 September 1781. In the Gendarmes d'Ordonnance 2 March 1807, dismissed with the corps 23 October 1807 and incorporated into the Dragoons of the Imperial Guard 17 December 1807. He was sub-lieutenant in the 8th Cuirassiers 3 June 1809, lieutenant 21 March 1812, several sabre wounds to his head at the Moskova 7 September 1812, lost five toes on his right foot from frostbite and taken prisoner during the retreat 1812. He returned and put in for retirement 25 August 1814, retired 29 October 1814. LH CH 11 October 1812.

AUBERT (Pierre François, 1781-?): born in Paris (Seine) on 16 April 1781. In the 1st Cuirassiers 30 December 1802, brigadier 22 March 1803, fourrier

20 June 1803, maréchal des logis 25 December 1806, incorporated into the 13th Cuirassiers 21 October 1808, sub-lieutenant in the suite 28 February 1812, took up the appointment 17 March 1813, lieutenant 5 March 1814, incorporated into the 10th Cuirassiers 6 August 1814, sabre wound to his head at Waterloo 18 June 1815. He dismissed with the corps 25 December 1815. LH CH 29 May 1810.

AUBERT (Pierre, 1771-?): born in Soufrière (Orne) on 5 January 1771. In the Manche Dragoons 6 March 1792, in the 1st Cavalry 7 February 1794, brigadier 12 July 1799, in the same regiment when it became the 1st Cuirassiers 10 October 1801, maréchal des logis 28 July 1807, maréchal des logis-chef 1 January 1808, sub-lieutenant in the 13th Cuirassiers 27 August 1813, lieutenant 27 March 1814. he was incorporated into the 9th Cuirassiers 9 August 1814, dismissed with the corps 26 November 1815. LH CH 29 December 1809.

AUBERTIN (Jean Pierre, 1784-?): born in Hagondange (Moselle) on 3 May 1784. In the 24th Dragoons 27 October 1805, brigadier 1 January 1807, maréchal des logis 16 February 1811, gendarme in the 1st Spanish Legion 16 September 1811, sub-lieutenant in the 9th Cuirassiers 1 March 1813, incorporated with his squadron into the 3rd Provisional Heavy Cavalry in Hamburg 11 September 1813, returned with the garrison Mai 1814 and incorporated into the Dauphin's Cuirassiers 22 September 1814 which became the 3rd Cuirassiers again April 1815, dismissed 25 November 1815.

AUBIGNAC (d'?-?): sub-lieutenant in the 8th Cuirassiers incorporated into the 3rd Provisional Heavy Cavalry in Spain 1808.

AUBIN (Michel, 1760-?): born in Limay (Seine-et-Oise) on 12 July 1760. In the Dauphin-Cavalerie 24 March 1782, brigadier 24 August 1787, in the same regiment when it became the 12th Cavalry 1 January 1791, maréchal des logis 1 April 1792, sub-lieutenant 16 February 1801. He was in the same regiment when it became the 12th Cuirassiers 24 September 1803, allowed to retire 19 September 1805.

AUBRIOT (Joseph Charles, 1765-1812): born in Void (Meuse) on 16 March 1795. In the Gendarmes of the Comte d'Artois from 26 October 1784 to 1 April 1788, maréchal des logis in the Gendarmes d'Ordonnance 1807, dismissed with the corps 23 October 1807, lieutenant in the 7th Cuirassiers 18 February 1808, rejoined his unit 7 May 1808, took up his appointment 8 June 1808, captain in the 6th Cuirassiers 7 April 1809, instated 1 May 1809, died in Russia 1812.

AUBUISSON (François d'1772-?): born in Saint-Germain-en-Laye (Seine-et-Oise) on 10 February 1772. In the 8th Cavalry 29 January 1794, brigadier 26 August 1800, in the same regiment when it became the 8th Cuirassiers 10 October 1801, maréchal des logis 6 August 1802, sub-lieutenant 9 August 1809, lance wound to his right arm near Moscow 4 October 1812, lieutenant 5 June 1813. Dismissed with the corps 5 December 1815 and retired 11 December 1815. LH CH 1 October 1807.

AUDEBAR FERUSSAC
see **DAUDEBAR FERUSSAC**

AUDENAERDE see **LALAING d'AUDERNAERDE**

AUDIGNE (Charles d', 1791-?): born in Paris (Seine) on 6 January 1791. Pupil at the Ecole Spéciale Militaire at Saint-Cyr 10 December 1808, sub-lieutenant in the suite of the 7th Chevau-Légers 22 June 1811, took up the appointment in the 8th Cuirassiers 25 September 1812. Instated 16 March 1812 or 1 July 1812, lieutenant 28 September 1813, aide de camp 11 July 1814, left 28 July 1814.

AUDINOT (Pierre, 1767-1807): born in Ambrière (Marne) on 7 November 1767. In the Cuirassiers du Roy 14 January 1788 which became the 8th Cavalry 1 January 1791, brigadier 3 August 1792, maréchal des logis 28 August 1793, maréchal des logis-chef 17 March 1800, sub-lieutenant by seniority 19 August 1800, in the same regiment when it became the 8th Cuirassiers 10 October 1801. He was elected lieutenant 6 June 1802, died April 1807.

AUDRY (?-1813): sub-lieutenant in the 5th Cuirassiers 16 May 1809, wounded at the Moskova 7 September 1812, lieutenant 22 May 1813, shot and taken prisoner at Hanau 30 October 1813, died of his wounds.

AUGE (Jean Pierre, 1774-?): born in Rosière (Aube) on 3 May 1774. Grenadier in the 10th Half-Brigade 20 October 1793, in the Grenadiers of the Garde du Directoire 10 January 1797, gendarme in the 14th Legion, Aube Company 6 January 1799, in the Legion

of the Gendarmerie d'Elite 17 January 1802, brigadier 1 May 1806, maréchal des logis 11 June 1808, lieutenant in the 1st Legion of the Gendarmerie à Cheval d'Espagne 20 July 1811. He was elected captain in the 4th Cuirassiers 28 February 1813, retired 21 December 1815. LH CH 7 May 1811.

AUGE (Pierre, 1755-?): born in Lamberville (Seine-Inférieure) on 8 April 1755. In the Artois-Cavalerie 7 February 1771, brigadier 1 May 1783, in the same regiment when it became the 9th Cavalry 1 January 1791, maréchal des logis 1 April 1792, maréchal des logis-chef 1 April 1793, sub-lieutenant 7 September 1793, lieutenant 26 November 1793, captain 13 March 1802. He was in the same regiment when it became the 9th Cuirassiers 24 September 1803, on retirement pay 2 July 1806.

AUGER (François, 1760-?): born in Vuy (Seine-et-Oise) on 8 August 1760. In the Volontaires Nationaux à Cheval from the Ecole Militaire 24 August 1792, brigadier 10 September 1792, brigadier-fourrier 7 October 1792, maréchal des logis-chef in the same regiment when it formed the 25th Cavalry 7 February 1793 which then became the 24th Cavalry 4 June 1793. He was elected quartermaster with rank of sub-lieutenant 4 November 1796, sub-lieutenant by exchange 25 April 1801, incorporated into the 1st Cuirassiers 1 January 1802, in the 2nd Cuirassiers 15 September 1802, left to join his unit 23 September 1802, instated 6 November 1802, lieutenant by seniority 21 August 1806, supernumerary 30 October 1806 and confirmed in the suite 6 November 1806, left for retirement 1 July 1809.

AUGER (Louis Pierre, 1791-?): born in Paris (Seine) in 1791. Child of the regiment in the pay of the 2nd Cuirassiers 10 July 1803, Cuirassiers 1 January 1808, brigadier 1 April 1809, brigadier-fourrier 14 May 1809, maréchal des logis 16 February 1811, maréchal des logis-chef 26 February 1813, sub-lieutenant 22 December 1813, shot in the left hand at Athies 9 March 1814, seconded to the school at Saumur 1 March 1815, struck off the rolls when the regiment was disbanded 10 December 1815.

AUGIER (Pierre Philippe, 1784-1812): born in Charente (Charente-Inférieure) on 30 September 1784. Boarder at the Ecole Spéciale Militaire 25 February 1804, sub-lieutenant in the 15th of the Line 23 October 1804, lieutenant 10 November 1807, captain 28 August 1808, aide de camp to General Raynaud 7 June 1808 then to General Cacault 22 March 1810, captain in the 7th Cuirassiers 1 February 1812, joined his unit 30 March 1812, wounded and disappeared at the Berezina 28 November 1812.

AURAUX (Jean, 1778-?): born in Chape (Ardennes) in 1778. In the 4th Cavalry 15 June 1799 which became the 4th Cuirassiers 12 October 1802, brigadier 1 October 1806, cannonball wound to his left hip and his horse killed under him at Essling 21 May 1809, maréchal des logis 1 September 1810, wounded by a Biscayan shot to his nose at Czaszniki 31 October 1812 and a lance wound to his neck at Borisov 23 November 1812, sub-lieutenant 18

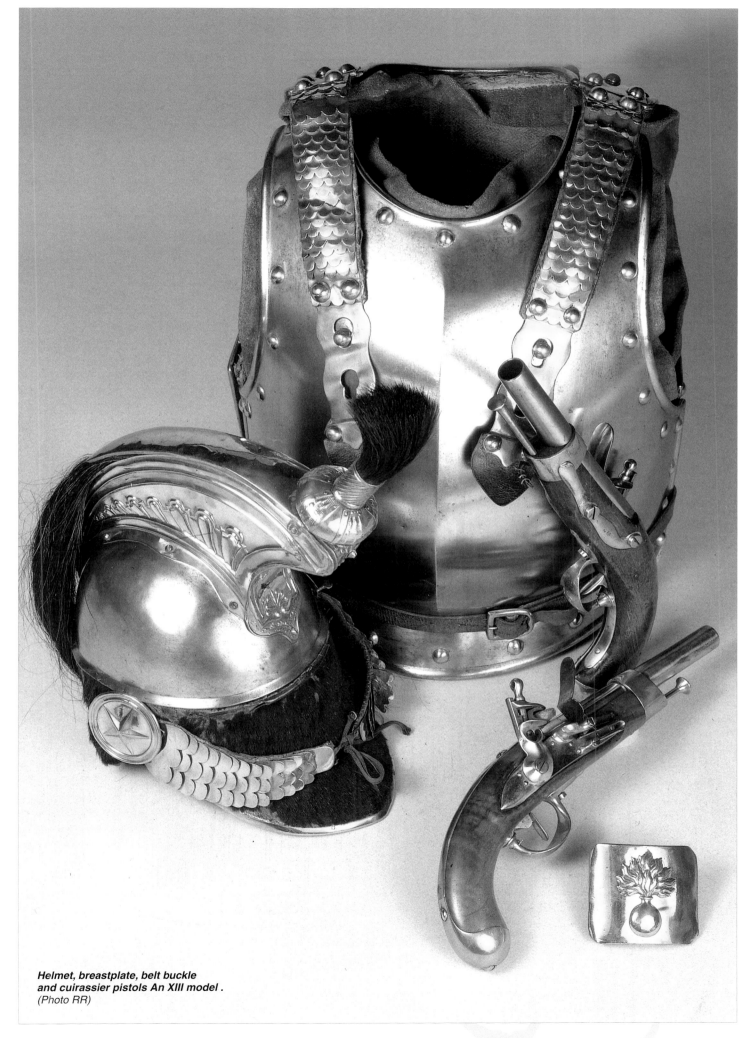

**Helmet, breastplate, belt buckle
and cuirassier pistols An XIII model .**
(Photo RR)

February 1815, shot in the arm at Waterloo 18 June 1815. Retired 21 December 1815. LH CH 4 December 1813.

AUSSIGNAC (Philippe Henry, 1754-?): born in Vaudray (Charente-Inférieure) on 29 July 1754. Trooper in the Royal-Etranger 30 April 1775, brigadier 13 March 1782, maréchal des logis 17 December 1785, in the same regiment when it became the 7th Cavalry 1 January 1791, maréchal des logis-chef 1 April 1792, adjutant 21 May 1792, sub-lieutenant 19 March 1793, lieutenant 16 November 1793, captain 11 May 1794, reassigned as lieutenant 6 August 1795. He was reinstated captain 31 January 1797, commissioned 2 May 1798, in the same regiment when it became the 7th Cuirassiers 23 December 1802, left with retirement pay 1 March 1806. LH CH 28 June 1805.

AVENAY see **RIOULT VILLAUNAY d'AVENAY**

AVOGARDO de QUINTO (Joachim, 1761-?): born in Verceil (Sésia) on 9 May 1761. Cadet in the service of the King of Sardinia in the Savoie-Cavalerie 23 December 1774, sub-lieutenant 11 May 1776, lieutenant 10 May 1781, captain-lieutenant, appointed captain 15 August 1790, first-captain 8 November 1796, shot in the shoulder at Verona 2 April 1799, taken prisoner with his division 28 April 1799, discharged 23 September 1801, commanded the Garde d'Honneur of the Sesia Department. He was elected first-lieutenant in the Gendarmes d'Ordonnance 30 October 1808, captain in the suite of the 7th Cuirassiers 16 July 1807, rejoined his unit 23 September 1807, took up his appointment 18 April 1808, squadron commander in the 2nd Cuirassiers 12 October 1808, left to join his regiment 1 December 1808, shot and wounded in the right hip at Regensburg 23 April 1809 and in the heel at Wagram 6 July 1809, second-major put at the disposal of the Minister of War and returned home 31 May 1811. LH CH 13 August 1808.

AVOINE (François Julien, 1756-?): born in Vaux (Eure) on 24 November 1756. In the Commissaire-Général-Cavalerie Regiment 3 October 1780, brigadier 1 January 1787, in the same regiment when it became the 3rd Cavalry 1 January 1791, maréchal des logis 1791, maréchal des logis-chef 1 August 1793, sub-lieutenant 21 December 1793, sabre wound to his right hand 21 April 1794, lieutenant 15 February 1799, sabre wound to his face at Alexandria 20 June 1799, in the same regiment when it became the 3rd Cuirassiers 12 October 1802, captain by seniority 11 December 1805, wounded at Friedland 14 June 1807, retired 9 May 1809.

AVRANGE d'HAUGE-RANVILLE (François Charles Jean Pierre Marie d', baron, 1782-1817): son of the general and a nephew of Berthier, was born in Versailles (Seine-et-Oise) on 15 October 1782. Hussar in the 5th Regiment, ordnance to Berthier 28 February 1799, sub-lieutenant in the suite of the 5th Hussars 31 January 1800, in the 12th Hussars 12 November 1800, shot in the left hand near Bassano December 18700, second-lieutenant in the Chasseurs à Cheval of the Guard 12 May 1801, commissioned 16 September 1801, captain in the 21st Dragoons 22 December 1802, captain in the suite of the 9th Dragoons 7 January 1802, aide de camp to General Léopold Berthier 21 July 1803, captain in the 16th Dragoons 24 March 185, squadron commander in the 1st Dragoons 1 May 1876, major in the 4th Dragoons 7 January 1807, aide de camp to the Grand Duke of Berg 23 May 1807, colonel of the 6th Cuirassiers 25 June 1807, wounded by a Biscayan shot to his left arm at Essling 22 May 1809, shot in the left leg at Wagram 6 July 1809, major of the Chasseurs à Cheval of the Guard 6 August 1811, brigadier-general 27 February 1813, in the 2nd Reserve Cavalry Corps of the Grande Armée 4 April 1813, commanded the 1st Brigade (Carabiniers and 1st Cuirassiers) of the 2nd division of Heavy Cavalry of the same corps 12 June 1813, cannonball wound to his right leg and taken prisoner at Leipzig 18 October 1813, freed on parole and returned to France December 1813, on convalescence leave 15 January 1814, lieutenant in the Gardes du Corps de Roi 1 June 1814, followed Louis XVIII to Ghent 20 March 1815. LH O 6 October 1808, Baron of the Empire d. 19 March 1808 and l.p. 10 September 1808.

AVRANGE DUKERMONT (François Eugène, baron d', 1784-1863): son of an Intendant-General, cousin of the above, husband of the adopted daughter of Maréchal Sérurier, born in Versailles (Seine-et-Oise) on 30 June 1784. Engaged in the 3rd Hussars 22 March 1800, cadet war commissioner with his father 20 July 1800, joined the 3rd Hussars then brigadier 23 October 1801, maréchal des logis 2 December 1801, sub-lieutenant 24 April 1802, lieutenant in the 21st Dragoons 5 September 1803, in the 16th Dragoons 23 September 1805. He was captain 8 December 1806, shot in the left shoulder at Bergfried 4 February 1807, aide de camp to General Clément 26 April 1807, wounded in the arm and side by a cannonball at Koenigsberg 14 June 1807, in the 6th Cuirassiers 11 July 1807, on the staff of the major-general of the Army of Spain 21 October 1808, in the suite of the 5th Chasseurs à Cheval 2 March 1809, on the staff of the major-general of the Army of Germany 29 March 1809. He was elected squadron commander in the 2nd Chasseurs à Cheval 30 April 1809. Bruised in the head and knocked off his horse by a cannonball at Raab 14 June 1809, wounded in the chest at Krasnoë 14 August and Smolensk 16 August 1812, colonel of the 9th Chasseurs à Cheval 3 March 1813, shot in the left shoulder at Goldberg 23 August 1813, kept during 1814, retired 2 May 1815.

LH CH 17 July 1809, O 13 September 1807, chevalier of the Empire l.p. May 1808, Baron d. 4 December 1813. Confirmed l.p. 28 November 1815.

ARRIGHI de CASANOVA (Jean Toussaint, Duke of Padua, 1778-1853) son of the Préfet, cousin of Napoleon and husband of Anne de Montesquiou-Fezensac, born in Ajaccio (Liamone) on 8 March 1778. Pupil of the King at the Rebais Military School near Meaux 1787, returned home when those schools were shut down 9 September 1793, sub-lieutenant in the 3rd Compagnie Franche of the Liamone Department levied in Corsica 30 November 1796, auxiliary lieutenant in the suite of the 75th Half-Brigade of the Line 17 April 1797, secretary of the legation with Joseph Bonaparte in Rome, deputy to the adjutant-generals in the suite of the staff of the Army of Italy 6 February 1798.

Named ieutenant 17 March 1798, retroactively 17 April 1797, deputy to the staff of the Army of the Orient 12 August 1798, sabre wound to his head at Salahieh 11 August 1798, promoted to captain on the battlefield 12 August 1798, shot in the carotid artery at Saint John of Acre March 1799, acting aide de camp to Berthier 19 February 1799, confirmed captain 17 March 1799, aide de camp to Berthier in the Reserve Army 2 May 1800, squadron commander 11 October retroactively on 14 June 1800, commissioned aide de camp to Berthier 1 January 1801, in the 1st Dragoons 3 November 1801, kept on as aide de camp 23 November 1801, brigade commander in the 1st Dragoons keeping his title of First Aide de Camp to the Minister of War 31 August 1803, replaced as aide de camp 1804,.He was major-colonel of the Dragoons of the Guard 19 May 1806.

He was brigadier-general while still maintaining his command 25 June 1807, major-general commanding the 3rd Cuirassier division 25 May 1809, bruised on his leg by a Biscayan shot at Wagram 6 July 1809, Inspector-General of cavalry 23 June 1810, commanded the 4th Mobile Column ordered to search for deserters and draft dodgers in the 27th and 28th Military Districts 18 March 1811, commanded the 3rd Cavalry Corps of the Grande Armée 22 March 1813, Governor of Leipzig 28 May 1813, at the head of the 1st Infantry Division of the Paris Reserve 15 February 1814, non-active 1 September 1814.

He was elected Governor of Corsica 14 April 1815, suspended and outlawed 24 July 1815. Holder of a Sabre of Honour at Saint John of Acre March 1799, LH CH 11 December 1802, O 14 June 1814, C 25 December 1804, Duke of Padua l.p. 24 April 1808.

On 8 October 1805 at Wertingen, at the head of the 1st and 2nd Dragoons, he charged and bowled over two Austrian cuirassier regiments, taking a battalion of Hungarian grenadiers and six flags. In the course of this action he was received several sabre wounds to his head.

General officers

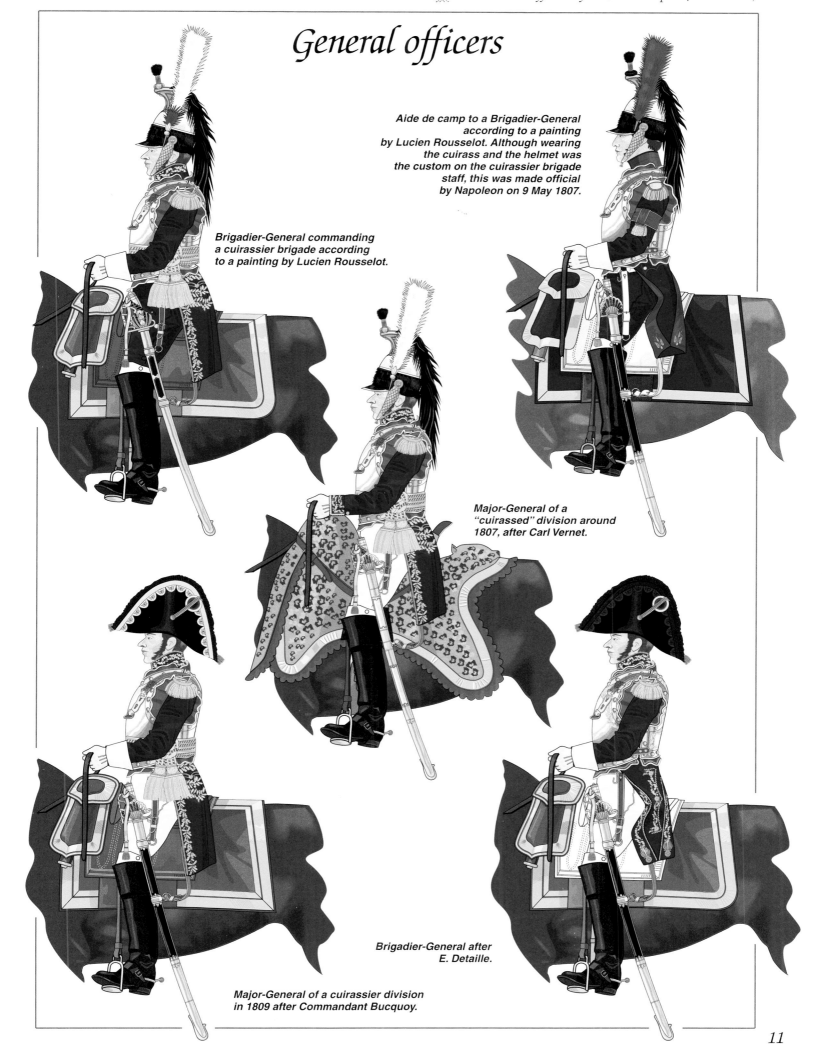

Aide de camp to a Brigadier-General according to a painting by Lucien Rousselot. Although wearing the cuirass and the helmet was the custom on the cuirassier brigade staff, this was made official by Napoleon on 9 May 1807.

Brigadier-General commanding a cuirassier brigade according to a painting by Lucien Rousselot.

Major-General of a "cuirassed" division around 1807, after Carl Vernet.

Brigadier-General after E. Detaille.

Major-General of a cuirassier division in 1809 after Commandant Bucquoy.

BABUT (Gaston Jean, 1767-1822): born in Nantes (Loire-Inférieure) on 4 April 1767. Trooper in the Légion Nantaise 22 September 1793, two sabre wounds in the head and arm at Machecoul 25 November 1793, sub-lieutenant in the 11th Cavalry 22 September 1794, in the suite 11 march 1796, took up his appointment 18 April 1800, lieutenant 19 August 1800, adjutant-major 13 March 1802, captain adjutant-major 9 September 1803.

He was in the same regiment when it became the 11th Cuirassiers 24 September 1803, bayonet wound to his thigh at Austerlitz 2 December 1805 and Biscayan shot wound to his head at Eylau 8 February 1807, aide de camp to General Fouler 7 May 1807.

He became squadron commander in the 3rd Cuirassiers 27 May 1809, second-major 8 February 1813, at the Hanau Cavalry Depot under Préval, adjutant-commander 6 November 1813, on the headquarters staff of the Grande Armée 1814, non-active 1 September 1814, recalled to the headquarters of the Army of the North 1815, then non-active again 1 September 1815. LH CH 5 November 1804.

BACHELEY (Claude, 1784-?): born in La Chassagne (Jura) on 21 July 1784. In the 2nd Cuirassiers 26 May 1804, brigadier 18 May 1809, gendarme in the 4th Squadron of the Gendarmerie d'Espagne 14 December 1809

He was in the 1st Legion of the Gendarmerie d'Espagne 1 January 1811, brigadier 1 March 1812, sub-lieutenant in the 1st Cuirassiers 28 February 1813, returned to his unit 12 March 1813, wounded and taken prisoner by the English at Waterloo 18 June 1815, struck off the lists 24 December 1815, went home 20 January 1816.

BADENER (Jacques Michel Marie, 1785-?): born in Rouen (Seine-Inférieure) on 12 June 1785. Volunteered for the 4th Light Infantry 4 November 1805, fourrier 23 May 1806, sergeant-major 31 August 1807, cuirassier in the 6th Regiment 31 August 1808.

He became fourrier 1 January 1809, maréchal des logis-chef 3 June 1809, adjutant-NCO 16 September 1809, sub-lieutenant 12 October 1811, in the Escadron Sacré during the retreat from Russia 1812, incorporated with his squadron into the 2nd Provisional Heavy Cavalry in Hamburg 11 September 1813, returned

with the garrison 30 May 1814, in service with the 6th Cuirassiers 4 August 1814, dismissed 21 November 1815.

BADES or BADEZ (Jean Louis, 1757-1809): born in Chalon-sur-Saône (Saône-et-Loire) on 2 July 1757. In the Royal-Picardie-Cavalerie 6 December 1777, brigadier 3 December 1787, in the same regiment when it became the 21st Cavalry 1 January 1791.

He was brigadier-fourrier 1 August 1791, maréchal des logis 10 February 1792, maréchal des logis-chef 3 May 1792, sub-lieutenant 1793, in the same regiment when it became the 20th Cavalry 4 June 1793, lieutenant 6 April 1795, discharged 7 April 1795, replacement lieutenant in the 24th Cavalry 19 June 1795, took up his appointment January 1798, dismissed with the corps 10 October 1801, incorporated as lieutenant in the suite of the 1st Cuirassiers 1 January 1802, captain by seniority 7 December 1802, wounded at Eylau 8 February 1807, retired 25 May 1807 and left 16 August 1807, died 1809. LH CH 14 March 1806.

BAGUE (Jean Baptiste, 1763-1809): born in Savoyeux (Haute-Saône) on 19 August 1763. Trooper in the Royal-Cravates 22 December 1788 which became the 10th Cavalry 1 January 1791, brigadier 20 November 1791, fourrier 15 September 1793.

He became maréchal des logis 26 August 1795, maréchal des logis-chef 3 June 1801, in the same regiment when it became the 10th Cuirassiers 24 September 1803, sub-lieutenant by seniority 20 December 1805, shot in the right leg and his horse killed under him at Hoff 6 February 1807, lieutenant 5 April 1807, captain 16 May 1809, killed after having his horse killed under him at Essling 22 May 1809. LH CH 14 April 1807.

BAILLEUL (Jean, 1778-?): born in Méry (Nord) on 10 August 1778. Chasseur à pied in a corps franc (irregular troops) September 1791, left it 1796, in the 11th Cavalry 9 May 1800 which became the 11th Cuirassiers 24 September 1803.

He became brigadier, gendarme à cheval in the 12th Escadron d'Espagne 16 December 1809, in the 1st Légion à Cheval "Burgos" 5 February 1811, dismissed with the corps and incorporated as sub-lieute-

nant in the 7th Cuirassiers 1 March 1813, returned 30 March 1813, non-active on half-pay 16 August 1814.

BAILLIENCOURT (Louis Archange Benoît de, 1777-1813): younger brother of the following, born in Béthune (Pas-de-Calais) on 8 May 1777. Volunteered for the 8th Cavalry 15 March 1793, brigadier 20 November 1798, fourrier 30 January 1799, maréchal des logis-chef 17 February 1800, adjutant NCO 26 August 1800, in the same unit when it became the 8th Cuirassiers 10 October 1801.

<April 1802, lieutenant by seniority 28 June 1805, captain 24 February 1807, wounded at Heilsberg 10 June 1807, wounded by a cannonball in his left side at Essling 22 May 1809 and by shrapnel to his left knee at the Moskova 7 September 1812, squadron commander 18 October 1812, wounded at Hanau 30 October 1813, major in the 2nd Carabiniers 4 November 1813, died of his wounds at Mainz 7 December 1813. LH CH 5 November 1804.

BAILLIENCOURT aka COURCOL (Charles François Joseph de, 1774-1826): older brother of the above, born in Béthune (Pas-de-Calais) on 22 November 1774. Volunteered for the 8th Cavalry 15 March 1793, brigadier-fourrier 4 June 1794, maréchal des logis-chef 30 October 1798, acting sub-lieutenant 30 June 1799, confirmed 8 February 1801, in the same unit when it became the 8th Cuirassiers 10 October 1801.

He became lieutenant 7 January 1802, adjutant-major 2 April 1802, captain 5 October 1803, went over to another company 16 May 1805, wounded at Essling 22 May 1809, squadron commander 12 September 1809, commanded the regiment at the Moskova contributing to the capture of the Great Redoubt, cannonball wound to his right leg 7 September 1812, colonel of the 1st Carabiniers 28 September 1813, commanded a provisional regiment made up of the remnants of the division (1st and 2nd Carabiniers, 1st, 5th 8th and 10th Cuirassiers) December 1813, serious Biscayan shot wound to his left hand and his horse killed under him at La Chaussée-près-Châlons 3 February 1814, on two months' sick leave on full pay 9 February 1814, left with retirement pension 18 May 1815, colonel in the Condé Cuirassiers N°6 13 September 1815. LH CH 5 November 1804, O 18 October 1812.

BAILLY (Claude Joseph, 1767-?): born in Besançon (Doubs) on 10 August 1767. In the Conti Regiment 11 March 1783.

He became corporal 4 June 1785, sergeant 17 October 1786, sergeant-major 13 September 1790, adjutant-major in the 3rd Battalion of the Somme 23 September 1793, unemployed 10 October 1794, trooper in the 12th Cavalry 14 July 1798, fourrier 17 September 1798, maréchal des logis-chef 24 February 1800, adjutant-NCO 27 December 1802, in the same regiment when it became the 12th Cuirassiers 24

September 1803, sub-lieutenant 12 December 1806, lieutenant 19 January 1808, captain 12 March 1812.

He was non-active 1814 returned to the regiment 1815 non-active again 3 August 1815, left 16 August 1815. LH CH 22 June 1804.

BAILLY (Edme Nicolas, 1782-?): born in Auxerre (Yonne) on 9 June 1782. In the 13 Dragoons 29 September 1798, brigadier 23 September 1801, maréchal des logis 9 May 1808, gendarme à cheval 25 December 1811, brigadier in the 1st Legion of the Gendarmerie à Cheval d'Espagne "Burgos" 8 June 1812.

He was dismissed with the corps 27 February 1813, incorporated sub-lieutenant in the 7th Cuirassiers the following day 28 February 1813, rejoined 6 March 1813, incorporated with his squadron into the 2nd Provisional Heavy Cavalry in Hamburg 11 September 1813, returned with the garrison 30 May 1814, non-active 16 August 1814, in service 6 April 1815, rejoined the regiment 24 April 1815, non-active again 26 August 1815.

BAILLY (François, 1784-?): born in Pierrefontaine (Doubs) on 18 February 1784. In the 4th Horse Artillery 1 September 1804, velite in the Grenadiers à Cheval of the Imperial Guard 3 March 1805, eight sabre wounds to the left hand and then maimed one finger at Eylau 8 February 1807, sub-lieutenant 11 July 1807, detached to the Versailles Riding School 2 February 1808, returned 1 September 1809.

He became lieutenant 8 October 1811, wounded by his horse's fall when it was killed under him at the Moskova 7 September 1812, and by a lance to the his right hand in front of Wiasma 4 November 1812, captain in the 4th Cuirassiers 14 March 1813, wounded and his horse killed under him at Leipzig 18 October 1813, on foot turned abandoned enemy artillery pieces against them forcing them to retreat 2 January 1814, wounded at La Rothière 1 February 1814, on six months' leave with pay 3 November 1814.

He, returned and wounded at Waterloo 18 June 1815, dismissed with the regiment 21 December 1815. LH CH 5 September 1813.

BAILLY (Pierre Antoine, 1780-?): born in Vesoul (Haute-Saône) on 22 February 1780. In the 8th Hussars 21 May 1802, fourrier 20 June 1802, maréchal des logis 28 August 1802, sub-lieutenant 26 May 1803, sabre wound to the left arm at Jena 14 October 1806 and shot in his left leg while reconnoitering near Morthausen 19 October 1806.

He became lieutenant 22 November 1806, aide de camp to General Marulaz 14 March 1807, captain 20 April 1809, shot in his right hand at Essling 22 May 1809, a cannonball wound to his chest and left hand at Wagram 6 July 1809, in the 3rd Cuirassiers 12 March 1812, instated 20 May 1812, in the Escadron Sacré during the retreat from Moscow December 1812, squadron commander following 14 May 1813, shot in his left arm at Dresden 27 August 1813, cannonball wound to his right leg at Leipzig 18 October 1813, took up his appointment 1814. He was dismissed with the regiment and retired 25 November 1815. LH CH 14 March 1807, O 28 September 1814.

BAILLY aka **EVRARD** (Charles Gabriel, 1769-1807): born in Favernay (Haute-Saône) on 3 February 1769. In the Royal-Cavalerie 6 March 1787 which became the 2nd Cavalry 1 January 1791, brigadier-fourrier 28 November 1792, sabre wound and a shot to his left arm 17 May 1793, maréchal des logis-chef 9 June 1797.

He became adjutant NCO 14 June 1800, in the same regiment when it became the 2nd Cuirassiers 12 October 1802, elected sub-lieutenant 24 September 1803, lieutenant 30 October 1806, died in the war squadrons 19 January 1807.

BANANS see **MARCHANT de la CHATELAINE de BANANS**

BAPTISTE see **CASENEUVE** aka **BAPTISTE**

BARATTE (Auguste Joseph, 1786-1812): born in Templeure (Nord) on 10 December 1786. Velite in the Grenadiers à cheval of the Guard 29 March 1806, sub-lieutenant in the suite of the 4th Cuirassiers 13 July 1813.

He was supernumerary lieutenant 7 April 1809, wounded at Essling 22 May 1809, took up his appointment 15 September 1809, shot and wounded in his shoulder at Polotsk 11 August 1812, retired 19 November 1812 and presumed to have died of his wounds during the retreat in 1812. LH CH 19 November 1812.

BARATTE (Joseph François Xavier, 1760-?): born in Besançon (Doubs) on 13 December 1760. Gunner in the Toul Regiment 10 April 1781, left 13 September 1789, assistant to the clerk then clerk to the Army of the Rhine's court martial 1 September 1792, left 25 July 1793.

He was at the head of the office for War Materiel 2 February 1794, Commissioner for War 13 June 1795 discharged 7 October 1800, deputy in the Inspection of Parades 5 January 1801, left 21 January 1802, captain-quartermaster of the 12th Cavalry 27 April 1802 which became the 12th Cuirassiers 24 September 1803, retired 14 March 1808.

BARBEYRAC de SAINT MAURICE (Frédéric Marie Aimé, 1793-1877): born in Sens (Yonne) on 3 January 1793. Admitted to the Ecole Impériale de Cavalerie in Saint-Germain 19 May 1810, passed out 10 July 1810, discharged for health reasons 19 December 1810, readmitted to the same school 2 September 1812.

He became sub-lieutenant in the 10th Cuirassiers 30 January 1813, in the 2nd Cuirassiers 5 March 18113, two sabre wounds to his head, taken prisoner and his horse killed under him at Leipzig 16 October 1813, returned and promoted to brigadier with the rank of captain in the Mousquetaires Noirs 1 July 1814.

He was captain commanding the 2nd Cuirassiers of the Royal Guard 12 October 1815. LH CH 5 September 1813.

BARLIER (Louis, 1773-1813): born in Pontault (Seine-et-Marne) in 1777. Corporal in the 50th Half-Brigade

BAGUET (Etienne, 1769- after 1833), born in Saulx (Haute-Saône) on 22 December 1769. Joined the 2nd Artillery 27 October 1788, emigrated and promoted to Sergent-fourrier in the artillery of the Mirabeau Legion 9 April 1791, in the service of Austria in the Rohan Hussars 1 July 1797, two sabre wounds and taken prisoner by the French near Guernecheim 14 May 1799, in the service of France as a chasseur in the 23rd Chasseurs à Cheval and lieutenant 25 December 1799, brigadier 21 April 1800.

He became adjutant NCO 7 December 1800, sub-lieutenant 22 April 1802, lieutenant aide de camp to General Saint-Germain 20 April 1807, instated as aide de camp 4 May 1807, adjutant-major in the 3rd Cuirassiers 14 May 1809, wounded by Biscayan shot in his right thigh and a shot in the head at Essling 21 May 1809, captain 14 November 1801, went to a company 16 July 1811, aide de camp to General Saint-Germain 20 January 1812.

He was shot in the right shoulder at the Moskova 7 September 1812, squadron commander 12 August 1812, non-active 1 January 1816 LH CH 14 May 1809, O 14 September 1813.

Promoted to Maréchal des Logis the previous day, he distinguished himself at Hohenlinden on 3 December 1800 by bringing the dismounted and wounded Lieutenant Pinson back to the French lines after charging by himself several Austrian Hussars, killing their officer and bringing back two prisoners.

This exploit earned him promotion to the rank of adjudant-NCO four days later.

2 January 1794, with the military teams of the Army 29 March 1798, in the 22nd Cavalry 16 September 1798.

He became brigadier 18 May 1800, dismissed with the corps 31 December 1802 and incorporated into the 2nd Carabiniers 31 January 1803, brigadier in the 2nd Cuirassiers 17 April 1803, maréchal des logis 10 October 1803, marécvhal des logis 10 October 1803, maréchal des logis-chef 30 October 1806, sub-lieutenant 12 March 1812, wounded at Ostrovno 25 July 1812, killed at Leipzig 16 October 18113. LH CH 5 September 1813.

BARNIQUE (1777-?): born in Bouillon (Forêts) on 28 December 1777. Maréchal des logis in the 6th Cuirassiers, sub-lieutenant 22 June 1809, wounded at Wagram 6 July 1809, amputated 27 August 1809, retired 14 December 1809.

BARON (Charles Pierre Emmanuel, ? -1813): Volunteered for the 9th Cuirassiers 1811, maréchal des logis, attached to the Veterinary School at Alfort, sub-lieutenant 20 September 1812, wounded at

Dresden 26 August 1813, died from his wounds at Dresden Hospital 30 August 1813.

BARROIN (François, 1761-?): born in Domcourt (Haute-Marne) on 6 January 1761. In the Ségur-Dragons 6 December 1782 which became the Hainaut Chasseurs à Cheval 17 March 1788, then 5th Chasseurs à Cheval 1 January 1791.

He became brigadier 1 July 1793, maréchal des logis 5 September 1793, sub-lieutenant on the battlefield at Catricum 18 October 1799, discharged 23 October 1800, confirmed sub-lieutenant 8 February 1801, appointed sub-lieutenant in the 10th Cavalry 15 September 1802 which became the 10th Cuirassiers 24 September 1803.

Retired 12 December 1804 and left 21 January 1805.

BARRY (Claude Auguste Brice, 1787-?): born in Tonnerre (Yonne) on 1 December 1787. In the 2nd Gardes d'Honneur 1 June 1813, shot and wounded in the thigh at Hanau 30 October 1813 and a sabre wound to his hand during the Mainz blockade 1814, non-active 181.

He became sub-lieutenant in the Berry Cuirassiers 20 January 1815 which became the 5th Cuirassiers once again April 1815, non-active on half-pay 24 December 1815.

BARTH (Jean Jules, 1791-?): born in Hanover on 28 July 1791. A volunteer in the 2nd Cuirassiers 21 February 1806, maréchal des logis, sub-lieutenant 9 August 1809, resigned 10 August 1810, resignation accepted 23 October 1810.

BARTHELEMI (Etienne, 1782-1813): born in Marseille (Bouches-du-Rhône) on 21 February 1782. In the 20th Dragoons 2 December 1803, brigadier-fourrier January 1804, maréchal des logis April 1804, maréchal des logis-chef 1805, adjutant NCO 1805, sub-lieutenant in the 22nd Dragoons 1806.

He became lieutenant in the 11th Dragoons 22 November 1808, adjutant-major 21 October 1809, captain 2 March 1811, aide de camp to General Dejean March 1812, squadron commander in the 10th Cuirassiers 21 March 1813, killed at Hanau 29 October 1813. LH CH 14 April 1814.

BARTHELEMY (Pierre, 1774-?): born in Vandœuvre (Aude) on 22 September 1774. In the 1st Saint-Denis Battalion 26 August 1793, in the 23rd Chasseurs à Cheval 20 February 1794, maréchal des logis in the 3rd Hussars 4 October 1796, sub-lieutenant 10 April 1799, lieutenant 7 April 1805, shot and wounded at

Jena 14 October 1806, captain 12 December 1806.

He was wounded by several lances and taken prisoner at Langheim 20 January 1807, returned 30 August 1807, wounded at Tudela 23 November 1808, captain (Old Guard) in the 1st Eclaireurs 21 December 1813, incorporated into the suite of the 3rd Hussars 8 June 1814, took up his appointment in the 6th Cuirassiers 1 August 1814, dismissed 21 November 1815. LH CH 4 December 1813, O 8 January.

BARTHES (Jean, 1762-1809): born in Lévignac (Haute-Garonne) on 27 October 1762. Trooper in the Royal-Champagne 7 May 1779, brigadier 9 July 1786.

He became fourrier in the same regiment when it became the 20th Cavalry the same day 1 January 1791, maréchal des logis 15 January 1792, sub-lieutenant 17 May 1793, in the same unit when it became the 19th Cavalry 4 June 1793, dismissed with the corps 31 December 1802 and incorporated as lieutenant in the 11th Cavalry 5 February 1803 which became the 11th Cuirassiers 24 September 1803, captain 15 May 1807, killed at Essling 21 May 1809.

BASCOP (Dominique Martin, 1783-?): born in Cassel (Nord) in 1783. In the 2nd Cuirassiers 21 March 1804, brigadier 1 August 1806, brigadier-fourrier in the suite 16 July 1807, maréchal des logis-chef 1 July 1809.

He became sub-lieutenant 14 May 1813, several sabre wounds to his right arm at La Rothière 1 February 1814, retired to the administration as of 6 August 1814.

BASOGE (Jean Hubert, 1757-1811): born in Saint-Mihiel (Meuse) on 8 April 1757. in the Royal-Cavalerie 10 April 1773, brigadier in the Chevau-Légers N°1 10 September 1780, maréchal des logis in the Orléans-Cavalerie 1 September 1784 which became the 13th Cavalry 1 January 1791, sub-lieutenant in the 23rd Cavalry 25 January 1792, lieutenant 17 May 1792.

He was confirmed 22 July 1792, captain 1 April 1793, in the same unit when it became the 22nd Cavalry 4 June 1793, commissioned 15 September 1793, with five troopers recaptured a canon at Grand-Rieux 13 May 1794, squadron commander on 2 January 1801 by governmental choice, dismissed with the corps 31 December 1802 and incorporated into the suite of the 9th Cavalry 25 January 1803 which became the 9th Cuirassiers 24 September 1803.

He took up his appointment in the 7th Cuirassiers 22 December 1803, joined his unit 31 January 1804, retired 25 June 1806, left 1 August 1806, died Nemours 2 February 1811. CH MLH 14 June 1804.

BASSET (François Marie, 1773-?): born in Paris (Seine) on 3 November 1773. In the 24th Cavalry 20

Captain's brevet belonging to Jean Basoge. (Author's collection)

Officers from the 3rd Cuirassiers in winter dress, 1804. Composition by Feist. (RR)

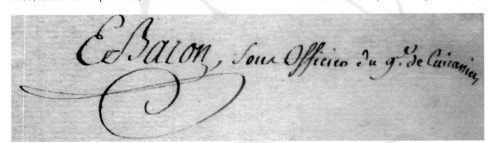

Senior officers

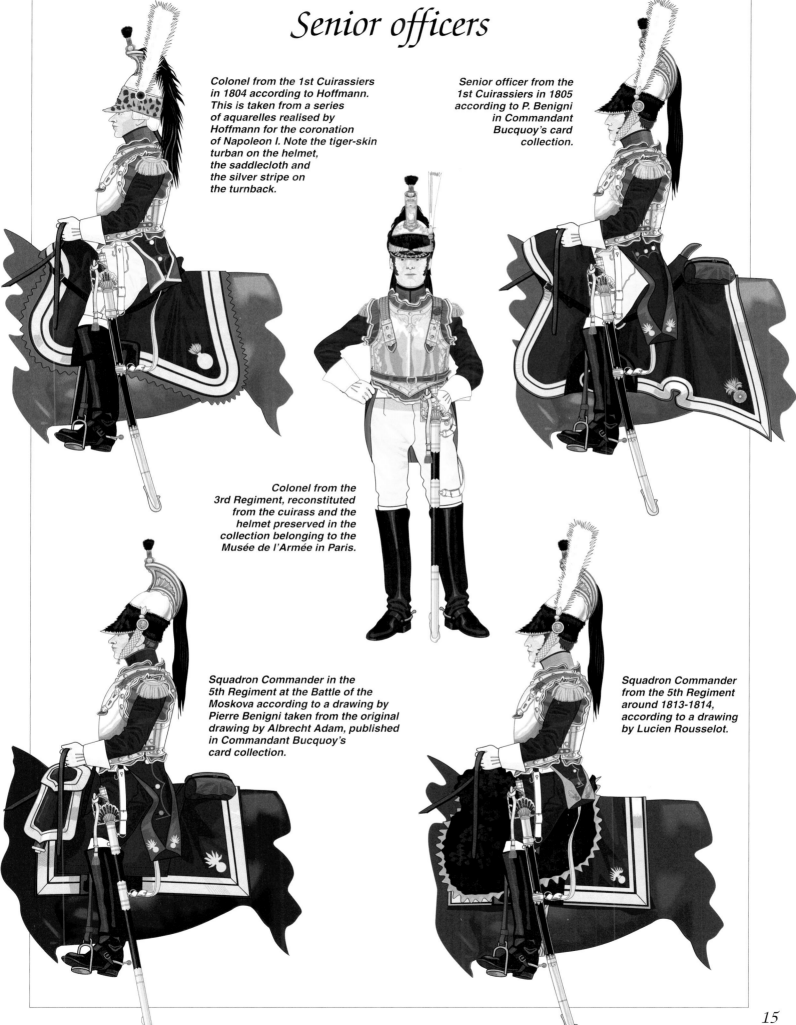

Colonel from the 1st Cuirassiers in 1804 according to Hoffmann. This is taken from a series of aquarelles realised by Hoffmann for the coronation of Napoleon I. Note the tiger-skin turban on the helmet, the saddlecloth and the silver stripe on the turnback.

Senior officer from the 1st Cuirassiers in 1805 according to P. Benigni in Commandant Bucquoy's card collection.

Colonel from the 3rd Regiment, reconstituted from the cuirass and the helmet preserved in the collection belonging to the Musée de l'Armée in Paris.

Squadron Commander in the 5th Regiment at the Battle of the Moskova according to a drawing by Pierre Benigni taken from the original drawing by Albrecht Adam, published in Commandant Bucquoy's card collection.

Squadron Commander from the 5th Regiment around 1813-1814, according to a drawing by Lucien Rousselot.

April 1794, brigadier 30 December 1796, maréchal des logis 1 March 1797, maréchal des logis-chef 1 November 1797.

He became sub-lieutenant 26 April 1799, quartermaster treasurer 24 April 1801, dismissed with the 24th Cavalry 10 October 1801 and incorporated into the suite of the 1st Cuirassiers as lieutenant 1 January 1802, confirmed lieutenant 18 July 1802, resigned 20 June 1804, resignation accepted 2 July 1804, left 8 July 1804.

BATAILLE de TANCAR-VILLE (Charles Antoine Benoît, baron, 1778-1864): born in Paris (Seine) on 21 May 1778. In the 4th Chasseurs à Cheval 27 December 1798, brigadier 29 April 1799.

He became maréchal des logis in the Compagnie Franche of the Calvados Dragoons 14 August 1799, acting sub-lieutenant 5 May 1800, aide de camp to General Kellermann 4 November 1800, Chasseurs à Cheval 24 November 1806, squadron commander 10 June 1809, adjutant-commandant chief of staff of the 4th Cavalry Corps 18 June 1813, chief of staff of the 6th Cavalry Corps 15 February 1814, on the staff of the Paris Government 15 May 1814, in the Inspection of Cavalry 13 July 1814, chief of staff of the 3rd and 4th Cavalry Corps 1 June 1815, joined 8 June 1815,.

He was colonel in command of the 3rd Cuirassiers 5 July 1815, dismissed with the regiment and returned home 25 November 1815. LH CH 1 April 1807, O 28 September 1813, Baron of the Empire d. 26 February 1814.

BAUCAIRE (-): in the 11th Chasseurs à Cheval 26 February 1804, in the 12th Chasseurs à Cheval 5 April 1805, brigadier 17 March 1806, maréchal des logis 16 March 1807.

He became sub-lieutenant in the 13th Cuirassiers 21 August 1809, lieutenant 6 November 1813, incorporated into the 7th Chasseurs à Cheval 9 August 1814, captain in the 4th Cuirassiers, allowed to go over to the 9th Cuirassiers 5 July 1815, dismissed with the corps 26 November 1815.

BAUDICHON (Pierre, 1757-?): born in Château-Meillan (Cher) on 8 August 1757. In the Roi-Cavalerie on 8 January 1778, brigadier 21 January 1784, maréchal des logis 26 September 1784, in the same regiment when it became the 6th Cavalry 1 January 1791, adjutant 14 March 1792.

He became sub-lieutenant 10 May 1792, lieutenant 11 September 1793, in the same unit when it became the 6th Cuirassiers 23 December 1802, captain by seniority 14 June 1805, wounded at Heilsberg 10 June 1807, retired 6 October 1808. LH CH.

BAUDOT (Basile Casimir, 1774-?): born in Ambly (Meuse) on 1 March 1774. In the 4th Ain Battalion on 8 September 1792, prisoner at Avesnes 12 September 1793, returned 19 January 1796, in the 10th Cavalry 18 August 1796, brigadier 25 July 1800, maréchal

des logis 30 April 30 April 1801, maréchal des logis-chef 28 June 1802, in the same unit when it became the 10th Cuirassiers 24 September 1803.

He became sub-lieutenant 24 November 1806, lieutenant 25 May 1807, captain 16 May 1809, wounded by a bullet in the head and his horse killed under him at Essling 22 May 1809, taken prisoner 12 November 1812. LH CH 1 October 1807.

BAUDOT (Pierre Joseph, 1766-1829): born in Ambly (Meuse) on 1 August 1766. In the Royal-Cravates on 15 April 1786 which became the 10th Cavalry 1 January 1791, brigadier 3 April 1791, brigadier-fourrier 20 November 1791, maréchal des logis 15 September 1793, adjutant 21 March 1797.

He became sub-lieutenant 21 December 1798, acting lieutenant 20 February 1801, confirmed 3 June 1801, adjutant-major 13 march 1802, captain adjutant-major 9 September 1803, in the same regiment when it became the 10th Cuirassiers 24 September 1803, captain commanding a company 24 November 1806, wounded at Longoreck 30 January 1807, squadron commander 16 May 1809.

He was wounded on the left thumb by a sabre at Eckmühl 22 April 1809, lance wound to his left arm at Moscow 4 October 1812, wounded by a Biscayan shot in the chest at Hanau 29 October 1813, retired 6 August 1814. LH CH 14 March 1806, O 28 September 1813.

BAUDOUIN (Jean Charles, 1763-1810): born in Tessy (Manche) on 11 January 1763. In the Royal-Infanterie on 12 November 1778, left 14 February 1799, in the 1st Cavalry 14 March 1791, brigadier-fourrier 28 August 1792, maréchal des logis 1 June 1793.

He became maréchal des logis-chef 19 January 1799, sub-lieutenant by seniority 2 May 1799, shot and wounded in his left leg and had his horse killed under him at Novi 15 August 1799, in the same regiment when it became the 1st Cuirassiers 10 October 1801, elected lieutenant 13 November 1802, captain 25 February 1807, retired 19 March 1808, left 1 May 1808, in the 2nd Half-Brigade of Veterans, died 23 October 1810. LH CH 14 June 1804.

BAUDOUIN (Jean Louis, 1772-?): born in Metz (Moselle) on 13 April 1772. In the Metz National Guard on 26 July 1789, in the 3rd Chasseurs à Cheval 22 February 1792, brigadier-fourrier 1 September 1793, sub-lieutenant on the battlefield then taken prisoner at Castelbar in Ireland 8 September 1798.

He returned to the regiment 22 October 1799, confirmed 20 July 1800, discharged 23 October 1801, appointed sub-lieutenant in the 10th Cuirassiers 30 November 1806, discharged 4 March 1808, left 6 April 1808.

BAUDOUX (Lucien, 1774-?): born in Caisne (Oise) on 24 January 1774. In the 7th Cavalry on 14 February 1794 which became the 7th Cuirassiers on 23 December 1802, brigadier 1 October 1806.

He became maréchal des logis 1 May 1809, shot

in the right thigh at Wagram 6 July 1809 and sabre wound to the right arm at Polotsk 18 October 1812, sub-lieutenant 19 November 1812, shot and wounded in the left foot at the Berezina 28 November 1812.

He left for Hamburg 10 July 1813, incorporated into the 2nd Provisional Heavy Cavalry in Hamburg with his squadron 11 September 1813, returned with the garrison 30 May 1814, retired 19 December 1815. LH CH 18 August 1814.

BAUER (Jean Christophe Gaspard, 1778-?): born in Amsterdam (Zuydersee) in 1778. Sub-lieutenant in the suite of the 14th French Cuirassiers 1 November 1810.

He took up his appointment 21 March 1812, resignation accepted 8 January 1813, left 25 January 1813.

BAURE (Jean Adam, 1760-?): born in Metelsheim (Mont-Tonnerre) on 22 September 1760. Trooper in the Royal-Guyenne 23 July 1776, brigadier 8 January 1787.

He was in the same regiment when it became the 23rd Cavalry 1 January 1791, maréchal des logis 20 May 1792, sabre wound to his left arm and a shell burst to his left knee at Trèves 1792, sub-lieutenant 1 April 1793, in the same regiment when it became the 22nd Cavalry 4 June 1793, lieutenant 11 October 1801, dismissed with the corps 31 December 1802.

He was incorporated into the 12th Cavalry 25 January 1803 which became the 12th Cuirassiers 24 September 1803, captain 30 October 1806, retired 29 January 1808.

BAUZIL (Hippolyte Thomas, 1778-?): born in Saint-Paul (Ariège) on 26 March 1778. In the 6th Landes Battalion on 23 September 1793, requisition officer for the Army of the Pyrénées-Orientales supply administration 7 August 1796, left 19 June 1798, in the 18th Dragoons 1 September 1798.

He became brigadier 2 October 1799, fourrier 4 October 1799, maréchal des logis 19 February 1802, maréchal des logis-chef 2 December 1802, sub-lieutenant 2 March 1805, lieutenant 20 November 1806, captain 20 September 1809, squadron commander in the 3rd Cuirassiers 10 April 1813, shot and wounded in his right foot at Leipzig 16 October 1813.

He was temporarily commanded the regiment November 1813 and during the whole of the 1814 Campaign, wounded by a shot to his left knee at La Rothière 1 February 1814, commanded the regiment provisionally after the colonel was wounded at Waterloo 18 June 1815 and until 5 July 1815, dismissed 25 November 1815. LH CH 1 October 1807, O 4 December 1813.

BAUZIL (Martin Théodore, 1786-?): born in Leran (Ariège) on 9 December 1786. Volunteer in the 18 Dragoons on 1 January.

He became deputy-veterinary 2 December 1807, with the 11th Chasseurs à Cheval 7 May 1809, in the 9th Cuirassiers 24 July 1911, first veterinary officer in the 9th Hussars 14 April 1812, in the 3rd Cuirassiers 20 September 1813, sub-lieutenant 22 December 1813, wounded at Champaubert 10 February 1814, dismissed 25 November 1815.

CUIRASSIERS OFFICERS' SADDLERY

The 1801 Regulations adopted the two flap holster cap for cavalry officers; these caps were abandoned progressively after Wagram. French harness of a cuirassier officer of the 8'h Regiment. The flat saddle, without a cantle, was covered with blue velvet. The whole ensemble had a simple blue cloth portmanteau cover with silver embroidery.

Junior officer's regulation saddle, early half of the Empire. The piping on the cover and the holster caps was the colour of the regimental distinctive. The regulation stipulated that the tips of the holsters should be made of silver metal.

The silver-thread embroidered grenade, visible in the rear corners was sometimes replaced by the number of the regiment. The saddle strap was made of strong yellowish canvas with blue and red cloth braid.

Regulation saddle of a junior officer wearing campaign dress and service dress. The cover was the same size and cut, the silver stripe being here replaced by a goat's hair stripe the same colour as the background.

The stirrups were bronze. All the buckles, the loops, the small head chain as well as the bit (half curved or straight) were silver.

The saddle straps were made of cloth on the French-style saddle; the silver stripe on the cover was a regulation 2 in (50 mm) for senior officers, 1 1/2 in (45 mm) for captains, 1 1/2 in (40 mm) for lieutenants and 1 1/3 in (35 mm) for NCOs. An additional 2/3 in (15-mm) stripe, also silver, was worn by colonels and majors. The piping was always the colour of the distinctive.

The sheepskin half-shabrack had several advantages for the campaigning officer; it enabled him in fact to carry his rolled up coat tied to the holsters; this was impossible with the configuration of the French-style saddle, which not having a cantle, could not use loading straps and a portmanteau could not be fastened to it.

The half-shabrack was held in place by a surcingle fitted with brown or black leather and a hoisting strap. Furthermore this half-shabrack protected the French-style saddle better.

Morning exercise saddle.

Regulation saddle belonging to a Cuirassier Major-General's aide de camp.

French saddle belonging to a cuirassier officer used during the Consulate and at the beginning of the Empire. This type of saddlery had been regulation issue for cavalry officers since 1786.

French regulation saddle for junior officers wearing campaign dress and service dress. Like the model on the left, the saddle is flat it is covered with stitched blue cloth according to the regulations. The seat and the quarters were edged with a stripe the same colour as the background.

Although the stirrup straps were red leather, the breast piece, the martingale, the crupper as well as the bridoon was made of black leather. This last element had loops and silver buckles; the reins and the filet, for the parade dress, had silver stripes.

Saddle in use at the end of the Empire with He black sheepskin half-shabrack and blue, silver-striped saddlecloth. The 3rd, 8th and 6th seem to have issued their officers with this harness, as early as 1804 for the first two, 1809 for the 6th. The serrated scallops were still the colour of the distinctive.

Like their opposite numbers in the light cavalry, certain cuirassier officers adopted a blue cloth shabrack with large points. A round portmanteau completed the whole.

BAUZIL (Pierre François, 1789-?): born in Leran (Ariège) on 4 January 1789. Volunteer in the 18th Dragoons on 1 July 1808, brigadier 4 May 1810, fourrier 11 May 1810.

He became maréchal des logis 16 June 1813, maréchal des logis-chef 9 February 1814, sub-lieutenant in the 16th Dragoons 12 March 1814, non-active 1 September 1814, took up his appointment in the Dauphin's Cuirassiers 20 January 1815, instated 31 January 1815, in the same when they became the 3rd Cuirassiers again in April 1815, dismissed with the corps 25 November 1815.

BAVAY see **DYVE de BAVAY**

BAVOILLOT (Jean, 1768-?): born in Paris (Seine) on 23 November 1768. Trooper in the Royal-Roussillon on 15 December 1784 which became the 11th Cavalry 1 January 1791, brigadier-fourrier 16 March 1791, maréchal des logis 1 December 1792.

He became maréchal des logis-chef 1 October 1793, adjutant 24 August 1794, adjutant sub-lieutenant 22 September 1794, lieutenant by seniority 2 march 1802, in the same regiment when it became the 11th Cuirassiers 24 September 1803, captain 24 November 1806, retirement pension 12 April 1810.

BAZILE (Frédéric David, 1791-?): born in Montpellier (Hérault) on 8 July 1791. In the 7th Cuirassiers on 7 October 1809, brigadier 21 December 1809, maréchal des logis 6 December 1810.

He became maréchal des logis-chef 3 March 1813, sub-lieutenant in the suite 14 May 1813, wounded by a bayonet at Dresden 26 August 1813, took up his appointment 16 March 1814, in the King's Cuirassiers 4 May 1814 which were the 1st Cuirassiers again in April 1815.

He was dismissed 24 December 1815. LH CH 5 September 1813.

BEASLAY (René, 1784-1815): born in 1784. In the 1st Cuirassiers 24 December 1801, brigadier 16 May 1804, fourrier 27 April 1806, maréchal des logis-chef 16 November 1806.

He became sub-lieutenant 16 May 1809, wounded in the right leg by a bullet at Znaïm 11 July 1809, lieutenant 5 November 1811, wounded by a Biscayan shot to his left keg at the Moskova 7 September 1812, killed at Waterloo 18 June 1815. LH CH 11 October 1812.

BEAUCHAMP (Louis François Achille, 1773-1812): born in Joucy (Saône-et-Loire) on 6 January 1773, sub-lieutenant cadet at the Engineers School at Mézières 1787.

He became sub-lieutenant in the Berri-Cavalerie 1787 which became the 18th Cavalry 1 January 1791, resigned because of illness 1791, lieutenant in the Company of Guides of the Army of the Pyrenees 8 July 1793, lieutenant in the Hussars of the Montagne 16 December 1793 which became the 12th Hussars 9

February 1794, aide de camp serving as acting adjutant-general in the Army of the West July 1795, retired without a job and discharged 20 June 1800, lieutenant in the 4th Cuirassiers 30 November 1806, captain 4 March 1812.

He became captain adjutant-major in the same regiment by changing with Captain Petitjean 24 May 1812, wounded at the Berezina 28 November 1812, died in a fire in Russia 10 December 1812. LH CH.

BEAUCHAMPS (?-1810): Sub-lieutenant in the 10th Cuirassiers, incorporated into the 2nd Provisional Heavy Cavalry December 1807, prisoner when the French surrendered at Baylen 22 July 1808, slaughtered by the inhabitants of Port-Mahon when escaping from the Cadiz prison hulks 14 March 1810.

BEAUCHART (Georges Louis Félix, 1785-1812): born in Grigny (Aisne) on 4 March 1785.

In the Gendarmes d'Ordonnance 1 November 1806, dismissed with the corps on 23 October 1807 and incorporated into the Grenadiers à Cheval of the Imperial Guard 24 November 1807, sub-lieutenant in the 10th Cuirassiers 3 June 1809, wounded at the Moskova 7 September 18712, died at Ghjat 3 October 1812.,

BEAUCHET (Eugène Gabriel Philippe, 1789-?): born in Paris (Seine) on 20 September 1789. Pupil at the Saint-Cyr Military Academy on 14 January 1809.

He became, sub-lieutenant in the 12th Cuirassiers

Squadron Commander from the 5th Cuirassiers at the Moskova. Composition by P. Benigni. (RR)

16 August 1810, lieutenant 12 June 1813, non-active 7 January 1815, resignation accepted 3 August 1815.

BEAUDINET de COURCELLES (Charles de, 1792-1846): born in Nancy (Meurthe) on 31 May 1792. In the 2nd Gardes d'Honneur on 22 June 1813, brigadier 30 June 1813, maréchal des logis-chef 18 July 1813, second-lieutenant 2 September 1813, lieutenant in the suite of the 6th Cuirassiers 4 August 1814, instated as sub-lieutenant only 31 January 1815,.

He was confirmed sub-lieutenant 4 February 1815, asked to resign 19 May 1815, left 6 July 1815.

BEAUDINET de COURCELLES (Victor, 1794-?): born in Metz (Moselle) on 2 March 1794. Pupil at the school in Saint-Germain on 15 June 1812, sub-lieutenant in the 5th Dragoons 30 March 1814, non-active 1814.

He was in the suite of the Dauphin's Cuirassiers 7 October 1814, took up his appointment 20 January 1815, in the same regiment when it became the 3rd Cuirassiers again April 1815, dismissed with his regiment 25 November 1815.

BEAUDOT (Ambroise, 1785-?): born in Wassy (Haute-Marne) on 5 June 1785. Velite on 20 February 1806, sub-lieutenant in the 3rd Cuirassiers 25 May 1809.

He became lieutenant 25 November 1811, incorporated with his squadron into the 1st Provisional Heavy Cavalry in Hamburg 3 July 1813, acting adjutant-major 20 April 1814, returned with the garrison to France 27 May 1814, replaced and confirmed in the Dauphin's Cuirassiers 16 August 1814 which became the 3rd Cuirassiers again April 1815, dismissed 25 November 1815.

BEAUJEAN (Gabriel, 1759-?): born in Presle (Oise) on 9 February 1859. Trooper in the Royal-Champagne on 27 February 1783, brigadier 11 September 1784, maréchal des logis 18 March 1787, in the same when it became the 20th Cavalry 1 January 1791, maréchal des logis-chef 21 December 1791.

He became sub-lieutenant 25 January 1792, lieutenant 17 May 1793, in the same unit when it became the 19th Cavalry 4 June 1793, captain 19 June 1799, incorporated into the 11th Cavalry 5 February 1803 which became the 11th Cuirassiers 24 September 1806, retired 25 May 1807.

BEAULIEU see **TREUILLE de BEAULIEU.**

BEAUMONT see **CARRIERE** aka **BEAUMONT**

BEAUREPAIRE (Urbain Jacques Dominique de, 1787-1859): born in Louvagny (Calvados) on 20 November 1787. In the Gendarmes d'Ordonnance 15 December 1806, brigadier 25 January 1807, dismissed with the corps 23 October 1807 and incorporated into the Dragoons of the Guard 24 November 1807.

He became sub-lieutenant in the 6th Cuirassiers 3 June 1809, slight bullet wound in the temple the bullet having spent itself against the chin strap, at Wagram 6 July 1809, cannonball wound to his arm at the Moskova 7 September 1793, in the "Escadron sacré" during the retreat 1812, lieutenant 18 March 1813, incorporated with his squadron into the 2nd Provisional Heavy Cavalry in Hamburg 1813.

He returned with the garrison 30 May 1814, one month's leave 17 July 1814, captain 7 August 1814, brigadier in the 2nd Musketeer Company retroactively 1 July 1814, followed Louis XVIII to Ghent, captain commanding the 2nd Cuirassiers of the Royal Guard 17 October 1815. LH CH 17 November 1814.

BECHELE (François Xavier, 1791-?): born in Wittelsheim (Haut-Rhin) on 19 June 1791. In the 2nd Gardes d'Honneur on 13 June 1813, sub-lieutenant in the Line 1 July 1814, in the suite of the 10th Cuirassiers 6 August 1814, confirmed in the suite 22 December 1814, took up his appointment 27 January 1815, dismissed with the regiment 25 December 1815.

BECKING (Sébastien, 1777-?): born in Sarrelouis (Moselle) on 25 September 1777, in the Moselle Gunners 28 July 1794, dismissed 29 August 1797, in the 9th Cavalry 19 December 1798. Brigadier 2 February 1802.

He became fourrier 17 March 1803, in the same regiment when it became the 9th Cuirassiers 24 September 1803, maréchal des logis 4 December 1806, sub-lieutenant 14 May 1809, wounded at Wagram 6 July 1809 and the Moskova 7 September 1812, lieutenant 21 May 1813, adjutant-major 21 December 1816, non-active 1814, back in the 9th Cuirassiers 12 May 1815 and non-active again 1 September 1815. LH CH 13 August 1809.

BEL (François, 1768-1815): born in Langres (Haute-Marne) on 12 October 1768. In the Dauphin-Dragons 23 January 1786 which became the 7th Dragoons 1 January 1791, left 11 July 1791.

He became captain in the 4th Morbihan Battalion 8 May 1794, auxiliary captain in the 163rd Half-Brigade 5 March 1796, took up his appointment in the 54th Half-Brigade 20 May 1796, in the 9th Dragoons 31 March 1800, went into the Gendarmerie 20 September 1801, in the 7th Cuirassiers 14 October 1806, joined 25 December 1806.

He was squadron commander in the 3rd Cuirassiers 19 August 1812, taken prisoner when Danzig capitulated 1 February 1814, returned to France 24 June 1814, non-active on half-pay, major in the 1st Carabiniers 28 March 1815, killed at Waterloo 18 June 1815. LH CH 1813.

BELIN (François Maximilien, 1769-?): born in Orléans (Loiret) on 28 March 1769. Quartermaster in the 1st Loiret Battalion 1 October 1791, war commissioner 1 December 1793, discharged 1 December 1796 but continued in his job for two years, divisional paymaster for the Treasury in the Armies of the Sambre and Meuse, Helvetia and Italy 29 October 1798, left 1 December 1804.

He became quartermaster of the 11th Battalion of the Artillery Train 14 December 1805, captain quartermaster of the 12th Cuirassiers 9 June 1908, dismissed with the corps 10 December 1815. LH CH 30 August.

BELLART (Pierre Anselme Isidore, 1777-1807): born in Abbeville (Somme) on 22 June 1777. In the 2nd Cavalry 2 August 1799, brigadier 22 March 1802, in the same regiment when it became the 2nd Cuirassiers 12 October 1802.

He became fourrier 24 May 1803, maréchal des logis-chef 13 October 1803, sub-lieutenant 30 October 1806, lieutenant 3 April 1807, killed at Friedland 14 June 1807.

BELLE (Aimé Gustave, 1776-?): born in Boulogne-sur-Mer (Pas-de-Calais) on 9 June 1776. In the Navy 1804, left 30 January 1807, lieutenant in the 1st Brest Regiment 16 February 1807, dismissed 27 July 1808, lieutenant in the 15th of the Line 17 August 1809.

He was aide de camp to General Gratien 2 October 1810, captain 23 April 1812, deputy on the general staff of the Grande Armée 29 July 1812, captain in the 9th Chevau-Légers 12 November 1813, in the 14th Cuirassiers 28 January 1814, dismissed with the corps and incorporated into the 12th Cuirassiers 13 July 1814, on the Jura Observation Corps staff with General Lecourbe 8 May 1815, left to join (Napoleon) 11 May 1815. LH CH 30 August 1814.

BELLEAU (Charles de, 1791-?): born in Angers (Maine-et Loire) on 11 May 1791. Pupil at the Saint-Cyr Military Academy 1809.

He became sub-lieutenant in the 121st of the Line 25 March 1811, three bayonet wounds and taken prisoner at Castalla 13 April 1813, commissioned lieutenant aide de camp during his captivity 12 May 1813, returned from enemy prison and non-active 28 May 1814, in the 1st Cuirassiers 26 May 1815, back on half-pay 1 September 1815.

BELLEGARDE de MAULEON
see DUPAS de BELLEGARDE ET DE MAULEON

 **BELLIARD** (Auguste Daniel, comte, 1769-1832): born in Fontenay-le-Comte (Vendée) on 25 May 1769. Volunteered in 1789, incorporated into the National Guard October 1791, Captain in the 1st Battalion of Vendée Volunteers when this was formed 8 December 1791, deputy to the adjutants-generals of Dumouriez's staff 22 August 1792.

He became adjutant-general battalion commander 8 March 1793, in the Army of the Côtes de La Rochelle May 1793, suspended 30 July 1793, volunteered for the 3rd Chasseurs à Cheval 15 August 1794, adjutant commanding a brigade 10 September 1795, in the Army of the West 15 September 1795, in that of the Côtes de l'Océan 1 January 1796, of Italy 22 February 1796, promoted to brigadier-general on the battlefield at Arcola 18 November 1796, confirmed 6 December 1796,

commanded the 9th Brigade of the 5th Division 14 June 1797, in the Army of England 12 January 1798, sent on a mission to Naples, then in the Army of Egypt 5 March 1798, commanded the 1st Brigade of Desaix's division 23 June 1798.

He was wounded in the lower abdomen when Cairo was captured again 8 April 1800, acting major-general 25 April 1800, Governor of Cairo 20 June 1800, confirmed 6 September 1800, returned to France and commanded the 24th Military Division 18 December 1800, chief of staff to Murat 30 August 1805, followed him to Spain 21 February 1808, joined Jourdan 22 August 1808, Governor of Madrid 4 December 1808, chief of staff of the Army of the Centre in Spain November 1810, available 1 October 1811, at the head of the 9th Infantry Division of the Elbe Observation Corps 25 December 1811 which became the 3rd division of the 2nd Corps of the Grande Armée 1 April 1812.

He became chief of staff of the Cavalry Reserve under Murat 12 June 1812, cannonball wound to his leg at Mojaïsk 10 September 1812, Colonel-General of the Cuirassiers in place of Gouvion-Saint-Cyr 4 December 1812, returned to France February 1813, left arm shattered by a cannonball at Leipzig 18 October 1813, commanded the Cavalry in Champagne 7 March 1814, then the two Roussel d'Hurbal and Berckheim divisions 17 March 1814, commanded at Metz 1 July 1814, Inspector-General of Cuirassiers 14 July 1814, major-general of the Duc de Berry's Corps 16 March 1815, accompanied Louis XVIII to Beauvais and ordered to return to France, Napoleon's plenipotentiary to Murat 22 April 1815.

He joined him 11 May 1815 commanded the 3rd and 4th Military Divisions 9 June 1815, commanded a corps of National Guards on the Moselle, arrested 22 November 1815 and shut up in l'Abbaye.

LH CH 11 December 1803, C 14 June 1804, GO 25 December 1805, GC 23 August 1814, Count of the Empire d.1808 and l.p. 9 March 1810.

General Belliard was Colonel-General of the Cuirassiers instead of Gouvion-Saint-Cyr, in 1812. (RR)

Colonel Sigismond de Berkheim, Colonel of the 1st Cuirassiers in 1809, and his brother Philippe. (RR)

BELLOQUET see **ROGET de BELLOQUET**

BELVAL (François, 1781-1813): born in Valenciennes (Nord) on 14 May 1781. Trooper in the Mestre-de-Camp-Général Regiment 1 December 1790, dismissed with the corps and placed in the 24th Cavalry of the so-called new levy the following day, 21 February 1791 which then became the 23rd Cavalry 4 June 1793.

He was dismissed with the corps 23 December 1802 and incorporated into the Grenadiers à Cheval of the Guard 3 January 1803, brigadier 20 February, maréchal des logis 14 September 1806, sub-lieutenant in the 13th Cuirassiers 23 April 1808, lieutenant 21 October 1808, supernumerary captain 13 May 1812, died in hospital in Jaca, Spain on 20 February 1813.

BENAY (Georges, 1775-?): born in Rothau (Vosges) on 3 June 1775. In the 3rd Hussars 4 March 1794, brigadier 9 June 1799, in the Grenadiers à Cheval of the Guard 23 April 1801, sub-lieutenant in the Line 1808, in the suite of the 3rd Cuirassiers 23 April 1808 and immediately detached to the 1st Provisional Heavy Cavalry in Spain which became the 13th Cuirassiers 21 October 1808.

He became lieutenant 18 September 1811, instated 21 October 1811, captain 5 March 1814, incorporated into the suite of the 9th Cuirassiers 9 August 1814, dismissed with the corps 25 November 1815 and left with his retirement pension 26 November 1815. LH CH 25 November 1807.

BENOIT (César, 1781-?): born in Nîmes (Gard) on 6 January 1781. In the 3rd Cuirassiers 154 January 1803, brigadier 1 June 1803.

He became maréchal des logis 21 May 1804, sub-lieutenant 14 May 1809, shot in the left leg and his horse killed under him at Essling 21 May 1809, lieutenant 11 March 1812, wounded at Fère-Champenoise 25 March 1814 and at Waterloo 18 June 1815, dismissed 25 November 1815. LH CH December 1813.

BERANGERER see **DUBOIS BERANGER**

BERBAIN (Nicolas, 1761-?): born in Thélod (Meurthe) on 25 January 1761. In the Reine-Cavalerie 20 April 1778, incorporated into the Chevau-Légers N°5 1779, which became the Quercy-Cavalry 30 March 1783, incorporated into the Languedoc Chasseurs à Cheval 10 May 1788 which became the 6th Chasseurs à Cheval 1 January 1791, left 30 March 1791, in the 24th Cavalry 16 June 1791, brigadier 18 July 1792.

He became maréchal des logis 1 April 1793, in the same regiment when it became the 23rd Cavalry 4 June 1793, maréchal des logis-chef 19 December 1793, adjutant NCO 26 August 1799, sub-lieutenant 7 June 1800.

He was dismissed with the corps 23 December 1802 and incorporated into the 6th Cuirassiers 11 January 1803, elected lieutenant 14 June 1805, wounded at Heilsberg 10 June 1807, captain 6 October 1808, retired 2 June 1809. LH CH.

BERCKHEIM (François Joseph Gérard de, 1782-?): born in Armentière (Nord) on 2 October 1792. In the 22nd Chasseurs à Cheval 13 October 1800, brigadier 5 January 1801.

He became maréchal des logis 6 June 1805, in the Grenadiers à Cheval of the Imperial Guard 28 October 1807, brigadier 13 November 1810, fourrier 15 February 1812, sub-lieutenant in the 2nd Cuirassiers 30 April 1812, lieutenant 27 September 1813, wounded and his horse killed under him, taken prisoner at Waterloo 18 June 1815, still held in England when the regiment was dismissed 10 December 1815. LH CH 4 September 1813.

BERCKHEIM (Philippe Gustave de, 1788-1812): brother of the colonel, born in Schoppenwihr (Haut-Rhin) on 1 March 1788. Volunteered for the 2nd Carabiniers 23 September 1802, brigadier 8 January 1803, maréchal des logis 26 March 1804, maréchal des logis-chef 30 October 1806, sub-lieutenant 8 May 1807.

He became lieutenant in the 1st Cuirassiers 16 May 1809, adjutant-major 19 May 1809, shot in the left thigh at Essling 22 May 1809, captain in the 2nd Carabiniers 8 August 1809, instated 24 September 1809, squadron commander 5 November 1811, killed at the Moskova 7 September 1812. LH CH 1 October 1807.

BERLAYMONT de BORMENVILLE (Henri Jules, 1790-1855): born in 1790. Pupil in the Prytanée of Saint-Cyr 1 August 1802, one of the Emperor's pages 15 November 1806, sub-lieutenant in the 1st Cuirassiers 15 August 1809.

He was wounded near Krasnoë 16 November 1812, prisoner in Russia 18 December 1812, married a countess and settled there, freed in 1814 but never returned to the regiment.

BERLIOZ (Henry Joseph, 1758-1840): born in Pont-de-Beauvoisin (Isère) on 12 July 1858. Cadet in the King of Sardinia's Bodyguards 18 October 1778, lieutenant 1 July 1789, returned to France 1 June 1793, lieutenant cavalry instructor in the Army of the Pyrenees 7 August 1793, deputy to the adjutants-generals 24 February 1794.

He was shot and wounded during the siege of Saint-Elme 1794, capitaine-adjoint in the suite of 18 June 1794, on foot in the 117th Half-Brigade 24 August 1795, aide de camp to General Frégeville 13 July 1796, squadron commander in the suite of the 2nd Hussars 30 July 1799, took up his appointment in the 5th Cavalry 2 January 1801 which became the 5th Cuirassiers 23 December 1802, major in the 7th Cuirassiers 29 October 1803, rejoined 23 December 1803, left waiting his retirement pay 1 January 1810, pensioned off 12 January 1810,. LH CH 25 March 1804.

BERMONT (Esprit François, 1770-?): born in 1770. In the Mestre-de-Camp de Cavalerie 6 October 1788 which became the 24th Cavalry 1 January 1791, dismissed with the corps 20 February 1791, reemployed in the 24th of the new levy 21 February 1791 took up his appointment 1 April 1791

He was brigadier 1 January 1792, maréchal des logis 1 April 1793, in the same when it became the 23rd Cavalry 4 June 1793, maréchal des logis-chef 2 July 1797, sub-lieutenant by seniority 20 April 1799, acting lieutenant 5 December 1800, confirmed 10 June 1801, dismissed with the corps 23 December 1802 and incorporated into the 6th Cuirassiers 11 January 1803, elected captain 14 June 1805, retired 2 June 1809. LH CH.

BERNARD (Antoine Claude, 1783-?): born in Châlons-sur-Saône (Saône-et-Loire) on 13 April 1783. Trooper in the 11th Regiment 5 November 1800 which became the 24 September 1803, brigadier 1 December 1806, maréchal des logis 3 April 1807, sub-lieutenant 6 November 1811, shot and wounded in the head at Winkovo 18 October 1812, lieutenant 3 September 1813.

He was wounded by a shell burst in the right arm at Lützen 3 May 1813 and by a lance to the right thigh 1 January 1814, in the King's Cuirassiers 1 May 1814, remained in Paris at the disposal of the Minister of War 20 January 1815, returned to the regiment which had become the 1st Cuirassiers 1 April 1815, two bullet wounds to his left hand and side and two sabre wounds on his right arm at Waterloo 18 June 1815, dismissed and retired 24 December 1815. LH CH 14 May 1813.

BERNARD (Florent Joseph, 1763-1825): born in Saint-Pol (Pas-de-Calais) on 15 May 1763. Trooper in the Royal-Etranger 17 November 1779, brigadier in the same regiment when it became the 7th Cavalry the same day 1 January 1791.

He was maréchal des logis 1 April 1792, sub-lieutenant 7 May 1793, sabre wound to the right hand near Cambrai 26 April 1794, lieutenant 27 April 1794, supernumerary 20 February 1796, took up his appointment 19 July 1798, lieutenant-adjutant-major 13 March 1802, in the same regiment when it became the 7th Cuirassiers 23 December 1802, on leave for six month's 22 November 1804, returned 3 February 1805, rank of captain 9 September 1803.

BERNARD LIANCOURT (? - ?): maréchal des logis in the 9th Cuirassiers, sub-lieutenant 30 October 1806, lieutenant 25 June 1807, retired 31 May 1810.

BERRET (Joseph Honoré, 1768-1832): born in Pignans (Var) on 26 October 1768. Sub-lieutenant in the 3rd Cavalry 15 September 1791, lieutenant 1 August 1793, captain 18 November 1794.

Acting squadron commander on the battlefield at la Trebbia 20 June 1799, confirmed 30 June 1799, in the 24th Cavalry 26 October 1800, dismissed with the corps 10 October 1801 and incorporated into the 8th Cuirassiers 11 February 1802, major in the 9th Cuirassiers 29 October 1809, sub-inspector of para-

des 17 February 1811, lost all his toes from frostbite in Russia 1812, took part in the 1813 and 1814 campaigns and retired 1 July 1814. LH CH 25 March 1804.

BERRUE (Augustin, 1785-?): born in Selles-sur-Cher (Loir-et-Cher) on 9 December 1785. Velite in the

BERCKHEIM (Sigismond Frédéric, baron de, 1775-1819): born in Ribeauville (Haut-Rhin) on 9 May 1775. Sub-lieutenant in the La Marck Regiment 12 May 1789, discharged 15 September 1791, lieutenant in the 44th Infantry 8 April 1795 and retroactively 15 September 1791, refused by the regiment, considered as having given up his job 1 November 1792, in the 1st Chasseurs à Cheval 11 October 1794, pupil at the Ecole Centrale des Travaux Publics 30 January 1795.

He became lieutenant in the 8th Chasseurs

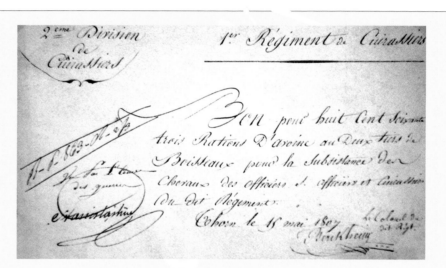

à Cheval 24 August 1795, aide de camp to General Duverger October 1795 then to General Férino 6 September 1798, deputy to the adjutant-General Plauzonne in the Army of the Rhine 19 June 1800, captain in the suite of the 2nd Carabiniers 9 July 1800, retroactively on 12 March 1800, accompanied his colonel (Caulaincourt) when he was Equerry to the Emperor 6 March 1805. He obtained the rank of squadron commander in the suite of the Dragoons 22 July 1807, brigadier-general 12 July 1809, commanded the 10th Brigade of Light Cavalry on the right wing of the Army of Italy 21 July 1809 then the 3rd Brigade (3rd and 12th Cuirassiers) of the 1st Heavy Cavalry Division 22 September 1809.

He, commanded a mobile column looking for deserters and draft dodgers in the 13th Military Division 18 March 1811 then the 1st Brigade of the 1st Heavy Cavalry Division April 1811, the 1st Brigade (4th and 7th

Cuirassiers, then the 4th Cuirassiers by itself) from the 3rd Cuirassiers Division 25 December 1811 and the 1st Brigade (1st, 3rd and 6th Cuirassiers) from the 1st Heavy Cavalry Division 1 March 1813, major-general 3 September 1813, commanded the 1st Division made up of the 4 regiments of Gardes d'Honneur 24 December 1813.

He commanded the mass levy in the Haut-Rhin 4 January 1814, then a division of Light Cavalry in the 2nd Cavalry Corps 19 February 1814, a new division in the 1st Cavalry Corps 4 March 1814, the division of grouping together the squadrons 13 March 1814, commanded the Haut-Rhin Department 24 May 1814.

He was at the head of the National Guards reserve division in the Army of the Rhine under Rapp 10 May 1815, non-active July 1815.

LH CH 25 March 1804, O 11 July 1807, C 14 May 1813, Baron of the Empire l.p. 9 May 1810.

Colonel Berkheim was made a Brigadier-General on 12 July 1809, following the Battle of Wagram. (RR)

Grenadiers à Cheval of the Guard 6 March 1806, sub-lieutenant in the 11th Cuirassiers 25 March 1809, resignation accepted 30 September 1811, left 21 October 1811.

BERSOLLE (Honoré Prosper, 1791,-?): born in Brest (Finistère) on 17 April 1791. Boarder at the Ecole Supérieure Militaire 3 April 1807.

He became sub-lieutenant in the 10th Cuirassiers 3 August 1809, lieutenant 8 July 1813 dismissed with the corps 25 December 1815. LH CH 2 November 1814.

BERTAUX (Jean Thomas, 1768-?): born in Tannerville (Manche) on 8 September 1768. In the 1st Carabiniers 8 April 1788, brigadier 9 January 1794.

He became maréchal des logis and maréchal des logis-chef on the same day 14 February 1797, elected sub-lieutenant 6 May 1800, lieutenant in the 8th Cuirassiers 25 August 1806, sabre wound to his right hand and his horse killed under him at Essling 21 May 1809, captain 3 June 1809, wounded at Vauchamps 14 February 1814 and Quatre-Bras 16 June 1815, dismissed with the corps 5 December 1815 and retired 11 December 1815. LH CH 1 October 1807.

BERTHE DEVILLERS (Jean Baptiste Auguste Ferdinand, 1797-?): born in Amiens (Somme) on 21 January 1797. In the 1st Gardes d'Honneur 9 July 1813, cavalry sub-lieutenant 31 July 1814, in the 7th Cuirassiers 16 August 1814 absent from 23 June 1815.

BERTHEMY (Pierre Augustin, chevalier, 1778-1855): born in Montier-en-Der (Haute-Marne) on 16 May 1778. In the 8th Cavalry Regiment 20 November 1798, honorary fourrier 30 March 1800.

He became honorary maréchal des logis 11 May 1800, acting sub-lieutenant and aide de camp to d'Hautpoul 14 August 1800, confirmed 8 February 1801, left service 24 September 1803, aide de camp to d'Hautpoul 3 March 1804, bullet wound in his left side at Austerlitz 2 December 1805, lieutenant 5 September 1806, wounded by a Biscayan shot to his left hip at Eylau 8 February 1807, captain ordnance officer to the Emperor on the death of d'Hautpoul 14 February 1807, squadron commander in the Line 10 July 1808, second major at the disposal of the Ministry of War 19 April 1812, aide de camp to Murat 10 May 1812, colonel 4 August 1812, wounded at the Moskova 7 September 1812.

He was maréchal de camp in Neapolitan service 14 December 1812, resigned 4 March 1815. LH C 5 December 1812, Chevalier of the Empire l.p. 14 April 1810.

BERTHENOT (Jean, 1761-1807): born in Toucy (Cote-d'Or) on 24 January 1761. Trooper in the Royal-Pologne 1 April 1794 which became the 5th Cavalry 1 January 1791, brigadier 1 April 1793, maréchal des logis 18 August 1798, maréchal des logis-chef 16 June 1799, adjutant NCO 23 October 1800.

He was in the same regiment when it became 5th Cuirassiers 23 December 1802, sub-lieutenant by seniority 21 February 1804, lieutenant 12 December 1806, killed at Eylau 8 February 1807. Holder of a Sabre of Honour 24 January 1803, LH CH by rights 24 September 1803.

BERTIN (Charles, 1754-1807): born in Ische (Vosges) on 4 November 1754. Soldier in the King's Regiment 7 September 1775, dismissed 7 September 1783, in the Roi-Cavalerie 23 January 1784.

He became brigadier in the 23rd Cavalry 1 January 1791, maréchal des logis 29 April 1792, sub-lieu-

tenant 1 April 1793, in the same regiment when it became the 22nd Cavalry 4 June 1793, lieutenant 18 August 1795, captain 11 May 1802, dismissed with the corps 21 December 1802 and incorporated into the 12th Cavalry 25 January 1803 which became the 12th Cuirassiers 24 September 1803, killed at Friedland 14 June 1807.

BERTRAND (Joseph, 1776-?): born in Gasse (Var) on 24 February 1776. In the 5th Var Battalion, brigadier 23 September 1804, sabre wound to the knee at Friedland 14 June 1807, maréchal des logis 7 October 1807. He became maréchal des logis-chef 14 May 1809, sub-lieutenant 12 August 1812, wounded by a shot to his nose at Waterloo 18 June 1815, dismissed with the regiment 25 November 1815.

BERVAL (André Louis Esprit de, 1789-?): born in Sotteville (Seine-Inférieure) on 30 August 1789. Volunteer in the 13th Cuirassiers 2 January 1811, instated the following day 3 January 1811, fourrier 16 March 1812.

He became maréchal des logis 1 May 1813, sub-lieutenant 27 August 1813, two sabre wounds to his right arm and his horse killed under him at the Col d'Orsal 13 September 1813, instated as sub-lieutenant 6 November 1813, incorporated into the 9th Cuirassiers 9 August 1814, dismissed with the corps and non-active 26 November 1815.

BERVILLER (Pierre, 1787-1815): born in Moyenvie in 1787. Velite in the Grenadiers à cheval of the Guard 3 March 1805, sub-lieutenant in the suite of the 2nd Cuirassiers 13 (15) July 1807. He was lieutenant 13 February 1812, in the 1st Cuirassiers 1 April 18714 having formed the King's Cuirassiers 1 July 1814, in the same regiment when it became the 1st Cuirassiers in March 1815, wounded, taken prisoner and disappeared at Waterloo.

BESNARD (?-1812): maréchal des logis-chef in the 12th Cuirassiers, sub-lieutenant 29 January 1808, lieutenant 9 August 1809.

He became captain 11 September 1812, wounded near Kaluga 24 October 1812 and died of his wounds 10 December 1812.

BESSIERES (Bertrand, baron, 1773-1854): brother of the maréchal, born in Prayssac (Lot) on 6 January 1773.

Engaged in the Berri-Cavalerie 15 August 1790 which became the 18th Cavalry 1 January 1791 then 17th Cavalry 4 June 1793, acting sub-lieutenant in the 22nd Chasseurs à Cheval 5 November 1793.

He rejoined March 1794, confirmed 19 January 1795, lieutenant 7 July 1795, captain in the guides of

ESTAGNES (Charles de, 1782-?) born in Asti (Marengo) on 24 June 1782. In the 3rd Cavalry 30 April 1801, brigadier 23 September 1801, in the same when it became the 3rd Cuirassiers 12 October 1802, maréchal des logis 11 November 1802.

He became sub-lieutenant 25 August 1806, lieutenant 2 March 1809, resignation accepted 24 February 1811

Maréchal des Logis in the 3rd Cuirassiers, Charles de Bestagne galvanised his neighbours in the row who were hesitating after a cannonball had removed two of their comrades. He was wounded thirteen times.

the Army of Italy commanded by his brother 4 June 1797, in the guides of the Army of Egypt 1798, squadron commander 1 August 1799, brigade commander of the 11th Chasseurs à Cheval 11 January 1800, shot and wounded in the head at Austerlitz 2 December 1805, brigadier-general 24 December 1805, commanded a brigade of Chasseurs à Cheval in the Army of Italy 17 June 1806, then the Cavalry Reserve 4 November 1806.

He commanded a provisional French brigade in the Western Pyrenees Observation Corps 23 December 1807, in the 5th Corps of the Army of Spain 7 September 1808, then in the 7th 20 October 1808, commanded a brigade of dragoons 7 December 1809, major-general 31 July 1811, turned the rank down and appointment cancelled 30 November 1811, beat a cavalry corps at Astorga, in the 1st Cuirassiers Division 5 December 1811, commanding the 1st Brigade 25 December 1811, then the 2nd Brigade 1 July 1812 . $He was wounded by grapeshot in the left shoulder at the Moskova 7 September 1812, commanded the 2nd Brigade of the 1st Division of the 1st Cavalry Corps 1 March 1813, sabre wound to his head at Leipzig 18 October 1813, available 13 January 1814, non-active 1 September 1814, commanded the Doubs Department then the Lot-et-Garonne 15 April 1815, at the disposal of the Minister of War to command a cavalry depot 3 June 1815, non-active 25 July 1815.

LH CH 11 December 1803, O 14 June 1804, C 28 November 1813, Baron of the Empire l.p. 16 December 1810.

BESSODES (Charles, 1781-?): born in Béthune (Pas-de-Calais) on 12 August 1781. In the 2nd Cavalry 19 June 1797, brigadier 21 May 1802, in the same regiment when it became the 2nd Cuirassiers 12 October 1802.

He became maréchal des logis 1 November 1806,

maréchal des logis-chef 1 August 1807, sub-lieutenant 9 August 1809, lieutenant in the 6th Cuirassiers 9 February 1813, left to join again 1 March 1813, dismissed 21 November 1815. LH CH 14 March 1806.

BETHMANN (Jacques Philippe, 1780-?): born in Bordeaux (Gironde) on 27 March 1780. In the Gendarmes d'Ordonnance 1 January 1807,

ETHUNE (François Joseph de, 1768-?): born in Bouchain (Nord) on 21 August 1768. Trooper in the Regiment des Cravates 19 February 1787 which became the 10th Cavalry 1 January 1791, brigadier 22 December 1791, maréchal des logis 20 July 1794, maréchal des logis-chef 16 April 1802, sub-lieutenant 8 June 1803, in the same regiment when it became the 10th Cuirassiers 24 September 1803, lieutenant 24 November 1806.

He became captain 25 May 1807, squadron commander 6 November 1811, commanded the regiment at the Moskova 7 September 1812, lance wound to the neck near Moscow 4 October 1812, major 28 September 1813, confirmed 24 September 1814, in the suite of the regiment 11 May 1815, non-active when dismissed 25 December 1815. LH CH 14 April 1807, O 2 November 1814.

During the fighting at Hoff on 6 February 1806 he received five bayonet wounds and had his horse killed under him after he had broken into the enemy's ranks at the head of the 1st Platoon of his regiment.

took on the job of brigadier, dismissed with the corps 23 October 1807 and put at the disposal of the Minister of War 24 November 1807, sub-lieutenant in the suite of the 12th Cuirassiers 18 February 1808.

He took up his appointment 16 May 1809, wounded at Wagram 6 July 1809 by a Biscayan shot to his left temple which caused deafness in his left ear, retired 31 May 1810.

BEUVERAND de LALOYERE (Nicolas Edouard Madeleine de, 1786-1813): brother of the following and Nansouty's nephew, born in Dijon (Côte d'Or) on 28 December 1786. Boarder in the Ecole Impériale Militaire in Fontainebleau instated 21 September 1805, fourrier 14 July 1806.

He became sub-lieutenant in the suite of the 5th Cuirassiers 23 September 1806, lieutenant in the 7th Cuirassiers 2 March 1809, remained a lieutenant in the 5th Cuirassiers by changing with Lieutenant Levillain 21 March 1809, lieutenant adjutant-major 16 May 1809, rank of captain 16 November 1810 went over to a company 6 November 1811, squadron commander aide de camp to General Nansouty 2 September 1813, killed at Leipzig October 1813. LH CH 1809.

BEUVERAND de LALOYERE (Pierre Joseph Armand Jean Baptiste Marie Catherine de, 1782-1857): older brother of the above and General Nansouty's nephew, born in Dijon (Côte d'Or) on 26 February 1782. Enrolled as a Chasseur in the 10th Regiment 6 November 1801, brigadier in the 11th Dragoons 20 June 1802, maréchal des logis 19 June 1803.

He became sub-lieutenant in the 12th Cavalry 29 August 1803 which became the 12th Cuirassiers 24 September 1803, lieutenant in the 6th Cuirassiers 5 September 1806, instated 1 October 1806, aide de camp to General Nansouty, his uncle, 24 January 1807, captain in the 2nd Carabiniers 14 May 1809, remained aide de camp 23 May 1809, squadron commander in the 2nd Cuirassiers 1 June 1811, rejoined October 1811, wounded at Lützen 2 May 1813, major in the 12th Cuirassiers 14 May 1813, commanded a regiment of heavy cavalry organised in Hamburg 1 October 1813.

He was adjutant-commandant 5 February 1814, chief of staff of the Cavalry of the Guard 1814, in the King's Musketeers, maréchal de camp 19 March 1815, non-active 1 October 1815. LH CH 14 March 1806, O 19 March 1815.

BEYLIE de DOUMET de SIBLAS (Louis César, 1769-?): born in Lorgues (Var) on 5 December 1769, sub-lieutenant in the 10th Cavalry 15 September 1791, lieutenant 15 September 1793 two sabre wounds to his head near Kreutznach December 1793, captain 6 May 1795, in the same regiment when it became the 10th Cuirassiers 24 September 1803, wounded by a bullet in the pelvis which penetrated his buttocks at Essling 21 may 1809, retired 25 April 1811, left 6 May 1811. LH CH 5 April 1807.

BEZENCOURT
see **CHIPAULT de BEZENCOURT**

BIARDE (Jean Baptiste, 1767-?): born in Raincourt (Haute-Saône) 1767. In the Royal-Cavalerie 30 September 1786 which became the 2nd Cavalry 1 January 1791, brigadier 12 July 1793, brigadier-fourrier 4 October 1793.

He became maréchal des logis-chef 21 May 1805, in the same regiment when it became the 2nd Cuirassiers 12 October 1802, sub-lieutenant 30 October 1806 wounded at Friedland 14 June 1807, retired 27 May 1809, left 1 June 1809, pensioned 2 June 1809.

BICAULT (Georges, 1772-?): born Ailli (Eure) on 10 November 1772. Grenadier in the 1st Eure Battalion 10 July 1791, in the 3rd Chasseurs à Cheval 1 August 1792, brigadier 20 May 1795, maréchal des logis 22 November 1796.

He became gendarme in the 5th Legion in Vendée 22 October 1798, brigadier 21 November 1798, maréchal des logis in the 5th Squadron of the Gendarmerie d'Espagne 19 January 1810, maréchal des logis-chef 15 February 1810, sub-lieutenant 21 January 1812, in the 1st Legion of the Gendarmerie à Cheval d'Espagne 'Burgos' 21 August 1812.

He was dismissed with the corps 27 February 1813 and placed as captain in the 10th Cuirassiers 28 February 1813, withdrawn when the regiment was dismissed 25 December 1815. LH CH 28 September 1813.

BICKER (Jean Bernard van, 1770-1812): born in Amsterdam (Zuydersee) on 2 April 1770. Captain in the 2nd Dutch Hussars 24 March 1807, lieutenant-colonel in the 2nd Dutch Cuirassiers 4 June 1808.

He became squadron commander in the same regiment when it was changed into the 14th French Cuirassiers 18 August 1810, killed in Russia 18 November 1812.

BIDAULT (Jean Victor, 1771-?): born in Hermaurupt (Marne) on 4 May 1771. In the 8th Cavalry 22 November 1792, brigadier 2 October 1797, fourrier 19 November 1798, maréchal des logis 17 March 1800, adjutant-NCO 11 May 1800, in the same regiment when it became the 8th Cuirassiers 10 October 1801.

He was sub-lieutenant 6 June 1802, lieutenant by governmental choice 8 July 1805, incorporated into the 3rd Provisional Heavy Cavalry with the rest of his company in Spain 1808, captain 12 April 1808, returned to the 8th Cuirassiers beginning of 1811, retired 1 July 1813.

BIDON (François Marie Pierre Théophile, 1790-?): born in Angers (Maine-et-Loire) on 22 May 1790. In the Navy 23 September 1805, cadet 2nd Class 1 June 1807, shell burst wound to his left foot and a bayonet wound in the right arm during the siege of Cadiz.

He became sub-lieutenant in the 96th Infantry 11

June 1810, in the 9th Cuirassiers 22 February 1813, lieutenant 27 July 1813, non-active 1814, put in the 7th Cuirassiers 9 June 1815, rejoined 30 June 1815, retired to his home on half-pay 24 August 1815.

BIENAIME (André Nicolas, 1759-?): born in Metz (Moselle) on 25 May 1759. Grenadier in the Royal Regiment 6 March 1778, in the Carabiniers 7 June 1783, in the same regiment when it formed the 2nd Carabiniers 1 January 1791, wounded in the left hand at Kaiserslauten 30 November 1793, brigadier 28 August 1794.

He became maréchal des logis 5 June 1800, sub-lieutenant in the 13th Cuirassiers 27 May 1808, lieutenant 13 February 1809, retired 22 December 1811.

BIGARNE (François, 1771-1829): born in Montbard (Côte d'Or) on 25 November 1771. In the Royal-Dragons 16 April 1787, in the national cavalry 24 July 1789 which formed the 29th Paris Gendarmerie Division 28 August 1791, brigadier 28 November 1792.

He became maréchal des logis 8 April 1793, adjutant NCO 1 January 1794, quartermaster treasurer December 1794, lieutenant 15 December 1795, captain in the Escaut Gendarmerie 20 August 1797, in the Deux-Nèthes Gendarmerie company 20 September 1801, senior deputy lieutenant-colonel in the Palace of the King of Holland 1 October 1806 squadron commander chief of staff of the captain-general of the King's Guards and colonel-general of the Dutch Gendarmerie 16 December 1806.

He was regimental colonel of the Dutch Gendarmerie Regiment 25 August 1808, on the staff of the Dutch Army 6 October 1809, returned to French service after Holland was united with France 9 July 1810, confirmed Major 11 December 1810, cavalry major in the Piedmont under Arrighi 23 December 1810, commanded a marching regiment of cavalry in Spain, took up his post in the 13th Dragoons 25 November 1811, colonel in the 13th Cuirassiers 28 June 18113, in the suite of the 9th Cuirassiers 9 August 1814, colonel of the regiment 28 September 1814.

He was commissioned 1 October 1814, on one month's leave with pay 26 December 1814, several sabre wounds to the head and right arm at Waterloo 18 June 1815, left and non-active at the disposal of the Government 26 November 1815. LH CH 12 March 1814, O 24 August 1814.

BIGNAULT (Louis, 1783-?): born in Claville (Eure) on 22 September 1783. In the 6th Cuirassiers 11 February 1804, brigadier 2 January 1808, maréchal des logis 5 October 1808.

He was wounded in the left wrist at Essling 21 May 1809, maréchal des logis-chef 16 September 1809, sub-lieutenant 29 September 1812, in the Escadron Sacré during the retreat from Russia 1812, wounded at Waterloo 18 June 1815, dismissed 21 November 1815. LH CH 5 September 1813.

BIGNON (Victor, 1792-?): born in Le Mans (Sarthe) on 28 May 1792. Pupil at the Saint-Germain Cuirassiers 30 January 1813, sixth months' leave 1 March 1815 and struck off the list as he did not reappear 1815. LH CH 5 September 1813.

LANCARD (Amable Guy, Baron, 1774-1853): brother of a Constituent and younger brother of the following, born in Loriol (Drôme) on 18 August 1774. Sub-lieutenant in the 11th Cavalry 15 September 1791.

He became lieutenant 5 October 1793, grapeshot wound to his right flank and broken right arm when he recaptured 2 artillery pieces at the head of 30 troopers at Marino near Rome 10 August 1799, captain 1800, in the Grenadiers à Cheval of the Guard 31 January 1804, squadron commander 5 September 1805, colonel of the 2nd Carabiniers 23 January 1807, instated 31 January 1807, shot wound at the Moskova 7 September 1812, wounded in the face and arm by a shot at Winkovo 18 October 1812, brigadier-general 28 September 1813, commanded the 1st Brigade (Carabiniers and 1st Cuirassiers) of the 2nd Division in the 2nd Cavalry Corps 2 December 1813, left for the remount depot at Versailles December 1813, returned to his brigade 12 February 1814, non-active 1 September 1814. He commanded a cavalry brigade 12 March 1815, then that of the Carabiniers in the Army of the Moselle 22 April 1815, wounded at Waterloo 18 June 1815, non-active 1 October 1815. Holder of the Sabre of Honour 25 December 1802, LH CH by rights 24 September 1803, O 14 June 1804, Baron of the Empire l.p. 17 May 1810.

At Homburg on 24 April 1796, the Wurmser Austrian Hussars got hold of the standards of his regiment, the 11th Cavalry. Putting himself at the head of fifteen horsemen, Second-Lieutenant Amable Blancard charged the enemy and recaptured the precious trophies.

BILLAUDEL (Claude Honoré, 1775-1814): born in Brignicourt-sur-Saux (Marne) on 10 June 1775. In the 11th Hussars 23 October 1793, brigadier 30 March 1798.

He became maréchal des logis 29 April 1798, in the horse guides of General in Chief Brune in the Army of Italy 1 November 1798 then in the Army of the West, adjutant NCO 21 January 1801, acting sub-lieutenant in the Hussar Guards of the General in Chief Murat 15 February 1802, confirmed 6 September 1802, in the Guard of the Governor of Paris – Murat - after he took up his appointment 1 January 1804.

He was dismissed with the corps 11 January 1804 and incorporated into the 13th Dragoons 17 May 1804, lieutenant 27 December 1805, second-lieutenant in the Grenadiers à Cheval of the Imperial Guard 1 May 1806, first-lieutenant 25 June 1809, captain 6 December 1811, squadron commander in the Line 9 February 1813, in the 5th Cuirassiers 1813, killed at Château-Thierry 14 March 1814. LH CH 14 March 1806.

BINANVILLE see **ABOS de BINANVILLE**

BIOT (François Antoine, 1774-after 1823): born in Strasbourg (Bas-Rhin) on 13 January 1774. In the 5th Artillery 26 February 1791, sub-lieutenant quartermaster in the Gendarmerie, lieutenant in the 2nd Cuirassiers 14 November 1807, under arrest for more than a year for fraudulent conduct and debauchery while in command of 150 army conscripts.

He changed regiment and went over to the 4th Cuirassiers 13 December 1808, instated 1 April 1809, wounded at Essling May 1809 and Wagram 6 July 1809, retired with pension 23 March 1810.

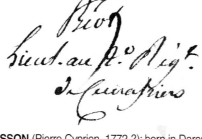

BISSON (Pierre Cyprien, 1772-?): born in Darental (Seine-Inférieure) on 17 October 1772. In the Royal-Bourgogne-Cavalerie 17 September 1789 which became the 17th Cavalry 1 January 1791 then 16th Cavalry 4 June 1793, in the Grenadiers à cheval of the Garde du Directoire Executif 20 April 1797.

He became brigadier when they formed up into the Grenadiers à cheval of the Consular Guard 3 January 1800, maréchal des logis 12 March 1801, sub-lieutenant in the 8th Cuirassiers 30 August 1805, lieutenant 27 April 1807, bayonet wound to the right foot at Essling 22 May 1809, captain 12 September 1809, lance wound to his neck at Winkovo 18 October 1812, Quatre-Bras 16 June 1815, dismissed with the corps 5 December 1815 and retired 11 December 1815. LH CH 14 March 1806.

BIZOT (Jean Auguste, 1789-?): born in Pont-Allier (Côte d'Or) on 5 July 1789. Velite in the Grenadiers à Cheval of the Guard 1 January 1808, sub-lieutenant in the 2nd Cuirassiers 2 May 1813, dismissed on half-pay 10 December 1815.

BLAISE (Joseph Dorothée, 1778-?): elder brother of the following, born in Lunéville (Meurthe) on 4 March 1778. In the 9th Cavalry 8 September 1798, fourrier 20 February 1802, in the same regiment when it became the 9th Cuirassiers 24 September 1803, maréchal des logis 12 December 1805.

He became maréchal des logis-chef 16 December 1805, sub-lieutenant 2 December 1806, lieutenant quartermaster 16 May 1808, captain quartermaster 30 April 1812, non-active at the disposal of the government 26 November 1815. LH CH 12 May 1812.

BLAISE (Nicolas, 1783-?): brother of the above, born in Lunéville (Meurthe) on 31 December 1783. In the 24th of the Line 5 September 1802, corporal 8 December 1805.

He became brigadier in the 9th Cuirassiers 9 may 1809, maréchal des logis 14 May 1809, Gendarmerie brigadier 14 May 1811, sub-lieutenant in the 9th

Cuirassiers 21 April 1813, taken prisoner 25 March 1814, returned 28 May 1814, non-active when the regiment was dismissed 26 November 1815. LH CH 19 March 1815.

BLAMONT (François, 1775-?): born in Petit-Mont (Meurthe) in 1775. In the 11th Cavalry 7 September 1795, sabre wound to the head 6 January 1799, in the same regiment when it became the 11th Cuirassiers 24 September 1803.

He became brigadier in the Berg Chevau-Légers 25 August 1807, maréchal des logis in the 1st Berg Chevau-Légers Lancers 12 November 1807, sub-lieutenant 15 February 1808, lieutenant 17 December 1811, captain 11 March 1813, in the 6th Cuirassiers 4 August 1814, retired 21 November 1815. LH CH 9 January 1813.

BLANC (Jules, 1779-?): born in Autrevaux (Hautes-Alpes) on 19 December 1779.

In the 8th Cavalry 14 July 1799 which became the 8th Cuirassiers 10 October, brigadier-fourrier 25 October 1801, maréchal des logis 1 October 1806, sub-lieutenant 9 August 1809, sabre wound to the left hand at Essling 21 May 1809, two sabre wounds to his head and right arm at the Moskova 7 September 1812, lieutenant 6 November 1813.

He became second-lieutenant (Old Guard) in the Chasseurs à Cheval of the Guard 21 December 1813, wounded at Laon 11 March 1814, in the suite of the Royal Corps of Chasseurs à Cheval de France 30 July 1814 which became the Chasseurs à Cheval of the Guard (Old Guard) 8 April 1815, dismissed and put on half-pay 21 October 1815. LH CH 30 April 1815.

BLANCARD (Jean Charles Marie Guy, 1773-1812): older brother of the general, born in Loriol (Drôme) on 28 June 1773. Sub-lieutenant in the 11th Cavalry 15 September 1791, lieutenant 1 September 1792 wounded when the lines were recaptured at Wissembourg 2 December 1793, captain 1797.

He was, in the same regiment when it became the 11th Cuirassiers 24 September 1803, acting squadron commander keeping command of his company 29 July 1806, shot in the right hand at Eylau 8 February 1807, confirmed squadron commander 25 May 1807, instated 10 November 1807, reconfirmed and appointed squadron commander by mistake 10 November 1808, shot in the left ear at Essling 21 May 1809, second-major at the disposal of the Minister of War 6 November 1811, left to be employed in the Grande Armée 1 December 1811, sent to the cavalry depot at Posen August 1812, disappeared in Russia. LH CH 5 November 1804.

BLANCHARD (Jean François Joseph, 1791-1812): born in Sèvres (Seine-et-Oise) on 15 October 1791. In the 5th Cuirassiers 3 April 1803, brigadier 1 January 1806, maréchal des logis 10 October 1806.

He became sub-lieutenant 15 May 1809, prisoner 4 December 1812 and disappeared. LH CH 1 October 1807.

BLANCHART (Etienne Jean Louis, 1767-1809): born in Troyes (Aube) on 7 March 1767. Volunteer in the Navy 14 December 1781, left 14 July 1783 in the Artois-Dragons 4 October 1784, left 1 September 1786, in the Swiss Guards 20 September 1786, officer in the National Guard 11 September 1790.

He became sub-lieutenant in the 22nd Cavalry 24 February 1793 which became the 21st Cavalry 4 June 1793, lieutenant 1 July 1793, director of the Strasbourg Military Hospital requisitioned by the Committee of Public Safety 21 November 1794, in the hospital at Landau 22 November 1795, unemployed when the hospital was closed 20 February 1803.

He was quartermaster treasurer at the Training School for Mounted Troops 26 February 1803, aide de camp to General Lahoussaye 8 March 1804, captain in the 2nd Cuirassiers 30 October 1806, squadron commander in the 3rd Cuirassiers 14 May 1809, killed at Essling 21 May 1809. LH CH 17 January 1805.

Senior officer's cuirass breastplate, probably a 1812 type. (RR)

BLANCHET (Toussaint, 1774-?): born in Meaux (Seine-et-Marne) on 1 November 1774. In the 5th Dragoons 14 September 1791, shot in the right leg in Luxemburg 12 June 1795, sabre wound to his right arm at Primolano 7 September 1796, brigadier 27 March 1798, in the Grenadiers à Cheval of the Guard 15 February 1800, brigadier 22 December 1801, wounded by a Biscayan shot in the back at Eylau 8 February 1807.

He became, maréchal des logis 22 December 1810, lieutenant in the 1st Cuirassiers 23 October 1811, adjutant-major 20 March 1813, captain adjutant-major 30 September 1814, retroactively to 20 September 1814, remained in Paris at the disposal of the Minister of War 20 January 1815.

He, returned to the regiment 1 April 1815, wounded at Waterloo 18 June 1815, retired 24 December 1815, holder of a Rifle of Honour 20 July 1800, LH CH 14 June 1804.

BLANDIN (Jacques, 1775-1807): born in Mehun-sur-Loire (Loiret) on 13 April 1775. In the 6th Cavalry 9 November 1798, fourrier 12 June 1800, maréchal des logis 5 July 1802, in the same regiment when it became the 6th Cuirassiers 23 December 1802.

He was maréchal des logis-chef 3 February 1803, adjutant NCO 14 June 1805, elected sub-lieutenant 22 March 1807, shot through the body at Heilsberg 10 June 1807 and died of his wounds at Neudorff 12 June 1807.

BLONDELLE (Jacques François, 1786-?): born in Paris (Seine) on 14 July 1786. Volunteered for the 3rd Cuirassiers 6 October 1803, brigadier 14 April 1807, fourrier 23 April 1809, maréchal des logis-chef 5 June 1809.

He was wounded by a shell burst to his head at Wagram 6 July 1806, sub-lieutenant 11 March 1812, wounded in the thigh by a cannonball at Moscow, amputated 4 October 1812, remained in Moscow and taken prisoner in October 1812 returned and retired with pay 11 November 1814.

BOCHARD (Charles, 1777-?): born in Bourg (Ain) on 18 December 1777. In the 10th Ain Battalion 22 October 1793, sergeant 24 December 1794, shot in the left arm 24 September 1795, in the Guides à Cheval under General Joubert 3 October 1798,.

He became brigadier 21 May 1799, in the Gendarmerie 20 June 1802, in the 1st Legion of the Spanish Gendarmerie à Cheval 1 April 1812.

He was sub-lieutenant in the 6th Cuirassiers 1 March 1813, retired 21 November 1815.

BOILLY (Jacques, 1774-?): born in Dommartin (Somme) on 25 July 1774. In the 25th Cavalry 26 January 1794, in the Grenadiers à Cheval of the Guard 17 March 1800, brigadier 30 April 1804, maréchal des logis 6 April 1811.

He became lieutenant in the 29th Chasseurs à cheval but went over to the 14th Cuirassiers 28 November 1813, confirmed 5 February 1814, dismissed with the corps and incorporated into the 12th Cuirassiers 13 July 1814, dismissed with the corps 10 December 1815. LH CH 1 May 1808.

BOISPINEL (Charles René Philippe, 1777-1812): born in Falaise (Calvados) on 29 September 1777. In the 2nd Carabiniers 15 February 1803, brigadier 25 December 1801, brigadier-fourrier 2 December 1803, in the 2nd Cuirassiers 9 January 1805.

He became maréchal des logis 17 July 1805, sub-lieutenant 30 October 1806, lieutenant 3 April 1807, captain 12 February 1812, wounded at the Moskova 7 September 1812, died 7 December 1812. LH CH 1 October 1807.

BOISSEAU (Claude, 1766-1821): born in Semur (Côte d'Or) on 5 November 1766. Trooper in the Royal-Etranger 20 October 1784 which became the 7th Cavalry 1 January 1791, shot in the right foot at La-Croix-au-Bois 14 September 1792.

He became brigadier-fourrier 7 May 1793, captured an artillery piece harnessed to four horses at Bamberg 6 September 1793, sabre wound to his right hand after putting four Dutch troopers out of action, took a horse at Tournai 10 May 1794, captured an ammunition caisson harnessed to four horses at Tourcoing 18 May 1794, maréchal des logis 4 October 1794, adjutant NCO 19 July 1799, in the same regiment when it became the 7th Cuirassiers 23 December 1802.

He was elected sub-lieutenant 25 August 1805, lieutenant 11 March 1807, acting captain 3 June 1809, sabre wound to his left hand at Wagram 6 July 1809, retired with pay 29 September 1811, left the war squadrons 8 October 1811. LH CH 14 June 1804.

BON (Joseph, 1793-?): born in Romans (Drôme) on 22 March 1793. Pupil at the Saint-Germain school 1 September 1811.

He became sub-lieutenant in the 5th Cuirassiers 5 January 1813, in the Cuirassiers du Roi 4 May 1814, standard-bearer 11 September 1814, in the same regiment when it became the 1st Cuirassiers April 1815, wounded at Waterloo 18 June 1815, dismissed and retirement planned 24 December 1815. LH CH 3 October 1814.

BONAFOUX (Pierre, 1786-1853): Murat's nephew, born in Montgesty (Lot) on 1 January 1786. In the Guides of the Army of Italy's General-in-Chief 16 November 1802.

He became maréchal des logis 22 July 1803, sub-lieutenant in the 10th Chasseurs à Cheval 25 January 1805, lieutenant aide de camp to Murat 21 May 1807, first lieutenant in the Grenadiers à cheval of the Imperial Guard 8 July 1807, in the 2nd Cuirassiers 1 June 1809.

He was captain in the 1st Cuirassiers 9 August 1809, aide de camp to Junot 23 January 1810, in the 7th Hussars 10 December 1811, in the 11th Hussars 20 May 1812, deputy at the general headquarters of the Grande Armée 18 June 1812, squadron commander 4 August 1812.

He was wounded at the Moskova 7 September 1812, colonel 22 October 1812, in the cavalry reserve in Saxony July 1813, in the service of Naples as aide to camp to the King, Murat, 3 October 1813, returned to France 1815, non-active 11 September 1813. LH CH 3 July 1807, O 15 October 1813.

BONARDI de SAINT SULPICE (Raymond Gaspard de, comte, 1761-1835): born in Paris (Seine) on 23 October 1761. Sub-lieutenant in Monsieur's Dragons 23 September 1777, captain 12 July 1781, in the same regiment when it became the 13th Dragoons 1 January 1791, lieutenant-colonel of the 2nd Dragoons 12 July 1792, colonel of the 12th Dragoons 26 October 1792.

He was suspended for being an aristocrat 3 September 1793, reinstated 8 May 1795, adjutant-general commanding a brigade 21 June 1795, in the Army of Italy 1 July 1795, resigned 27 August 1795, brigade commander in the 5th Chasseurs à Cheval 30 March 1797, brigade commander of the 19th Cavalry 5 may 1799, brigadier-general 24 March 1803, non-active 2 April 1803, available 26 May 1803, commanded the mounted troops in the Bayonne camp 8 August 1803, Ecuyer Cavalcadour of the Empress 20 November 1804, allowed to return to the camp at Brest 4 April 1805.

He commanded the 1st Brigade (3rd and 5th Cuirassiers) of the 2nd Cuirassier Division 1 September 1805, called back to Paris to continue his service as Ecuyer Cavalcadour 5 February

1806, commanded the 2nd Brigade (10th and 11th Cuirassiers) of the 2nd Heavy Cavalry Brigade of the Grande Armée 20 September 1806, commanded the 1st Brigade 1st and 5th Cuirassiers in the same division 18 October 1806, wrist wound at Eylau 8 February 1807, commanded the 2nd Division of Cuirassiers after d'Hautpoul was wounded 9 February 1807.

He became major-general 14 February 1807, in the Army of the Rhine 12 October 1808, in the reserve of the Army of Germany's cavalry 30 March 1809, colonel commanding the Dragoons of the Imperial Guard 12 July 1809, commanded a mobile column ordered to track down deserters and draft dodgers in the 1st, 2nd, 4th and 5th Military Divisions 18 march 1811, commanded the 2nd Cuirassier Division in the 2nd Cavalry Reserve Corps 10 January 1812.

He commanded the Dragoons of the Guard in Russia 25 March 1812, recalled to France 11 January 1813, governor of the palace at Fontainebleau 2 March 1813, colonel of the 4th Regiment of Gardes d'Honneur organised at Lyon 8 April 1813, served in Saxony then at Lyon under Augereau March 1814, commanded the 22nd Military Division may 1815, replaced 26 May 1815, retired 18 October 1815. LH CH 11 December 1803, C 14 June 1804, GO 23 August 1814, Count of the Empire l.p. 6 June 1808.

BONIFACE (Joseph, 1758-?): born in Saint-Côme (Aveyron) on 2 January 1758. In the Royal-Navarre-Cavalerie 15 December 1777, brigadier 5 October 1784, maréchal des logis 1 April 1788, in the same regiment when it became the 22nd Cavalry 1 January 1791.

He was maréchal des logis-chef 20 June 1792, sub-lieutenant 1 April 1793, in the same regiment when it became the 21st Cavalry 4 June 1793, lieutenant 1 July 1793, sabre wound to the left arm at Bornheim 22 July 1793, incorporated into the 2nd Carabiniers 10 February 1803, in the 7th Cuirassiers 8 June 1803, rejoined 9 July 1803, captain by seniority 12 December 1804, left with his pension 26 December 1808. LH CH 5 November 1804.

*Fragment from "**Before the charge, 1805**" – Oil on canvas by Meissonier. (RMN)*

BONNAIR (Auguste Joseph, ?-1808): Born in Cambrai (Nord). One of the Emperor's pages, sub-lieutenant in the 1st Cuirassiers 23 February 1808, in the 1st Provisional Heavy Cavalry in Spain December 1807, killed at Logrono 1 September 1808.

BONNAIRE (Léopold, 1786-1815): born in Charmes (Vosges) on 14 November 1786. In the 9th Cuirassiers 11 July 1805, fourrier 1 November 1806.

He became maréchal des logis-chef 14 May 1809, sub-lieutenant 1 August 1812, shot in the right thigh at Leipzig 16 October 1813, in the 11th Cuirassiers 1 September 1814, wounded at Waterloo 18 June 1815 and died of his wounds at Limoges Hospital 25 August 1815. LH CH 14 May 1813.

BONNECARRERE (Jean Pierre Alexis, 1768-?): born in Muret (Haute-Garonne) on 16 October 1768. In the Turenne Regiment 5 April 1785, left 14 August 1787, sub-lieutenant in the 28th Infantry 12 January 1792, lieutenant 18 July 1792.

He was shot in the right knee at Laperoza 17 April 1793, two bayonet wounds in the chest during the siege of Toulon November 1793, incorporated into the 55th Half-Brigade of the Line, captain 25 April 1795, aide de camp to General Menou 6 May 1798, squadron commander 11 January 1800, retroactively in the suite of the 7th Cavalry 20 January 1802, returned to the regiment 11 June 1802, on convalescence leave for two months 4 August 1802.

He was in the same when it became the 7th Cuirassiers 23 December 1802, took up his post in the 12th Cuirassiers 21 February 1804, commandant d'armes 4th Class 12 December 1806. LH CH.

BONNEFIN (Daniel, 1792-?): born in Amiens (Somme) on 7 August 1792. Boarder at Saint-Cyr 14 February 1811, then at Saint-Germain school 9 September 1811.

He became sub-lieutenant in the 4th Cuirassiers 30 January 1813, in the 1st Cuirassiers 30 April 1814 which then became Cuirassiers du Roi 1 July 1814, seconded to the school at Saumur 1815, dismissed and put on the active list 24 December 1815.

BONNEFOY (Claude, 1770-?): born in Villefranche (Rhône) on 2 march 1770. In the Picardy Chasseurs à Cheval which became the 7th Chasseurs à Cheval 1 January 1791, brigadier 11 September 1792.

He became maréchal des logis-chef 15 August 1793, sub-lieutenant 2 October 1794, in the Légion des Francs 28 June 1796, lieutenant 22 September 1796, captain 8 July 1797, incorporated into Augereau's Guides 22 October 1797, incorporated into the suite of the 7th Hussars 29 July 1798, discharged 27 August 1800, left 23 October 1800, captain in the 7th Cuirassiers 12 December 1806, rejoined 12 January 1807, at the head of 50 cuirassiers recaptured a convoy, two artillery pieces and a howitzer, taking 60 prisoners near Gironne 24 September 1810, on retirement pay 9 September 1811, left 15 November 1811.

BONNET aka **VINET** (Antoine Joseph, 1771-1809): born in Myon (Doubs) on 25 December 1771. Trooper

BOUDAILLE (Jean Antoine, 1757-1807): born in Sainte-Ménéhould (Marne) on 6 April 1757. In the Royal-Cavalerie 10 February 1779 which became the 2nd Cavalry 1 January 1791, brigadier-fourrier 21 March 1791, maréchal des logis 27 December 1792, maréchal des logis-chef 6 January 1793, adjutant 1 April 1793, sub-lieutenant 25 June 1793, saved Colonel Radal who had been left for dead at Heidenheim 11 August 1796.

He became lieutenant 19 June 1799, adjutant-major 13 March 1802, confirmed 22 March 1802, in the same regiment when it became the 2nd Cuirassiers 12 October 1802, rank of captain 9 September 1803, wounded at Austerlitz 2 December 1805, left while waiting for his retirement 26 October 1806, retired 30 October 1806, died at Sainte-Ménéhould end 1807. LH CH 14 June 1804.

*Heindeheim, 11 August 1797, Sous-Lieutenant Jean Boudaille saved Colonel Radal's life; he had been left for dead. With 12 Tirailleurs, he also charged 25 Prussian Hussars escorting the teams of French émigrés, killed one himself, got the remaining 24 to surrender and brought them back to head*quarters with the teams.

in the Royal-Roussillon 28 February 1789 which became the 11th Cavalry 1 January 1791, brigadier 3 December 1793,.

He became maréchal des logis 14 July 1794, maréchal des logis-chef 27 August 1794, adjutant 1 September 1802, in the same regiment when it became the 11th Cuirassiers 24 September 1803, sub-lieutenant by seniority 24 October 1804, lieutenant wounded at Essling 21 May 1809 and died of his wounds 31 May 1809.

BONNOT (Claude, 1765-?): born in Roanne (Loire) on 31 July 1765. Trooper in the Royal-Cravates 20 June 1785 which became the 10th Cavalry 1 January 1791, brigadier 21 March 1791, maréchal des logis 10 August 1792, maréchal des logis-chef 15 September 1793, sub-lieutenant 11 August 1794.

He became lieutenant 21 April 1797, two sabre wounds to his head and his horse killed under him near Erbach 16 May 1800, in the same regiment when it became the 10th Cuirassiers 24 September 1804, captain 8 October 1806, two sabre wounds on his right leg and his horse killed under him at Hoff 6 February 1807, retired 16 May 1809. LH CH 5 November 1804.

BONTEMPS (Louis, 1775-?): born in Berville (Seine-et-Oise) on 24 December 1775. In the 22nd Cavalry 1 December 1793, sabre wound to his right hand at Fleurus 26 June 1794, brigadier 16 January 1799.

He became maréchal des logis 5 November 1800, lance wound on his right thigh in the Tyrol 1801, incorporated into the 15th Cavalry 24 January 1803 which became the 24th Dragoons 24 September 1803, dra-

goon in the Dragoons of the Paris Guard 23 July 1806, brigadier 13 July 1807, maréchal des logis 22 October 1808, lieutenant in the 11th Cuirassiers 8 February 1812, in the 2nd Chevau-Légers Lancers of the Guard 18 March 1813, in the 4th lancers 10 June 1814, retired 28 July 1814.

HE was captain in the 11th Cuirassiers 25 April 1815, wounded at Waterloo 18 June 1815, returned home 25 August 1815.

BONVALET (François, 1773-?): born in Saint-Gand (Haute-Saône) on 22 June 1773. In the 1st Cavalry 21 March 1794, brigadier 26 October 1798, fourrier 20 January 1799, wounded by a shot in his right leg at La Trebbia 8 June 1799, maréchal des logis 11 April 1800.

He became maréchal des logis-chef 16 April 1800, took five prisoners at Sainte-Maxime near Verona 2 January 1801, sub-lieutenant in the 5th Cavalry 19 September 1801 which became the 5th Cuirassiers 23 December 1802, lieutenant 1 March 1804, sabre wound to his head and bayonet wound in the lower abdomen at Hoff 6 February 1807, captain 25 May 1807, retired 5 August 1813 with pay 14 August 1813. Holder of a Rifle of Honour 14 June 1801, commissioned 30 May 1803, LH CH by rights 24 September 1803.

BORDENAVE (Jean, 1771-1832): born in Pau (Basses-Pyrénées) on 2 January 1771. Brigadier-fourrier in the 12th Hussars 20 April 1794, maréchal des logis 22 April 1794, maréchal des logis-chef 25 January 1796.

He became adjutant NCO 18 March 1797, sub-lieutenant 31 July 1798, prisoner on the ship, le Hoche, during the Irish Expedition 12 October 1798, dischar-

The order appointing Captain Duchatelet to the rank of aide de camp to General Bordessoulle. (Private Collection)

ged 27 January 1799, returned to France on parole 20 March 1799, sub-lieutenant in the suite of the 2nd Cuirassiers 7 February 1807, rejoined 25 April 1807.

He was, confirmed 30 June 1807, retroactively 31 August 1806, retired 18 September 1807, left 1 October 1807.

BORDES DUCHATELET (Jean Louis François de, 1786-1850): born in Oyonnax (Ain) on 21 December 1786. In the 11th Cuirassiers 23 August 1805, brigadier 18 July 1806, maréchal des logis 1 December 1806, sub-lieutenant 16 May 1809, wounded at Essling 21 May 1809, lieutenant 14 May 1813.

He became deputy captain on the staff of the 1st Cuirassier Division 19 July 1813, aide de camp to General Bordessoulle 22 February 1814, commissioned 9 May 1814, unemployed because he did not leave France with his general 20 March 1815, aide de camp to the same 9 July 1815. LH CH 16 June 1809.

BORDESSOULLE see **TARDIF de POMMEROUX de BORDESSOULLE**

BORE VERRIER (Louis Pierre, 1784-?): born in Paris (Seine) on 5 April 1784. In the 3rd Cuirassiers 3 March 1803, brigadier 6 August 1803, maréchal des logis 24 November 1803, maréchal des logis-chef 7 March 1804, sub-lieutenant 25 June 1807.

He became lieutenant in the 13th Cuirassiers 20 September 1809, adjutant-major 7 August 1810, rank of captain 7 February 1812, first lieutenant in the grenadiers à Cheval of the Guard 9 February 1813, wounded at Altenburg 28 September 1813, in the suite of the Royal Corps of Cuirassiers of France 19 November 1814, first lieutenant adjutant-major in the same when they became the Grenadiers à cheval of the Imperial Guard 14 April 1815. LH CH 1 October 1807.

BOREL (Pierre Aimé, 1748-1824): born in Caen (Calvados) on 12 November 1748. In the Lyonnais-Infanterie 10 September 1766, left 6 March 1772, in the La Rochefoucauld-Dragons 28 March 1773, in the Chasseurs à cheval N°5 20 July 1779, brigadier 7 January 1780, in the same regiment when it became the Gévaudan Chasseurs 8 August 1784, maréchal des logis 17 October 1784.

He was in the same regiment when it became the Normandy Chasseurs à Cheval 17 March 1788, left 19 July 1789, in the Pont-l'Evêque National Guard 3 September 1789, sub-lieutenant in the 1st Orne Battalion 14 September 1791, adjutant-major in the 2nd Eure Battalion 22 October 1791, in the 11th Dragoons 3 June 1792, deputy to the adjutant-generals 27 August 1793.

He became squadron commander in the 8th Dragoons 24 July 1794, discharged 21 December 1795, employed in levying horses 25 March 1796, on the war council of the 17th Military Division, then deputy on the headquarters staff of the 2nd Reserve Army 16 March 1800, commanded the Arona stronghold in Italy.

He became squadron commander in the 6th Cavalry 13 January 1802 which became the 6th Cuirassiers 23 December 1802, wounded at Heilsberg 10 June 1807, retired 11 July 1807. LH CH 14 June 1804, O 3 April 1807.

BORGHESE (François Cajetan Dominique Philippe André Antoine Vincent Nicolas Louis Gaspard Melchior Balthazar, prince Aldobrandini, 1776-1839): brother of Prince Camille, the husband of Pauline Bonaparte, born in Rome on 9 June 1776.

Officer in the Rome National Guard, ordnance officer to MacDonald 1798, of General Watrin and MacDonald again, taken prisoner at la Trebbia 20 June 1799, called to Spain, rank of squadron commander in the Imperial Guard 1807, colonel of the 4th Cuirassiers 25 June 1808, two months' leave without pay 6 February 1809, shot in the shoulder at Wagram 6 July 1809, First Equerry to the Empress 24 February 1810, brigadier-general 2 January 1812, retained among the active generals 26 April 1814, one year's leave 22 October 1814.

LH CH 9 March 1809.

BORITIUS (Barthold Theodor Alhard, 1787-?): born in Vianen on 21 May 1787. NCO cadet in the service of Holland 2 February 1807, maréchal des logis in the Hussars of the king of Holland's Guard 4 April 1807, maréchal des logis-chef in the Cuirassiers of the Guard 20 September 1809.

He became sub-lieutenant in the King of Holland's bodyguard 26 October 1809, in the 2nd Dutch Cuirassiers 12 May 1810 which became the 14th French Cuirassiers 18 August 1810, in the suite of the regiment with the new reorganisation 5 December 1810, in post 25 March 1811, entered Indesbruck Hospital 1812 and prisoner 20 December 1812.

BORMENVILLE
see **BERLAYMONT de BORMENVILLE**

BOSSU (Claude, ? -1809): born in Salins (Jura). Maréchal des logis in the 3rd Cuirassiers, sub-lieutenant 14 May 1809, killed at Essling 21 May 1809.

BOTTU (Louis Charles, 1785-?): born in Valence (Drôme) on 30 August 1785. In the Gendarmes d'Ordonnance 15 December 1806, sub-lieutenant in the suite of the 12th Cuirassiers 16 July 1807, instated 10 September 1807, en pied 29 January 1808.

He became lieutenant 14 May 1809, wounded at Essling 22 May 1809, two months' leave without pay 13 October 1810, left 1 January 1811, resigned 11 October 1811, resignation accepted 1812.

BOUDIER (Jean Baptiste Michel, 1787-?): born in Epegards (Eure) on 16 September 1787. In the 5th Cuirassiers 2 March 1807, shot in the right shoulder at Essling 22 May 1809, brigadier 25 January 1811, shot in the right leg at Winkovo 18 October 1812.

He became brigadier-fourrier 1 January 1813, maréchal des logis-chef 1 October 1813, sub-lieutenant 27 January 1815, wounded at Waterloo 18 June 1815, dismissed 23 December 1815. LH CH 3 November 1814.

BOUDIN (Jacques Nicolas, 1768-?): born in Honfleur (Calvados) on 25 December 1768. Sub-lieutenant in the 22nd Chasseurs à Cheval 23 June 1793, lieutenant 16 July 1793, discharged 10 December 1793, at the disposal of the general commanding the 14th Military Division 26 July 1799, captain of the Compagnie Franche of the Calvados Dragoons 14 August 1799.

He was incorporated into the suite of the 5th Dragoons 21 May 1800, retired to his home as an officer in the suite 27 August 1800, discharged 26 October 1800, lieutenant in the 3rd Cuirassiers 30 November 1806, captain 14 May 1809, wounded at Wagram 6 July 1809, retired and pensioned off 1810.

BOUESDENOS
see **MANCEL de BOUESDENOS**

BOUILLARD aka **NEROUX** (Barthélémy, 1770-?): born in Néroux (Haut-Rhin) on 1 August 1770. In the Royal-Etranger-Cavalerie 3 October 1787 which became the 7th Cavalry 1 January 1791, brigadier 7 May 1793.

He became maréchal des logis 20 July 1802, in the same regiment when it became the 7th Cuirassiers 23 December 1802, maréchal des logis-chef 13 June 1805, sub-lieutenant in the suite 8 October 1811, in

B̸OYER (Etienne, 1770-?): born in Gray (Haute-Saône) on 3 March 1770. In the Bresse-Infanterie Regiment 28 November 1790 which became the 26th Infantry 1 January 1791, fourrier 10 August 1792.

He returned to the 52nd Light Infantry Half-Brigade, sergeant 1 September 1795, in the same regiment when it became the 27th Light June 1796, health officer in the 2nd Light 21 March 1797, maréchal des logis in the 9th Cavalry 22 May 1802, maréchal des logis-chef 23 October 1802, in the same regiment when it became the 9th Cuirassiers 24 September 1803, adjutant NCO 1 November 1806, sub-lieutenant 3 April 1807, lieutenant 14 May 1809, lieutenant adjutant-major 15 April 1812, captain 1 August 1812, retired 25 November 1815, left 26 November 1815. LH CH 14 June 1804.

Stationed in Corsica, Etienne Boyer was taken prisoner by the English on 17 February 1794. Imprisoned at Gibraltar he managed to get away with some comrades on 30 December of the same year by taking an English ship and forcing them to disembark them at Lorient, taking the opportunity to take seven prisoners.

post 4 March 1812, lieutenant 9 February 1813, retired 19 December 1815. LH CH 5 September 1813.

BOULANGER (Jean Claude, 1780-?): born in Vanjoutin (Haut-Rhin) on 30 November 1780. In the 17th of the Line 6 May 1798, lance wound to his right shoulder and taken prisoner by the Austrians at Plaisance 1799.

He returned to the 3rd Cavalry 12 April 1801 which became the 3rd Cuirassiers 12 October 1802, brigadier 11 November 1803, lance wound to his right hand at Austerlitz 2 December 1805, maréchal des logis 1 November 1806, shot wound at Essling 22 May 1809,, sub-lieutenant 5 June 1809, lieutenant 9 February 1813.

G.Rava 07

He saved Colonel Delacroix during a charge in Saxony 1813, shot and wounded in his right hand at Champaubert 10 February 1814, retired 25 November 1815. LH CH 25 February 1814.

BOULLAND (François, 1773-1805): born in Saint-Dizier (Haute-Marne) on 2 July 1776. In the 24th Cavalry of the new levy in his constitution 21 February 1791, brigadier-fourrier 7 August 1792, in the same regiment when it became the 23rd Cavalry 4 June 1793.

He became maréchal des logis 29 December 1793, confirmed 8 January 1794, maréchal des logis-chef 17 January 1794, sub-lieutenant 20 April 1799, employed at headquarters 22 February 1800, returned to the suite of the 23rd Cavalry 6 April 1801, confirmed 15 June 1801.

He was dismissed with the corps 23 December 1802 and incorporated into the 5th Cuirassiers 3 January 1803, lieutenant by seniority 1 November 1803, killed at Austerlitz 2 December 1805.

BOULLIERS see **JACQUET de BOULLIERS**

BOUR (François Pierre Nicolas, 1776-?): born in Metz (Moselle) on 23 September 1776. In the 24th Cavalry 25 April 1799, dismissed with the corps 10 October 1801 and incorporated into the 8th Cuirassiers 6 January 1802.

He became brigadier-fourrier 21 January 1803, maréchal des logis-chef 1 June 1806, sub-lieutenant 9 August 1809, lieutenant 12 September 1809, Gendarmerie lieutenant in the company from the Jemmapes Department 23 October 1811.

BOURBON (Jacques, 1766-1831): born in Flégnieux (Ardennes) on 15 October 1766. Trooper in the Colonel-Général Regiment 13 November 1787 which became the 1st Cavalry 1 January 1791.

He became fourrier 16 September 1793, maréchal des logis 14 May 1799, maréchal des logis-chef 31 May 1799, in the same regiment when it became the 1st Cuirassiers 10 October 1801, sub-lieutenant 24 December 1805, lieutenant 23 February 1807, retired with pension 22 May 1809. LH CH 18 December 1803.

BOURDON (Jean Baptiste Guillaume Ferdinand, 1776-?): born in Roissy (Seine-et-Oise) on 22 June 1776. Second-lieutenant in the 4th Gendarmerie Legion in Saint-Domingo 16 December 1802, shot wound to his right arm 14 February 1803.

He was discharged with the corps and took up his appointment as deputy-lieutenant in the Saint-Domingo headquarters 11 March 1803, lieutenant in the Chasseurs à Cheval in Saint-Domingo 2 August 1803, adjutant of the district 3 January 1804, deputy to the Adjutant-General Devaux 2 August 1804, commanded the place 5 October 1804, shot in the back during a sally 21 August 1805, returned to France 21 August 1805, confirmed as sub-lieutenant 15 January 1807 retroactively on 16 December 1802, in the 1st Carabiniers 17 February 1807, in the suite 13 April 1807, in post in the 13th Cuirassiers 21 October 1808, lieutenant 13 February 1809.

Following page.
Cuirassier saddles and sabres.
*(Collections Musée de l'Empéri,
Photograph Raoul Brunon, RR)*

He became captain 18 September 1811, instated 21 October 1811, dismissed with the corps and incorporated into the 9th Cuirassiers 9 August 1814, left thigh broken by a shot and taken prisoner at Waterloo 18 June 1815, dismissed 25 November 1815.

BOURGET see **CHOLLET de BOURGET**

BOURGOIN (Valère Martin, 1775-?): born in Esnoms (Haute-Marne) on 10 October 1775. In the 11th Cavalry 17 September 1792 which became the 11th Cuirassiers 24 September 1803, brigadier 17 November 1805.

He became maréchal des logis 1 December 1806, sub-lieutenant 6 November 1811, wounded at the Moskova 7 September 1812, lieutenant 19 June 1813, incorporated with his squadron into the 3rd Provisional Heavy Cavalry Regiment in Hamburg 11 September 1813.

He returned with the garrison May 1814, dismissed with the corps 16 December 1815.

BOURGUIGNON (Dieudonné, 1780-?): born in Sarreguemines (Moselle) on 29 February 1780. Volunteer in the 2nd Carabiniers 4 January 1798, dismissed by replacement 8 May 1802, lieutenant in the 2nd Etranger 17 November 1806, taken prisoner near Corfu, returned on parole and exchanged 25 May 1812.

He became captain in the 4th Etranger 9 August 1812, deputy at the headquarters of the 1st Corps 14 February 1814, supernumerary captain in the 7th Cuirassiers 4 October 1814, rejoined 9 November 1814, non-active on half-pay 19 December 1815.

BOURLON (Jean François, 1751-1821): born in Révigny (Meuse) on 10 December 1751. In the Royal-Cavalerie 13 June 1774, brigadier 1 September 1782, maréchal des logis 1 September 1784.

He became maréchal des logis-chef 15 September 1791, sub-lieutenant 10 May 1792, taken prisoner at Kreuznach 26 March 1793, freed end 1795, sabre wound to his head at Neubourg 15 September 1796, lieutenant 5 September 1797, in the same regiment when it became the 2nd Cuirassiers 12 October 1802.

He retired 21 August 1806, left 15 September 1806, underequerry instructor at the Saint-Germain school 1809, retired 1 October 1814. LH CH 14 June 1804.

BOURLON de CHEVIGNE (François Louis Charles, 1780-?): born in Cruas (Ardèche) on 9 April 1780. In the 1st Cuirassiers 18 February 1803, fourrier 6 December 1803, maréchal des logis 1 January 1806, sabre wound to his head at Jena 14 October 1806, maréchal des logis-chef 25 November 1806, adjutant NCO 10 July 1807, sub-lieutenant 16 May 1809, shot wound in the left thigh at Essling 22 May 1809.

He became lieutenant 15 October 1809, adjutant-major 25 September 1812, captain adjutant-major 28 September 1813, shot in the left hip in

front of Paris 30 March 1814, in the same regiment when it became the King's Cuirassiers 1 July 1814, aide de camp to Maréchal Moncey 15 February 1815, rejoined 1 March 1815. LH CH 1 October 1807.

BOURZAC (François Ignace de, 1789-?): born in Angoulême (Charente) on 17 August 1789. Velite in the Grenadiers à Cheval of the Guard 3 March 1807, shot and wounded in his right leg at Valladolid 1 March 1809, bayonet wound to his hip at Salinas 20 May 1810.

He became grenadier à cheval 1 January 1812, sub-lieutenant in the 1st Cuirassiers 17 December 1811, rejoined 14 March 1812, sabre wound on his right arm at Winkovo 18 October 1812 and another at Leipzig 16 October 1813, wounded at Paris 30 March 1814, in the King's Cuirassiers 1 July 1814 which became the 1st Cuirassiers again in March 1815, dismissed 24 December 1815.

BOUSIES de ROUVEROY (Philippe René de, 1790-1875): born in Mons (Jemmapes) on 9 March 1790. In the Gendarmes d'Ordonnance 9 November 1806, brigadier 7 August 1807, dismissed with the corps 23 October 1807, sub-lieutenant in the 7th Cuirassiers 18 February 1808, rejoined 23 April 1808.

He became lieutenant 4 March 1812, instated 11 April 1812, captain in the 4th Cuirassiers 19 November 1812, incorporated with his squadron into the 1st Provisional Cuirassiers in Hamburg 11 September 1813, wounded at Schwerin 25 November 1813 and near Hamburg 9 February 1814, returned with the garrison 27 May 1814 and non-active 1814, resigned 19 October 1814, replaced April 1815, did not join up again in May 1815. LH CH April 1815.

BOUSSIRON (Charles Philippe, 1784-?): born in Angoulême (Charente) on 20 December 1784. In the 3rd Gardes d'Honneur 4 June 1813, brigadier 12 June 1813.

He became maréchal des logis 5 July 1813, adjutant-NCO 15 August 1813, second-lieutenant 5 November 1813, lieutenant in the Dauphin's Cuirassiers 14 July 1814, three month's leave on half-pay 16 January 1815, in the same regiment when it became the 3rd Cuirassiers again April 1815, dismissed with the regiment 25 November 1815.

BOUTELET (Jean Vincent, 1763-?): born in Montrond (Orne) on 19 May 1763. Trooper in the King's Regiment 1 February 1782, brigadier 9 May 1784, maréchal des logis 1 May 1786, in the same regiment when it became the 6th Cavalry 1 January 1791.

He became maréchal des logis-chef 12 June 1791, adjutant 10 May 1792, confirmed 1 July 1792, sub-lieutenant 22 October 1792, prisoner at Ypres 10 September 1793, returned 1 February 1796, lieutenant 3 June 1799, adjutant-major 12 April 1802, in the same regiment when it became the 6th Cuirassiers 23 December 1802, rank of

As a Light Cavalry general, Bruyères commanded a division of the heavy cavalry for a short time. (RR)

captain 15 October 1803, in post in a company 11 April 1806, wounded at Heilsberg 10 June 1807, retired 7 January 1808.

BOUTROUX (Etienne Séverin, 1781-?): born in Coulon (Loiret) on 22 November 1781. In the 8th Cuirassiers 4 March 1804, brigadier-fourrier 5 June 1806, maréchal des logis-chef 9 July 1809, sub-lieutenant 8 July 1813.

He was incorporated into the 2nd Provisional Heavy Cavalry with his squadron in Hamburg 11 September 1813, returned with the garrison May 1814, dismissed with the corps 5 December 1815.

BOUVIER (Pierre Marie Eléonor, 1766-?): born in Grenoble (Isère) on 21 July 1766. Trooper in the Royal-Champagne 22 February 1787 which became the 20th Cavalry 1 January 1791, brigadier 15 September 1791, fourrier 21 December 1792, maréchal des logis 1 May 1793, sub-lieutenant 17 May 1793, in the same regiment when it

Officers in social dress, 1812. Composition by Benigni. (RR)

became the 19th Cavalry 4 June 1793, lieutenant 27 March 1794, shot wound at Rousselaer 13 June 1794, captain 19 June 1799, dismissed with the corps 31 December 1802 and incorporated into the 10th Cavalry 11 February 1803 which became the 10th Cuirassiers 24 September 1803, retired 16 May 1809. LH CH 5 November 1804.

BOUVIER des ECLATZ (Joseph, baron, 1759-1830): born in Belley (Ain) on 3 December 1759. In the la Rochefoucauld Dragoons 7 November 1778, brigadier 4 April 1782.

He became maréchal des logis 13 September 1784, maréchal des logis-chef 10 May 1786, in the same regiment when it became the Angoulême Dragoons 1788, adjutant NCO 1 March 1789, in the same regiment when it became the 11th Dragoons 1 January 1791, lieutenant 3 June 1792, captain 8 March 1793, sabre wound to his head at Fleurus 26 June 1794, squadron commander in the suite 12 January 1797, chief of staff of Klein's division 1797.

He was confirmed squadron commander 16 February 1799, major in the 17th Dragoons 29 October 1803, colonel of the 14th Dragoons 20 September 1806, shot wound at Eylau 8 February 1807, and wounded by a shell burst at Heilsberg 10 June 1807, acting CO of the brigade made up of his regiment and the 26th Dragoons, brigadier general 8 October 1810.

He was confirmed in his post, returned to France 18 December 1811, commanded the 1st Brigade (1st Carabiniers) of the 4th Cuirassier Division 31 January 1812, replaced temporarily for illness November 1812,

RUGUIERE aka **BRUYERES** (Jean Pierre Joseph, baron de, 1772-1813): General César Berthier's son-in-law born in Sommières (Gard) on 22 June 1772. Son of a surgeon-major who became chief-surgeon in the Army of Italy, student surgeon, took up his appointment in 1786, aide-major to the Army of Italy 1 July 1793, chasseur in the 15th Light Infantry 8 February 1794, deputy to the adjutant-generals 21 December 1794, sub-lieutenant in the 15th Light 4 February 1795, lieutenant 5 February 1796, deputy to the adjutant–generals 17 February 1797, aide de camp to Berthier 8 March 1797, acting captain at the head of the 7th bis Hussars 7 August 1797, confirmed 13 November 1797, aide de camp to Joubert 5 November 1798, captain in the 6th Hussars 21 March 1799, aide de camp to Joubert 2 August 1799, returned to the 6th Hussars when Joubert died, aide de camp to Berthier 6 March 1800, left to fetch Desaix and brought him back to the battlefield at Marengo 14 June 1800.

He became squadron commander in the 7th bis Hussars 8 August 1800, retroactively to 14 June 1800, major of the 5th Hussars 29 October 1803, keeping his functions of aide de camp, colonel of the 23rd Chasseurs à Cheval 16 February 1805, shot in the right thigh at Vicence 3 November 1805 and when crossing the Tagliamento 13 November 1805, aide de camp to Berthier October 1806, brigadier-general 30 December 1806, commanded the 3rd Brigade, Lasalle's division 31 December 1806.

He commanded a brigade of light cavalry in the Army of Germany 12 October 1808 then the 3rd Brigade, Dupas' division (13th and 24th Chasseurs à Cheval) 1 January 1809 which became the 1st Brigade of the 2nd Division of the Grande Armée 30 March 1809, then Lasalle's division 19 May 1809, shot twice in the left shoulder near Wagram 10 July 1809, replaced Marulaz at the head of the Light Cavalry division of the Rhine Army Observation Corps 11 July 1809, major-general 14 July 1809, allowed to return to France to be cared for 28 August 1809, commanded the 1st division of Heavy Cavalry of the Army of Germany 17 October 1809 then that of the Light Cavalry 8 April 1811, commanded the 1st Division of Light Cavalry of the 1st Cavalry Corps 15 February 1812, wounded by his horse falling on him when it was killed under him at the Moskova 7 September 1812, in the same corps under Latour-Maubourg 15 February 1813, both thighs blown off by a cannonball at Reichenbach 22 May 1813 and died of his wounds at Gœrlitz 5 June 1813. LH CH 25 March 1804, O 11 July 1807, C 14 June 1809, Baron of the Empire l.p. 1808.

At Eylau on 8 February 1806, Jean-Pierre Bruyères, at the head of his two light cavalry regiments, took a column of 6 000 Russian Grenadiers from behind; they were threatening to carry away the centre of the French line; it was wiped out entirely. During this action, he was wounded by Biscayan shot which passed between his chest and his left arm.

lieutenant 2 September 1813, non-active lieutenant in the Line on half-pay 24 July 1814. He was lieutenant in 2nd Cuirassiers 14 May 1815, He was dismissed and non-active 20 October 1815.

BRAINVILLE see **DELISLE de BRAINVILLE**

 **BRANCAS** (Antoine Constant Dioville de, baron, 1764-1809): born in Paris (Seine) on 16 October 1764. Sub-lieutenant in the 104th Infantry 22 January 1792 wounded at Maulde 30 August 1792, in the 5th Hussars 20 October 1792, deputy to the adjutant-generals of the Army of the North 31 October 1792.

He was wounded while defending the mortally wounded General, Dampierre, with a trumpet-major at Saultain near Valenciennes 8 May 1793, adjutant-general battalion commander 25 May 1793, suspended and imprisoned as a suspect 26 August 1793, freed 29 August 1794, reinstated as captain in the suite of the 5th Hussars 11 February 1795.

He became squadron commander in the 9th hussars 12 October 1797, captured 4 cannon and considerable booty in Switzerland 24 September 1798, major in the 7th Hussars 29 October 1803, colonel in the 11th Cuirassiers 31 December 1806, wounded then died at Essling 21 May 1809. LH CH 25 March 1804, O 11 July 1807, Baron of the Empire l.p. 15 January 1809.

BRANCOURT (Joseph, 1780-?): born in Ribemont (Aisne) on 1 April 1790. In the 11th Cavalry 30 March 1800 which became the 11th Cuirassiers 24 September 1803.

He became brigadier 1 December 1806, maréchal des logis 29 August 1809, Biscayan shot wound in the right forearm at Eylau 8 February 1807, sub-lieutenant 14 May 1813, wounded at Leipzig 16 October 1813 and remained a prisoner there until 18 October 1813, not included in the organisation of the 1 August 1814, returned and retired 1814. LH CH 5 September 1813.

BRANDICOURT MONTMOLIN (Louis Marie, 1781-?): born in Domard (Somme) on 31 March 1781. Sub-lieutenant in the 2nd Legion of the Somme National Guard from 1 January to 1 May 1807, at the Veterinary School at Alfort, left to join up 17 March 1809, supernumerary sub-lieutenant in the 7th Cuirassiers 13 February 1809, rejoined 3 June 1809, lieutenant 4 March 1812, instated 11 April 1812.

He was wounded at Polotsk 18 October 1812, captain in the suite 5 October 1813, wounded at Leipzig 18 October 1813 and at Craonne 8 March 1814,

He took up his appointment 16 March 1814, discharged 19 December 1815. LH CH 5 September 1813.

BRANDZAUX see **BRUNDSAUX**

BRAY (?-1812): Sub-lieutenant in the 3rd Cuirassiers 14 May 1809, lieutenant 12 March 1812, died 18 November 1812.

authorised to return to France for health reasons 3 March 1813, left beginning of May 1813, commanded the Frise Department 17 July 1813 then the Bouches-de-la-Meuse Department 7 September 1813, capitulated during the uprising 17 November 1813, arrested and interrogated 7 December 1813.

He was non-active January 1814, commanded the National Guards of the 6th Military Division 14 April 1815, retired 15 November 1815. LH CH 25 March 1804, O 14 May 1807, C 6 August 1811, Baron of the Empire l.p. 22 November 1808.

BOUVIER DESTOUCHES (Urbain Mathurin Marie, 1773-?): born in Rennes (Ille-et-Vilaine) on 10 September 1773. Sub-lieutenant in the 71st Infantry 15 May 1792, lieutenant aide de camp April 1793, discharged 31 July 1793.

He became lieutenant in the 9th Cuirassiers 30 July 1804, second-lieutenant in the Grenadiers à cheval of the Guard 1 May 1806, first-lieutenant 11 April 1809, lost all his fingers from frost bite 1812, retired 9 February 1813, at the disposal of the major-general to be employed as headquarters adjutant 2nd class in the suite 11 August 1813, order revoked and he retired 6 October 1813, returned as lieutenant (Old Guard) in the Grenadiers à cheval of the Imperial Guard 20 February 1814, two bullet wounds at taken prisoner at Craonne 7 March 1814, retired again 22 July 1814.

BOYER (Jacques Marie, 1768-1809): born in Paris

(Seine) on 19 February 1768. In the Alsace Chasseurs à Cheval 4 January 1789 which became the 1st Chasseurs à Cheval 1 January 1791, maréchal des logis-chef 11 July 1793, adjutant sub-lieutenant 13 March 1794, sub-lieutenant 16 march 1795, shot in the leg near Wetzlar 15 June 1796, lieutenant 19 July 1799, captain 1 April 1800, three sabre wounds at Obertzbalzberg 5 June 1800, shot and wounded at Schwanstadt 18 December 1800, went over to the 10th Cuirassiers by exchanging with Capitaine Rambourgt 13 October 1803. He became squadron commander 25 May 1807, killed after having two horses killed beneath him at Essling 21 May 1809. LH CH 5 November 1804, O 18 May 1809.

BOYER (Jean Fleury, 1763-?): born in Saint-Quentin (Aisne) on 30 June 1763. In the King's Cuirassiers 17 April 1784 which became the 8th Cavalry 1 January 1791, brigadier 27 August 1793, maréchal des logis the following day 28 August 1793, in the same regiment when it became the 8th Cuirassiers 10 October 1801, sub-lieutenant 4 October 1801.

He was elected lieutenant 21 January 1805, captain 26 April 1807, wounded at Essling 21 May 1809, left with his pension 9 August 1809. LH CH 18 October 1807.

BRACKERS de HUGO (Guillaume Charles, 1793-1835): born in Colmar (Haut-Rhin) on 26 February 1793. He was in 2nd Guards of Honour 13 June 1813.

He became maréchal des logis-chef 27 Jne 1813, sub-

BRUNO de SAINT GEORGES (Charles Gaudens Aloîse Marie, Baron, 1775-1842): born in Tortone (Stura) on 4 February 1775. Pupil at the royal Academy in Turin 8 October 1790, sub-lieutenant in the Royal-Cavalerie of the Piedmont 23 September 1792, lieutenant 11 January 1798.

He was captain French service in the 4th Piedmont Dragoons 9 December 1798, correspondence officer for General Montrichard 10 December 1798, captain in the suite of the 1st French Dragoons 9 March 1799, acting squadron commander 28 July 1798, shot in the left foot at Moesskirch 5 May 1800, in the 1st Piedmont Dragoons 29 March 1801, in the 21st French Dragoons 26 October 1801, confirmed 26 April 1802, allowed to return home for family business 10 August 1802, squadron commander in the 1st Provisional Dragoon Regiment 31 March 1808, ordered to watch over army teams in Madrid 17 December 1808, in the 13th Cuirassiers 1 May 1809, acting commander regularly and for a long time, taking 1 500 prisoners with a single squadron at Vimaros.

Leading the regiment at Sagonte and crushing the enemy centre 25 October 1811, supernumerary colonel 25 November 1813, commanded the 27th Chasseur à Cheval 16 December 1813, in the suite of the 9th Cuirassiers 18 November 1814, commanded the 6th Cuirassiers provisionally 21 July 1815, instated 1 August 1815, non-active 21 November 1815.

LH CH 29 May 1810, O 16 March 1812, Baron d. 3 April 1814.

BRAYELLE (Siméon Thimothé, 1751-?): born in Mézières (Ardennes) on 24 December 1751. In the King's Cuirassiers 2 January 1778, brigadier 17 March 1784, maréchal des logis 12 September 1784, in the same regiment when it became the 1 January 1791, maréchal des logis-chef 10 May 1792.

He became sub-lieutenant by choice 10 February 1793, lieutenant 26 September 1793, captain by seniority 30 April 1796, commanded the Elite Company of the regiment in 1799, went to another company 1800, in the same regiment when it became the 8th Cuirassiers 10 October 1801, retired 24 February 1807. LH CH June 1805.

BRECHET (Antoine, 1758-?): born in Clermont-Ferrand (Puy-de-Dôme) on 23 August 1758. Grenadier in the Royal Regiment of the Navy 11 March 1775, dismissed 11 March 1783, lieutenant in the Grenadiers

12 October 1791, sub-lieutenant in the 21st Cavalry 10 February 1793.

He became lieutenant in the 4th Dragoons 24 August 1795, deputy to the adjutant-generals 1 March 1796, captain 30 April 1797, in the suite of the 14th Dragoons 4 May 1798, under-adjutant-general commanding the regimental depot in Milan 1798.

He was squadron commander 3 September 1799, took up his post in the 21st Cavalry 13 February 1800, discharged 25 March 1801, in the 1st Provisional Heavy Cavalry in Spain 30 March 1808 which became the 13th Cuirassiers 21 October 1808, retired 17 February 1810.

BRESSE (Etienne, 1769-?): born in Semur-en-Auxois (Côte-d'Or) on 3 October 1769, emigrated August 1791. Volunteer in Mirabeau's Legion, artillery sub-lieutenant 17 February 1792, second-lieutenant 28 June 1795, returned to French service as a volunteer in the 3rd Chasseurs à Cheval 12 October 1797.

He became brigadier 5 February 1799, fourrier 25 February 1800, shot in the thigh crossing the Mincio 25 December 1800, in the 3rd Cavalry 21 May 1801, maréchal des logis 31 May 1801, sub-lieutenant 3 November 1801, in the same regiment when it became the 3rd Cuirassiers 12 October 1802.

He was elected lieutenant 18 February 1804, captain 24 June 1807, wounded in the leg and unhorsed at Essling 22 May 1809, wounded and unhorsed at Leipzig 16 October 1813, retired 25 November 1815.

BRETON (Jean Pierre, 1754-?): born in Cintrey (Meurthe) on 8 April 1754. In the Dauphin-Cavalerie 1 April 1777, brigadier 1 September 1794, in the same regiment when it became the 12th Cavalry 1 January 1791.

He became maréchal des logis 1 November 1792, maréchal des logis-chef 1 April 1793, sub-lieutenant 22 October 1796, lieutenant 4 December 1798, in the same regiment when it became the 12th Cuirassiers 24 September 1803, retired 30 October 1806.

BREY (François, 1769-?): born in Sélestat (Bas-Rhin) on 28 September 1769. In the National Volunteers à Cheval of the Ecole Militaire 20 August 1792 which formed the 26th Cavalry 212 February 1793 which became the 25th Cavalry 4 June 1793.

He was brigadier 25 November 1800, dismissed with the corps 12 October 1802 and incorporated into the 2nd Cuirassiers 24 November 1802, maréchal des logis 23 September 1804, in the Berg Chevau-Légers 1 September 1807, sub-lieutenant 15 February 1808, Gendarmerie lieutenant in the Grand-Duchy of Berg 1 May 1800.

He returned to French service and entered the Imperial Gendarmerie 7 September 1812, non-active on half-pay 1 November 1814, in the 2nd Cuirassiers 23 June 1815, went home, non-active again 20 October 1815.

BRIFFOTEAU (Nicolas, 1776-?): born in Hardoye (Ardennes) on 2 February 1776. In the 4th Cavalry 13 March 1800, brigadier 17 March 1802, in the same regiment when it became the 4th Cuirassiers 12 October 1802, fourrier 22 December 1804.

He became maréchal des logis 1 October 1806, maréchal des logis-chef 25 June 1807, sub-lieutenant 3 July 1808, lieutenant 22 December 1813, retired 21 December 1815. LH CH 5 September 1813.

BRINK (Egbert, 1761-?): born in Eppen (Yssel) on 23 February 1761. Trooper in the Hesse-Philipstadt Regiment 54 January 1785, brigadier 12 September 1788, fourrier in the 1st Dutch Cavalry 13 March 1793, maréchal des logis-chef 16 March 1794.

He was sub-lieutenant in the 1st Light Dragoons 23 October 1804 which became the 1st Batavian Dragoons 25 June 1805 then the 3rd Dutch Hussars 14 July 1806 and formed the 2nd Chevau-Légers Lancers of the Imperial Guard 23 September 1810, lieutenant in the 14th French Cuirassiers 5 December 1810, captain 4 March 1812, resignation accepted 9 June 1815.

BRISSET (Jacques François, 1771-?): born in Fontenay (Seine-et-Oise) on 8 June 1771. In the 10th Light Half Brigade 4 January 1794; left 28 March 1798, in the 8th Cavalry 21 September 1798 which became the 8th Cuirassiers 10 October 1801.

He became brigadier 6 October 1803, maréchal des logis 1 October 1803, wounded at Heilsberg 10 June 1807, sub-lieutenant 6 November 1811, wounded at Quatre-Bras 16 June 1815, dismissed with the regiment. LH CH 25 February 1814.

BRISSOTAUX (? - ?): maréchal des logis-chef in the 4th Cuirassiers, sub-lieutenant 3 July 1809, wounded at the Berezina 28 November 1812, lieutenant 22 December 1813, dismissed with the corps 21 December 1815.

BROCHAND (Marie Théodore, 1790-?): born in Dreux (Eure-et-Loir) on 12 January 1790. In the 13th Cuirassiers 25 June 1809, fourrier 16 March 1610.

He became maréchal des logis 1 April 1813, sub-lieutenant 21 August 1813, in the suite of the 11 Cuirassiers 9 August 1814, instated 1 September 1814, three months' leave on half-pay 7 December 1814, wounded at Waterloo 18 June 1815, dismissed with the corps.

BRODT (Louis François, 1784-?): born in Strasbourg (Bas-Rhin) on 9 May 1784. Child of the regiment on half-pay in the Artois-Cavalerie 21 September 1790 which became the 9th Cavalry 1 January 1791.

He was enrolled as a volunteer 9 May 1793, in the same regiment when it became the 9th Cuirassiers 24 September 1803, maréchal des

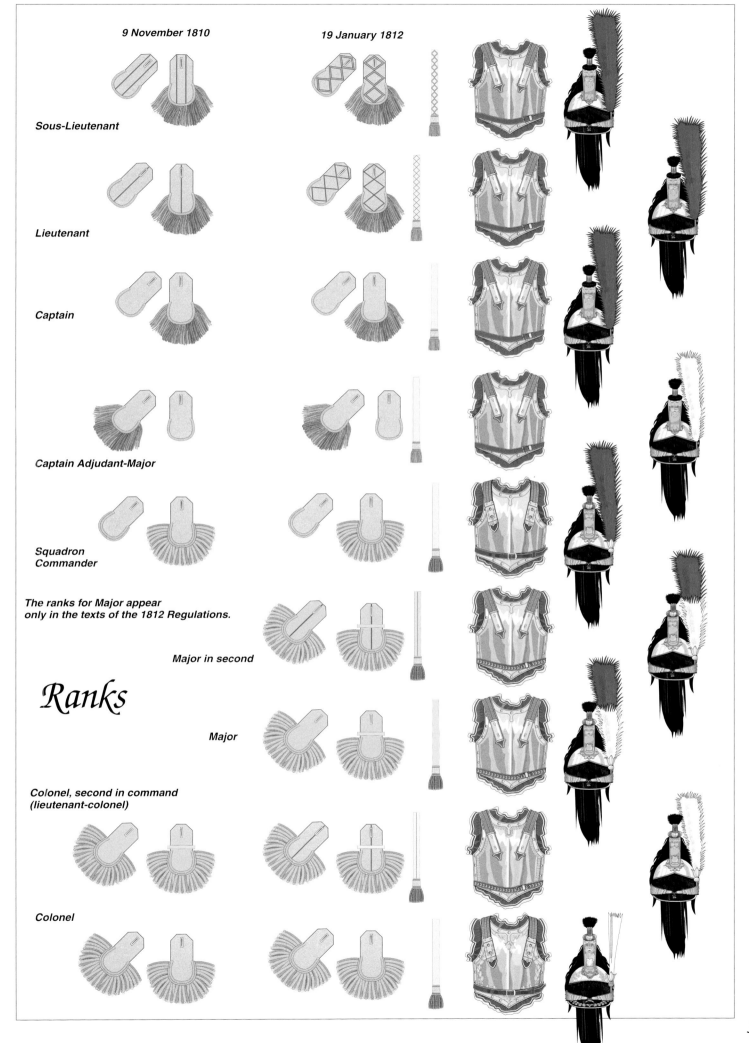

9 November 1810

19 January 1812

Sous-Lieutenant

Lieutenant

Captain

Captain Adjudant-Major

Squadron
Commander

The ranks for Major appear
only in the texts of the 1812 Regulations.

Major in second

Ranks

Major

Colonel, second in command
(lieutenant-colonel)

Colonel

logis 16 September 1809, sub-lieutenant 14 May 1813, remained behind after Waterloo, struck off the lists 26 November 1815. MH CH 4 December 1813.

BROQUET (Jean Baptiste, 1761-?): born in Montainville (Seine-et-Oise) on 22 June 1761. Trooper in the Royal-Pologne 29 November 1785 which became the 5th Cavalry 1791, brigadier 1 April 1791.

He became maréchal des logis 1 April 1793, maréchal des logis-chef 21 November 1793, sub-lieutenant 22 March 1800, in the same regiment when it became the 5th Cuirassiers 23 December 1802, elected lieutenant 21 February 1804, captain in the 7th Cuirassiers 25 February 1809, rejoined 18 May 1809, left with his retirement pay 23 March 1810. LH CH 1 April 1809

BROUILHAC (Charles André, 1785-1809): born in Saint-Maurice (Vienne) on 19 December 1785. Velite in the Grenadiers à Cheval of the Imperial Guard 9 March 1806, sub-lieutenant in the 10th Cuirassiers 7 January 1808, killed at Essling 21 May 1809.

BROUSSE (Jean Baptiste, 1768-1834): brother of the following, born in Nîmes (Gard) on 7 May 1768. in the Chartres-Dragons 24 November 1785, fourrier 4 February 1789.

He was in the same regiment when it became the 14 Dragoons 1 January 1791, dismissed 31 March 1791, captain in the 2nd Gard Battalion 25 September 1793, captured three Portuguese soldiers including one officer, wounded in the right leg by a bullet at Villelongue 2 November 1793, brigadier in the guides of the General in chief of the Army of the Pyrénées Orientales 10 January 1794, brigadier-fourrier 11 December 1794, sub-lieutenant in the Alp Hussars when they were formed 31 January 1795, lieutenant quartermaster 20 March 1795, in the same regiment when it became the 13th Hussars 1 September 1795, dismissed with the regiment and put up for temporary war commissioner but incorporated into the N°2 7th Hussars 16 May 1796, temporary deputy to Adjutant-General Partouneaux 29 September 1796, appointed deputy to the adjutant-generals and retroactively in the 7th bis Hussars 15 January 1797, captain 27 June 1798.

He was wounded by a piece of caisson which exploded at la Trebbia 19 June 1799, acting squadron commander 30 June 1799, returned to the suite of the 7Th bis Hussars 13 July 1802, confirmed 2 January 1801, in the same regiment when it became the 28th Dragoons 24 September 1803, major of the Chevau-Légers of the King of Naples' Guard 30 September 1806, then of the King of Spain 1808, colonel of the Chevau-Légers of the Royal Guard 19 November 1810, returned to serve for France end of 1813 and colonel again in the suite of the Chevau-Légers Lancers of the Guard 1 February 1814.

He was non-active 22 December 1814, in the Royal French Corps of Cuirassiers 5 January 1815 which became the Grenadiers à Cheval of the Imperial Guard again March 1815, remained in the

depot during the Hundred Days, dismissed end 1815. LH CH 14 June 1804, O 1 September 1814.

BROUSSE (Joachim, 1793-?): brother of the above, born in Nîmes (Gard) 1793. In the Chevau-Légers of the King of Spain's Guard 4 August 1808, brigadier 1 July 1810, maréchal des logis 1 January 1811, shot wound to his left leg at Salamanca, adjutant NCO 1 September 1812.

He became lieutenant 2 April 1813, second-lieutenant (Young Guard) in the Chasseurs à Cheval of the Imperial Guard 1 February 1814, incorporated with his squadron into the 9th Chasseurs à cheval, sub-lieutenant in the Angoulême Cuirassiers 10 August 1814, in post 4 January 1815, non-active lieutenant in the suite of the same regiment 10 February 1815, took up his post in the same regiment when it became the 4th Cuirassiers once again April 1815, wounded at Waterloo 18 June 1815, dismissed with the corps 21 December 1815.

BROUVILLE (Jean de, 1787-?): born in Clermont (Haute-Marne) on 7 July 1787. In the 5th Cuirassiers 23 February 1807, brigadier 1 May 1807, maréchal des logis 1 July 1807, maréchal des logis-chef 28 January 1808, adjutant NCO 19 May 1810, sub-lieutenant 6 November 1811, lieutenant 21 April 1813, captain adjutant-major 28 September 1813.

He was wounded at Hanau 30 October 1813 and Waterloo 18 June 1815, dismissed 23 December 1815. LH CH 30 September 1814.

BRUGNON (Michel, 1767-1815): born in Vatigny (Aisne) on 10 December 1767.

Trooper in the Royal-Roussillon 8 February 1788 which became the 11th Cavalry 1 January 1791, brigadier 9 July 1794, maréchal des logis 11 August 1794, in the same regiment when it became the 11th Cuirassiers 24 September 1803, sub-lieutenant in the suite 14 February 1807, in post 3 April 1807, lieutenant 25 May 1807, two sabre wounds to his head and left arm at Regensburg 23 April 1809, captain 6 November 1811.

He died at hospital at Fontenay-le-Comte 10 November 1815. LH CH 14 February 1807.

BRULE (Zéphirin, 1780-?): born in Ribemont (Aisne) on 22 July 1780. In the 11th Cavalry 19 December 1800 which became the 11th Cuirassiers 24 September 1803,

He became brigadier 5 October 1804, maréchal des logis 15 August 1805, maréchal des logis-chef 16 May 1809, sub-lieutenant 13 August 1809, wounded at Smolensk 9 November 1812, lieutenant 19 June 1813, aide de camp to General Duclaux his former colonel 3 December 1813, left 9 December 1813. LH CH 16 June 1809.

BRUNDSAUX (Nicolas, 1790-?): born in Essey (Meurthe) on 28 August 1790. Velite in the Dragoons of the Guard 8 November 1808, sub-lieutenant in the 7th Cuirassiers 13 March 1813, rejoined 27 May 1813.`

He became lieutenant adjutant-major 16 March 1814, on four months' leave 1 September 1814, non-active 19 December 1815. LH CH 18 August 1814.

BRUNEAU (Etienne François, 1781-1813): born in Tours (Indre-et-Loire) on 15 November 1791. In the 8th Cuirassiers 19 April 1803, brigadier 10 May 1804, maréchal des logis 23 October 1804.

He became sub-lieutenant in the suite 2 March 1809, wounded at Essling 22 May 1809, in post 23 May 1809, lieutenant 9 August 1809, aide de camp to General Bourcier 23 January 1810, in the 23rd Chasseurs à Cheval 23 October 1811.

He became second-lieutenant in the Grenadiers à cheval of the Imperial Guard 6 December 1811, died in the hospital at Fulda 6 March 1813.

BRUNET (Jacques, 1770-?): born in Pont-de-Vaux (Ain) on 19 March 1770. In the 24th Cavalry 6 July 1791 which became the 23rd Cavalry 4 June 1793, fourrier 5 July 1794, maréchal des logis 20 August 1800.

He became maréchal des logis-chef 15 December 1800, dismissed with the corps 23 December 1802 and incorporated into the 6th Cuirassiers 3 January 1803, sabre wound to his left shoulder at Heilsberg 10 June 1807, sub-lieutenant 6 October 1808, lieutenant 3 June 1809, in the Escadron Sacré during the retreat from Moscow 1812, retired 21 November 1815. LH CH 1 October 1807.

BRUNO (Adrien François, baron de, 1771-1861): born in Pondichéry (India) on 10 June 1771. Brought to France with his uncle Law de Lauriston, artillery officer cadet 1790 in the Nièvre Cavalry 1792, incorporated into the 4th Hussars 1 September 1793, sub-lieutenant aide de camp to General Saint-Rémy 3 July 1795, in the 1st Hussars 24 August 1795, lieutenant 3 July 1797, captain 4 January 1798, aide de camp to Boyé 11 April 1801.

He became squadron commander in the 12th Hussars 14 December 1801, which became the 30th Dragoons 24 September 1803, major in the 10th chasseurs à cheval 29 October 1803, aide de camp to the King Louis 10 July 1806, colonel of the 2nd Dutch Hussars 27 September 1806, commanded the Hussars of the Royal Guard 20 December 1806, Dutch general-major 6 April 1807, lieutenant-general 2 November 1808, brigadier-general in French service 11 November 1810, commanded a brigade of the 1st Heavy Cavalry Division In the Army of Germany 14 February 1811, commanded the 2nd Brigade of the same division 25 December 1811, then the 1st Brigade 1 July 1812.

He commanded the division at the Moskova 7 September 18125, commanded the cavalry of the Elbe Observation Corps 20 January 1813, then the 5th Corps 4 April 1813 and the 2nd corps 1 July 1813, taken prisoner near Freyberg 18 September 1813, returned to France 26 June 1814, in the 16th Military Division 30 December 1814, commanded the 1st Brigade of Jacquinot's Light Cavalry division in the 1st Corps of the Army of the North 6 April 1815, commanded the Hérault Department 1 September 1815. LH CH 25 March 1804, O 11 October 1812, C 23 August 1814, Baron of the Empire 10 June 1811.

BRUYERES see **BRUGUIERES** aka **BRUYERES**

Senior officer from the 7th cuirassiers.
(Private collection)

d'après Ed. Detaille.

BRYAS (Alexandre François Ferdinand Guislain Marie de, 1781-1828): brother of the following, born in Morialmé (Sambre-et-Meuse) on 1 October 1781. Ordnance officer to Louis Bonaparte 31 November 1800.

He became second-lieutenant in the Gendarmes d'Ordonnance 31 October 1806, lieutenant in the suite of the 1st Cuirassiers 16 July 1807, took up his appointment in the 6th Cuirassiers 18 November 1807, instated 31 December 1807, shot in the left leg, his horse killed under him at Essling 21 May 1809, returned.

He was captain 12 September 1809, wounded and unhorsed at the Moskova 7 September 1812, in the Escadron Sacré during the retreat, bayonet wound to his right side at Leipzig 16 October 1813, intended for promotion 10 January 1814.

He was squadron commander 19 February 1814, shrapnel wound to his right side in front of Paris 30 March 1814, confirmed squadron commander 3 April 1814, in the suite of the King's Cuirassiers 24 May 1814, two months' leave with pay 15 June 1814, confirmed when regiment formed 1 July 1814, two months' leave on half-pay 11 September 1814, returned 31 October 1814, in the suite 3 March 1815, resignation accepted 18 April 1815. LH CH 11 October 1812.

BRYAS (Charles Raymond Louis Alphonse de, 1786-1828): brother of the above, born on 8 February 1786. Sub-lieutenant in the cavalry in French service 21 January 1810, in the suite of the 6th Cuirassiers 28 February 1811, resignation accepted 13 July 1811.

BUCHOUAT (François, 1774-1813): born in Sommerson (Seine-et-Marne) on 10 July 1774. In the 23rd Cavalry 4 April 1794, lance wound in his armpit at Offemburg 21 April 1799, in the Grenadiers à Cheval of the Guard 16 April 1800, brigadier 12 March 1801, fourrier 15 October 1802.

He became maréchal des logis 20 June 1805, maréchal des logis-chef 29 September 1805, second-lieutenant 16 February 1807, captain in the suite of the 10th Cuirassiers 23 October 1811, presumed killed at Elbing 23 January 1813. LH CH 14 June 1804.

BUFFET (Louis, 1791-?): born in Tendon (Vosges) on 22 June 1791. Velite in the Dragoons of the Imperial Guard 12 March 1809.

He became sub-lieutenant in the 11th Cuirassiers 13 March 1813, incorporated into the 3rd Provisional Heavy Cavalry in Hamburg with his squadron 11

September 1813, returned with the garrison May 1814, resignation accepted 13 March 1815.

BUIRET (? - ?): maréchal des logis in the Gardes d'Honneur, sub-lieutenant in the 2nd Cuirassiers 12 May 1815, wounded at Waterloo 18 June 1815, appointment cancelled 1 August 1815, sent home.

BUISSON (Michel, 1753-?): born in Lyon (Rhône) on 21 January 1753. In the Rouergue-Infanterie 11 January 1768, left 11 January 1777, trooper in the Franche-Comté Regiment 28 February 1784.

He became brigadier 11 October 1786, incorporated into the Roi-Cavalerie 14 June 1788, maréchal des logis 18 August 1790, in the same regiment when it became the 6th Cavalry 1 January 1791, maréchal des logis-chef 1 July 1792, adjutant 22 February 1793.

He was lieutenant 28 June 1794, discharged 1796, in post 24 November 1798, in the same regiment when it became the 6th Cuirassiers 23 December 1802, on retirement pay 4 May 1805, left the regiment May 1805.

BUNO (Dirk Christophe, 1788-?): born in Del-Loosen (Yssel) on 6 December 1788. Cadet in the 1st Batavian Light Dragoons 4 January 1805, sub-lieutenant in the 2nd Dutch Cuirassiers 26 February 1807 which became the 14th Cuirassiers 5 December 1810, lieutenant 8 October 1811.

He was captain 15 May 1813, blocked in Hamburg, left with the garrison May 1814 and resigned from French service August 1814.

BUNO (Guillaume Charles, 1791-?): born in Whyé (Yssel) on 16 May 1791. In the 14th Cuirassiers 25 May 1811.

He became brigadier 16 June 1811, maréchal des logis 11 October 1811, sub-lieutenant during the siege of Hamburg 13 September 1813, left with the garrison May 1814 and resigned from French service August 1814.

BUOB (Grégoire André, 1777-?): born in Ohnenheim (Bas-Rhin) on 30 November 1777. In the 8th Cavalry, brigadier 6 August 1802, maréchal des logis 19 June 1806.

He became adjutant NCO 27 July 1807, shot in the left leg and his horse killed under him at Essling 22 March 1809, sub-lieutenant 3 June 1809, shot in the head at Wagram 6 July 1809, lieutenant 12 September 1809, several lance wounds near Moscow 4 October 1812, captain 5 June 18113, dismissed with the corps 5 December 1815 and put in for the Gendarmerie 11 December 1815. LH CH 11 October 1812.

BUSSETTI DE BERZANO (Bonifert, 1786-1812): born in Tortone (Stura) on 19 December 1786. In the Guard of Honour of the Viceroy of Italy 18 December 1806.

He became brigadier 10 September 1808, sub-lieutenant in the suite of the 12th Cuirassiers 5 November 1810, in post 25 February 1812, disappeared in Russia.

CABROL de MONTE (Pierre, chevalier, 1769-1819): born in Nîmes (Gard) on 28 August 1769. Sub-lieutenant in the 54th Infantry 15 September 1791, lieutenant 12 May 1792, captain in the 15th Chasseurs à Cheval 13 March 1793, aide de camp to General Déprez-Crassier 17 June 1795.

He became squadron commander in the 10th Dragoons 24 August 1795, deputy at the general headquarters of the Army of the Rhine 21 January 1797, aide de camp to General Gudin 30 August 1801, wounded falling off his horse at Pultusk 26 December 1806, major at headquarters of the Army 7 July 1807, in the 3rd Cuirassiers 3 March 1809, commanded the regiment's war squadrons 29 December 1813, retired 17 January 1814, pensioned 19 February 1814. LH CH 14 June 1804, Chevalier of the Empire d. 15 August 1809 and l.p. 16 December 1810.

CACATTE (Nicolas, 1774-?): born in Limoges (Haute-Vienne) on 6 September 1774. In the 3rd Haute-Vienne Battalion 17 October 1792, in the 1st Chasseurs à Cheval 22 May 1794.

He was in the 6th Cavalry 2 February 1799, brigadier 11 April 1799, maréchal des logis 8 June 1800, sub-lieutenant 12 March 1802, instated 29 May 1802, in the same regiment when it became the 6th Cuirassiers 23 December 1802, lieutenant 16 May 1806, shot twice in the right thigh and left ear and taken prisoner at Essling 21 May 1809, reappointed as supernumerary sub-lieutenant during his captivity 3 June 1809, lieutenant in post 30 November 1810.

He became captain 21 March 1812, retired 25 November 1815, left 26 November 1815. LH CH 11 October 1812.

CACQUERAY (Edouard de, 1790-?): born in Chartres (Eure-et-Loir) on 16 October 1790. Pupil at Saint-Cyr 4 May 1808.

He became sub-lieutenant in the suite of the 2nd Cuirassiers 14 August 1810, rejoined his regiment 19 September 1810, took up his appointment 25 January 1812, wounded and taken prisoner at Kovno 12 December 1812, returned home 1814.

CADE (Virgile, 1794-?): born in Florac (Lozère) on 5 April 1794. In the 4th Gardes d'Honneur 5 May 1813, brigadier June 1813, maréchal des logis December 1813, dismissed May 1814, sub-lieutenant in the suite of the 1st Cuirassiers 12 May 1815, struck off the rolls and appointment cancelled 1 September 1815.

CADEROUSSE
see **GRAMONT de CADEROUSSE**

CADET DEVAUX (Antoine Charles, 1774-1836): born in Paris (Seine) on 21 April 1774. Sub-lieutenant in the 46th Infantry 12 January 1792, amalgamated into the 92nd Half-Brigade, lieutenant 28 April 1792, resigned 30 July 1795, employed in the

ADE (André, 1794-?): born in Uzès (Gard) on 20 June 1774. In the 2nd Gard Battalion 15 August 1792, left 8 September 1793, volunteer in the same regiment 23 September 1793, in the Guides à Cheval of the Army of the Pyrenees 21 December 1793.

He was incorporated into the Guides of the Army of the Alps 29 March 1794, left 16 April 1796, in the 1st Cavalry 11 October 1799, brigadier 9 April 1800, maréchal des logis 1 May 1800, in the same regiment when it became the 1st Cuirassiers 10 October 1801, maréchal des logis-chef 20 June 1802, adjutant-NCO 1 April 1803, sub-lieutenant 3 January 1806.

He was lieutenant 3 April 1807, captain 13 October 1809, shot and wounded at Krasnoë 12 August 1812 and again at Smolensk 18 August 1812, kept in the King's Cuirassiers 1 July 1814 which became the 1st Cuirassiers again March 1815, dismissed and put on the active list 24 December 1815. LH CH 3 April 1807.

At Hoff on 6 February 1807, Sous-Lieutenant André Cade of the 1st Cuirassiers took a Russian flag and was wounded in action. He was made a lieutenant and chevalier of the Légion d'Honneur on the following 3 April for his brilliant action.

Versailles arms factory 9 February 1796 left to follow riding lessons at the National Riding School at Versailles from 19 June 1796 to 19 June 1797, aide de camp to General Jourdan 24 October 1798, deputy to the Adjutant-General Defrance 9 April 1799.

He was in the suite of the headquarters staff of the Army of the Rhine and the Danube 9 November 1799, captain 23 April 1800, in the 7th Dragoons 31 May 1800, in the 8th Dragoons 23 October 1800, wounded at Eylau 8 February 1807, squadron commander 18 September 1808, in the same regiment when it became the 3rd Chevau-Légers 18 June 1811, wounded in front of Polotsk 31 October 1812, second-major 8 February 1813, designated to command the 11th Chasseurs à Cheval depot, in the meantime appointed major in the 2nd Provisional Cuirassiers in Hamburg 3 July 1813, instated when the regiment was formed 11 September 1813.

He returned with the garrison 30 May 1814, major in the suite of the Dragoons N° 14 20 November 1814, on two months' leave on half-pay 7 January 1815, in the same regiment when it became the 19th Dragoons again in April 1815, non-active on half-pay 10 November 1815. LH CH 14 April 1807.

CAGNARD (?-1807): maréchal des logis in the 3rd Cuirassiers, sub-lieutenant by seniority 11 December 1805, died 30 March 1807.

CAGNON (Louis Antoine, 1771-1853): born in Togny-aux-Boeufs (Marne) on 15 Janaury 1771.

In the 20th Cavalry 2 September 1793, sabre wound to his right hand at Rousselaer 8 June 1794, brigadier 20 January 1799, fourrier 19 February 1799.

He became adjutant NCO 20 April 1800, shot and wounded in his left thigh at Marengo 14 June 1800, on four months' leave 15 August 1801, dismissed with the corps 31 December 1806 and incorporated into the suite of the 12th Cuirassiers 25 January 1803, sub-lieutenant 30 October 1806, lieutenant 29 January 1808, lieutenant adjutant-major 9 August 1809, acting captain 9 February 1811, went over to a company 25 February 1812, confirmed in post 16 March 1812, sabre wound to his head and taken prisoner 21 November 1812, returned 16 November 1814 and put on the non-active list. LH CH 14 March 1806.

CAGNY (Louis de, 1788-?): born in Caen (Calvados) on 22 September 1788. At the Ecole Spéciale Militaire, sub-lieutenant in the 6th Cuirassiers 12 July 1807.

He became lieutenant 8 October 1811, taken prisoner in Russia 15 November 1812, returned 1 September 1814, in the Musketeers 1 March 1815. LH CH 28 September 1814.

CAILLAUD (Pierre Etienne, 1777-?): born in Ars (Charente-Inférieure) on 17 May 1777. In the 19th Cavalry 22 July 1799, sabre wound to his left hand 10 August 1800, dismissed with the corps 31 December 1802 and incorporated into the 9th cavalry 25 January 1803 which became the 9th Cuirassiers 24 September 1803, brigadier 23 October 1805.

He was maréchal des logis 14 May 1809, adjutant NCO 1 May 1813, sub-lieutenant 22 December 1813, left with retirement pay 26 November 1815. LH CH 19 March 1815.

CAILLEUX (Simon, 1774-?): born in Loguy (Oise) on 28 October 1774. In the 10th Cavalry 2 December 1793, brigadier 24 June 1803, in the same regiment when it became the 10th Cuirassiers 24 September 1803.

He became maréchal des logis 1 December 1806, two bayonet wounds to his hand and left thigh at Hoff 6 February 1807, sub-lieutenant 16 May 1809, right arm shattered by a bullet while charging Hungarian grenadiers then amputated at Znaîm 11 July 1809 and retired.

CAIMO (Hyacinthe Ferdinand François, 1795-?): born in Schele (Deux-Nèthes) on 15 November 1795. Pupil at the Ecole Impériale de Cavalerie at Saint Germain 15 October 1812, sub-lieutenant 30 March 1814, in the suite of the 4th Cuirassiers 12 June 1814 which became the Angoulême Cuirassiers 6 August 1814, resignation accepted November 1814.

CALLERY (Joseph, 1784-?): born in Caron (Stura) on 17 April 1786. In the 3rd Cuirassiers

2 December 1803, brigadier 1 June 1807, wounded by a Biscayan shot to his right arm 6 July 1809.

He became maréchal des logis 1 October 1809, sub-lieutenant 23 September 1812, shot in the left thigh at Leipzig 18 October 1813, lieutenant 22 December 1813, permitted to leave the corps to go to Paris 7 May 1814, resigned 16 May 1814 and not included in the 20 August 1814 re-organisation.

CALLORY (Antoine Bonaventure Ferdinand, 1795-?): born in Chartres (Eure-et-Loir) on 24 July 1794. Pupil at the Ecole Spéciale Militaire at Saint-Cyr 23 May 1813, brigadier 26 June 1814, fourrier 31 June 1814, maréchal des logis 21 August 1814, maréchal des logis-chef 13 November 1814.

He became sub-lieutenant in the 7th Cuirassiers 3 March 1815, seconded to the Saumur School 15 March 1815, took up his post without passing by the regiment, dismissed with the corps whilst still at Saumur 19 December 1815.

CAMP (Pierre, 1757-1807): born in Aquaize (Gard) on 5 October 1757. In the Sarre-Infanterie 11 January 1776, corporal in the Grenadiers 1781, dismissed 11 January 1784, trooper in the Royal-Cravates 17 May 1786 which became the 10th Cavalry 1 January 1791.

He became brigadier-fourrier 20 November 1791, maréchal des logis 27 August 1792, maréchal des logis-chef 1 October 1793, sub-lieutenant 11 December 1798, lieutenant 28 June 1802, in the same regiment when it became the 10th Cuirassiers 24 September 1803, wounded at Hoff 6 February 1807 and died of his wounds at Soldau in Poland 21 April 1807.

CAMPARIOL (Pierre Victor 1770-after 1845), born in Toulouse (Haute-Garonne) on 27 July 1770. In the 1st Carabiniers 20 February 1789, brigadier-fourrier 1 April 1791, maréchal des logis in the 1st Carabiniers 23 May 1794, maréchal des logis-chef 24 July 1794, sub-lieutenant 2 May 1800, in the Grenadiers à

Captain Cagnon's proposal for active service in the 12th Cuirassiers.
(Author's collection)

Cheval of the Guard 13 October 1802, second-lieutenant 23 September 1804, under-adjutant-major 22 November 1804.

He became captain adjutant-major 18 December 1805, captain commanding a company 25 June 1809, major in the 5th Cuirassiers 20 February 1811, confirmed 9 September 1814, non-active when the regiment was disbanded 24 December 1815.

CAMPEN (Abraham Théodor van, 1783-?): born in Gravesante (Bouches-de-la-Meuse) on 11 May 1783. Dutch cadet NCO 4 February 1807, fourrier in the Cuirassiers of the Royal Dutch Guard 4 August 1807.

He became maréchal des logis 26 February 1808, sub-lieutenant in the suite 25 September 1809, in the 2nd Dutch Cuirassiers 6 October 1809 which became the 14th French Cuirassiers after the annexation 18 August 1810, lieutenant adjutant-major 17 February 1811, rank of captain 17 August 1812, prisoner at Halberstadt 31 May 1813.

Legion d'Honneur medals.
(RR)

CAMUS (Pierre, 1762-?): born in Villegardin (Yonne) on 31 March 1762. In the Chasseurs à Cheval N°1 8 December 1780 which became the Chasseurs des Alpes 8 August 1784 then the Picardy Chasseurs à Cheval 17 March 1788 and the 7th Chasseurs à Cheval 1 January 1791, brigadier 23 March 1791.

He was dismissed and struck of the rolls 27 May 1792, in the Volontaires Nationaux à Cheval 23 August 1792, lieutenant in the same regiment when it became the 26th Cavalry 21 February 1793 which became the 26th Cavalry 4 June 1793, confirmed 22 June 1793, shot in the right thigh at le Mans 10 December 1793, seconded to the Versailles riding school 1796. He returned to the regiment 1797, captain 21 March 1798, in the suite of the 4th Cuirassiers when the corps was disbanded 23 November 1802, retired 2 June 1809.

CANAVASSI (Hyacinthe, 1764-?): born in Turin (Pô) on 19 November 1764. Employed riding in the service of the King of Sardinia 1778, lieutenant instructor in the 1st Piedmont Dragoons 1799.

He became captain attached to the staff of the general commanding the Army of Italy, attached to the 21st Dragoons 31 March 1801, discharged 23 September 1801, attached to the French Legation in Constantinople 1803, on Maréchal Brune's staff 1805, aide de camp to the maréchal with the rank of cavalry captain in the service of France 26 July 1807, captain in the 1st Cuirassiers 6 August 1808, retired 29 December 1811.

CANDELLE de KNYFF
see **LECANDELLE de KNYFF**

CANTU (?-?): velite in the Grenadiers à Cheval of the Imperial Guard, sub-lieutenant in the 5th Cuirassiers 13 March 18131, incorporated with his squadron into the 2nd Provisional Heavy Cavalry in Hamburg 11 September 1811, returned with the garrison 30 May 1814, does not appear on the rolls on 11 August 1814.

CAPDEVILLE (Désiré Jean, 1785-1852): born in Barsac (Gironde) on 12 August 1785. Velite in the Dragoons of the Guard 15 March 1806, sub-lieutenant in the 29th Dragoons 9 June 1809 sabre wound to his head and his horse killed under him at Wagram 6 July 1809.

He was in the same regiment when it became the 6th Chevau-Légers 18 June 1811, lance wound to his thigh and a sabre wound to his arm at the Moskova 7 September 1812, lieutenant 26 September 1812, captain on the staff of Major-General Exelmans 28 September 1803, captain on the staff of the Old Guard 15 February 1814, shot in the lower belly while carrying despatches near Craonne 26 February 1814, in the King's Cuirassiers 1 July 1814, remained at the disposal of the Minster of War in Paris 20 January 1815, returned to the same regiment which had become the 1st Cuirassiers again 1 April 1815, dismissed and put on the active list 24 December 1815. LH CH 28 September 1813.

CARDET (Louis Pierre, 1772-?): born in Champelan (Seine-et-Oise) on 17 February 1772. In the 8th Cavalry 1794 which became the 8th Cuirassiers 10 October 1801, brigadier 1 October 1806.

He became maréchal des logis 25 March 1807, maréchal des logis-chef 3 June 1809, shot in the left hand at Wagram 6 July 1809, sub-lieutenant 4 September 1812, wounded 15 February 1814 while escorting the general in command, dismissed with the corps 5 December 1815.

CARDOT (Louis, 1775-?): born in Guise (Aisne) on 15 March 1775. In the 6th Cavalry 9 December 1793, fourrier 16 June 1800, in the same regiment when it became the 6th Cuirassiers 23 December 1802, maréchal des logis-chef 26 April 1803.

He became sub-lieutenant 25 June 1807, lieutenant 6 October 1808, captain 3 June 1809, non-active on half-pay while waiting for the adjutancy of a stronghold to be free 24 July 1814, retired 1 August 1814, in the 5th Cuirassiers 10 April 1815, joined the regiment 19 April 1815, on half-pay 1 August 1815 LH CH 1 October 1807.

CAREL (Alexandre, 1785-?): born in Raneville (Calvados) on 18 December 1785. Velite in the Grenadiers à cheval of the Guard 27 January 1806, sub-lieutenant in the suite of the 3rd Cuirassiers 13 July 1807.

He became lieutenant 3 June 1809, captain 12 August 1812, shot in the left shoulder at Waterloo 18 June 1815, dismissed 25 November 1815. LH CH 4 December 1813.

CARIGNAN see **SAVOIE CARIGNAN**

CARLIER (Camille Alexandre, 1782-?): younger brother of the following, born in La-Ferté-en-Braye (Seine-Inférieure) on 5 January 1782. In the 6th Cavalry 1 January 1798, brigadier 23 September 1802, in the same regiment when it became the 6th Cuirassiers 23 December 1802, fourrier 20 February 1803,.

He became maréchal des logis 26 January 1805, maréchal des logis-chef 1 January 1807, sub-lieutenant 25 May 1807, confirmed 11 July 1807, lieutenant 3 June 1809, captain 29 September 1812, eleven lance and two sabre wounds at Voronov 21 November 1812, lost two horses killed under him at Waterloo 18 June 1815, disbanded with the corps 21 November 1815. LH CH 12 October 1811.

CARLIER (Pierre Jérôme, 1774-1809): elder brother of the above, born in La-Ferté-en-Braye (Seine-Inférieure) on 28 June 1774. In the 6th Cavalry 17 October 1793.

He became brigadier 21 November 1798, fourrier 7 April 1794, maréchal des logis 21 May 1800, maréchal des logis-chef 5 July 1800, sub-lieutenant, in the same regiment when it became the 6th Cuirassiers 23 December 1802, adjutant NCO 25 February 1803, lieutenant 22 March 1807 adjutant-major 10 November 1807, shot at point blank range and seriously wounded in the lower belly at

ARRIERE aka **BEAUMONT** (Louis Chrétien, baron de Beaumont, 1771-1813): born in Malplacey (Somme) on 14 April 1771. In the Queen's Dragoons 1 April 1788 which became the 6th Dragoons 1 January 1791, sub-lieutenant in the 7th Hussars 23 November 1792.

He was lieutenant 20 April 1793, in the same regiment when it became the 6th Hussars 4 June 1793, aide de camp to General Dumas 23 September 1793, acting squadron commander and aide de camp to Murat 14 August 1799, confirmed 21 April 1800, brigade commander 17 April 1801, colonel of the 10th Hussars 1 February 1805.

He became brigadier-general 24 December 1805, aide de camp to Murat, temporarily commanded a light cavalry brigade 16 October 1806, commanded the light cavalry of the 1st Corps of the Grande Armée 14 Mai 1807, at the head of the 4 cavalry regiments of the 1st Corps in Spain 7 September 1808, wounded at Talavera-de-la-Reyna 28 July 1809, commanded the 1st Brigade of the 2nd Cuirassier Division 1811, same division in the 2nd Corps of the Grande Armée 15 January 1812, commanded a cavalry brigade on foot 18 October 1812, major-general 4 December 1812, commanded the Light Cavalry Division of the 3rd Corps 22 March 1813, then that of the 6th Corps 5 May 1813, and finally that of the 12th Corps 15 August 1813.

He commanded the 5th Cavalry Division of the 5th Corps 2 December 1813, died 16 December 1813 at Metz. LH CH 14 June 1804, O 14 May 1807, Baron de Beaumont l.p. 26 October 1808.

Wertingen, 8 October 1805: the Colonel of the 1st Hussars, Louis Carrière captured an Austrian captain in the middle of his regiment by himself and killed several cuirassiers who came to rescue their officer. He was made a Brigadier-General in the 24 December 1806 promotions.

Essling 22 May 1809 and died from his wounds 20 June 1809.

CARLIER DE LAGARDE (Georges Constant, 1774-1813): born in Pontséricourt (Aisne) on 23 April 1774. Volunteer in the 5th Dragoons 11 May 1792, in the Grenadiers à cheval of the Consular Guard 15 February 1800.

He became brigadier 12 March 1801, maréchal des logis 12 October 1802, sub-lieutenant in the 6th Cuirassiers 30 August 1805, took up his appointment 21 June 1806, lieutenant 6 October 1808, confirmed 1808, sabre wound to his wrist at Essling May 1809, captain 3 June 1809, squadron commander in the 12th Cuirassiers 3 September 1813, lost a leg at Leipzig 16 October 1813 and died from the amputation 19 October 1813. LH CH 14 June 1804

CAULAINCOURT (Auguste Jean Gabriel, Count, 1777-1812): younger brother of the Duke of Vicence and nephew of General d'Harville, born in Caulaincourt (Aisne) on 16 September 1777. Volunteered for the 8th Cavalry 6 January 1792, struck off the rolls because on leave 1 April 1793, sub-lieutenant aide de camp to General Aubert Dubayet 28 March 1795, in the 12th Dragoons 24 August 1795, lieutenant in the 1st Carabiniers 21 January 1796.

He became captain in the 21st Dragoons 28 January 1797, in the suite of the 1st Dragoons 12 December 1797, in post 22 January 1798, aide de camp to General Klein 8 May 1799, acting squadron commander 30 June 1799, lance wound at Muotathal 1 October 1799 and shot in the head at Marengo 14 June 11800, confirmed in the 1st Dragoons 8 December 1799 and by decree dated 17 December 1799, took 400 prisoners with only forty dragoons at Vedolago 13 January 1801, brigade commander in the 19th Dragoons 24 August 1801, aide de camp to Louis Bonaparte while keeping his command 9 June 1804.

He went into service with the King of Holland 5 June 1806, Grand Equerry and aide de camp to the King Louis 21 June 1806, general-major 30 August 1806, ambassador of Holland to Naples 19 December 1807, Lasalle's division 12 January 1808, brigadier-general in French service in the Poitiers cavalry division 11 February 1808, in Spain March 1808, in the suite of the general staff of the Army of Spain 15 November 1808, commanded the 2nd Brigade of Lahussaye's Dragoon Division 24 December 1808, got hold of Amarantha and commanded the rearguard when it was evacuated 12 May 1809, victor at the Puent-del-Arzobispo 8 August 1809.

He commanded the 5 brigades of dragoons which formed the 8th Corps Cavalry in the Army of Spain 29 November 1809, on sick leave 28 February 1810,

returned to France, Governor of the Pages, in Russia 1812, commanded the Imperial General Headquarters 7 July 1812.

He replaced Montbrun at the head of the 2nd Cavalry Corps at the Moskova and captured the Great Redoubt having assured Napoleon that they would find him there dead or alive, killed by a cannonball when he entered it at the head of the 5th Cuirassiers 7 September 1812. LH CH 11 December 1803, O 14 June 1804, C 25 December 1805, Baron of the Empire l.p. 19 May, Count 1810.

At the Moskova on 7 September 1812, the artillery cannonades were terrible. General Montbrun had just been killed at the head of the 2nd Cavalry Corps. Napoleon entrusted these proud horsemen to Auguste de Caulaincourt with the mission to capture the Great Redoubt. The general announced to the Emperor they would find him there dead or alive. The charge was launched and the redoubt was taken at very heavy cost. Auguste de Cauilaincourt, at the forefront of the 4th Cuirassiers was hit by a cannonball and killed at the entrance of the redoubt. He had kept his word.

of Spain 25 December 1809, in the 1st Legion of the Gendarmerie à Cheval d'Espagne 'Burgos' 1 January 1811.

He became brigadier 10 June 1812, dismissed with the corps 27 February 1813 and posted sub-lieutenant in the 6th Cuirassiers 1 March 1813, incorporated with his 4th Squadron into the 2nd Provisional Heavy Cavalry in Hamburg 11 September 1813, returned with the garrison 30 May 1814, wounded at Waterloo 18 June 1815 dismissed 21 November 1815.

CARTIER (Jean Baptiste, 1777-?): born in Hanvoile (Oise) on 21 March 1777. In the 19th Cavalry 25 January 1800, shot in the right thigh at Hohenlinden 3 December 1800, brigadier 22 March 1802, in the Grenadiers à Cheval of the Guard 9 February 1803, fourrier 22 December 1805, maréchal des logis 3 July 1809, maréchal des logis-chef 1 September 1809, lieutenant in the 1st Cuirassiers 13 March 1813, rejoined the regiment 20 June 1813, incorporated with his regiment into the 1st Provisional Heavy Cavalry in Hamburg 11 September 1813.

He was returned with the garrison 27 May 1814, in the King's Cuirassiers 1814, remained in Paris at the disposal of the Minister of War 20 January 1815, returned to the same regiment which had become the 1st Cuirassiers again 1 April 1815, dismissed and put in retirement 24 December 1815. LH CH 14 March 1806.

CASENEUVE aka **BAPTISTE** (Jean, 1773-?): born in Commercy (Meuse) on 8 February. Child of the regiment in the Royal-Cavalerie 2 February 1780, paid by the corps 1 July 1780, trooper 8 February 1790, in the same regiment when it became the 2nd Cavalry 1 January 1791.

He was brigadier 7 June 1799, brigadier-fourrier 14 June 1800, maréchal des logis 3 November 1800, maréchal des logis-chef 22 December 1800, in the

CARPENTIER (Louis Joseph, 1779-?): born in Arras (Pas-de-Calais) on 24 December 1779. Hussar in the 3rd Regiment 212 May 1798, brigadier 27 June 1802, grenadier in the Grenadiers à Cheval of the Guard 18 June 1805, brigadier 22 December 1805.

He became maréchal des logis 1 August 1806, lieutenant in the 20th Dragoons 28 November 1813, in the 14th Cuirassiers 14 February 1814, dismissed with the corps and incorporated into the 12th Cuirassiers 13 July 1813, dismissed with the corps 10 December 1815. LH CH 25 November 1807.

CARRE (Jacques, 1777-1842): born in Marles (Aisne) on 14 February 1777. In the 1st chasseurs à Cheval 7 October 1792, Health Service Officer 3rd Class in the 19th Cavalry 25 September 1797, trooper in the same regiment 8 October 1799, in the Grenadiers à Cheval of the Consular Guard 15 March 1800, brigadier 11 August 1800, maréchal des logis 12 March 1801, maréchal des logis-chef 22 December 1801.

He became adjutant sub-lieutenant 13 October 1802, second-lieutenant 26 November 1804, captain in the Line 18 December 1805, supernumerary in the 10th Cuirassiers 31 December 1805, in post in the 9th Cuirassiers 11 April 1806, sabre wound to his head at Friedland 14 June 1807, shot in the neck at the Moskova 7 September 1812.

He was squadron commander in the 2nd Cuirassiers 14 May 1813, left on half-pay when the regiment was disbanded 10 December 1815. LH CH 22 June 1804.

CARRE (Simon, 1777-après 1833): born in Beugnuex (Aisne) on 17 August 1777. In the 16th Dragoons 30 February 1801, brigadier 26 March 1802, gendarme in the 6th Legion of the Indre Company 29 September 1804, in the 14th Squadron

same regiment when it became the 2nd Cuirassiers 12 October 1802, sub-lieutenant 30 October 1806, confirmed 6 November 1806, incorporated into the 13th cuirassiers 21 October 1808, lieutenant 13 February 1809, captain 18 September 1811, instated 21 October 1811, replaced 5 March 1814 and retired 9 August 1814.

CASTAGNOLA (Barthélémy, 1786-?): born in la Spezzia (Apenines) on 29 April 1786. In the Grenadiers à Cheval of the Imperial Guard 15 January 1807.

He became sub-lieutenant in the 8th Cuirassiers 3 July 1809, lieutenant-adjutant-major 5 June 1813, captain 28 September 1813, in the suite 12 may 1814, dismissed with the regiment 5 December 1815. LH CH 25 February 1814.

CASTAGNON (?-1807): adjutant NCO in the 5th Cuirassiers, sub-lieutenant 12 December 1806, killed at Hoff 6 February 1807.

CASTELLANI DE MERLANI (Pierre Laurent Michel Hyacinthe Auguste Louis Marie, 1790-1812): born in Alexandria (Marengo) on 29 September 1790. Pupil at Saint-Cyr 12 July 1808.

He passed out 19 September 1808, sub-lieutenant in the suite of the 3rd Cuirassiers 14 August 1810, in post 15 November 1811, disappeared at the Berezina 28 November 1812.

CASTINEL (Joseph Louis, 1785-?): born in Aix (Bouches-du-Rhône) on 31 May 1785. Grenadier in the 32nd of the Line 1 January 1811, corporal 1 April 1811, fourrier 14 May 1811, maréchal des logis in the team train of the Guard 5 April 1812, taken prisoner when trying to save a caisson of the Royal Neapolitan Artillery during the retreat in 1812.

He became maréchal des logis-chef 2 February 1814, dismissed 16 May 1814, in the Gardes du Corps of the King 16 June 1814, cavalry sub-lieutenant 22 December 1814, in the 3rd Cuirassiers 19 May 1815, rejoined his regiment 7 June 1815, left 1 September 1815 to return to his position of the previous 20 March. LH CH 3 November 1814.

CATRIN (Guillaume, 1785-?): born in Andernack (Rhin-et-Moselle) on 1785. Velite in the Grenadiers à Pied of the Guard 6 September 1806, velite in the Grenadiers à Cheval of the Guard 2 October 1806, sub-lieutenant in the suite of the 1st Cuirassiers 20 June 1809, in post 31 July 1811, in the King's cuirassiers 1 July 1814.

He became captain by mistake 25 March 1815, rectified to lieutenant 30 March 1815, in the 2nd Cuirassiers 23 May 1815, rejoined his regiment 2 June 1815, instated 6 June 1815, left as a foreign national when the regiment was disbanded 10 December 1815. LH CH 29 July 1814.

CATUFFE (Raymond, 1765-?): born in

Layrac (Aude) on 15 August 1765. In the 22nd Chasseurs à Cheval 16 November 1792, lieutenant 16 January 1793, captain 5 September 1793, wounded at Réart 14 September 1793, in Bonaparte's Guides 8 July 1796 returned to the 22nd Chasseurs à Cheval 18 June 1797.

He became squadron commander in the suite 20 December 1800, in post at the headquarters of the Army of Spain 11 April 1808, deputy on the staff of the Grand-Duke of Berg 24 May 1808, in the General Cavalry Depot of the Army of Germany 2 June 1809, squadron commander in the 30 Dragoons 29 September 1809, in the 31st Chasseurs à Cheval 5 October 1811, cavalry major 28 June 1813, in the suite of the 11th Cuirassiers 2 May 1815, returned home 25 August 1815. LH CH.

CAUVIGNY (François Gustave Frédéric, 1792-1812): born in Caen (Calvados) on 22 July 1792. Pupil at the Saint-Germain school, sub-lieutenant 7 June 1811, supernumerary in the 6th Cuirassiers 25 June 1811, in post 21 February 1812, wounded at the Moskova 7 September 1812 and died from his wounds 18 October 1812.

CAVAILHON (Philippe, 1769-?): born in Exidueil (Dordogne) on 15 August 1769. In the 14th Dragoons 25 April 1791, brigadier 22 September 1794, brigadier-fourrier 20 April 1795, two sabre wounds to his head and one to his left arm 10 July 1796.

He became maréchal des logis 25 November 1798, shot in the right thigh at Abukir 25 July 1799, maréchal des logis-chef 23 September 1799, shot and wounded at Alexandria 21 March 1801, maréchal des logis in the Gendarmerie 28 March 1802, lieutenant 5 December 1809 in the 1st Legion of Gendarmerie à Cheval 1 January 1811, captain in the 6th Cuirassiers 28 February 1813, Gendarmerie captain 19 July 1813.

CAYEN aka **MARIN** (François, 1760-?): born in Thonon (Mont-Blanc) on 3 March 1760. In the Piedmont Dragoons 19 October 1772, brigadier 1 October 1787, dismissed 1 June 1790, in the Volontaires Nationaux à Cheval of the Ecole Militaire 20 September 1792.

He became brigadier October 1792, brigadier-fourrier October 1792, maréchal des logis November 1792, sub-lieutenant in the 35th Cavalry when it was formed from the Volontaires Nationaux 7 February 1793 which became the 24th Cavalry 4 June 1793, lieutenant 10 September 1798, incorporated into the 1st Cuirassiers 1 January 1802, captain 24 November 1806, retired 9 May 1808, left 1 June 1808, in the 6th Battalion of Veterans 30 September 1811, in the suite of the 13th Company of Veterans 1 August 1814, retired 21 October 1814, in the 12th Company of Veterans 25 February 1815, dismissed with pension 9 December 1815. LH CH 14 April 1807.

CAZENEUVE see **DEBATE** aka **CAZENEUVE**

CEGLAS (Sébastien, 1763-1805): born in Chalons-sur-Saône (Saône-et-Loire) on 6 January 1763.

Fusilier in the Provence-Infanterie 13 August 1780, left 15 October 1788, in the 1st Cavalry 22 March 1791, brigadier 3 August 1794, brigadier-fourrier 21 June 1798.

He became maréchal des logis 14 May 1799, shot in the right shoulder at la Trebbia 19 June 1799, maréchal des logis-chef 11 April 1800, in the same regiment when it became the 1st Cuirassiers 10 October 1801, adjutant-NCO 3 April 1803, elected sub-lieutenant 21 April 1804, killed by a cannonball at Austerlitz 2 December 1805. LH CH 18 December 1803.

CELARD (Jean Antoine, ?-1812): in the velites of the Imperial Guard, sub-lieutenant 17 December 1811, in the suite of the 3rd Cuirassiers 25 January 1812, took up his appointment 21 February 1812, killed at the Moskova 7 September 1812.

CERNAY see **QUINETTE** de **CERNAY.**

CEYRAT (Jean Baptiste, 1777-?): born in Clermont-Ferrand (Puy-de-Dôme) on 3 November 1777. In the 21st Cavalry 7 October 1798, brigadier 31 December 1798, fourrier 10 January 1799, maréchal des logis 28 April 1800, incorporated into the Carabiniers 10 February 1803, in the 8th Cuirassiers 31 March 1803, maréchal des logis-chef 28 December 1803, sub-lieutenant 27 April 1807, cannonball wound to his right leg and his horse killed under him at Essling 22 May 1809, lieutenant 3 June 1809, lieutenant adjutant-major 9 August 1809, acting captain 9 February 1811.

He was shot in the neck during the taking of the Great Redoubt at the Moskova 7 September 1812, lance wound to his left arm and his horse killed

Anselme Chalendar towards 1840.

under him at Mojaïsk 4 October 1812, went as captain to a company 14 April 1813, seconded with his squadron to the 2nd Provisional Heavy Cavalry in Hamburg 11 September 1813, acting squadron commander 24 March 1814, returned with the garrison 30 May 1814, non-active 25 August 1814.

He was confirmed as squadron commander, non-active, on 4 February 1815, returned in the suite of the 8th Cuirassiers 14 April 1815, confirmed in post 19 May 1815, wounded at Waterloo 18 June 1815, non-active again 1 September 1815. LH CH 13 August 1809, O 18 October 1812.

CHABANNE see **TANDEAU de CHABANNE.**

CHABOT see **ROHAN CHABOT.**

CHABRILLAN see **MORETON de CHABRILLAN**

CHAILLOT (François Hyacinthe, 1779-1867): born in Châlons (Marne) on 21 December 1779. In the 16th Cavalry 24 June 1803 which became the 25th Dragoons 24 September 1803, brigadier 24 October 1803.

He became fourrier 7 December 1804, maréchal des logis 1 September 1809, maréchal des logis-chef 16 September 1809, sub-lieutenant, 21 April 1813, taken prisoner 27 September 1813, returned to the 2nd Cuirassiers 3 September 1814, wounded at Waterloo 18 June 1815, dismissed with the corps and non-active on half-pay 10 December 1815.

CHALENDAR (Anselme Frédéric Joseph Vincent de, 1791-after 1846): born in Vaudoncourt (Vosges) on 21 January 1792. Pupil at the Ecole Spéciale Impériale de Cavalerie in Saint-Germain 7 January 1810, sub-lieutenant in the 9th Cuirassiers 11 March 1812, shrapnel wound to his left hip at Leipzig 16 October 1813, lieutenant 22 December 1813.

He became captain in the 2nd Company of the King's Musketeers 1 July 1814, first-lieutenant in the 2nd Cuirassiers of the Garde Royale 12 October 1815, captain adjutant-major 2 November 1815. LH CH 5 September 1813.

CHALUS (Jean, 1764-1809): born in Mauzun (Puy-de-Dôme) on 30 August 1764. Volunteer in the Royale-Dragons 25 May 1782, brigadier 18 September 1784, fourrier 21 May 1787, maréchal des logis 1 May 1788, maréchal des logis-chef 1 January 1790, in the same regiment when it became the 1st Dragoons 1 January 1791, resigned 6 April 1791.

He commanded the Mauzun National Guard 19 May 1791, elected captain in the 1st Battalion of the Puy-de-Dôme Volunteers 21 September 1791, sub-lieutenant in the 6th Cavalry 25 January 1792, lieutenant 1 September 1792, captain 28 April 1794, two sabre wounds near Maubeuge 13 May 1794, discharged 9 April 1796, captain in the 6th Cavalry 2 September 1798.

He became squadron commander 19 September 1804, in the same regiment when it became the 6th Cuirassiers 23 December 1802, adjutant-commandant 11 July 1807, in the Ocean Coast Observation Corps 9 November 1807, in Spain with the 4th Corps 11 April 1809, died of fever at Palencia 19 Mai 1809. LH CH 14 June 1804.

CHAMBARLHAC (Jean Antoine Joseph, 1778-après 1824): born in le Puy (Haute-Loire) on 29 June 1778. In the 1st Haute-Loire Battalion 1 January 1793, in the 12th Infantry of the Line 14 February 1794, sergeant 24 February 1798, sub-lieutenant 13 October 1798, lieutenant in the 78th Half-Brigade 5 October 1799, in the 15th Cavalry 14 March 1800, in the 20th Cavalry 21 July 1801.

He was dismissed with the corps 31 December 1802, incorporated in the suite of the 1st Carabiniers 6 February 1803, took up his appointment in the 8th Cuirassiers 8 June 1803, instated 19 June 1803, aide de camp to General Girardon 16 November 1805, in the 5th Dragoons 27 February 1807, captain 13 November 1810

He became squadron commander in the 10th Chasseurs à Cheval 25 November 1813, in the 1st Chasseurs à Cheval 16 December 1813, non-active on half-pay 16 September 1815.

CHAMBELLANT (Antoine Jules, 1781-?): born in Paris (Seine) on 23 July 1781. Soldier in the Navy 20 April 1794, in the 2nd Cuirassiers 18 September 1806, brigadier 24 October 1803, maréchal des logis 2 December 1803, confirmed 2 January 1804, sub-lieutenant 3 April 1807, lieutenant 10 March 1809, wounded at Wagram 6 July 1809.

He was confirmed 9 August 1809, captain 13 February 1812, sabre wound to his head at Leipzig 18 October 1813, in the 1st Cuirassiers 30 April 1814, kept in his unit in the King's Cuirassiers 1 July 1814, non-active on half-pay 16 January 1815. LH CH 11 October 1812.

CHAMBON (Louis Charles, 1788-?): born in Lesraux (Ardèche) on 24 May 1788.

Velite in the Dragoons of the Imperial Guard 31 May 1808, sub-lieutenant in the 12th Cuirassiers 8 February 1813, lost his index finger of his right hand at Leipzig 18 October 1813, resigned 1814.

General Joachim Chamorin.

CHAMORIN (Joachim Vital, baron de, 1773-1811): born in Bonneles (Seine-et-Oise) on 16 August 1773. Engaged in the Champagne-Infanterie 23 December 1788, instated 17 January 1789.

He was in the same regiment when it became the 7th Infantry 1 January 1791, corporal 11 March 1792, caporal-fourrier 26 April 1792, left 30 June 1792, in the 6th Hérault Battalion, adjutant NCO 15 July 1793, sub-lieutenant 24 October 1793, wounded by a Biscayan shot to his left leg, and promoted acting captain on the battlefield for having been the first to enter a redoubt at le Boulou 30 April 1794, confirmed at the 8th Côte-d'Or Battalion 8 September 1794, in the 60th Battle 30 June 1795, grenadier captain 24 April 1796, in the 12th of the Line 25 May 1796.

He became aide de camp to General Sauret 7 March 1800, acting aide de camp to General Watrin 12 May 1800, shot in the right hip at Montebello 9 June 1800, in the suite of the 6th Hussars and kept in his job 10 June 1800, confirmed 8 September 1800, shot in the chest at Pozzolo while crossing the Mincio 25 December 1800, acting squadron commander in the 11th Hussars and kept on as aide de camp 25 December 1800, confirmed 22 December 1801, available 15 December 1802, took up his appointment in the 3rd Cuirassiers 23 January 1804, squadron commander in the Grenadiers à Cheval of the Guard 5 September 1805, colonel in the 26th Dragoons 15 February 1807, shot in the right leg continuing nonetheless to lead all the charges until 11 pm at Heilsberg 10 June 1807.

He was killed by a sabre blow to his head after being unhorsed and refusing to surrender at Campo Mayor 25 March 1811, had not received

Mem ody [signature]

CHAMPION de NANSOUTY (Etienne Marie Antoine Charles, Count, 1768-1815): born in Bordeaux (Gironde) on 30 May 1768. Pupil at the school in Brienne then in Paris 21 October 1782, gentleman cadet with the rank of sub-lieutenant 30 May 1783, sub-lieutenant in the Bourgogne-Cavalerie 26 March 1785.

He was , replacement captain in the

General Nansouty reviews his Cuirassier division at Cologne on 24 November 1811. Composition by J. Girbal.
(Private collection)

General Nansouty wearing his Major-General's uniform.
(RR)

Franche-Comté-Cavalerie 6 April 1788, replacement captain in the Lauzun Hussars 24 May 1788, deputy to the Adjutant-General Poncet 20 December 1791, aide de camp to Luckner, lieutenant-colonel in the 2nd Chasseurs à Cheval 5 March 1792, in the 9th Cavalry 4 April 1792, colonel of the regiment 9 November 1793, brigadier-general 29 August 1799, under Ney September 1799, in the cavalry reserve October 1799.

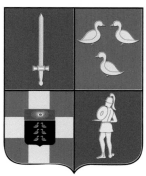

He commanded the four cavalry regiments intended for the Reserve Army 9 March 1800, commanded a brigade of dragoons on the right wing of the Army of the Rhine 15 March 1800, Gudin's division 4 July 1800, commanded the cavalry reserve of the corps on the right from 23 September 1800 until 10 March 1801, in the 1st Gironde Observation Corps 1

June 1801, available 1 January 1802, in the 22nd Military Division 19 March 1802, major-general 24 March 1803, commanded the Seine-et-Oise Department in the 1st Military division 25 march 1803, in the Nijmegen Camp 28 April 1803.

He commanded the cavalry in the Army of Hanover 3 May 1803, called back to Paris 31 January 1804, commanded the heavy cavalry division in the corps of Prince Louis at Boulogne 3 August 1805 then the 1st Cuirassier and Carabinier Division in the cavalry reserve of the Grande Armée 24 August 1805, First Chamberlain to the Empress 1805, First Equerry to the Emperor 1808, commanded the 1st Heavy Cavalry Division in the Army of the Rhine 12 October 1808, in Spain as First Equerry to Napoleon November 1808.

He returned with him at the end of January 1809, accompanied him to Germany April 1809, took up command of the 1st Heavy Cavalry Division again in the cavalry reserve of the Army of the Rhine 17 April 1809, replaced 17 October 1809, First Inspector-General of Dragoons, commanded the 2nd and 4th

Murat orders Nansouty to attack.
Composition by Victor Huen.
(Unterlinden Museum, RR)

Cuirassier Divisions 19 October 1811 then the 2nd alone 15 January 1812, commanded the 1st Reserve Cavalry Corps of the Grande Armée 15 February 1812, shot in the knee at the Moskova 7 September 1812, Colonel-General of Dragoons 14 January 1813, Commander-in-Chief of the Cavalry of the Imperial Guard 10 January 1814.

He was wounded at Montmirail 11 February 1814 and at Craonne 7 March 1814, aide de camp to the Comte d'Artois April 1814, member of the commission of general officers for the Guard 20 April 1814, the King's Extraordinary Commissioner in the 18th Military Division 22 April 1814, Captain-Lieutenant in the Musketeers 6 July 1814, Inspector-General of Dragoons 14 July 1814, died in Paris as a result of his wounds and fatigue from the war 12 February 1815.

LH CH 11 December 1803, C 14 June 1804, GO 25 December 1805, GA 11 July 1807, Count of the Empire l.p. 27 July 1808.

Nansouty charging at the head
of his cuirassiers. He remained faithful
to the Emperor and only death prevented
him from taking part in the Hundred Days.
Composition by P. Benigni. (RR)

his appointment to the rank of brigadier-general on 5 March 1811. LH CH 14 June 1804, O 14 March 1806, C 11 December 1808, Baron of the Empire l.p. 10 February 1809.

CHAMOY
see **ROUSSEAU de CHAMOY**

CHAMPAGNAC (Joseph, 1772-?): born in Paulhenc (Cantal) on 2 May 1772. In the 3rd Cavalry 20 November 1793, brigadier-fourrier 25 May 1797, maréchal des logis-chef 20 May 1798, sabre wound to is left hand at Valence 1799, sub-lieutenant 21 May 1800, lieutenant 24 May 1802, in the same regiment when it became the 3rd Cuirassiers 12 October 1802, captain 12 March 1804, wounded by a Biscayan shot which broke his left shoulder at Friedland 14 June 1807.

He became squadron commander in the 5th Cuirassiers 13 February 1809, shot in the right arm at Essling 22 may 1809, second-major 6 April 1811, commanded the 2nd Marching Regiment of Dragoons of the Army of the Midi in Spain from 14 September 1811 to 1 November 1812, appointed major of the 8th Cuirassiers 26 February 1813, confirmed 28 September 1814, dismissed with the corps and put on the non-active list 5 December 1815, left 12 February 1816. LH CH 14 March 1806.

CHANAUD (Pierre, 1764-?): born in Saint-Vallier (Drôme) on 22 November 1794. In the Roi-Infanterie 15 March 1786, dismissed 15 April 1790, sergeant-major in the 2nd Drôme Battalion 12 October 1791, sub-lieutenant 5 April 1792, lieutenant 22 November 1793, shot at Saorgio 27 May 1794.

He was in the Guides à Cheval of the Army of Naples 11 December 1798, in the same regiment when it became the Dragons-Gardes of the general in command of the Army of Italy 13 March 1800, captain 21 May 1800, shot and wounded at Genoa 28 May 1800, Gendarmerie captain 16 May 1802, discharged 1 January 1811,

Standard belonging to the 1st Squadron of the 12th Cuirassiers. (RR)

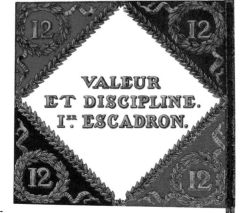

reappointed captain in the 10th Cuirassiers 3 July 1813, retired 6 August 1814.

CHANDEBOIS (Pierre Louis, 1784-?): born in Courcerault (Orne) on 11 August 1784. In the 10th Cuirassiers 12 May 1805, fourrier 11 January 1807, maréchal des logis-chef 9 October 1808, several sabre wounds, his horse killed under him and taken prisoner at Eckmühl 22 April 1809, freed when Regensburg was taken the following day 23 April 1809.

He became adjutant 16 May 1809, sub-lieutenant 6 November 1811, wounded by a Biscayan shot to his left side at the Moskova 7 September 1812, lieutenant 8 July 1812, shot and wounded in his left thigh at Waterloo 18 June 1815, dismissed with the corps 25 December 1815. LH CH 2 November 1814.

CHANDRU (Pierre François, 1783-?): born in Chartres (Eure-et-Loir) on 18 July 1783. In the 3rd Cuirassiers 11 November 1803, fourrier 3 December 1805, three sabre wounds to his face, one to the neck and another to his left calf at Friedland 14 June 1807, maréchal des logis 2 January 1808.

He became maréchal des logis-chef 14 May 1809, sub-lieutenant 5 June 1809, lieutenant 12 August 1812, left hand fractured by a bullet at Waterloo 18 June 1815, dismissed 25 November 1815. LH CH 25 February 1814.

CHANOINE de SAINT THIBAULT (Sulpice, 1776-?): born in Troyes (Aube) on 20 March 1776. In the infantry of the Nord Legion 21 November 1792, caporal-fourrier 14 February 1793, shot in the left thigh at Mainz, in the 11th Hussars 4 September 1797, brigadier-fourrier 4 April 1798, maréchal des logis 10 May 1799, grapeshot wound to his right knee while crossing the Neckar.

He was discharged because of his wound 1 July 1799, in the same regiment when it became the 29th Dragoons 24 September 1803, sub-lieutenant in the 7th Hussars 4 August 1804, wounded at Heilsberg 10 June 1807.

He became lieutenant 12 October 1809, aide de camp to General Gauthrin 10 January 1812, captain 18 October 1812, shot in the left hip in front of Smolensk August 1812, deputy on the general staff of Danzig 1 January 1813, captain commanding the Imperial Gendarmerie in Danzig 15 February 1813.

He became director of the Police and commanded the depot of prisoners of war during the siege 1813, taken prisoner with the town 1814, in the 2nd Cuirassiers 23 June 1815, returned home 20 October 1815.

CHANZY (Bertrand Nicolas, 1789-?): born in Grivy (Ardennes) on 20 October 1789. In the 3rd Cuirassiers 12 February 1807, fourrier 1 May 1808, three sabre wounds and hurt by his horse when it was killed under him by a cannonball at Essling May 1809.

HIPAULT de BEZENCOURT (François Clément, 1765-1809): born in Orléans (Loiret) on 8 December 1765. Dragoon in the Colonel-Général Regiment 10 August 1781, dismissed 31 May 1787, in the Loiret National Guard 1789, captain in the 1st Corps of Hussards de la Liberté when it was created 2 September 1792 which became the 7th bis Hussars 28 November 1792, squadron commander 17 February 1794, captured 22 Hussars during a reconnaissance mission 23 February 1794, discharged 26 August 1794, reinstated in the suite of the same regiment 1 May 1794.

He took up his appointment 17 February 1795, unemployed 3 April 1796, squadron commander in the 18th Cavalry 11 March 1802 which became the 27th Dragoons 24 September 1803, in the 4th cuirassiers 22 January 1804, shot and wounded after having two horses killed under him when, accompanied by three squadrons of the cavalry vanguard, he chased the enemy out of the town and pursued them without letting up over four leagues taking 260 prisoners at Marienwerder 11 February 1807. Wounded at Friedland 14 June 1807, major in the 6th Chasseurs à Cheval 22 March 1808, died of illness in Venice 24 February 1809. LH CH 14 June 1804, O 15 January 1808.

At Lavauzone on 3 December 1794, Squadron Commander François Chipault de Bezencourt of the 7th Bis Hussars captured forty Hussars including a colonel and seven other officers, a flag and two cannon. He was wounded by a bayonet in his left thigh and his horse killed under him in the action. He joined the 4th Cuirassiers, was shot and wounded and had two horses killed under him while at the head of two squadrons of the cavalry vanguard pursuing the enemy out of the town of Marienwerder and chasing them without respite for four leagues taking 260 prisoners on 11 February 1807. On the following 10 June at the Battle of Heilsberg, he was wounded fifty-four times by swords and daggers etc., and was wounded again at Friedland on 14 June. He was made an Officer of the Légion d'Honneur on 8 January 1808.

He became maréchal des logis-chef 5 June 1809, regimental pay officer 1812, sub-lieutenant pay officer 14 May 1813, wounded by a cannon-ball in his back at Leipzig 16 October 1813 and by a Biscayan shot to his shoulder 18 October 1813, sabre wound to is left arm at Fère-Champenoise 25 March 1814, dismissed 25 November 1815. LH CH 4 December 1813.

CHANZY (Pierre Nicolas, 1768-?): born in Grivy (Ardennes) on 16 April 1768. Trooper in the Commissaire-Général Regiment 9 September 1789

HOUARD (Claude Louis, Baron, 1771-1843): born in Strasbourg (Bas-Rhin) on 15 August 1771. Cadet at the artillery school in Metz 28 September 1789, lieutenant in the 1st Bas-Rhin Battalion 7 September 1791, sub-lieutenant in the 9th Cavalry 25 January 1792, sabre wound to his left arm at Alzey 30 March 1793.

He became lieutenant 1 April 1793, several sabre wounds of which one to his left hand at Landau 22 July 1793, captain 19 November 1793, aide de camp to Delmas 5 November 1798, squadron commander on the battlefield at Magnano 5 April 1799, aide de camp to Moreau 11 May 1799 then Delmas April 1800.

He was deputy on the general staff of the Army of the Rhine, retroactively in the suite of the 1 Carabiniers since 2 March 1801, appointed squadron commander in the 1st Carabiniers 19 August 1801, acting commanding officer of the 1st Carabiniers from 21 October 1805 to 3 December 1805, wounded by a Biscayan shot in his chest and four sabre wounds and his horse killed under him at the head of his regiment at Austerlitz 2 December 1805, colonel of the 2nd Cuirassiers 27 December 1805, rejoined his unit and instated 18 January 1806, as the obstacles on the terrain prevented his regiment from following him he crossed several ditches and threw himself almost alone against a village occupied by the enemy where the regiment then took 200 prisoners near Regensburg 25 April 1809, allowed to retire 3 May 1810, kept in command of his regiment 20 August 1810, on prolonged leave for a month June 1811, brigadier-general 6 July 1811, in Cologne 19 October 1811, struck off the regimental rolls 1 November

1811, commanded the 2nd Carabinier Brigade (2nd Carabiniers) in Defrance's Division May 1812, wounded twice by Biscayan shot and shot and wounded in the arm at the Moskova 7 September 1812, dismissed for health reasons and returned to France 24 February 1813, commanded a brigade of the 21st Dragoons Division 13 April 1813, on leave because of his wounds, major in the Dragoons of the Guard 6 October 1813, commanded the mass levy in the Bas-Rhin 4 January 1814, commanded at Huningue 5 September 1814, on leave 1815.

He commanded a cavalry brigade of the Army of the Moselle 23 April 1815 then two lancer regiments of the Bas-Rhin National Guard 11 May 1815, retired 6 October 1815. LH CH 14 June 1804, O 14 May 1807, C 23 August 1814, Baron of the Empire l.p. 27 November 1808.

Landshut, 27 June 1800. The Alsatian Squadron Commander Claude Chouard charged into the town capturing two cannon and 150 prisoners including several officers. His horse was killed under him.

On 23 April 1808, as Colonel of the 2nd Cuirassiers he distinguished himself not very far away from there, near Regensburg. Some obstacles had prevented his regiment from following him and he crossed several ditches to throw himself almost alone into an enemy-occupied village where the regiment then took 200 prisoners.

12th Cavalry, paid by the corps 22 October 1797, in the same regiment when it became the 12th Cuirassiers 24 September 1803, maréchal des logis 5 January 1804.

He became maréchal des logis-chef 20 February 1808, adjutant NCO 1 May 1808, seconded to the Veterinary School at Alfort for the year 1809, sub-lieutenant 15 March 1812, died at Vilna 8 December 1812. LH CH 1 October 1807.

CHARDOILLET (François Christophe, 1766-1804): born in Essers (Haut-Rhin) on 21 January 1766. In the Royal-Etranger-Cavalerie 31 July 1784, brigadier 29 September 1786, maréchal des logis 17 February 1788 in the same regiment when it became the 7th Cavalry 1 January 1791.

He became quartermaster-treasurer 10 March 1792, rank of lieutenant 1 November 1792, rank of captain 16 November 1793 and squadron commander 7 December 1793, in the same regiment when it became the 7th Cuirassiers 23 December 1802, died of illness in Verdun 29 September 1804. LH CH 14 June 1814.

CHARET (Auguste de, 1773-1815): born in Saint-Marc (Saint-Domingo) on 4 February 1773. Sub-lieutenant in a corps of volunteer dragoons 1 February 1793 incorporated into the Chasseurs à Cheval des Côtes 7 March 1793 which became the 15th Chasseurs à Cheval 4 June 1793, aide de camp to General Cambray January 1795, staff officer to General Lavalette in Saint Domingo 1801.

He was shot in the left knee in Saint Domingo, in the Gendarmes d'Ordonnance 16 October 1806, maréchal des logis 18 October 1806, maréchal des

which became the 3rd Cavalry 1 January 1791.

He became brigadier-fourrier 16 September 1791, wounded in the left wrist when falling from his horse in Famars Camp 23 May 1793, maréchal des logis 21 June 1793, adjutant sub-lieutenant 1 August 1793, lieutenant quartermaster treasurer 23 April 1794, acting captain 30 May 1798, in the same regiment when it became the 3rd Cuirassiers 12 October 1802, retired 25 November 1815. LH CH 28 September 1814.

CHAPELLE (Alphonse Constant, 1786-?): officer in a company of cavalry levied in Sambre-et-Meuse, sub-lieutenant in the suite of the 1st Cuirassiers 7 March 1810, in post 31 July 1811, taken prisoner in Russia 15 December 1815.

CHARBAUT (Ambroise, 1780-1813): born in Fère-Champenoise (Marne) on 9 June 1780. In the 1st Cuirassiers 22 August 1803, shot in the forearm at Jena 14 October 1806, brigadier-fourrier 5 April 1807, maréchal des logis-chef 11 March 1809, foot bruised by a cannonball at Essling 22 May 1809, sub-lieutenant 5 November 1811, died at the hospital at Kustrin 29 January 1813.

CHARCELLAY de LAROBERDIERE (Achille, 1782-?): born in Amboise (Indre-et-Loire) on 6 July 1782. Gendarme in the Army of the West 20 May

1803, brigadier in the Pô Company 9 June 1803.

He became maréchal des logis in the Genoa Company 20 June 1805, lieutenant in the 4th Squadron of the Gendarmerie d'Espagne 5 December 1809, in the 1st Legion of the Gendarmerie à Cheval d'Espagne 'Burgos' 1 January 1810, dismissed with the legion 27 February 1813, captain in the 1st Cuirassiers the following day 28 February 1813, in the King's Cuirassiers 1 July 1814, remained in Paris at the disposal of the Minister of War 20 January 1815, returned to the corps 1 April 1815, dismissed and put on the active list 24 December 1815. LH CH 1 March 1813.

CHARDARD (Claude, 1768-?): born in Vittouville (Moselle) on 8 August 1768. In the Artois-Cavalerie 16 December 1784 which became the 9th Cavalry 1 January 1791, brigadier 7 September 1793, fourrier 10 May 1799, maréchal des logis 20 February 1802, in the same regiment when it became the 9th Cuirassiers 24 September 1803.

He was sub-lieutenant 4 March 1812, wounded and taken prisoner near Moscow 22 September 1812, returned 18 December 1814, sent home to await his pension 10 January 1815.

CHARDIN (Louis François, 1787-1812): born in Joigny (Yonne) in 1787. Child of the regiment in the

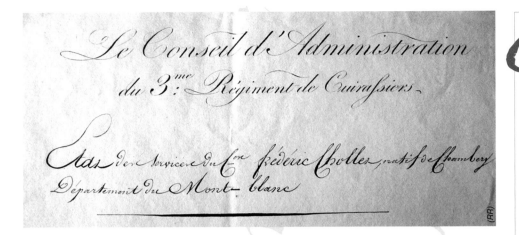

logis-chef 24 January 1807, second-lieutenant 20 April 1807, lieutenant in the suite of the 11th Cuirassiers 16 July 1807, took up his appointment in the 10th Cuirassiers 10 December 1807, captain 16 May 1809, aide de camp to General Richter 23 December 1812, died in Metz 8 April 1815. LH CH 16 April 1807.

CHARLES (Lambert, 1780-?): born in Fouèche (Ardennes) on 18 September 1780. In the 11th Cavalry 11 July 1800 which became the 11th Cuirassiers 24 September 1803, brigadier 1 December 1806, maréchal des logis 8 June 1809, sub-lieutenant 15 March 1812, wounded and taken prisoner at Laon 9 March 1814.

CHARMI (Pierre, 1781-?): born in Saint-Bresson (Haute-Saône) on 16 November 1781. In the 2nd Cavalry 28 April 1800 which became the 2nd Cuirassiers 12 October 1802, brigadier 3 July 1805.

He was maréchal des logis 17 December 1806, in the 1st Provisional Heavy Cavalry in Spain which became the 13th Cuirassiers 21 October 1808, sabre wound to his right hand at Maria 15 June 1809, shot in the head at Sagonte 25 October 1811.

He became sub-lieutenant 11 January 1812 dis-

General Chouard, a Carabinier General. Figurine painted by Ivo Préda.
(Figurines Magazine)

charged 22 May 1813, placed back in the same regiment 6 September 1813, lieutenant 26 November 1813, confirmed 5 March 1814, shot in the right thigh at Villefranche-sur-Saône 18 March 1814, dismissed with the corps and incorporated into the 9th Cuirassiers 9 August 1814, shot in the hand at Waterloo 18 June 1815 retired when the corps was disbanded 26 November 1815. LH CH 29 December 1809.

CHARMONT see **LEMARCHANT de CHARMONT**

CHARNIER (Jean François, 1766-?): born in Liesle (Doubs) on 16 December 1766. In the Royal-Roussillon-Cavalerie 27 June 1782, brigadier 2 December 1789, in the same regiment when it became the 11th Cavalry 1 January 1791, fourrier 16 March 1791, maréchal des logis 25 June 1792,.

He became maréchal des logis-chef 14 July 1792, sub-lieutenant 5 October 1793, lieutenant 23 November 1793, in the suite 11 March 1796, took up his appointment again 25 July 1800, captain but not confirmed 1801, lieutenant-adjutant-major 13 March 1802, in the same regiment when it became the 11th Cuirassiers 24 September 1803, rank of captain 9 September 1803, lieutenant in the 1st Legion of the Gendarmerie 2 June 1804.

CHARROIS (François, 1775-?): born in Ancerville (Meuse) on 8 February 1775. In the 9th Cavalry 15 June 1793, in the 2nd Carabiniers 16 June 1798, brigadier 20 December 1806.

He became maréchal des logis in the 13th Cuirassiers 21 October 1808, sub-lieutenant 12 June 1813, dismissed with the corps and incorporated into the 9th Cuirassiers 9 August 1814, left with a pension when the corps was disbanded 26 November 1815. LH CH 5 November 1804.

CHARTIER (Michel, 1777-?): born in La-Queux (Seine-et-Oise) on 8 October 1777. In the 8th Cavalry 1 December 1798, shot in the left foot while crossing the Danube 19 June 1801, in the same regiment when it became the 8th Cuirassiers 10 October 1801, brigadier 1 January 1802, maréchal des logis 23 June 1805.

He was shot in the right leg at Essling 22 May 1809, shot in the head and his horse killed under

LERC (Antoine Marguerite, Baron, 1774-1846): born in Lyon (Rhône) on 19 July 1774. In the Bretagne Chasseurs à Cheval 1 November 1790 which became the 10th Chasseurs à Cheval 1 January 1791, brigadier-fourrier 16 May 1793, sabre wound to his left wrist at Landau 17 May 1793.

He was second-lieutenant in the Chasseurs à Cheval 18 July 1800, first lieutenant 26 October 1800, captain adjutant-major 1 October 1801, captain in a company 28 July 1802, squadron commander 5 September 1805, commanded the Velites of the regiment when they were created 19 September, with 106 chasseurs took a Russian column and an eight-piece battery at Austerlitz 2 December 1805, colonel in the Line 5 June 1809, in the suite of the Cuirassiers to take over the first commander-less regiment 15 June 1809, appointed colonel commanding the 1st Cuirassiers 16 July 1809.

He was wounded by a shell burst to his right thigh and private parts at Hanau 30 October 1813, wounded in the head by a shell burst in front of Paris 30 March 1814, on leave for a month with pay 19 April 1814, maréchal de camp 23 August 1814, non-active 1 September 1814, confirmed 10 June 1815, did not serve during the Hundred Days. He commanded the Drôme Department 8 December 1815. LH CH 14 June 1804, O 14 March 1806, Chevalier of the Empire l.p. 20 August 1808, Baron d. 15 August 1809 and l.p. 4 June 1810.

He became maréchal des logis-chef 3 April 1794, shot through the body 28 August 1804, sabre wound to his right hand while capturing the grand-Garde of the Wurmser Hussars and 200 infantrymen near Mannheim 3 April 1795, sub-lieutenant 5 January 1797, with four chasseurs captured 300 soldiers and three Austrian officers in the headquarters at Bellune 13 March 1797, in the Grenadiers à cheval of the Consular Guard 3 January 1800.

him at Wagram 5 July 1809, sub-lieutenant 9 August 1809, lieutenant 8 July 1813, wounded at Quatre-Bras 16 June 1815, dismissed with the regiment 1815.

CHASSAIGNE DE LARIBIERE (Antoine Marie François Eugène, 1789-?): born in Limoges (Haute-Vienne) on 4 July 1789. Boarder at the Ecole Militaire at Fontainebleau 11 January 1806.

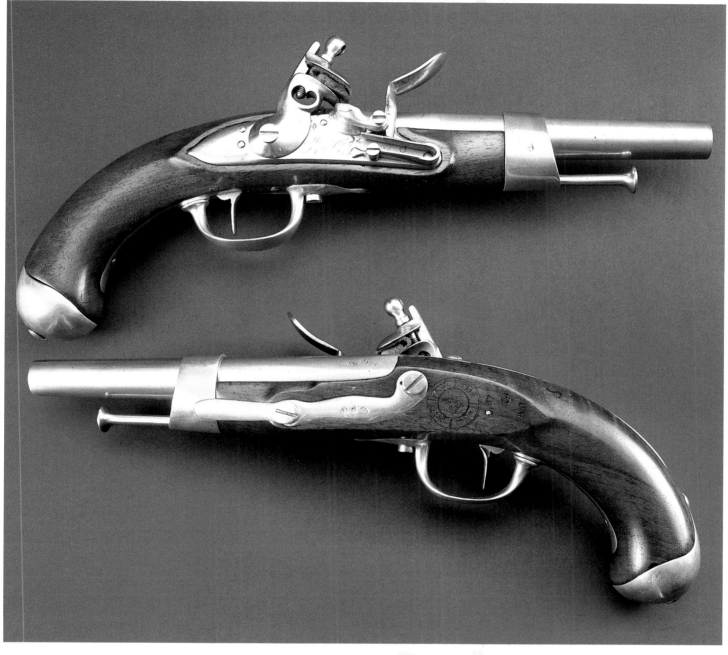

An An-XIII-Model cavalry pistol.
(Photograph © Jean-Louis Viau)

He became sub-lieutenant in the suite of the 2nd Cuirassiers 14 December 1806, took up his appointment, lieutenant 9 August 1809, captain 29 September 1812, two sabre wounds to his head and a lance wound to his thigh and taken prisoner at Leipzig 16 October 1813, returned 1814, six months' leave on half-pay 20 October 1814, returned to the corps, non-active on half-pay when the regiment was disbanded 10 December 1815.

CHASELIER de MOULBAIX
see DUCHASTELIER de MOULBAIX

 **CHATELAIN** (René Julien, baron, 1771-1836): born in Versailles (Seine-et-Oise) on 15 March 1771.
In the Angoulême-Infanterie 2 March 1788, left 27 January 1791, in the

Garde Constitutionelle of the King, dismissed with the corps June 1792, in the Volontaires Nationaux à Cheval from the Ecole Militaire when they were formed 19 August 1792, brigadier 26

August 1792, maréchal des logis 1 February 1793, sub-lieutenant 13 February 1793, in the same regiment when it formed the 27th Cavalry 21 February 1793 and then became the 26th

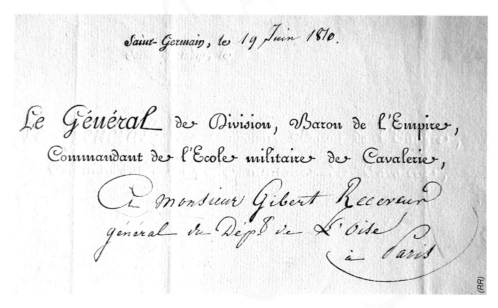

Saint-Germain, le 19 Juin 1870.

Le Général de Division, Baron de l'Empire,
Commandant de l'Ecole militaire de Cavalerie,

A monsieur Gibert Receveur
général de Dept de L'Oise
à Paris

Cavalry 4 June 1793, lieutenant 17 December 1793, arrested with the regiment 28 January 1794 then dismissed with the corps 30 August 1794, in the suite of the Dragoons 29 January 1795, at the head of a platoon routed two enemy battalions supported by 5 cannon at Arcola 17 November 1796.

He became captain 8 October 1798, in the 9th Dragoons 27 July 1799, squadron commander in the 9th Cuirassiers 17 April 1807, second-major 12 January 1812, took up his appointment in the 13th Cuirassiers 19 February 1814, in the suite of the 9th cuirassiers 5 November 1814, colonel 5 May 1815, left 16 May 1815, non-active as a major 1 September 1815. LH CH 14 June 1804, O 15 May 1809, Chevalier of the Empire l.p. 14 June 1810, Baron l.p. 5 May 1815.

CHATELAINE de BANANS see **MARCHANT de la CHATELAINE de BANANS**

CHATILLON
see **REGNAULT CHATILLON**

CHATRY DE LAFOSSE (Jacques Louis, 1776-1854): eldest brother of the President of the Corps Législatif, born in Caen (Calvados) on 8 December 1776. In the 9th Dragoons 18 August 1799, brigadier 29 September 1799, fourrier 14 October 1799.

He became maréchal des logis 30 December 1799, maréchal des logis-chef 2 April 1800, shot and wounded in the left arm at Marengo 14 June 1800, sub-lieutenant 23 October 1800, lieutenant 27 February 1804, aide de camp to General Marmont 7 May 1805, on Maréchal Berthier's staff March 1808, captain 13 Mai 1809, aide de camp to General Saint-Sulpice 1811, squadron commander in the 4th Cuirassiers 23 August 1812, captain in the Dragoons of the Guard 28 March 1813, left to join again 14 April 1813, wounded at Château-Thierry 12 February 1814.

He was squadron commander 17 March 1814, wounded at Waterloo 18 June 1815, non-active 1 December 1815. LH CH 14 March 1804.

CHAUVIN (Alexis Marie, 1770-1805): born in Paris (Seine) on 15 August 1770. Soldier in the Paris Provincial Regiment 25 September 1785, left 1791, in the Volontaires Nationaux à Cheval from the Ecole Militaire 1 September 1792 which formed the 26th Cavalry 21 February 1793 and then became the 25th Cavalry 4 June 1793, sub-lieutenant 22 June 1793, lieutenant 25 August 1797, dismissed with the regiment and incorporated into

the 9th Cuirassiers 22 December 1802, captain by seniority 18 February 1804, killed at Austerlitz 2 December 1805.

CHAUVIN DESORIERES (Charles René Eusèbe François, 1786-?): born in Romazy (Ille-et-Vilaine) on 7 December 1786. Velite in the Grenadiers à Cheval of the Imperial Guard 3 March 1808, sub-lieutenant in the 13th Cuirassiers 20 February 1811, lieutenant 27 August 1813, instated 6 November 1813.

He became adjutant-major 22 November 1813, confirmed 5 March 1814, incorporated into the 9th Cuirassiers 6 August 1814, captain adjutant-major 13 May 1815, wounded at Ligny 16 June 1815, shot and wounded in the right arm at Waterloo 18 June 1815, non-active at the disposal of the government 26 November 1815.

CHAYRON (Raymond, 1758-?): born in Rogendet (Lot-et-Garonne) on 15 September 1758. In the

LE GÉNÉRAL COMTE CLÉMENT DE LA RONCIÈRE
ET SON OFFICIER D'ORDONNANCE
LE CAPITAINE WEIGEL, DU 19ᵉ CHASSEURS
1810

General Clément de la Roncière lost his left arm after receiving 12 wounds at the Battle of Eckmühl. (RR)

Royal-Cravates 11 February 1782, brigadier 6 September 1784.

He became maréchal des logis 22 June 1788, in the same regiment when it became the 10th Cavalry 1 January 1791, quartermaster-treasurer 17 June 1792, rank of lieutenant 6 July 1794, cap-

tain quartermaster-treasurer 21 April 1797, in the same regiment when it became the 10th Cuirassiers 24 September 1803, retired 1 October 1812. LH CH 5 November 1804.

CHAZAUD (Pierre Philippe, 1795-?): born in Confolens (Charente) on 20 October 1795. Supernumerary sub-lieutenant in the 7th Cuirassiers 3 November 1814, rejoined his unit 20 November 1814.

He took up his appointment in the 12th Cuirassiers 18 February 1815, left for the school at Saumur 14 March 1815, reconfirmed as being in the suite of the 7th Cuirassiers 1 April 1815, sent home 9 April 1815, left for home 15 May 1815, returned to the corps 27 August 1815, non-active at the disposal of the Minister of War 19 December 1815.

CHAZOURNES (Jean, ?-1809): born in Aurec (Haute-Loire). Velite in the Grenadiers à Cheval of the Imperial Guard, sub-lieutenant in the suite of the 8th Cuirassiers 13 July 1807, killed at Essling 22 May 1809.

CHEF (Jean Baptiste, 1784-?): born in Stéville (Ardennes) on 17 June 1784. In the 5th Cuirassiers 25 April 1805, brigadier 1 September 1807.

He became maréchal des logis 7 June 1809, shot and wounded in the chest at the Moskova 7 September 1812, adjutant NCO 1 February 1814, sub-lieutenant 27 January 1815, dismissed 23 December 1815. LH CH 30 September 1814.

CHERBONNIER (René Pierre, 1770-1809): born in Montmorillon (Vienne) on 16 July 1770. In the 6th Cavalry 28 August 1791, brigadier-fourrier 1 May 1794, three bullet wounds at Liptingen 25 March 1799, brigadier.

He became maréchal des logis 27 July 1799, adjutant- NCO 17 April 1800, wounded in the left leg by a cannonball 23 June 1800, in the same regiment when it became the 6th Cuirassiers 23 December 1802, sub-lieutenant 3 February 1803, lieutenant 22 March 1807, captain 1808, killed at Essling 22 May 1809. Sabre of Honour 30 May 1803, LH CH by rights 24 September 1803.

CHERON see **SAINT CHERON**.

CHESNARD de DEVINZELLES (Pierre Charles, 1781 - ?): born in Metz (Moselle) on 19 April 1781. Brigadier in the Gendarmes d'Ordonnance 20 November 1806, sub-lieutenant in the suite of the 10th Cuirassiers 16 July 1807, lieutenant 16 Mai 1809,.

He became adjutant-major 6 November 1811, rank of captain 10 April 1813, aide de camp to General Marcognet 17 April 1815. LH CH 11 October 1812.

COULAC (Jean Labadie, 1760-1841), born in Ausserain (Basses-Pyrénées) on 17 September 1760. Trooper in the Royal-Etranger 1 May 1784, brigadier 26 August 1786, in the same regiment when it became the 7th Cavalry 1 January 1791, maréchal des logis 1 April 1792, maréchal des logis-chef 10 May 1792, charged 5 Austrian hussars who had captured three unhorsed troopers from the regiment and killed two of them and took the remainder prisoner with their horses near Cateau 7 April 1793,.

He became sub-lieutenant 7 May 1793, lieutenant 27 April 1794, captain 20 February 1800, in the same regiment when it became the 7th Cuirassiers 23 December 1802, squadron commander 28 June 1807, retired with orders to present himself to the Imperial Headquarters 2 June 1809, pensioned off 29 October 1809. LH CH 14 June 1804.

Near Cateau on 7 April 1796, five Austrian Hussars had captured three dismounted troopers of the 7th Cavalry. Jean Coulac, Maréchal des logis chef in the regiment charged the enemy, killed two of them and brought the others back prisoner as well five of heir horses.

CHEUZEVILLE (César, 1765-1814): born in Belmont (Rhône) on 28 September 1795. In the Cuirassiers du Roi 10 August 1786, brigadier-fourrier in the same regiment when it became the 8th Cavalry the same day 1 January 1791, maréchal des logis 19 December 1791, maréchal des logis-chef 25 January 1792, sub-lieutenant 28 august 1793.

He became lieutenant 13 February 1794 shot and wounded in the chest near Nivelles 6 July 1794, wounded his legs crushed by his horse at Bamberg 6 August 1796, his legs henceforth being in a varicose state necessitating the use of skin gaiters to stop the haemorrhages, captain 3 August 1797, in the same regiment when it became the 8th Cuirassiers 10 October 1801, aide de camp to General Espagne 18 April 1807, shot and wounded at Heilsberg 10 June 1807, squadron commander 19 February 1809, in the 6th Cuirassiers 26 May 1809, in the Escadron Sacré during the retreat from Moscow 1812, died at Metz 14 January 1814. LH CH 5 November 1804.

[signature: Cheuzeville]

CHEVALIER (François, 1762-?): born in Grenoble (Isère) on 8 January 1762. Trooper in the Royal-Roussillon 15 May 1778, went over to the Roi-Cavalerie 1 January 1784, brigadier 6 January 1785, in the same regiment when it became the 6th Cavalry 1 January 1791, maréchal des logis 6 January 1791, adjutant 22 October 1792.

He became sub-lieutenant 1 April 1793, lieutenant 28 January 1798, wounded at Julier 1795, discharged 27 February 1796, reassigned 3 October 1797, in the same regiment when it

became the 6th Cuirassiers 23 December 1802, retired 14 January 1806.

CHEVALIER (Jean Baptiste, 1765-?): born in Labonneville (Eure) on 23 March 1765. Trooper in the Franche-Comté Regiment 1 August 1784, incorporated into the Colonel-Général-Cavalerie 21 May 1788 which became the 1st Cavalry 1 January 1791, fourrier 16 September 1793, maréchal des logis 16 February 1794.

He was captured 27 artillery pieces at the head of a detachment of eight men at Waterloo 26 April 1794, sub-lieutenant by seniority 5 March 183, in the same regiment when it became the 1st Cuirassiers 10 October 1801, returned to the depot whilst waiting to retire December 1805, retired 28 august 1806, left 1 October 1806. Sabre of Honour 24 January 1803, LH CH by rights 24 September 1803.

CHEVALLIER see **LECHEVALLIER.**

CHEVIGNE see **BOURLON de CHEVIGNE**

CHEVRIERES de SAYVE
see **LACROIX CHEVRIERES de SAYVE**

CHICARD (Jean Nicolas, 1764-?): born in Vocé (Ille-et-Vilaine) on 10 April 1794. Child of the regiment in the pay of the Royal-Champagne-Cavalerie 1 February 1772, trooper 11 April 1780, brigadier 11 September 1784, maréchal des logis 1 March 1785, maréchal des logis-chef 1 May 1788, in the same regiment when it became the 20th Cavalry 1 January 1791, in the Garde du Roi 21 December 1791, returned to the 20th Cavalry 21 August 1792.

He became sub-lieutenant 21 December 1792, wounded in the left eye by the tip of a sabre at Pont-à-Marcq 1 May 1793, in the same regiment when it became the 19th Cavalry 4 June 1793, lieutenant 16 November 1793, sabre wound to his head at Ingolstadt 1 July 1800.

He was dismissed with the corps 31 December 1802 and incorporated into the 10th Cavalry 11 February 1803 which became the 10th Cuirassiers 24 September 1803, retired 23 December 1805, left 21 May 1806.

CHOBRIAT (Etienne, 1766-?): born in Revigny (Meuse) on 30 September 1766. In the Artois-Cavalerie 14 March 1786 which became the 9th Cavalry 1 January 1791, brigadier-fourrier 29 April 1792, maréchal des logis 1 April 1793, wounded in his right arm 22 July 1793, adjutant 5 May 1795, sub-lieutenant 4 September 1802, in the same regiment when it became the 9th Cuirassiers 24 September 1803, wounded at Austerlitz 2 December 1805, lieutenant 25 August 1806, adjutant-major 11 December 1806, joined a company 25 June 1807, retired 12 February 1812.

CHOLET (Jean Victor, 1757-1808): born in Sablé-sur-Sarthe (Sarthe) on 23 February 1757. In the royal-Dragons 28 July 1776, brigadier 8 June 1781, fourrier 17 May 1782, adjutant 18 September 1784.

He was in the same regiment when it became

A sword guard belonging to a cuirassier officer.
(Tradition Magazine, photo Jean-Louis Viau)

the 1st Dragoons 1 January 1791, lieutenant 25 October 1792, captain 6 June 1793, discharged with pay 20 May 1799, in the 3rd cuirassiers 30 November 1806, died at Jerichow in Prussia 28 November 1808.

CHOLLET de BOURGET (Frédéric, ?-?): born in Chambéry (Mont-Blanc). Cadet in the service of Sardinia in the Savoie-Cavalerie 12 May 1796, brigadier in the auxiliary Piedmont Army 31 January 1799, maréchal des logis 5 July 1799, taken prisoner at Cremona June 1800 and held for two years in Austria.

He returned home 1802, in the service of France in the 3rd Cuirassiers 3 April 1803, maréchal des logis 31 July 1803, sub-lieutenant 16 July 1805, lieutenant 25 June 1807, aide de camp to General Bron 5 November 1808 then to General Pachtod.

1812 Model Standard belonging to the 12th Cuirassier Regiment.
(DR).

CHOMEL (Joseph Henry, 1787-?): born in Dunkirk (Nord) on 13 November 1787. In the Navy 1802, naval cadet and apprentice helmsman January 1803, taken prisoner by the English July 1803, escaped from the Barbados prison and landed in France October 1803, in the military schools in Dunkirk and Boulogne 1803, instated as midshipman 2nd Class July 1804, passed out as midshipman 1st Class February 1806.

He became cavalry sub-lieutenant in Dutch service 6 February 1807, lieutenant in the 1st Light Dragoons of the Army of Java 16 May 1808, captain 29 November 1809, taken prisoner by the English in Java 10 September 1811, set sail for Bengal 15 November 1811, set sail for Europe 28 September 1813.

He landed in France 2 August 1814, commissioned and confirmed as captain in French service and placed in the suite of the 12th Cuirassiers 23 October 1814, dismissed 22 November. 1815.

CHOMEL (Samuel Charles, 1787-?): born in Amsterdam (Zuydersee) on 24 March 1787, NCO cadet in the service of the King of Holland 25 March 1807, dismissed 25 June 1808, sub-lieutenant in the King of Holland's Bodyguard 26 October 1809, in the 2nd Dutch Cuirassiers 12 May 1810 which became the 14th French Cuirassiers 18 August 1810, seconded to the school at Alfort, left to join the war squadrons of the regiment 12 April 1812, wounded and prisoner at the Berezina 28 November 1812.

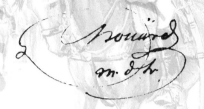

CHOUARD (Gaspard, 1789-?): born in Bourbonne-les-Bains (Haute-Marne) on 8 February 1789. Volunteer in the 36th of the Line, corporal 20 December 1806, fourrier 11 January 1807, in the 2nd Cuirassiers 11 October 1809, instated 6 December 1809.

He became maréchal des logis 1 October 1810, sub-lieutenant 14 May 1813 but in the meantime appointed sub-lieutenant in the 9th Cuirassiers 21 April 1813, left for the 9th Cuirassiers, does not appear on the new rolls dated 9th August 1814.

CHOUARD DE MAGNY (?-1813): pupil in the Saint-Germain school, sub-lieutenant in the 6th Cuirassiers 30 January 1813, killed by a shot at Weissenfeld 9 September 1813.

CHRETIEN (Jean Baptiste, 1777-?): born in Lalin (Nord) on 2 May 1777. In the 54th Chasseurs à Cheval 5 July 1799.

He was in the guides of General-in-chief Murat 8 November 1799, in the Grenadiers à Cheval of the Guard 27 December 1801, brigadier 1 August 1806, maréchal des logis 19 May 1808, lieutenant in the 11th Cuirassiers 25 November 1813, wounded at Waterloo 18 June 1815, dismissed with the corps 16 December 1815. LH CH 25 November 1807.

CHRISTOPHE (Benoît, 1756-?): born in Quimperlé (Finistère) on 17 July 1756. In the Penthièvre-Infanterie, dismissed 1 July 1780, trooper in the Royal-Etranger 15 May 1781, trumpet-major in the same regiment when it became the 7th Cavalry on the same day 1 January 1791.

He became maréchal des logis-chef 23 December 1794, sub-lieutenant by seniority 20 January 1799, commissioned 11 March 1799, in the same regiment when it became the 7th Cuirassiers 23 December 1802, lieutenant by choice 25 December 1804, captain in the 2nd Cuirassiers 27 March 1809, instated 1 May 1809, wounded at Essling 22 May 189, left to benefit from his pension 1 January 1810. LH CH 1 October 1807.

CHRISTOPHE de LAMOTTE GUERY (Charles Auguste, 1795 -?): son of the following, born in Les Petites Armoises (Ardennes) on 15 November 1795. In the 5th Cuirassiers where his father was the colonel 19 April 1813, brigadier 6 May 1813.

He became maréchal des logis 28 May 1813, sub-lieutenant 8 July 1813, adjutant-major 3 April 1814, lieutenant adjutant-major in the suite 4 February 1815, commissioned the same day, dismissed 23 December 1815.

CHRISTOPHE de LAMOTTE GUERY (Philippe, baron, 1769-1848): elder brother of the two generals, born in Nancy (Meurthe) on 11 February 1769. Lieutenant aide de camp to Chevalier Basquinet of the Army of the Rhine 2 September 1792.

He became lieutenant in the Fabrefonds Scouts 9 January 1793 which became the 9th Hussars 26 February 1793 and 8th hussars 4 June 1793, captain 18 July 1793, squadron commander 7 May 1794, charged the Austrian cuirassiers at the head of his squadron and captured a column of teams, several horses and General Klinglin's luggage at Anspach 21 April 1797, squadron commander commanding the regiment at la Trebbia.

He was brigadier, maréchal des logis le 19 June 1799, in the 12th cavalry 29 August 1799, after disengaging a chasseur regiment, captured 150 dragoons off an Austrian regiment which he surrounded at the head of his regiment at Hohenlinden 3 December 1800, in the same regiment when it became the 12th Cuirassiers 24 September 1803, major 29 October 1803, incorporated in the 2nd Provisional Heavy Cavalry November 1807, second-colonel commanding the regiment 31 march 1808, commanded the cavalry in the vanguard of General Dupont in Spain, prisoner because of the capitulation at Baylen 22 July 1808, held on the Vieille Castille hulk ship, led the revolt on 15 May 1810, succeeded in grounding the hulk and escaping from it 16 May 1810, in the suite of the 12th Cuirassiers August 1810.

He became colonel of the 5th Cuirassiers 7 September 1811, he was the very first to enter the great Redoubt at the head of his regiment ay the

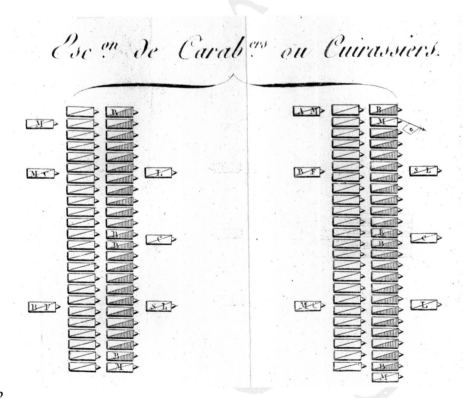

Deployment of a Squadron, in line, by platoons. (RR)

Moskova 7 September 1812, colonel of the 1st Cuirassiers 11 May 1812 which became the King's Cuirassiers 1 July 1814, reassigned 25 March 1815, in the Remount Depot at Versailles 23 May 1815, Gendarmerie colonel 29 August 18415. LH CH 25 March 1804, O 12 August 1813, retroactively to 11 October 1812, C 18 July 1814, Baron of Lamotte Guéry d. 28 September 1813; l.p. 26 February 1814.

CHUSTAIT (Philippe, 1769-?): born in Corcelle (Côte d'Or) on 16 May 1769. In the Beauce-Infanterie 29 January 1785 which became the 68th Infantry 1 January 1791, grenadier in the 2nd Paris battalion 20 July 1791, brigadier in the 6th Hussars 20 September 1792, maréchal des logis 4 January 1793.

He became maréchal des logis-chef 10 February 1793, prisoner at Marchiennes 3 October 1793, escaped and returned 1795, adjutant 26 April 1796, sub-lieutenant 13 October 1796, in the 11th Cuirassiers 12 December 1806, wounded and took a flag at Baylen 19 July 1808, prisoner by capitulation 22 July 1808, returned to France 27 February 1813.

He was, lieutenant 16 October 1813, dismissed with the corps 16 December 1815.

CINGLANT (Fidèle Joseph Amable, 1769-?): born in Priche (Nord) on 15 January 1769. In the Royal-Pologne-Cavalerie 18 May 1786 which became the 5th Cavalry 1 January 1791, brigadier-fourrier 1 April 1791, maréchal des logis-chef 31 March 1792, quartermaster-treasurer 30 July 1792.

He obtained rank of sub-lieutenant 1 December 1792, rank of lieutenant 1 April 1793 then captain 21 November 1796, in the same regiment when it became the 5th Cuirassiers 23 December 1802, deputy 2nd Class in the Inspection of Parades 3 January 1814, returned to his regiment July 1814, retired 23 December 1815. LH CH 1 October 1807.

CLARY see **LAVAL de CLARY**

CLEMENDOT (François, 1786-?): born in Château-Chinon (Nièvre) on 21 March 1786. In the 1st Cuirassiers 1 June 1805, maréchal des logis 18 June 1807.

He became sub-lieutenant 10 April 1813, in the King's Cuirassiers 1 July 1814, non-active on full pay 1 October 1814, returned to the regiment 1 April 1815 which became the 1st Cuirassiers again, put on half-pay 1 September 1815.

CLEMENT (Joseph Augustin, 1784-1813): born in Montrevieux (Vosges) on 17 April 1784. In the 1st Cuirassiers 8 April 1805, brigadier 20 December 1806.

He was maréchal des logis 16 May 1809, maréchal des logis-chef 11 June 1809, sub-lieutenant 10 April 1813, killed Leipzig 10 October 1813.

CLEMENT de la **RONCIERE** (François Marie, baron, 1773-1854): born in Amiens (Somme) on 2 February 1773. In the Chasseurs à Cheval of Rosenthal's Legion 1 March 1793, maréchal des logis 15 May 1793, sub-lieutenant in the same regiment when it formed the 19th chasseurs à Cheval 10 June 1793, lieutenant 1 September 1793.

He became quartermaster, captain 27 September 1795, on Lefebvre's staff, returned to the corps 30 June 1796, squadron commander 19 February 1797, shot in the right leg at la Trebbia 19 June 1799, brigade commander in the suite of the regiment 20 June 1799, commissioned temporarily 30 June 1799, appointed to command the 16th Dragoons 7 July 1799, instated 10 July 1799, brigadier-general commanding the 1st Brigade (1st and 5th cuirassiers) of the 2nd Cuirassier Division 31 December 1806, in the Army of the Rhine 15 October 1808, in that of Germany 1 April 1809 eleven sabre wounds and one shot wound to his left arm causing its amputation at Eckmühl 22 April 1809.

He became major-general 11 June 1809, commanded the cavalry school in Saint-Germain when it was formed 8 August 1809, on leave with pay 20 August 1812, commanded the 27th Military Division 8 September 1812, commanded the Piedmont 27 April 1814, retired 6 October 1815. LH CH 11 December 1803, O 14 June 1804, C 25 December 1805, Baron of the Empire d.17 March 1808 and l.p. 28 July 1808.

CLER (Jean Baptiste, 1765-?): born in Chalons-sur-Saône (Saône-et-Loire) on 21 October 1765. chasseur à cheval in the Normandie Regiment 29 January 1789 which became the 11th Chasseurs à Cheval 1 January 1791, brigadier-fourrier 21 January 1792, maréchal des logis 16 May 1793.

He became , maréchal des logis-chef 11 August 1793, wounded at Fleurus 26 June 1794, sub-lieutenant 3 June 1795, discharged 11 January 1796, remained in the corps then went home 21 March 1797, sub-lieutenant in the 1st Cuirassiers 12 December 1806, rejoined his unit 2 January 1807, in the 13th Cuirassiers 21 October 1808, lieutenant 13 February 1809.

He was captain 13 April 1812, in the 1st Cuirassiers 1 February 1813, rejoined the regiment 19 May 1813, retired 16 August 1814. LH CH 29 July 1814.

CLERET (Jean Charles Marie, 1787-1853): born in Ranchicourt (Pas-de-Calais) on 8 September 1787, cuirassier officer. LH CH.

CLERMONT TONNERRE (Jules Marie Louis, 1793-?): born in Amiens (Somme) on 16 May 1793. Pupil at the Ecole Spéciale Militaire in Saint-Germain 13 March 1810, sub-lieutenant in the 13th cuirassiers 29 June 1810.

He was retired to his home with the permission of the Minister of War, leave prolonged 25 August 1814, in the suite of the 9th cuirassiers 9 June 1815, dismissed with the corps 26 November 1815.

CLERMONT see **HOLDRINET** aka **CLERMONT**

CLEVENOT (Jean Baptiste Henry, 1772-?): born in Sainte-Marie-aux-Mines (Haut-Rhin) on 19 January 1772. In the Cevennes Chasseurs 9

G. Rava 07 53

July 1787, incorporated into the Bretagne Chasseurs à Cheval 17 March 1788, left 17 January 1789, grenadier lieutenant in the 1st Haut-Rhin Battalion 3 October 1791, grenadier captain 11 April 1793, deputy to Adjutant-General Espagne 23 October 1793, aide de camp to General Espagne 2 September 1799.

He was confirmed 16 September 1799, in the 13th Dragoons 12 June 1800, aide de camp to General Amey then to General Mermet 23 October 1804, squadron commander in the 23rd Dragoons 28 May 1807, major 17 July 1813, wounded at Leipzig 16 October 1813, in the suite of the 10th Cuirassiers 16 November 1814, took up his appointment 11 May 1815, dismissed 25 December 1815. LH CH 17 July 1809, O 28 June 1813.

CODERE (François, 1781-1813): born in Cayes-Saint-Louis (Saint-Domingo) on 18 October 1781. Sub-lieutenant in the 1st legion of the South 23 October 1795, lieutenant 25 May 1799 wounded 7 May 1800, Gendarmerie captain the same day.

He became adjutant of the stronghold at Cayes-Saint-Louis 22 March 1802, adjutant on the staff of General Brunet 21 April 1803, captain in the Colonial Dragoons, discharged 26 November 1806, sub-lieutenant in the 1st Carabiniers 31 May 1806, lieutenant in the 7th Cuirassiers 2 March 1809, joined the war squadrons 1 April 1809, wounded at Essling 21 May 1809, captain 3 June 1809.

He was squadron commander 27 April 1811, wounded at the Berezina 28 November 1812 and died at the hospital of Danzig 18 February 1813. LH CH 13 August 1809.

COFFIN (Jacques Michel, 1767-?): born in Ablon-sur-Seine (Seine-et-Oise) on 25 September 1767. In the Royal-Vaisseaux 13 November 1783, in the Paris National Guard 21 March 1789, left 5 September 1789, maréchal des logis in the Volontaires Nationaux à Cheval from the Ecole Militaire 1 February 1793 which formed the 26th Cavalry 21 February 1793 which became the 25th Cavalry 4 June 1793.

He was surrounded by three enemy hussars killed two of them with his own hands and took the other prisoner 1 July 1794, maréchal des logis-chef 30 August 1796, sub-lieutenant 24 March 11803, lieutenant 19 December 1806, wounded at Heilsberg 10 June 1807, allowed to retire 2 January 1809, pensioned 1 March 1809, Sabre of Honour 30 May 1803, LH CH by rights 24 September 1803.

COGNEL (Jean François, 1790-1812): born in Vic (Meurthe) on 24 June 1790. Pupil at the Ecole Impériale de Cavalerie in Saint-Germain.

He became sub-lieutenant in the 5th Cuirassiers 19 April 1812, wounded at Studianka 26 November 1812, remained under control of the enemy at Gumbinge hospital and disappeared 1812.

COINTE (Jean-Baptiste, ? -1812) born in Hary (Aisne). In the 6th Cuirassiers 9 December 1793, brigadier 4 August 1803, maréchal des logis 1 October 1806,

sub-lieutenant 3 June 1809, prisoner in Russia 22 September 1812 and disappeared.

COINTE de LAFANGERAYE
see **LECOINTE de LAFANGERAYE**

COLAS (Joseph, 1761-?): born in Fossieux (Meurthe) on 24 December 1791. In the Royal-Etranger-Cavalerie 1 April 1783, brigadier 12 March 1788, brigadier-fourrier in the same regiment when it became the 7th Cavalry the same day 1 January 1791.

He became maréchal des logis 5 July 1792, maréchal des logis-chef 7 May 1793, sub-lieutenant 17 November 1793, lieutenant 20 February 1800, prisoner 25 May 1800, exchanged 28 October 1800 returned to the forward positions 27 January 1801, in the same regiment when it became the 7th Cuirassiers 23 December 1802, left with retirement pay 6 July 1807.

COLETTE (Louis, 1785-?): born in Bourth (Eure) on 30 June 1785. In the 12th Dragoons 8 December 1805, in the Dragoons of the Imperial Guard 1 June 1812.

He became sub-lieutenant in the 10th Cuirassiers 8 February 1813, incorporated into the 3rd Provisional Heavy Cavalry in Hamburg with his squadron, returned with the garrison May 1814, dismissed with the corps 25 December 1815.

COLINET (Alexandre Pierre Jacques, 1784-1812): born in Bruxelles (Dyle) on 17 January 1784. Conscripted into the 12th Cuirassiers 4 June 1805, brigadier 1 December 1806, fourrier 20 December 1806.

He became maréchal des logis-chef 1 March 188, sabre wound at Eckmühl 22 April 1809, shot and wounded at Wagram 6 July 1809, sub-lieutenant 9 August 1809, on three months' leave 13 October 1810, left 1 January 1811, lieutenant 11 September 1812, wounded and taken prisoner at Kovno 21 November 1812 and disappeared.

COLLARD (Claude Alpin, 1764-?): born in Chalons-sur-Marne (Marne) on 5 September 1764. In the Royal-Pologne-Cavalerie 16 October 1782, brigadier 24 January 1789, in the same regiment when it became the 5th Cavalry 1 January 1791.

He was fourrier 8 November 1791, maréchal des logis 20 August 1792, maréchal des logis-chef 1 April 1793, sub-lieutenant 21 November 1796, lieutenant 22 March 1800, in the same regiment when it became the 5th Cuirassiers 23 December 1802, captain by seniority 1 November 1803, retired 16 May 1809, ill so he remained in the regimental depot, captain in the 1st Provisional Dragoons 13 October 1809, did not join his unit as he was appointed a member of the Permanent War Council 27 October 1809, in the suite of the army staff 14 November 1809, commanded the town of Haag, at the disposal of the Minister of War in Strasbourg 17 January 1812. LH CH 14 March 1806.

COLLAS (Jean Augier, 1790-?): born in Béthelainville (Meuse) on 18 October 1790. Velite in the Dragoons of the Imperial Guard 1 June 1808, sub-lieutenant

in the 10th Cuirassiers 13 March 1813.

He was incorporated into the 3rd Provisional Heavy Cavalry with his squadron in Hamburg 11 September 1813, returned with the garrison May 1814, wounded by a shot which pierced his left arm at Waterloo 18 June 1815, dismissed with the regiment 25 December 1815.

COLLAS (Michel, 1775-1813): born in Antheux (Côte d'Or) on 2 January 1775. In the 6th Cavalry 6 December 1793, brigadier 7 April 1799, fourrier 23 April 1800, maréchal des logis 14 August 1802, in the same regiment when it became the 6th Cuirassiers 23 December 1802, adjutant NCO 25 March 1807, sub-lieutenant 25 March 1808.

He became lieutenant adjutant-major 8 October 1808, sabre wound to his left arm at Essling 21 May 1809, squadron commander 29 September 1812, in the Escadron Sacré during the retreat from Russia November 1812, killed at Leipzig 18 October 1813. LH CH 1 October 1807.

COLLET (Antoine Ferdinand, 1791-1812): born in Versailles (Seine-et-Oise) on 14 January 1791. Boarder at the Ecole Spéciale Militaire in Fontainebeleau 4 June 1807, claimed back by his parents and struck from the rolls 14 June 1808, in the 9th Dragoons 24 August 1808, brigadier-fourrier 1 September 1808, maréchal des logis 15 December 1808.`

He became sub-lieutenant in the 13th Cuirassiers 17 August 1809, in the suite of the 5th Cuirassiers 9 January 1810, instated 22 January 1810, on convalescence leave for three months 10 December 1811, took up his appointment 21 February 1812, treated for ophthalmia, disappeared in Russia 26 November 1812.

COLLIGNON (Auguste, 1795-?): born in Metz (Moselle) on 30 October 1795. Cuirassier in the 1st Westphalia Regiment 15 January 1812, brigadier 21 March 1812, maréchal des logis 27 September 1812.

He became sub-lieutenant 9 April 1813, in the service of France 26 February 1814, in the 6th Cuirassiers 4 August 1814, seconded to the school in Saumur 4 March 1815, dismissed with the regiment 21 November 1815.

COLLIN (Jacques Noël, 1788-1815): born in Biesles (Haute-Marne) on 25 July 1788. In the 10th Cuirassiers 29 June 1807, brigadier 30 October 1807, fourrier 16 May 1809, maréchal des logis-chef 3 June 1809, adjutant 6 November 1811.

He became sub-lieutenant 12 August 1812, two lance wounds to his left side at Winkovo 18 October 1812, lieutenant adjutant-major 28 September 1813, in the suite 6 August 1814, wounded and left for dead at Waterloo 18 June 1815. LH CH 28 September 1813.

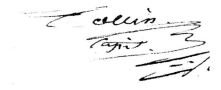

COLLIN (Pierre, 1769-?): born in Ambly (Meuse) on 14 December 1769. In the 2nd Meuse Battalion 28 August 1791, left 26 January 1793, in the 23rd Cavalry 12 October 1793, brigadier 12 December 1797, maréchal des logis 30 November 1801, dismissed with the corps 23 December 1802 and incorporated into the 54th Cuirassiers 3 January 1803.

He became maréchal des logis-chef 30 July 1804, confirmed 2 September 1804, adjutant NCO 21 December 1805, instated 14 January 1806, sub-lieutenant 24 November 1806, lieutenant 20 February 1807, captain 16 May 18090, retired 23 December 1815. LH CH 5 November 1804.

COLLIN de VERDIERE (Jean Christophe, 1754-1806): born in Paris (Seine) on 18 January 1754. In the Mestre-de-Camp-Général des Dragons 1 April 1767, supernumerary in the Gardes du Corps du Roi 15 December 1770, bodyguard and instructor-equerry in the Gardes du Corps de Monsieur 1 April 1771, captain in the Lauzun Hussars 18 September 1778, lieutenant-colonel of the Paris Cavalry and entrusted with setting it up 6 September 1789, colonel of the corps 14 November 1789, discharged and retired 12 August 1792.

He became brigadier-general, first inspector of the riding school 13 June 1795, drove off the insurrectionists from the Pont de la Concorde 13 Vendémiaire (5 October 1795), took up his appointment in the Army of Italy 28 September 1796, but kept in the 17th Military Division 4 December 1796, commanded Paris 14 August 1797, authorised to bear distinctive markings and to receive a general's pay 26 May 1798, major-general 5 February 1799, commanded the 15th Military Division 22 July 1799 then the Côte de la Manche September 1799.

He was employed with the troops stationed in Batavia 18 November 1799, discharge pay 30 December 1799, in the army of the Rhine 24 March 1800, brigadier-general in the reorganisation of the staff dated 29 March 1801, non-active 23 September 1801, in the 22nd Military Division 23 September 1802, commanded the light cavalry of the 4th Corps, decision put off to 5 September 1805.

He commanded the 3rd Brigade of the 4th division of Dragoons in the Grande Armée 21 September 1805, assigned to command the depot of the Heavy Cavalry at Marburg 8 October 1805, returned to the 4th Dragoon Division November 1815, commanded the 1st Brigade (1st and 5th Cuirassiers) of the 2nd Division of Heavy Cavalry 20 September 1806, temporarily replaced 5 October 1806, died at Sonderhausen 18 October 1806. LH CH 11 December 1803, C 14 June 1804.

COLLOT (Antoine François, 1781-?): born in Thiaucourt (Meurthe) on 25 December 1781. In the 8th Cuirassiers 25 April 1802, maréchal des logis 25 November 1803.

He became maréchal des logis-chef 20 June

Sous-Lieutenant Scipion Corvisart.
(RR, Liège Museum)

1805, sub-lieutenant 25 March 1807, wounded at Essling May 1809, put in the suite and replaced 3 June 1809, retired 22 February 1810.

COLPIN (Jean Baptiste François Joseph, 1784-?): born in le Cateau (Nord) on 18 November 1784. In the 11th Cuirassiers 14 November 1804, brigadier 11 March 1805, fourrier 4 September 1805, maréchal des logis 1 December 1806.

He became maréchal des logis-chef 25 May 1807, sub-lieutenant 16 May 1809, lieutenant 25 September 1812, taken prisoner at Toloschinn 21 November 1812, returned 22 October 1814 and retired 1 November 1814. LH CH 1 October 1807.

COMBES (François Julien, 1764-?): born in Monfrin (Gard) on 30 December 1764. In the Commissaire-Général-Cavalerie 8 June 1783 which became the 3rd Cavalry 1 January 1791.

He became brigadier-fourrier 18 January 1792, maréchal des logis-chef 1 August 1793, sub-lieutenant 21 December 1793, lieutenant 20 May 1798, elected captain 15 October 1801, in the same regiment when it became the 3rd Cuirassiers 12 October 1802, wounded at Austerlitz 2 December 1805, retired 15 June 1809.

COMTE (François Barthélémy Joseph, 1790-?): born in Rivesalte (Pyrénées-Orientales) on 14 September 1790. In the 12th Cuirassiers 26 November 1808, brigadier 1 February 1811, fourrier 6 February 1812.

He became sub-lieutenant 8 July 18131, resigned 1 June 1814, resignation accepted 24 January 1815. LH CH 4 December 1813.

COMTE or **LECOMTE** (?-1809): maréchal des logis in the 3rd Cuirassiers, sub-lieutenant in the 10th Cuirassiers 14 April 1807, kept as sub-lieutenant in the 3rd Cuirassiers 2 May 1807, wounded at Eckmühl 22 April 1809 and died of his wounds in Augsburg 25 May 1809.

CONDAT (Jean Marie, 1794-?): born in Pouzac (Hautes-Pyrénées) on 1 February 1794. Pupil at the Ecole Spéciale Militaire de Cavalerie in Saint-Germain-en-Laye 21 April 1813, sub-lieutenant 30 March 1814, in the 10th Cuirassiers 12 June 1814, dismissed with the corps 25 December 1815.

CONNAUX (Alexandre, 1778-?): born in Rilly (Ardennes) on 27 February 1778. In the 23rd Cavalry 21 November 1798.

He was dismissed with the corps 23 December 1802 and incorporated into the 5th Cuirassiers with his company 3 January 1803, shot in the left foot and his horse killed under him near Eylau 7 February 1807, brigadier 9 February 1807, maréchal des logis 16 May 1809, sabre wound to his right arm at Essling 21 May 1809 and cannonball wound to his lower belly and thigh at Wagram 6 July 1809.

He became sub-lieutenant 28 September 1813, sabre wound at Hanau 30 October 1813, dismissed 23 December 1815. LH CH 13 August 1809.

CONRAD (Jean David, 1774-1813): born in Gries (Bas-Rhin) on 22 March 1774. In the 9th Cavalry 7 July 1792, brigadier 7 May 1795, maréchal des logis 21 April 1801, in the same regiment when it became the 9th Cuirassiers 24 September 1803.

He was maréchal des logis-chef 1 November 1806, sub-lieutenant 25 June 1807, assigned to the 2nd Provisional Heavy Cavalry, prisoner by capitulation at Baylen 22 July 1808, escaped from the hulks off Cadiz 16 May 1810 and returned to be in the suite of the 9th Cuirassiers, took up his appointment 25 January 1812, lieutenant 21 March 1812, adjutant-major 1 August 18121, killed at Leipzig 16 October 1813. LH CH 14 April 1807.

CONROT REMACLE (1768-?): born in Logny-Magny (Ardennes) on 3 January 1768. Trooper in the Colonel-Général Regiment 21 February 1787 which became the 1st Cavalry 1 January 1791.

He became brigadier-fourrier 16 September 1793, maréchal des logis 31 May 1793, maréchal des logis-chef 221 June 1798, in the same regiment when it became the 1st Cuirassiers 10 October 1801, sub-lieutenant by seniority 12 November 182, elected lieutenant 24 February 1804, captain in the 27 March 1809, left 30 April 1809, in the 4th Cuirassiers 16 August 1810, captain in the Gendarmerie 8 October 1811.

Retired 15 November 1815. Holder of the Sabre

of Honour 4 March 1803, LH CH by rights 24 September 1803.

CONSTANT see **RILLIET de CONSTANT**

CONTADES (Gaspard de, 1785-?): son of one of Napoleon's chamberlains born in Angers (Maine-et-Loire) on 6 April 1785. Boarder at the Ecole Spéciale Militaire in Fontainebleau 19 July 1804, corporal 30 November 1806, sub-lieutenant in the suite of the 4th Cuirassiers 14 January 1807,.

He took up his appointment 25 June 1807, 5 sabre wounds to his arm, forearm and right hand and head at Essling 21 May 1809, lieutenant 10 September 1809, on 3 months' convalescence leave 5 November 1809, retired 27 November 1810. LH CH 3 December 1809.

CONTI di GROPPELLO (Vittorio Figarolo dei, ?-?): sub-lieutenant in the 19th Chasseurs à cheval 31 January 1813, in the 5th Cuirassiers 20 March 1813, incorporated with his squadron into the 2nd Provisional Heavy Cavalry in Hamburg 11 September 1813, returned with the garrison 30 May 1814.

COQUELET (Martin, 1761-?): born in Marcelcave (Somme) on 7 November 1761. Trooper in the Royal-Pologne 1 November 1777, brigadier 6 September 1785, in the same regiment when it became the 5th Cavalry 1 January 1791.

He became maréchal des logis 1 May 1793, maréchal des logis-chef 16 July 1793, sub-lieutenant 2 April 1799, sabre wound to his head and taken prisoner but then freed by his own troopers at la Trebbia 18 June 1799, lieutenant 21 June 1800 in the same regiment when it became the 5th Cuirassiers 23 December 1802, retired 25 May 1807.

CORRA (Joseph, 1786-after 1832): born in Nantes (Loire-Inférieure) on 28 October 1786. In the 10th Chasseurs à Cheval 1 August 1802, in the 1st Dragoons 18 June 1803.

He became velite in the Grenadiers à Cheval of the Imperial Guard 10 February 1806, two sabre wounds to his head and a bayonet wound to his left side at Eylau 8 February 1807, sub-lieutenant in the suite of the 3rd Cuirassiers 13 July 1807, took up his appointment 14 May 1809, Gendarmerie Lieutenant in the Deux-Sèvres Company 15 March 1812.

He was in the Côtes-du-Nord Company 29 November 1814 then in that of the Sarthe 16 October 1815. LH CH 13 August 1809.

CORVISART (Scipion Charles Louis, 1790-1866): nephew then adopted son of Napoleon's famous doctor, born in Dixmont (Yonne) on 30 August 1790. One of Napoleon's pages 15 January 1804.

He became sub-lieutenant in the 2nd Carabiniers 15 October 1808, wounded by a Biscayan shot in the lower abdomen at Wagram 6 July 1809, lieutenant in the 1st Cuirassiers 12 November 1809, adjutant-major 5 November 1811, captain in the

3rd Cuirassiers 6 October 1812, aide de camp to General Exelmans 12 October 1812, in the 12th Cuirassiers 19 March 1813, squadron commander 21 February 1814, dismissed with the corps 16 July 1815 and put on the non-active list. LH CH 11 October 1812, O 14 February 1815.

COTTIN (François Firmin, 1785-?): born in Francy (Yonne) on 25 September 1785. in the 3rd Dragoons 28 June 1801.

He became brigadier 1 June 1802, fourrier 30 July 1803 wounded by a Biscayan shot to his foot at Eylau 8 February 1807 and two sabre wounds at Friedland 14 June 1807, in the Dragoons of the Guard 17 June 1808, brigadier 21 December 1811, maréchal des logis 1 January 1813, sub-lieutenant in the 1st Cuirassiers 23 March 1813, rejoined his unit 13 May 1813.

He was captain by mistake 25 March 1815, rectified 30 March 1815, in the 4th Cuirassiers 23 May 1815, rejoined the unit 6 June 1815, appointed lieutenant 1 August 1815, dismissed with the regiment 21 December 1815.

COUCHAUD (Victor, 1781-1809): born in Lyon (Rhône) on 23 April 1781. In the Gendarmes d'Ordonnance 25 October 1806, maréchal des logis 7 August 1807, dismissed with the corps 23 October 1807.

He became lieutenant in the suite of the 7th Cuirassiers 18 February 1808, joined 14 April 1808, took up his appointment in the 8th Cuirassiers 8 June 1808, left to join his unit 15 August 1808, wounded and taken prisoner at Essling 22 May 1809, no news received and struck off the rolls 3 June 1810.

COURANT (Claude Louis Henry, 1763-?): born in Saint-Germain-en-Laye (Seine-et-Oise) on 9 January 1763. In the Gendarmes of the King's Household 31 January 1781, discharged with the corps and went over to the Gardes de la Porte du Roi 1785, sub-lieutenant in the 1st Hussars 10 Mars 1792.

He became lieutenant 10 May 1792, taken prisoner, escaped and returned, given leave 24 May 1793, correspondence officer for General Taponier in the Army of the Moselle and captain in the suite of the 2nd Hussars 17 November 1795.

He was unemployed when the correspondence officers were disbanded, attached to the 3rd Hussars 1797, discharged 28 June 1800, captain in the 2nd Carabiniers 12 December 1806.

He was incorporated into the 1st Provisional Heavy Cavalry in Spain December 1807, struck off the rolls and returned to the Carabiniers 1 December 1808, in the suite of the 4th cuirassiers 16 august 1810, took up his appointment in the 7th Cuirassiers 9 March 1811, joined 10 April 1811, in the 7th Battalion of Veterans 19 July 1811, left to join his unit 16 August 1811.

COURCELLES
see **BEAUDINET de COURCELLES**

COURDEL (?-1809): sub-lieutenant in the 11th Cuirassiers 25 May 1807, killed at Regensburg 23 April 1809.

COURTEFOY (Jean, 1770-?): born in Condé-sous-Suippes (Aisne) on 3 November 1770. In the 13th Dragoons 7 March 1794, brigadier in General Masséna's Guides 15 March 1799, maré-chal des logis 4 February 1801, brigadier in the Gendarmerie d'Elite 25 February 1802, maréchal des logis in the 1st Company of Dordogne Gendarmes, sub-lieutenant in the 8th Squadron of the Gendarmerie d'Espagne 5 December 1809, lieutenant in the 1st Legion of the Gendarmerie à Cheval d'Espagne "Burgos" 20 July 1811.

He was dismissed with the corps 27 February 1813, captain in the 5th Cuirassiers 28 February 1813, shot in the chest at Champaubert 10 February 1814 and a lance wound to his lower lip near Troyes 4 March 1814, in the 6th Cuirassiers 4 August 1814, instated 11 August 1814, retired 21 November 1815. LH CH 10 February 1813.

COURTIER (Eléonore Ambroise, chevalier, 1772-1837): born in Charmantry (Seine-et-Marne) on 28 May 1772. Sub-lieutenant in the 16th Chasseurs à Cheval 10 March 1793, lieutenant 12 December 1794, captain 23 June 1795, resigned 19 July 1796, reinstated as captain 4 August 1799.

He became deputy to Adjutant-General Maurin 18 August 1799, available 13 May 1802, deputy on the staff of the 11th Military Division 20 November 1802, on the staff of the Camp at Bayonne 21 September 1803, aide de camp to General Maurice Mathieu in Brest 8 November 1803 then in the 2nd Division of the 7th Corps of the Grande Armée 1805, deputy on the staff at the Prince of Neuchatel's headquarters 7 November 1806, squadron commander in the 24th Chasseurs à Cheval 17 April 1807, major 26 May 1809, in the 1st Chasseurs à Cheval 4 September 1809, colonel 29 March 1813, in the 28th Chasseurs à Cheval 16 June 1813, lance wound at Hamburg 6 December 1813.

He was in the suite of the 11th Chasseurs à Cheval 5 November 1814, colonel of the 1st Cuirassiers at the same time as Ordener and remained in the suite of the 11th Chasseurs à Cheval 25 March 1815, colonel of the 11th Cuirassiers 13 April 1815, wounded at Waterloo and his horse killed under him 18 June 1815, non-active 1 October 1815.

LH CH 14 March 1806, O 10 September 1807, Chevalier of the Empire l.p. 25 February 1809.

COURTILLOLES (Auguste de, 1784-?): born in Alençon (Orne) on 4 February 1784. In the 6th Cuirassiers 1 January 1805, brigadier 7 June 1805, maréchal des logis 1 October 1806, wounded at Barcelona 12 June 1808.

Junior officers

Officer from the 1st Cuirassiers wearing full dress around 1806, according to L. Rousselot.

Officer wearing a greatcoat towards 1806-1808 according to drawing by L. Rousselot.

Officer wearing a frock coat around 1806, according to a drawing by P. Benigni in Commandant Bucquoy's card collection.

Officer wearing morning dress.

Officer from the 3rd Regiment in social dress and winter town dress, after Commandant Bucquoy's set of cards.

Officer from the 4th Regiment towards 1809, according to L. Rousselot.

Officer from the 3rd Regiment mounted, wearing service dress about 1805 according to a drawing by P. Benigni.

He became sub-lieutenant in the 13th Cuirassiers 29 June 1810, wounded in Catalonia 26 December 1811 and retired 1 September 1812.

COURTOIS (Charles François, 1757-?): born in Malesherbes (Loiret) on 25 January 1757. In the Noailles-Dragons 16 August 1784, left 1790, in the Volontaires Nationaux à Cheval from the Ecole Militaire 7 September 1792, fourrier October 1792.

He became maréchal des logis-chef October 1792, lieutenant in the same regiment when they formed the 25th Cavalry 7 February 1793 then 24th Cavalry 4 June 1793, captain 11 February 1795, discharged 1 October 1796, took up his appointment 5 April 1799, discharged again 30 March 1802, captain in the 5th Cuirassiers 16 November 1806, retired 16 May 1809.

COURTOT (Albin, 1766-1807): born in Vailly (Pas-de-Calais) on 22 January 1766. In the Royal-Champagne-Cavalerie 6 November 1786 which became the 20th Cavalry 1 January 1791, fourrier 1 November 1792, in the same regiment when it became the 19th Cavalry 4 June 1793, in the 12th Cavalry 6 October 1793, captured 3 Hussars when he had his horse killed under him at Fleurus 26 June 1794.

He became maréchal des logis-chef 3 July 1794, with great determination charged 200 Uhlans at the head of 10 troopers routing them at Engen 3 May 1800, in the same regiment when it became the 12th Cuirassiers 24 September 1803, sub-lieutenant 30 October 1806, killed at Friedland 14 June 1807.

Holder of a Sabre of Honour 29 May 1803, LH CH by rights 24 September 1803.

COUSIN (Pierre Alexandre, 1770-?): born in Paris (Seine) on 11 May 1770. Soldier in the Poitou-Infanterie Regiment 25 August 1785, left 22 February 1786, in the Dauphin-Dragons 10 August 1789, left 7 October 1790, in the Garde Constitutionelle du Roi from its creation in November 1791 to its disbanding 5 June 1792.

He was chasseur à cheval in the 19th Regiment 13 June 1793, adjutant 1 November 1793, sub-lieutenant aide de camp to General Olivier, in the suite of the regiment 1 November 1795, lieutenant aide de camp 14 May 1797, captain 15 November 1798, in the 1st Cuirassiers 29 May 1802, in the Mont-Blanc Gendarmerie Company by exchanging with Captain Fribis 24 February 1805, instated 17 March 1805.

CRAVE (François, 1776-1809): born in Granges (Haute-Saône) on 17 September 1776. In the 12th Cavalry 18 April 1791, shot in the left arm at Strasbourg 1 December 1793, brigadier 30 July 1800.

He became maréchal des logis 21 April 1803, in the same regiment when it became the 12th Cuirassiers 24 September 1803, sub-lieutenant 14 May 1809, wounded at Essling 22 May 1809, killed at Wagram 6 July 1809.

CRESTAULT de LAMOTHE (Louis Marie, 1769-?): born in Saint-Florent-le-Vieil (Mayenne) on 20

August 1769. Sub-lieutenant in the 6th Cavalry 25 January 1792.

He became lieutenant 18 October 1792, lost his fingers with a cannonball at Charleroi 12 June 1794, captain by seniority 24 November 1798, in the same regiment when it became the 6th Cuirassiers 24 September 1803, squadron commander 11 July 1807, retired 12 September 1809. LH CH.

CREVEAUX (Nicolas Joseph, 1782-?): born in Menneville (Aisne) on 31 October 1782. Sub-lieutenant in the 3rd Cuirassiers 14 May 1809, wounded when his horse was killed under him, taken prisoner and presumed dead at Essling 22 May 1809, returned 15 August 1809, in the 2nd Carabiniers 23 October 1809, wounded at Winkovo 18 October 1812.

He was in the Escadron Sacré during the retreat from Moscow November 1812, lieutenant 5 November 1812, lieutenant adjutant-major 12 May 1813, rank of captain 12 November 1814, dismissed with the corps 1815. LH CH 11 October 1812.

CREVEL (Jacques Georges Désiré, 1769-?): born in Rouen (Seine-Inférieure) on 24 May 1769. In the Gendarmes d'Ordonnance of the Guard, sub-lieutenant in the Line 16 July 1807, in the 6th Cuirassiers 10 September 1807, lieutenant adjutant-major 3 June 1809, rank of captain 3 December 1811.

He became aide de camp to General Valence 24 June 1812, squadron commander in the 6th Cuirassiers 16 December 1813, aide de camp to Valence again 5 February 1814. LH CH.

CUENIN (Joseph, 1790-?): born in Dunkirk (Nord) on 18 May 1790. In the Gardes d'Honneur 11 May 1813, brigadier 1 September 1813.

He became sub-lieutenant in the suite of the 2nd Cuirassiers 26 February 1814, pupil at the Ecole Royale de Cavalerie in Saumur 1 March 1815, struck off the rolls when the 2nd Cuirassiers were disbanded 10 December 1815, retired home.

CURELY (Jean Nicolas, 1774-1827): born in Avillers-Sainte-Croix (Meuse) on 26 May 1774. Engaged in the 8th Hussars 5 April 1793 which became the 7th Hussars 4 June 1793, fourrier 6 March 1794.

He became maréchal des logis 13 September 1800, bruised in the hip by a cannonball which also broke his sword scabbard at Salzburg 14 December 1800, in the Elite Company when it was formed beginning of 1802, adjutant-NCO 17 June 1802, captured 300 infantrymen and charged 500 troopers with only 20 Hussars at Afflentz December 1805, sub-lieutenant in the Elite Company 8 January 1806 commanded Demmin 2 November 1806 returned 20 November 1806.

He was lieutenant in the Elite Compnay 26 March 1807, adjutant-major 8 May 1807, shot and wounded at Deppen 8 June 1807, lance wound at Guttstadt 9 June 1807, commanded the town but kept his job at Radomsk from 1 September 1807 to 7 October 1807, Konieckpol 8 October 1807 and

Ratibor from 13 July to 18 November 1808, captain 8 November 1808, aide de camp to Colbert his former colonel 18 April 1809, took up his appointment 10 May 1809, sabre wound to his cheek and left arm at Karako 11 June 1809, shot in the knee before Wagram 5 July 1809.

He became squadron commander in the 20th Chasseurs à Cheval 21 September 1809, commanded a marching regiment June to August 1812, at the head of 350 troopers with Colonel Saint-Chamans and drove off the assaults made by 1 500 Russians 24 October 1812, colonel of the 10th Hussars 17 August 1813, joined them the same day, several lance and sabre wounds to his back, fell off his horse and taken prisoner, shot in the head before being recovered by his own Hussars at Leignitz 18 August 1813, convalesced then took up his command again 25 August 1813.

He took 450 prisoners with his regiment at Dessau 12 October 1813, brigadier-general 12 February 1814, left the corps 1 March 1814, at general headquarters 5 March 1814, commanded the 11th Brigade (Dragons d'Espagne) 8 March 1814, ordered to form a brigade of squadrons gathered together into what became the 2nd Light Cavalry Brigade, Berckheim's Division 14 March 1814, in the suite of the Imperial Headquarters 21 March 1814.

He commanded a brigade of Dragoons from the Roussel d'Hurbal Division from 3 April to 10 May 1814, non-active 1 September 1814, commanded a brigade of dragoons from the Jacquinot Division 29 April 1815, at headquarters when the brigade was disbanded 6 June 1815.

He joined and assigned to Maréchal Ney's staff 17 June 1815, commanded a brigade of chasseurs à cheval on the eve of Waterloo 18 June 1815, then one of Cuirassiers from the Roussel d'Hurbal Division 26 June 1815, opened a passage through the Prussian lines at Senlis 27 June 1815, temporary cavalry inspector commanding the 3rd and 9th Cuirassiers.

He was confirmed 3 August 1815, allowed to return home 22 October 1815, left the army 1 November 1815, non-active 3 November 1815. LH CH 14 March 1806.

CURIN LECLERC aka CUNY (Cyril, 1778-?): born in Metz (Moselle) on 18 June 1778. Child of the regiment in the Royal-Cavalerie 21 July 1788 which became the 2nd Cavalry 1 January 1791, trooper 17 June 1794, brigadier 24 March 1799, maréchal des logis-chef 28 April 1800, in the same regiment when it became the 2nd Cuirassiers 12 October 1802, sub-lieutenant 30 October 1806.

lieutenant in the 3rd Cuirassiers 27 March 1809, instated 1 May 1809, adjutant-major in the 2nd Cuirassiers 21 November 1809, instated 15 December 1809, appointed captain 29 September 1813, wounded at Waterloo 18 June 1812, retired 10 December 1815. LH CH 1 October 1807.

CURNIEU see **MATHEVON de CURNIEU**

Wounded officer retreating. Oil on canvas by Géricault.
(© RMN. Photograph by Gérard Blot)

DABADIE APATIN (Barthélémy Mathieu, 1783-?): born in Maubourgues (Hautes Pyrénées) on 20 May 1783. In the 7th Cuirassiers 16 August 1805, brigadier 16 May 1808, fourrier 18 May 1808, shot in the left knee at Wagram 6 July 1809.

He became maréchal des logis 12 November 1810, maréchal des logis-chef 1 June 1811, 9 lance wounds and taken prisoner near Leipzig 24 May 1813, escaped 30 May 1813 and returned to the corps 8 June 1813, adjutant-NCO 5 September 1813, incorporated with his squadron into the 2nd Provisional Heavy Cavalry in Hamburg 11 September 1813, returned with the garrison 30 May 1814, arrived July 1814.

He, put back as adjutant sub-lieutenant 16 August 1814, confirmed as sub-lieutenant 1815, wounded at Waterloo 18 June 1815, non-active when the corps was disbanded 19 December 1815. LH CH 16 May 1813.

DADIER (Simon, 1778-?): born in Paris (Seine) on 25 January 1778. In the 20th Cavalry 26 October 1798, brigadier 23 September 1800, fourrier 12 March 1802, maréchal des logis 21 January 1803, dismissed with the corps 31 December 1802 and incorporated into the 12th Cavalry 25 January 1803 which became the 12th Cuirassiers 24 September 1803.

He became maréchal des logis 30 October 1806, sub-lieutenant 7 February 1808, wounded at Essling 22 May 1809, shot and wounded at Essling 22 May 1809, amputated, lieutenant 9 August 1809, in the suite August 1811 then retired 19 September 1811, left 29 October 1811. LH.

DAIGREMONT see **AIGREMONT**

DAIN (Jean Antoine Gabriel, 1764-?): born in Monchâlons (Aisne) on 22 March 1764. In the Roi-Cavalerie 14 October 1785 which became the 6th Cavalry 1 January 1791.

He became brigadier 1 January 1793, maréchal des logis 30 June 1795, adjutant 17 July 1799, sub-lieutenant 25 May 1800, in the same regiment when it became the 6th Cuirassiers 23 December 1802, lieutenant by seniority 14 June 1805, captain in the 3rd Cuirassiers 27 March 1809, in the 6th Provisional Dragoons 13 October 1809.

DALBAN see **VERGNETTE d'ALBAN**

DALBIGNAC see **RIVET d'ALBIGNAC.**

DAMBRUN (Charles François, 1784-?): brother of below, born in Nuit-Saint-Georges (Côte-d'Or) on 18 March 1784. In the 20th Cavalry 21 April 1801, in the 3rd Cavalry 14 September 1802 which became the 3rd Cuirassiers 12 October 1802, maréchal des logis 3 April 1803, in the 12th Cavalry 18 May 1803, maréchal des logis-chef 3 September 1804, sub-lieutenant 14 May 1809, his horse killed under him and a cannonball blew his foot off at the Moskova 7 September 1812,.

He became lieutenant, ill en route 10 January 1813 and stayed behind, returned to the depot and then retired 22 July 1813, aide de camp to General Creutzer commanding the military district of Bitche 11 May 1815. LH CH 25 November 1813.

DAMBRUN (François, 1773-1812): brother of the above, born in Nuit-Saint-Georges (Côtes-d'Or) on 1 July 1773. In the Côte-d'Or Chasseurs 24 July 1793, lieutenant 1 September 1793, in the 4th Chasseurs à cheval 6 April 1794, in the Côte-d'Or Chasseurs 20 February 1795.

He was incorporated with the corps into the 15th Chasseurs à Cheval 25 August 1796, with Sub-Lieutenant Lemaire freed Squadron Commander Lepic who was commanding the regiment and seriously wounded, enabling him to be transported to the ambulance at Pastrengo near Verona 26 March 1799, captain 29 July 1799, in the 20th Cavalry 2 May 1800, incorporated into the 12th Cavalry 25 January 1803.

He was in the same regiment when it became the 12th Cuirassiers 24 September 1803, wounded at Eckmühl 22 April 1809, squadron commander 26 December 1811, wounded at the Moskova 7 September 1812 and killed at Wilna 10 December 1812.

DANCOURT (Auguste César Thomas, 1786-?): born in Villeneuve-Saint-Georges (Seine-et-Oise) on 6 June 1786. Velite in the Grenadiers à Cheval of the Guard 11 February 1806, sub-lieutenant in the suite of the 7th Cuirassiers 13 July 1807, joined them 15 July 1807.

He was in service 21 November 1808, wounded at Essling 21 May 1809, lieutenant 3 June 1809, employed at divisional headquarters 1812, captain 4 March 1812, returned to the regiment and instated as captain 12 April 1812, squadron commander 16 March 1814, returned home on half-pay 1 December 1814.

He returned to the corps 24 April 1815, in the 4th Cuirassiers 19 May 1815, remained in the 7th Cuirassiers and confirmed 14 June 1815, replaced on half-pay 1 August 1815, left 24 August 1815. LH CH 8 October 1811, O 25 February 1814.

DANDIGNE see **ANDIGNE**

DANIS (Hubert, 1769-?): born in Anore (Nord) on 3 November 1769. In the 8th Cavalry 1 November 1783, brigadier 19 February 1801, in the same regiment when it became the 8th Cuirassiers 10 October 1801.

He was maréchal des logis 29 May 1802, detached to the 3rd Provisional Heavy Cavalry in Spain 1807, sub-lieutenant 3 July 1809, returned to the corps February 1811, remained ill in Königsberg and prisoner 1813. LH CH 5 November 1804.

DARGENT (Florimond, 1752-1816): born in Collemay (Moselle) on 9 August 1752. In the Royal-Etranger-Cavalerie, brigadier 31 January 1782, maréchal des logis 6 September 1784.

He was maréchal des logis-chef 1 October 1788, in the same regiment when it became the 7th Cavalry 1 January 1791, adjutant-sub-lieutenant 1 May 1792, recaptured one of his regiment's standards at Neerwinden 18 March 1793, lieutenant 7 May 1793, captain 27 April 1794, supernumerary 20 February 1796, in his post 18 May 1796, prisoner in the citadel of Wurzburg 4 September 1796, acting squadron commander 30 June 1799, confirmed 21 October 1800.

He was in the same regiment when it became the 7th Cuirassiers 23 December 1802, major in the 7th Dragoons 29 October 1803, left to join up 23 November 1803, retired 13 November 1805. LH CH 25 March 1804.

DARGET (Bertrand, 1756-?): born in Labeyrie (Basses-Pyrénées) on 8 January 1756. In the Royal-Champagne-Cavalerie 21 October 1778, brigadier 29 September 1781, maréchal des logis 1 February 1788, in the same regiment when it became the 20th Cavalry 1 January 1791.

He became sub-lieutenant 22 September 1792, in the same regiment when it became the 19th Cavalry 4 June 1793, lieutenant 31 March 1794, captain 20 July 1800, incorporated into the 11th Cavalry 5 February 1803 which became the 11th Cuirassiers 24 September 1803, retired 12 April 1810.

DARNAL (Benjamin François, 1781-1807): born in Lyon (Rhône) on 21 March 1781. In the 21st Cavalry April 1799, in the 3rd Cavalry 4 July 1801, maréchal des logis 6 February 1802, sub-lieutenant 29 May 1802.

He was, in the same regiment when it became the 3rd Cuirassiers 12 October 1802, lieutenant by seniority 11 December 1805, killed at Friedland 14 June 1807.

DARROT (Jean Baptiste, 1772-?): born in Thiers (Puy-de-Dôme) on 25 March 1772. In the 14th Cavalry 18 March 1792, brigadier-fourrier 1 April 1793, maréchal des logis 28 September 1795, brigadier à cheval in the Bouches-du-Rhône Gendarmerie 23 August 1799.

He became maréchal des logis 30 July 1803, sub-lieutenant quartermaster 25 March 1807, lieutenant in the 7th Squadron of the Gendarmerie d'Espagne 5 December 1809.

He was captain in the 2nd Cuirassiers 28 February 1813, incorporated with his squadron into the 2nd Provisional Heavy Cavalry in Hamburg 11 September 1813, left the regiment when the town capitulated 27 May 1814.

DAUCHE (Jean François, 1761-1807): born in Lafond-de-Roche (Dordogne) on 6 January 1761. In the Royal-Roussillon-Cavalerie 3 March 1785 which became the 11th Cavalry 1 January 1791, brigadier 21 September 1792.

He became maréchal des logis 1 October 1793, in the same regiment when it became the 11th Cuirassiers 24 September 1803, sub-lieutenant by seniority 30 April 1806, killed at Eylau 8 February 1807, lieutenant in the 1st Carabiniers 27 October 1808 by mistake.

DAUDEBAR FERUSSAC (Jacques Achille, 1790-1813): born in Bordeaux (Gironde) on 30 august 1790. Boarder at the Ecole Militaire at Saint-Cyr 4 February 1809, corporal 28 July 1809, sergeant 8 October 1808, sub-lieutenant in the 9th Cuirassiers 14 August 1810, died at Danzig in around April 1813.

DAUDIES (Michel Jean Paul, chevalier, 1763-1839): born in Perpignan (Pyrénées-Orientales) on 29 September 1763. In the Vermandois-Infanterie 3 June 1785,.

He became corporal 25 April 1786, fourrier 11 March 1787, sergeant-major 1 January 1791, in the same regiment when it became the 61st Infantry 1 January 1791, sub-lieutenant 12 February 1792, lieutenant 15 October 1792, taken prisoner by the Spaniards after 54 days' siege at the Fort des Bains where he was in command 3 June 1793, returned June 1794 and promoted to captain in the 122nd Half-Brigade 1 July 1794, wounded by a shot to his left arm near Cologne 11 November 1795.

He was deputy to the adjutant-generals of the Army of Italy 17 January 1796 wounded by a shell burst in his left leg near Bassano 6 August 1796, captain in the suite of the 1st Cavalry 22 September 1797, in service 19 June 1799, in the same regiment when it became the 1st Cuirassiers 10 October 1801, squadron commander in the 10th Cuirassiers 5 October

1806, instated 7 October 1806, major in the 12th Cuirassiers 7 April 1809, left to join them 1 May 1809, acting CO of the regiment from 17 January to 1 September 1810, colonel 29 March 1813. He commanded the regimental brigade temporarily and until 27 June 1813, commanded the 2nd Brigade, 1st Division of the Cuirassiers from August to November 1813 and in January 1814, confirmed and commissioned 28 September 1814, returned home by order of the minister 25 April 1815, maréchal de camp and allowed to retire 12 May 1815, retired on a colonel pension 9 September 1815. LH CH 14 June 1804, O 14 May 1813, Chevalier of the Empire l.p. 9 January 1810.

DAUPHIN (Jean François, 1773-?): born in Han-sur-Seille (Meurthe) on 8 March 1773. In the 43rd Half-Brigade 15 March 1793, in the 24th Cavalry 23 November 1798, in the Grenadiers à Cheval of the Guard 9 November 1800, brigadier 22 December 1801, fourrier 29 December 1801, maréchal des logis-chef 23 September 1802.

He became sub-lieutenant in the suite of the 1st Cuirassiers 30 August 1805, in service 24 December 1805, bayonet wound to his right shoulder at Hoff 6 February 1807, lieutenant 23 February 1807, sabre wound to his right arm at Eckmühl 22 April 1809, captain 16 May 189, wounded at Essling May 1809, lance wound to his nose at Winkovo 187 October 1812.

He was shot and wounded in the back at Hanau 30 October 1813 and by a Biscayan shot to his right shoulder at la Chaussée-près-Châlons 3 February 1814, dismissed 24 December 1815. LH CH 14 March 1806.

DAVENAY see **RIOULT de VILLAUNAY d'AVENAY**

DAVID (Claude Antoine Frédéric, 1785-?): born in Montbrison (Loire) on 1 January 1785. In the Gendarmes d'Ordonnance 22 November 1806, dismissed with the corps and incorporated into the Grenadiers à Cheval of the Guard 24 November 1807.

He became sub-lieutenant in the 3rd Cuirassiers 3 June 1809, wounded by a cannonball in the thigh at the Moskova 7 September 1812, lieutenant 14 May 1813, dismissed with the regiment 25 November 1815. LH CH 1 October 1812.

DAVID (François Eugène, 1784-?): born in Paris (Seine) on 27 April 1784. In the 5th Dragoons 3 March 1804, brigadier 26 April 1804.

He became maréchal des logis 21 April 1805, sub-lieutenant 8 January 1807, instated 21 January 1808, wounded by a Biscayan shot in his left shoulder near Baza 3 November 1810, sabre wound to his right arm at Chiclana 20 March 1810, lieutenant aide de camp to General Meunier 7 October 1810, captain in the 2nd Cuirassiers 8 February 1813, three sabre wounds to his head and three other to his left arm and hand and taken prisoner at Leipzig 16 October 1813.

He escaped immediately and returned home 3 April 1814, put on the non-active list 1 March 1815, squadron commander in the 1st Cuirassiers 8 May 1815, commanded the regiment after the colonel was wounded July 1815, put on half-pay 1 September 1815. LH CH 1 October 1807.

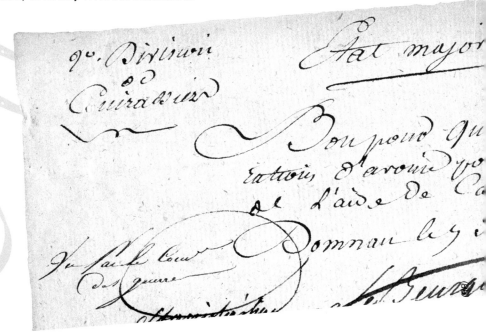

DAVID see **SIBER aka DAVID**

DAZOLS (Jean, 1774-?): born in Saint-Projet (Tarn-et-Garonne) on 24 March 1774. In the 9th Dragoons 1 December 1793.

He became brigadier 18 July 1794, in General Joubert's guides 24 January 1794, gendarme in the 11th Legion of the Lot Department 10 January 1800, in the 4th Squadron of the Gendarmerie d'Espagne 10 January 1809, incorporated into the Légion of the Gendarmerie à Cheval d'Espagne "Burgos" 2 January 1810.

He was brigadier 11 December 1810, maréchal des logis 1 March 1812, dismissed with the corps 27 February 1813, put as lieutenant in the 14th Cuirassiers 28 February 1813, remained in Hamburg during the siege, returned to France May 1814, dismissed with the corps and put in the suite of the 10th Cuirassiers 6 August 1814, retired 4 January 1815. LH CH 10 February 1813.

DAZY (Benoît Gabriel, 1784-?): born in Servizy (Meuse) on 28 august 1784. In the 7th Cuirassiers 2 November 1803, brigadier-fourrier 23 March 1806.

He became maréchal des logis 3 June 1809, maréchal des logis-chef 18 August 1809, adjutant-NCO 5 February 1812, sub-lieutenant 5 September 1813, lieutenant 16 March 1814, non-active when the regiment was disbanded 19 December 1815. LH CH 19 November 1812.

DAZY (Jean Baptiste, 1776-?): born in Sedan (Ardennes) on 27 March 1776. In the 1st Chasseurs à Cheval 4 November 1792, fourrier 18 July 1793, maréchal des logis 24 July 1795, sub-lieutenant on the battlefield 14 June 1800, commissioned 17 May 1803, lieutenant 8 November 1806.

He became adjutant-major in the 12th Chasseurs à Cheval 22 January 1807, rank of captain 22 July 1808, went over to a company 13 August 1809, several lance wounds at Leipzig 16 October 1813, in the suite of the 8th Cuirassiers 25 August 1814, took up his appointment 14 February 1815, dismissed with the corps and put on the active list 11 December 1815. LH CH 11 October 1812.

DEBASTARD (Jean François, 1793-?): born in Nogaro (Gers) on 11 December 1793. Pupil in the school in Saint-Germain 16 January 1810, sub-lieutenant in the 2nd Cuirassiers 30 January 1813, wounded at Dresden 30 August 1813.

He was shot and wounded in the left arm and several sabre wounds one of which lost him the use of two fingers of his right hand, taken prisoner at Leipzig 16 October 1813, returned to France 1814.

DEBATZ aka **CAZENEUVE** (Jean, 1773-1815): born in Auch (Gers) on 24 October 1773. In the 72nd Infantry 23 April 1792, in the 12th Hussars 1794, fourrier 6 December 1798, maréchal des logis-chef 21 May 1800, adjutant 2 April 1801, sub-lieutenant 13 June 1802, in the same regiment when it became the 30th Dragoons 24 September 1803.

He became lieutenant 18 September 1806, adjutant-major 27 November 1807, sabre wound to his head, his horse killed under him and himself taken prisoner at Villanova near San Bonifacio 29 April 1809, escaped 3 May 1809, captain adjutant-major 1 June 1809, shot and wounded in the left arm at the Moskova 7 September 1812.

He was squadron commander in the 9th Cuirassiers 5 September 1813, wounded at Waterloo 18 June 1815 and died of his wounds at the military hospital in Philippeville 30 July 1815. LH CH 29 July 1809.

DEBEURGES (Louis François, 1782-?): born in Trémont (Meuse) on 25 September 1782. In the 16th Dragoons 31 October 1799, brigadier 3 January 1801, fourrier 12 March 1801, maréchal des logis 18 October 1802.

He became sub-lieutenant 30 June 1804, lieutenant 8 December 1806, aide de camp to General Clément 25 March 1807, commissioned as captain 16 May 1809, in the 5th Cuirassiers 3 June 1809, squadron commander 21 March 1813, AWOL 1 July 1815. LH CH 13 August 1809, O 3 September 1814.

DEBLOU (Jean Nicolas Bruno, 1772-?): son of General Deblou de Chadenac, born in Nancy (Meurthe) on 25 May 1772. Sub-lieutenant in

DECOPPIN (Antoine, 1787-?): born in Canne (Meuse-Inférieure) on 20 October 1787. In the 3rd Cuirassiers 9 March 1805, fourrier 3 December 1805, maréchal des logis 21 April 1807, sub-lieutenant 14 May 1809,.

He became lieutenant 9 February 1813, in the Grenadiers à Cheval of the Guard (Young Guard) 8 July 1813.

21 May 1809, Essling: the battle had been raging for some hours already. Sous-Lieutenant Antoine Decoppin had been shot and wounded. Nevertheless he returned to the rear and assembled thirty-two dismounted cuirassiers who although wounded, were made to get some abandoned horses and led them back into combat.$ The following day he was again shot and wounded his left foot. In the course of the three days, three horses were killed under him.

the Piémont-Infanterie 20 June 1787, in the same regiment when it became the 3rd Infantry 1 January 1791, lieutenant 15 September 1791, captain 1 May 1792, aide de camp to his father 15 November 1792.

He was wounded by a Biscayan shot to his right thigh and a shot in the left thigh 1793, with only 20 men captured 2 cannon defended by an entire battalion at the siege of Mainz 1793, adjutant-general 6 October 1793, in the Army of the Côtes de Cherbourg, suspended because suspect February 1794, reinstated as lieutenant in the 23rd Chasseurs à Cheval 17 November 1794, appointment cancelled and he went to another company 10 March 1795, captain in the 2nd Chasseurs à Cheval 6 April 1795, discharged 1796, remained in the army as Murat's correspondence officer.

He captured a flag with his horse killed under him at Marengo 14 June 1800, captain in the 6th Cavalry 3 November 1801 which became the 6th Cuirassiers 23 December 1802, retired 7

December 1805. Holder of a Sabre of Honour 2 January 1801, LH CH by rights 24 September 1803, O 14 June 1804.

DEBONNE (Louis Honoré Marie, 1778-1809): born in Saint-Quentin (Aisne) on 16 May 1778. In the 4th Pas-de-Calais Battalion 12 June 1792, in the 22nd Light Infantry 5 November 1793, in the 19th Cavalry 22 October 1796, in the Chasseurs à Cheval of the Guard 31 March 1800, brigadier 12 March 1801.

He became maréchal des logis 11 October 1802, sub-lieutenant in the suite of the 10th Cuirassiers 30 August 1805, joined them 22 December 1805, in post 22 March 1806, lieutenant 24 November 1806, captain 25 May 1807, died in Hanover 22 March 1809. LH CH 14 April 1807.

DEBOULIERS (Aimé Jean Baptiste Louis Jacques, 1783-?): born in Paris (Seine) on 1 February 1783. Gendarme d'Ordonnance 21 January 1807.

He was dismissed with the corps and incorporated into the Grenadiers à Cheval of the Guard 22 November 1807, sub-lieutenant in the 3rd Cuirassiers 26 March 1810, lieutenant 10 September 1812, gave up his job after Waterloo and went into the Royal Guard.

DEBOUSIES (Philippe René, 1790-?): born in Ferrière-la-Petite (Nord) on 9 March 1790. Gendarme d'Ordonnance 9 November 1806, brigadier 7 August 1807, dismissed with the corps 24 November 1807, sub-lieutenant in the 7th Cuirassiers 8 February 1808, lieutenant 4 March 1812.

He became captain in the 4th Cuirassiers 19 November 1812, in the 1st Provisional Heavy Cavalry in Hamburg 3 July 1813, returned with the garrison 27 May 1814 and kept in the same regiment when it became the Angoulême Cuirassiers 6 August 1814, resigned March 1815. LH CH 1814.

DEBRAINE (?-1809): maréchal des logis in the 1st Cuirassiers, sub-lieutenant 16 May 1809, killed by a cannonball at Essling 21 May 1809.

DEBRUGES (Marie Frédéric Adolphe, 1783-?): born in Muttersholz (Bas-Rhin) on 19 December 1783. In the 10th Cuirassiers 23 March 1804, brigadier 1 December 1806, maréchal des logis 25 January 1811.

He became sub-lieutenant in the 2nd Foreign Regiment 18 September 1813, at the disposal of the Minister of War when the regiment was disbanded 26 May 1815, in the 3rd Cuirassiers June 1815, left 1 September 1815.

DECAUX (?-1812): sub-lieutenant in the 6th Cuirassiers 16 August 1809, in the suite and detached to Spain, killed at Vronovo 21 November 1812.

DECAUX (Antoine Elie, 1779-1812): born in Versailles (Seine-et-Oise) on 30 November 1779.

Velite in the Grenadiers à Cheval 18 February 1806.

He became sub-lieutenant in the 2nd Carabiniers 25 March 1809, in the suite of the 4th Cuirassiers 12 July 1810, instated 16 August 1810, granted leave of absence 1 January 1811 until 1 May 1811, in post 21 February 1812, lieutenant 17 June 1812, prisoner in Russia 15 December 1812, disappeared.

DECORNOIS (Nicolas François, baron, 1765-1845): born in Fontaine-bleau (Seine-et-Marne) on 7 March 1765. In the Aunis-Infanterie 6 December 1784 which became the 31st Infantry 1 January 1791.

He was dismissed 1 September 1791, maréchal des logis in the Volontaires Nationaux à Cheval from the Ecole Militaire 12 September 1792, lieutenant 13 October 1792, in the same regiment when it became the 26th Cavalry 21 February 1793 which became the 25th Cavalry 4 June 1793, commissioned as lieutenant 22 June 1793, sabre wound to his head at Fleurus 26 June 1794, wounded when he fell off his horse when he was General Souham's ordnance near Aresdorff in Switzerland June 1798, in the suite of the 2nd Cuirassiers when the corps was disbanded 23 November 1802.

He joined them the following day 24 November 1802, captain 30 October 1806, retired with his pension 17 October 1811, left 9 November 1811.

LH CH 1 October 1807, Baron of the Empire l.p. 30 October 1810.

Senior officer in the 12th Cuirassiers.
(Private collection. RR)

Troupes Françaises

Pl. 209

CUIRASSIERS
Officier Superieur
12. Régiment

DECREST DE SAINT GERMAIN (Antoine Louis, comte, 1761-1835): born in Paris (Seine) on 8 December 1761. In the Lunéville Gendarmerie 15 February 1778, cavalry lieutenant in the Foreign Legion aka Waldner's 20 October 1781, in the Petite Gendarmerie 25 February 1783, struck off the rolls for indiscipline 1 August 1784.

He was in the Paris National Guard 30 March 1790, captain in the mounted troops 22 July 1790, lieutenant-colonel commanding the Hussars of the Ardennes Legion 16 December 1792, brigade commander 23 January 1793 in the same regiment when it became the 23rd Chasseurs à Cheval 10 September 1793, suspended 25 September 1793, under orders to be arrested as suspected of "non-public-spiritednes"s 18 April 1794.

He was reinstated as brigade commander of the 23rd Chasseurs à Cheval 13 August 1795, wounded with his right foot shattered by a cannonball 20 September 1796, wounded with two broken ribs and his left arm fractured at Wiesbaden near Mainz 22 April 1797, brigadier-general 1 February 1805, in the 20th Military Division 2 March 1805, commanded the 3rd Brigade (3rd and 12th Cuirassiers) of the 1st Cuirassier Division 7 June 1805, acting CO of the same division from 30 March 1809, returned to his brigade May 1809.

He became major-general commanding the 2nd Cuirassier Division 12 July 1809, returned to France with his division 24 April 1810, commanded the 1st Cuirassier Division in the Elbe Observation Corps, took up command of his division 18 August 1811 when it became the 1st Cuirassier Division of the 1st Reserve Cavalry Corps of the Grande Armée 15 February 1812, wounded at the Moskova 7 September 1812, lieutenant in the Escadron Sacré during the retreat from Russia.

He put back at the head of his division 15 February 1813, acting CO of the 2nd Cavalry Corps at Mainz 31 March 1813, commanded the 1st Cavalry Marching Division of the 2nd Cavalry Corps in the Army of Germany 4 April 1813, commanded the 2nd Heavy Cavalry Division under Sebastiani 15 August 1813, commanded the 2nd Cavalry Corps 2 December 1813 then the 2nd Heavy Cavalry Division of the same corps under Grouchy 7 February 1814 and again the 2nd Cavalry Corps 26 February 1814.

He became inspector-general of cavalry May 1814, inspector-general of cavalry for 1815 30 December 1814, ordered to inspect and organise the cavalry in the Army of the Alps 7 June 1815, non-active 1 August 1815. LH CH 11 December 1803, O 14 June 1804, C 10 May 1807, GO 27 December 1814, Baron of the Empire l.p. 15 January 1809, Count d. 28 September 1813 Confirmed l.p. 26 October 1816.

DEFAWERS (Henri Joseph, 1778-?): born in Verviers (Ourthe) on 16 March 1778. In the 2nd Carabiniers

DELACROIX (Adolphe, 1782 - 1814) born in Hemestroff (Moselle) on 8 March 1782. Child of the regiment on the roll of the Nassau-Infanterie 11 October 1790 which became the 96th Infantry 1 January 1791, sub-lieutenant in the 37th Infantry 14 May 1797, suspended 8 January 1799 until he was eighteen, reinstated 8 August 1799, bayonet wound at Zurich 26 September 1799, with a single hussar captured a position with 20 lost Austrians 11 May 1800, seven sabre wounds and ten lance wounds when he charged 2 Austrian squadrons with 30 Carabiniers of the 2nd Regiment to disengage the 84th of the Line at the crossing of the Danube 20 May 1800, deputy to the adjutant-generals 25 May 1800.

He became aide de camp to General Grenier 23 September 1800, lieutenant in the 12th Cavalry 7 January 1802, at the disposition of the general in chief Rochambeau in San Domingo 25 March 1803, in the 1st Company of Coastguard Gunners 20 June 1803, in the 3rd Cuirassiers 30 June 1804, adjutant-major 18 April 1807.

He obtained the rank of captain 18 October 1808, at the disposal of the Minister of War 6 November 1809, captain in the 13th Cuirassiers 7 May 1811, shot and wounded in the thigh at Sagonta 25 October 1811, aide de camp to Maréchal Marmont attached to the 6th Corps but not commissioned 6 November 1813, wounded at Meaux 27 February 1814. He died of his wounds in Paris 24 March 1814. LH CH 7 May 1807.

On 11 May 1800, with the help of one other Hussar, Adolphe Delacroix captured twenty Austrians who were wandering around lost. Several days later on 20 May, he received seven sabre wounds and ten lance wounds while with only thirty Carabiniers he was charging two Austrian squadrons to disengage the 84th of the Line during the crossing of the Danube.

The following year on 19 June 1801, he swam across the Danube at the head of 180 volunteers in front of an enemy battery, got hold of it, killed the officer commanding it and a guard, carried on into the village of Blintheim and with two captured cannon loaded with grapeshot, drove off several charges made by enemy dragoons. This brilliant action earned him the rank of Lieutenant on 29 July 1801.

Adolphe Delacroix was appointed Adjudant-Major of the 3rd Cuirassiers on 18 April 1807 and was made Chevalier of the Légion d'Honneur the following 8 May; he honoured his new status at Friedland on 14 June 1807 by saving one of his cuirassiers who was surrounded, killing two Hussars himself and disengaging a dismounted Maréchal des Logis and bringing him back from within an enemy square on his own horse.

He gave him a new mount by retaking a 12th Cuirassiers' horse back off a Cossack. During this act of bravery he received five sabre wounds and one from a lance.

Defrance in general clothing. *(RR)*

23 June 1799, left 23 October 1801, in the 11th Cavalry 5 August 1802 which became the 11th Cuirassiers 24 September 1803, brigadier 14 October 1803, maréchal des logis 1 December 1806, sub-lieutenant 25 September 1812, resigned 9 August 1814.

DEFLECHINS (Charles Armand Alexandre, 1787-?): born in Noyelles-en-Chaussée (Somme) on 9

January 1787. Gendarme d'Ordonnance 24 November 1806, brigadier 8 June 1807.

He became sub-lieutenant in the suite of the 11th Cuirassiers 16 July 1807, in post 16 May 1809, lieutenant 15 October 1809, captain adjutant on Maréchal Ney's staff 20 July 1812, put back in the 11th Cuirassiers 16 April 1813, instated 3 May 1813, in the King's Cuirassiers N°1 1 July 1814, remained at the disposal of the Minister of War in Paris 20 January 1815.

He returned to the suite of the 1st Cuirassiers 1 April 1815, in the 2nd Cuirassiers of the Garde Royale 1 October 1815. LH CH 16 June 1809.

DEFRANCE (Jean Marie Antoine, comte, 1771-1855): son of the member of the Convention, born in Wassy (Haute-Marne) on 21 September 1771. Pupil at the Rebais military school where his father was a doctor, volunteered for the Rebais National Guard end July 1789, volunteered in the Cap Dragoons August 1791, in the 3rd Battalion of the Fédérés Nationaux 10 June 1792, sub-lieutenant 25 July 1792.

He was ordnance officer to General Duhoux, elected quartermaster treasurer of the battalion 17 February 1793, sub-lieutenant in the 7th Cavalry 10 April 1793, retroactively to 10 February 1793, did not rejoin them, captain in the 1st Seine-Inférieure Squadron 20 August 1793, commissaire of the inspection of the light cavalry depot with the Saint Mihiel Army of the Ardennes 4 November 1793 then Verdun 11 April 1793, adjutant-general brigade commander in the Army of the Interior 13 June 1795, discharged 26 September 1796, in the 6th division of the Army of Mainz 1 February 1799, brigade commander of the 12th Chasseurs à Cheval 7 April 1799,

He became chief of staff of the Army of the Danube and Helvetia 20 April 1799, refused the rank of general 22 September 1799, acting brigade commander of the 11th Chasseurs à Cheval 29 November 1799, adjutant-general in the Army of Italy 12 March 1800, brigade commander of the 12th Chasseurs à cheval 14 March 1800, Ecuyer Cavalcadour to Napoleon keeping his functions 17 July 1814, brigadier-general kept as ordinary Equerry to the Emperor 1 February 1805.

He commanded the 1st Brigade (Carabiniers) of the 1st Heavy Cavalry Division of the Grande Armée 21 September 1806, wounded by the second of his horses to be killed under him falling at Wagram 6 July 1809, available 19 July 1810.

He commanded a mobile column ordered to search for draft dodgers in the 11th and the 20th Military Divisions 18 March 1811, in Spain 22 March 1811.

He became inspector of the cavalry depots in Niort and Saintes 1 June 1811, major-general 31 July 1811, commanded the 4th Cuirassiers Division 9 January 1812, captain in the Escadron Sacré during the retreat from Moscow 1812, in Mainz 2 February 1813, commanded the 3rd Division of the Heavy Cavalry (Dragoons) of the 3rd Cavalry Corps being formed in Metz 15 February 1813, inspector general of remounts 29 November 1813, commanded the Division of the Gardes d'Honneur 3 January 1814, inspector general of cavalry in the 12th Military Division 3 June 1814, retired 26 March 1815,.

He commanded the Troyes Cavalry depot 12 May 1815, then that of Gien 23 June 1815 and of Moulins July 1815, non-active 1 September 1815.

LH CH 11 December 1803, O 14 June 1804, C 14 April 1807, Count of the Empire l.p. 2 July 1808.

DEHEZ (Pierre Philippe Joseph, 1771-?): born in Cambria (Nord) on 27 June 1771. In the Vintimille-Infanterie from 15 September 1788 to 16 March 1790, in the Bourbonnais-Infanterie 15 October 1790, in the 22nd Chasseurs à Cheval 13 August 1793?He became brigadier 19 January 1794.

He became maréchal des logis 6 February 1794, sub-lieutenant 11 July 1795, lieutenant in Bonaparte's Guides à Cheval 9 May 1797, in the Guides à Cheval of the Army of Helvetia 19 May 1799, discharged when the corps was disbanded 23 September 1801, in the Cambrai Garde Nationale Sédentaire August 1801, in the 1st Cuirassiers 12 December 1806, joined them 9 January 1807, sabre wound to his nose at Ulm 1805, sabre wound to his left hand at Jauer 26 August 1813, captain in the suite 28 September 1813.

He was shot and wounded in his left hip at Hanau 30 October 1813, remained at the disposal of the Minister of War 20 January 1815, returned to the corps 1 April 1815, dismissed and put up for retirement 24 December 1815. LH CH 29 July 1814.

DEJACE (Hubert Joseph, 1779-?): born in Liège (Ourthe) on 2 September 1779. In the 19th Cavalry 27 November 1801, incorporated into the 9th Cavalry 25 January 1803 which became the 9th Cuirassiers 24 September 1803, brigadier 28 November 1804, fourrier 1 November 1806, maréchal des logis 1 May 1807.

He became maréchal des logis-chef 1 June 1807, sub-lieutenant March 1812, wounded at Leipzig 16 October 1813, lieutenant 22 December 1813, in the suite of the 11th Cuirassiers 1 September 1814, dismissed with the corps 16 December 1815.

LH CH 14 May 1813.

DEJEAN (Pierre François Marie Auguste, baron, 1780-1845): son of the General of Engineers, born in Amiens (Somme) on 10 August 1780. Temporary aide de camp to his father March 1795, sub-lieutenant keeping his functions 5 August 1796.

He became lieutenant 5 August 1797, discharged and put in the suite of the Army of the North, in the 8th Half-Brigade of the Infantry of the Line 3 October 1797, in the suite of the 28th of the Line 30 September 1798, aide de camp to his father 6 May 1800, captain 2 January 1801, in the 20th dragoons 3 October 1803, squadron commander in the 3rd Dragoons 23 September 1805, colonel in the 11th Dragoons 13 February 1807, brigadier-general 6 August 1811.

He was in the Montbrun Division in Spain October 1811, commanded the 3rd Brigade of the 5th Cuirassier Division of the Army of Germany 25 December 1811, in the 2nd Brigade of the same division 16 February 1812 (11th Cuirassiers) then the 1st Brigade (1st Carabiniers) of the 4th Division provisionally November 1812, commanded the brigade made up of the 1st and 3rd Polish Lancers 6 February 1813, aide de camp to the Emperor 20 February 1813.

He commanded the 1st Brigade of the Gardes d'Honneur 6 August 1813, senior commander at Huningue 21 December 1813, in Lorraine for the mass levy 9 January 1814, major-general 23 March 1814, sent to King Joseph whom he reached 30 March 1814, unable to prevent the capitulation, confirmed as lieutenant-general 23 July 1814, aide de camp to the Emperor during the Hundred Days, suspended from his functions and exiled by the decree of 15 July 1815 because he had refused the evening before to sign an act of submission to Louis

DELACROIX (Jean Guillaume, 1778-1815): born in Bourgoin (Charente) on 27 January 1778. Volunteer in the 11 Hussars 14 January 1794, with 15 comrades recaptured 2 cannon from the Légion de Rohan-Emigré at Braga in Spanish Cerdagna 23 October 1794, shot and wounded in the leg at Quibéron 21 July 1795, fourrier 11 August 1796, maréchal des logis 17 August 1798.

He became sub-lieutenant 20 April 1799, aide de camp to General Laboissière 20 May 1799, lieutenant 24 June 1801, lieutenant-adjutant-major in the 2nd Chasseurs à Cheval 16 December 1803, captain adjutant-major 15 July 1805, sabre wound to the head and a shot at Abensberg 20 April 1809, squadron commander 25 May 1809, unhorsed and wounded by a shot to his head at Wagram 6 July 1809, major 12 August 1812.

He was wounded in the hand at Smolensk 17 August 1812, in the Escadron Sacré during the retreat from Moscow, colonel of the 3rd Cuirassiers 13 May 1813, cannonball wound to his left leg at Leipzig 18 October 1813, confirmed 28 September 1814, on four months' leave on half-pay 19 November 1814, wounded by a Biscayan shot in the head at Waterloo 18 June 1815 and died of his wounds in Paris 30 June 1815. LH CH 14 June 1804, O 5 September 1813, C 26 November 1813.

Jean Delacroix was Captain Adjutant-Major in the 2nd Chasseurs à Cheval. At Auerstadt on 14 October 1806, he captured 40 dragoons after having charged two squadrons with only his own squadron then, after the senior officers were wounded, he commanded the regiment taking a two-gun battery.

XVIII, included moreover in the ordnance of 24 July 1814, left for Styria, Dalmatia and Croatia. LH, Baron of the Empire l.p. 1 June 1808.

DELACHAISE see **TERRIER DELACHAISE**

DELAISTRE (Pierre, 1771-?): born in Verneuil (Oise) on 19 February 1771. In the 10th Cavalry 10 January 1794, brigadier 23 March 1799, maréchal des logis 14 February 1801. He became maréchal des logis-chef 12 November 1802, in the same regiment when it became the 10th Cuirassiers 24 September 1803, sub-lieutenant 7 June 1806, lieutenant 26 June 1807, quartermaster treasurer 7 September 1812, rank of captain 1 April 1813, disbanded with the corps 25 December 1815. LH CH 14 April 1807.

DELAISTRE de TILLY (François Hilaire Louis, 1787-?): eldest son of the general, born in Caen (Calvados) on 28 June 1797. In the Prytaneum at Saint-Cyr.

He became sub-lieutenant in the 6th Cuirassiers 2 March 1805, wounded and his horse killed under him at Heilsberg 10 June 1807, lieutenant 11 July

1807, captain adjutant-major 22 June 1809, wounded and his horse killed under him at Wagram 6 July 1809, sabre wound to his right wrist at Winkovo 18 October 1812 and three lance wounds to his right hand, a sabre blow cut off his nose and seriously damaged his right eye, two horses killed under him during the day at Leipzig 16 October 1813, on leave extended by 3 months with pay 7 January 1814.

He was supernumerary squadron commander 10 January 1814, in post 2 March 1814, instated 15 March 1814, in the suite 4 August 1814, wounded by a shell burst at Waterloo 18 June 1815, dismissed 21 November 1815. LH CH 1 October 1807.

DELAISTRE de TILLY (Gustave, 1788-?): second son of the general, born in Caen (Calvados) on 28 October 1788. In the 10th Dragoons 14 March 1805, brigadier in the 22nd Dragoons 1 June 1807, in the 1st Provisional Dragoons 4 February 1808, maréchal des logis 7 June 1808, three sabre wounds to his right shoulder, left knee and back at Baylen 19 July 1808 and prisoner by capitulation 22 July 1808?

He returned to France 19 May 1814, in the Body Guards 15 June 1814, resigned in order to go into the Line 20 September 1814, cavalry lieutenant on half-pay 16 November 1814, temporary sub-lieutenant in the 6th Cuirassiers 23 March 1815, on leave in Paris 1 August 1815, struck off the rolls 1 September 1815.

DELAMARRE (Louis Guillaume, 1773-1838): born in Orval (Manche) in 1776. Volunteer in the Manche Dragoons 8 July 1793, incorporated into the 17th Cavalry 7 February 1794, adjutant- NCO 21 December 1798, in the same when it became the 26th Dragoons 24 September 1803, sub-lieutenant 5 October 1803.

He became lieutenant 8 November 1806, adjutant-major 8 May 1807, first-lieutenant in the Dragoons of the Guard 8 July 1807, captain in the 5th Cuirassiers 11 December 1811, retired 1815. LH CH 1 October 1807.

DELAMOTTE (Jacques Philippe, 1785-?): born in Enqueteville (Seine-Inférieure) on 13 May 1785. In the 6th Cuirassiers 27 August 1806, brigadier 26 May 1807.

He became maréchal des logis 5 October 1808, maréchal des logis-chef 19 July 1813, sub-lieutenant 22 December 1813, wounded and his horse killed under him at Waterloo 18 June 1815, dismissed 21 November 1815. LH CH 14 May 1813.

DELANGE see **VERGNIAUD de LANGE**

DELANNOY (Adrien, 1783-1854): born in Liège (Ourthe) on 7 July 1783. In the Gendarmes d'Ordonnance 4 October 1806, joined them 3 November 1806, brigadier 25 January 1807, sub-lieutenant in the suite 2 July 1807.

He was in the 7th Cuirassiers 16 July 1807, joined them 12 September 1807, lieutenant 8 October 1811, aide de camp 1 June 1812, in the 6th Cuirassiers 7 June 1813, incorporated with his squadron into the

ELORT (Jacques Antoine Adrien, Baron, 1774 - 1846): brother of the above, born in Arbois (Jura) on 16 November 1774. Volunteer in the 4th Jura battalion 14 August 1791, sub-lieutenant in the 8th Infantry 16 June 1792, lieutenant 17 September 1792, deputy to the adjutant-generals 15 June 1793, commissioned as a cavalry captain 28 August 1793, discharged 10 January 1797, on Sérurier's staff and attached to the 24th Cavalry 21 October 1797, in service and commanded a company 8 January 1798, deputy on the staff 21 November 1798 and rank of squadron commander on the battlefield 29 March 1799, confirmed 23 April 1799, attached to the 22nd Cavalry 30 June 1799, in service 21 January 1800, dismissed with the corps 31 December 1802 and incorporated into the suite of the 2nd Cuirassiers 7 February 1803, joined them 18 March 1803, major of the 9th Dragoons 29 October 1803, left to join 23 November 1803, acting CO of the regiment during the end of the campaign instead of Colonel Maupetit wounded 8 October 1805, two lance wounds and his horse killed under him, seized that of a seriously wounded squadron commander to continue leading the regiment until the end of the battle in spite of his loss of blood at Austerlitz 2 December 1805, colonel of the 25th Dragoons 8 May 186, shot and wounded in his right leg and several sabre wounds at Valls in Catalonia 25 February 1809, sabre wound to his left leg at Cespina 16 January 1810, brigade commander 21 July 1811, victor at Villareal, Torrente and Alcira, commanded the vanguard cavalry in the Army of Aragon 1812 then a cavalry brigade of the Paris Reserve Division 9 January 1814, wounded in the leg at Montereau 18 February 1814, major-general commanding the 2nd Division of the 2nd Cavalry Corps 26 February 1814, non-active 1 September 1814, commanded the 14th Cavalry Division (5th, 6th, 9th and 10th Cuirassiers), in the 4th Cavalry Reserve Corps of the Army of the North 23 April 1815, shot and wounded in the leg, a sabre wound to his arm, his hat and coat riddled with bullets at Waterloo 18 June 1815, non-active 15 August 1815. LH CH 25 March 1804, O 7 March 1810, C 16 March 1812, Chevalier of the Empire d. 19 March 1808 and l.p. 30 October 1810, Baron d.15 August 1810 and l.p. 4 June 1811.

At Montereau on 18 February 1814, General Jacques Delort led one of the most spectacular and decisive charges of the Empire. For several hours the French were gradually pushing back the Wurtemburgers towards the town of Montereau, an important road junction at the meeting of the Seine and the Yonne. General Pajol then ordered his subordinate to take his light cavalry brigade and take the bridges of the town. These three regiments were made up of mainly young recruits who could barely ride and had no real knowledge of how to wield a sabre. Delort therefore gave the only order possible; form up into a column on the road and charge at the gallop. He took the lead of this curious column and in spite their lack of assurance, the young troopers bowled over everything in their way, throwing over the enemy battalions one after the other. The bridges were taken and the battle won. During the charge the general was wounded in the left leg. He was soon promoted to Major- General.

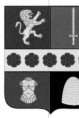

2nd Provisional Heavy Cavalry in Hamburg 11 September 1813.

He returned with the garrison 30 May 1814, on 6 months' leave 11 September 1814, leave extended 18 February 1815 until 1 April 1815 and he did not reappear in the corps.

DELARCHAND (Pierre Jean François, 1760-1830): born in Vassy (Calvados) on 4 March 1760. In the Berry-Infanterie 22 September 1778, corporal 3 February 1780, dismissed 1 December 1786, in the Commissaire-Général-Cavalerie 6 December 1786, brigadier 26 august 1787, brigadier-fourrier 1 January 1791, in the same regiment when it became the 3rd Cavalry on the same day.

He became, maréchal des logis-chef 17 January 1792, sub-lieutenant 1 August 1793, lieutenant 1 April 1795, when the brigade commander and most of the main officers were killed he took command of the regiment 8 August 1796 and the general commanding kept him there until the end of the campaign, captain by seniority 11 June 1801, in the same regiment when it became the 3rd Cuirassiers 12 October 1802, retired 8 May 1807. LH CH 14 June 1804.

DELAROCHE (François, 1767-1815): born in Honfleur (Calvados) on 5 July 1767.

Captain in the 18th Chasseurs à Cheval 23 November 1792, in the 14th Dragoons 26 June 1794, 14 sabre and lance wounds at Huterath 19 June 1796, in the Gendarmerie 12 January 1799, arbitrarily dismissed 22 June 1804, reinstated 10 November 1807, in the 17th Dragoons 12 January 1808, squadron commander in the Line and captain adjutant-major in the 1st Chevau-Légers Lancers of the Guard the same day 17 February 1811, in the Berri Cuirassiers 11 August 1814 which became the 5th Cuirassiers April 1815, killed at Waterloo 18 June 1815. LH CH, O 30 September 1814.

EMONGIN (Louis François, 1758 - ?): born in Mont-les-Fresnois (Haute-Saône) on 25 August 1778. Trooper in the Colonel-Général Regiment 2 December 1778, brigadier 1 March 1787, in the same regiment when it became the 1st Cavalry 1 January 1791, maréchal des logis 16 April 1792, with five other troopers managed to get a 6000-strong enemy column to withdraw after pretending to be a sentinel's position in full view of the enemy and holding the position with bravura making the enemy believe that their unit was bigger than it was 29 September 1792.

He bacame sub-lieutenant on the battlefield for this feat of arms 9 October 1792, confirmed 30 October 1792 and instated the following day 31 October 1792, lieutenant 16 September 1793, a sabre wound to his head near Maubeuge 26 September 1793, captain 11 September 1794, squadron commander 17 July 1799, wounded by a Biscayan shot to his left shoulder and his horse killed under him at Coni 28 October 1799, in the same regiment when it became the 1st Cuirassiers 10 October 1801, wounded at Austerlitz 2 December 1805, retired and left 1 January 1809. LH CH 15 June 1804, O 11 July 1807.

On 29 September 1795, Louis Demongin was a maréchal des logis in the 1st Cavalry Regiment. A 6000-men strong column was approaching. With five troopers he managed in full view of the enemy to halt this enemy column of 6 000 men by pretending to be a guard post and held the position with assurance, pretending that the unit present was stronger than it was. He was promoted on the battlefield on 9 October 1792 for this act of bravery.

DELAVERGNE (Paul Joseph Rémi, 1788-?): born in La Rochelle (Charente-Inférieure) on 18 May 1788. Pupil at the Ecole Militaire in Fontainebleau 24 October 1804, sub-lieutenant on the staff of the Grande Armée 7 November 1806, sub-lieutenant in the 69th of the Line 21 April 1807, wounded at Wagram 6 July 1809, in the 13th Cuirassiers 6 August 1810.

He disengaged Colonel Klicki from a group of Spanish Hussars killing one himself at Blancas 3 September 1810, captured a Spanish colonel while getting the enemy out of the town of Castala

Heavy Cavalry General.
(Composition by Patrice Courcelle, Private collection RR)

with his squadron 21 July 1812, lieutenant 12 June 1813, instated 14 July 1813, wounded at Leipzig 18 October 1813, captain 25 February 1814, dismissed with the corps and incorporated into the suite of the Queen's Cuirassiers July 1814, in post with the 4th Cuirassiers 30 October 1814, kept in the Queen's Cuirassiers 4 January 1815, which became the 2nd Cuirassiers again April 1815, dismissed and left on half-pay 10 December 1815. LH CH 12 February 1813.

DELBARRE (Jean François Guislain, 1777-?): born in Béthune (Pas-de-Calais) on 9 October 1777. In the 7th Cavalry 26 November 1798, brigadier 26 August 1801, brigadier-fourrier 13 March 1802, in the same which became the 7th Cuirassiers 23 December 1802, maréchal des logis 1 October 1806.

He became maréchal des logis-chef 11 March 1807, adjutant-NCO 1 May 1809, sub-lieutenant 9 August 1809, lieutenant 9 February 1813, wounded at Waterloo 18 June 1815, dismissed with the corps 19 December 1815. LH CH 1 October 1807.

DELBETZ (Pierre, 1789-?): born in Eymet (Dordogne) on 31 August 1789. Velite in the Grenadiers à Cheval of the Guard 22 February 1806, supernumerary sub-lieutenant in the 4th Cuirassiers 25 March 1809, lieutenant 9 June 1812, wounded at the Berezina 28 November 1812.

He was on convalescence leave with three months' pay 5 April 1815, dismissed 21 December 1815. LH CH 4 December 1813.

DELEAU (Ulrich Louis, 1777-1812): born in Versailles (Seine-et-Oise) on 3 June 1777. In the 1st Cuirassiers 14 June, brigadier 6 January 1803, fourrier 6 July 1803. He became maréchal des logis 6 January 1806, wounded shot in the right arm at Hoff 6 February 1807, sub-lieutenant 16 May 1809, lieutenant 25 September 1812, prisoner in Russia 10 December 1812 and disappeared.

DELESPINE (Gabriel Edouard, 1781-1809): born in Saint-Omer (Pas-de-Calais) on 15 June 1781. In

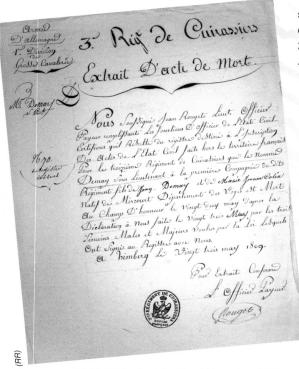

(RR)

the 16th Half-Brigade of the Line 1 November 1797, left 23 January 1799, maréchal des logis in the 1st Cuirassiers 29 April 1803, maréchal des logis-chef 18 January 1806.

He became sub-lieutenant 20 February 1807, lieutenant 25 May 1807, confirmed 18 February 1808, in the 13th Cuirassiers 21 October 1808, captain 13 February 1809, wounded at Tudela 23 November 1808 and died of his wounds at Henesca 22 April 1809.

DELESSART (Adrien François Louis Joseph, 1769-?): born in Avesnes (Nord) on 14 November 1769. In the Royal-Roussillon-Cavalerie 16 September 1784 which became the 11th Cavalry 1 January 1791.

He became brigadier-fourrier 1 May 1791, maréchal des logis 25 June 1792, maréchal des logis-chef 14 July 1792, adjutant 5 October 1793, rank of sub-lieutenant 27 October 1793, prisoner at Kaiserlautern 23 May 1794, managed to get away alone through enemy lines and rejoin his regiment, sub-lieutenant 24 August 1794, lieutenant 26 August 1794, quartermaster treasurer 20 April 1799, confirmed 2 January 1801.

He obtained the rank of captain 30 July 1802.

He was in the same regiment when it became the 11th Cuirassiers 24 September 1803, deputy to the sub-inspectors of parades 9 October 1813, left 9 November 1813. LH CH 5 November 1804.

DELETAILLE (Pierre Auguste Benoît, 1773-1809): born in Lyon (Rhône) on 25 August 1773. In the Queen's Dragoons 28 February 1787 which became the 6th Dragoons 1 January 1791, dismissed 28 February 1791, in the Volontaires Nationaux à Cheval from the Ecole Militaire 23 August 1792, brigadier 8 September 1792.

He became maréchal des logis 1 February 1793, in the same regiment when it became the 26th Cavalry 4 June 1793, saved 2 artillery pieces at the head of his platoon and shot and wounded in the heel 15 October 1793, assigned to the Versailles riding school from 4 February 1797 to 20 July 1800,

sub-lieutenant 8 October 1800, dismissed with the corps 12 October 1802 and incorporated into the 2nd Cuirassiers 24 November 1802, lieutenant 23 August 1805, in the 7th Cuirassiers 13 November 1805.

He was adjutant-major 9 September 1806, captain 11 March 1807, burnt alive in the fire which destroyed the hamlet of Brünn in the night of 7-8 May 1809. LH CH 1 October 1807.

DELISLE de BRAINVILLE (Jean Baptiste Charles, chevalier, 1770-1831): born in Brainville (Haute-Marne) on 6 July 1770. Replacement sub-lieutenant in the Artois-Cavalerie 23 February 1786, in service 31 May 1786, in the same regiment when it became the 9th Cavalry 1 January 1791.

He became lieutenant 25 January 1792, captain 29 October 1792, relieved of his command 11 November 1793, reinstated 5 March 1795, in the same regiment when it became the 9th Cuirassiers 24 September 1803, squadron commander 12 December 1806, major of the 2nd Cuirassiers 7 April 1809.

He was confirmed 28 September 1814, retired 11 October 1815. LH CH 14 June 1804, O 17 March 1815, Chevalier of the Empire l.p. 9 September 1810.

DELITEAU (Jean Claude, 1759-?): born in Antorpes (Doubs) on 4 June 1759. In the Dauphin-Cavalerie 2 December 1777 which became the 12th Cavalry 1 January 1791.

He became brigadier 26 March 1793, maréchal des logis 1 April 1793, maréchal des logis-chef 3 November 1793, alone charged two Austrian hussars freeing a trooper from the 9th Regiment at Spire 19 June 1794, elected sub-lieutenant 21 November 1798, lieutenant 21 March 1802, in the same regiment when it became the 12th Cuirassiers 24 September 1803.

He was second-lieutenant in the Grenadiers à Cheval of the Imperial Guard 1 May 1806, wounded at Eylau 8 February 1807, retired 7 February 1808.

DELITOT see **DELITEAU.**

DELMAS de LACOSTE (Antoine, 1774 -after 1840): brother of the general, born in Argentat (Corrèze) on 23 January 1774. In the 1st Corrèze Battalion 14 September 1791, corporal 18 September 1791, lieutenant in the Hussards de la Liberté 30 June 1793.

He became aide de camp to his brother, General Delmas, 1 July 1793, captain in the 6th Saône-et-Loire Battalion 2 May 1794, squadron commander 23 April 1799, in the 3rd Cavalry 14 December 1801 which became the 3rd Cuirassiers 12 October 1802, major 29 October 1803, retired 20 June 1807 and pensioned off 10 September 1807, returned as major in the 12th Cuirassiers 21 April 1813, on two months' leave with pay 2 July 1814.

He was squadron commander in the Gendarmerie 5 September 1814. LH CH 25 March 1804, O 8 July 1813.

DELOBEL (Henry Adrien, 1794-1815): born in Lille (Nord) on 26 June 1794. In the Ecole Spéciale

EMORELLE (Robert Charles, 1788-1866): born in Falaise (Calvados) on 18 April 1788. Pupil in the Ecole Impériale Militaire in Fontainebleau 13 August 1805, sub-lieutenant in the 6th Cuirassiers 23 September 1806, lieutenant in the 4th Cuirassiers 2 March 1809, adjutant-major 3 May 1809, wounded by a Biscayan shot to his knee at Wagram 6 July 1809, captain 12 September 1809, lance wound at the Berezina 28 November 1812.

He became squadron commander 5 September 1813, lance wound at Vauchamps 14 February 1814, in the same regiment when it became the Angoulême Cuirassiers 6 August 1814 and 4th Cuirassiers again in April 1815, resigned 12 May 1815, resignation refused 30 May 1815, wounded at Waterloo 18 June 1815, sent home to await further orders 14 July 1815, dismissed with the corps 21 December 1815. LH CH 8 October 1811, O 17 February 1814.

Squadron Commander Robert Demorelle distinguished himself at Brienne on 29 January 1814 by taking a Hungarian battalion with only 60 men from the 4th Cuirassiers. Less than to weeks later on 10 February during the Battle of Champaubert, he charged with three Cuirassier platoons with which he broke through a Russian division and got hold of six artillery pieces. These exploits earned him the Officer of the Légion d'Honneur on 17 February 1814.

Militaire at Saint-Cyr. He became sub-lieutenant in the 12th Cuirassiers 10 April 1815, disappeared at Waterloo 18 June 1815 and struck off the rolls 1 July 1815.

DELOBEL (Simon Jean Baptiste Joseph, 1781-1856): born in Tournai (Escaut) on 24 June 1781. In the Aremberg Chevau-Légers 22 March 1807 which became the 27th Chasseurs à Cheval 29 May 1808, shot and wounded in the right hip at Mohernando November 1809 and shot in the left leg at Huelva 1810.

He became sub-lieutenant 22 May 1812, wounded by a cannonball in the left leg and his horse killed under him at Vittoria 21 June 1813, shot and wounded in his right thigh at Naunbourg 9 October 1813, lieutenant in the 2nd Cuirassiers 8 January 1814, wounded and his left arm broken by a shell burst at Vitry-le-François 21 March 1814, left 26 August 1814, lieutenant in the Carabiniers in the service of Holland,.

He was wounded by a sabre on the forehead by a cuirassier squadron commander who left his ranks to challenge an officer of his regiment at Waterloo 18 June 1815. LH CH 4 December 1813.

DELORGERIL (Louis Toussaint, 1789-?): born in Parigny (Manche) on 27 July 1789. Pupil at the Saint-Germain military school 2 September 1812, sub-lieutenant in the 5th Chevau-Légers 30 January 1813, in the suite of the 4th Cuirassiers 15 March 1813, in post 20 January 1814, in the same regiment when it became the Angoulême Cuirassiers 13 March 1815, dismissed 21 December 1815.

DELORT (Augustin Ozias, 1777-?): the brother of the general, born in Arbois (Jura) on 25 February 1777. Corporal in the 12th Jura Battalion September 1792, in the Guides à Cheval of the Army of the Alps 9 November 1793, discharged 8 July 1795 and allowed to return home, trooper in the 22nd Cavalry 10 October 1799, brigadier-fourrier 25 December 1799, maréchal des logis 20 July 1800.

He became sub-lieutenant 21 April 1801, dismissed with the corps 31 December 1802 and incorporated into the 18th Cavalry 25 March 1803, in the 2nd Cuirassiers 7 July 1803, lieutenant in the 12th Cuirassiers 25 August 1806, instated 1 October 1806, two sabre wounds to his forehead, one behind the head, on his right hand one on his left hand and two lance wounds to his right arm and left thigh and left for dead at Friedland 14 June 1807, captain 12 April 1808, retired as he had lost the use of his right elbow 18 August 1808. LH CH 1 October 1807.

DELPECHE (Benjamin Barthélémy, ?-1809): Born in Rodez (Aveyron), maréchal des logis in the 1st Cuirassiers, sub-lieutenant 16 May 1809, killed by a cannonball at Essling 21 May 1809.

DEMAISON (Baptiste Constant, 1775-?): born in Harbonnière (Somme) on 27 March 1775. In the 2nd Cavalry 6 February 1794, brigadier 11 August 1800, fourrier 18 July 1801.

He was in the same regiment when it became the 2nd Cuirassiers 12 October 1802, maréchal des logis 20 December 1806, sub-lieutenant 9 August 1809, lieutenant 11 March 1812, retired 10 December 1815. LH CH 29 September 1814.

DEMANGES (Charles Antoine, 1786-?): born in Vesoul (Haute-Saône) on 4 July 1786. Maréchal des logis in the 5th Cuirassiers having captured a flag during the 1806 Campaign.

He became sub-lieutenant 16 May 1809, lost an arm at Essling 22 May 1809, retired 2 November 1809. LH CH 6 May 1807.

DEMARAIS (? - ?): sub-lieutenant, In the 12th Cuirassiers, incorporated with his squadron into the 2nd Provisional Heavy Cavalry in Hamburg 11 September 1813. He returned with the garrison 30 May 1814.

DEMAY (?-1809): Born in Mirecourt, sub-lieutenant in the 3rd Cuirassiers and killed at Essling 22 May 1809.

DEMELE (Yves, 1774-1812): born in Bouseuil (Côtes-d-Nord) in 1774. In the 4th Cavalry 26 May 1794, brigadier 17 August 1800, in the same regiment when it became the 4th Cuirassiers 11 January 1803.

He became maréchal des logis 27 December 1802, maréchal des logis-chef 22 December 1804, supernumerary sub-lieutenant 5 March 1809, in service 1 May 1809, sabre wound to his head, his horse killed under him and taken prisoner at Essling 21 May 1809.

He Returned 12 August 1809, lieutenant 4 March 1812, killed at the Berezina 28 November 1812. LH CH 1 October 1807.

DEMENGEL (Nicolas Antoine, 1771-?): born in Vézelise (Meurthe) in 1771. In the 24th Cavalry 23 July 1791, brigadier-fourrier 1 October 1792, in the same regiment when it became the 23rd Cavalry 4 June 1793, maréchal des logis 19 December 1793, sub-lieutenant 13 July 1794, put in as adjutant-NCO 21 March 1797.

He became sub-lieutenant by choice 13 December 1800, several sabre wounds near Salzburg 14 December 1800, confirmed 10 June 1801, dismissed with the corps 23 December 1802 and incorporated into the 7th Cuirassiers 15 January 1803, on leave for six months 9 November 1802, returned 11 May 1803.

He was lieutenant by seniority 24 December 1805, discharged without pay 26 December 1807.

DEMICHY (Antoine Auguste, 1773-1814): born in Beaumont (Oise) on 19 September 1773. In the 7th Cavalry 6 December 1793, prisoner 26 May 1800, returned 5 March 1801, in the same regiment when it became the 7th Cuirassiers 23 December 1802, brigadier 2 January 1803.

He became maréchal des logis 23 October 1804, maréchal des logis-chef 26 April 1807, sub-lieutenant 7 April 1809, temporary lieutenant 3 June 1809, captain 15 May 1813, killed at Brienne 30 January 1814. LH CH 8 October 1811.

DEMULDER (Augustin Joseph, 1785-1815): born in Nivelles (Dyle) on 30 August 1785. Velite in the Grenadiers à Cheval of the Guard 12 February 1806, bayonet wound at Eylau 8 February 1807.

He became sub-lieutenant in the 5th Cuirassiers 7 January 1808, cannonball wound at Essling 22 May 1809, lieutenant 6 November 1811, several sabre wounds to his left arm at Hanau 30 October

Sabre belonging to Squadron Commander Dequevauvillier. *(Private collection, photograph Bertrand Malvaux)*

EQUEVAUVILLIER (Charles Louis Marie Auguste, 1782-1852): born in Besançon (Doubs) on 22 March 1782. In the 23rd Cavalry 28 December 1797, brigadier 19 April 1800, brigadier-fourrier 11 August 1800, maréchal des logis 15 November 1802, dismissed with the corps 23 December 1802, promoted meanwhile to maréchal des logis-chef 2 January 1803, incorporated into the 7th Cuirassiers 1 January 1803, detached to the veterinary school in Lyon 25 August 1804, returned and adjutant-NCO 3 May 1805.

He became sub-lieutenant by governmental choice 13 June 1805, lieutenant in the 10th Cuirassiers 20 August 1808, instated 25 September 1808.

He became adjutant-major 14 May 1811, rank of captain 6 November 1811, squadron commander 28 September 1813, dismissed with the regiment and put in the new Orléans Cuirassiers 25 December 1815. LH CH 16 June 1809, O 2 November 1814.

Eckmühl, 22 April 1809: Lieutenant Charles Dequevauvillier from the 10th Cuirassiers faced the Austrian cavalry. Wounded by a sabre in the head and bruised on his left knee, he continued charging and got hold of a flag. Separated from his men and surrounded by twenty or so enemy who wounded him again six times with their sabres, he was forced to abandon his prize.

He was made chevalier of the Légion d'Honneur on the following 16 June.

1813, killed at Waterloo 18 June 1815. LH CH 28 September 1813.

DENIS (Jean, 1766-?): born in Bonnetable (Sarthe) on 14 May 1766. In the 7th Dragoons 28 May 1794, in the Grenadiers à Cheval of the Guard 14 March 1800, brigadier 22 December 1801, maréchal des logis 26 February 1806.

He became lieutenant in the 1st Cuirassiers 8 February 1813, joined them 25 March 1813, meanwhile appointed to the 1st Carabiniers 15 February 1813, rejoined the depot at Lunéville 3 April 1813, incorporated with a detachment into the 2nd Provisional Cavalry Regiment in Magdeburg beginning of August 1813, wounded and taken prisoner during a sally from Lübnitz 27 August 1813.

He returned to the 1st Carabiniers 1 October 1814 and authorised to go home, non-active 1 November 1814, back in activity in the 1st Carabiniers 12 April 1815, joined them at the depot at Lunéville and placed as lieutenant in the suite 28 April 1815, non-active again 1 August 1815, left 21 August 1815. LH CH 14 March 1806.

DENNEFERT (Pierre Charles Bruno, 1771-?): born in Péronne (Somme) on 7 October 1771. In the Royal-Normandie-Cavalerie 22 September 1789 which became the 20th Cavalry 1 January 1791, fourrier 18 May 1793, in the regiment when it became the 19th Cavalry 4 June 1793, adjutant 16 November 1793.

He became adjutant sub-lieutenant 2 April 1795, lieutenant 28 August 1800, lieutenant adjutant-major, incorporated into the suite of the 9th Cuirassiers 25 January 1803, rank of captain 9 September 1803, captain adjutant-major in the 1st Cuirassiers 16 March 1804, captain in post in a company 24 November 1806.

He was wounded at Eylau 8 February 1807, squadron commander 13 January 1809, wounded at Essling May 1809, retired 6 November 1811. LH CH 14 April 1807.

DENONCIN (Jean Baptiste, 1767-1807): born in Sapoyne (Ardennes) on 6 May 1767. In the Forez-Infanterie 27 June 1785 which became the 14th of the Line 1 January 1791, chief instructor in the 2nd Béthune Battalion 25 September 1793, in the 21st Chasseurs à Cheval 8 January 1794, brigadier 14 December 1794.

He became maréchal des logis 15 March 1795, brigadier in the Garde à Cheval of the Directoire 21 December 1796, maréchal des logis 2 June 1798, incorporated into the Grenadiers à Cheval of the Consular Guard 3 January 1800, sub-lieutenant in the 5th Cuirassiers 30 August 1805, killed at Eylau 8 February 1807. Holder of a Rifle of Honour 22 July 1800, LH CH by rights 24 September 1803.

DENORMANDIE (Louis, 1787-?): born in Paris (Seine) on 3 November 1787. In the Ecole Militaire 14 June 1803, fourrier 24 July 1805, sub-lieutenant in the 4th Light Infantry 14 September 1805, lieute-

nant 28 June 1808, aide de camp 1 January 1810. He became captain 1 November 1811, in the suite of the 8th Cuirassiers 5 November 1814, in post April 1815, dismissed with the corps and put on the non-active list 5 December 1815. LH CH 21 November 1814.

DENOUE (? - ?): lieutenant aide de camp to General Reynaud, captain in the 6th Cuirassiers 3 June 1809, wounded at Wagram 6 July 1809, amputated 17 August 1809 and retired 1 January 1810.

DENY (Jean Baptiste, 1762-1805): born in Rouvre-en-Woëvre (Meuse) on 21 March 1762. Soldier in the Anjou Regiment 24 March 1781, dismissed 24 March 1789, chasseur on the payroll of the Paris National Guard 10 April 1789, dismissed 30 December 1791.

He became brigadier-fourrier in the Volontaires Nationaux à Cheval from the Ecole Militaire 20 November 1792, elected captain in the 26th Cavalry when it was created from the volunteers 21 February 1793, commissioned 22 June 1793, in the same regiment when it became the 25th Cavalry 1793, wounded with his thigh broken when he fell from his horse during a charge 19 April 1794.

He was dismissed with the corps 12 October 1802, incorporated into 3rd Cuirassiers 22 December 1802, killed at Austerlitz 2 December 1805.

DEPAIX de CŒUR (Alexandre, 1782-1813): born in Dugleville (Seine-Inférieure) in 1782. In the 5th Cuirassiers 28 January 1804, brigadier 5 July 1804, maréchal des logis 1 May 1806, maréchal des logis-chef 15 December 1806, adjutant NCO 1 July 1807.

He became sub-lieutenant 15 May 1809, lieutenant 12 July 1812, prisoner in the hospital at Gumbingen 31 January 1813 and disappeared.

DEPERREAUD (Jean Pierre Marie, 1786 -after 1839) born in Caudiès (Basses-Pyrénées) on 17 September 1786. In the 1st Cuirassiers 31 October 1803, brigadier 16 December 1805, maréchal des logis 16 November 1806, adjutant-NCO 3 June 1809.

He became sub-lieutenant 5 November 1811, acting lieutenant during the siege of Magdeburg 14 November 1813, in the King's Cuirassiers 1 July 1814, non-active on full pay 1 October 1814, returned to the regiment 1 April 1815 which had become the 1st Cuirassiers, on half-pay again 1 September 1815. LH CH 16 June 1809.

DEPRECOURT (Jean Marc Félix, 1777-?): born in Paris (Seine) on 23 June 1777. In the 19th Cavalry 6 May 1799, brigadier 23 October 1799, fourrier 24 January 1800.

He became maréchal des logis 28 August 1800, maréchal des logis-chef 23 September 1802, dismissed with the corps 31 December 1802 and incorporated into the 11th Cuirassiers 5 February 1803, adjutant-NCO 1 December 1804, wounded by a Biscayan shot to his right shoulder at Eylau 8 February 1807, sub-lieutenant 3 April 1807.

He was lieutenant 16 May 1809, adjutant-major 6 November 1811, captain 25 September 1812, in

the Escadron Sacré during the retreat from Moscow December 1812, squadron commander 3 September 1813, wounded by a cannonball in the left leg at Leipzig 16 October 1813, in the suite of the Cuirassiers du Dauphin 1 August 1814 which became the 3rd Cuirassiers again April 1815.

DEREPERE (Jacques Antoine, 1765-?): born in Senozan (Saône-et-Loire) on 29 March 1765. In the Mestre-de-Camp-Général-Cavalerie 20 April 1782, brigadier 6 May 1785, in the same regiment when it became the 24th Cavalry 1 January 1791, dismissed with the corps 20 February 1791 and promoted to maréchal des logis in the 24th Cavalry of the so-called new levy the following day 21 February 1791, maréchal des logis-chef 7 May 1792.

He became sub-lieutenant 1 October 1792, in the same regiment when it became the 23rd Cavalry 4 June 1793, quartermaster treasurer 12 December 1793, rank of lieutenant 3 April 1795 then of captain 21 September 1798, dismissed with the corps 23 December 1802 and placed as supernumerary in the suite of the 7th Cuirassiers 3 January 1803, in the Secretariat of War for winding up the accounts of the Army of the Orient from 22 April 1803 to 4 September 1803.

He was captain quartermaster treasurer of the 6th Cuirassiers 19 September 1803, left to join them 29 September 1803, retired 21 November 1815. LH CH 19 June 1815.

DERIM (?-1813): maréchal des logis in the 5th Cuirassiers, sub-lieutenant 9 August 1809, remained under enemy control in Interburg hospital July 1813.

DERMONCOURT (Paul Ferdinand Stanislas, baron, 1771-1847): born in Crécy-au-Mont (Aisne) on 3 March 1771. Took part in the taking of the Bastille 14 July 1789, in the Grenadiers of the Paris National Guard end of July 1789.

He was in the 3rd Aisne Battalion 4 September 1791, sergeant 4 April 1792, sergeant-major 3 July 1792, lieutenant 19 December 1792, captain 28 December 1792, returned from San Domingo 11 June 1794 and assigned to General Dumas end of June 1794, adjutant of the military area of Brest, aide de camp to Dumas 12 April 1796, sabre wound to his right shoulder at Brixen bridge 23 March 1797, captain in the 3rd Dragoons 27 October 1797, acting captain of the brigade 3 June 1799.

He was wounded in the chest and left ankle by a shot at Abukir 25 July 1799, acting squadron commander in the 14th Dragoons 23 June 1800, shot and wounded in the throat at Canope 21 March 1801, confirmed 6 March 1802, in the 22nd Cavalry 4 June 1802, in the 21st Dragoons 7 February 1803, major of the 11th Cuirassiers 15 December 1803, colonel of the 1st Dragoons 5 April 1807, wounded by a shot which went through his thigh at Talavera-de-la-Reyna 29 July 1809 and by a shot to his right knee at Sierra-Morena 29 December 1809,.

He was confirmed as regimental colonel 9 October 1811 which became the 1st Chevau-Légers Lancers 18 June 1811, commanded a cavalry marching regiment joining the Grande Armée April 1813, brigadier-general 22 July 1813, commanded the 3rd Light Cavalry Brigade of the 1st Cavalry Corps 15 August 1813 (2nd, 3rd and 6th Chasseurs à Cheval) then the 5th Corps Cavalry at the end of August 1813, ordered to organise the defence of Neuf-Brisach 25 December 1813.

He became commanded the 2nd Brigade of the 9th Light Cavalry Division 5 January 1814 but had not joined them because he stayed back to defend Neuf-Brisach which he defended until peace was proclaimed, acting CO of the Haut-Rhin troops keeping his functions end of April 1814, in the 5th Military Division 23 September 1814, commanded at Neuf-Brisach October 1814, replaced 2 January 1815, reinstated 25 March 1815, went through another blockade, non-active on half-pay 6 October 1815.

LH CH 25 March 1804, O 4 October 1808, C 4 December 1813, Baron of the Empire d.14 March 1808 and l.p. 16 September 1808.

DEROISIN (François Joseph Léopold Marie, 1791-1812): born in Rongy (Jemappes) on 11 March 1791. Pupil at the Ecole Impériale Militaire de Cavalerie 9 July 1810.

He became velite in the Grenadiers à Cheval of the Guard 3 January 1811, brigadier 15 September 1811, sub-lieutenant in the 4th Cuirassiers 24 April 1812, lieutenant 1812, wounded at Polotsk 20 October 1812, prisoner 24 October 1812 and disappeared.

DEROST (Nicolas, 1765-1812): born in Percey-le-Grand (Haute-Saône) on 6 June 1765. In the Dauphin-Cavalerie 11 January 1785, fourrier 1 January 1791, in the same regiment when it became the 12th Cavalry on the same day, maréchal des logis 11 November 1792, sub-lieutenant 1 April 1793.

He became lieutenant quartermaster 21 June 1795, relieved of his command 10 April 1796, reinstated lieutenant 22 July 1796, quartermaster treasurer 20 November 1801, adjutant-major 13 March 1802, rank of captain 9 September 1803, in the same regiment when it became the 12th Cuirassiers 24 September 1803, went over to a company 12 December 1806, killed at Orcha 21 November 1812.

DEROUSSE (Didier, 1792-?): born in Sarreguemines (Moselle) on 24 April 1792. In the 9th Cuirassiers 7 July 1808, fourrier 14 May 1809, maréchal des logis 1 February 1812, adjutant-NCO 1 August 1812, wounded at the Moskova 7 September 1812, sub-lieutenant 20 September 1812, prisoner in Russia 10 December 1812, returned to the regiment 3 September 1814, dismissed with the corps and put on the non-active list 26 November 1815.

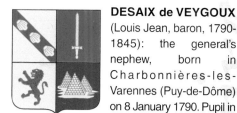

DESAIX de VEYGOUX (Louis Jean, baron, 1790-1845): the general's nephew, born in Charbonnières-les-Varennes (Puy-de-Dôme) on 8 January 1790. Pupil in the Elite Company of the military prytaneum of saint-Cyr 23 January 1806, sub-lieutenant in the 10th Light Infantry 20 September 1806, wounded by a Biscayan shot in the stomach at Heilsberg 10 June 1807, lieutenant in the 10th Light 10 February 1808, aide de camp to his uncle, General Beker, 31 May 1808 then to General Suchet 8 November 1808,.

He became captain 10 February 1810, in the 13th Cuirassiers 21 March 1810, aide de camp to Suchet 20 January 1812, wounded in the leg at Tarragone 28 June 1811, ordnance officer to the Emperor 29 February 1812, left Valence to go to Kovno 10 May 1812, squadron commander in the 2nd Gardes d'Honneur 5 August 1813, sous-aide-major in the 2nd Musketeer Company of the King's Guard 1 July 1814.

He was maréchal des logis of the Palace April 1815, major in the suite of the 6th Chasseurs à Cheval 4 May 1815, on the general staff of the Army of the North 13 May 1815, colonel 21 June 1815, chief of staff of the 11th Division of the 3rd Cavalry Corps 5 July 1815, non-active with the rank of lieutenant-colonel 8 August 1815. LH CH 10 March 1809, O 28 November 1813, Baron of the Empire d. 2 March 1811 and l.p. 12 February 1812.

DESARBRES (Charles, 1786-après 1819): born in Chalon-sur-Saône (Saône-et-Loire) on 16 June 1786. Velite in the Grenadiers à Cheval of the Imperial Guard 16 December 1806, sub-lieutenant in the suite of the 5th Cuirassiers 17 December 1811, in post 21 February 1812, first lieutenant in the 1st Gardes d'Honneur 3 September 1813, lance wound at Reims 13 March 1814, non-active on half-pay 1 September 1814. LH CH 19 February 1814.

DESARGUS (Jean Baptiste Pierre Martin, baron, 1776-1851): born in Amiens (Somme) on 8 October 1776. In the 2nd Battalion of Paris Volunteers 20 July 1791, in the 10th Battalion of the Fédérés Nationaux 20 October 1792.

He became sergeant-major 11 June 1793, lieutenant 8 March 1794, in the 178th Half-Brigade of the Line 20 December 1794,

supernumerary in the 17th Half-Brigade of the Line 11 February 1796, in the suite of General Julienne de Belair's staff 10 November 1798, on that of the Army of Naples 16 May 1799, acting captain on the battlefield at la Trebbia 30 June 1799, deputy to Adjutant-General Villet 12 April 1800, confirmed captain 5 May 1800.

He was aide de camp to Generals Watrin and Jablonowski 30 November 1800 and commissioned 29 April 1802, aide de camp to Saint-Sulpice 3 June 1804, battalion commander 14 February 1807, wounded at Essling 21 and 22 May 1809, adjutant-major 8 August 1809, chief of staff of the 3rd Cuirassier Division, colonel in the suite of the 7th cuirassiers 14 September 1809, joined them 29 September 1809, detached in a mobile column to Bordeaux 1811, in service in the 20th Dragoons 14 October 1811, struck off the rolls of the 7th Cuirassiers 1 December 1811.

He became colonel in the same regiment when it became the Dragoons N°15 in 1814 and 20th Dragoons again April 1815, allowed to retired 19 April 1815, chief of staff of a division which was in the process of being formed 31 May 1815, non-active 1 September 1815. LH CH 14 March 1806, O 16 January 1809, Chevalier of the Empire 15 August 1809, Baron d. 19 November 1813 and l.p. 11 November 1814.

DESAVOYE (Jean Baptiste Joseph, 1776-1815): born in

Cuirassier General Officer
(Figurines Magazine)

Pouy-l'Hôpital (Somme) on 19 August 1776. In the 5th Dragoons 22 October 1798, brigadier 23 December 1799, fourrier 16 October 1800, maréchal des logis 29 August 1803.

He became maréchal des logis-chef 8 January 1804, gendarme in the Somme Company 27 July 1804, maréchal des logis in the 14th Cuirassiers 20 March 1813, maréchal des logis-chef 21 March 1813, sub-lieutenant 22 December 1813.

He was dismissed with the corps and incorporated into the 12th cuirassiers 13 July 1814, wounded then disappeared at Waterloo 18 June 1815.

DESAYVE
see **LACROIX de CHEVRIERES de SAYVE**

DESBORDES (François, 1790 -after 1819): born in Firbeix (Dordogne) on 17 August 1790. Velite in the Dragoons of the Imperial Guard 29 March 1809, sub-lieutenant in the 6th Cuirassiers 13 March 1813, prisoner 5 December 1813, on half-pay with the new 1 July 1814 re-organisation.

He returned 6 December 1814, confirmed as non-active 15 December 1814, allowed to go home 26 December 1814, left 1 January 1815, returned to the corps 1 July 18151 and non-active again 26 August 1815.

DESBROSSES (Frédéric Jean Louis, 1781-?): born in Confolens (Charente) on 12 October 1781. In the 1st Cuirassiers 14 September 1801, brigadier 18 June 1802.

He became maréchal des logis 16 November 1806, shot and wounded in the shoulder at Eckmühl 22 April 1809, sub-lieutenant 3 June 1809, arrested 16 May 1815. LH CH 1 October 1807.

DESCAMPS (Pierre, 1771-?): born in Thil (Landes) on 22 September 1771. In service 1 March 1794, sabre wound to his left arm at Castillon 12 June 1796, brigadier 7 October 1797.

He became maréchal des logis 4 February 1799, shot and wounded in his right thigh at Novi 15 August 1799, sub-lieutenant in the Ionian Chasseurs à Cheval 1 January 1808, lieutenant in the 19th Chasseurs à Cheval 28 June 1813, non-active 1 September 1814, put back into the 12th Cuirassiers 1815, dismissed 3 August 1815, went home 16 August 1815.

DESCHAMPS (Jean Baptiste, 1789-?): born in Chanceaux (Côte-d'Or) on 11 December 1789. In the 10th Dragoons 23 March 1801, brigadier 1 August 1807, gendarme in the 5th Escadron d'Espagne 1 January 1811.

He was in the 1st Légion de Gendarmerie à Cheval d'Espagne "Burgos" 1 March 1811, brigadier 1 March 1812, dismissed with the corps 27 February 1813, incorporated as sub-lieutenant in the 11th cuirassiers 28 February 1813, in the King's Cuirassiers 1 May 1814, confirmed 1 July 1814, in the same regiment when it became the 1st Cuirassiers again April 1815, captain by mistake 25 March 1815, rectified to lieutenant 30 March

1815, in the 3rd cuirassiers 23 May 1815, left 1 June 1815, instated 6 June 1815.

He was dismissed as a sub-lieutenant and retired 25 November 1815. LH CH 25 February 1814.

DESCOURS (Jacques Emmanuel Casimir Eugène, 1786-?): born in Saint-Just (Hérault) on 26 May 1786. In the 1st Carabiniers 20 November 1806, brigadier 20 august 1807, maréchal des logis 10 January 1808, in the 1st Provisional Heavy Cavalry in Spain which became the 13th Cuirassiers 21 October 1808, adjutant-NCO 1 January 1812.

He became sub-lieutenant 28 February 1812, instated 16 March 1812, lieutenant 27 August 1813, incorporated into the 9th Cuirassiers 9 August 1814, shot in the knee at Ligny 16 June 1815 or Waterloo 18 June 1815, dismissed and non-active at the disposal of the Minister of War 26 November 1815. LH CH 29 May 1810.

DESEQUE (17?8-1809): Born in Bailleul-Cornailles (Pas-de-Calais) on 10 January 17?8. In the 8th Cavalry 1796, brigadier 23 September 1799, in the same regiment when it became the 1st Cuirassiers 10 October 1801, maréchal des logis 6 June 1802.

He became, maréchal des logis-chef 30 October 1803, sub-lieutenant 3 June 1809, killed by a bullet at Wagram 5 July 1809.

DESFOSSES (Michel Charles, 1775-?): born in Coucy (Aisnes) on 14 February 1775. In the 2nd Dragoons 4 September 1793, discharged 17 December 1795, captain instructor for the artillery wagon train 20 March 1800, left 18 August 1802, taken back into service as sub-lieutenant 2 May 1804.

He became aide de camp to General Dulauloy 14 December 1804, lieutenant in the 1st Cuirassiers 30 May 1807, captain 29 April 1809, wounded at Essling May 1809, retired and pensioned off 9 October 1811. LH CH 4 January 1807.

DESFRANCS (Louis Henry, 1787-?): born in Prègne (Deux-Sèvres) on 23 March 1787. In the Grenadiers à Cheval of the Imperial Guard 2 February 1807, sub-lieutenant in the 8th Cuirassiers 3 July 1809.

He became lieutenant 1 June 1812, shot and wounded in the right hand at the Moskova 7 September 1812, captain 5 June 1813, non-active September 1814.

DESHAYES (Edouard, 1781-?): born in Villemont (Orne) in 1781. In the Velites à Cheval of the Guard 20 March 1806, discharged for health reasons 12 August 1810, sub-lieutenant in the 1st Foreign Battalion 8 February 1811.

He became second-lieutenant in the 2nd Gardes d'Honneur 26 May 1813, non-active on half-pay 26 July 1814, lieutenant in the 3rd Cuirassiers 14 May 1815, non-active again 1 September 1815.

DESISLES see **PERRIN DESISLES**

DESMAREST (Charles Louis, 1777-?): born in Argicourt (Ain) on 17 June 1777. In the 11th Cavalry 21 April 1800 which became the 11th Cuirassiers 24 September 1803, in the 11th Squadron of the Gendarmerie d'Espagne 9 March 1810, in the 1st Légion de Gendarmerie à Cheval d'Espagne "Burgos" 16 December 1810.

He became sub-lieutenant in the 12th Cuirassiers 1 March 1812, incorporated with his squadron into the 2nd Provisional Heavy Cavalry in Hamburg 3 September 1813, returned with the garrison 30 May 1814, dismissed with the corps 10 December 1815.

DESMARETS (Guillaume Joseph, 1773-?): born in Douai (Nord) on 11 May 1773. In the 4th Hussars 30 November 1791, fourrier 12 August 1793, shot and wounded in the right leg 5 March 1793, maréchal des logis 21 March 1793, maréchal des logis-chef 1 November 1798, shot in the chest 26 May 1799, adjutant-NCO 10 April 1800, sub-lieutenant 10 December 1801, lieutenant 30 January 1806, lieutenant adjutant-major 17 September 1806, sabre wound to his shoulder at Schleitz 8 October 1806.

He became captain 30 March 1807, squadron commander in the suite 15 October 1808, in post in the 10th Hussars 10 January 1810, acting CO of the regiment and the vanguard of the army pushed aside 2000 Spanish troopers who lost 400 men and 6 cannon September 1810, major 1 May 1813, major in the 5th Hussars 20 January 1814, provisional major in the same regiment 11 August 1814, non-active 6 November 1814.

He was in the suite of the 12th Cuirassiers 19 November 1814, in service 11 May 1815, instated 8 June 1815, dismissed with the corps 10 December 1815. LH CH 14 March 1806, O 10 November 1810.

DESMENARD (Jean Baptiste Pierre, 1772-?): sub-lieutenant in the Vexin-Infanterie 15 September 1790, lieutenant in the Vermandois Regiment 1 August 1792, deputy captain on the staff of the Grand Duke of Berg 6 April 1808, on the staff of the 6th Corps of the Army of Spain 13 November 1809.

He was wounded by a Biscayan shot in the shoulder at Santiago 26 May 1810, squadron commander 24 April 1814, in the suite of the King's Cuirassiers 1 August 1814, confirmed as squadron commander 19 august 1814 and commissioned 14 September 1814, remained in Paris at the disposal of the Minister of War 20 January 1815.

DESMONTS (Jacques, 1770-1822): born in Laneuville (Calvados) on 20 April 1770. In the Champagne Chasseurs à Cheval 27 January 1789 which became the 12th Chasseurs à Cheval 1 January 1791, wounded by a shell burst in the right leg at Valmy 20 September 1792.

He became brigadier 1 July 1793, maréchal des logis 5 May 1794, maréchal des logis-chef 27 December 1798, sub-lieutenant 26 July 1799, four sabre wounds to his right arm, head and left shoulder at Marengo 14 June 1800, confirmed 20 July

Le 8ᵉ Cuirassiers 1786-1815

Cuirassiers du Roi according to the 1786 Regulations. The saddle cover as well as the portmanteau stripe and the holster caps bore the regimental livery. The Cuirassiers were 8th in seniority in the King's cavalry.

Trooper from the 8th Cavalry Regiment towards 1800 according to a drawing by Kobell taken up by P. Benigni in Commandant Bucquoy's Card collection.

Brigadier from the 8th Cavalry Regiment towards 1800, according to a drawing by Rigo. Note the change in the colour of the collar.

Trooper from the 1st Cuirassiers, formerly the 8th Cavalry Regiment towards 1801, after a manuscript in J. and R. Brunon's archives. It was an initiative taken by Brigade Commander Merlin who wanted his regiment to be N°1 since as it had been wearing a cuirass for more than a century. But the Republic had no intention of giving way and remained steeped in the tradition with in the royal regiments.

Officer from the Elite Company of the 1st Cuirassier Regiment towards 1801, according to Brigade Commander Merlin's proposals.

Trooper from the 8th "Cuirassed" Cavalry Regiment, an uniform put forward in 1802.

1800, in the Grenadiers à Cheval of the Guard 13 October 1802, second-lieutenant 5 September 1803, first-lieutenant 23 September 1804, sabre wound to his right arm at Schaffenburg November 1805, captain 16 February 1807, major in the 13th Cuirassiers 16 October 1811, relieved of his command 19 February 1814, dismissed with the corps July 1814, one month's leave with pay 5 November 1814.

He was in the suite of the Angoulême Cuirassiers n°4 16 November 1814, major in the suite of the 7th Cuirassiers 18 November 1814, one month's leave on half-pay 20 December 1814, rejoined 30 January 1815, on half-pay again 1 November 1815. LH CH 18 December 1803, O 14 March 1806.

DESMOULINS (Etienne, 1773-?): born in Blanzy (Ardennes) on 14 July 1773. In the 19th Cavalry 30 August 1798, dismissed with the corps 31 December 1802 and incorporated into the 11th Cavalry 5 February 1803 which became the 11th Cuirassiers 24 September 1803, brigadier 1 December 1806, maréchal des logis 8 October 1807.

He became sub-lieutenant 6 November 1811, several lance wounds to his head and taken prisoner at Winkovo 18 October 1812, returned 14 November 1813, non-active on half-pay 1 December 1814.

DESORIERES see **CHAUVIN DESORIERES**

DESPONT (Louis Antoine, 1750-1819): born in Nouvion (Aisne) on 12 December 1750. In the Royal-Cravates 1 December 1767, maréchal des logis 25 December 1775, maréchal des logis-chef 7 September 1785, in the same regiment when it became the 10th Cavalry 1 January 1791, sub-lieutenant 10 September 1791, lieutenant 26 October 1792, captain 21 March 1794.

He was wounded having killed the CO of the enemy cavalry at Gosselles near Charleroi 18 June 1794, squadron commander 22 April 1797, major of the 11th Cuirassiers 29 October 1803, refused and allowed to keep his post as squadron commander in the 10th Cuirassiers 15 December 1803, retired 5 October 1806, left 21 October 1806, pensioned 20 November 1806. LH CH 14 June 1804.

DESPORTES (Michel, 1783-1809): born in Paris (Seine) on 19 May 1783. In the 3rd Hussars 31 August 1803, in the 2nd Cuirassiers 20 September 1803.

He became brigadier 23 September 1804, maréchal des logis 20 November 1806, sub-lieutenant 14 May 1809, wounded at Essling 22 May 1809 and killed at Wagram 6 July 1809.

DESRUES (Guillaume Thomas, 1774-?): born in Gommencourt (Pas-de-Calais) on 3 May 1774. In the 6th Chasseurs à Cheval 22 April 1794, gendarme in the 15th Legion 23 September 1800, brigadier with the provosts of the Army of Spain 1 December 1806, brigadier in the 7th Squadron of

the Gendarmerie d'Espagne 1 December 1809, brigadier-chef in the 1st Légion of the Gendarmerie à Cheval d'Espagne 21 December 1810.

He became, maréchal des logis-chef 1 June 1812, lieutenant in the 4th Cuirassiers 28 February 1813, incorporated with his squadron into the 1st Provisional Heavy Cavalry in Hamburg 11 September 1813, returned with the garrison 27 May 1814, non-active on half-pay 6 August 1814.

DESSAIGNES (Jean Antoine, 1771-?): born in Puy (Haute-Loire) on 16 March 1771. In the Colonel-Général-Cavalerie 17 November 1787 which became the 1st Cavalry 1 January 1791, two sabre wounds to his eye and left shoulder at Neerwinden 18 March 1793, brigadier 1 June 1793, fourrier 23 June 1798.

He became maréchal des logis 19 January 1799, maréchal des logis-chef 23 March 1799, adjutant-NCO 11 April 1800, in the same regiment when it became the 1st Cuirassiers 10 October 1801, sub-lieutenant 5 March 1803, shot and wounded in the right hip at Austerlitz 2 December 1805, lieutenant by seniority 6 January 1806, lieutenant adjutant-major 24 November 1806, captain 25 May 1807, squadron commander 5 November 1811, wounded by a Biscayan shot in the left hip at the Moskova 7 September 1812.

He commanded one of the two regiments of dismounted cavalry (3 000 men) during the retreat October 1812, kept in the corps which had become the King's Cuirassiers 1 July 1814 and which became the 1st Cuirassiers again March 1815, in the Seine Dragoons N°10 13 December 1815. Holder of a Sabre of Honour 15 September 1802, commissioned 5 March 1803, LH CH by rights 24 September 1803, O 29 July 1814.

DESTEZ (Joseph, 1789-?): born in Avesnes (Meuse) in 1789. In the Gendarmes d'Ordonnance 1 December 1806.

He was dismissed with the corps 23 October 1807 and incorporated into the Grenadiers à Cheval of the Guard 24 November 1807, sub-lieutenant in the 1st Cuirassiers 3 June 1809, discharged without pay 29 March 1811, left 27 April 1811.

DESTOMBES (Joseph, 1791-?): born in Lille (Nord) on 6 April 1791. Volunteer in the war squadrons of the 13th Cuirassiers 1 September 1810, brigadier 8 December 1810, fourrier 1 January 1811, maréchal des logis-chef 1 January 1812.

He became sub-lieutenant 27 August 1813, dismissed with the corps and incorporated into the 9th Cuirassiers 9 August 1814, shot in the right leg breaking his tibia, his horse killed under him at Waterloo 18 June 1815, non-active at the disposal of the Minister of War when the corps was disbanded 26 November 1815.

DESTOMBES (Louis Joseph, 1778-?): born in Roubaix (Nord) on 28 November 1778. Volunteer in the 4th Dragoons 20 June 1800, fourrier 28 August 1800, maréchal des logis 11 April 1801.

He became sub-lieutenant 5 January 1802, lieu-

OULLEMBOURG (Stanislas Marie Joseph Ignace Laurent, Baron, 1766-1833): son of a baron who was a Hussar colonel, born in Landau (Bas-Rhin) on 10 August 1766. In the Chamborant Hussars 21 February 1779, sub-lieutenant in the Nassau-Sarrebruck-Cavalerie 8 July 1779, second-lieutenant 8 April 1783, sub-lieutenant in the Gévaudan Chasseurs losing his rank in order to remain active 30 January 1785, in the same regiment when it became the Normandie Chasseurs à Cheval 17 March 1788, then the 11th Chasseurs à Cheval 1 January 1791, lieutenant 25 January 1792, captain 25 May 1792, shot in the right leg at Jemmapes 6 November 1792.

Acting squadron commander 23 September 1795, confirmed 14 March 1800, major of the 10th Hussars 29 October 1803, adjutant-major first aide de camp to Bessières 12 September 1805, colonel of the 1st Dragoons 19 June 1806, wounded at Jena 14 October 1806, brigadier-general 4 April 1807, commanded the 2nd Brigade (4th and 14th Dragoons) of the 1st Dragoon Division 14 May 1807, in Spain 7 September 1808, commanded the cavalry depot at Versailles 9 November 1809, commanded the Seine-et-Oise Department 3 July 1810 then a cuirassier brigade Doumerc's division in Germany 16 September 1811 then the 3rd Brigade same division in the Elbe Observation Corps 28 December 1811, in Russia 1812, commanded the depots of the 1st Cavalry Corps in Leipzig February 1813, allowed to return to France 3 March 1813, commanded the Seine-et-Oise 5 May 1813, in the 10th Cavalry Division of the Army of the Alps 23 May 1815, retired 1 August 1815. LH CH 25 March 1804, O 18 February, C 23 august 1814, Baron of the Empire l.p. 26 October 1808.

Altenhowen, 1 March 1793: Captain Stanislas Doullembourg and his squadron were surrounded by enemy cavalry. Launching a charge he managed to break through taking on the way two cannon and freeing a battalion which had already laid down its arms. Putting himself at the head of this motley group he succeeded in rejoining the main part of the French troops.

tenant 6 March 1807, aide de camp to General Wathiez 21 May 1807, captain in the 13th Cuirassiers 17 April 1809, acting squadron commander in the suite of the 9th Cuirassiers 9 August 1814, non-active 4 February 1815, returned as squadron commander in the 9th Cuirassiers 10 April 1815, put back on the non-active list 3 August 1815. LH CH 18 July 1809.

DESTOUCHES see **BOUVIER DESTOUCHES**

DESVERGNES see **LAJARTHE DESVERGNES**

DEVANSSAY (Charles, 1783-1809): brother of below, born in Coudreau (Sarthe) on 14 October 1783. Volunteered for the colonies, set off for San Domingo, incorporated into the 5th of the Line 17 May 1802, corporal 2 June 1802, sergeant 22 July 1802.

He became sub-lieutenant 18 January 1803, returned to France carrying despatches 24 July 1803, sub-lieutenant in the 24th Dragoons 30 June 1804, lieutenant in the 4th Cuirassiers 12 April 1808, killed at Essling 21 May 1809.

DEVANSSAY (Louis Armand, 1787-?): brother of the above, born in le Mans (Sarthe) 1787. Velite grenadier 27 June 1804, fourrier in the 65th Infantry 4 April 1805.

He became sergeant 2 June 1806, sub-lieutenant 1 December 1806, lieutenant 25 February 1809, aide de camp to General Vaufreland 12 September 1809, in the 2nd Cuirassiers 5 March 1810, retired 23 December 1813.

DEVILLE (Antoine Raymond, 1777 -after 1845): born in Soissons (Aisne) on 21 April 1777. In the Chasseurs à Cheval of the National Legion of the Pyrenees 7 November 1792, requisitioned to be employed with the national printers 29 December 1793, in the 7th Hussars 12 September 1795.

He became brigadier 13 September 1800, simple chasseur in the Chasseurs à Cheval of the Guard 31 July 1800, brigadier 3 June 1802, brigadier-fourrier 15 October 1802, maréchal des logis 17 October 1802, maréchal des logis-chef 18 December 1805, second-lieutenant 28 October 1808.

He was first- lieutenant under-adjutant-major 6 December 1811, captain (Old Guard) 27 February 1813, left the corps without leave 11 April 1814, squadron commander in the suite of the 11th Cuirassiers 23 June 1814, confirmed 2 June 1815, wounded by a bayonet at les Quatre-Bras 16 June 1815, wounded at Waterloo 18 June 1815, dismissed and non-active 18 December 1815. LH CH 14 June 1804, O 27 September 1814.

DEVILLERS see **BERTHE DEVILLERS**

DEVINZELLES
see **CHESNARD de DEVINZELLES**

DEVISE (André, 1772-?): born in Lantermange (Belgium) in 1772. Trooper in the 1st Batavian Regiment 25 October 1796, shot and wounded in his left leg in Holland 1799, dragoon in the Cape of Good Hope Squadron 22 May 1802, in the Royal Dutch Guard 1 August 1806, brigadier 24 June 1808.

He became maréchal des logis 3 April 1810, incorporated into the Imperial Guard 1 October 1810, lieutenant in the 1st Cuirassiers 8 February 1813, joined them 29 March 1813, dismissed as a foreign national 6 July 1814.

DEVOCEY (François Paul Etienne, 1784-1813): born in San Domingo on 7 February 1784. Velite in the Grenadiers à Cheval of the Guard 15 February 1806, sub-lieutenant in the suite of the 1st Cuirassiers 13 July 1807, lieutenant 15 October 1809, prisoner of war in Russia 24 December 1812, died of fever in Danzig Hospital 13 February 1813. LH CH 16 June 1809.

DEWILDERMOUTH (Frédéric Auguste Ernst Henry, 1791-?): born in Obenheim (Bas-Rhin) on 20 March 1791. Sub-lieutenant in the grenadiers in the infantry regiment of the King of Wurtemberg 15 March 1809, aide de camp to General Scherb 8 May 1812, lieutenant 8 August 1812, shot and wounded in his left foot during the retreat from Russia.

He returned to the Wurtemberg regiment 21 February 1813, resigned to return to France 9 November 1813, lieutenant in the 11th French Hussars 5 February 1814, non-active on half-pay 1 September 1814, lieutenant in the 10th Cuirassiers 28 April 1815, as he did not rejoin the corps, put on the non-active list 1 September 1815. LH CH April 1815.

DEY (Antoine Joachim, 1761-?): born in Sedan (Ardennes) on 29 November 1761. In the Deux-Ponts-Dragons 17 April 1780, bought leave 17 April 1780, trooper in the Artois Regiment 13 November 1785, left 30 September 1790.

He was volunteer in the 1st Ardennes Battalion 7 October 1792, maréchal des logis 1 March 1793, in the same regiment when it became the 23rd Chasseurs à Cheval 10 September 1793, sub-lieutenant 25 September 1793, two sabre wounds to his left arm and prisoner at Altenkirchen 18 September 1796, exchanged 28 June 1797, lieutenant 13 September 1800, discharged 23 September 1805.

He became, lieutenant in post in the 10th Cuirassiers 30 November 1806, incorporated in the 2nd Provisional Heavy Cavalry in Spain 1808, prisoner with the capitulation at Baylen 22 July 1808, returned 23 January 1812, retired 1 September 1813.

DEZEREINES (Godefroy Charles, 1789-1815): born in Cateau-Cambrésis (Nord) on 31 March 1789. Two years' service in the infantry, in the Chasseurs à Cheval of the Guard 25 September 1807.

He was wounded at Wagram 6 July 1809, maréchal des logis in the 13th Cuirassiers 9 November 1810, sub-lieutenant 6 November 1813, incorporated into the 4th Cuirassiers 9 August 1814, killed at Waterloo 18 June 1815.

DIBON (Jean Baptiste William, 1793 -after 1857): born in Louviers (Eure) on 8 April 1793. in the school in Saint-Germain 11 November 1812, left 27 December 1813, sub-lieutenant in the Chasseurs à Cheval of the Guard 29

December 1813, instated (Young Guard) 19 February 1814, in the King's Cuirassiers 10 July 1814.

He was in the same regiment when it became the 1st Cuirassiers again in March 1815, captain by mistake 25 March 1815 rectified to lieutenant 30 March 1815, in the 5th Cuirassiers 19 May 1815 then in the 2nd Chasseurs à Cheval of the Guard 21 May 1815 and once again in the 5th Cuirassiers 23 May 1815, instated 1 June 1815, aide de camp to General Exelmans 27 June 1815. LH CH 5 July 1815.

DIEFFENBRUCKER (Jean Simon, 1769-1841): born in Strasbourg (Bas-Rhin) on 3 February 1769. In the Artois-Cavalerie 22 November 1786 which

Senior officer.
(Private collection.
RR)

became the 9th Cavalry 1 January 1791, brigadier 10 February 1795, shot and wounded twice in the head and left thigh.

He became maréchal des logis 23 October 1802, in the same regiment when it became the 9th Cuirassiers 24 September 1803, maréchal des logis-chef 21 January 1805, sub-lieutenant 14 May 1809, lieutenant 11 March 1812, captain 20 March 1813, retired 4 January 1815. LH CH 14 June 1804.

DIEN (Jean André, 1788-?): born in Richelieu (Indre-et-Loire) on 26 June 1788. In the 5th Cuirassiers 24 June 1807, brigadier 10 August 1807.

He became maréchal des logis 10 August 1808,

(RR)

in the 2nd Provisional Heavy Cavalry in Spain December 1807, prisoner with the regiment with the capitulation at Baylen 22 July 1808, escaped from the Spanish hulks, incorporated into the 1st Provisional Heavy Cavalry which became the 13th Cuirassiers 21 October 1808, sub-lieutenant in the 8th Cuirassiers 10 April 1813, incorporated with his squadron into the 2nd Provisional Cuirassiers in Hamburg 11 September 1813.

He was wounded at Willemburg near Hamburg 9 February 1814, acting lieutenant adjutant-major 20 April 1814, left for France with the garrison 30 May 1814, returned July 1814 and put on the non-active list as sub-lieutenant 25 August 1814, confirmed lieutenant adjutant-major, non-active 4 February 1815.

DIETRICH (Evrard Louis Philippe Chrétien, 1787-1812): born in Strasbourg (Bas-Rhin) on 2 March 1787. In the Bas-Rhin National Guard 1 October 1805, brigadier in the Gendarmes d'Ordonnance 31 October 1806, maréchal des logis 17 June 1807, sub-lieutenant in the Line 16 July 1807.

He was in the suite of the 1st Cuirassiers 10 September 1807, wounded by a shell burst to his right thigh at Ebersdorff near Essling 22 May 1809, lieutenant 3 June 1809, aide de camp to General Berckheim 19 September 1809, instated 1 November 1809, captain in the 2nd Carabiniers 29 October 1811, wounded at the Moskova 7 September 1812, died in Russia 6 December 1812. LH CH 16 June 1809.

DIGEON (Honoré, 1773-1815): born in Rouppy (Aisne) on 6 December 1773. In the 10th Cavalry 28 July 1792, brigadier 20 January 1799, maréchal des logis 30 April 1801, maréchal des logis-chef 6 January 1803, in the same regiment when it became the 10th Cuirassiers 24 September 1803, adjutant 21 January 1805.

He became sub-lieutenant 26 November 1806, lieutenant in the 5th Cuirassiers 27 March 1809, adjutant-major in the 10th Cuirassiers 16 May 1809, rank of captain 16 November 1810, joined a company 6 November 1811, squadron commander 19 February 1814, wounded and taken prisoner at Waterloo 18 June 1815.

He died of his wounds in Brussels Hospital 29 September 1815. LH CH 5 November 1804, O 28 September 1813.

DIJOLS (François Etienne Marie, 1785-?): born in Rodez (Aveyron) on 7 November 1785. Velite in the Chasseurs à Pied of the Guard 21 April 1804.

He became brigadier in the 25th Dragoons 11 December 1805, maréchal des logis 14 October 1806, shot and wounded in Poland 24 December 1806, sub-lieutenant in the 12th Cuirassiers 29 January 1808, lieutenant 9 August 1809, adjutant-major 15 March 1812, lance wound to his chin in Russia 24 November 1812, captain 8 July 1813, shot and wounded in the head at Leipzig 18 October 1813, on leave 21 January 1814, in the King's Cuirassiers 1 May 1814.

He was in the suite with the 1 July 1814

D UBOIS (Jacques Charles, Baron, 1762-1847): brother of Dubois-Thainville, born in Reux (Calvados) on 27 November 1762. In the Colonel-Général-Dragons 3 March 1781, brigadier 17 March 1784, dismissed by seniority 2 March 1789, sub-lieutenant in the 16th Dragoons 25 January 1792, sent to San Domingo 12 June 1792, lieutenant 17 December 1792, captain 12 June 1793, returned end 1794.

He was confirmed 30 December 1794, wounded September 1796, squadron commander in the 3rd Dragoons 3 October 1803, attached to the 2nd Regiment of the 1st Brigade of the Dragons à Pied Division 26 August 1805, major of the 5th Dragoons 24 September 1806, colonel of the 7th Cuirassiers 25 June 1807, instated the same day, commanded the 2nd Brigade of the 3rd Cuirassiers Division at Essling 22 May 1809 as all the generals had been killed or wounded the previous day.

He became brigadier-general 7 February 1813, commanded the general cavalry depot in Brunswick 1 April 1813, non-active 1 September 1814, commanded a brigade (1st and 4th Cuirassiers) of the 3rd Cavalry Reserve Division 7 April 1815 which became the 1st Brigade of the 13th Cavalry Division of the 4th Cavalry Reserve Corps, sabre wound while supporting the retreat at Waterloo 18 June 1815, retired 6 October 1815. LH CH 14 June 1804, O 8 October 1811, Baron of the Empire d.17 March 1808 and l.p. 2 August 1808.

Wagram, 6 July 1809: Colonel Jacques Dubois of the 7th Cuirassiers took the first platoon from his regiment and charged an Austrian square. He was shot and wounded in the right hip during the skirmish.

On 28 November 1812 on the right bank of the Berezina he led the regiment's famous charge thus ensuring the security of the bridges and during which out of the 22 officers present two were killed and fourteen wounded.

reorganisation, remained at the disposal of the Minister of War in Paris 20 January 1815, squadron commander in the Chevau-Légers of the King's Household 27 June 1815, in the 1st Cuirassiers of the Royal Guard 10 October 1815. LH CH 11 October 1812.

DIQUELON (?-1809): maréchal des logis in the 5th Cuirassiers, sub-lieutenant 16 May 1809, wounded at Essling 22 May 1809, died of his wounds in Vienna Hospital 12 June 1809.

DOMBAL (Jean Baptiste, 1775-1809): born in Dugny (Meuse) in 1775. In the 10th Cavalry 6 May 1793, brigadier 20 June 1800, maréchal des logis 11 April 1802, in the same regiment when it became the

G. Rava 07

Junior officers

Officer from the 7th Regiment wearing full dress and mounted, wearing an overcoat according to the 1812 regulations.

Officer wearing social dress towards 1813-1814 according to L. Rousselot.

Officer from the 7th Regiment mounted and wearing full dress towards 1807, after L. Rousselot.

Officer from the 11th Regiment at Waterloo, from a plate by P. Courcelle.

Officers from the 14th former Dutch Regiment in 1810 after a drawing by H. Boisselier.

Officer from the 14th Regiment in 1811 after Rigo, wearing social dress.

10th Cuirassiers 24 September 1803, sub-lieutenant 16 May 1809, killed at Essling 22 May 1809.

DONOP (Claude Frédéric, 1796-?): born in Nancy (Meurthe) on 23 February 1796. Sub-lieutenant in the 3rd Cuirassiers 18 June 1815, instated 30 June 1815, left 1 September 1815.

DONOP (Frédéric Guillaume de, 1773-1815): born in Cassel (Hesse-Cassel) on 3 June 1773. In the Esterhazy Hussars 17 March 1789, brigadier 21 November 1789, maréchal des logis 16 June 1790.

He was in the same regiment when it became the 3rd Hussars 1 January 1791, replacement sub-lieutenant 5 June 1791, in post 10 March 1792, lieutenant 10 February 1793, relieved of his functions for non-public-spiritedness 15 November 1793, clerk in the wood department for the Nancy communities, clerk of the review council for the 17th Military Division, acting aide de camp to General Tharreau 20 February 1801.

A cting deputy on the staff of the Tuscany Division 29 August 1801, adjutant of the military area at Livorno 21 May 1802, in the 2nd Regiment pf the Paris Guard 28 March 1805, deputy on the staff of the cavalry reserve of the Grande Armée 22 September 1805, captain in the 9th Hussars 25 August 1806, deputy captain on Murat's staff 18 March 1807, squadron commander aide de camp to Lahoussaye 5 July 1807, adjutant-commandant chief of staff of the 4th Dragoon Division 21 August 1810, interim chief of staff of the army of the Centre in Spain from 15 to 30 November 1812.

He became brigadier-general in the 13th Division of the 4th Corps of the Grande Armée 25 December 1813, unable to join them, at the Versailles cavalry depot 12 January 1814, commanded the Chasseurs à Cheval in Caen April 1814, non-active 1 July 1814, in the 2nd Reserve Cavalry Division 7 April 1815, commanded the 2nd Brigade (2nd and 3rd Cuirassiers) of the 12th Division of the 3rd Cavalry Corps of the Army of the North 3 June 1815, disappeared after being seriously wounded and thrown off his horse at Waterloo 18 June 1815. LH O 8 February 1813.

DONZE (François Joseph Gabriel, 1788 -after 1817): born in Salins (Jura) on 7 April 1788. Pupil at the Ecole Polytechnique 12 October 1806.

He became sub-lieutenant 12 October 1806, in the suite of the 4th Cuirassiers 2 January 1807, in service 8 January 1807, assigned to the riding school in Versailles, lieutenant 2 March 1809, ordered to take a detachment to be incorporated into the 3rd Provisional Heavy Cavalry and left for Spain 26 February 1810, returned July 1810, cannonball wound at the Drissa 1 August 1812. He was relieved of his command upon the advice of the administrative council for misconduct and moral weakness in the face of the enemy 19 September 1813.

DOR (Léonard Pierre, 1767-?): born in Paris (Seine) on 13 January 1767. In the Royal-Picardie-Cavalerie 16 May 1786, left 29 September 1788, trooper in the Royal-Etranger 7 September 1789 which became the

7th Cavalry 1 January 1791, brigadier-fourrier 10 May 1792, maréchal des logis 7 May 1793, maréchal des logis-chef 10 May 1794, sub-lieutenant 20 June 1794, placed as maréchal des logis-chef 6 August 1795.

He was elected sub-lieutenant 22 January 1799, commissioned 11 March 1799, in the same regiment when it became the 7th Cuirassiers 23 December 1802, lieutenant by governmental choice 2 March 1805, captain in the 2nd cuirassiers 27 March 1809, left to join them 1 May 1809, retired 15 May 1810, left 16 June 1810.

DORNEROND (Claude, 1775-?): born in Irigny (Rhône) on 18 March 1775. In the 8th Dragoons 10 July 1794, sabre wound to his head 29 March 1799, sabre wound to his head at Marengo 14 June 1800, brigadier 22 September 1800, in the Grenadiers à Cheval of the Guard 24 April 1803, brigadier 22 June 1805,.

He became maréchal des logis 14 September 1806, in the Grenadiers of the King's Household 7 August 1814, sous-brigadier with rank of sub-lieutenant 12 November 1814, returned in subsistence with the Grenadiers à Cheval of the Guard 1 April 1815, confirmed sub-lieutenant in the cavalry 22 April 1815, in the 2nd Cuirassiers 5 May 1815, dismissed and left the regiment 20 October 1815. Holder of a Rifle of Honour 2 January 1800, LH CH by rights 24 September 1803.

DORNES (Joseph Philippe Marie, baron, 1760-1812): born in Saint-Georges-de-Camboulas (Aveyron) on 28 January 1760. In the Royal-Navarre-Cavalerie 5 August 1778, brigadier 15 September 1784, adjutant-NCO 5 October 1784, in the same regiment when it became the 22nd Cavalry 1 January 1791, sub-lieutenant 25 January 1792, lieutenant 17 June 1792, captain 26 January 1793, in the same regiment when it became the 21st Cavalry 4 June 1793, squadron commander 1 July 1793, in the 23rd Cavalry 23 July 1801, joined them 20 August 1801.

He was dismissed with the corps 23 December 1802 and discharged 3 January 1803, placed in the 1st Cuirassiers 5 February 1803, major 23 October 1803, colonel of the 12th Cuirassiers 27 December 1805, left to join them 16 February 1806, brigadier-general 3 August 1809, commanded the Forêts Department 26 September 1806.`

He commanded the 3rd Brigade of the 2nd Cuirassier Division 25 December 1811 then the 2nd Brigade of the same division May 1812, remained prisoner of the enemy because he was ill then died at Wilna of exhaustion 29 November 1812.

LH CH 25 March 1804, O 14 May 1807, Baron d. 19 March 1808 and l.p. 10 September 1809.

DOUBLET (Jean Baptiste, 1787 -) born in Domart (Somme) on 15 April 1787. In the 12th Cuirassiers 10 March 1807, brigadier 1 October

1808, maréchal des logis 16 August 1809, sublieutenant 14 May 1813, sabre wound to his head 28 May 1813, shot in the foot at Dresden 27 August 1813, shot in the lower abdomen at Sézanne 25 March 1814, on half-pay 13 July 1814.

DOUMENGE (François, 1774-1845): born in Allemans (Dordogne) on 9 October 1774. In the Jemmapes Hussars 12 December 1792 which became the 10th Hussars 4 June 1793, two sabre wounds under his left eye and on the wrist at Courtrai 26 April 1794, in the Chasseurs à Cheval of the Guard 12 February 1800, brigadier 25 September 1801.

He was maréchal des logis 15 October 1802, maréchal des logis-chef 29 May 1803, adjutant sub-lieutenant 24 September 1803, second-lieutenant 23 September 1804, first-lieutenant underadjutant-major 18 December 1805, captain 6 December 1811, major in the Line 27 February 1813,.

He became major of the 1st Cuirassiers 2 July 1813, instated 13 July 1813, confirmed in the suite 6 November 1814 in the same regiment when it became the King's Cuirassiers 1 July 1814 then the 1st Cuirassiers again April 1815.

He was in service 4 May 1815, instated 11 May 1815, dismissed and put up for retirement 24 December 1815. LH CH 14 June 1804, O 28 March 1815.

DOUMERC (Jean Pierre, comte, 1767-1847): born in Montauban (Tarn-et-Garonne) on 7 October 1767. In the Dauphin-Dragons 23 December 1783, dismissed 3 January 1788, left with the ambassadors of Typpo-Sahib September 1788 and returned to Paris 27 July 1790, in the Paris National Guard, commissioned as sublieutenant in the 4th Chasseurs à Cheval 15 September 1791, admitted 15 December 1791, lieutenant 17 September 1792.

He became aide de camp to Pichegru 4 December 1793, rank of squadron commander 25 September 1794, in the 11th Cavalry 8 November 1794, in the 4th Chasseurs à Cheval 7 December 1795, supernumerary 5 March 1796, in service 5 March 1797, brigade commander of 9th Cavalry replacing Nansouty 3 September 1799, in the same regiment when it became the 9th Cuirassiers 24 September 1803, brigadier-general in the 2nd Dragoon division of the Cavalry Reserve of the Grande Armée 31 December 1806, commanding the 2nd Cuirassier Brigade Nansouty's division 1 April 1807.

He was inspector of the cavalry depots of the 5th military Division 31 March 1810, acting CO of the 1st Heavy Cavalry Division in the Army of Germany 4 September 1810, major-general commanding the 3rd Cuirassier Division 30 November 1811, in the 3rd Cavalry Corps 10 January 1812 then detached to the 2nd May 1812, keeping command of the 3rd Division in the 1st Cavalry Corps in Germany 15

(RR)

February 1813, same division in Saxony 15 August 1813, commanded the division made up of 1st Cavalry Corps 3 January 1814, inspector general of cavalry in the 9th and 10th Military Divisions May 1814 then of the 3rd Military Division 30 December 1814.

He became inspector general in the 1st Military Division chairing the commission examining the appointments made under the First Restoration 20 April 1815, ordered to gather together a cavalry corps made up of different detachments in Saint-Denis 23 June 1815, non-active 1 September 1815. LH CH 11 December 1803, O 14 June 1804, C 25 December 1805, GO 17 January 1815, Baron of the Empire l.p. 20 August 1808, count d. 3 September 1813.

DOUMET de SIBLAS
see **BEYLIE de DOUMET de SIBLAS**

DOURTRE (Jean Baptiste, 1770-?): born in Landres (Ardennes) on 22 May 1770. In the Reine-Cavalerie 9 June 1788 which became the 4th cavalry 1 January 1791, being on ordnance duty he carried General Moreau's orders several time through the fire of the enemy lines, alone rallied a platoon and brought it back to the fight at Rodalf 1793, alone disengaged his captain from enemy hands at Kreutznach 31 December 1793, brigadier 6 April 1794, maréchal des logis 21 May 1795, adjutant-NCO 20 February 1799, in the same regiment when it became the 4th Cuirassiers 12 October 1802.

He was elected sub-lieutenant 8 September 1803, lieutenant 8 January 1807, lieutenant adjutant-major 19 July 1808, captain in service 4 March 1812, in the Gendarmerie 19 November 1812, in the 3rd Legion of the Gendarmerie d'Espagne 1 June 1813, commanded the 1st Gendarmerie Battalion attached to the Old Guard 11 January 1814.

He was in the Gendarmerie depot in Vincennes 26 April 1814, commanded the Indre Company 16 December 1814, in that of the Basses-Pyrénées then of the Indre-et-Loire 1815. Holder of a Sabre of Honour 24 January 1803, LH CH by rights 24 September 1803.

DOUZE see **DONZE.**

DREUX NANCRE (Hyacinthe Louis Ernest de, 1787-1848): the son of a cavalry captain, born in Paris (Seine) on 30 March 1787. Volunteer in the 24th Light 13 December 1803, corporal 23 January 1804.

He became sergeant 21 February 1804, two sabre wounds at Austerlitz 2 December 1805, sub-lieutenant 31 December 1805, disarmed and mastered a Russian infantryman who had been forgotten and who was on duty at the Eylau cemetery when Napoleon approached 8 February 1807, lieutenant 27 May 1807, right thigh shattered by a cannonball which left him with a limp at Friedland 14 June 1807, inapt for the infantry and retired because of his wounds 7 February 1808, lieutenant in the 12th Cuirassiers 9 June 1808, deputy on the staff of General Vandamme in the 8th Corps 1809, captured a battery at the head of an infantry brigade at Urfar, aide de camp to General Gudin 21 July 1809, captain 5

August 1809, unemployed at the death of Gudin 21 August 1812, lost his right toe from frostbite during the retreat December 1812.

He was squadron commander in the 24th Chasseurs à Cheval 14 February 1813, major 5 October 1813, deputy on the staff of the Minister of War 12 October 1814, accompanied the King to the frontier 20 March 1815, on the staff of the 18th Military Division April 1815, returned to the staff of the Minister of War 10 July 1815. LH CH 1 October 1807, O 28 September 1813.

DROGUE (Jean Nicolas, 1761-1827): born in Avignon (Vaucluse) on 16 December 1791. In the Cuirassiers du Roy 28 may 1781, brigadier 7 February 1786, maréchal des logis 25 November 1786, in the same regiment when it became the 8th Cavalry 1 January 1791, maréchal des logis-chef 14 December 1792, sub-lieutenant 28 August 1793.

He became lieutenant 22 October 1798, in the same regiment when it became the 8th Cuirassiers 10 October 1801, captain 29 January 1802, retired because of rheumatic pains 12 September 1809. LH CH 28 June 1808.

DRON (Marius Félix, 1794-?): born in 1794. In the 1st Cuirassiers, brigadier-fourrier 29 May 1813, maréchal des logis, sub-lieutenant 25 March 1815, struck off the rolls and his appointment cancelled 1 September 1815.

DRONE (François Chrisostôme, 1778-1813): born in Nancy (Meurthe) on 27 January 1778. In the 10th Cavalry 22 December 1795.

He became brigadier 6 May 1802, in the same regiment when it became the 10th Cuirassiers 24 September 1803, maréchal des logis 23 June 1806, sub-lieutenant 16 May 1809, died at the Berlin military hospital 29 January 1813.

DROZ (Jean Pierre, 1777-?): born in Paris (Seine) on 4 May 1777. In the 9th Hussars 20 February 1801, brigadier 1 February 1807, maréchal des logis 15 august 1809, gendarme in the 3rd Escadron d'Espagne 25 June 1810, in the 1st Légion of the Gendarmerie à Cheval d'Espagne 16 December 1810, dismissed with the corps 28 February and placed as sub-lieutenant in the 2nd cuirassiers 1 March 1813.

He was shot in the right shoulder at Athies 9 March 1814, wounded at Waterloo 18 June 1815, prisoner

6 July 1815, returned from captivity in Holland after the regiment was disbanded 4 January 1816 and sent home. LH CH 29 September 1814.

DUBIEN (Pierre Marie, 1770-1813): born in Montmarie (Puy-de-Dôme) on 1 November 1770. In the Royal-Etranger-Cavalerie 1 April 1788 which became the 7th Cavalry 1 January 1791, brigadier-fourrier 1 May 1792, maréchal des logis 19 March 1793, adjutant-NCO 7 May 1793.

He saved two artillery pieces, bringing them back and giving them to the regiment they belonged to near Cambrai 24 April 1794, lieutenant 1 July 1799, on six months' leave 19 August 1801, in the same regiment when it became the 7th Cuirassiers 23 December 1802, retired 11 March 1807, left 12 April 1807.

He became lieutenant in the 11th Cuirassiers 29 April 1809, captain 21 March 1812, cannonball wound at Leipzig 16 October 1813 and died of his wounds 26 October 1813. LH CH 28 June 1805.

DUBOIS (Armand, 1784-?): born in Bayonne (Basse-Pyrénées) on 4 July 1784. Hussar in the 3rd Regiment 11 October 1797, sub-lieutenant aide de camp to General Lannes and placed in the suite of the Chasseurs à Cheval of the Consular Guard 28 July 1800.

He became lieutenant in the 2nd Cavalry 19 September 1801, joined them 12 November 1801, in the same regiment when it became the 2nd Cuirassiers 12 October 1802, elected captain 28 September 1805, resigned 30 July 1806, resignation accepted 22 August 1806.

DUBOIS (Charles Louis, 1772-1826): born in Paris (Seine) on 4 November 1772. Volunteer in the 1st Paris Battalion 20 July 1791.

He was in the Garde Constitutionnelle du Roi 5 January 1792, dismissed with the corps and promoted to sub-lieutenant in the 2nd Carabiniers 1 June 1792, two sabre wounds to his left arm at Duttweiler 14 September 1793, captured a cannon June 1794, wounded by several sabre blows to his head and taken prisoner at Mannheim 18 October 1795, lieutenant 4 March 1797, instated 6 April 1797, captain by seniority 29 January 1799, confirmed 6 February 1799, squadron commander in the 2nd Cuirassiers 27 April 1807, joined up 1 May 1807, wounded and his horse killed under him at the Moskova 7 September 1812, second-major 9 October 1812.

He commanded one of the two regiments of dismounted cavalry (4 000 men) during the retreat October 1812, major commanding the 3rd Provisional

Heavy Cavalry during the siege of Hamburg 3 July 1813, instated when the corps was formed 11 September 1813, left for France with the garrison May 1814, non-active on half-pay 25 October 1814, in the suite of the 8th Cuirassiers 1 December 1814, dismissed with the corps and put up for retirement 11 December 1815. LH CH 14 June 1804.

DUBOIS (Jean, 1791-?): born in Pont-l'Evêque (Calvados) on 30 July 1791. In the 7th Cuirassiers 27 January 1809, brigadier 30 April 1809.

He became maréchal des logis 22 May 1809, wounded by a shot to his wrist and his helmet pierced by a Biscayan shot at Wagram 6 July 1809, sub-lieutenant 9 August 1809, lieutenant 15 May 1813, wounded at Waterloo 18 June 1815, on six months' leave when the corps was disbanded 19 December 1815. LH CH 13 August 1809.

DUBOIS (Louis Félix, 1787-?): born in Privas (Ardèche) on 20 November 1787. Boarder in the Ecole Militaire in Fontainebleau 11 October 1806, sub-lieutenant in the suite of the 5th Cuirassiers 11 April 1807, in post 1 July 1807, lieutenant 15 May 1809.

He became adjutant-major 1812, wounded at the Moskova 7 September 1812, captain of a company 11 October 1812, wounded at Waterloo 18 June 1815, dismissed and put on the non-active list 23 December 1815. LH CH 16 June 1809.

DUBOIS (Nicolas Joseph Gabriel, 1789-?): born in Bruges (Lys) on 20 June 1789. NCO cadet in the Guard of the King of Holland 10 July 1807, in the Cuirassiers of the Guard of the King of Holland 10 July 1808, sub-lieutenant in the 2nd Dutch Cuirassiers 25 August 1809.

He was in the same regiment when it became the 14th French Cuirassiers 18 August 1810, lieutenant 9 February 1813, confirmed 22 December 1813, dismissed with the corps July 1814. LH CH 5 December 1813.

DUBOIS BERANGER (Eugène, 1784-?): born in Rennes (Ille-et-Vilaine) on 8 October 1784. Velite in the Grenadiers à Cheval of the Guard 20 February 1806.

He became sub-lieutenant in the 12th Cuirassiers 3 June 1809, lieutenant 11 September 1812, adjutant-major 18 May 1813, captain adjutant-major 26 January 1815, retroactively 18 November 1814, dismissed 22 November 1815. LH CH 4 December 1813.

DUBORD see **PREVOST du BORD.**

DUBOULOZ (Gaspard Philibert, 1788-1812): born in Thonon (Léman) on 2 November 1788. In the Gendarmes d'Ordonnance 2 November 1806, shot and wounded twice at Colberg 20 March 1807, in the Dragoons of the Imperial Guard 17 September 1807.

He became sub-lieutenant in the 8th Cuirassiers 3 June 1809, lieutenant 21 February 1812, instated 1 April 1812, killed by a cannonball at the Moskova 7 September 1812.

DUBREUIL (Louis Charles Heuvrard, 1781-?): born in Châlon (Marne) on 10 January 1781. In the Bourbon-Hussards in the service of Prussia 15 February 1793, cadet maréchal des logis 1 March 1798, returned to France, maréchal des logis in the 5th French Dragoons 15 January 1804.

He became adjutant sub-lieutenant in the 2nd Dutch Cuirassiers 15 April 1808 which became the 14th French Cuirassiers 18 August 1810, sub-lieutenant 5 December 1810, retired 7 February 1811.

DUBUSSE (Pierre Joseph, 1771-?): born in Illy (Nord) on 27 January 1771. In the 22nd Cavalry 19 February 1794, incorporated into the 12th Cavalry 25 January 1803.

He became brigadier 14 January 1799, maréchal des logis 31 May 1802, in the same regiment when it became the 12th Cuirassiers 24 September 1803, sub-lieutenant 14 May 1809, sabre wound to his cheek at Essling 22 May 1809, lieutenant 9 August 1812, shot and wounded twice at Dresden 27 August 1813, in the suite 14 July 1814, dismissed with the corps 10 December 1815. LH CH 1 October 1807.

DUCHAMBON (Camille, 1794-?): born in Ris (Puy-de-Dôme) on 9 October 1794. In the Ecole Spéciale Militaire de Cavalerie 30 August 1812.

He became sub-lieutenant 30 March 1814, in the suite of the 5th Cuirassiers 12 June 1814, wounded and taken prisoner at Waterloo 18 June 1815, returned 1815.

DUCHASTELER de MOULBAIX (Albert François, 1794-1836): born in Wurtzburg (Bavaria) on 16 December 1794. In the cavalry school in Saint-Germain 21 January 1810, page to the Emperor 15 February 1811, sub-lieutenant in the 19th Dragoons 12 December 1811.

He became lieutenant in the 6th Cuirassiers 10 February 1812, instated 15 May 1812, wounded by a shot in his left foot at Frankenthal 1 January 1814, aide de camp to General Darriule 12 February 1814, captain aide de camp to General Lemarois March 1814, resigned 7 May 1814, in the service of Holland in the Crooy Hussars 20 December 1814, captain 12 February 1815.

He was wounded at the Quatre-Bras 16 June 1815 and a cannonball which grazed his chest at Waterloo 18 June 1815. LH CH 4 December 1813.

DUCHATELET see **BORDES DUCHATELET.**

DUCHENNE (Jeant Gilbert, 1773-?): born in Flein (Ardennes) on 12 August 1773. In the 22nd Cavalry 16 September 1793, gendarme à cheval in the 16th Legion 31 December 1798, brigadier 16 July 1803, brigadier-chef in the 17th Squadron of the Gendarmerie d'Espagne 15 January 1810, maréchal des logis in the 1st Légion of the Gendarmerie à Cheval d'Espagne 16 December 1810.

He became maréchal des logis-chef 4 September 1811, dismissed with the corps 27 February 1813, lieutenant in the 3rd Cuirassiers the following day 28 February 1813, incorporated with his squadron into the 1st Provisional Heavy Cavalry in Hamburg 11 September 1813, returned with the garrison 27 May 1814.

He was lieutenant quartermaster in the suite 20 August 1814, resignation accepted 27 September 1814, left 7 October 1814. LH CH 1 March 1813.

DUCHESNE (Jean Baptiste, 1770 -between 1828 and 1845): born in Chatillon-sur-Barre (Ardennes) on 9 January. In the Reine-Cavalerie 20 April 1788.

He became brigadier-fourrier in the same regiment when it became the 4th Cavalry 1 January 1791, maréchal des logis 13 May 1792, adjutant-NCO and adjutant sub-lieutenant the same day 1 August 1793, lieutenant 20 February 1799, lieutenant adjutant-major 13 March 1802, in the same regiment when it became the 4th Cuirassiers 12 October 1802, rank of captain 9 September 1803.

He went over to a company 19 July 1808, retired 2 June 1809, pensioned off 23 November 1809. LH CH 28 June 1809.

DUCHEYLARD (Evrard Victor, 1788-?): born in Besançon (Doubs) on 15 June 1788. Boarder in the Ecole Militaire in Fontainebleau 3 January 1805, sub-lieutenant in the 12th Cuirassiers 14 December 1806, sabre wound at Eckmühl 22 April 1809, lieutenant 29 April 1809, captain 26 December 1811.

He was shot and wounded in the thigh at Görlitz 26 May 1813, aide de camp to General d'Aigremont end 1815. LH CH 10 October 1812.

DUCLAUX (Pierre Alexis, 1786-?): brother of the following, born in Duravel (Lot) on 20 September 1786. In the 12th Chasseurs à Cheval 5 February 1802, brigadier 23 September 1804, maréchal des logis 22 September 1805, in the Grenadiers à Cheval of the Guard 4 May 1808.

He became brigadier 1 October 1808, brigadier-fourrier 3 July 1809, sub-lieutenant in the 11th Cuirassiers 15 October 1809, wounded at the Moskova 7 September 1812, prisoner 31 December 1812, returned 4 November 1814, dismissed with the corps 16 December 1815.

DUCLAUX (Pierre Alexis, baron, 1775-1828): brother of the above, born in Duravel (Lot) on 2 December 1775. Requisitions officer in the 22nd Chasseurs à Cheval 3 April 1794.

He became maréchal des logis in Bonaparte's Guides 22 September 1796, sub-lieutenant 9 May 1797, in the guides of the Army of Egypt 1798, lieutenant 22 August 1798, lance wound to his left foot at Heliopolis 20 March 1800, captain 2 April 1801, in the Grenadiers à Cheval of the Consular Guard 2 October 1801, squadron commander 5 September 1805, colonel of the 11th Cuirassiers 1 June 1809, lost his nose affected by bone caries due to the severe cold he suffered in Russia 1812, convalescing 1813, brigadier-general 3 September 1813, left 6 October 1813, commanded the Forêts Department 6 December 1813, non-active 1 September 1814.

He commanded the Meuse Department 22 April 1815, non-active 10 August 1815. LH CH 25 March 1804, O 14 March 1806, Chevalier of the Empire l.p. 20 August 1808, Baron l.p. 21 November 1810.

DUCLOS (Jean Charles Henri, 1773-?): born in Bernot (Aisne) on 15 February 1773. In the 10th Cavalry 25 May 1793, brigadier-fourrier 20 January 1799, maréchal des logis-chef 11 December 1801, in the same regiment when it became the 10th Cuirassiers 24 September 1803, sub-lieutenant 25 May 1807.

He became lieutenant 16 May 1809, shot and wounded in the thigh and his horse killed under him at Essling 21 May 1809, captain 6 November 1811, lost

Aide de camp to General Nansouty.
(Composition by P. Courcelle, Private collection RR)

Duclos, cuirassier Colonel.
(Composition by P. Conrad for Le Cimier, RR)

his right leg blown off by a cannonball and amputated at the Moskova 7 September 1812, on retirement pay 4 February 1813. LH CH 5 November 1804

DUCOUDROY (Jean, 1785-?): born in Marmande (Lot-et-Garonne) on 24 June 1785. In the 11th Cuirassiers 4 October 1804, brigadier-fourrier 10 October 1804, maréchal des logis 1 December 1806, maréchal des logis-chef 25 May 1807, sub-lieutenant 16 May 1809, lieutenant 1 July 1811.

He was in the 2nd Carabiniers 31 July 1811, aide de camp to General Gault 5 September 1811, then to General Tarayre 14 December 1811, returned to the 2nd Carabiniers 30 January 1813, captain in the 10th Cuirassiers 10 April 1813, dismissed with the corps 25 December 1815. LH CH 1 October 1807.

DUCREY (Jean Pierre Aimé, 1788-?): born in Sallanches (Mont-Blanc) on 1 January 1788. In the 23rd of the Line 15 April 1807, grenadier 1 May 1807, grenadier fourrier 21 October 1807, gendarme à pied in the 14th Escadron d'Espagne 1 January 1810.

He became gendarme à cheval in the same unit 31 October 1810, in the 1st Légion of the Gendarmerie à Cheval d'Espagne "Burgos" 15 December 1810, brigadier 1 March 1812, dismissed with the corps 27 February 1813[1] and promoted to sub-lieutenant in the 2nd cuirassiers the following day 28 February 1813, incorporated with his squadron into the 1st Provisional Heavy Cavalry in Hamburg 11 September 1813.

He returned with the garrison 27 May 1814, went home 31 December 1814, non-active 24 February 1815.

DUCROCQ (François Joseph, 1765-1821): born in Metz-en-Couture (Pas-de-Calais) on 23 April 1765. In the Royal-Etranger-Cavalerie 24 February 1785, brigadier in the same regiment when it became the 7th Cavalry the same day 1 January 1791.

He became maréchal des logis 1 April 1792, maréchal des logis-chef 7 May 1793, sub-lieutenant 11 May 1794, with his platoon charged a detachment of English dragons killing the CO and capturing two can-

non, two howitzers and several carriages 18 May 1794, supernumerary 20 February 1796, in post 20 January 1799, instated 9 February 1799, in the same regiment when it became the 7th Cuirassiers 23 December 1802, elected lieutenant 24 October 1803, discharged for disciplinary reasons 30 January 1805, left 28 February 1805.

He took part in the 1809 Campaign in the cohort of the Meuse National Guard then returned to his original post, retired 6 June 1811. Sabre of Honour 24 May 1803, LH CH by rights 24 September 1803, O 15 June 1804.

DUCROS (Jean Baptiste, 1782-?): born in Seurey (Charente-Inférieure) on 10 December 1782. Velite in the Grenadiers à cheval of the Imperial Guard 12 March 1806, sub-lieutenant in the 4th Cuirassiers 3 June 1809.

He became lieutenant 14 May 1813, in the same regiment when it became the Angoulême Cuirassiers 6 August 1814, resignation accepted 26 January 1815; request to return to service refused 14 April 1815. LH CH 17 February 1814.

DUFOURG (Maurice Xavier, 1773-?): born in Chaussin (Jura) on 18 June 1773. Trooper in the Royal-Etranger 6 September 1789 which became the 7th Cavalry 1 January 1791.

He became brigadier 6 December 1791, maréchal des logis 7 May 1793, elected sub-lieutenant 11 May 1794, captured a senior English officer 26 May 1794, lieutenant by choice 19 June 1794, placed as sub-lieutenant 6 August 1795, supernumerary 20 February 1796, in post 20 January 1799, lieutenant 18 December 1801, in the same regiment when it became the 7th Cuirassiers 23 December 1802.

He was confirmed lieutenant 8 June 1803, adjutant-major in the 6th Cuirassiers 9 November 1805, rank of captain 8 May 1807, second-lieutenant in the Grenadiers à Cheval of the Imperial Guard 25 June 1807, first-lieutenant 25 June 1809, captain 20 August 1809, major in the suite of the 19th Dragoons 9 February 1813, non-active September 1814. LH CH 26 May 1808.

DUGUEN (Auguste, 1788 -after 1847): born in Saint-Malo (Ille-et-Vilaine) on 4 July 1788. Boarder in the Ecole Militaire in Fontainebleau 20 April 1807, sub-lieutenant in the 7th Cuirassiers 24 July 1809, left to join 5 August 1809, joined them 3 September 1809.

He was incorporated into a provisional regiment in Spain 28 February 1810, returned to the 7th Cuirassiers 9 January 1811, lieutenant 8 March 1812, instated 11 April 1812, adjutant-major 19 November 1812, lance and sabre wounds to his face and crotch with two horses killed under him at the Berezina 28 November 1812, sabre wound to his left hand and two lance wounds to his head and right arm at Goldberg 27 March 1813.

He became captain 14 March 1813, wounded and his horse killed under him at Leipzig 18 October 1813, six lance wounds and five sabre wounds and his horse killed under him and himself taken prisoner at Neustadt 1 January 1814, returned 12 May

1814, dismissed and placed at the disposal of the Minister of War 19 November 1815. LH CH 14 May 1813, O 4 December 1813.

DUJONC see MENOU DUJONC

DULONGVAL (Jean Baptiste François, 1783-?): born in Lisieux (Calvados) on 2 July 1783. In the 1st Cuirassiers 20 July 1803, fourrier 28 September 1806, maréchal des logis 16 November 1806, shot and wounded in the right foot at Eylau 8 February 1807, maréchal des logis-chef 1 March 1807. He became sub-lieutenant in the 13th Cuirassiers 15 October 1809, trench adjutant during the siege of Valencia, discharged with a bonus 15 July 1812. LH CH 1 October 1807.

DULUDE see LOIR DULUDE

DUMAIGNEAUX see LASALLE DUMAIGNEUAX

DUMANOIR see DUVAL DUMANOIR

DUMAS (Christophe, 1771-?): born in Busset (Allier) on 19 July 1771. In the 9th Cavalry 22 February 1791, brigadier 1 April 1793, fourrier 24 May 1797, maréchal des logis 4 May 1800, maréchal des logis-chef 5 May 1800.

He became sub-lieutenant by governmental choice 8 June 1803, in the same regiment when it became the 9th Cuirassiers 24 September 1803, retired 8 July 1807.

DUMAS (Jean, chevalier, 1772-1833): born in Pouillon (Landes) on 27 October 1772. Requisitions officer in the 18th Dragoons 10 March 1794, brigadier 1798, fourrier 18 October 1798, maréchal des logis 24 April 1800, adjutant 23 May 1800, shot and wounded in his left hand at Abukir 8 March 1801, sub-lieutenant 9 August 1801, shot and wounded at Austerlitz 2 December 1805, lieutenant 22 December 1805, adjutant-major 17 October 1806, captain 20 November 1806.

He became aide de camp to Lefebvre-Desnoëttes his former colonel 30 November 1806, took two cannon and 150 prisoners at Glatz 19 March 1807, in post with his rank in the Guard 15 November 1808, aide de camp to Durosnel 22 February 1809, squadron commander in the 23rd Chasseurs à Cheval 28 May 1809, shot and wounded in the heel at Wagram 6 July 1809, commanded a provisional regiment of Chasseurs à Cheval in the Hautes-Pyrénées 1811, major at the disposal of the Minister of War 29 October 1811, in service in the 5th Chevau-Légers 26 February 1813.

He was wounded at Culm 30 August 1813 and then again three more lance wounds and taken prisoner at Fraunstein 22 September 1813, returned 16 June 1814, in the suite of the 13th Dragoons 16 November 1814, colonel 10 April 1815, non-active 18 April 1815, recalled 18 June 1815, in the suite of the 10th Cuirassiers 23 July 1815, confirmed in the suite 25 August 1815, non-active as a major 25 December 1815. LH CH 14 June 1804, O 13 August 1809, Chevalier of the Empire d. 15 August 1809, and l.p.

22 October 1810.

DUMAS de la MARCHE (Louis Etienne Hipolythe, 1789-?): born in Lons-le-Saulnier (Jura) on 8 February 1789. In the Navy 6 January 1805, midshipman 7 June 1807, acting ensign 9 September 1808.

He was wounded by shrapnel in the foot at the Karlstaadt battery 8 September 1809, sub-lieutenant in the 15th Chasseurs à Cheval 18 September 1811, sabre wound at Villadrigo 23 October 1812 and shot and wounded in the shoulder at Mondragon 6 January 1813, lieutenant in the 10th Chasseurs 10 August 1813, lance wound to his left leg in Paris 30 March 1814, non-active on half-pay 1 September 1814, lieutenant in the 10th Cuirassiers 2 may 1815, non-active 1 September 1815.

DUMAUVOIR see LODIN DUMAUVOIR

DUMEGNOT see MARTIN DUMEGNOT

DUMONT (Jacques François, 1759-?): born in Blincourt (Somme) on 16 May 1759. Trooper in the Royal-Pologne 1 March 1778, brigadier 1 September 1765, in the same regiment when it became the 5th Cavalry 1 January 1791.

He was wounded in the left leg at Toulon November 1793, maréchal des logis 5 May 1795, adjutant-NCO 22 September 1796, sub-lieutenant 13 March 1800, lieutenant 11 February 1802, in the same regiment when it became the 5th Cuirassiers 23 December 1802, retired 6 June 1808.

DUMORTIER (Jean, 1772-?): born in Faussemagne (Dordogne) on 19 January 1772. Gendarme à cheval in the Dordogne Company 9 June 1794, in the Legion of the Gendarmerie d'Elite 22 December 1801, brigadier in the Dordogne Company 4 February 1804, maréchal des logis in the 2nd Squadron of the Gendarmerie d'Espagne 1 January 1810.

He became sub-lieutenant in the 1st Légion of the Gendarmerie à Cheval d'Espagne 11 April 1812, dismissed with the corps 27 February 1813 and placed as captain in the 12th Cuirassiers 28 February 1813, incorporated with his squadron into the 3rd Provisional Heavy Cavalry in Hamburg 11 September 1813.

He returned with the garrison May 1814, returned to the corps 1815 and placed on the non-active list 3 August 1815, left 16 August 1815.

DUMOULIN (Etienne, 1783-?): born in Metz (Moselle) on 29 August 1783. In the 6th Cavalry 19 August 1800, brigadier 26 May 1801, maréchal des logis in the 12th Cavalry 30 March 1802, sub-lieutenant in the 11th Cavalry 2 October 1802 which became the 11th Cuirassiers 24 September 1803, lieutenant 25 may 1807.

He was in the 13th Cuirassiers 11 July 1810, shot and wounded in the shoulder and the left hand at Mora 19 June 1811, adjutant-major 13 July 1811, confirmed 1 August 1811, captain adjutant-major 13 January 1813, captain commanding a company 25 May 1813. He became adjutant on the staff 30 December 1813, deputy of a military area January 1814. LH CH 16 March 1812.

DUMOUTIER (Louis Joseph, 1782-?): born in Bouhain

UVERNOY (Jacques Frédéric, 1768-1820) born in Héricourt (Haute-Saône) on 20 February 1768. Trumpeter in the Conti-Dragons 1 July 1782 which became the 4th Dragoons 1 January 1791, brigadier-fourrier 1 August 1793, maréchal des logis 8 June 1794, maréchal des logis-chef 4 August 1794, adjutant-NCO 10 May 1795.

He became sub-lieutenant 22 September 1796, at the Versailles riding school 14 April 1800, lieutenant 15 June 1801, returned to the regiment 20 July 1801, second-lieutenant in the Chasseurs à Cheval of the Guard 3 February 1804, first-lieutenant 23 September 1804, captain in the Dragoons of the Guard 13 September 1806, adjutant-major 15 September 1806, supernumerary major in the 5th Cuirassiers 23 October 1811, in service in the 6th Cuirassiers 5 May 1812, confirmed 28 September 1814, retired 21 November 1815. LH CH 14 June 1804, O 28 September 1814.

Adjutant-NCO, Jacques Duvernois charged with his platoon enabling an infantry battalion to retreat in good order; and during the same day he alone charged five Uhlans, killing one and putting the others to flight near Kaiserlauten in 1795.

(Aisne) on 9 April 1782. In the 3rd Cuirassiers 18 January 1804, brigadier 5 June 1809, maréchal des logis 1 December 1809, sub-lieutenant 14 May 1813, dismissed 25 November 1815.

DUMOUTIER see LEMARCHANT DUMOUTIER

DUNAND (Laurent Louis, 1769 -after 1818): born in Paris (Seine) on 11 September 1769. In the Agenois Regiment 20 November 1787, in the Paris National Guard 25 September 1790, in the 17th Infantry 13 September 1791, in the 13th Chasseurs à Cheval 25 January 1793, brigadier 15 April 1793, maréchal des logis 1 August 1793.

He was shot and wounded in the thigh at Breda and promoted to maréchal des logis-chef the same day 26 October 1793, shot and wounded in the head at Dunkirk 1796, shot and wounded in the right leg at Verona 6 November 1798, prisoner 26 April 1799, returned 6 January 1801, in the Gendarmerie 23 May 1804, maréchal des logis-chef in the 14th Cuirassiers 18 March 1813, stuck in Hamburg 1813.

Acting sub-lieutenant 20 April 1814, returned with the garrison May 1814, dismissed with the 14th Cuirassiers and put in the suite of the 12th Cuirassiers 13 July 1814, confirmed 4 February 1815, non-active on half-pay 1 March 1815, placed back in the regiment 14 June 1815, non-active again 3 August 1815 and went home 16 August 1815. LH CH 18 March 1815.

DUPAS de BELLEGARDE et de MAULEON (César,?-1809): Born in Belfort (Haut-Rhin). Sub-lieutenant in the 3rd cuirassiers 14 May 1809, killed at Essling 22 May 1809.

DUPERROIR (Nicolas Joseph Philippe, 1768-?): born in Torigny (Manche) on 2 February 1768. In the Mestre-de-Camp-Général-Cavalerie 11 March 1787 which became the 24th Cavalry 1 January 1791, fourrier 22 January 1791.

He became maréchal des logis in the Garde Constitutionnelle du Roi 21 January 1792, sub-lieutenant in the Volontaires Nationaux à Cheval from the Ecole Militaire 4 September 1792, captain in the 26th Cavalry when it was formed from the volunteers 21 February 1793, commissioned 22 June 1793, in the same regiment when it became the 25th Cavalry 4 June 1793, deputy to the adjutant-generals 21 November 1797 and aide de camp to General Micas, returned to the 25th Cavalry 19 February 1798, employed as instructor at the depot 1799, dismissed with the corps 12 October 1802 and incorporated into the 2nd cuirassiers 24 November 1802.

He was wounded by a Biscayan shot to his right leg and his horse killed under him at Friedland 14 June 1807, wounded by another Biscayan shot in the left hip and his horse killed under him at the Moskova 7 September 1812, in the Escadron Sacré during the retreat from Moscow 1812, squadron commander 14 May 1813, wounded by a bayonet to this right arm and his horse killed under him at Dresden 27 August 1813, wounded in the right arm at Athies near Laon 9 March 1814, retired 6 August 1814.

LH CH 14 March 1806, O 22 August 1813.

DUPIN (Antoine Joseph Janvier, 1774-?): born in Pernas (Hérault) on 1 January 1774. In the 12th Cuirassiers 27 November 1802, brigadier-fourrier 21 March 1804.

He became maréchal des logis 1 October 1807, sub-lieutenant in the suite 2 March 1809, wounded at Essling 22 May 1809, in post 23 May 1809, retired because of a dry cough and chronic rheumatic pains coming from the exhaustion of war 29 March 1810, pensioned as adjutant-NCO 8 April 1810.

DUPORT de SAINT VICTOR (Honoré Victor Alexandre, 1786-?): born in Grenoble (Isère) on 18 January 1786. In the 19th Dragoons 1 December 1803, brigadier 7 April 1804, fourrier 17 September 1804, maréchal des logis 26 March 1806, maréchal des logis-chef 1 April 1806,.

He became sub-lieutenant 3 March 1807, lieutenant aide de camp to General Rioult d'Avenay 4 October 1808, aide de camp to Caffarelli on the death of Rioult d'Avenay 27 May 1809, in the 6th Cuirassiers 17 August 1809, captain 8 October 1811.

He was wounded and his horse killed under him at Leipzig 16 October 1813, incorporated into the King's Cuirassiers when they were formed 21 July 1814, in the 2nd Cuirassiers of the Royal Guard 23 October 1815. LH CH 1 October 1807.

DUPRADELET see **TEYNIER DUPRADELET.**

DUPRE (Gervais Joseph Pierre, 1787 - 1876) born in Namur (Sambre-et-Meuse) on 1 April 1787. In the Gendarmes d'Ordonnance 26 October 1806, dismissed with the corps 23 October 1807 and incorporated into the Grenadiers à Cheval of the Imperial Guard

Junior officer's helmet and cuirass (Photograph by Jean-Louis Viau. RR)

21 November 1807, instated 10 December 1807.

He became sub-lieutenant in the 5th Cuirassiers 21 April 1809, shot and wounded at Essling 22 May 1809, admitted into the 5th Cuirassiers 3 June 1809, wounded by a Biscayan shot to his head and two horses killed under him at the Moskova 7 September 1812, several lance wounds at Winkovo 4 October 1812, in the Escadron Sacré during the retreat.

He was lieutenant 21 April 1813, wounded by a shell burst to his side and unhorsed at Laon 9 March 1814, resigned from French service 6 November 1814, adjutant-major in the Belgian Carabiniers 11 November 1814, captain instructor 5 June 1815. LH CH 21 October or 30 September 1814.

DUPUGET see **DURAND DUPUGET.**

DUPUY (Antoine, 1781-?): nephew of a state counsellor, born in Clermont Ferrand (Puy-de-Dôme) on 20 April 1781. Pupil at the Prytaneum paid by the government, pupil in foreign relations, sub-lieutenant in the 12th Dragoons 5 October 1806, lieutenant 1 November 1806, aide de camp to General Beker 5 April 1807.

He became first-lieutenant in the Dragoons of the Guard 8 July 1807, captain 18 June 1813, shot and wounded in the shoulder at Château-Thierry 12 February 1814, squadron commander in the suite of the 8th Cuirassiers 24 May 1814, in post aide de camp to General Letort 10 May 1815 then to General Beker 3 July 1815, dismissed 1 September 1815. LH CH 13 October 1812, O 27 February 1814.

DURAND (Nicolas Antoine, 1773-?): born in Paris (Seine) on 10 March 1773. In the 5th Chasseurs à Cheval 31 March 1792, brigadier 1 October 1794, fourrier 21 January 1796, maréchal des logis 9 September 1800, sub-lieutenant in the 26th Chasseurs à Cheval 23 September 1801, lieutenant adjutant-major 4 January 1806.

He became captain 5 July 1807, aide de camp to General Legrand 7 July 1807, bruised left thigh and chest at Essling 22 May 1809, squadron commander 20 June 1809, major 18 June 1812, at general headquarters 26 August 1812, wounded five times in the arms and head and taken prisoner defending a convoy including his general in Russia 4 December 1812, returned 18 August 1814 and placed in the suite of the 7th Cuirassiers, in the 3rd Cuirassiers 26 May 1815.

He left to join his unit at its 20 March position on 1 September 1815. LH CH 5 May 1809, O 9 August 1812.

DURAND aka **de SAINTE ROSE** (Denis Louis Rose, 1763-1837): born in Paris (Seine) on 12 March 1763. In the Estaing Volunteers 29 June 1779, left 1 January 1781, in the Normandy Regiment 28 June 1781, dismissed 13 April 1787, sergeant-major in the Chasseurs à Cheval of the Paris National Guard 1 November 1789, sub-lieutenant in the 14th Light Infantry Battalion 3 August 1791, deputy to Adjutant-General Huard 31 October 1795, lieutenant 30 October 1796.

He became captain 28 April 1798, deputy to Adjutant-General Reubell 8 September 1800, captain in the 8th cavalry 3 December 1800, deputy squadron commander on the staff of the 1st Military Division 25 March

1801, in the 8th Cuirassiers when it was formed 27 December 1801, adjutant-major at the cavalry depot in Versailles 21 January 1814, chief of staff of the Paris military area, non-active 20 March 1815, took up his functions again 1 July 1815. LH CH 14 June 1804.

DURAND DUPUGET (Pierre Jean Baptiste Marie Antoine, 1786 -after 1844): born in Saint-Martin (Tarn) on 24 December 1786. Velite in the Grenadiers à Cheval of the Guard 5 August 1806, pupil at the Ecole Militaire in Fontainebleau 16 December 1806, corporal 15 January 1807, sub-lieutenant in the suite of the 3rd Cuirassiers 16 May 1807, in post in the 13th Cuirassiers 21 October 1808.

He became lieutenant 18 September 1811, instated 21 October 1811, captain 27 August 1813, instated 6 November 1813, dismissed with the corps and incorporated into the 9th Cuirassiers 9 August 1814, dismissed with the corps 25 November 1815 and put at the disposal of the Minister of War 26 November 1815. LH CH 12 February 1813.

DUSSERRE (François Charles Camille, 1783-1809): born in Joyeuse (Ardèche) on 13 January 1783. In the 1st Cuirassiers 4 July 1803, brigadier 6 November 1804, maréchal des logis.

He became sub-lieutenant 16 May 1809, wounded at Essling 21 May 1809 and died of his wounds in the Austrian hospital 22 May 1809.

DUTAUZIN (Joseph Auguste, 1784-?): born in Symphorine (Gironde) on 22 April 1784. In the 7th Cuirassiers 12 July 1805, brigadier 1 October 1806, fourrier 14 January 1807, maréchal des logis 1 July 1809.

He became maréchal des logis-chef 15 February 1812, shot and wounded in the right knee in Russia 12 August 1812, sub-lieutenant 16 March 1814, wounded by a shell burst to his left cheek and a sabre blow to his right hand at Waterloo 18 June 1815, non-active 19 December 1815. LH CH 16 May 1813.

DUTERRAGE (Joseph, 1779-?): born in Treillin (Seine-et-Oise) on 2 December 1779. In the 5th Dragoons 23 July 1799, brigadier 6 February 1803, in the 3rd Escadron de Gendarmerie d'Espagne 5 December 1809, in the 1st legion de Gendarmerie à Cheval d'Espagne "Burgos" 16 December 1810, dismissed with the corps, dismissed with the corps 27 February 1813 and incorporated as maréchal des logis into the 12th Cuirassiers 18 March 1813, maréchal des logis-chef 23 March 1813, sub-lieutenant 14 May 1813.

He was wounded at Könnern 24 May 1813, prisoner 30 May 1813, returned and put on the non-active list 1814, returned to the 12th Cuirassiers 20 April 1815, put back on the non-active list 3 August 1815 and sent home 16 August 1815.

DUTREUX (François, 1773-1809): born in Metz (Moselle) on 26 July 1773. In the Hussars of the Ardennes Legion 23 December 1792 which formed the 23rd Chasseurs à Cheval 10 September 1793, shot and wounded at Wissemburg, brigadier 22 October 1794, fourrier 29 June 1795.

He became maréchal des logis 12 May 1798, sub-

lieutenant 5 May 1799, prisoner of war 4 August 1800, exchanged 14 August 1800, lieutenant 6 August 1805, aide de camp to General Saint-Germain 27 December 1807, captain in the 3rd Cuirassiers 14 May 1809, killed at Essling 21 May 1809.

DUVAL (Théodore, 1774-?): born in Le Mans (Sarthe) in 1774. In the 3rd Cavalry 23 April 1801, brigadier 17 November 1801, fourrier 27 December 1801, in the same regiment when it became the 3rd Cuirassiers 12 October 1802, maréchal des logis 31 July 1803.

He became maréchal des logis-chef 24 October 1803, in the 13th Cuirassiers 21 October 1808, adjutant-NCO 25 February 1810, sub-lieutenant 11 November 1810, paying officer, retired 1 January 1814.

DUVAL DUMANOIR (Paul Émile Gisbert Guillaume Marie, 1795-?): born in Paris (Seine) on 25 March 1795. One of the Emperor's pages 14 September 1810, lieutenant in the 8th Cuirassiers 5 February 1813.

He was aide de camp to Maréchal MacDonald 22 July 1813, captain 7 November 1813, in the Dragoons of the Royal Guard 10 October 1815. LH CH 3 April 1814.

DUVIGNAUX (Jean Baptiste Achille,?-1808): Born in Saint-Bertrand (Haute-Garonne) on 28 February. Boarder in the Ecole Militaire Impériale in Fontainebleau 13 October.

He became sub-lieutenant in the 10th Cuirassiers 14 December 1806, died in the army by falling off his horse and breaking his spine 12 January 1808.

DUVIVIER (Vincent Marie Constantin, 1774-1851): brother of the above, born in Mons (Jemmapes) on 12 Dec.1774. In the Army of the Brabant Patriots, volunteer in the Jemmapes Hussars 18 January 1793, sub-lieutenant 22 February 1793, in the same regiment when it became the 10th Hussars 4 June 1793, in the 3rd Dragoons 24 May 1796, lieutenant 22 January 1799. He was wounded by a sabre on his left shoulder at Abukir 7 March 1801 and shot and wounded in the right hand at Alexandria 13 March 1801, captain 16 January 1800, squadron commander in the 3rd Cuirassiers 30 October 1803, confirmed 15 December 1803, in the 21st Dragoons 23 January 1804, instated 5 March 1804, reformed and pensioned off because of his wounds, retired 2 July 1807, pensioned 29 August 1807.

He commanded the Legion of the Jemmapes National Guards 1813, battalion commander in the service of Holland commanding the Mons military district 16 December 1814. LH CH 14 June 1804.

DYVE de BAVAY (Charles Louis Marie Joseph Nepomucène Felix, 1793-1814): born in Mons (Jemmapes) on 15 June 1793.

At the Ecole Spéciale de Cavalerie 1 March 1810, grenadier 15 September 1811, sub-lieutenant 24 April 1812, prisoner in Russia 21 November 1812, replaced 31 December 1812, died January 1814.

The wounded cuirassier. Oil on canvas by Géricault. *(© RMN. Photograph by Gérard Blot)*

EBERLIN (Jean Chrétien, 1770-?): born in Pfaffenhoffen (Bas-Rhin) on 6 May 1770. In the Volontaires Nationaux à Cheval from the Ecole Militaire 4 September 1792 which formed the 26th Cavalry 21 February 1793 which itself became the 25th Cavalry 4 June 1793, saved two cannon thanks to the good reaction of the detachment he took command of on the death of their lieutenant who was in command of the retreat from the camp at César 8 August 1793, shot in the knee while disengaging General Osten from the hands of the enemy 22 October 1793, shot and wounded in the face 22 May 1794, sabre wound to his little finger on his left hand October 1794, brigadier 28 December 1797, maréchal des logis 22 December 1799.

He was incorporated with his squadron into the 3rd Cuirassiers 22 December 1802, elected sub-lieutenant 24 October 1803, lieutenant 31 May 1806, incorporated with his company into the 1st Provisional Heavy Cavalry December 1807 which formed the 13th Cuirassiers 21 October 1808, adjutant-major 13 February 1809, captain 17 August 1809, squadron commander 18 January 1814, confirmed 15 March 1814, chest wound and sprain when he fell under his horse at Lyon 20 March 1814, in the 9th Cuirassiers 9 August 1814, left with his pension 26 November 1815. Sabre of Honour 30 May 1803, LH CH by rights 24 September 1803, O 6 October 1814.

ECARTS (Pierre, 1776-?): born in Saint-Silardoux (Charente) on 10 August 1776. In the Carabiniers 9 May 1799, in the Grenadiers à cheval of the Guard 14 May 1802, brigadier 22 December 1805, maréchal des logis 16 February 1807.

He was elected lieutenant in the 2nd Cuirassiers 13 March 1813, adjutant-major 6 August 1814, wounded and left for dead at Waterloo 18 June 1815, left on half-pay 10 December 1815. LH CH 25 November 1807.

ECHELLES see **MILLIOT des ECHELLES.**

ECLATZ see **BOUVIER des ECLATZ**

ECQUEVILLY (Alfred Frédéric Armand d', 1787-?): born in Ecquevilly (Seine-et-Oise) on 7 July 1787. Pupil at the Ecole Militaire in Fontainebleau, sub-lieutenant in the suite of the 7th cuirassiers 14 January 1807, joined his unit 6 June 1807, in service 3 October 1808, lieutenant 13 February 1809, captain 8 October 1811, on one month's leave 7 May 1814, six months' leave 1 September 1814, squadron commander aide de camp 8 February 1815. LH CH 13 January 1809, O 18 August 1814.

ECUBARD (Pierre, 1788-?): born in Etaule (Charente-Inférieure) on 2 March 1788. In the Gendarmes d'Ordonnance 1 May 1807, dismissed with the corps 23 October 1807 and incorporated into the Grenadiers à Cheval of the Guard 24 November 1807, brigadier 6 April 1811, brigadier-fourrier 11 June 1811, sub-lieutenant in the 11th Cuirassiers 17 December 1811, lieutenant 25 December 1813, dismissed with the corps 16 December 1815. LH CH 5 September 1813.

EGUETHER (Jean, 1773-1840): born in Grosfrederching (Moselle) on 17 January 1773. In the 12th Cavalry 11 May 1793 which became the 12th Cuirassiers 24 September 1803, brigadier 1 January 1806, maréchal des logis 1 December 1806, vaguemestre 14 May 1809, sub-lieutenant 12 June 1813, wounded at Leipzig 18 October 1813, and regimental standard-bearer 14 July 1814, dismissed with the corps 10 December 1815. LH CH 1 October 1807.

EHRET (Antoine, 1772-1815): born in Massevaux (Haut-Rhin) in 1772. In the 4th Cavalry 20 February 1794, brigadier 21 March 1799, brigadier-fourrier 21 April 1800, maréchal des logis 6 April 1802, in the same regiment when it became the 4th Cuirassiers 12 October 1802, maréchal des logis-chef 1 November 1806, sub-lieutenant 3 June 1809, lieutenant 4 March 1812.

He was, in the 1st Cuirassiers 30 April which formed the Cuirassiers du Roi 1 July 1814 and which became the 1st Cuirassiers again in April 1815, killed at Waterloo 18 June 1815. LH CH 3 October 1814.

ELBEE (Charles Louis d', 1783-?): born in Paris (Seine) on 3 July 1783. In the 1st Cavalry 30 July 1801, brigadier 3 September 1802, maréchal des logis in the suite of the 2nd Cuirassiers 2 March 1803, sub-lieutenant in the 11th Cuirassiers 7 April 1804, lieutenant in the 2nd Cuirassiers 12 July 1808, aide de camp to General Tilly 30 May 1809

He was captain 8 February 1813, supernumerary maréchal de logis in the 2nd Company of the King's Musketeers 28 August 1814, squadron commander 8 July 1815, in the Dauiphin's Cuirassiers 29 November 1815.

Right.
General Espagne was one of the most famous cuirassiers officers. He was deadly wounded by a cannonball while charging at Essling 21 May 1809.
(Photo and Collection from Municipality of Auch, RR)

ESPAGNE (Jean-Louis-Brigite) COMTE DE L'EMPIRE, GÉNÉRAL

General Espagne at the head of his division charging the Austrian artillery at the Battle of Essling.
(Composition by J. Girbal, private collection, RR)

EMOURGEON (François, 1766-1813): born in Bitche (Moselle) on 6 February 1766. In the Reine-Cavalerie 15 January 1783, brigadier 1 October 1790, in the same regiment when it became the 4th Cavalry 1 January 1791, brigadier-fourrier 21 January 1792, maréchal des logis 1 August 1793, at the regimental depot from 16 April 1794 to 16 September 1796, maréchal des logis-chef 19 June 1797, sub-lieutenant 15 July 1800, in the same regiment when it became the 4th Cuirassiers 12 October 1802, elected lieutenant 8 May 1806. He was lieutenant adjutant-major 25 June 1807, rank of captain 25 December 1808, joined a company 5 March 1809, wounded and his horse killed under him at Essling 21 May 1809, died at Caen 15 December 1813. LH CH 13 April 1809.

EMPEREUR (Auguste, 1780-?): born in Melun (Seine-et-Marne) on 12 May 1780. In the 11th Cavalry 11 April 1800 which became the 11th Cuirassiers 24 September 1803, brigadier 28 September 1805, maréchal des logis 1 December 1806, sub-lieutenant 15 March 1812, resignation accepted 27 February 1815, left 31 March 1815. LH CH 13 August 1809.

ENGELMANN (Jean Baptiste Valentin, 1771-?): born in Sirck (Moselle) on 24 February 1771. Hussar in the Lauzun Regiment 18 October 1786 which became the 6th Hussars 1 January 1791, fourrier 23 October 1792, in the same regiment when it became the 5th Hussars 4 June 1793, maréchal des logis 30 June 1793, sub-lieutenant 1 July 1793, lieutenant 4 October 1796, staff captain 20 April 1798, in the service of Holland as captain adjutant-major in the 1st Dutch Cuirassiers 22 September 1808, in the Grenadiers of the Royal Dutch Guard January 1807, adjutant-major 1807, squadron commander in the 2nd Dutch cuirassiers 3 August 1808, bayonet and sabre wounds at Straalsund 31 May 1809, with 10 Cuirassiers forced 300 Hussars and infantry to capitulate 1809, major 25 August 1809.

He was in French service with his regiment which had become the 14th Cuirassiers 18 August 1810, acting CO of the 2nd Provisional

Cuirassier Regiment in Hamburg 11 September 1813, colonel of the same regiment 25 November 1813.

Returned with the garrison May 1813, non-active August 1814, retired 1 April 1815, retired 9 December 1815. OH LH 17 January 1815.

ERARD (? -1807): elected sub-lieutenant in the 2nd Cuirassiers 4 October 1803, lieutenant 30 October 186, died in hospital 1807.

ESPAGNE (Jean Baptiste Paul Emile, 1795-?): son of the general, born in Reims (Marne) on 19 February 1795. Pupil in the Ecole Militaire in Saint-Germain 17 July 1811, sub-lieutenant in the 8th Cuirassiers 14 April 1813, resignation refused 27 July 1814, on six months' leave on half-pay 20 December 1814, wounded at Waterloo 18 June 1815, on leave 25 November 1815, dismissed with the corps 5 December 1815.

ESPAGNE (Jean Louis Brigitte, comte, 1769-1809): born in Auch (Gers) on 16 February 1769. In the Queen's Dragoons 6 July 1787, brigadier 21 April 1788, in the same regiment when it became the 6th Dragoons 1 January 1791, maréchal des logis 10 January 1792, maréchal des logis-chef 16 February 1792, sub-lieutenant in the 6th Chasseurs à Cheval 2 August 1792.

He was captain in the Hussards Défenseurs de la Liberté et de l'Egalité when they were formed 2 September 1792 which then became the 7th Hussars 23 November 1792, second lieutenant-colonel 30 November 1792, in the same regiment when it became the 6th Hussars 4 June 1793, adjutant-general brigade commander in the Army if the Pyrénées Occidentales 23 September 1793, aide de camp to Dumas in the Army of the Alps 22 May 1794, on a mission for the Comité de Salut Public 24 June 1794, in the Army of the Sambre-et-Meuse 9 August 1794 then in that of the Côtes de Brest 24 October 1794, on a mission in Paris 26 November 1794, on the staff of the Army of the Sambre-et-Oise 17 December 1794, colonel of the 8th Cavalerie-Cuirassiers 16 December 1796, commanded the 3rd Brigade (4th and 8th Cavalry) in d'Hautpoul's Division March 1799, brigadier-general 10 July 1799, in the Army of the Bas-Rhin 25 July 1799, then of the Rhine 25 September 1799. He commanded the 2nd Brigade (8th and 98th Cavalry) in d'Hautpoul's division 25 April 1800, wounded in the arm at Neubourg 27 June 1800, commanded a brigade in Montrichard's division 4 July 1800 then the 1st Brigade (Carabiniers) of the Reserve Cavalry Division July 1800, non-active 23 September 1801, commanded the Haute-Vienne Department 28 October 1801, major-general 1 February 1805, commanded the 4th Division of the Army of Italy 2 March 1805, then a Chasseurs à Cheval division 18 October 1805, commanded a cavalry division in the 8th Corps 11 December 1805, in the 1st Corps of the army of Naples 20 February 1806, commanded the Labour Province 12 August 1806, commanded the 3rd Cuirassiers Division of the Grande Armée 22 November 1806, four lance wounds at Heilsberg 10 June 1807, returned to France for convalescence beginning July 1807, dismissed 5 December 1807.

he commanded a division of cuirassiers in the Army of the Rhine 12 October 1808, then the 3rd Cuirassier Division in the 2nd Corps under Lannes, wounded by a cannonball while charging at Essling 21 May 1809, taken to the island of Lobau and died in the evening. LH CH 11 December 1803, C 14 June 1804, GO 11 July 1807, Count of the Empire d. April 1808 and l.p. 26 April 1810.

EUCHE (Jean Baptiste, 1761-1807): born in Languendorff on 3 July 1791. Child of the regiment in the Dauphin-Cavalerie, on the regimental payroll 7 August 1770, trooper 20 August 1778, in the same regiment when it became the 12th cavalry 1 January 1791.

He was elected sub-lieutenant 19 August 1803, in the same regiment when it became the 12th Cuirassiers 24 September 1803. He was killed at Friedland 14 June 1807.

EULER (Jacques, 1766-?): born in Vibersviller (Moselle) on 24 April 1766. In the Alsace-Infanterie from 19 December 1780 to 27 August 1786, volunteer in the Colonel-Général-Cavalerie 1 April 1787 which became the 1st Cavalry 1791, sabre wound at Neerwinden 18 March 1793, brigadier 5 March 1796, fourrier 8 August 1796, maréchal des logis 7 September 1799, in the same regiment when it became the 1st Cuirassiers 10 October 1801, maréchal des logis-chef 20 June 1802, maréchal des logis at his own request 2 July 1803, sabre wound at Austerlitz 2 December 1805, sub-lieutenant 16 May 1809, lieutenant 15 October 1809, left his regiment to go home and wait for his retirement pension 18 May 1812. LH CH 3 April 1807.

ELOGE see **LABRETONNIERE EULOGE.**

EYQUEM (Jean, 1787-?): born in Saint-Médard (Gironde) on 1 April 1787. Velite in the Grenadiers à cheval of the Guard 21 March 1807, sub-lieutenant in the 4th Cuirassiers 3 July 1809, lieutenant 22 December 1813 and aide de camp to General Curto 28 April 1814.

FADAT (Victor François, 1781-?): born in Nant (Aveyron) on 24 June 1781. In the 7th Chasseurs à Cheval 29 September 1802, brigadier 23 December 1803, maréchal des logis 12 January 1807, maréchal des logis-chef 1 April 1809, gendarme in the Aveyron Company 5 February 1811.

He was in the 1st Legion à Cheval of the Gendarmerie d'Espagne 15 September 1812, sub-lieutenant in the 12th Cuirassiers 28 February 1813, non-active July 1814.

FAGNY (Pierre, 1777-?): born in Carignan (Ardennes) on 17 August 1777. In the 6th cavalry 16 October 1798, brigadier-fourrier 25 November

AILLE (Séraphin Joseph, 1763-1808): born in Trouville (Pas-de-Calais) on 27 September 1763. In the Gardes Françaises 10 August 1780, left 27 September 1783, in the Cuirassiers du Roy 10 December 1783 which became the 8th Cavalry 1 January 1791, brigadier 17 September 1791, maréchal des logis and adjutant-sub-lieutenant the same day 28 August 1793, lieutenant 31 January 1800.

He was in the same regiment when it became the 8th Cuirassiers 10 October 1801, elected captain 4 June 1805, died of fever in Prussia 9 January 1808. Sabre of Honour 15 September 1802, LH CH by rights 24 September 1803, O 14 June 1804.

A Lieutenant in the 8th Cavalry, Séraphin Faille got 640 Austrians commanded by a colonel and fourteen officers to lay down their arms with only his platoon at Hochstaedt on 19 June 1800.

1802, in the same regiment when it became the 6th Cuirassiers 23 December 1802, maréchal des logis 20 July 1805.

He was maréchal des logis-chef 7 August 1805, sub-lieutenant 3 June 1809, lieutenant 2 September 1812, captain 6 October 1813, dismissed 21 November 1815.

FAILLY (Gabriel Victor Marie de, 1791-1812): born in Grand-Failly (Moselle) on 11 May 1791. Boarder at the Ecole Militaire 8 November 1808, corporal 28 July 1809, sub-lieutenant in the 11th Cuirassiers 14 August 1810.

He disappeared with three other officers from the same regiment during fighting on the other side of the Niemen after crossing the Berezina 31 December 1812.

FANGERAY
see **LECOINTE de LAFANGERAYE**

FARINE DU CREUX (Pierre Joseph, baron, 1770-1833): born in Damprichard (Doubs) on 2 October 1770. Sub-lieutenant in the 2nd Doubs Battalion 9 October 1791, shot twice and wounded in the head and thigh at Saverna December 1793, lieutenant in the 41st Battle 25 September 1794.

He was deputy to Adjutant-General Heudelet 20 January 1795, captain 22 February 1795, confirmed 29 December 1795, several sabre wounds to his left arm and taken prisoner at Engen 3 October 1796, exchanged April 1797, returned to France May 1797, acting aide de camp to General Michaud 3 December 1797, confirmed 31 January 1798, battalion comman-

der 10 September 1799, supernumerary squadron commander in the 14th Cavalry 18 November 1800.

He was deputy on the staff of the Army of Italy 12 March 1801, appointed to the 14th Cavalry 30 December 1801 which became the 23rd Dragoons 24 September 1803, commanded the Salerno arrondissement 1806, major in the 29 Dragoons 7 January 1807, left to join his unit 23 February 1807, colonel in the 4th Dragoons 7 April 1809, taken prisoner at Usagre 25 May 1811, landed in England 28 July 1811, locked up in a humid cell then escaped 21 December 1811, commanded the General Cavalry and Remount Depot of the Grande Armée in Warsaw 22 February 1812 then Elbing, rejoined the army 25 March 1812, brigadier-general in the 10th Corps at Danzig 26 June 1813.

He was chief of staff to Rapp, taken prisoner after the capitulation 2 January 1814 and taken to Russia whence he returned July 1814, non-active 8 September 1814, Cavalry Inspector in the 5th Military Division 30 December 1814, commanded the 1st Brigade (5th and 10th Cuirassiers) of the 3rd Reserve Cavalry Corps 10 April 1815 which became the 14th Cavalry Division of the 4th Cavalry Corps 3 June 1815, sabre wound to his left shoulder at Ligny 16 June 1815.

He was shot and wounded in the head at Waterloo 18 June 1815, in Paris during the retreat to look after his wounds, responsible for disbanding the cavalry in the 21 Military Division 11 October 1815. LH CH 14 June 1804 O 26 November 1810, C 23 August 1814, Chevalier of the Empire l.p. 28 January 1809 and Baron d. 6 August 1811 and l.p. 12 February 1812.

General Farine distinguished himself at Waterloo at the head of his brigade of cuirassiers. (RR)

FARJON (Pierre Charles, 1764-?): born in Maastricht (Meuse-Inférieure) on 8 January 1764. Sub-lieutenant in the 2nd Dutch Cuirassiers 23 July 1795, lieutenant in the 1st Dutch Light Dragoons 21 November 1804.

He was named captain in the 2nd Dutch Cuirassiers 27 February 1807 which became the 14th French Cuirassiers 18 August 1810, resigned 5 December 1810.

12th Cuirassier Regiment charging. (RR)

FAUCONNET (Joseph Emmanuel Auguste François, chevalier, 1778-?): the eldest of the five sons of the general in service, born in Lunéville (Meurthe) on 27 November 1778. In the Carabiniers 1 November 1791 left 25 May 1792, in the 2nd Carabiniers 1 October 1793, in the 6th Dragoons 26 February 1795, sub-lieutenant 5 September 1795, sabre wound to his left parietal when crossing the Rhine 24 June 1796, saved the lives of General Beaupuy and his father who was a colonel in the 6th Dragoons both of whom were wounded and killed 2 Anspach Cuirassiers with his own hands at Göritz near Kehl 26 June 1796, aide de camp to his father 10 July 1796, lieutenant 10 July 1797, deputy to Adjutant-General Garabuau 23 January 1798, commissioned captain in the suite 11 January 1799.

He was aide de camp again to General Fauconnet this time 14 May 1800, shot and wounded in his left leg 22 June 1800, appointed captain in the 1st Carabiniers 27 November 1800 and confirmed 8 February 1801, seconded to General Bourcier the Inspector General of Cavalry from 6 March 1804 to 21 January 1805, squadron commander 8 May 1807, fell from his horse and crushed under foot at Friedland 14 June 1807, wounded in the right buttock and head by a cannonball at Wagram 6 July 1809, second-major in the cavalry 3 August 1811, appointed to the 2nd Dragoons 1811, wounded at Maëstricht 7 February 1814, acting CO of the cavalry brigade to which his regiment was attached April 1814.

He was in the suite of the 9th Cuirassiers 5 July 1814, confirmed 28 September 1814, non-active at the disposal of the government 26 November 1815. LH CH November 1804, O 6 October 1814, Chevalier of the Empire l.p. 2 September 1810.

FAUCONNET (Renaud Philippe, 1784-1814): third of the general's sons, born in Lunéville (Meurthe) on 18 April 1784. In the 6th Dragoons 10 August 1796, in the 1st Carabiniers 5 June 1801, brigadier 16 January 183, maréchal des logis 25 April 1802, sub-lieutenant in the 8th Cuirassiers 8 June 1803, lieutenant 24 February 1807.

He was shot in the right thigh at Heilsberg 10 June 1807, wounded when two horses fell beneath him at Essling 21 May 1809, captain 3 June 1809, shot in the right hand at Winkovo 18 October 1812, killed at La Chaussée near Châlons-sur-Marne 3 February 1814. LH CH 1 October 1807.

FAULCON (Etienne, 1792-?): born in Montmorillon (Vienne) on 18 April 1792. Gendarme à cheval in the 14th Escadron d'Espagne 24 February 1810, in the 1st Legion à Cheval "Burgos" 1 January 1811, brigadier 9 June 18112.

He was dismissed with the corps 23 February 1813 and took up his appointment as sub-lieutenant in the 6th Cuirassiers 28 February 1813, dismissed 21 November 1815.

FAURE (Claude, 1764-1813): born in Féline (Haute-Loire) on 28 March 1764. Trooper in the Colonel-Général-Régiment 23 April 1785 which became the 1st Cavalry 1 January 1791, brigadier 1 June 1793, maréchal des logis 16 September 1763, wounded by a Biscayan shot to his left shoulder at Tournai 22 May 1794, maréchal des logis-chef 19 January 1799, shot in the neck at la Trebbia 24 June 1799, sub-lieutenant 10 August 1799.

He was in the same regiment when it became the 1st Cuirassiers 10 October 1801, lieutenant by governmental choice 13 April 1804, wounded at Nordlingen 17 October 1805, captain 3 April 1807, killed at Hanau 30 October 1813. LH CH 14 April 1807.

FAURE (Eloi, 1780-?): born in Paris (Seine) on 3 June 1780. Volunteer in the 22nd Cavalry 28 May 1799, brigadier 19 August 1800, shot in the right leg at Zürich 2 September 1801, wounded by a Biscayan shot to his right thigh at Biberach 13 August 1802, in the Grenadiers à Cheval of the Guard 22 November 1802, maréchal des logis in the 24th Dragoons 20 July 1805, shot in the left shoulder at Ivitello 3 March 1806, brigadier in the Gendarmerie Royale of the Two Sicilies 30 July 1806. He was maréchal des logis 20 November 1808, in the cuirassiers 22 April 1813, sub-lieutenant 5 February 1814, non-active on half-pay 1814, in the 5th French Cuirassiers 18 April 1815, confirmed 2 May 1815, appointment cancelled and put back on half-pay 1 August 1815.

FAYET (Louis, 1777-?): born in Reims (Marne) on 27 October 1777. In the 25th Cavalry 21 November 1798, brigadier 23 September 1802, dismissed with the corps 12 October 1802 and incorporated into the 4th Cuirassiers 23 November 1802, maréchal des logis 1 July 1806, sub-lieutenant 4 March 1812, non-active on half-pay 6 August 1814.

He was elected sub-lieutenant again 4 January 1815 in the same regiment when it became the Cuirassiers d'Angoulême then the 4th Cuirassiers again April 1815, retired 21 December 1815.

FAYNOT (Frédéric, 1767-?): born in Montbéliard (Haut-Rhin) on 24 December 1767. In service with a Swiss regiment 14 March 1786, in the 3rd Hussars February 1798, Gendarme in the 10th Sqaudron of the Army of Spain 25 November 1809.

He was in the 1st Legion of Gendarmerie à Cheval "Burgos", dismissed with the corps 27 February 1813 and appointed sub-lieutenant in the 11th Cuirassiers 1 March 1813.

He was incorporated with his squadron into the 3rd Provisional Heavy Cavalry in Hamburg 11 September 1813. He returned after the capitulation with the garrison May 1814, wounded at Waterloo 18 June 1815 and dismissed with the regiment 1815.

FAYOLLE (Nicolas Augustin Savinien, ?-1813): born in Nogent (Seine-et-Marne). In the 12th Cuirassiers 22 March 1804, brigadier-fourrier 23 October 1805, maréchal des logis 1 December 1806, maréchal des logis-chef 1 March 1808, adjutant-NCO 14 May 1809, sub-lieutenant 15 March 1812.

He was wounded at Orcha 21 November 1812. He was lost during the retreat, presumed taken prisoner near Ebling 1 January 1813. He died of fever in Danzig hospital 15 Februar 1813.

FERRAGU (François Joseph, 1773-?): born in le Quesnoy-sur-Arrain (Somme) on 10 March 1773.

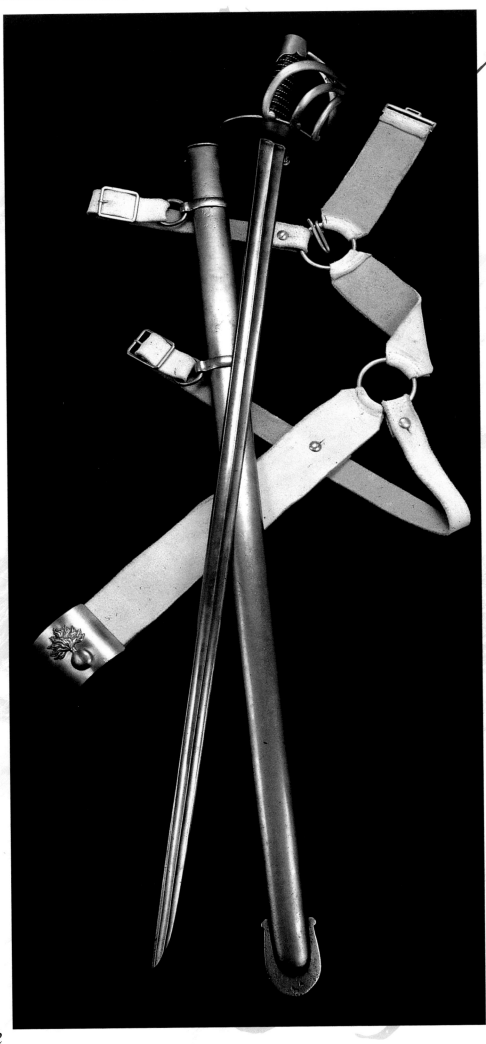

LEURY (Anne Pierre Louis, 1761-1823): born in Florac (Lozère) on 22 May 1761. In the Roi-Cavalerie 31 March 1777, brigadier 18 August 1781, maréchal des logis 26 September 1784, fourrier 19 April 1787, maréchal des logis-chef 15 August 1789.

He was in in the same regiment when it became the 6th Cavalry 1 January 1791, adjutant 1 April 1791, lieutenant 14 March 1792, wounded in the left shoulder near Lille 1792, captain 18 October 1792, squadron commander 30 June 1799.

He was confirmed 8 February 1801

He was in the same regiment when it became the 6th Cuirassiers 23 December 1802, major in the 10th Cuirassiers 29 October 1803, instated 26 May 1804, retired 9 July 1807.

LH CH 26 March 1804.

On 19 June 1800, Squadron Commander Fleury of the 6th Cavalry repulsed a charge made by fourteen squadrons of enemy cuirassiers enabling the infantry and the rest of the regiment to cross over onto the other side of the Rhine.

Captain of a company of requisition officers for the Amiens District 17 September 1793, soldier in the 71st Half-Brigade 12 April 1794, ordnance officer to General Bernadotte 1795, sub-lieutenant in General Bernadotte's Company of Guards in the Army of the West 20 June 1800, second-lieutenant in the same unit under Brune 12 October 1800, confirmed 6 September 1801, discharged 20 June 1802.

He was lieutenant in the 11th cavalry which became the 11th Cuirassiers 24 September 1803, captain 13 April 1804, appointed 4 September 1810, in the suite 12 August 1804, dismissed with the corps 16 December 1815. LH CH 27 September 1814.

FERRENHOLZ (Georges, 1790-?): born in Cologne (Röer) on 23 April 1790. Velite in the Dragoons of the Guard 20 June 1807, sub-lieutenant in the 4th Cuirassiers 13 March 1813, returned home as a foreign national (no longer French) 6 August 1814.

FERRIERE (Jean Baptiste, 1754-?): born in Saint-Chely-d'Apcher (Lozère) on 13 July 1754. Trooper in the Royal-Cravates 19 October 1775, brigadier 20 August 1782, maréchal des logis 20 September 1784, maréchal des logis-chef 1 April 1789, in the same regiment when it became the 10th Cavalry 1 January 1791, sub-lieutenant 15 September 1792, lieutenant 14 November 1793, sabre wound to his head near Kreutznach January 1794. He was captain 21 March 1794, in the same regiment when it became the 10th Cuirassiers 24 September 1803, retired 27 August 1805 and left 8 October 1805.

Cuirassier sabre, scabbard and leather beltwork. *(Photo Jean-Louis Viau)*

FERROUSSAT (Jean Louis, 1780-1850): born in London (England) on 3 July 1780. In the 14th Dragoons 14 November 1799, brigadier 4 June 1800, maréchal des logis 20 September 1800, sub-lieutenant 15 January 1802, lieutenant 30 January 1806, aide de camp to General Maupetit 10 January 1807, captain 6 July 1807, squadron commander in the 9th Cuirassiers 18 September 1811.

He was wounded at the Moskova 7 September 1812, major in the 10th Chasseurs à Cheval 16 August 1813, wounded at Provins 29 February 1814, colonel 3 April 1814, confirmed 6 December 1814, chief pf staff of the 2nd Cavalry Corps 15 May 1815, in the suite of the 2nd Lancers July 1815, non-active 22 September 1815. LH 14 May 1807, O 12 March 1814.

FERROUSSAT (Louis Claude Félix, 1795-?): born in Paris (Seine) on 23 January 1795. Volunteer in the 9th Cuirassiers 26 December 1811, maréchal des logis 2 February 1812, sub-lieutenant 25 May 1813, on two months' leave without pay 6 September 1814, prolonged by three months on half-pay 15 June 1815, struck off the rolls for long absence and for not getting in touch 26 November 1815.

FERRY see **TESTOT FERRY.**

FERTE (Christophe, 1773-?): born in Condé (Aisne) on 1 September 1773. Velite in the Gendarmes à Cheval of the Imperial Guard 7 November 1805, sub-lieutenant in the 2nd Carabiniers 7 January 1808, instated 6 March 1808, in the 4th Cuirassiers 16 August 1810, appointed 13 May 1811.

He was lieutenant 4 March 1812, lance wound to on the right side of his jaw at the Berezina 28 November 1812, wounded on the Vilna road 1 December 1812, retired 6 August 1814.

FERUSSAC see **DAUDEBAR FERUSSAC**

FEUILLADE (Jean, 1766-1812): born in Clermont-Ferrand (Puy-de-Dôme) on 26 December 1766. In the Cuirassiers du Roy 31 March 1786 which became the 8th Cavalry 1 January 1791, brigadier 25 January 1792, fourrier 20 September 1792, maréchal des logis-chef 28 August 1793, sub-lieutenant 7 February 1794, lieutenant by choice 28 July 1795, captain 9 May 1800, in the same regiment when it became the 8th Cuirassiers 10 October 1801, squadron commander 25 January 1807.

He was wounded at Heilsberg 10 June 1807, acting CO of the regiment in the absence of Colonel Merlin who was wounded in June and until 15 July 1807, commanded the regiment after the same colonel was wounded at Essling 21 and 22 May 1809, acting CO of another regiment whose colonel was wounded at Wagram 6 July 1809, second-major 3 August 1811, kept in the 8th Cuirassiers 30 October 1811, wounded at the Moskova 7 September 1812 and disappeared.

FEZENSAC
see **MONTESQUIOU FEZENSAC**

FONTAINE (François Xavier Octave aka Louis Octave, Baron, 1762-1812): born in Saint-Rémy (Haute-Saône) on 5 November 1762. In the Poitou-Infanterie 19 November 1778, with five of his comrades captured a position defended by 25 Englishmen at Pensacola in America 1781, corporal 1 May 1785, in the 6th Battalion of the Paris National Guard 17 September 1789.

Ddismissed 1 September 1791, brigadier-fourrier in the 32nd Gendarmerie Division 7 August 1792, bayonet wound in his chest at Menin, adjutant in Rosenthal's Legion 1 May 1793.

He was first adjutant sub-lieutenant in the same regiment when it became the 19 Chasseurs à Cheval 10 June 1793, acting deputy to the adjutant-generals 22 September 1793, confirmed with Beaufort 18 November 1793, confirmed lieutenant 18 June 1794, adjutant-general brigade commander 13 June 1795, prisoner on 13 Vendémiaire (5 October 1795), discharged 22 September 1796, under Augereau on 18 Fructidor (4 September 1797), active again 23 July 1798.

He was taken prisoner with the expedition 8 September 1798, exchanged and returned to France 24 December 1798, chief of staff for Lefebvre's division in the Army of the Danube March 1799 and of the 4th Division of the Army of the Danube and Helvetia 4 May 1799, noticed because of his services on 18 Brumaire (6 November 1799), in the 26th Military Division 1800 and then the 24th 1802, in Saint-Omer Camp 4 November 1803 then that of Brest December 1803, chief of staff of the 3rd Heavy Cavalry Division (d'Hautpoul) 1805.

Confirmed 20 December 1805, in the reserve cavalry division 15 March 1808, Lasalle's division in the Army of Spain 17 March 1808, at Berthier's headquarters in Germany 15 March 1809.

He was back in Spain 19 May 1810, Dorsenne's division 1811, returned to France for health reasons and employed with Bailly de Monthion, aide major-general of the army, died in Paris 17 May 1812. Sabre of Honour 1799. LH CH 16 October 1803, O 25 December 1805, Baron of the Empire l.p. 20 March 1810.

Irish Expedition, 6 September 1798: At Castlebar, François Fontaine at the head of forty troopers from the 3rd Chasseurs à Cheval took an English regiment and four artillery pieces.

He was made Brigadier-General on the battlefield.

(RR)

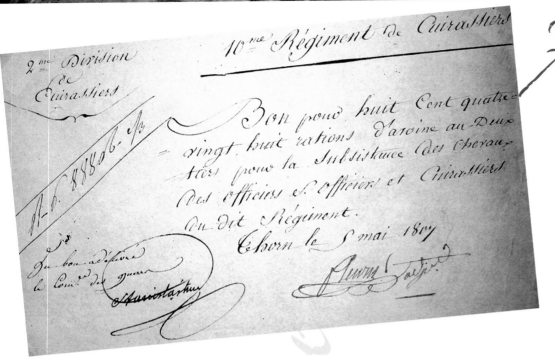

Purchase note for fodder signed by Captain François Fleury.
(Author's collection)

RANCOLLIN (Louis François, 1784-?): born in Issoudun (Indre) on 25 August 1784. In the 8th Cuirassiers 22 May 1804, fourrier 15 October 1806, in the 13th Cuirassiers 5 April 1809, maréchal des logis 15 August 1809, maréchal des logis-chef 2 February 1810, temporary sub-lieutenant 27 August 1813, confirmed 6 November 1813.

He was dismissed with the corps and left on half-pay 9 August 1814.

Between Saint-Amour and Lons-le-Saulnier on 6 March 1814, Sous-Lieutenant Louis Francollin completely defeated a detachment of sixty Cossacks with only twelve recently-recruited Cuirassiers mounted on new horses, taking eleven prisoners and fifteen horses.

FITEAU (Edme Nicolas, comte de Saint-Etienne, 1772-1810): born in Saint-Léger-le-Petit (Cher) on 9 August 1772. In the Franche-Comté Chasseurs à Cheval 19 August 1789 which became the 4th Chasseurs à Cheval 1 January 1791, brigadier-fourrier for the Army of the Rhine partisans 15 July 1793, maréchal des logis 7 January 1794, lieutenant quartermaster 29 January 1794, noticed when with 4 other troopers he broke through 15 enemy Hussars holding the pass and routed them in the Kaiserlauten Wood 24 February 1794.

He was incorporated lieutenant into the 7th bis Hussars 30 May 1794, with a 25-man platoon routed two Neapolitan squadrons and captured their CO Prince Cutto near Valeggio 31 May 1797, captain 19 February 1798, acting squadron commander in Egypt 12 October 1798, acting brigade commander of the 3rd Dragoons 23 September 1800, shot twice in the right arm at Canope 21 March 1801, confirmed squadron commander and brigade commander of the 3rd Dragoons 3 October 1803, colonel-major of the Dragoons of the Guard 13 October 1806, wounded 5 February 1807, brigadier-general commanding the 1st Brigade (1st and 5th Cuirassiers) of the 2nd Cuirassier Division 25 May 1809.

He was wounded at Wagram 6 July 1809, commanded the Léman Department while still convalescing 5 August 1810, occupied the Valais November 1810, shot himself when the balance of his mind was temporarily disturbed in Geneva 14 December 1810.

LH CH 11 December 1803, O 14 June 1804, Comte de Saint-Etienne l.p. 14 April 1810.

FLAGEAC see **LENORMAND FLAGEAC.**

FLAVIER (Jean, 1778-?): born in Mainevalle (Eure) on 12 September 1778. In the 10th Dragoons 21 March 1799, brigadier 1 July 1807, gendarme in the Meaux Depot 20 January 1812, brigadier 13 August 1812, sub-lieutenant in the 10th Cuirassiers 28 February 1813.

He was dismissed on half-pay 6 August 1814, in the 7th Cuirassiers 9 May 1815, rejoined 22 May 1815, returned home on half-pay 24 August 1815.

FLEURENT (Jean Baptiste Vincent Athanase, 1783-1812): born in Tillé (Bas-Rhin) on 22 January 1783. In the 10 Cuirassiers 24 September 1803, brigadier 15 January 1806, maréchal des logis 16 July 1806, maréchal des logis-chef 1 January 1808, adjutant 3 June 1809.

He was named sub-lieutenant 21 March 1812, wounded and disappeared around Borisov 25 November 1812.

FLEURY (François Hippolyte Hilarion Casimir, 1783-?): born in Florac (Lozère) on 15 January 1783. In the 6th Cavalry 23 June 1798, brigadier 7 October 1802, maréchal des logis 20 April 1802, in the 10th Cuirassiers 20 January 1804, instated 22 January 1804, sub-lieutenant 31 March 1806, lieutenant 25 May 1807.

He was captain 3 June 1809, shot in the right thigh, seven lance wounds to his stomach, left groin, hip, back and left shoulder and three sabre wounds to his right hand, left elbow and head and taken prisoner at Moscow 4 October 1812, returned to the suite of the regiment 21 September 1814, appointed captain 20 January 1815, dismissed with the corps 25 December 1815.

LH CH 1 October 1807.

FLEURY (Nicolas Martin, 1773-?): born in Tille (Oise) on 6 October 1773. In the 10th Cavalry 10 January 1794, brigadier 20 January 1799, fourrier 8 August 1799, maréchal des logis 22 March

1800, in the same regiment when it became the 10th Cuirassiers 24 September 1803, maréchal des logis-chef 22 January 1804, adjutant 24 November 1806, sub-lieutenant 25 May 1807, lieutenant 16 May 1809.

He was shot and wounded in his right leg, his horse killed under him, and taken prisoner at Essling 21 May 1809, returned to France 8 August 1809, retired 9 October 1811. LH CH 5 November 1804.

FLOQUET (Jean Pierre Florentin, 1774-?): born in Montigny (Aisne) on 2 February 1774. In the 7th Cavalry 1 June 1793 which became the 7th Cuirassiers 23 December 1802, brigadier 12 February 1806, maréchal des logis 1 October 1806, six sabre wounds to his head at Essling 21 May 1809.

He was sub-lieutenant 17 June 1812, shot in the left foot at the Berezina 28 November 1812, lieutenant 16 March 1814, retired 19 December 1815. LH CH 16 May 1813.

FLOTARD de MONTAGU LOMAGNE (Armand Jean, 1787-1858): born in Paris (Seine) on 12 June 1787. Boarder at the Ecole Militaire in Fontainebleau 23 November 1806, corporal 28 January 1807, sub-lieutenant in the 5th Cuirassiers 19 February 1807, lieutenant 16 May 1809, wounded at Essling 22 May 1809, adjutant-major 15 June 1809, rank of captain 2 December 1810, went to a company 21 February 1812,

He was wounded at Fère-Champenoise 25 March 1814, squadron commander on half-pay 20 January 1815, in the 1st Cuirassiers of the Garde Royale 10 October 1815. LH CH 16 June 1809.

FLOURY (Louis François Joseph, 1784-?): born in Amiens (Somme) on 22 August 1784. In the 8th Cuirassiers 11 July 1806, lance and sabre wounds at Essling May 1809, gendarme in the Frise Department 2 October 1811, in the Legion of the Gendarmerie d'Elite of the Guard 4 March 1813, maréchal des logis in the Chevau-Légers Lancers of the Guard 28 April 1813.

He was named sub-lieutenant in the 13th Cuirassiers 24 May 1813, lieutenant 25 February 1814, non-active on half-pay 6 August 1814.

FOECHE (Martin, 1783-1809): born in Rixheim (Haut-Rhin) in 1786. In the 2nd Cavalry 20 December 1792, brigadier 21 March 1798, fourrier 22 November 1800.

He was maréchal des logis 25 June 1802, in the same regiment when it became the 2nd Cuirassiers 12 October 1802, sub-lieutenant 14 May 1809, died 31 December 1809.

FOLKERS (Lambertus Jacobus, 1784-?): born in Gronigen (Ems-Occidental) on 27 March 1784. In the 2nd Dutch Cuirassiers 16 October 1806, brigadier 17 January 1807, maréchal des logis 21 May 1807 in the same regiment when it became the 14th French Cuirassiers 18 August 1810. He was maréchal des logis-chef 1 February 1811, sub-lieutenant 19 November 1812, dismissed with the corps 13 July 1814.

FONTAINE (Antoine Marie de, 1788-?): born in Morissel (Somme) on 21 June 1788. In the Gendarmes d'Ordonnance 2 June 1807, in the Dragoons of the Imperial Guard 24 November 1807, sub-lieutenant in the 8th cuirassiers 3 June 1809, seconded to the 3rd Provisional Heavy Cavalry in Spain. He returned to the 8th Cuirassiers February 1811, lieutenant 15 October 1813, taken prisoner 1814, appointed 4 February 1815, dismissed with the corps 5 December 1815.

FONTAINE (Joseph, 1772-1809): born in Verviers (Ourthe) on 16 September 1772. Trooper in the Colonel-Général Regiment 21 April 1789 which became the 1st Cavalry 1 January 1791, brigadier-fourrier 1 June 1793, maréchal des logis 19 January 1799, maréchal des logis-chef 2 May 1799, in the same regiment when it became the 1st Cuirassiers 10 October 1801, adjutant NCO 7 December 1802, sub-lieutenant 5 March 1803, commissioned 11 April 1803, lieutenant by choice of the corps 28 September 1806, adjutant-major 23 February 1807.

He was captain 20 August 1808, wounded at Wagram 6 July 1809, died of his wounds in Vienna Hospital 10 August 1809. LH CH 18 December 1803.

FONTANEAU (François, 1792-?): born in Ardilleux (Deux-Sèvres) on 14 May 1792. Pupil at the school in Saint-Germain 20 April 1810, sub-lieutenant in the 14th Cuirassiers 30 January 1813, blocked inside Hamburg 1813.

FONTIGNY see **GAGELIN de FONTIGNY**.

FORCEVILLE (Julien Alphonse Joseph, 1791-?): born in Lille (Nord) on 22 October 1791. Velite in the Dragoons of the Guard 20 July 1809, lance wound to his right hand near Moscow 17 September 1812, sub-lieutenant in the 12th Cuirassiers 13 March 1813, incorporated with his squadron into the 3rd Provisional Heavy Cavalry in Hamburg 11 September 1813.

He returned with the garrison May 1814, dismissed with the corps 10 December 1815.

FORCEVILLE (Pierre Michel, 1774-1815): born in Ainville (Oise) on 4 July 1774. In the 7th Cavalry 26 January 1794, brigadier 21 April 1802, in the same regiment when it became the 7th Cuirassiers 23 December 1802, maréchal des logis 4 February 1806, maréchal des logis-chef 1 May 1809, adjutant-NCO 16 October 1811, sub-lieutenant 4 March 1812, bayonet wound and his breastplate broken by a shot at the Berezina 28 November 1812, left with his squadron for Hamburg 17 July 1813.

He was incorporated into the 2nd Provisional Heavy Cavalry in Hamburg 11 September 1813, returned with the garrison 30 May 1814, disappeared at Waterloo 18 June 1815. LH CH 18 August 1814.

FORCEVILLE see **MARCOTTE de FORCEVILLE**

FORGEOT (Etienne, 1787-?): born in Occy (Haute-Marne) on 28 January 1787. In the 6th Cuirassiers 14 March 1807, brigadier 16 March 1809, maréchal des logis 17 October 1810, maréchal des logis-chef 26 February 1813, adjutant-NCO 25 October 1813, sub-lieutenant 22 December 1813,.

He was wounded and his horse killed under him at Waterloo 18 June 1815, dismissed 21 November 1815. LH CH 5 September 1813.

FORQUIGNON (Jean Nicolas, 1770-?): born in Haudicourt (Meuse) on 20 December 1770. In the 24th Cavalry 20 April 1793 which became the 23rd 4 June 1793, brigadier 20 April 1799, dismissed with the corps 23 December 1802 and incorporated into the 5th Cuirassiers 3 January 1803, maréchal des logis 1 January 1806, maréchal des logis-chef 20 January 1806, bayonet wound at Hoff 6 February 1807, sub-lieutenant 23 February 1807. He was lieutenant 15 May 1809, captain 12 August 1812, lance wound to his right arm at the Moskova 7 September 1812, wounded at Waterloo 18 June 1815, retired 23 December 1815. LH CH 5 November 1804.

FOULER DE RELINGUE (Albert Louis Emmanuel, count, 1769-1831): son of the Mayor of Lille and brother of an adjutant-general killed at Saint John of Acre, born in Lille (Pas-de-Calais) on 9 February 1769. Page to the King in the Petite Ecurie (small stables) 1 April 1786, replacement sub-lieutenant in the Navarre-Infanterie 12 September 1787.

Appointed 1 May 1788, in the same regiment

REGEVILLE de GAU (Charles Louis Joseph de, 1762-1841): born in the Chateau at Frégeville (Tarn) on 1 November 1762, substituted for his elder brother as a cadet in the Condé-Dragons 1774, sub-lieutenant 11 July 1779, captain 12 July 1781, replacement captain 24 May 1785, commanded the Montpellier Garde à Cheval 17 May 1790, captain in the 3rd Chasseurs à Cheval 20 January 1792, lieutenant-colonel in the 2nd Hussars 13 April 1792.

the first lieutenant-colonel and 8 officers keeping temporary command of the regiment August 1792, brigadier-general 15 May 1793, commanded the vanguard of the Pyrénées-Orientales, prisoner 3 September 1793 returned 1 November 1795 and retired to Montpellier where he put down an insurrection, in the 9th Military Division 1797, deputy for l'Hérault in the Cinq-Cents 14 April 1799, took an active part in 18 Brumaire, removing Lucien Bonaparte from his seat with two of his colleagues, deputy for l'Hérault in the Corps Legislatif 25 December 1799, major-general 28 March 1800, organised 25 Regiments for Italy, Inspector-General of Cavalry in the Army of Italy 3 November 1800, commanded the 9th Military Division 27 April 1801, retired with active service pay 1 July 1801, commanded a brigade (7th and 8th Cuirassiers) under Pully in the Army of Italy 20 September 1805, commanded the cavalry of the Army of Naples 1 February 1806, governor in Puoille, sent to the Grande Armée for misuse of authority 28 March 1807, discharged and put on the non-active list because of his friendship with Lucien Bonaparte 10 September 1807, active again 4 July 1814, in the 1st Military Division 17 March 1815, available 23 March 1815, entrusted with the inspection of the 25th Chasseurs à cheval 17 June 1815, commanded the cavalry of the 2nd Observation Corps of the Pyrénées-Orientales being formed, refused to carry out the order given by the Duke d'Angoulême to dismiss the cavalry he was in command of, removed from his command, Inspector-General of Cavalry for the Army of the Loire, retired 18 October 1815. LH CH 11 December 1803, C 14 June 1804, GO 27 December 1814.

13 April 1792. Having learnt during the night that four of his officers had gone over to the enemy, Charles Frégeville de Gau, Lieutenant-Colonel of the 2nd Hussars, resisted the incitation of Colonel Malzan and exhorted the regiment not to go over to the enemy. Being unable to prevent a hundred men from following their colonel, he had the rest of the regiment put in battle order and sounded the rally soon after, seeing thus most of the Hussars who had left with their colonel returning to him, limiting this particular act of emigration to the colonel alone.

when it became the 5th Infantry 1 January 1791, lieutenant 1 September 1791, captain 1 May 1792, aide de camp to General Pully 19 September 1792, commissioned 23 March 1793, deputy to the adjutant-generals Drouet and Mortier 16 March 1795, shot in the right foot at Schweinfurt 24 July 1796.

He was captain in the 19th Cavalry 16 March 1799, taken prisoner at Meinbischoffsheim near Mainz 16 May 1799, exchanged, squadron commander in the 21st Chasseurs à Cheval 20 November 1799, brigade commander of the 24th cavalry 26 October 1800, dismissed with the corps 10 October 1801 and became brigade commander of the 11th Cavalry 20 November 1801 which became the 11th Cuirassiers 24 September 1803, Equerry commanding the Empress's stables 1804.

He was brigadier-general in the 3rd cuirassiers Division 31 December 1806, joined his unit 1 February 1807, lance wound at Heilsberg 10 June 1810, commanded the 2nd Brigade (7th and 8th Cuirassiers) Espagne's division in the Army of Germany 1 January 1809, several sabre wounds and taken prisoner at Essling 22 May 1809, returned 22 July 1809, commanded the cavalry of the 8th Corps 11 August 1809, entrusted with forming the 21st Reserve Cavalry division of the Army of Spain 30 October 1809, commanded the 4th Brigade of the 3rd Dragoon division in Spain 27 January 1810, Equerry to the Emperor 12 February 1810, commanded the stables 17 April 1810, major-general 23 March 1814.

He was non-active May 1814, commanded a squadron of the 1st Company of the Musketeers 6 July 1814, confirmed major-general 29 July 1814, Equerry to the Emperor in the Army of Belgium June 1815, retired 9 September 1815.

LH C H 11 December 1803, O 14 June 1804, C 25 December 1805, GO 19 March 1815, Comte de Relingue l.p. 16 September 1808.

General Fouler de Relingue. (RR)

FOULON (Pierre, 1766 -) born in Bissey-la-Côte (Côte-d'Or) on 17 May 1766. In the Septimanie-Cavalerie 29 January 1795, incorporated into the Chamborant Hussars 17 March 1788, in the Royal-Etranger-Cavalerie 29 May 1789 which became the 7th Cavalry 1 January 1791, brigadier 2 May 1792, maréchal des logis 24 November 1793, maréchal des logis-chef

15 May 1794, sub-lieutenant by seniority 20 March 1802, appointment cancelled 24 April 1802, in the same regiment when it became the 7th Cuirassiers 23 December 1802.

He was made sub-lieutenant by governmental choice 30 December 1802, lieutenant 29 December 1806, wounded at Essling 21 May 1809, left with his retirement pay 23 March 1810. LH CH 13 August 1809.

FOUPERINE (?-1809): adjutant-NCO, two sabre wounds at Eylau 8 February 1807, sub-lieutenant in the 5th cuirassiers 23 February 1807.

He was lieutenant adjutant-major 25 May 1807, rank of captain 25 November 1809, died at Osterdorff in Hanover 1809.

FOUQUIER (Charles François Louis, 1770-?): born in Muille-Villette (Somme) on 12 June 1770. Trooper in the Septimanie Regiment 17 October 1787, incorporated into the Alsace Chasseurs 20 May 1788 which became the 1st Chasseurs à Cheval 1 January 1791, fourrier 4 March 1792, maréchal des logis-chef 11 July 1793, sub-lieutenant 7 May 1794, shot and wounded in the right shoulder at Altenkirchen 3 June 1796, prisoner by capitulation in Wurtzburg Citadel 21 August 1796, lieutenant 30 June 1799.

He was shot and wounded in the left thigh when with only his platoon he routed a whole squadron of Austrian dragoons at Wichtel 25 April 1800, captain by choice 28 December 1805, shot in the left thigh, took up his appointment 13 October 1808, aide de camp to General Desbarreaux 5 December 1809, in the 4th Chevau-Légers 19 April 1813, squadron commander in a provisional cuirassiers regiment in Hamburg 13 August 1813.

Appointed squadron commander in the 9th Cuirassiers 16 December 1813, wounded at Waterloo 18 June 1815, left with his retirement pay 16 November 1815. LH CH 1 October 1807.

FOUR (Hypolite, 1788-1813): born in Saint-Hypolite (Haut-Rhin) on 27 July 1788. Boarder

at the Ecole Speciale Militaire in Fontainebleau 12 November 1806, sub-lieutenant in the 32nd of the Line 11 April 1807.

He was leutenant 8 November 1809, in the suite of the 13th Cuirassiers 8 October 1811, left to join his unit 27 December 1811.

Appointed 16 January 1812, wounded in Spain 20 April 1813 and died of his wounds 23 April 1813 without knowing that his appointment as adjutant-major had been accepted 25 May 1813.

FOURNIER (Jean François, 1774-1812): born in Francastel (Oise) on 27 January 1774. In the 10th Cavalry 10 January 1794, brigadier 3 May 1800, fourrier 2 November 1802, in the same regiment when it became the 10th Cuirassiers 24 September 1803, maréchal des logis-chef 8 October 1806.

Wounded by a Biscayan shot in the back at Eylau 8 February 1807, sub-lieutenant 16 May 1809, killed at Winkovo 18 October 1812. LH CH 14 April 1807.

FOURNIER (Jean Pierre, 1787-?): born in Ardecourt-aux-Bois (Somme) on 17 December 1787. In the 12th Cuirassiers 10 March 1807, brigadier 13 June 1809, wounded at the Moskova 7 September 1812, maréchal des logis 30 January 1813, sub-lieutenant 14 May 1813, dismissed with the corps 10 December 1815.

FOURNIER (Joseph Léopold, 1790-1813): born in Lunéville (Meurthe) on 19 June 1790. Volunteer in the 12th Cuirassiers 23 October 1805, brigadier 1 March 1807, fourrier 1 March 1808, sabre wound in the face at Eckmühl 22 April 1809 and a Biscayan shot wound to his right hand at Essling 22 May 1809, maréchal des logis 4 June 1809, maréchal des logis-chef 16 August 1809, adjutant-NCO 21 April 1812, sub-lieutenant 31 August 1812.

Wounded by a shell burst to his forehead at the Moskova 7 September 1812, killed at Leipzig 18 October 1813.

FOURRIER (Henri, 1785-1812): born in Hesdin (Pas-de-Calais) on 13 August 1785. In the 19th Cavalry 23 September 1801, brigadier May 1802 incorporated into the 11th Cavalry 31 December 1802 which became the 11th Cuirassiers 24 September 1803, fourrier 7 October 1803, maréchal des logis 1 December 1806, maréchal des logis-chef 3 April 1807.

He was sub-lieutenant 3 June 1809, wounded by a cannonball hitting his leg at Essling 22 May 1809, wounded at the Moskova 7 September 1812, died of fever and his wounds 15 November 1812.

FOUX (Balthazard, 1769-?): born in Notre-Dame-des-Ermites (Switzerland) on 17 September 1769. In the Royal-Guyenne-Cavalerie 4 June 1789 which became the 23rd Cavalry 1 January 1791, sabre wound to his right arm at Neerwinden 18 March 17936, sabre wound to his chest in Famar Camp 23 May 1793, in the same regiment when it became the 22 Cavalry 4 June 1793, sub-lieutenant 17 December 1793, lieutenant 22 December 1801.

Dismissed with the corps 31 December 1802 and incorporated into the 18th Cavalry 25 March 1803 which became the 27th Dragoons 24 September 1803, captain adjutant-major in the 4th Swiss Regiment 12 November 1803, lieutenant in the 8th cuirassiers 25 July 1807, incorporated into the 3rd Provisional Heavy Cavalry in Spain 1808, returned to the corps with his squadron into the 8th Cuirassiers February 1811, captain in the suite 21 March 1812.

Wounded by a shot to the right of his chest which pierced his breastplate at Vauchamps 14 February 1814, dismissed with the corps 5 December 1815 and retired 11 December 1815.

FRANC (Joseph, 1772-?): born in Saumières (Gard) on 29 November 1772. In the 1st Gard Battalion 15 September 1792 which formed the 13th Half-Brigade, in the Garde Constitutionelle 2 February 1798, in the Garde du Directoire 21 April 1799 which became the Consular Guard, sabre wound to his head 5 May 1800, brigadier in the 8th Chasseurs à Cheval 3 September 1800, fourrier 30 December 1803, maréchal des logis 8 September 1805, maréchal des logis-chef 6 August 1807, sabre wound to his right thumb at la Piava 9 May 1809.

Wounded by a Biscayan shot in his left leg at Wagram 5 July 1809, adjutant 1809, sub-lieutenant 23 August 1809, lance wound to his left hand and his horse killed under him at the Moskova 7 September 1812, with 25 men captured an enemy position held by 80 Cossacks by charging the Prussian squadron which was supporting them three times April 1813, lieutenant 15 May 1813, wounded at Chemnitz 6 October 1813.

Franc was captain 22 December 1813, wounded at Hanau 30 October 1813, sabre wound to his right hand near Toulouse 6 April 1814, reti-

red 1814, put back in the 5th Cuirassiers 2 May 1815, instated 16 May 1815, on half-pay 31 August 1815. LH CH 18 June 1813.

FRANÇOIS (Jean Marie, 1785-?): born in Fontenay (Seine-et-Marne) on 4 September 1785. In the 6th Cuirassiers 10 February 1806, lance wound to his head at Heilsberg 10 June 1807, brigadier-fourrier 1 July 1807.

He was maréchal des logis 11 July 1807, maréchal des logis-chef 3 June 1809, adjudant-NCO 16 September 1809, sub-lieutenant 12 June 1813, resigned 1 December 1814.

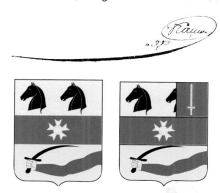

FRANCQ (Louis Bernard, baron, 1766-1818): born in Auxonne (Côte d'Or) on 25 August 1766. In the Chasseurs à cheval N° 5 27 August 1782 which became the Gévaudan Chasseurs 8 August 1784, brigadier 11 February 1785.

Francq was in the same regiment when it formed the Normandy Chasseurs à Cheval 17 March 1788 which then became the 11th Chasseurs à cheval 1 January 1791, brigadier-fourrier 25 March 1791, maréchal des logis 1 January 1793, maréchal des logis-chef 1 June 1793, sub-lieutenant 11 August 1793, shot and wounded in the left foot at Fleurus 26 June 1794, lieutenant 1 April 1800, first-lieutenant in the Chasseurs à Cheval of the Guard 26 October 1800.

He was captain 13 October 1802n squadron commander 18 December 1805 shot in his left foot at Wagram 6 July 1809, colonel in the Line 6 August 1809, colonel of the 10th Cuirassiers 10 August 1809, on retirement pay 21 May 1812, left 1 June 1812.

LH CH 14 June 1804, O 14 March 1806, Chevalier of the Empire l.p. 20 August 1808, Baron d. 15 August 1809 and l.p. 26 April 1810.

FRANKARD (Cornélius Joseph, 1781-1839): born in Soiron (Ourthe) on 4 November 1781. In the 6th Cavalry 17 September 1798, brigadier 26 September 1801, maréchal des logis 29 May 1802.

He was in the same regiment when it became the 6th Cuirassiers 23 December 1802, maréchal des logis-chef 1 October 1806.

He recaptured a cannon, several sabre wounds and taken prisoner after getting through three enemy lines with his platoon in order to open the way for a column of infantry at Moliette 21 January 1810, freed when Lerida was captured April 1810, sub-lieutenant 2 September 1812, in the Escadron Sacré during the retreat from Moscow November 1812, wounded at Waterloo 18 June 1815.

He was dismissed 21 November 1815, sub-lieutenant in the service of the Netherlands December 1815. LH CH 12 October 1811.

FRANQUEFORT (Paul Ulrich Aristide, ?-1812): born in Charente. Pupil in the school in Saint-Germain, brigadier, sub-lieutenant in the suite of the 5th Cuirassiers 24 April 1812, appointed 25 August 1812, killed at Smolensk 9 November 1812.

Senior officer wearing full dress. Composition by P. Benigni. (RR).

FREMEAUX (Nicolas, 1767-?): born in Mont-d'Origny (Aisne) on 2 January 1767. In the Artois-Cavalerie 6 January 1785 which became the 9th Cavalry 1 January 1791, fourrier 1 April 1793, maréchal des logis 10 May 1795, maréchal des logis-chef 10 July 1800, in the same regiment when it became the 9th Cuirassiers 24 September 1803.

He was adjutant NCO 21 January 1805, sub-lieutenant 30 October 186, wounded in Poland 23 April 1807, lieutenant 8 May 1807, adjutant-major 14 May 1809, rank of captain 14 November 1810, aide de camp to General Paultre his former colonel 25 September 1811, shot in the right hand at Winkovo 18 October 1812, non-active because of retirement of his general 28 June 1813.

Fremmeaux was temporary aide de camp to General Richter, put back into the 9th Cuirassiers 28 January 1814, non-active 1 February 1815, adjutant-major of the Aisne National Guard Chasseurs 30 May 1815, left non-active 10 December 1815. LH CH 14 April 1807.

FRERE (Jean Ferdinand, 1778-?): born in Paris (Seine) on 28 September 1778. In the 15th Chasseurs à Cheval 13 June 1793, in the 6th Dragoons 20 May 1798, shot and wounded in the left thigh at Kehl 1799, brigadier 27 March 1800, maréchal des logis 8 September 1800, in the Grenadiers à Cheval of the Imperial Guard 6 July 1806.

He was named brigadier 14 September 1806, maréchal des logis 16 February 1807, lieutenant in the 14th Cuirassiers 17 February 1811, adjutant-major 4 March 1812, cannonball wound to this left foot at Lepel 24 October 1812, rank of captain 4 September 1813.

He was madeprisoner, incorporated into the 10 Cuirassiers 6 August 1814, shot and wounded at Waterloo 18 June 1815, dismissed 25 December 1815.

LH CH 25 November 1807.

FRESIA (Maurice Ignace, Baron of Oglianco, 1746-1826): born in Saluces (Stura) on 1 August 1746. In the Turin Military School 25 October 1757, cornet in the King of Sardinia's Dragoons 17 April 1766, aide-major 27 April 1776, captain 7 August 1776.

He was named major 27 September 1787, lieutenant-colonel of the Chablais-Dragons 3 August 1790, colonel 15 March 1793, brigadier-general commanding the Chevau-Légers of the King of Sardinia 16 March 1796.

Fresia was assimilated as brigadier-general and commanded the Piedmont cavalry in the service of France 14 December 1798, commanded a brigade of dragoons in Hatry's division, with two weak squadrons took an Austrian regiment 5 April 1798, taken with Sérurier at Verdorio 28 April 1799, exchanged 20 May 1799, brigadier-general in the service of France 3 April 1802, commanded the Haute-Loire Department in the 19th Military Division

23 September 1802, organised the Legion du Midi at Montpellier June 1803, in the 18th Military Division 1804, CO of the 1st Brigade of the Division of Mermet Dragoons 11 September 1805, commanded the 2nd Brigade (4th and 6th Cuirassiers) of the 3rd Heavy Cavalry Division 18 October 1805, commanded the 2nd Brigade of the 1st Heavy Cavalry Division 18 March 1807, major-general 3 June 1807, commanded the Cavalry Division of the 8th Corps then that of the 2nd Observation Corps of the Gironde 6 December 1807.

Prisoner by capitulation at Baylen 22 July 1808, boarded at Cadiz 5 September 1808, landed in France 21 September 1808, commanded the 18th Military Division 28 October 1807, given a mission to Tuscany 4 April 1809, entrusted with the organisation a cavalry reserve in Verona 23 July 1809, commanded the 1st Dragoon Division in the Army of Italy 20 October 1809, commanded the 4th Division of the Kingdom of Italy end of 1809, temporary governor of Venice end of July 1810, CO of the 1st Division active in Italy 27 May 1812, commanding a cavalry division under Bertrand which became the 4th Corps Of the Grande Armée 27 February 1813, commanded the cavalry depots in Dresden 18 May 1813.

He was named military commandant of the Illyrian Provinces 17 July 1813, evacuated Trieste 27 September 1813, organised a reserve division in Genoa December 1813 given the defence of Genoa 1 February 1814, held the siege until 18 April, coming out with the honours of war and bringing back his troops to France, retired 24 December 1814, at the disposal of the Minister of War as Inspector-General of Cavalry 3 June 1815.

Retired 29 August 1815 and naturalised French 7 December 1815.

LH CH 11 December 1803, GO 14 June 1804, Baron d'Oglianco l.p. 7 June 1808.

FREUND (Jean Henri, 1776-1812): born in La Haye – den Haag - (Zuydersee) on 21 January 1776. Bodyguard in the service of Holland 6 May 1793, cadet in the 1st Dutch Cavalry 20 February 1795, sub-lieutenant 11 November 1799, lieutenant 28 June 1805, captain adjutant-major in the 2nd Dutch Cuirassiers 26 February 1807.

Back as captain in the same regiment when it became the 14th French Cuirassiers 18 August 1810, wounded at the Berezina 28 November 1812 and died at Tilsitt 12 December 1812.

FREUNDSTEIN
see **WALDNER de FREUNDSTEIN**

FRIBIS (Jean Baptiste, 1771-1809): born in Saint-Martin (Bas-Rhin) on 24 June 1771. Hussar in the Colonel-Général Regiment 28 May 1787 when it became the 5th Hussars 1 January 1791, brigadier 12 February 1792, maréchal des logis 20 March 1793.

He was sub-lieutenant in the 7th Hussars 20 April 1793 which became the 6th Hussars 4 June 1793, lieutenant 4 August 1794, captain in the Guard of the general in chief of the Army of Batavia 23 September 1799.

He was in General Murat's Guards in the Observation Army of the Midi 6 September 1801 then in that of Italy, captain of the Mont-Blanc Gendarmerie Company when the corps was dismissed 2 June 1804.

He was captain in the 1st Cuirassiers by exchanging with Captain Cousin 24 February 1805, left to join his unit, instated 29 March 1805, wounded at Hoff 6 February 1807 and at Eylau 8 February 1807, killed at Hollabrünn 9 June 1809. LH CH 14 April 1806

FRISSON (Louis, 1765-?): born in Saint-Martin (Seine-et-Marne) on 8 February 1795. In the 19th Cavalry Regiment 10 December 1793, brigadier 20 January 1799, fourrier 29 June 1799, maréchal des logis 3 September 1800, maréchal des logis-chef 21 January 1803.

He was dismissed with the regiment 31 December 1802 and incorporated into the 10th Cavalry 11 February 1803 which became the 10th Cuirassiers 24 September 1803, sub-lieutenant 16 May 189, shot and wounded in the right thigh at Essling 22 May 1809.

Frisson died 10 June 1812. LH CH 5 November 1804.

FROIDEFOND (?-1809): Velite in the Grenadiers à Cheval of the Guard, sub-lieutenant in the suite of the 12th Cuirassiers 25 March 1809, appointed 23 May 1809.

He was killed at Wagram 6 July 1809.

FROMAND (Claude Romain, 1784-1813): born in Viry (Jura) on 30 July 1784. In the 2nd Cuirassiers 18 May 1805, brigadier 20 November 1806, maréchal des logis 16 June 1809, sub-lieutenant 14 May 1813.

He was killed by a cannonball at Leipzig 18 October 1813. LH CH 11 October 1812.

FYARD de MERCEY (Charles Louis Catherine de, 1786-?): born in Vesoul (Haute-Saône) on 4 July 1786. In the 5th Cuirassiers 30 September 1805, brigadier 14 December 1805, maréchal des logis 1 May 186.

He was shot and wounded in the left leg at Eylau 8 February 1807, maréchal des logis-chef 9 February 1807, sub-lieutenant 15 May 1809, eight sabre wounds to his head, left arm and left thigh and taken prisoner at Essling 21 May 1809.

Escaped 6 July 1809, lieutenant 12 August 1812; lost the first knuckle of his right thumb during the retreat from Moscow 1812, incorporated with his squadron into the 2nd Provisional Heavy Cavalry in Hamburg 11 September 1813, returned with the garrison 30 May 1814.

He was dismissed 23 December 1815. LH CH 30 September 1814.

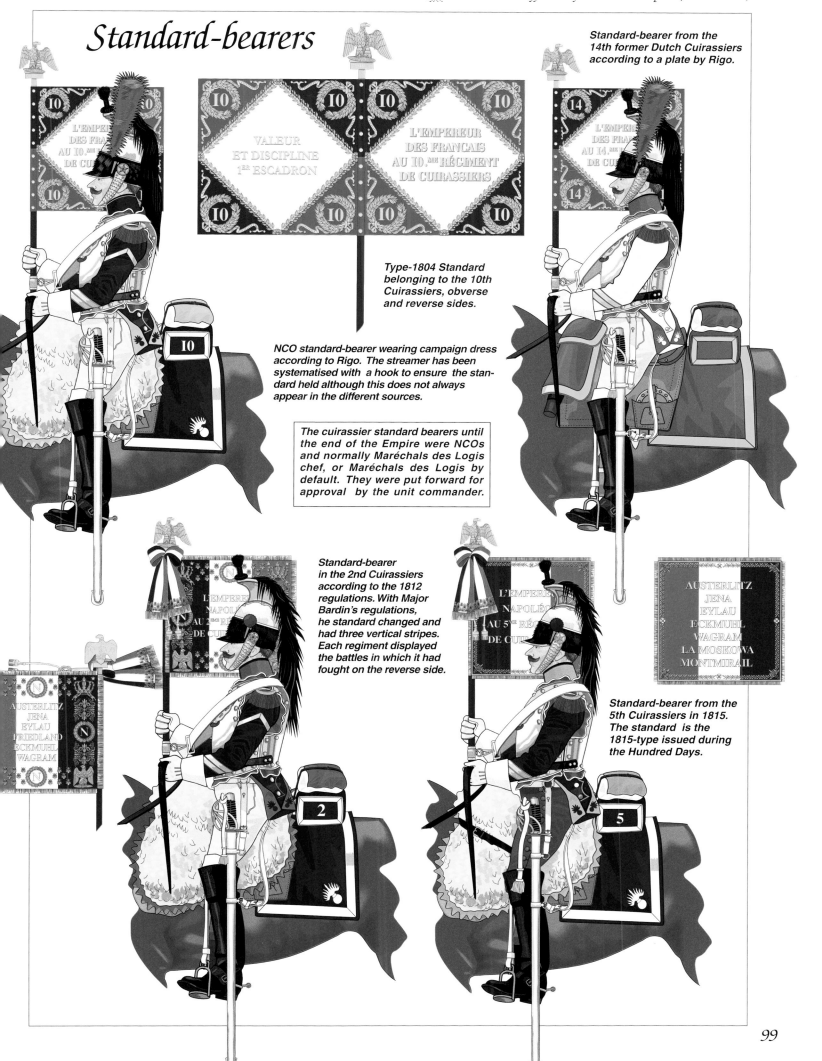

Standard-bearers

Type-1804 Standard belonging to the 10th Cuirassiers, obverse and reverse sides.

Standard-bearer from the 14th former Dutch Cuirassiers according to a plate by Rigo.

NCO standard-bearer wearing campaign dress according to Rigo. The streamer has been systematised with a hook to ensure the standard held although this does not always appear in the different sources.

The cuirassier standard bearers until the end of the Empire were NCOs and normally Maréchals des Logis chef, or Maréchals des Logis by default. They were put forward for approval by the unit commander.

Standard-bearer in the 2nd Cuirassiers according to the 1812 regulations. With Major Bardin's regulations, he standard changed and had three vertical stripes. Each regiment displayed the battles in which it had fought on the reverse side.

Standard-bearer from the 5th Cuirassiers in 1815. The standard is the 1815-type issued during the Hundred Days.

GACHET (Auguste, 1787-1812): born in Paris (Seine) on 16 June 1787. Engaged as a volunteer in the 9th Cuirassiers and reached the corps 20 August 1804, fourrier 4 December 1803.

He was maréchal des logis-chef 14 May 1809, having already had 3 horses killed under him, mounted a fourth so as not to abandon command of the platoon for which he had been made responsible at Wagram 6 July 1809, sub-lieutenant 11 March 1812. He was wounded near Moscow 22 September 1812 and died of his wounds at Vilna 6 December 1812.

At Wagram on 6 July 1809, Maréchal des logis Gachet of the 9th Cuirassiers having already had three horses killed under him mounted a fourth and returned to the fight in order not leave the command of the platoon which had been entrusted to him.

GACON (Philibert, 1784-?): born in Villeurbanne (Isère) on 24 March 1784. In the 11th Cuirassiers 31 May 1805, brigadier 1 December 1806.

He was maréchal des logis 16 April 1809, in the 13th Cuirassiers 1 February 1810, sub-lieutenant 28 August 1813, instated 6 November 1813.

Dismissed with the corps and incorporated into the 9th Cuirassiers 9 August 1814, non-active when the corps was dismissed 26 November 1815.

GADRAD (Gabriel Sylvestre, 1786-?): born in Boscamnant (Charente-Inférieure) on 31 December 1786, sub-lieutenant in the 8th Cuirassiers 8 July 1813, lieutenant adjutant-major 28 September 1813.

He was wounded at Hanau 30 October 1813, rank of captain 28 March 1815, wounded at les Quatre-Bras 16 June 1815, dismissed with the corps 5 December 1815 and non-active at home 11 December 1815. LH CH 23 September 1814.

GAGELIN de FONTIGNY (Michel Opportun Henri Marie, 1789-?): born in Bordeaux (Gironde) on 22 April 1789. Volunteered for the 1st Cuirassiers 28 February 1808, brigadier 1 May 1809, fourrier 11 March 1809, sabre wound to his head at Essling 22 May 1809.

He was maréchal des logis 15 January 1811, maréchal des logis-chef 5 September 1811, lance wound at Winkovo 18 October 1812, adjutant-NCO 12 September 1813, temporary sub-lieutenant in the 1st Provisional Cuirassiers in Hamburg 20 April 1814, non-active on half-pay 1 July 1814.

Confirmed sub-lieutenant on half-pay 13 November 1813, went home 1 December 1814.

GAGNEMAILLE (Jean Baptiste, 1765-1811): born in Brilleul (Ardennes) on 8 June 1765. In the Commissaire-Général-Cavalerie 13 November 1786 which became the 3rd Cavalry 1 January 1791.

He was brigadier 2 October 1792, sabre wound to his right arm at Famars Camp 23 May 1793, recaptured a canon and two caissons with 16 comrades at Landrecies 17 April 1794, maréchal des logis 23 April 1794, discharged for health reasons 11 November 1796, returned to service 19 July 1797, sabre wound in his back at Marengo 14 June 1800, sub-lieutenant 16 November 1800.

Gagnemaille was in the same regiment when it became the 3rd Cuirassiers 12 October 1802, lieutenant 12 March 1804, wounded at Friedland 14 June 1807, captain 6 September 1808, died 5 December 1811. LH CH 14 June 1804.

GAIDIOZ (Charles André, 1767-?): born in Bettonet (Mont-Blanc) on 17 February 1767. In the Volonatires Nationaux à Cheval from the Ecole Militaire aka the Dragons de la République 24 August 1792.

He was fourrier 7 February 1793, in the same regiment when it became the 25th Cavalry 7 February 1793, then the 24th Cavalry 4 June 1793, maréchal des logis 8 November 1797, adjutant-NCO 14 April 1798, dismissed with the corps 10 October 1810 and incorporated into the suite of the 1st Cuirassiers 1 January 1802, seconded to the Versailles riding School 22 March 1802, seconded to take part in the Louisiana Expedition 7 December 1802.

Returned to the 1st Cuirassiers 19 September 1803 after the expedition was cancelled, sub-lieutenant in the 9th Cuirassiers 15 December 1803, lieutenant 30 October 1806, allowed to retire 1 October 1809.

GAILLET (Jean Baptiste Louis, 1780-1812): born in Bar-le-Duc (Meuse) on 14 September 1780. In the 9th Chasseurs à Cheval 8 October 1798, brigadier 25 June 1800, maréchal des logis in the Gardes à cheval of the general in chief 23 October 1800, sub-lieutenant in the 2nd Cavalry 6 November 1800, rejoined his unit 29 May 1801.

He was confirmed 24 August 1801, in the same regiment when it became the 2nd Cuirassiers 12 October 1802, lieutenant 30 October 1809, captain 27 May 1809, wounded at Wagram 6 July 1809.

Orisoner and presumed dead in Russia 3 December 1812. LH CH 14 April 1807.

GALANT (Jean Baptiste, 1792-?): born in Espelette (Basses-Pyrénées) on 24 March 1792. Vélite in the Dragoons of the Imperial Guard 18 December 1809. He was sub-lieutenant in the 2nd Cuirassiers 13 March 1813, dismissed and left on half-pay 10 December 1815.

GALLANT (Jean, 1774-?): born in Ille (Marne) on 29 November 1774. In the 1st Marne Battalion 4 September 1791, in the 15th Cavalry 29 February 1794.

Charge by the 7th Cuirassier Regiment. Aquarelle by Lucien Rousselot. (RR)

He was shot and wounded in the shoulder at Kehl 4 September 1795, brigadier 7 November 1800, gendarme in the 14th legion, Marne Company 21 January 1803, brigadier in the 1st Legion of the Gendarmerie d'Espagne 10 June 1812.

Named sub-lieutenant in the 11th Cuirassiers 28 February 1813, standard-bearer 1 August 1814. LH CH 4 December 1813.

GALLIEE (?-?): maréchal des logis in the 9th Cuirassiers, sub-lieutenant 30 October 1806, lieutenant 8 May 1807, retired 18 May 1809, left 29 May 1809.

GARAND (Jean François, 1769-?): born in Bouligny (Meuse) on 28 August 1769. In the 23rd Cavalry 6 February 1794, shot and wounded in his left leg and his horse killed under him at Philisburg 12 November 1799, brigadier 23 April 1802. He was dismissed with the corps 23 December 1802 and incorporated into the 6th Cuirassiers 3 January 1803, fourrier 23 August 1804, maréchal des logis 1 July 1806, two lance wounds to his neck and lower lip at Heilsberg 10 June 1807, maréchal des logis-chef 1 July 1807.

He was sub-lieutenant 3 June 1809, wounded on the left part of his face and his horse killed under him at Essling 21 May 1809, lieutenant 12 June 1813, retired 21 November 1815. LH CH 8 October 1811.

GARAVAQUE (Antoine Laurent Marie, chevalier, 1778-1836): born in Marseilles (Bouches-du-Rhône) on 10 August 1778. In the 1st Battalion of the Volontaires des Bouches-du-Rhône 8 June 1793.

He was 1st class deputy in the Engineers 22 September 1794, lieutenant at the headquarters of the Army of Italy 24 November 1798, temporary captain 4 April 1799, deputy to Adjutant-General Bacciochi 19 July 1799, confirmed 10 February 1800, in the 6th Dragoons 12 December 1800, wounded at Hoff 6 February 1807, squadron commander in the 11th Dragoons 20 February 1807, major in the 10th Dragoons 18 October 1809.

He was kept in the corps which became the 5th Chevau-Légers 18 June 1811, colonel in the 14th Hussars 8 February 1813, taken prisoner after the capitulation at Dresden 11 November 1813, returned April 1814, in the suite of the 2nd Chasseurs à Cheval 18 November 1814, colonel in the 8th Cuirassiers 19 April 1815. Non-active 5 December 1815.

LH CH 5 November 1804, O 3 August 1813, Chevalier of the Empire l.p. 2 September 1810.

GARELLE (Antoine Marie Joseph, 1768-?): born in Paris (Seine) on 11 October 1768. Sub-lieutenant in the 2nd Cavalry 25 January 1792, instated 10 March 1792, lieutenant 7 May 1795, assigned to the Riding School 1799 to 1801.

He was, lieutenant adjutant-major 13 March 1802, confirmed 22 March 1802, in the same regiment when it became the 2nd Cuirassiers 12 October 1802, captain adjutant-major 9 September 1803, left to retire 5 October 1809, pensioned off 23 October 1809.

He was returned as a captain to the regiment 12 March 1812, joined the Gendarmerie 29 March 1812.

GARNIER (Claude Etienne Alexandre, 1786-1855): born in Montcey (Haute-Saône) on 8 December 1786. Volunteer in the 3rd Dragoons 18 November 1802, brigadier 13 December 1802, fourrier 1 June 1806, two sabre wounds to his head at Eylau 8 February 1807, maréchal des logis 12 June 1807, maréchal des logis-chef 14 June 1807, sabre wound to his wrist and taken prisoner near Lisbon 11 April 1811.

He was escaped 13 August 1811, sub-lieutenant in the 13th Chasseurs à Cheval 21 March 1812, second-lieutenant (Old Guard) in the Eclaireurs of the Guard 21 December 1813, first-lieutenant 2 April 1814, lieutenant adjutant-major in the 6th Cuirassiers 6 August 1814, dismissed 21 November 1815.

LH CH 27 October 1807.

GARNIER (Athanase, 1792-?): born in 1792. Maréchal des logis in the 3rd Gardes d'Honneur 1 May 1813.

He was put on lieutenant's half-pay 3 September 1814, sub-lieutenant in the 1st Cuirassiers 10 May 1815, non-active again 1 September 1815.

GARNIER (Pierre, 1770-?): born in Carpentras (Vaucluse) on 29 April 1770. Grenadier in the Ile-de-France Regiment 2 October 1788 which became the 39th of the Line 1 January 1791, gunner in the 5th Artillery 12 November 1793, shot and wounded in the left leg at Cholet 1794, dragoon in the 3rd Regiment 7 April 1796, sabre wound to his head and shot and wounded while taking a canon near Alexandria 10 March 1801.

He was brigadier 8 August 1802, maréchal des logis 6 December 1802, gendarme in the 24th Hérault Department Legion 9 November 1804, detached to Spain 1808, taken prisoner by capitulation at Baylen 23 July 1808, escaped from Spanish prisons with General Verdier 20 October 1808, brigadier 11 June 1809, in the 2nd Squadron of the Gendarmerie d'Espagne 25 December 1809, in the Legion of the Gendarmerie d'Espagne "Burgos" 16 December 1810.

He was maréchal des logis 1 March 1812, dismissed with the corps 27 February 1813, became lieutenant in the 8th Cuirassiers the following day 28 February 1813, no longer appears on the rolls 11 September 1814.

GASCARD (Pierre Auguste, 1786-?): born in Metz (Moselle) on 20 December 1786. In the 12th Cuirassiers 31 August 1805, fourrier 1 December 1806, maréchal des logis 6 April 1809, maréchal des logis-chef 16 May 1809, sub-lieutenant 21 March 1812, regimental paying officer, in the Cuirassiers du Roi 1 May 1814, rejoined his unit 4 May 1814, in the Musketeers 1 July 1814. LH CH 5 September 1813.

GASNES (Louis, 1773-1809): born in Valliers (Creuse) in 1773. In the 2nd Cavalry 1 July 1798, brigadier 22 November 1800, maréchal des logis 10 June 1802, in the same regiment when it became the 2nd Cuirassiers 12 October 1802.

He was adjutant sub-lieutenant 23 September 1804, sub-lieutenant in the suite 8 May 1807, took up his appointment 11 April 1809, lieutenant 14 May 1809, killed at Wagram 6 July 1807.

GASPARD (Charles Joseph, 1796-?): eldest son of an adjutant-commandant who had become an Inspector of Parades, born in Saint-Valéry (Somme) on 24 January 1796. Passed the entrance exam to, but not accepted at, the Ecole Polytechnique 28 August 1813, self-taught at his own expense in the depots of the 1st Hussars and 31st Chasseurs à Cheval for military training then riding in the suite of the depot of the 13th Cuirassiers.

He was sub-lieutenant in the 13th Cuirassiers 26 February 1814, incorporated into the 4th Cuirassiers 6 August 1814, assigned to the Ecole Royale de Saumur 7 March 1815, arrived 16 March 1815, dismissed from the corps 21 December 1815 and kept in Saumur until 1 June 1816 before entering the Cuirassiers d'Orléans 3 July 1816.

GASSE (Edme Charles, 1791-?): born in Paris (Seine) on 11 September 1791. In the 5th Cuirassiers 14 May 1811, brigadier-fourrier 7 June 1812, maréchal des logis-chef 1 February 1813, sub-lieutenant quartermaster and paying officer in the suite 27 January 1815, dismissed 23 December 1815.

GAU see **FREGEVILLE de GAU**

GAUDINOT (François, 1778-?): born in Nevers (Nièvre) on 3 July 1778. In the 16th Cavalry Regiment 3 May 1798, in the Grenadiers à Cheval of the Guard 23 April 1801, fourrier 15 October 1805, maréchal des logis 29 September 1805, maréchal des logis-chef 22 December 1805, second-lieutenant 16 February 1807, first-lieutenant 6 December 1811, captain (Old

Seal belonging to the 5th Cuirassier Regiment.
(Author's collection)

101

Guard), paying officer in the Eclaireurs of the Imperial Guard 21 December 1813, non-active on half-pay of a squadron commander 22 July 1814, left 1 September 1814, squadron commander in the 6th Cuirassiers 25 April 1815, in the 3rd Cuirassiers 19 May 1815, instated 23 May 1815, non-active again 1 September 1815. LH CH 14 March 1806.

GAULTHIER (Pierre Arsène, 1781-?): born in Saint-Dizier (Haute-Marne) on 18 November 1781. In the 6th Cavalry 9 June 1802.

He was fourrier 4 August 1802, in the same regiment when it became the 6th Cuirassiers 23 December 1802, maréchal des logis 5 February 1805, sub-lieutenant 25 June 1807, seconded to the Riding School from 1807 to 1809, lieutenant 12 October 1811.

Six lance wounds to his behind, hip and left cheek, right arm and chest and also taken prisoner at Winkovo 18 October 1812, returned 24 December 1814, captain on half-pay 27 February 1815, active again 30 April 1815, half-pay again 29 August 1815.

GAUTHIER (?-1807): resigned as sub-lieutenant from the 10th Dragoons, sub-lieutenant in the 6th Cuirassiers, rejoined the war squadrons 2 May 1807, killed at Heilsberg 10 June 1807.

GAUTRON (Jean Louis, 1776-1809): born in Luzarche (Seine-et-Oise) on 24 October 1773. Child of the regiment taken in by the Royal-Roussillon-Cavalerie 23 September 1791 which became the 11th Cavalry 1 January 1791.

Engaged as a trooper 24 October 1792, brigadier 15 August 1800, maréchal des logis 22 November 1801, maréchal des logis-chef 12 October 1802, in the same regiment when it became the 11th Cuirassiers 24 September 1803, elected sub-lieutenant 2 April 1805, lieutenant 3 April 1807, killed at Essling 21 May 1809.

GAUTRON (Laurent, 1780-?): born in Clermont-Ferrand (Puy-de-Dôme) on 14 August 1780. Child of the regiment taken on by the Royal-Roussillon-Cavalerie 8 July 1785 which became the 11th Cavalry 1 January 1791, brigadier 30 January 1802.

He was brigadier-fourrier 8 January 1803, in the same regiment when it became the 11th Cuirassiers 24 September 1803, maréchal des logis 1 December 1806, wounded by a Biscayan shot to his right shoulder at Eylau 8 February 1807, maréchal des logis-chef 25 May 1807, sub-lieutenant 15 October 1809.

Named lieutenant 9 February 1813, dismissed with the corps 16 December 1815. LH CH 4 December 1813.

GAVORY (Germain François, 1762-?): born in Rebreuville (Pas-de-Calais) on 15 February 1762. In the Royal-Cavalerie 5 July 1781 which became the 2nd Cavalry 1 January 1791, brigadier 26 June 1792, maréchal des logis 1 April 1793, sub-lieutenant 18 March 1795, elected lieutenant 22 March 1802, in the same regiment when it became the 2nd Cuirassiers 12 October 1802, captain in the

3rd Cuirassiers 6 September 1808, instated 1 October 1808, wounded at Eckmühl 22 April 1809, retired 11 July 1811.

GENIN (François, 1766-?): born in Nouville (Vosges) on 10 July 1760. In the Royal-Cavalerie 26 September 1784.

He was brigadier 9 September 1787, in the same regiment when it became the 2nd Cavalry 1 January 1791, brigadier-fourrier 21 March 1791, maréchal des logis 15 September 1791, maréchal des logis-chef 1 June 1792, adjutant-NCO 4 January 1793.

He was sub-lieutenant 1 April 1793, lieutenant quartermaster –treasurer 28 November 1793, rank of captain 27 July 1794, in the same regiment when it became the 2nd Cuirassiers 12 October 1802, retired 22 January 1808, left 31 May 1808.

GENOT (Nicolas, 1778-?): born in Longueville (Moselle) on 18 August 1778. In the 6th Cavalry 16 October 1798, brigadier 9 December 1801, maréchal des logis.

He was in the same regiment when it became the 6th Cuirassiers 23 December 1802, maréchal des logis-chef 25 March 1807, sub-lieutenant 12 September 1809, lieutenant 15 March 1812, captain 3 September 1813, dismissed 21 November 1815. LH CH 5 September 1813.

GEORGES (Amant, 1762-?): brother of the following, born in Mousson-sur-Meuse (Ardennes) on 3 May 1762. In the Royal-Guyenne-Cavalerie 18 June 1781, brigadier 1 March 1785, in the same regiment when it became the 23rd Cavalry 1 January 1791, maréchal des logis 20 May 1792.

He was maréchal des logis-chef 1 April 1793, in the same regiment when it became the 22nd Cavalry 4 June 1793, taken prisoner 2 November 1793, sub-lieutenant during his captivity 18 August 1795, returned 23 October 1795, lieutenant 21 April 1801, dismissed with the corps 31 December 1802 and incorporated into the 2nd Carabiniers as a supernumerary 10 February 1803, in the 4th Cuirassiers 6 April 1803,.

Captain 27 October 1808, left in order to retire 23 May 1810.

GEORGES (Jean Baptiste Auguste, 1770-?): brother of the above, born in Mousson-sur-Meuse (Ardennes) on 25 February 1770. In the 22nd Cavalry where his brother was maréchal des logis-chef 23 December 1793, sabre wound to his neck 11 May 1794, gendarme in the 16th Legion 22 January 1797.

He was brigadier 5 February 1800, shot and wounded in the left shoulder in Spain 19 May 1810, brigadier-chef 8 December 1810, maréchal des logis 25 December 1810.

Lieutenant in the 11th Cuirassiers 28 February 1813, incorporated with his squadron into the 3rd Provisional Heavy Cavalry in Hamburg 11 September 1813.

Returned with the garrison May 1814, dismissed with the corps 16 December 1815.

GEORGES see **SAINT-GEORGES**

GERARD (Charles, 1771-1809): born in Cernay (Marne) on 26 September 1771. In the 1st Cavalry 7 February 1794, brigadier 14 May 1799, in the same regiment when it became the 1st Cuirassiers 10 October 1801, fourrier 20 June 1802, maréchal des logis 13 August 1803, maréchal des logis-chef 6 January 1806, adjutant-NCO 8 January 1806, sub-lieutenant 24 November 1806.

He was wounded at Eylau 8 February 1807, lieutenant 25 May 1807, captain adjutant-major 16 May 1809, wounded in the advanced posts 9 July 1809 and died from his wounds in Strausdorf in Austria 3 September 1809. LH CH 14 April 1807.

GERARD (Charles, 1772-?): born in Perthes (Haute-Marne) on 18 October 1772. In the 1st Vosges Battalion 11 May 1793, in the 4th Cavalry 24 February 1794, brigadier 21 April 1800, wounded before 1802, fourrier 9 April 1802, in the same regiment when it became the 4th Cuirassiers 12 October 1802.

He was maréchal des logis 17 April 1806, maréchal des logis-chef 4 July 1809, sub-lieutenant in the suite 8 October 1811, appointed to the 3rd Cuirassiers 21 February 1812, instated 1 May 1812.

Named lieutenant 14 May 1813, wounded at Leipzig 16 October 1813 and taken prisoner 18 October 1813.

GERARD (Louis Gaspard, 1783-?): born in Jouy-le-Châtel (Seine-et-Marne) on 15 April 1783. In the 12th Cuirassiers 22 March 1804, fourrier 30 October 1806, sabre wound at Eckmühl 22 April 1809, maréchal des logis-chef 7 July 1809.

He was sub-lieutenant 11 September 1812, lieutenant 14 May 1813, wounded in the leg by a cannonball and his horse killed under him at Leipzig 16 October 1813, wounded at Waterloo 18 June 1815 and returned home.

GERARD (Michel Ambroise, 1773-?): son of General François Joseph Gérard, born in Merlot (Marne) on 13 August 1773. In the 23rd Cavalry 14 January 1795, brigadier 12 February 1801.

He was dismissed with the corps 23 December 1802 and incorporated into the 5th Cuirassiers 3 January 1803, maréchal des logis 10 October 1806, maréchal des logis-chef 25 May 1807.

Named as sub-lieutenant 8 July 1813, retired 23 December 1815. LH CH 14 April 1807.

GERBU (Antoine Sébastien, 1787-?): born in Paris (Seine) on 10 March 1787. In the 2nd cuirassiers 27 December 1802, brigadier-fourrier 23 September 1804, maréchal des logis 1 January 1806, shot and wounded at Smolensk 17 August 1812.

He was sub-lieutenant 4 September 1812, shot and wounded again at Smolensk 13 November 1812, bayonet wound at Dresden 27 August 1813, wounded at Troyes 25 February 1814, sabre and lance wounds at Fère-Champenoise

25 March 1814, left on half-pay 10 December 1815. LH CH 14 May 1815.

GERMAIN (Gaspard, 1788-?): born in Monthiers (Mont-Blanc) on 17 August 1788. In the 1st Piedmont Hussars 4 September 1800 which became the 26th French Chasseurs à Cheval 26 October 1801, bayonet wound to his chin at Austerlitz 2 December 1805, brigadier 8 November 1806, lance wound to his forehead at Liebstadt 24 January 1807, fourrier 15 May 1807, in the Chasseurs à Cheval of the Guard 15 July 1807, brigadier 18 January 1809, sabre wound to his right hand at Wagram 16 July 1809, maréchal des logis 7 May 1812.

He was second-lieutenant (Old Guard) in the 1st Eclaireurs 21 December 1813, non-active on half-pay 1814, in the 2nd Cuirassiers 26 April 1815, dismissed and non-active again 20 October 1815. LH CH 27 January 1814.

GESELSCHAP (Henri Louis, 1786-?): born in Wesel (Roer) on 10 March 1786. In the 2nd Batavian Light Dragoons 5 October 1805.

He was brigadier 9 December 1805, maréchal des logis 1 May 1806, in the same regiment when it became the 2nd Dutch Cavalry 14 July 1806 then the 2nd Dutch Cuirassiers 7 October 1807 and finally the 14th French Cuirassiers 18 August 1810, adjutant-NCO 11 September 1810.

Named as sub-lieutenant 4 March 1812, wounded at the Berezina 28 November 1812, stuck in Hamburg until the end of the siege May 1814.

GHILINI (Raymond, 1793-1812): born in Alexandria (Marengo) on 1 July 1790. One of the Emperor's pages, sub-lieutenant in the suite of the 12th Cuirassiers 14 July 1811.

He arrived in the depot 16 February 1811, on six weeks' leave to go to his family, equip himself and find a horse 26 February 1811, took up his appointment 25 February 1812, left at Vilna and disappeared 8 December 1812.

GIGNOUX (François André de, 1788-1812): born in Griningen (Ems-Occidental) on 6 December 1788.

Cadet in the Batavian Light Dragoons 4 January 1805, sub-lieutenant in the 2nd Dutch Cuirassiers 26 February 1807 which became the 14th French Cuirassiers 18 August 1810 confirmed 5 December 1810, lieutenant 4 March 1812, shot and killed by a bullet in the forehead at the Berezina 28 November 1812.

GIGNOUX (Samuel de, 1784-1812): born in Groningen (Ems-Occidental) on 18 November 1784. Cadet in the 1st Dutch Cavalry 1 November 1797, sub-lieutenant 4 December 1804, lieutenant in the 1st light Dragoons 26 February 1807, lieutenant in the 2nd Dutch Cuirassiers 29 September 1809 which became the 14th French Cuirassiers when the kingdom was annexed 18 August 1810, lieutenant adjutant-major 25 March

1811, captain commanding a company 4 March 1812, killed at the Berezina 27 November 1812.

GIHS (François Antoine, 1775-?): born in Molsheim (Bas-Rhin) on 9 March 1775. In the 19th Cavalry 3 June 1799, brigadier 22 March 1800, fourrier 14 August 1800, dismissed with the corps 31 December 1802 and incorporated into the 10th Cavalry 11 February 1803, maréchal des logis and maréchal des logis-chef on the same day 24 June 1803.

He was in the same regiment when it became the 10th Cuirassiers 24 September 1802, sub-lieutenant 16 May 1809, taken prisoner in Russia 26 December 1812 returned and non-active 30 December 1814, appointed to the regiment 24 February 1815, dismissed with the corps 25 December 1815.

GILET (Jean Charles, 1781-1813): born in Houille (Seine-et-Olse) on 11 October 1784. Vélite in the Grenadiers à Cheval of the Imperial Guard 8 January 1807, sub-lieutenant in the 4th Cuirassiers 3 July 1809, wounded when he drove off a column of enemy cavalry with only his platoon at Uezacz near Polotsk 24 October 1812, lieutenant 29 August 1813, wounded at Leipzig 16 October 1813, prisoner in the town hospital and died of his wounds 19 October 1813. LH CH 5 September 1813.

GILLARDIN (François, 1780-1812): born in Wittemont (Forêts) in January 1780. In the 2nd Chasseurs à Cheval 15 January 1799.

He was in the Grenadiers à cheval of the Guard

20 July 1802, brigadier 26 February 1806, maréchal des logis 19 May 1808, sub-lieutenant in the suite of the 2nd Cuirassiers 17 February 1811, titular 13 February 1812, wounded at the Moskova 7 September 1812, prisoner and presumed dead in Russia 3 December 1812.

GILLE (Jacques François, 1770-?): born in Paris (Seine) on 29 June 1770. In the chasseurs des Barrières de Paris 2 December 1789, dismissed 15 January 1792, in the Volontaires Nationaux à Cheval from the Ecole Militaire 13 September 1792 which formed the 26th Cavalry 21 February 1793 which in turn became the 25th Cavalry 4 June 1793, brigadier 13 September 1793, fourrier 5 March 1794.

He was maréchal des logis 16 November 1798, dismissed with the regiment 12 October 1802 and incorporated into the 4th Cuirassiers 24 November 1802, maréchal des logis-chef 7 March 1803, sub-lieutenant 27 April 1806, several sabre wounds to his head at Marienwerder 11 February 1807.

Named as lieutenant 25 June 1807, wounded and his horse killed under him at Essling 21 May 1809, captain 3 July 1809, wounded at Polotsk 24 October 1812, retired 19 November 1814. LH CH 8 October 1812.

GILLES (Nicolas, 1782-?): born in Villers-les-Mangiennes (Meuse) on 12 March 1782. In the 7th Cuirassiers 21 December 1803, brigadier 11 June 1807.

He was maréchal des logis 22 January 1811, sub-lieutenant 16 March 1814, on six months' leave 1 September 1814, non-active on half-pay 19 December 1815. LH CH 14 May 1813.

GILLES see **SAINT-GILLES**

GILLON (François Hyppolite, 1784-1813): born in Saint-Mihiel (Meuse) on 5 April 1784. Volunteer in the 12th Cuirassiers 25 April 1805, brigadier 1 December 1806, maréchal des logis 1 August 1807.

He was maréchal des logis-chef 14 May 1809, sub-lieutenant 9 August 1809, lieutenant 9 February 1813, wounded at Leipzig 18 October 1813 and died from his wounds 8 December 1813.

GILSON (Jacques de, 1766-1814): born in Melun (Seine-et-Oise) on 30 November 1766. In the Dragons d'Angoulême 12 May 1784 which became the 11th Dragoons 1 January 1791, dismissed by seniority 11 February 1792.

He was maréchal des logis in the Volontaires Nationaux à Cheval from the Ecole Militaire, sub-lieutenant in the same

Brigadier-General wearing full dress.
(Composition by P. Benigni. RR)

regiment when it formed the 26 Cavalry 21 February 1793 which became the 25th Cavalry 4 June 1793, confirmed 22 June 1793, commissioned 24 June 1793, lieutenant by seniority 19 July 1798, adjutant-major 23 March 1802, dismissed with the corps 12 October 1802 and became supernumerary in the suite of the 2nd Cuirassiers 23 November 1802.

He obtained the rank of captain adjutant-major in the suite 25 September 1803, took up his appointment in the 11th Cuirassiers 15 July 1804, left to join them 21 July 1804, shot and wounded through his thigh at Essling 22 May 1809, squadron commander 6 November 1811, in the 14th Cuirassiers 29 April 1813, left 5 May 1813, instated 14 May 1813.

He was wounded at Leipzig 18 October and died of his wounds at Mannheim 6 January 1814. LH CH 14 April 1807.

GIRARDIN (?-1807): maréchal des logis in the 3rd Cuirassiers, sub-lieutenant 30 October 1806, killed at Friedland 14 June 1807.

GIRARDIN (Georges Célestin François Xavier, 1783-?): born in Delle (Bas-Rhin) on 19 August 1783. In the 2nd Gardes d'Honneur 13 June 1813, dismissed with the corps 1 August 1814, cavalry sub-lieutenant 31 July 1814, in the 11th Cuirassiers 1 August 1814.

He was wounded at Les Quatre-Bras 16 June 1815, dismissed with the regiment.

Senior officer wearing campaign dress. Composition by P. Benigni. (RR)

GIRAUD (Georges, 1789-?): born in Paris (Seine) on 2 august 1789. In the 9th Cuirassiers 1 July 1807, brigadier 1 August 1807, fourrier 1 April 1808, maréchal des logis 16 February 1809, maréchal des logis-chef 9 July 1809, adjutant-NCO 11 March 1812, sub-lieutenant 1 August 1812.

He was wounded by a shell burst to his right arm and his horse killed under him at the Moskova 7 September 1812, several lance wounds and his horse killed under him and himself taken prisoner 24 May 1813, returned to France 10 September 1814, shot twice and wounded, his horse killed under him at Waterloo 18 June 1815, dismissed with the corps and left, non-active at the disposal of the government 26 November 1815.

GIRAUDEAU (Joseph, 1791-?): born in Cezilly (Allier) on 1 October 1791. In the Ecole Militaire de Cavalerie in Saint-Germain 15 October 1809, sub-lieutenant in the 9th Cuirassiers 30 January 1813, non-active when the regiment was dismissed 26 November 1815.

GIRAUDOT (Claude Sigisbert, 1771-?): born in Dammarie-sur-Saux (Meuse) on 7 December 1771. In the 24th Cavalry 1 June 1791 which became the 23rd Cavalry 4 June 1793, brigadier 30 December 1797.

He was brigadier-fourrier 29 April 1799, maréchal des logis-chef 15 December 1800, dismissed with the corps 23 December 1802 and incorporated into the 5th Cuirassiers 3 January 1803, elected sub-lieutenant 30 December 1805, lieutenant 3 April 1807, captain 17 May 1811, retired 27 July 1811. LH CH 5 November 1804.

GIROD de NOVILLARD (Charles Justin Casimir, chevalier, 1776-1824) : born in Besançon (Doubs) on 16 December 1776. In the 4th Hussars 19 July 1799, brigadier 30 January 1800, maréchal des logis 22 February 1800, adjutant 17 April 1800,

Sabre of Honour belonging to General Girod de Novilard. Private collection.
(Photo by Bernard Malvaux)

wounded three times of which one was a sabre blow to his head at Neresheim May 1800.

He was sub-lieutenant on the battlefield at Neuburg 27 June 1800, confirmed 13 August 1800, shot and wounded twice, sabre blow to his head and a Biscayan shot shattered his left leg while he captured several batteries at Hohenlinden 3 December 1800, lieutenant in the 24th Cavalry 19 September 1801, dismissed with the corps 10 October 1801 and incorporated into the suite of the 1st Cuirassiers when they were disbanded

Brevet for a Weapon of Honour awarded to Girod de Novilard by Bonaparte, at the time First Consul. (Author's collection)

Le 8ᵉ Cuirassiers 1786-1815

Sous-Lieutenant wearing town dress towards 1800-1803 according to a drawing by Commandant Bucquoy.

Junior officer mounted and wearing full dress around 1800-1803 according to a drawing by Commandant Bucquoy.

Captain mounted wearing full dress in around 1808.

Brigadier wearing going-out dress around 1806. The Cuirassiers returned to the coat with lapels which will be abandoned in 1809 because it was too fragile.

Lapels was unsuccessfully tried out – it wore out too quickly because it was in constant contact with the cuirass and the padding inside – they were re-tailored as overcoats.

Captain wearing town dress.

Trooper wearing a greatcoat.

1 January 1802, adjutant-major in the suite 11 February 1802, took up his appointment 7 June 1803, on three months' leave with pay 8 July 1803, rank of captain 10 August 1803, aide de camp to General Margaron his former colonel 13 September 1803.

He returned from leave 28 September 1803, left the 1st Cuirassiers to join his general 8 October 1803, bayonet wound at Austerlitz 2 December 1805, wounded in the chest when crossing the Lech 5 November 1806, squadron commander in the 21st Chasseurs à Cheval 16 January 1807, retired because of his wounds 25 August 1807. Holder of a Sabre of Honour 7 February 1803, LH CH by rights 24 September 1803, O 14 June 1804, Chevalier of the Empire l.p. 9 March 1810.

GISCARD (Guillaume Barthélémy, 1778-?): born in Saint-Geniès (Dordogne) on 3 April 1778. In the 8th Hussars 4 April 1799, in the 21st Chasseurs à Cheval 4 July 1802, brigadier 1 March 1806, maréchal des logis 10 May 1807, in the Grenadiers à Cheval of the Imperial Guard 19 July 1807, brigadier 19 May 1808, discharged for reasons of exhaustion due to the war 15 December 1808; once his health was better returned as maréchal des logis in the 13th Cuirassiers 2 March 1813, sub-lieutenant 27 March 1814.

He was dismissed with the corps and incorporated into the suite of the 9th Cuirassiers 9 August 1814, confirmed in the post 22 December 1814, took up his appointment 27 January 1815, in the Imperial Guard 28 April 1815, in the cavalry regiment of the Young Guard 25 May 1815 which became the 2nd Chasseurs à Cheval of the Guard (Young Guard) 27 May 1815.

Dismissed 16 October 1815.

GLACIER (Henri, 1774-?): born in Tours (Indre-et-Loire) on 15 September 1774. In the Indre-et-Loire Battalion 8 October 1791 which became the 33rd Half-Brigade then the 69th of the Line, wounded at Philisburg 8 October 1796, gendarme à pied in the Léman Department 24 May 1797.

He was gendarme à cheval 24 December 1797, in the 13th Squadron of the Gendarmerie d'Espagne 16 December 1809 which formed the 1st Legion "Burgos" 16 December 1810, dismissed with the corps 27 February 1813, sub-lieutenant in the 14th Cuirassiers 28 February 1813, lieutenant 22 December 1813, wounded at Troyes 25 February 1814, dismissed with the corps and incorporated into the 12th Cuirassiers 13 July 1814. He was dismissed with the regiment after the Belgian Campaign 1815. LH CH 25 February 1814.

GLAURON (Jean Claude, 1775-?): born in Bargville (Doubs) on 24 December 1775. In the 1st Haute-Saône Battalion 18 July 1792, left 25 July 1794, in the 1st Dragoons 4 February 1794, struck off the rolls as he was a prisoner of war 12 April 1799, returned to France, put in the 22nd Cavalry 24 June 1800, brigadier 21 April 1801.

He was maréchal des logis 20 February 1802, dismissed with the corps 31 December 1802 and incorporated into the 2nd Carabiniers 10 February 1803, maréchal des logis-chef 1 July 1806, adjutant-NCO 1 May 1807, sub-lieutenant 25 June 1807, confirmed 12 January 1808, lieutenant 8 October 1811.

Second-lieutenant in the Grenadiers à Cheval of the Imperial Guard 18 February 1812, first-lieutenant 20 November 1813, non-active 22 July 1814, returned to the corps 1815, non-active again 1 August 1815 and retired 24 November 1816.

 **GOBERT** (Armand Louis, baron, 1785-1816): born in Auteuil (Seine) on 5 June 1785. Volunteer in the 7th Hussars 14 June 1805, brigadier 5 November 1805, maréchal des logis 27 November 1805.

He was sub-lieutenant 19 April 1806, three sabre wounds at Steyer 4 November 1805, lieutenant January-February 1808, aide de camp to Murat 3 March 1808, captain of the velites of the Royal Neapolitan Guard 15 November 1808, squadron commander 25 January 1809, colonel 31 December 1809, captain of the Naples Gardes du Roi 21 January 1810, aide de camp 12 July 1812, wounded at Winkovo 27 October 1812, shot and wounded in the foot at Lowenberg 19 August 1812.

He was colonel of hussars in the service of France 5 March 1814, Colonel of the Berri Cuirassiers 9 September 1814, one month's leave on half-pay 20 January 1815, extended by one month still on half-pay 6 March 1815, returned to the same regiment when it became the 5th Cuirassiers again April 1815, wounded at Waterloo 18 June 1815, non-active 23 December 1815, died as a result of his wounds 21 February 1816.

LH CH 10 July 1810, O 5 December 18121, C 15 October 1813, Chevalier of the Empire l.p. 24 February 1809, Baron d. 3 April 1814 and confirmed l.p. 3 February 1815.

GOBERT (Jean Jacques, 1776-1814): born in Dontrin (Marne) on 30 January 1776. In the 7th Cavalry 22 June 1799, brigadier-fourrier 3 January 1802, in the same regiment when it became the 7th Cuirassiers 23 December 1802.

He was maréchal des logis 25 January 1806, maréchal des logis-chef 17 March 1806, adjutant-NCO 12 March 1807, sub-lieutenant 9 August 1809, lieutenant 19 November 1812, adjutant-major 17 July 1813, prisoner and disappeared at Neustadt 1 January 1814. LH CH 19 November 1812.

GOBIN (Jean Baptiste, 1783-?): born in Villevenard (Marne) on 20 June 1783. Conscript in the 8th Cuirassiers 25 February 1804, brigadier-fourrier 20 June 1805, shot and wounded in his right foot at Heilsberg 10 June 1807, maré-

chal des logis-chef 3 June 1809, adjutant-NCO 9 August 1809, sub-lieutenant 12 August 1812, wounded at Essling May 1809, bayonet wound to his right arm at the Moskova 7 September 1812.

He was incorporated with his squadron into the 2nd Provisional Heavy Cavalry in Hamburg 11 September 1813, temporary adjutant-major 20 April 1814, returned with the garrison 30 May 1814, in service in the 7th Cuirassiers 5 August 1814, non-active on half-pay 19 December 1815.

GODARD (François Joseph, 1795-?): born in the Vosges c. 1795. In the 3rd Gardes d'Honneur, commissioned as a cavalry sub-lieutenant 1 August 1814.

Godard was in the suite of the 11th Cuirassiers 4 February 1815, dismissed with the corps 16 December 1815.

GODDE de MONTHIERES (Augustin, 1789-1809): born in Abbeville (Somme) on 14 September 17898. Boarder in the Ecole Spéciale Militaire in Fontainebleau 17 December 1805.

He was sub-lieutenant in the suite of the 11th Cuirassiers 14 December 1806, took up his appointment 30 August 1808, instated 15 October 1808.

Lieutenant 16 May 1809, wounded then died on the evening of Essling 21 May 1809.

GODEBOUT (Henry, 1790-?): born in Le Havre (Seine-Inférieure) on 20 February 1790. In the 1st Carabiniers 18 June 1809.

He was gendarme in the 1st Escadron d'Espagne 19 December 1809, in the 1st Legion of the Gendarmerie à Cheval d'Espagne "Burgos" 15 December 1810, brigadier 30 January 1812, sub-lieutenant in the 14th Cuirassiers 1 March 1813, dismissed with the corps and incorporated into the 12th Cuirassiers 13 July 1814. Dismissed with the regiment 1815.

GOLDEMBERG (Frédéric, 1779-1809): born in Gundesblum (Mont-Tonnerre) on 10 January 1779. Sub-lieutenant in the Wolfrath Hussars in the service of Prussia, resigned when his country joined France, in the 2nd (French) Hussars 20 October 1798, brigadier, maréchal des logis.

He was sub-lieutenant in the Chasseurs à Cheval of the Francs du Nord 23 October 1800, wounded with a broken arm and taken prisoner at Hohenlinden 3 December 1800, still in the 2nd Hussars, rejoined them when he returned from captivity April 1801, discharged 26 June 1801, deputy on General Boivin's staff 10 June 1805, left 27 January 1806.

Goldemberg was in the Gendarmes d'Ordonnance 13 November 1806, maréchal des logis 24 December 1806.

Promoted meanwhile to sub-lieutenant in the 12th Cuirassiers 12 December 1806. He left 31 December 1806 and joined them 2 January 1808, wounded at Essling 22 May 1809 and died of his wounds 24 May 1809.

GONNEVILLE see **HARIVEL de GONNEVILLE**

GOSSE (François, 1773-?): born in Saint-Germain-en-Laye (Seine) on 6 January 1773. In the Paris National Guard and on the payroll 28 October 1789.

He was maréchal des logis in the 32nd Gendarmerie à Pied Division 2 November 1792, shot and wounded in the left arm at Fleurus 26 June 1794, in the 16th Légion Départementale of the Dyle 16 December 1797, brigadier in the provost's in Hanover 3 November 1802, in the 14th Squadron of Gendarmerie d'Espagne 1 January 1810, brigadier-chef in the 1st legion of Gendarmerie à Cheval d'Espagne "Burgos" 5 February 1812.

He was dismissed with the legion 27 February 1813 and went over to the 4th Cuirassiers 28 February 1813 as a sub-lieutenant, retired 21 December 1815.

GOUJON de LAREYNERIE (Charles Philibert, 1757-?): born in Paris (Seine) on 5 July 1757. Volunteer 30 April 1779, Gentleman-Cadet in the Colonel-Général-Cavalerie 6 April 1780, discharged during the 1788 reorganisation.

He was sub-lieutenant in the 7th Chasseurs à Cheval 15 September 1791, lieutenant 15 August 1793, captain 13 June 1795, resigned 13 October 1796, resignation accepted 6 November 1796, reinstated with his rank in the 21st Dragoons 22 January 1797, in the suite of the 7th Chasseurs à Cheval 26 February 1797, discharged because he was supernumerary 2 March 1798, active again 24 May 1798, sabre wound to his right hand at Modena 12 June 1799 and shot in the right knee at la Trebbia 18 June 1799, returned home and put in the suite of the corps 23 September 1800, back in his post in the 19th Cavalry 6 December 1801.

He was dismissed with the corps 31 December 1802 and incorporated into the 10th Cavalry which became the 10th Cuirassiers 24 September 1803, retired 9 August 1807.

GOUPIL de PREFELN (Alexandre, 1787-1815): born in Argentan (Orne) on 13 May 1787. In the Gendarmes d'Ordonnance 19 November 1806, brigadier 10 January 1807.

He was maréchal des logis 4 February 1807, dismissed with the corps 23 October 1807, lieutenant in the suite of the 4th Cuirassiers 18 February 1808, in service 4 March 1808, aide de camp to General César Berthier 6 December 1808, wounded and his horse killed under him at Wagram 6 July 1809, joined the 4th Cuirassiers 18 July 1809, confirmed 20 July 1809, captain 8 October 1811, lance wound to his thigh at the Drissa 11 August 1812, shot and wounded in the right shoulder at the Berezina 28 November 1812, four sabre

wounds and taken prisoner at Epinal 11 January 1814.

He returned to the regiment 29 April 1814 which became the Cuirassiers d'Angoulême 6 August 1814 only to become the 4th Cuirassiers again April 1815, killed at Waterloo 18 June 1815.

LH CH 25 September 1812, O 9 November 1814 and confirmed 11 April 1815.

GOUTTES (Jean François Louis Auguste, 1784-?): born in Revel (Haute-Garonne) on 12 February 1784. In the 11th Cuirassiers 3 November 1804, brigadier 27 January 1805, fourrier 2 April 1805, maréchal des logis 1 December 1806, shot and wounded in the right thigh at Eylau 8 February 1807, maréchal des logis-chef 27 May 1807, sub-lieutenant 16 May 1809, lieutenant 15 March 1812, captain 14 May 1813, dismissed with the corps 16 December 1815. LH CH 13 August 1809.

GOUVIGNAUX (Louis, 1788-?): born in Balant (Ardennes) on 17 November 1788. In the 9th Cuirassiers 19 July 1807, brigadier 16 September 1809.

He was maréchal des logis 1 September 1811, maréchal des logis-chef 1 February 1812, adjutant-NCO 1 March 1813, sub-lieutenant 21 April 1813, non-active when the corps was dismissed 26 November 1815.

GOUY (de, ?-?): second-lieutenant in the Gardes d'Honneur, in the suite of the 7th Cuirassiers, non-active as a sub-lieutenant 20 January 1815.

GRADY (Albert de, 1787-?): born in Liège (Ourthe) on 12 october 1787. Vélite in the Grenadiers à Cheval of the Guard 25 February 1807.

He was sub-lieutenant in the 6th Cuirassiers 17 December 1811, sabre wound to his head and two lance wounds to his right side and his horse killed under him at Leipzig 16 October 1812, lieutenant 22 December 1813, dismissed as a foreign national 21 November 1815. LH CH.

GRAMONT de CADE-ROUSSE (Marie Pierre Félix Isidor Emmanuel de, count, 1783-?): born in Paris (Seine) on 15 July 1783. Sub-lieutenant in the 5th Cuirassiers 30 March 1809, detached from Antwerp and sent to Spain August 1809, returned to France March 1810, chamberlain to the Emperor 21 December 1809, captain in the suite of the 10th Cuirassiers 25 November 1811, rejoined his unit December 1811, took up his appointment 25 February 1812.

He was squadron commander in the 5th Hussars 23 February 1813, left to join his unit 30 March 1813. Count of the Empire.

GRAMONT de VILLEMONTES (François Louis de, 1786-1812): born in Calignac (Lot-et-Garonne) on 4 May 1786. In the Gendarmes d'Ordonnance 4 December 1806, dismissed with the corps 23 October 1807 and incorporated into the Grenadiers à Cheval of the Imperial Guard 24 November 180.

He was sub-lieutenant in the Line 17 December 1811, in the suite of the 9th Cuirassiers 24 January 1812, took up his post 25 February 1812, cut in two by a cannonball at the Moskova 7 September 1812.

GRANDCOURT (Claude Pierre, 1768-?): born in Revigny (Meurthe) on 6 April 1768. In the Artois-Cavalerie 14 March 1786 which became the 9th Cavalry 1 January 1791, brigadier-fourrier 20 July 1793. He was maréchal des logis 12 September 1794, maréchal des logis-chef 8 May 1795, adjutant-NCO 23 October 1802, sub-lieutenant by seniority 18 August 1803, in the same regiment when it became the 9th Cuirassiers 24 September 1803.

Leutenant 30 October 1806, adjutant-major 8 May 1807, rank of captain 8 November 1808, captain commanding a company 14 May 1809, wounded Borisov 23 November 1812, retired 20 September 1813.

GRANDEAU (Jean François, 1777-1815): born in Dieulouard (Meurthe) on 7 November 1777. In the Mars School 30 April 1794, dismissed along with the school 3 December 1794.

He was in the 1st Carabiniers 14 October 1798, fourrier 7 February 1800, maréchal des logis-chef 22 December 1800, adjutant-NCO 24 October 1802, sub-lieutenant by governmental choice 17 February 1805, confirmed 24 March 1805, lieutenant 30 October 1806, captain in the 2nd Cuirassiers 2 April 1807, joined his unit 3 April 1807.

He was squadron commander in the 11th Cuirassiers 14 May 1813, wounded at Leipzig 18 October 1813, wounded and disappeared at Waterloo 18 June 1815. LH CH 1 October 1807, O 5 September 1813.

GRANDIDIER (Joseph Pierre, 1784-?): born in Paris (Seine) on 1 January 1784. In the 2nd Carabiniers 14 May 1805.

He was brigadier 29 April 1807, fourrier 1 January 1808, maréchal des logis 15 January 1808, maréchal des logis-chef 21 October 1808, sub-lieutenant in the 13th Cuirassiers 14 July 1813.

He was dismissed with the corps and incorporated into the 4th Cuirassiers 9 August 1814, dismissed 21 December 1815. LH CH 19 March 1815.

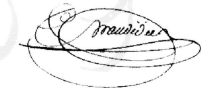

GRANDIDIER (Nicolas, 1776-?): born in Pont-à-Mousson (Meurthe) on 21 June 1776. Child of the regiment in the Artois-Cavalerie 29 July 1786 which became the 9th Cavalry 1 January 1791, enrolled 21 June 1792, brigadier 7 March 1803, in the same regiment when it became the 9th Cuirassiers 24 September 1803. He was maréchal des logis 1 May 1807, sub-lieutenant 14 May 1809, wounded at Wagram 6 July 1809, lieutenant 9 June 1812, taken prisoner near Kaluga 26 September 1812, returned to France 15 January 1815 left with his pension when the corps was disbanded 26 November 1815. LH CH 13 August 1809.

GRANDIN (Pierre, 1773-?): born in Biaché (Somme) in 1773. In the 2nd Cavalry 24 January 1799, brigadier 4 December 1802, in the same regiment when it became the 2nd Cuirassiers 12 October 1802, maréchal des logis 14 May 1809, in the 13th Cuirassiers 10 September 1811.

He was sub-lieutenant 26 February 1814, dismissed with the corps and incorporated into the Cuirassiers d'Angoulême 6 August 1814 which became the 4th Cuirassiers again April 1815, retired 21 December 1815. LH CH.

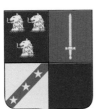

GRANDJEAN (Louis Stanislas François, baron, 1777-1821): born in Nancy (Meurthe) on 25 January 1777. In the 8th Dragoons 18 August 1794.

He was brigadier 9 December 1796, in the 3rd Cavalry 23 January 1799, maréchal des logis 5 February 1799, sub-lieutenant in the Guides à Cheval of the Army of Italy 8 February 1799, lieutenant in the 3rd Cavalry on the battlefield 20 April 1799, lance wound in the left leg at Cassano 27 April 1799.

promoted captain in the suite on the battlefield 30 May 1800, took up his appointment in the 15th Cavalry 23 October 1800 which became the 24th Dragoons 24 September 1803, in the Grenadiers à Cheval of the Imperial Guard 5 September 1805, bayonet wound to his left arm and his horse killed under him at Eylau 8 February 1807, squadron commander in the Dragoons of the Guard 8 July 1807, wounded by a Biscayan shot to his right leg and his horse killed under him at Medina del Rio Seco 14 July 1808, colonel of the 8th Cuirassiers 5 June 1809.

He was shot and wounded in the right shoulder in front of the Great Redoubt at the Moskova 7 September 1812.

He was retired because of his wounds 2 July 1813, at the General Cavalry Depot in Versailles 18 January 1814, colonel of the Queen's Cuirassiers 28 September 1814 which became the 2nd Cuirassiers April 1815, wounded by a Biscayan shot to his right shoulder at Waterloo 18 June 1815, returned home and put in for retirement 10 December 1815.

LH CH 14 March 1806, O 4 September 1808, Chevalier of the Empire l.p. 28 May 1809, Baron d. 15 August 1809 and l.p. 25 March 1810.

GRANDVAUX (François Bon, 1790-?): born in Poligny (Jura) on 12 December 1790. In the 5th Cuirassiers 30 November 1807, brigadier 22 May 1808. He was maréchal des logis 21 September 1808, maréchal des logis-chef 5 May 1813, sub-lieutenant 27 January 1815, non-active 23 December 1815.

GRENIER (Adrien Jean, 1782-1812): born in Angiens (Seine-Inférieure) in June 1782. In the 5th Cuirassiers 20 January 1804, brigadier 1 January 1806.

He was maréchal des logis 10 October 1806, maréchal des logis-chef 20 February 1807, sub-lieutenant 12 August 1812, taken prisoner 10 December 1812 and disappeared.

GRENIER (Benoît, 1761-?): born in Brioude (Haute-Loire) on 30 October 1761. Sub-lieutenant in the Legion of the Centre when it was created 31 May 1792, left 7 May 1793, cavalry captain aide de camp to General Mirabel in the Army of the Pyrénées Orientales December 1793, rank not accepted by the government, sent to the Ligurian Republic to form a corps of 150 men in order to make up a Gendarmerie unit October 1797.

He was captain in service and temporarily attached to the 7th bis Hussars 13 September 1798, captain in service in the 11th Cavalry 24 April 1802, in the same regiment when it became the 11th Cuirassiers 24 September 1803,.

Wounded at Austerlitz 2 December 1805, retired 24 November 1806.

GRENIER (Jean Claude, 1769-?): born in La Chaux (Doubs) in 1769. In the Roi-Cavalerie 23 November 1789 which became the 6th Cavalry 1 January 1791, in the Légion de Police Générale 28 July 1794, in the Grenadiers à Cheval of the Garde du Directoire 21 December 1796, incorporated as a brigadier in the Grenadiers à Cheval of the Consular Guard 3 January 1800.

He was maréchal des logis 24 June 1802, sub-lieutenant in the suite of the 9th Cuirassiers 30 August 1805, remained in the Grenadiers à Cheval for the 1805 Campaign only joining the Cuirassiers on 15 January 1806, took up his appointment 17 July 1806, put up for retirement 29 November 1807 and allowed to return home to wait for his pension 12 January 1808, pensioned-off 21 February 1808.

GRENIER (Pierre André Alexandre, 1797-?): born in Amiens (Somme) on 24 February 1797. Pupil at Saint-Cyr 25 August 1814.

He was sub-lieutenant in the 7th Cuirassiers 10 April 1815, reached the corps 2 May 1815, appointment cancelled and returned home 24 August 1815.

GRENU (Jean, 1788-?): born in Remilly (Moselle) on 19 June 1788. In the 10th Cuirassiers 16 June 1806, brigadier 9 July 1807, fourrier 16 September 1807.

He was maréchal des logis-chef 16 May 1809, sub-lieutenant 28 September 1813, 13 sabre and lance wounds at Hanau 29 October 1813, not mentioned on the rolls as of 6 August 1804.

GREZES SAINT LOUIS (Jacques, 1782-1814): born in Domme (Dordogne) on 15 January 1782. In General Augereau's guides 24 September 1797, brigadier 1 March 1798, fourrier 4 July 1798, incorporated into the 8th Hussars 7 September 1798, simple chasseur in the Chasseurs à Cheval of the Guard 19 February 1802, fourrier 15 October 1801, sub-lieutenant in the 22nd Chasseurs à Cheval 23 September 1805, wounded on the index finger of his right hand at Heilsberg 10 June 1807,.

He was aide de camp to General Bourdessoulle with rank of lieutenant in the 8th Cuirassiers April 1808, captain 9 August 1809, squadron commander in the 12th Cuirassiers 14 May 1813, killed near Brienne 2 February 1814. LH CH 30 June 1807.

GRILLOT (Nicolas, 1777-1810): born in Gray (Haute-Saône) on 1 May 1777. In the Grenadiers à Cheval of the Guard 6 May 1802, in the 5th Cuirassiers 23 April 1804.

He was brigadier 21 December 1805, maréchal des logis, wounded at Eylau 8 February 1807, adjutant-NCO 20 February 1807, sub-lieutenant 16 May 1809. Wounded at Wagram 6 July 1809, died of his wounds at Linz Hospital 20 April 1810.

GRIMAULT (Jacques Paul, 1771-?): born in Saint-Hilaire (Eure-et-Loir) on 25 March 1771. In the 4th Eure-et-Loir Battalion 12 February 1794, incorporated into the 60th Half-Brigade 28 February 1795.

He was shot and wounded in the right foot when crossing the Mincio 26 December 1800, in the 3rd Cavalry 10 July 1801, brigadier 29 December 1801, fourrier 3 September 1802, in the same regiment when it became the 3rd Cuirassiers 12 October 1802, maréchal des logis 31 July 1803, maréchal des logis-chef 20 July 1804, shot and wounded in the left hand at Essling 22 May 1809.

He was sub-lieutenant 3 June 1809, lieutenant 6 August 1813, taken prisoner and sent to Russia 1 January 1814, returned October 1814, retired 25 November 1815. LH CH 14 April 1807.

GRIMM (Pierre, 1779-1812): born in Breda (Deux-Nèthes) on 28 March 1779. Cadet in the 1st Batavian Cavalry 12 June 1795.

He was sub-lieutenant 12 May 1800, lieutenant 27 October 1806, with three other cuirassiers captured 14 Russians with their weapons and luggage at Friedland 14 June 1807, captain in the 2nd Dutch Cuirassiers 26 August 1809 which became the 14th French Cuirassiers 18 August 1810, disappeared at the Berezina 28 November 1812. LH CH 1 October 1807.

Pl. 202.

Troupes Françaises

A Paris chez Martinet, libraire rue du Coq. N°13 et15

CUIRASSIERS
Officier Supérieur
1. Régiment

GROGNET (Charles Emmanuel, 1792-?): born in Pont-de-Vaux (Ain) on 8 May 1792. In the Chasseurs à Pied of the Guard 27 August 1808, corporal in the 1st Tirailleurs of the Guard 5 September 1809.

He was sergeant 8 October 1810, discharged for illness 9 September 1811, sub-lieutenant of an Elite Company in the Ain National Guard 6 January 1814, lieutenant in the Damas Legion and dismissed 5 May 1814, enrolled as a volunteer in the 7th Cuirassiers 10 July 1814, sub-lieutenant 16 August 1814, assigned to the Saumur School 14 March 1815, absent when the 7th Cuirassiers were disbanded 19 December 1815, as still away on assignment.

GROOTEMAY (Pierre Johan van, 1764-?): born in Beesch on 17 October 1764. Cadet in the van Reftherm Regiment 1778, quartermaster 18 May 1785.

He was lieutenant of Dragoons 17 July 1787, retired with pension 5 August 1795, lieutenant in the King of Holland's Gendarmerie 26 February 1807, in the 2nd Dutch Cuirassiers 18 August 1809 which became the 14th French Cuirassiers 18 August 1810, left with pension 30 May 1811.

GROSSELIN (Robert, 1774-?): born in Vendresee (Ardennes) on 16 October 1774. In the 20th Cavalry 2 April 1793.

He was shot and wounded in the left leg at

GUERY (Didier Antoine, 1765-1825): born in Troyes (Aube) on 17 January 1765. In the Roi-Infanterie Regiment 8 February 1780, dismissed 31 January 1785, in the Chartres-Dragons 12 May 1785, brigadier 1 May 1787, maréchal des logis 1 January 1791, in the same corps when it became the 14th Dragoons on the same day sabre wound at Dammartin 20 September 1792, adjutant sub-lieutenant in the 21st Chasseurs à Cheval 16 February 1793.

He was lieutenant 1 June 1793, captain 14 August 1793, squadron commander 18 November 1793,

hurt his left shoulder when his horse was killed under him at Saint-Marck 28 September 1793, shot twice and wounded in his left shoulder and a shell burst to his thigh at Ypres 31 May 1794, discharged 22 September 1796, squadron commander in the 21st Dragoons 23 August 1797, dismissed with the corps and incorporated into the suite of the 2nd Dragoons 21 December 1797.

He mortally wounded the Russian general-major, Count Hiszel at Zurich 26 September 1799, in service in the 7th Cavalry 12 October 1800, joined them 2 November 1800, confirmed 8 February 1801, on convalescence leave for two months 14 June 1801, major in the 8th Cuirassiers 29 October 1803, left to join his unit 23 November 1803, commissioned

16 March 1804, commanded the 3rd Provisional Cuirassiers in the Army of Catalonia when it was formed 1808, colonel commanding the regiment 3 September 1808.

He was taken prisoner when his horse was killed under him at Mollit 21 January 1810, returned to France and retired because he allowed himself be surprised 19 June 1811. LH CH 25 May 1804.

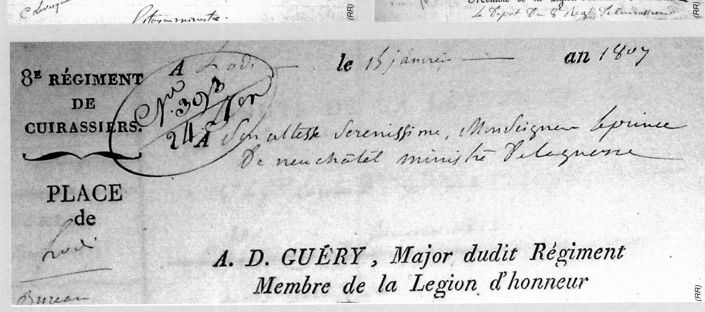

***Officer from the 12th Cuirassier Regiment.** (RR)*

Menin 26 April 1794, in the Grenadiers à Cheval of the Garde du Directoire 26 April 1797, brigadier in the Grenadiers à Cheval of the Consular Guard 3 January 1800, maréchal des logis 12 March 1801, maréchal des logis-chef 22 December 1805, shot and wounded in the back at Eylau 8 February 1807.

Second-lieutenant standard-bearer 16 February 1807, captain in the 1st Cuirassiers 23 October 1811, joined them 29 December 1811, lance wound at Winkovo, in the Cuirassiers du Roi 1 July 1814, remained in Paris non-active and at the disposal of the Minister of War 20 January 1815.

He was returned to the corps 1 April 1815, dismissed and put up for retirement 24 December 1815. Holder of a Sabre of Rifle of Honour 22 July 1800, LH CH by rights 24 September 1803 and 14 June 1804.

GROULT (Pierre, 1774-?): born in Monfiquet (Calvados) on 11 September 1774. In the 11th Cavalry 15 May 1794, brigadier 11 December 1799, brigadier-fourrier 25 December 1799.

He was maréchal des logis-chef 30 June 1802, in the same regiment when it became the 11th Cuirassiers 24 September 1803, sub-lieutenant 3 April 1807, lieutenant 25 May 1807, captain 6 November 1811, incorporated into the 3rd Provisional Heavy Cavalry in Hamburg 11 September 1813, returned to the regiment with the garrison May 1814, dismissed with the corps 16 December 1815. LH CH 14 April 1807.

GROUT de SAINT PAER (Léopold, 1784-1853): born in Cergy (Seine-et-Oise) on 4 September 1784. In the 5th cavalry 5 September 1802 which became the 5th Cuirassiers 23 December 1802, brigadier 21 January 1803.

He was brigadier-fourrier 24 October 1803, maréchal des logis 23 September 1804, shot and wounded in the left side at Austerlitz 2 December 1805, maréchal des logis-chef 4 February 1806, sub-lieutenant 23 February 1807, lieutenant 16 May 1809, retired 12 April 1810,

lieutenant under-adjutant-major in the 1st Gardes d'Honneur 14 June 1813, captain 11 September 1813, incorporated into the Royal Corps of the Chasseurs à Cheval de France 13 August 1814 which became the Chasseurs à Cheval of the Guard (Old Guard) 8 April 1815, at the disposal of the Minister of War the same day 8 April 1815.

He was squadron commander in the suite of the 5th Cuirassiers 1 May 1815, at the Duke of Angoulême's headquarters 19 August 1815, in the Hérault Dragoons 20 December 1815. LH CH 1 October 1807.

GUASCO (François Charles, 1784-?): born in Vauquemont (Meuse-Inférieure) on 8 December 1784. In the 12th Cuirassiers 13 May 1805, brigadier 1 March 1808, maréchal des logis 6 July 1809.

He was sub-lieutenant 30 August 1812, shot four times and wounded at Könnern 24 May 1813, incorporated with his squadron into the 3rd Provisional Heavy cavalry in Hamburg 3 July 1813, returned with the garrison May 1814, left as a foreign national 14 July 1814.

GUEDON (François, 1772-?): born in Lay-Saint-Christophe (Meurthe) in 1772. In the 11th Cavalry 2 February 1794, serious sabre wound to his head at Biberach 1797, sabre wound to his left hand and broke his left arm falling from his horse at Albano 1799, in the Grenadiers à Cheval of the Guard 3 May 1800, brigadier 1 August 1806, maréchal des logis 6 April 1811

Guedon was lieutenant in the 1st Cuirassiers 8 February 1813¹, joined his unit 29 March 1813, left with his squadron for Hamburg May 1813, incorporated with it into the 1st Provisional Heavy Cavalry 11 September 1813, returned with the garrison 27 May 1814, retired home on full pay 1 October 1814, returned to the 1st Cuirassiers 14 June 1815,.

He was non-active on half-pay 1 September 1815. LH CH 1 August 1805.

GUELTON (Albert Joseph, 1787-1839): born in Tournay (Jemmapes) on 29 May 178. Vélite in the Grenadier à Cheval of the Imperial Guard 7 March 1806.

He was sub-lieutenant in the suite of the 10th Cuirassiers 13 July 1807, in service 13 February 1812, lieutenant 9 February 1813, retired 1814. LH CH.

GUEPRATTE (Pierre, 1769-1834): born in Moivron (Moselle) on 23 July 1769. In the Royal-Cavalerie 27 October 1787 which became the 2nd Cavalry 1 January 1791, brigadier-fourrier 1 April 1793, maréchal des logis 21 March 1795, maréchal des logis-chef 9 June 1797, adjutant-NCO 22 November 1800, in the same regiment when it became the 2nd Cuirassiers 12 October 1802.

He was sub-lieutenant 24 December 1805, supernumerary lieutenant, lieutenant 1 October 1808, captain 28 December 1809, confirmed 25

January 1810, detached with his company to Hamburg and incorporated there into the 1st Provisional Heavy Cavalry 11 September 1813, returned with the garrison, wounded at Waterloo 18 June 1815, retired 10 December 1815. LH CH 14 June 1804.

GUERARD (Cyr Eugène, 1781-?): born in Montbard (Côte-d'Or) on 16 April 1781. Volunteer in the 8th Cavalry 1 January 1800, brigadier-fourrier 26 August 1800, in the same regiment when it became the 8th Cuirassiers 10 October 1801, maréchal des logis 6 May 1802.

Guerard was adjutant-NCO 1 April 1807, sabre wound to his head at Heilsberg 10 June 1807, detached to the 3rd Provisional Heavy Cavalry in Spain 1808, sub-lieutenant 3 July 1809, wounded at Barcelona 15 July 1810, returned to the 8th Cuirassiers February 1811.

Lieutenant 1 June 1812, wounded at Les Quatre-Bras 16 June 1815, dismissed with the regiment 1815. LH CH 1 October 1807.

GUERARD (Jean Nicolas, 1768-1808): born in Flyret (Meurthe) on 5 April 1768. Trooper in the Royal –Roussillon 16 February 1787 which became the 11th Cavalry 1 January 1791, brigadier-fourrier 1 October 1793.

He was maréchal des logis 19 August 1800, adjutant 2 November 1801, sub-lieutenant 30 June 1802, in the same regiment when it became the 11th Cuirassiers 24 September 1803, elected lieutenant 16 April 1804, wounded at Eylau 8 February 1807, captain 3 April 1807, died of illness 23 December 1808.

GUERARD (Nicolas François, 1754-?): born in Thiaucourt (Meurthe) on 11 September 1754. Trooper in the Royal-Roussillon 14 January 1772, brigadier 10 January 1780, fourrier-scribe (clerk) 21 September 1784.

He was maréchal des logis-chef 1 February 1787, in the same regiment when it became the 11th Cavalry 1 January 1791, sub-lieutenant 15 September 1791, lieutenant 1 December 1792, captain 28 October 1793, prisoner at Cholet 1793, in the same regiment when it became the 11th Cuirassiers 24 September 1803.

He was retired 24 November 1806.

GUERARD (Paul Sauveur, 1753-?): born in Bausset (Var) on 20 june 1753. In the Cuirassiers du Roy 24 March 1782. He was brigadier 1 January 1791, in the same regiment when it became the 8th Cavalry the same day, maréchal des logis 28 August 1793,

He was shot and wounded in the right hand near Bouin 17 April 1794, in the same regiment when it became the 8th Cuirassiers 10 October 1801, sub-lieutenant by seniority 1 June 1806, retired 25 March 1807. LH CH 5 November 1804.

GUERIN (?-?): sub-lieutenant In the 3rd Cuirassiers 14 May 1809, lieutenant 13 February 1812, wounded at the Moskova 7 September 1812 and retired 1814.

GUERIN (Charles, 1777-?): born in Orléans (Loiret) on 19 May 1777. In the 24th Cavalry 17 June 1799, incorporated into the 1st Cuirassiers 1 January 1802, brigadier 3 April 1803, maréchal des logis 10 June 1804, shot and wounded losing a finger at Eylau 8 February 1807, sub-lieutenant 16 May 1809, shot through the left foot at Essling 22 May 1809.

He was lieutenant 5 November 1811, lance wound to his head at Winkovo 128 October 1812 and shot in the left leg at Krasnoë 17 November 1812, remained in Paris at the disposal of the Minister of War 20 January 1815, returned to his regiment 1 April 18151, dismissed and put up for retirement 24 December 1815. LH CH 11 October 1812.

GUERY see **CHRISTOPHE de LAMOTTE GUERY**

GUICHARD (Jean François, 1760-1823): born in Prouilly-sur-Meuse (Ardennes) on 8 February 1760. Trooper in the Commissaire-Général Regiment 11 April 1780.

He was brigadier 24 August 1784, in the same regiment when it became the 3rd Cavalry 1 January 1791, maréchal des logis 15 August 1791, broke his shoulder when he fell from his horse during a charge at Cambrai 1793, sub-lieutenant 22 September 1796, lieutenant 29 August 1799, adjutant-major 13 March 1802,.

He was in the same regiment when it became the 3rd Cuirassiers 12 October 1802, captain adjutant-major 9 September 1803, retired 7 July 1809. LH CH 14 June 1804.

GUILBERT (Michel, 1781-?): born in Beaumesnil (Eure) on 14 November 1781. In the 9th Dragoons 11 February 1804, brigadier 15 August 1805, fourrier 1 January 1810, maréchal des logis 2 May 1812.

He was maréchal des logis-chef 9 March 1813, sub-lieutenant 14 July 1813, lance wound and his horse killed under him by a cannonball near Dresden 25 August 1813, in the Cuirassiers du Dauphin 8 September 1814 which became the 3rd Cuirassiers again April 1815.

Dismissed 25 November 1815.

GUILHON (Jacques, 1778-1813): born in Loriol (Drôme) on 14 July 1778. In the 11th Cavalry 30 June 1799, brigadier 31 May 1802, in the same regiment when it became the 11th Cuirassiers 24 September 1803.

He was maréchal des logis 28 January 1804, maréchal des logis-chef 25 June 1806, sub-lieutenant 16 May 1809, lieutenant 6 November 1811, captain 16 August 1813, wounded and taken prisoner at Leipzig 18 October 1813, died of his wounds 9 December 1813. LH CH 14 April 1807.

GUILLAUME (Henry, 1786-?): born in Chaumont (Haute-Marne) on 6 May 1786. In the Ecole Militaire in Fontainebleau 20 November 1802.

He was sub-lieutenant in the 82nd of the Line 10 January 1804, sub-lieutenant in the 14th Dragoons 27 June 1805, lance wound to his head at Heilsberg 10 June 1807, lieutenant 9 November 1808, shot through the leg at Medellin 28 March 1809.

He was captain 9 August 1809, squadron commander in the 7th Dragoons 24 March 1812, commanded the regiment in the battles of Bautzen and Leipzig and during the retreat of 1813, wounded and taken prisoner at La Rothière 1 February 1814, returned and put on the non-active list then in the 8th Cuirassiers 4 October 1814.

He was wounded at les Quatre-Bras 16 June 1815, sent home to await governmental orders concerning the disbanding of the corps 5 December 1815. LH CH 7 May 1810, O 9 October 1814.

GUILLEMAUX (Jean Nicolas, 1760-?): born in Pont-à-Mousson (Meurthe) on 5 December 1760. Trooper in the Royal-Champagne Regiment 9 November 1780, brigadier 2 June 1785.

He was maréchal des logis 1 January 1791, in the same regiment when it became the 20th Cavalry on the same day, maréchal des logis-chef 21 December 1792, sub-lieutenant 18 May 1793, in the same regiment when it became the 19th Cavalry 4 June 1793.

He was lieutenant 19 June 1799, dismissed with the corps 31 December 1802 and incorporated into the 9th Cavalry 15 February 1803 which became the 9th Cuirassiers 24 September 1803, wounded at Austerlitz 2 December 1805, captain 30 October 1806, retired 4 July 1808.

GUILLEMINOT (Charles Prudent, 1766-?) born in Clermont (Oise) on 22 October 1766. In the Volontaires Nationaux à cheval from the Ecole Militaire 26 August 1792, brigadier 1 February 1793, in the same regiment when it formed the 26th Cavalry 21 February 1793 which became the 25th cavalry 4 June 1793, maréchal des logis 5 July 1799.

He was maréchal des logis-chef 7 September 1799, incorporated into the 2nd Cuirassiers 23 November 1802, sub-lieutenant 3 April 1807, lieutenant 24 May 1809, wounded at Wagram 6 July 1809, commissioned 25 January 1810, captain 13 March 1812.

Retired 10 December 18151. LH CH 14 March 1806, O 29 September 1814.

GUILLEMY (Nicolas, 1772 - 1812) born in Bourbonne (Haute-Marne) on 25 October 1772.

In the 7th Cavalry 14 February 1794, sabre wound to his head at Courtrai 10 March 1794 and shot in the left thigh at Cassel 21 August 1796, brigadier 2 March 1801.

He was maréchal des logis 25 April 1802, in the same regiment when it became the 7th Cuirassiers 23 December 1802, maréchal des logis-chef 23 October 1804, adjutant-NCO 18 January 1807, sub-lieutenant 11 March 1807, lieutenant adjutant-major 3 June 1809, rank of captain 3 December 1810, captain in service 8 October 1811, cannon ball took off one of his legs, amputated and admitted to the hospital at Polotsk 18 October 1812.

Remained a prisoner at the hospital and never reappeared afterwards, probably deceased. LH CH 14 June 1804.

GUILLET (Aimé Joseph, 1784-?): born in Annecy (Mont-Blanc) on 15 September 1784. In the 11th Cuirassiers 22 June 1805, brigadier-fourrier 1 December 1806.

He was maréchal des logis 1 April 1808, adjutant- NCO 16 May 1809, sub-lieutenant 6 November 1811, wounded and taken prisoner at Toloschinn 21 November 1812, returned 8 September 1814, prolonged leave 18 February 1815 until 1 September 1815, active again as a captain 12 March 1815.

He was dismissed with the corps 16 December 1815. LH CH 16 June 1809.

GUINAND (Jean Alexandre Charles, 1787-?): born in Versailles (Seine-et-Oise) on 5 September 1787. In the 6th Cuirassiers 1 October 1806, brigadier 16 May 1807.

He was fourrier 1 July 1807, wounded in the right arm at Essling 22 May 1809, maréchal des logis-chef 3 June 1809, sub-lieutenant 22 June 1809, shot and wounded in the right cheek at Wagram 6 July 1809, incorporated with his squadron into the 2nd Provisional Heavy Cavalry in Hamburg 11 September 1813, returned with the garrison 30 May 1814.

He was dismissed 21 November 1815. LH CH 28 September 1814.

GUINECAGNE (Denis François, 1780-?): born in Villiers-sur-Marne (Seine-et-Oise) in 1780. In the 5th Cuirassiers 31 January 1803, bayonet wound to his left leg at Austerlitz 2 December 1805..

He was brigadier 10 October 1806, maréchal des logis 1 January 1807, detached with his company to the 2nd Provisional Heavy Cavalry in Spain December 1807, adjutant-NCO 16 July 1808, prisoner with the capitulation at Baylen 22 July 1808, escaped from the hulk "Vieille Castille" with his colonel 16 May 1810. Sub-lieutenant 21 February 1812, wounded at the Moskova 7 September 1812, retired 5 August 1813.

GUINET (François Louis, 1772-?): born in Hallois (Oise) on 1 April 1772. In the 2nd Oise Battalion 18 September 1791, sergeant 3 May 1793, sergeant-major 29 July 1795, chasseur in the 15th Chasseurs à Cheval 13 October 1799, brigadier 19 August 1800.

He was maréchal des logis 10 April 1803, in the Grenadiers à cheval of the Imperial Guard 20 September 1806, sub-lieutenant in the Line 4 April 1808, in the 10th Cuirassiers 23 April 1808, incorporated into the 2nd Provisional Heavy Cavalry in Spain, prisoner because of the capitulation at Baylen 22 July 1808, escaped from the hulks off Cadiz 15 May 1810, returned to the regiment 21 October 1810.

He was lieutenant 13 February 1812, captain 8 July 1813, incorporated with his squadron into the 3rd Provisional Heavy Cavalry in Hamburg 11 September 1813, returned with the garrison May 1814, shot and wounded in the right leg at Waterloo 18 June 1815, retired when the corps was dismissed 25 December 18151. LH CH 25 November 1807.

GUINOT (Philippe, 1774-?): born in Sauvoy (Meuse) on 13 May 1774. In the 7th Cavalry 17 June 1793 sabre wound to his left hand near Juliers 3 October 1794 and shot in the right leg near Weslau November 1795, in the same regiment when it became the 7th Cuirassiers 23 December 1802.

He was brigadier 12 February 1806, maréchal des logis 15 October 1806, maréchal des logis-chef 27 April 1808, sub-lieutenant 6 March 1813, retired 19 December 1815.

GUITON (Adrien Marie François, baron, 1761-1819): born in Corvolle-Lorgueilleux (Nièvre) on 8 June 1791.

He was in the Colonel-Général-Dragons 1 October 1779, dismissed 1 October 1787, in the Nièvre National Guard July 1789, captain in the 1st Ardennes Battalion 11 October 1791, in the Hussars of the Ardennes Legion 14 October 1792 which formed the 23rd Chasseurs à Cheval 10 September 1793, squadron commander 24 June 1794, in the Grenadiers à Cheval of the Consular Guard 2 December 1800, colonel of the 1st Cuirassiers 31 August 1803, brigadier-general 1 April 1807.

He commanded the 2nd Brigade (10th and 11th Cuirassiers) of the 2nd Cuirassier Division 12 April 1807, then the 1st Brigade (4th and 6th Cuirassiers) of the 3rd Cuirassier Division 25 August 1809, commanded the Ems-Occidental Department 22 December 1810, in the 31st Military Division 4 June 1811, in the General Cavalry Depot in Hanover 14 January 18121, commanded that in Berlin 20 March 1812, under Bourcier May 1812, in the Grande Armée end of 1812.

He was employed in Hamburg 1813, besieged there and commanded the brigade of the 3rd Provisional Cuirassier Regiment September 1813, left for France with the garrison at the end of the siege 27 May 1814, returned to France July 1814,

retired 24 December 1814, under Pajol at Orléans 25 March 1815, commanded the cavalry reserve of the Army of the Moselle then the 2nd Brigade (8th and 11th Cuirassiers) of the 11th Cavalry Division in the 3rd Cavalry Corps of the Army of Belgium 3 June 1815.

Wounded at Waterloo 18 June 1815, returned to Paris 25 June 1815, retired 1 August 1815.

LH CH 11 December 1803, O 15 June 1804, C 25 December 1805, Baron of the Empire l.p. 2 July 1808.

GUSLER (Pierre Georges, 1780-1847): born in Pont-à-Mousson (Meurthe) on 12 October 1780. Child of the regiment in the Royal-Allemand-Cavalerie 10 September 1787, in the same regiment when it became the 15th Cavalry 1 January 1791.

He was, incorporated as a trumpeter in the Kellermann Legion when the regiment deserted 1792, incorporated into the 7th Hussars 19 June 1794, taken prisoner 27 May 1799, returned, brigadier 22 December 1799, maréchal des logis 13 September 1800, maréchal des logis-chef 23 September 1801, adjutant-NCO 18 July 1802, sub-lieutenant 19 July 1803.

Lieutenant 8 May 1807, shot and wounded in the left shoulder at Deppen 8 June 1807, lieutenant adjutant-major in the 11th Cuirassiers 28 August 1807, rank of captain 28 February 1809, shot and wounded in the right arm at Essling 21 May 1809.

He was captain in service in a company 28 September 1809, squadron commander 6 November 1811, major 3 September 1813, shot in the back at Leipzig 18 October 1813, confirmed 28 September 1814, non-active as lieutenant-colonel 16 December 1815. LH CH 14 April 1807, O 28 November 1813.

GUYARD (Louis François, 1775-?): born in Meley (Maine-et-Loire) on 24 September 1775. In the 10th Cavalry 11 august 1791, brigadier 17 January 1799.

He was maréchal des logis 22 March 1802, in the same regiment when it became the 10th Cuirassiers 24 September 1803, sub-lieutenant 26 June 1807, lieutenant 3 June 1809, retired 7 August 1812. LH CH 16 June 1809.

GUYOT (Joseph, 1778-1809): born in Pierrefitte (Meuse) on 10 August 1778. 23rd Cavalry 22 September 1798, brigadier 24 August 1801, brigadier-fourrier 4 February 1802.

He was maréchal des logis-chef 20 February 1802, dismissed with the corps 23 December 1802, incorporated into the 5th Cuirassiers 3 January 1803, elected sub-lieutenant 24 October 1803.

He was lieutenant 24 November 1806, captain 25 May 1807, killed at Essling 22 May 1809.

Officer from the 7th or the 10th Cuirassier Regiment. Weiland Manuscript. *(RR)*

HABERT (Jean Baptiste Nicolas, 1774-1842): born in Nyon (Haute-Marne) on 27 October 1774. In the 4th Cavalry 6 January 1794, brigadier-fourrier 21 March 1795, maréchal des logis 30 January 1799

He was maréchal des logis-chef 21 April 1800, adjutant-NCO 26 April 1800, sub-lieutenant 5 June 1800, confirmed 12 December 1800, elected lieutenant 20 July 1802, in the same regiment when it became the 4th Cuirassiers 112 October 1802, confirmed 8 September 1803, at the Versailles riding school 24 October 1803, adjutant-major of the 6th Cuirassiers 11 April 1806.

He was replaced in the 4th Cuirassiers 20 July 1806, wounded by a bayonet in the lower abdomen and a lance in the right arm at Heilsberg 10 June 1807, captain commanding a company 6 October 1808, wounded in the foot by his horse which was killed under him, and captured at Essling 21 May 1809, squadron commander 12 September 1809, major in the 9th Cuirassiers 7 September 1812, regimental colonel 3 September 1813.

Wounded in the left foot and his horse killed under him by the same cannonball at Leipzig 16 October 1813, non-active 25 October 1814, colonel of the 4th Cuirassiers 8 May 18151, accepted 11 May 1815.

Non-active on half pay 21 December 1815. LH CH 1 June 1807, O 28 November 1813.

HAINGUERLOT (Edouard, 1794-1813): born in Versailles (Seine-et-Oise) on 19 January 1794. Boarding pupil at the Ecole Spéciale Militaire de Cavalerie 26 October 1811, entered 7 November 1811, Grenadier 6 September 1812.

He was sub-lieutenant in the 10th Cuirassiers 30 January 1813, killed at Hanau 29 October 1813.

HAMAIDE (Louis Joseph, 1785-?): born in Maestricht (Meuse-Inférieure) on 28 April 1785.

Volunteer in the 19th cavalry 9 August 1802, brigadier-fourrier 23 September 1802, dismissed with the corps 31 December 1802, maréchal des logis 25 January 1803.

Incorporated into the 10th cavalry 11 February 1803, in the 3rd Cuirassiers 19 September 1803, maréchal des logis-chef 3 December 1805, sub-lieutenant 12 March 1812.

He was wounded at the Moskova 7 September 1812 and in front of Moscow 8 October 1812, lieutenant 16 August 1813, adjutant-major 16 August 1814, dismissed 25 November 1815. LH CH 1 October 1807.

HAMEL (Jean Baptiste, 1774-1846): born in la Romagne (Ardennes) on 27 February 1774. In the 3rd Battalion of the Ardennes 15 September 1792, left 25 January 1794, in the 4th Cavalry 2 February 1794, brigadier 19 June 1797, maréchal des logis 18 September 1800, in the same regiment when it became the 4th Cuirassiers 12 October 1802, maréchal des logis-chef 1 May 1807, adjutant NCO 1 May 1809, sub-lieutenant 3 June 1809, wounded at Wagram 6 July 1809, supernumerary lieutenant 12 September 1809, in service 31 December 1810, captain 17 June 1812, retired 19 November 1812. LH CH 14 June 1804.

HANEUR (Louis Constant Armand, 1786-after 1824): born in La-Ferté-sous-Jouarre (Seine-et-Marne) on 24 May 1786. In the 1st Cuirassiers 25 June 1803, brigadier 1 October 1808, fourrier 15 May 1809, in the Grenadiers à Cheval o f the Guard 1 October 1809, in the 2nd Cuirassiers 8 August 1812, brigadier 22 October 1812, fourrier 29 January 1813, maréchal des logis-chef 14 May 1813, adjutant-NCO 3 September 1813, acting sub-lieutenant 28 March 1814.

He was confirmed sub-lieutenant and assigned to the suite of the Queen's Cuirassiers 4th February 1815, took up his appointment

2 February 1815, in the same regiment when it became the 2nd Cuirassiers in April 1815, dismissed on half pay 10 December 1815.

HANIN (Gervais, 1792-?): born in Joinville (Haute-Marne) on 17 February 1792. At the school in Saint-Germain 25 October 1809, grenadier 5 August 1811, sub-lieutenant in the 7th Cuirassiers 24 April 1812, rejoined 6 May 1812, left with his squadron for Hamburg 17 July 1813.

He was incorporated into the 2nd Provisional Heavy Cavalry in Hamburg 11 September 1813, returned with the garrison 30 May 1914, six-months' leave 1 September 1814, wounded at Waterloo 18 June 1815, dismissed with the corps 19 December 1815.

HANNE (Paul Auguste Amelin, 1795-?): born in Amel (Meuse) on 3 July 1795. At the Ecole Spéciale Impériale de Cavalerie in Saint-Germain 10 August 1812, sub-lieutenant 30 March 1814, rejoined the 7th Cuirassiers 15 May 1814 and confirmed 12 June 1814, non-active when the corps was dismissed 19 December 1815

HANNOTIN (Jean Joseph, 1786-?): born in Bar-le-Duc (Meuse) on 6 April 1786. In the 21st Dragoons 29 October 1803, wounded by a sabre blow to the right arm at Ulm in October 1805 and by a lance in the back at Eylau 8 February 1807.

Named brigadier 1 March 1808, shot in the right knee in Madrid 2 May 1808, maréchal des logis 12 September 1810, retired 14 March 1813, maréchal des logis in the Gardes d'Honneur 19 June 1813, second-lieutenant standard-bearer in the 8th Cuirassiers 25 August 1814,

He was replaced in April 1815 by a decision dated 3 March 1815 for drunkenness and unbecoming conduct, in the suite of the 4th Cuirassiers 16 May 1815, lieutenant commanding the 1st Auxiliary Team Company of the Meuse 31 May 1815, non-active 29 August 1815, left 30 August 1815.

HANSWYK (Guillaume Jean Amma van, 1788-?): born in Leuwarden (Holland) on 18 January 1788. Cadet in the 1st Batavian Dragoons 1 January 1805, sub-lieutenant in the 2nd Dutch Cuirassiers 26 February 1807, shot and wounded in the right shoulder at Friedland 14 June 1807, in the same regiment when it became the 14th French Cuirassiers 18 August 1810, lieutenant 9 February 1813, wounded and two horses killed under him at Leipzig 16 and 18 October 1813, left February 1814. LH CH 1 October 1807.

HARDY (Augustin, 1767-?): born in Auth (Ardennes) on 28 October 1767. In the Reine-Cavalerie 18 May 1788 which became the 4th Cavalry 1 January 1791, brigadier-fourrier 14 May 1792, maréchal des logis 1 August

ARIVEL de GONNEVILLE (Aymar Olivier le, 1783-1872): born in Caen (Calvados) on 9 October 1783.

Messenger in the Armée Royale de Normandie under Bruslart from 1794 to 1796, engaged in the 20th Chasseurs à Cheval 23 October 1804, brigadier in the Elite Company 23 January 1805, maréchal des logis 24 February 1805, sub-lieutenant in the 6th Cuirassiers 18 June 1805, shot and wounded above the right hip and taken prisoner when he charged a platoon of Black Hussars and a squadron of Prussian Dragoons with 23 men 3 February 1807, exchanged March 1807.

He was made lieutenant 5 April 1807, aide de camp to General Rioult d'Avenay 16 July 1807 then to General Caffarelli when Riuolt d'Avenay died 27 May 1809, captain in the 6th Cuirassiers 17 August 1810, disengaged a three-cannon battery at the head of a squadron, captured five others with their caissons and a general at Sagonte 25 October 1811, returned to France to fetch horses August 1812, in the 1st Cuirassiers 26 January 1813, returned after leave 23 April 1813, left with his squadron for Hamburg May 1813.

He was incorporated with the squadron into the 1st Provisional Heavy Cavalry 11 September 1813, squadron commander 20 April 1814, returned to France in the 1st Cuirassiers June 1814, in the suite of the same regiment when this became the Cuirassiers du Roi 10 July 1814.

He was nommed chief of staff to General Bruslart in the 23rd Military Division 27 August 1814, left to return to service 1 September 1814, resigned 7 May 1815, with the Cuirassiers de Condé N°6 29 November 1815.

LH CH 1 October 1807.

Aymar Harivel de Gonneville. *(RR).*

Sous-Lieutenant in the 6th Cuirassiers, Aymar Harivel de Gonneville was shot and wounded above his right hip and was taken prisoner when charging a platoon of Black Hussars and a squadron of Prussian Dragoons with 23 men on 3 February 1807. He was exchanged in March 1807 and made a Lieutenant on 5 April 1807.

1793, maréchal des logis-chef 27 June 1794, adjutant-NCO 6 July 1794, sub-lieutenant 6 April 1795, lieutenant by seniority 19 June 1799, in the same regiment when it became the 4th Cuirassiers 12 October 1802, elected captain 1 August 1806, wounded at Essling 21 May 1809, retired 23 May 1810.

HARDY (Jean, 1779-?): born in Plessy (Seine-et-Oise) on 19 November 1779. In the 3rd Cuirassiers 3 January 1804, fourrier 21 May 1804, maréchal des logis-chef 4 December 1805, sub-lieutenant 14 May 1809.

He was wounded by Biscayen shot in the left leg at Essling 22 May 1809, lieutenant 9 June 1812, in the Escadron Sacré during the retreat from Moscow December 1812, non-active and retired 25 November 1815. LH CH 1 October 1807.

HASTRON (François Isaac, 1787-?): born in Couché (Vienne) on 24 February 1787. In the 1st Cuirassiers 13 September 1807 and detached immediately to the 1st Provisional Heavy Cavalry in Spain, fourrier 1 January 1808, in the same regiment when it formed the 13th Cuirassiers 21 October 1808, maréchal des logis then adjutant-NCO 15 March 1812, sub-lieutenant 27 August 1813n admitted 6 November 1813, incorporated into the 9th Cuirassiers 9 August 1814, resigned 1 October 1815. LH CH 19 March 1815.

HATRY (Alexandre Jacques Christophe, 1778-?): born in Strasbourg (Bas-Rhin) on 25 September 1778. Aide de camp 9 January 1795, cavalry lieutenant 3 July 1796, aide de camp to his father 1 September 1796, captain in the 12th Cavalry 4 January 1798, in the suite of the 23rd Cavalry 1 February 1800, took up his appointment 18 April 1800, dismissed with the corps 23 December 1802 and incorporated

(Private collection.RR)

the 6th Chasseurs à Cheval 1 January 1791, captain 10 March 1792, lieutenant-colonel 15 August 1792, dismissed because he was a noble but then retained on the insistence of his own men, brigade commander 21 March 1794, acting brigadier-general in the Army of the North 3 April 1794. He commanded the vanguard of the light cavalry in the Army of the Ardennes 17 May 1794, in the Army of the Sambre-et-Meuse 2 July 1794, confirmed 13 June 1795, wounded by a shot in the right shoulder at Altenkirchen 4 June 1796.

He was major-general 10 October 1796, commander in chief of the heavy cavalry in the Army of the Sambre-et-Meuse 23 January 1797, in the « Armée d'Angleterre » 12 January 1798, commanded the 7th Division (Cavalry) in the Army of Mainz 29 July 1798, in the Army of the Danube 6 March 1799.

He was suspended after a complaint by Jourdan for disobedience and missing a charge at Stockach 30 April 1799, acquitted and brought back into service 27 July 1799. He commanded the cavalry reserve 25 September 1799, in the reserve corps 1 April 1800, Inspector-General of the Cavalry 24 July 1801, at the Compiègne Camp 30 August 1803.

He commanded the cavalry at the Saint-Omer Camp 17 November 1803, CO of the 2nd Cuirassier Division in the cavalry reserve of the Grande Armée 24 August 1805, drove in the Russian centre with a charge on the Pratzen Plateau at Austerlitz 2 December 1805, Senator 19 March 1806, in the same division in the 2nd Cavalry Corps 13

D'HAUTPOUL.

HAUTPOUL (Jean Joseph d', 1754-1807): born in the Chateau de Salette at Cahuzac-sur-Vèrre (Tarn) on 13 May 1754.

Volunteered for the Dragoons of the Dauphiné-Légion 14 September 1771, brigadier 1744, maréchal des logis and gentleman-cadet 24 November 1775. He was sub-lieutenant in the suite of the Languedoc Dragoons 29 December 1777 which became he Languedoc Chasseurs 17 March 1788, then

December 1806, then in the cavalry reserve 12 January 1807, wounded by a Biscayen shot which shattered his right thigh after he charged several times at Eylau 8 February 1807.

He died from his wounds in the chateau at Wozin between Eylau and Landsberg 14 February 1807. LH CH 11 December 1803, O 14 June 1804, GA 8 February 1806.

Inspection générale de Cavalerie.

N°. 22.

LIBERTÉ.

ÉGALITÉ.

Au Quartier-général à Besançon le 7 Ventose an 10 de la République française.

Le Général de Division d'Hautpoul,

Inspecteur-général de Cavalerie.

au Ministre de la Guerre.

béard Dutaillis
é de 27 ans offi^{er} au
Rég^t de Cuirass^{ers}
peint en 1810

(RR)

**Michel Héard,
Sous-Lieutenant in
the 8th Cuirassier
Regiment.**
*(Private collection,
photograph J.-L. Viau)*

Senior Cuirassier Officer.
(Aquarelle by Michel Pétard, RR)

117

OLLE (Nicolas, 1746-1807): born in Morinville (Moselle) on 25 February 1746. Trooper in the Artois Regiment 21 March 1759, brigadier 15 June 1758, maréchal des logis 1 January 1770, maréchal des logis-chef 1 September 1784.

He was nommed standard-bearer 24 April 1786, elected sub-lieutenant 1 January 1791, in the same regiment when it became the 9th Cavalry the same day, lieutenant 10 May 1792, held 600 Prussians at bay with a platoon of 30 men at Oberfloersheim 31 March 1792, captain the following day 1 April 1793.

Suspended because he was a former Chevalier of Saint-Louis 11 November 1793, reinstated 20 June 1794, in the same regiment when it became the 9th Cuirassiers 24 September 1803, on retirement pay 13 November 1805

He died at Lunéville 22 October 1807. LH CH 14 June 1804.

At Oberfloersheim, Lieutenant Nicolas Holle held 600 Prussians at bay with a platoon of thirty men. For this feat of arms he was promoted to captain the following morning, 1 April 1793.

into the 5th Cuirassiers 3 January 1803, squadron commander in the 7th Cuirassiers 10 November 1807, wounded at Essling 21 May 1809, left with retirement pay 9 June 1811, commanded the 8th Cohort 8 May 1812.

He was second-major in the cavalry 21 April 1813, in the suite of the 14th Dragoons 11 May 1815 but did not join them. LH CH 54 November 1804.

HAUTELIN (Guillaume Nicolas, 1774-?): born in Paris (Seine) on 30 October 1774. In the 25th Cavalry 21 February 1793 which became the 24th Cavalry 4 June 1793, in the Grenadiers à Cheval of the Garde du Directoire 10 December 1798, brigadier in the grenadiers à Cheval of the consular guard 3 January 1800, maréchal des logis 11 October 1802, sub-lieutenant in the suite of the 11th Cuirassiers 30 August 1805, took up his post 22 March 1806.

He received a sabre wound on his upper lip, a shot to his left leg and was taken prisoner at Eylau 8 February 1807, lieutenant during his captivity in Russia 3 April 1807, returned 6 August 1807, adjutant-major 16 May 1809, rank of captain 16 November 1810, lieutenant in the Gendarme Company of the Puy-de-Dôme 22 June 1811, left for service 1 August 1811. LH CH 1 October 1807.

HAVARD (Pierre René Jean, 1788-?): born in Vaars (Sarthe) on 22 June 1788. In the 5th Cuirassiers 27 June 1807, brigadier 20 September 1807, maréchal des logis 25 January 1811.

He was maréchal des logis-chef 11 April 1812, adjutant-NCO 1 February 1813, sub-lieutenant 22 December 1813, dismissed 23 December 1815.

HAZOTTE aka **MASSON** (Nicolas, 1776-?): born in Jallaucourt (Meurthe) on 22 August 1776. In the 7th Cavalry 23 March 1797, returned to the 7th Cuirassiers 23 December 1802, brigadier 212 January 1805, maréchal des logis 23 March 1806, maréchal des logis –chef 21 January 1807, sabre wound to his face at Essling 21 May 1809, adjutant-NCO 18 August 1809.

He was sub-lieutenant 8 October 1811, lieutenant 15 May 1813, wounded by shot in the thigh and taken prisoner at Leipzig 18 October 1813, returned to the corps 24 June 1814 and dismissed with it 19 December 1815. LH CH 8 October 1811.

HEARD (Michel, 1783-?): born in Saintes (Charente-Inférieure) on 28 April 1783. In the 8 Cuirassiers 22 February 1803, brigadier-fourrier 29 March 1804, maréchal des logis 19 June 1806, shot and wounded in his left hand at Wagram 6 July 1809, sub-lieutenant 12 September 1809, lance wound to his head at Winkovo 18 October 1812, in the 2nd Provisional Hamburg Cuirassiers 1814, returned with the garrison May 1814, resignation refused 19 May 1815, dismissed with the corps 5 December 1815.

HEIN (Pierre, 1771-?): born in Magern (Moselle) on 9 March 1771. In the Chamborant Hussars 5 December 1788 which became the 2nd Hussars 1 January 1791.

He was brigadier June 1796, gendarme in the Dyle Department 30 November 1802, brigadier 2 June 1807, in the 10th Squadron of the Gendarmes d'Espagne 5 December 1809, in the 1st Legion of the Gendarmerie à Cheval d'Espagne 'Burgos' when it was formed 16 December 1810, maréchal des logis 25 October 1811.

Hein was ismissed with the corps 27 February 1813, lieutenant in the 7th Cuirassiers 28 February 1813, returned 6 March 1813, wounded at La Rothière 1 February 1814.

He was amputated and taken prisoner near Brienne 3 February 1814. LH CH 1 March 1813.

HELFERT (Joseph, 1772-?): born in Hittenheim (Bas-Rhin) on 22 March 1772. In the Boulonnais-Infanterie 17 August 1789, in the 7th Cavalry 7 January 1801, brigadier 7 October 1803, maréchal des logis 11 October 1803, in the same regiment when it became the 7th Cuirassiers 23 December 1802, maréchal des logis-chef 18 December 1805, sub-lieutenant 10 January 1807.

He was in the 3rd Provisional Heavy Cavalry in Spain, wounded in the Mollit Gorge 21 January 1810, lieutenant 8 October 1811, aide de camp to General Offenstein 20 January 1812, left 21 February 1812, captain 12 March 1814, non-active on half-pay 1 September 1814, captain in the reserve squadron of the Bas-Rhin 18 March 1815, in the Bas-Rhin Lancers 17 May 1815, dismissed 24 August 1815.

HENNEZEL (Sosthène Romarie d', 1796-?): born in Neufchateau (Vosges) on 14 June 1796. Pupil in the Ecole Spéciale Militaire de Cavalerie at Saint-Germain 20 August 1813, went to the school at Saint-Cyr 1 August 1814, brigadier 30 August 1814, maréchal des logis 10 January 1815.

He was sub-lieutenant in the 10th Cuirassiers 3 March 1815, assigned to the Saumur Riding School 1 June 1815, dismissed with the regiment 25 December 1815.

HENRIONNET (Jean Hippolite, 1782 -after 1834): born in Châlons-sur-Marne (Marne) on 13 August 1782. In the 8th Cuirassiers 24 September 1803, medical officer 3rd Class 5 April 1804, sub-lieutenant in the suite 26 April 1807, several sabre and lance wounds of which one cost him the use of his elbow, taken prisoner at Heilsberg 10 June 1807.

He was exchanged and on leave for four months with pay to recover 17 January 1708, appointed 30 April 1809, wounded at Essling 22 May 1809, instated 3 June 1809, shot and wounded in his left leg at Wagram 6 July 1809, lieutenant 9 August 1809, retired 12 September 1809, lieutenant in the 25th Legion of the Roër Department Gendarmerie 25 March 1811, Seine-et-Oise company 9 October 1814, non-active on half-pay 25 February 1816.

HENRIOT (?-?): Pupil at the Ecole Polytechnique, sub-lieutenant in the suite of the 4th Cuirassiers 9 June 1815, dismissed with the corps on 5 December 1815.

HENRY (Alexandre, 1775-?): born in Baissey aux Hauts-de-Vingeanne (Haute-Marne) on 4 April 1775. In the 24th Cavalry 20 January 1799, brigadier 29 May 1801, dismissed with the corps 10 October 1801, and incorporated into the 1st Cuirassiers on 1 January 1802, fourrier 26 November 1802, maréchal des logis-chef 28 September 1806, wounded in the right foot by a shell burst at Eylau 8 February 1807, shot and wounded in the right hand and his horse killed under him at Eckmühl, 22 April 1809.

He was sub-lieutenant 16 May 1809, shot twice in the left leg and thigh at Essling 21 and 22 May 1809, lieutenant 9 February 1813, in the King's Cuirassiers 1 July 1814 which became the 1st Cuirassiers once again April 1915, intended to go to the 9th Cuirassiers but remained with the 1st Cuirassiers 9 June 1815, dismissed and put on the active list 24 December 1815. LH CH 13 August 1809.

HERBAULT (Fulgent, baron, 1760-1808): born in Chennevelle (Vienne) on 1 August 1760. In the Mestre-de-Camp-Général-Cavalerie 26 April 1789 which became the 24thh Cavalry 1 January 1791, disbanded with the regiment and dismissed 20 February 1791, not reemployed in the new levy formed the following day, in the Parisian National Guard 11 April 1791 having formed the

OREAU (Xavier, 1775-?): born in Stenvoorde (Nord) on 3 September 1775. Sub-lieutenant in the Ypres Dragoons in the Belgian Legion 1 January 1791, in the Jemmapes Hussars 1 January 1793 which became the 10th Hussars 4 June 1793, lieutenant 1 September 1793, captain 1 September 1799, shot in the right forearm at Cholet 1796 shot in the chest at Lorenzo in Piedmont 4 November 1799, in the 22nd Cavalry 22 November 1800.

He was dismissed with the corps 31 December 1802 and incorporated into the 15th Cavalry 25 January 1803 which became the 24th Dragoons 24 September 1803, recaptured an artillery piece in Spain 21 December 1808, squadron commander 28 December 1809.

He was with the 1st Squadron captured 2 000 prisoners, two cannon and 4 flags at Castalla 24 August 1812, major 3 November 1812, in the 30th Dragoons 28 June 1813, incorporated into the 14th Dragoons 1 August 1814

He was placed in non-active on half-pay 1 November 1814, engaged in the 4th Cuirassiers 4 May 1815, put back on half-pay 1 August 1815. LH CH 10 March 1810.

At Castella on 24 August 1812, Squadron Commander Horeau charged at the head of the 1st Squadron of the 24th Dragoons and captured 2 000 men, two cannon and four flags. He was made a major shortly afterwards.

102nd Infantry, left 17 April 1792, in the Volontaires Nationaux à Cheval from the Ecole Militaire, sub-lieutenant 18 October 1792, lieutenant 7 February 1793 with the same regiment when it formed the 25th cavalry 7 February 1793 which became the 24th Cavalry 4 June 1793, elected captain 19 February 1798, adjutant-major in the Garde à Cheval du Directoire 24 May 1798, squadron commander in the same regiment which became the Grenadiers à Cheval of the Consular Guard 3 January 1800, colonel in the 4th Cuirassiers 31 August 1803.

He was wounded in the head by a sabre at Heilsberg 10 June 1807, died at Bayreuth in Bavaria 112 May 1808. LH CH 11 December 1803, O 14 June 1804, Baron of the Empire d. 19 March 1808 without l.p

HERBAULT (Henry, 1783-1809): born on 18 June 1783. In the 2nd Cuirassiers 12 September

1803, brigadier 12 January 1804, maréchal des logis 3 August 1805, in the 4th Cuirassiers 21 January 1805, maréchal des logis-chef 9 January 18070, sub-lieutenant 3 April 1807, wounded at Heilsberg 10 June 1807.

He was supernumerary lieutenant 5 March 1809, took up his appointment 18 April 1809, wounded at Essling 21 May 1809 and died of his wounds 5 June 1809.

HERBET (Jean Baptiste, 1766-?): born in Villers-Autreaux (Nord) on 18 September 1766. In the Reine-Cavalerie 23 May 1788 which became the 4th Cavalry 1 January 1791, brigadier 16 February1792, maréchal des logis 1 August 1793, maréchal des logis-chef 20 February 1799, in the same regiment when it became the 4th Cuirassiers 12 October 1802.

He was sub-lieutenant by seniority 18 December 1802, wounded at Heilsberg 10 June 1807, retired 20 February 1808.

HERBIGNY
see **LAMBERT SAINT-MARC D'HERBIGNY**

HERBILLON (Philippe, 1776-?): born in Varmont (Marne) on 8 September 1776. In the 7th cavalry 22 June 1799 which became the 7th Cuirassiers 23 December 1802, seconded to the school at Hyppiatrique 4 January 1811, sub-lieutenant 4 March 1812, returned to the army, wounded by a shell burst to his left shoulder at Yacht 30 October 1812 and a bayonet wound in the groin at the Berezina 28 November 1812.

He was lieutenant 22 December 1813, dismissed with the corps 19 December 1815. LH CH 13 August 1809.

HERBULOT (Charles, 1777-?): born in Yvoy-Carignan (Ardennes) on 3 December 1777. In the 4th Cavalry 26 November 1798 which became the 4th Cuirassiers 12 October 1802, fourrier 1 October 1806, maréchal des logis 21 October 1808, maréchal des logis-chef 4 June 1809, adjutant-NCO 20 October 1812, sub-lieutenant 19 November 1812, shot in the right leg at Waterloo 18 June 1815, retired 21 December 1815. LH CH 4 December 1813.

HERGAT (Claude, 1766-?): born in Thionville (Moselle) on 8 January 1766. In the Conti-Infanterie 16 July 1784 which became the 81st Infantry 1 January 1791, left 22 February 1793, supernumerary sub-lieutenant in the 4th Cavalry March 1793.

He was appointed 7 April 1793, lieutenant 20 January 1798, in the same regiment when it became the 4th Cuirassiers 12 October 1802, cap-

tain by seniority 8 May 1806, Dismissed 21 March 1807.

HERISSANT (Jean François Denis, 1761-?): born in Paris (Seine) on 21 May 1791. In the Ségur-Dragons 15 August 1782, left January 1787, lieutenant in the Volontaires Nationaux à Cheval from the Ecole Militaire 5 September 1792, captain when they were formed into the 25th Cavalry on the same day 7 February 1793 which then became the 24 Cavalry 4 June 1793.

He was dismissed 12 October 1797, captain in the 1st Hussars, took up his appointment 8 April 1800, incorporated into the 45th of the Line and discharged 23 January 1801, captain in the 5th Cuirassiers 13 April 1804, wounded at Eylau 8 February 1807, retired 7 March 1811.

HERMANN (1775-?): born in Geneva (Léman) on 2 June 1775. In the Allobroges Legion 1 October 1793, in the 15th Dragoons 1 May 1798, brigadier-fourrier 262 October 1799, maréchal des logis 20 June 1801, in the Grenadiers à Cheval of the Imperial Guard 16 September 1805, brigadier-fourrier 2 March 1806, sub-lieutenant in the 13th Cuirassiers 4 April 1808, lieutenant 23 April 1808, retired 5 September 1810.

HERVILLY (?-?): Caulaincourt's brother-in-law, sub-lieutenant in the 9th Cuirassiers 24 August 1808, lieutenant aide de camp to Nansouty 3 August 1811.

He took up his appointment 1812, squadron commander 1814. LH CH 1812.

HEYDEN (Jacobus van der, 1768-1812): born in Nijmegen (Bouches-du-Rhin) on 9 February 1768. In the Batavian Dragoons 28 December 1790, brigadier 10 December 1792, shot in the right leg 1793, fourrier 12 May 1797, maréchal des logis 28 December 1804, sabre wound to his head 1805, in the same regiment when it became the 2nd Dutch Cavalry 14July 1806, sabre wound to his head at Straalsund 1809.

He was in the same regiment when it became the 14th French Cuirassiers 18 August 1810, sub-lieutenant 19 November 1812, killed at the Berezina 28 November 1812.

HIBERT (Jacques, 1778-?): born in Greminvilliers (Oise) on 25 January 1778. In the 6th Cavalry 29 November 1798, brigadier 20 April 1802, in the same regiment when it became the 6th Cuirassiers 23 December 1802, fourrier 20 July 1805, maréchal des logis 25 March 1807, maréchal des logis-chef 6 October 1808, adjutant NCO 28 June 1809.

He was sub-lieutenant 12 September 1809, bayonet wound to his left hip at Essling May 1809.

FROM THE CAVALRY TO THE CUIRASSIERS

January 1791: there were 29 cavalry regiments including the carabiniers. They lost their Ancien Regime appellation in favour of the more Republican numbering system (obviously ranging from 1 to 29). The carabiniers became independent in April 1791.

In 1800, during the Battle of Marengo, the cavalry's charge inspired the First Consul to reform the arm. 10 October 1801: the 1st Cavalry Regiment became the 1st Cuirassier Regiment, adopting the breastplate and embrigading with the 8th Cavalry Regiment (which had been issued with a breastplate ever since 1768) according to the wishes of the First Consul and under the authority of the Commission entrusted with studying the tactics and the organisation of the cavalry.

12 October 1802: at the end of the commission's work, the 2nd, 3rd and 4th Cavalry Regiments became the 2nd, 3rd and 4th Cuirassier Regiments respectively.

23 December 1802: the 5th, 6th and 7thCavalry Regiments in turn were changed into Cuirassier Regiments.

24 September 1803: apart from two carabinier regiments the reorganised cavalry comprised twelve cuirassier regiments.

October 1803: the 9th, 10th, 11th and 12th Regiments were created.

The cavalry regiments numbered 23 to 25 were disbanded after those numbered 19 to 22.

1807: Creation in Spain of the 1st Provisional Heavy Cavalry Regiment (troopers from the 1st, 2nd and 3rd Cuirassiers and from the 1st and 2nd Carabiniers).

22 June 1808: still in Spain, creation of the 2nd Provisional Heavy Cavalry Regiment (troopers from the 5th, 9th, 10th, 11th and 12th). This disappeared with the capitulation at Baylen in July.

End of 1808: the 1st Provisional became the 13th Cuirassiers Regiment.

11 September 1810: creation of the 14th

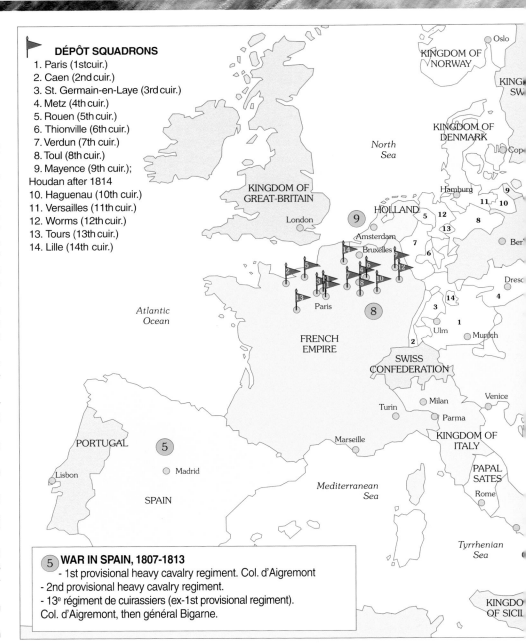

DÉPÔT SQUADRONS
1. Paris (1stcuir.)
2. Caen (2nd cuir.)
3. St. Germain-en-Laye (3rd cuir.)
4. Metz (4th cuir.)
5. Rouen (5th cuir.)
6. Thionville (6th cuir.)
7. Verdun (7th cuir.)
8. Toul (8th cuir.)
9. Mayence (9th cuir.); Houdan after 1814
10. Haguenau (10th cuir.)
11. Versailles (11th cuir.)
12. Worms (12th cuir.)
13. Tours (13th cuir.)
14. Lille (14th cuir.)

5 WAR IN SPAIN, 1807-1813
- 1st provisional heavy cavalry regiment. Col. d'Aigremont
- 2nd provisional heavy cavalry regiment.
- 13e régiment de cuirassiers (ex-1st provisional regiment). Col. d'Aigremont, then général Bigarne.

---

1 1st CAMPAIGN FOR AUSTRIA, 1805 MURAT'S CAVALRY RESERVE

— NANSOUTY'S DIVISION
● **Piston's Brigade**
- *1st Carabiniers Regiment. Colonel Cochois.*
- *2nd Carabiniers Regiment. Colonel Morin.*
● **Brigade Lahoussaye's Brigade**
- 2nd Cuirassiers Regiment. Colonel Yvendorf
- 9th Cuirassiers Regiment. Colonel Doumerc
● **Saint-Germain's Brigade**
  3rd Cuirassiers Regiment. Colonel Préval
- 12th Cuirassiers Regiment. Colonel Belfort
— D'HAUTPOUL'S DIVISION
● **Saint Sulpice's Brigade**
- 1st Cuirassiers Regiment. Colonel Guiton
- 5th Cuirassiers Regiment. Colonel Noirot
● **Fontaine's Brigade**
- 10th Cuirassiers Regiment. Colonel La Taye
- 11th Cuirassiers Regiment. Colonel Fouler
These regiments did not fight in Austria:
— ESPAGNE'S DIVISION
● **Reynaud's Brigade**
- 4th Cuirassiers Regiment. Colonel Herbault
- 6th Cuirassiers Regiment. Rioult-Davenay
● **Fouler's Brigade**
- 7th Cuirassiers Regiment. Col. Offenstein
- 8th Cuirassiers Regiment. Colonel Merlin

2 CAMPAIGN FOR PRUSSIA 1806 MURAT'S CAVALRY RESERVE

— NANSOUTY'S DIVISION
● *Defrance's Brigade*
- *1st Carabiniers Regiment. Col. de La Roche.*
- *2nd Carabiniers Regiment.Colonel Morin.*
● **Lahoussaye's Brigade**
- 2nd Cuirassiers Regiment.Colonel Chouard
- 9th Cuirassiers Regiment. Colonel Doumerc
● **Saint-Germain's Brigade**
- 3rd Cuirassiers Regiment. Colonel Richter
- 12th Cuirassiers Regiment. Colonel Dornes
— D'HAUTPOUL'S DIVISION
● **Verdière's Brigade**
- 1st Cuirassiers Regiment. Colonel Guiton
- 5th Cuirassiers Regiment. Colonel Noirot
● **Saint-Sulpice's Brigade**
- 10th Cuirassiers Regiment. Colonel Lhéritier
- 11th Cuirassiers Regiment. Colonel Brancas
These regiments did not fight in Prussia
— ESPAGNE'S DIVISION
● **Reynaud's Brigade**
- 4th Cuirassiers Regiment. Colonel Herbault
- 6th Cuirassiers Reg. Col. Rioult d'Avenay
● **Fouler's Brigade**
- 7th Cuirassiers Regiment. Colonel Offenstein
- 8th Cuirassiers Regiment.Colonel Grandjean

3 CAMPAIGN FOR POLAND, 1807 MURAT'S CAVALRY RESERVE

— NANSOUTY'S DIVISION
● *Defrance's Brigade*
- *1st Carabiniers Regiment. Col. de La Roche.*
- *2nd Carabiniers Regiment. Colonel Morin.*
● **Lahoussaye then Doumerc's Brigade**
- 2nd Cuirassiers Regiment. Colonel Chouard
- 9th Cuirassiers Reg. Col. Paultre de Lamotte
● **Saint-Germain's Brigade**
- 3rd Cuirassiers Regiment. Colonel Richter
- 12th Cuirassiers Regiment. Colonel Dornes
— D'HAUTPOUL'S DIVISION
● **Clément's Brigade**
- 1st Cuirassiers Regiment. Col. Berckheim
- 5th Cuirassiers Regiment. Colonel Noirot
● **Guitton's Brigade**
- 10th Cuirassiers Regiment. Colonel Lhéritier
- 11th Cuirassiers Regiment. Colonel Brancas
— ESPAGNE'S DIVISION
● **Reynaud's Brigade**
- 4th Cuirassiers Regiment. Colonel Herbault
- 6th Cuirassiers Regiment. Rioult-Davenay
● **Fouler's Brigade**
- 7th Cuirassiers Regiment. Col. Offenstein
- 8th Cuirassiers Regiment. Colonel Merlin

1. Bavaria
2. Baden
3. Wurtemberg
4. Saxony
5. Berg
6. Hesse-Cassel
7. Nassau
8. Hanover
9. Swedish Pomerania
10. Mecklenberg
11. Hanover
12. Oldenberg
13. Hesse
14. Thuringe

6 **CAMPAIGN FOR RUSSIA, 1812**
MURAT'S CAVALRY RESERVE
NANSOUTY'S 1st CORPS
— SAINT-GERMAIN'S DIVISION
● **Bruno's Brigade**
- 2nd Cuirassiers Regiment.Colonel Rolland
● **Bessière's Brigade**
- 3rd Cuirassiers Regiment. Colonel
● **Queunot's Brigade**
- 9th Cuirassiers Reg. Col. Murat-Sestrières
- *1st chevau-légers Regiment.*
— VALENCE'S DIVISION
● **Reynaud's Brigade**
- 6th Cuirassiers Regiment. Colonel Martin
● **Dejean's Brigade**
- 11th Cuirassiers Regiment. Colonel Duclaux
● **Lagrange's Brigade**
- 10th Cuirassiers Regiment.
- *5th chevau-légers Reg. Major Guérin*
MONTBRUN'S 2nd CORPS
— WATIER DE SAINT-ALPHONSE'S DIVISION
● **Beaumont's Brigade**
- 5th Cuirassiers Regiment. Col. Christophe
● **Dorne's Brigade**
- 8th Cuirassiers Regiment.Col. Grandjean
● **Richter's Brigade**
- 10th Cuirassiers Regiment. Colonel Franck
- *2nd chevau-légers Reg. Colonel Berruyer*
— DEFRANCE'S DIVISION
● *Paultre de la Motte's Brigade*
- *1st Carabiniers Regiment. Colonel Laroche*
● *Chouard's Brigade*
- *2nd Carabiniers Regiment. Colonel Blancard*
● **Bouvier des Eclaz' Brigade**
- 1st Cuirassiers Regiment.Colonel Clerc
- *4th chevau-légers Reg. Col. Deschamps*
These regiments did not fight in Russia
- 4th Cuirassiers Regiment. Colonel Dujon
- 7th Cuirassiers Regiment. Colonel Ordener

7 **CAMPAIGN FOR PRUSSIA, 1813**

LATOUR-MAUBOURG's 1st CAVALRY CORPS
— BORDESSOULLE'S 1st HEAVY CAVALRY DIV.
● **Berkheim's 1st Brigade**
- 2nd Cuirassiers Regiment. Colonel Rolland
- 3rd Cuirassiers Regiment. Colonel Lacroix
- 6th Cuirassiers Regiment. Colonel Martin
● **Bessières's 2nd Brigade**
- 9th Cuirassiers Reg. Col. Murat-Sestrières
- 11th Cuirassiers Regiment. Colonel Duclos
- 12th Cuirassiers Regiment. Colonel Dandies
— DOUMERC 'S 3rd HEAVY CAVALRY DIV.
● **Oudenarde's 1st Brigade**
- 4th Cuirassiers Regiment.
- 7th Cuirassiers Regiment. Colonel Ordener
- 14h Cuirassiers Regiment. Colonel Tripp
- *Napoléon's Dragoons. Colonel Gualdi (It.)*

SEBASTIANI's 2nd CAVALRY CORPS
— SAINT-GERMAIN'S 2nd HEAVY CAVALRY DIV.
● **Haugéranville's 1st Brigade**
- *1st Carabiniers Regiment.*
- *2nd Carabiniers Regiment.*
- 1st Cuirassiers Regiment. Colonel Clerc
● **Thiry's 2nd Brigade**
- 5th Cuirassiers Regiment. Col. Christophe
- 8th Cuirassiers Regiment. Col. Grandjean
- 10th Cuirassiers Reg. Col. de la Huberdière

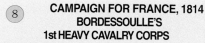

Cuirassier Regiment from the 2nd Dutch Cuirassier Regiment.
1812: for the campaign, single cuirassier regiment brigades were formed to which were attached a lancer regiment.
12 May 1814: a Royal ordnance reduced the cuirassier regiments to 12.
July 1814: the 13th Regiment was disbanded.
1814: the 13th Regiment left Spain and joined the Army of Lyon.
August 1814: the 14th Regiment in turn was disbanded.
January 1815: the 6th Cuirassier Regiment became the Régiment des Cuirassiers du Roi.

8 **CAMPAIGN FOR FRANCE, 1814**
BORDESSOULLE'S
1st HEAVY CAVALRY CORPS
● **Thiry's Brigade**
- 2nd Cuirassiers Regiment. Colonel Morin
- 3rd Cuirassiers Regiment. Colonel Préval
- 6th Cuirassiers Regiment. Colonel Martin
- 9th Cuirassiers Regiment. Colonel Habert
- 11th Cuirassiers Regiment. Colonel Lefèvre
- 12th Cuirassiers Regiment. Colonel Daudiès
● **Laville's Brigade**
- 4th Cuirassiers Regiment. Colonel Dujon
- 7th Cuirassiers Regiment. Colonel Richardot
- 14th Cuirassiers Regiment.Colonel Martin
- *7th, 28th and 12th dragoons Regiments Colonels Leopold, Hodrinet and Ordener*
SAINT-GERMAIN'S 2nd HEAVY CAVALRY CORPS
● **Blancard's Brigade**
- 1st Cuirassiers Regiment. Colonel Clerc
- *1st Carabiniers Regiment. Colonel Courcol*
- *2nd Carabiniers Regiment. Colonel Desève*
● **Sopransi's Brigade**
- - 5th Cuirassiers Regiment.Colonel Christophe
- 8th Cuirassiers Regiment. Colonel Lefaivre
- 10th Cuirassiers Reg. Col. de la Huberdière
- 13th Cuirassiers Regiment. Colonel Bigarne

9 **CAMPAIGN FOR BELGIUM, 1815**
KELLERMANN'S 3rd CAVALRY CORPS
—L'HÉRITIER'S 11th DIVISION
● **Picquet's Brigade**
- *2nd Dragoons Regiment*
- *7th Dragoons Regiment*
● **Guiton's Brigade**
- 8th Cuirassiers Regiment.
- 11th Cuirassiers Regiment.
—HURBAL'S 12th DIVISION
● *Blanchard's Brigade*
- *1st Carabiniers Regiment.*
- *2nd Carabiniers Regiment.*
● **Donop's Brigade**
- 2nd Cuirassiers Regiment.
- 3rd Cuirassiers Regiment.
MILHAUD'S 4th CAVALRY CORPS
—WATHIER'S 13th DIVISION
● **Dubois' Brigade**
- 1st Cuirassiers Regiment.
- 4th Cuirassiers Regiment.
● **Travers's Brigade**
- 7th Cuirassiers Regiment.
- 12th Cuirassiers Regiment.
—DELORT'S 14th DIVISION
● **Vial's Brigade**
- 5th Cuirassiers Regiment.
- 10th Cuirassiers Regiment.
● **Farine's Brigade**
- 6th Cuirassiers Regiment.
- 9th Cuirassiers Regiment.

4 **2nd CAMPAIGN FOR AUSTRIA, 1809**
BESSIERES' CAVALRY RESERVE

— NANSOUTY'S DIVISION
● **Defrance's Brigade**
- *1st Carabiniers Regiment. Col. de La Roche.*
- *2nd Carabiniers Regiment. Col. Blancard.*
● **Doumerc's Brigade**
- 2nd Cuirassiers Regiment. Colonel Chouard
- 9th Cuirassiers Reg.Col. Paultre de Lamotte
● **Saint-Germain's Brigade**
- 3rd Cuirassiers Regiment. Colonel Richter
- 12th Cuirassiers Regiment. Colonel Dornes
— SAINT-SULPICE'S DIVISION
● **Fiteau's Brigade**
- 1st Cuirassiers Regiment. Col. Berckheim
- 5th Cuirassiers Regiment. Colonel Quinette
● **Guitton's Brigade**
- 10th Cuirassiers Regiment. Colonel Lhéritier
- 11th Cuirassiers Regiment. Colonel Duclaux
— ARRIGHI'S DIVISION (ex-Espagne)
● **Reynaud's Brigade**
- 4th Cuirassiers Regiment. Colonel Borghèse
- 6th Cuirassiers Regiment. Col. d'Haugéranville
● **Bordessoulle's Brigade**
- 7th Cuirassiers Regiment. Colonel Dubois
- 8th Cuirassiers Regiment. Colonel Merlin

UMBERT (Charles, 1786-?): born in Belot (Côte-d'Or) on 26 March 1786. In the 1st Cuirassiers 25 October 1806, fourrier 1 April 1808, maréchal des logis-chef 16 May 1809.

He was sub-lieutenant 10 April 1813, wounded on the left breast by Biscayan shot near Leipzig 17 October 1813.

Returned 1 June 1814, in the King's Cuirassiers 1 July 1814, remained in Paris at the disposition of the Minister of War 20 January 1815

He returned to the corps 1 April 1815 when it became the 1st Cuirassiers again, dismissed and intended for activity 24 December 1815.

LH Ch 29 July 1814.

Sous-Lieutenant Charles Humbert was wounded by Biscayan shot on his left breast near Leipzig on 17 October 1813. the following day he was wounded again by a shot which went through his left wrist, by a sabre blow to the same left hand and three lance blows to his thigh and buttocks, and taken prisoner the following day, only returning on 1 June 1814.

He was lieutenant 14 May 1813, cannonball wound to his left leg and unhorsed at Leipzig 18 October 1813, on leave 14 January 1814, returned to his regiment.

He was wounded at Waterloo 18 June 1815, dismissed 21 November 1815. LH CH 14 May 1813.

HOLDRINET aka **CLERMONT** (Pierre, 1766-1831): born in Barécourt (Meuse) on 12 December 1766. Child of the regiment in the Chasseurs à Cheval N° 6 1 July 1772, volunteer 14 September 1782, in the same regiment when it became the Ardennes Chasseurs 1784 then Champagne Chasseurs à Cheval 17 March 1788 and 12th Chasseurs à Cheval 1 January 1791.

He was brigadier-fourrier 1 September 1792, maréchal des logis-chef 1 July 1793, sub-lieutenant, 7 December 1793, shot twice in the right leg at Fleurus 26 June 1794, shrapnel wound broke his left leg at Maestricht 2 December 1794 and two lance wounds to his left hand and forehead at Camberg 13 June 1796, lieutenant in the Grenadiers à cheval of the Guard 3 January 1800, captain 26 October 1800, in the velite squadron, cavalry major in the Line 26 June 1809, commanded a provisional cavalry regiment 16 February 1810.

Clermont was in service in the 4th Cuirassiers 18 December 1810, colonel in the suite 19 November 1812; at the disposition of the Minister of War at Mainz 13 May 1813, in the 3rd Cuirassiers 18 June 1813, had not yet rejoined when he was appointed to his command of the 28th Dragoons 5 August 1813, seven lance wounds to the left knee, left side, right side and to his face and taken prisoner at Dürkheim 2 January 1814.

He returned and put in the suite of the Berri-Dragons N°6 18 October 1814 which became the 11th Dragoons April 1815, retired 9 December 1815. LH CH 14 June 1804, O 14 March 1806.

HONNE (Théodore Jean, 1788-?): born in Herrequais (Meuse-Inférieure) on 29 December 1788. In the 1st Cuirassiers 17 June 1807, seconded to the 1st Provisional Heavy Cavalry in Spain end 1807 then forming the 13th Cuirassiers 21 October 1808, brigadier 1 June 1812, maréchal des logis 12 July 1813.

He was assigned as ordnance to Delort, placed as a guard had his horse killed under him and mounted the first horse he could take off the enemy o that he could charge with his regiment killing an English officer and bringing back his horse to the Ordal Pass 13 September 1813, sub-lieutenant 4 December 1813, instated 18 December 1813.

Dismissed with the corps and incorporated into the 9th Cuirassiers 9 August 1814, wounded in the left shoulder and shot in the right leg at Waterloo 18 June 1815, on non-active pay 26 November 18151 LH CH 27 May 1810.

 **HOOGENDORP** (Charles Sirandus Guillaume van, baron, 1788-1856): born in Bengal (India) on15 August 1788. Volunteer cadet in the Dutch navy 11 April 1806, ordnance officer to the King of Holland 22 October 1806.

He was lieutenant in the 2nd Dutch Cuirassiers 20 December 1806, resigned 8 July 1808, volunteer captain on the headquarters staff of General Dumonceau 16 August 1809, on the staff of the Duke of Reggio 27 July 1810.

He was captain in the 14th French Cuirassiers 1 April 1811, aide de camp to Gouvion-St-Cyr 11 November 1812, squadron commander 17 June 1813, prisoner when Dresden capitulated 11 November 1813.

He returned to France 15 March 1814, in the suite of the 7th Cuirassiers 18 May 1814, joined the regiment 26 May 1814, on six month's dismissal leave when the regiment was disbanded 19 December 1815 and returned home to Holland.

LH CH 1 October 1807, Baron of the Empire l.p. 24 August 1811.

HOUDETOT (d', 1790-1810): born in 1790. One of the Emperor's pages, sub-lieutenant in the suite of the 3rd Cuirassiers 2 February 1808 and went over to the 1st Provisional Heavy Cavalry in Spain.

He took up his appointment in the same regiment when it was formed into the 13th Cuirassiers 21 October 1808, two bayonet wounds at Lerida 23 April 1810

Died of his wounds the following day 24 April 1810. LH CH end 1809 beginning 1810.

HOUDRE (Jean Claude, 1775-?): born in Coulommier (Seine-et-Marne) on 17 January 1775. In the 10th Cavalry 16 Janaury 1794, shot in the back at Flessing 1794, brigadier 20 January 1799, maréchal des logis 28 June 1802, in the same regiment when it became the 10th Cuirassiers 24 September 1803.

He was sub-lieutenant 25 May 1807, sabre wound to his face at Eckmühl 22 April 1809, lieutenant 6 November 1811, shot in the right arm at Essling 22 May 1809, shrapnel wound to his left knee at the Moskova 7 September 1812, captain 8 July 1813, incorporated into the 3rd Provisional Heavy Cavalry in Hamburg with his squadron 11 September 1813.

He returned with the garrison May 1814, seven lance and two sabre wounds at Ligny 16 June 1815, retired after the regiment was disbanded 25 December 1815. LH CH 1 October 1807.

HOURCADE (Théophile, 1760-1831): born in Saint-Martin (Basses-Pyrénées) on 12 October 1760. In the Bourbon-Infanterie 20 December 1777, dismissed by favour 11 September 1780, trooper in the Royal-Etranger 31 December 1783 which became the 7th Cavalry 1791.

He was brigadier-fourrier 1 April 1792, maréchal des logis 3 October 1792, two sabre wounds to his left hand and nose when he freed the regimental standard-bearer who had fallen into enemy hands at Neerwinden 18 March 1793, adjutant sub-lieutenant 19 March 1793, charged four Austrian cuirassiers killing one and wounding another to disengage a trumpeter and a fourrier in the regiment near Cateau 26 April 1794.

Named lieutenant 27 April 1794, sabre wound to his right arm near Tournai 10 May 1794 and shot in the left leg with his horse killed under him at Wurtzburg 3 September 1796, captain 19 July 1799, prisoner at Donnaschingen 25 May 1800, exchanged 28 December 1800, in the same regiment when it became the 7th Cuirassiers 23 December 1802.

He retired because of his wounds and ordered to present himself to the Imperial Quartermaster 2 June 1809, employed as acting commandant of strongpoints until 31 December 1809, pensioned off 10 August 1810. LH CH 14 June 1804.

HOURS (Joseph Aimé, 1784-?): born in Bourg-Saint-Andéol (Ardèche) on 4 July 1784. In the 4th Cuirassiers 20 June 1805, brigadier 1 October 1806, maréchal des logis 15 May 1807, maréchal des logis-chef 1 May 1809.

He was adjutant NCO 3 June 1809, wounded by Biscayan shot which pierced his thigh at Wagram 6 July 1809, sub-lieutenant 8 October 1811, lost a calf muscle at the Drissa 11 August 1812,, lieutenant 19 November 1812.

Retired 6 August 1814. LH CH 25 September 1812.

HOUSSAYE see **LEBRUN de LAHOUSSAYE**

HUBLER (Nicolas Aimé, 1779-1845): born in Saint-Amé (Vosges) on 12 April 1779. In the 10th Cavalry 3 October 1800 which became the 10th Cuirassiers 24 September 1803.

He was brigadier 20 December 1805, brigadier-fourrier 5 October 1806, maréchal des logis-chef 1 September 1807, sub-lieutenant 16 May 1809. Dismissed with the regiment 25 December 1815.

HUG (Gaspard, chevalier, 1772-1820): born in Thann (Haut-Rhin) on 7 January 1772, captain in the 1st battalion of the Belfort National Guard 1 September 1793.

He was in the 2nd Hussars 4 April 1794, brigadier-fourrier 12 September 1794, maréchal des logis 19 July 1796, adjutant-NCO 15 January 1797, in the suite of the headquarters staff of the Irish Expedition 22 July 1798, take prisoner and taken to England 13 October 1798.

He was freed on parole 4 January 1799, exchanged 26 August 1799, returned to the 2nd Hussars, acting sub-lieutenant 28 July 1800, aide de camp to General Bonet 25 August 1800, rank confirmed 22 November 1800 and his post 2 December 1800, lieutenant 24 August 1801, adjutant-major of the 5th Hussars 18 December 1801, captain's rank 15 October 1803.

Named quadron commander in the 8th Chasseurs à Cheval 18 January 1807, shot and wounded in the head and a sabre wound to his right hand at Wagram 5 July 1809, major in the 30th Chasseurs à Cheval 14 March 1811 which became the 9th Chevau-Légers 18 June 1811, colonel 26 September 1811, organised and commanded a provisional light cavalry regiment in Hamburg 1814, in the suite of the 11th Cuirassiers 16 November 1814, colonel of the 2nd Regiment of Bas-Rhin National Guards 1 May 1815.

Non-active 1 August 1815. LH CH 14 March 1806, O 27 July 1809, Chevalier of the Empire l.p. 27 September 1810.

HUGO see **BRACKERS de HUGO**

HUGUET (Martin, 1763-?): born in Gugny (Haute-Saône) on 2 April 1763. In the Cuirassiers du Roy 21 January 1785 which became the 8th Cavalry 1 January 1791, maréchal des logis 28 August 1793, in the same regiment when it became the 8th Cuirassiers 10 October 1801, sub-lieutenant by seniority 7 October 1802.

He was lieutenant 25 March 1807, retired 22 February 1810. LH CH 1 October 1807.

HUMBERT (Antoine Joseph, 1775-?): born in Hannapes (Aisne) on 1 March 1775. In the 6th Dragoons 15 September 1792, brigadier 2 July 1796.

He was gendarme à cheval in the 16th Escaut Legion 11 March 1800, brigadier in the 16th Squadron of the Gendarmerie d'Espagne 16 January 1810, in the 1st Legion of the Gendarmerie d'Espagne 'Burgos' 15 December 1810, maréchal des logis 7 march 1812, dismissed with the corps 27 February 18113 and posted lieutenant in the 6th Cuirassiers 1 March 1813, lost a leg at Ligny 16 June 1815.

Retired because of wounds 21 November 1815. LH CH 15 September 1813.

HUMBERT (Jean Baptiste, 1793-?): born in Nancy (Meurthe) on 12 June 1793. Velite in the Grenadiers à Cheval of the Guard 5 April 1811, sub-lieutenant in the 14th Cuirassiers 13 March 18113, dismissed with the corps and posted to the 12th Cuirassiers 13 July 1814, dismissed with the corps 10 December 1815.

HUMBERT (Lambert, 1777-1834): born in Vagney (Vosges) on 21 September 1777. In the 24th Cavalry 1 August 1799, brigadier 23 September 1801, dismissed with the corps 10 October 1801 and incorporated into the 1st Cuirassiers 1 January 1802.

He was maréchal des logis 1 April 1804, shot and also wounded by a lance in the right thigh at Eylau 8 February 1807, maréchal des logis-chef 1 July 1808, wounded by shrapnel in his right thigh at Eckmühl 22 April 1809, sub-lieutenant 16 May 1809, shot in the left leg at Essling 22 May 1809, lieutenant in the 6th Team Train Battalion 23 January 1812, left to join his regiment 19 February 1812.

He was adjutant-major 1812, incorporated with the depot of the regiment into the artillery train 20 January 1814 which became the 13th Principal Battalion 23 February 1814.

LH CH 1 October 1807.

HUOT (Mathurin Marie François, 1780-1812): born in Coulommiers (Seine-et-Marne) on 24 September 1780. In the 23rd Cavalry 30 December 1802, dismissed with the corps and incorporated into the 7th Cuirassiers 15 January 1803, brigadier 22 March 1804, maréchal des logis 20 January 1805, maréchal des logis-chef 24 March 1805, sub-lieutenant 26 April 1807, left to join the riding school at Versailles 10 November 1807, returned 28 July 1809.

He was lieutenant 8 October 1811, lost a calf muscle with a cannonball at Polotsk 18 October 1812, admitted to the hospital at Borisov 1 November 1812 and disappeared. LH CH 8 October 1811.

HUQUET (Jean, ?-1810): born in Versailles (Seine-et-Oise). Captain in the 3rd Paris Battalion 1 July 1791, deputy to the adjutant-generals 1 April 1793.

Employed in Guadeloupe with General Aubert, shell burst wound at Morne-Mascot, dismissed April 1795, landed in France 18 June 1805 and kept at the disposition of the Minister of War, paid

UBERT (Pierre Louis d', 1763-?), born in Laneuville-Garnier (Oise) on 6 December 1763. In the King's Cuirassiers 1 June 1786 which became the 8th Cavalry 1 January 1791, brigadier-fourrier 28 August 1793, maréchal des logis 5 February 1794.

He was maréchal des logis-chef 26 June 1794.

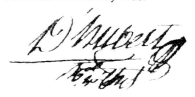

He was named sub-lieutenant by seniority 22 December 1804, lieutenant 17 April 1807, shot and wounded in the head at Heilsberg 10 June 1807, several sabre wounds which cost him his right hand and the loss of his little finger on the left hand at Essling May 1809, retired 9 August 1809.

Sabre of Honour 15 September 1802, commissioned 30 May 1803, LH CH by rights 24 September 1803.

Maréchal des Logis chef, Pierre Hubert received several sabre wounds and his horse was killed under him while trying to disengage General Jourdan and his staff who were about to be taken at Schweinfürth on 28 July 1796.

as a discharged infantry captain 7 January 1807.

He was captain in the 4th Cuirassiers 1 March 1807, assigned to the 3rd Provisional Cuirassiers in Spain discharged without pay 28 May 1809, entered the military hospital at Atarazanas 17 February 1810.

Appointed to work on the staff of the stronghold 20 August 1810, died in the same hospital 1 September 1810.

HURBAL see **ROUSSEL d'HURBAL**

HUSS (Florent, 1770-?): born in Veyenheim (Bas-Rhin) on 26 March 1770. Trooper in the Royal-Etranger 3 September 1786 which became the 7th Cavalry 1 January 1791, brigadier-fourrier 7 May 1793, maréchal des logis 11 December 1793.

He was adjutant sub-lieutenant 27 April 1794, lieutenant by choice 11 March 1797, adjutant-major 13 March 1802, acting captain 9 September 1803, captain commanding a company 9 January 1809, in the King's Cuirassiers when they were formed 1 July 1814 and when they became the 1st Cuirassiers again April 1815.

He was wounded at Waterloo 18 June 1815, dismissed and made to retire 24 December 1815. LH CH 19 November 1812.

JACQUEMIN (François, 1757-1807): born in Lagarde (Moselle) on 14 October 1757. Trooper in the Royal-Lorraine 8 December 1744, brigadier 27 August 1781.

He was maréchal des logis 1 September 1784, adjutant 5 September 1784, in the same regiment when it became the 16th Cavalry 1 January 1791, lieutenant 10 May 1792, captain 17 June 1792, in the same regiment when it became the 15th Cavalry 4 June 1793, squadron commander in the 5th Cavalry 22 February 1800 which became the 5th Cuirassiers 23 December 1802.

He captured a standard at Austerlitz with Colonel Sénilhac 2 December 1805, killed at Eylau on 8 February 1807. LH CH on 14 June 1804, O 1805.

JACQUET (Pierre, 1757-?): born in Grivy (Ardennes) on 10 May 1757. With the Commissaire-Général-Cavalerie 11 January 1778, brigadier 26 August 1784, maréchal des logis 15 June 1785, in the same regiment when it became the 3rd Cavalry 1 January 1791, maréchal des logis-chef 13 August 1791, adjutant-NCO 18 January 1792.

He was adjutant sub-lieutenant 27 April 1792, lieutenant 1 August 1793, commissioned captain 21 December 1793, sabre wound to the left hand and bullet wound to the left thigh on 24 April 1794, broke his arm falling off his horse while charging at Biberach in October 1796, in the same regiment when it became the 3rd Cuirassiers 12 October 1802, squadron

commander 30 October 1806. He was wounded at Friedland 14 June 1807, retired 5 July 1807. LH CH.

JACQUET de BOULLIERS (Anne Jean Baptiste Marie Louis de, 1783-?): born in Paris (Seine) on 1 February 1783.

With the Gendarmes d'Ordonnance 12 March 1807, dismissed with the corps 23 October 1807 and incorporated into the Grenadiers à Cheval of the Guard 24 November 1807, supernumerary sub-lieutenant in the 3rd Cuirassiers 13 April 1810, appointed 26 November 1810, wounded at the Moskova 7 September 1812.

He was lieutenant 10 September 1812, wounded at Waterloo 18 June 1815, dismissed with the corps on 25 November 1815.

JACQUETOT (?-1809): maréchal des logis-chef in the 8th Cuirassiers, sub-lieutenant 3 June 1809, wounded at Wagram 6 July 1809, died of his wounds in the hospital in Vienna 31 July 1809. LC CH 18 October 1807.

JALLAND see **LACROIX JALLAND**

JAMIN (Jean Baptiste Augustin Marie, baron, 1775-1815): born in Louvigné-au-Désert (Ille-et-Vilaine) on 15 May 1775. Sub-lieutenant in the 9th Cavalry 17 June 1792, lieutenant 5 Mai 1795, aide de camp to Nansouty, his former colonel 8 September 1799, acting captain in the suite of the 9th Cavalry 31 August 1800.

He was appointed captain 14 January 1801, in the suite of the 8th Cavalry 21 April 1801, appointed 3 June 1801, retroactively to 21 April 1801, in the same regiment when it became the 8th Cuirassiers 10 October 1801, squadron commander 27 December 1801, appointed 21 January 1802, aide de camp to Masséna September 1805

then to Joseph Bonaparte in his post 4 June 1806, Major in the Chevau-Légers of the Royal Neapolitan Guard 6 July 1806, regimental colonel 30 October 1807, maréchal de camp in Spanish service 17 November 1810, commanded the two cavalry regiments of the Spanish Royal Guard 19 November 1810.

He was accepted February 1811, acting CO of the Cavalry Brigade of the Spanish Royal Guard from 16 July until he was dismissed on 25 November 1813, major-general in French service 20 January 1814, Central Cavalry Depot at Versailles 8 February 1814, commanded a light cavalry brigade in the 2nd Corps, Major in the Grenadiers à cheval of the Imperial Guard 16 March 1814, followed Napoleon to Fontainebleau and stayed with him until he abdicated, remained with the same regiment when this became the Corps Royal des Cuirassiers de France 24 November 1814.

He was confirmed as major of the same regiment when it became the Grenadiers à Cheval of the Imperial Guard on 14 April 1815, killed at Waterloo 18 June 1815. LH CH 14 June 1804, O 14 February 1815, Baron of the Empire l.p. 26 April 1811.

JANSEN (Evers, 1779-?): born in Epée (Upper Yssel) on 8 January 1779. In the 1st Batavian Cavalry 6 March 1794, brigadier 1 July 1798.

He was maréchal des logis in the 2nd Dutch Cavalry 18 December 1803, maréchal des logis-chef 11 January 1807, in the same regiment when it became the 14th French Cuirassiers 18 August 1810, sub-lieutenant 4 March 1812,.

He was dismissed with the corps in 1814.

JANSON (Jean Christian, 1763-?): born in Zutphen (Upper Yssel) on 13 March 1736. Sub-lieutenant in the 2nd Batavian Dragoons 11 July 1795, lieutenant 4 November 1796, cap-

Opposite page.
Officer from the 10th Cuirassier Regiment.
(Private collection, photograph Bertrand Malvaux)

ANSON (Pierre, 1756-?): born in Bois-le-Duc (Meuse) on 19 April 1756.

Sub-lieutenant in the 2nd Batavian Dragoons 11 July 1795, lieutenant 8 May 1800.

He was captain in the 2nd Dutch Cavalry 26 February 1807 which became the 14th French Cuirassiers 18 August 1810, five lance and five sabre wounds at Polotsk 18 October 1812.

He was dismissed with the corps in 1814. LH CH 1807.

At Bamberg on 7 December 1800, Lieutenant Pierre Janson charged three times with twenty-five dragoons against a squadron of Blankenstein Hussars forcing them to retreat and taking several prisoners.

tain in the Cuirassiers of the King of Holland's Guard 26 February 1807.

He was, captain in the 2nd Dutch Cavalry which became the 14th French Cuirassiers 18 August 1810, resigned 5 December 1810.

JARLEAUD (Claude Bernard, 1773-?): born in Autun (Saône-et-Loire) on 14 March or 12 May 1773. In the Chasseurs de Bretagne in September 1789 which became the 10th Chasseurs à Cheval 1 January 1791.

He was adjutant NCO in the 1st Côte-d'Or Battalion 18 October 1793, adjutant sub-lieutenant December 1793, Gendarmerie lieutenant 4 February 1795, discharged with pay 10 June 1797, lieutenant quartermaster in the Nice Colonial Depot 26 February 1803,.

He was Gendarmerie lieutenant in the Police Company with the Army of Italy 30 June 1803, discharged 8 February 1805, lieutenant with the 1st Cuirassiers 14 November 1806, returned 1 December 1806, wounded by a cannonball at Essling 22 May 1809, captain on the headquarters staff of the 6th Military Division 15 August 1809. LH CH 16 June 1809.

JARRE (Jean Pierre, 1775-?): born in Arbois (Jura) on 10 March 1775. Brigadier 29 May 1802, fourrier 4 August 1802, in the same regiment when it became the 6th Cuirassiers 23 December 1802.

He was maréchal des logis 29 April 1804, maréchal des logis-chef 20 July 1805, adjutant-NCO 16 July 1807, sub-lieutenant 3 June 1808, lieutenant 12 September 1809, adjutant-major 2 September 1812, captain 25 September 1812,

Standard belonging to the 1st Cuirassier Regiment.
(Figurines Magazine)

wounded and his horse killed under him at Leipzig 16 October 1813, dismissed 21 November 1815. LH CH 5 September 1813.

JARSAILLON (Pierre Eugène de, 1777-1807): born in Cercy-la-Tour (Nièvre) on 2 May 1777. In the 21st Chasseurs à Cheval 9 June 1799, left 3 January 1800, in the 1st Cavalry 21 January 1800, brigadier 12 April 1800, fourrier 18 April 1800, in the same regiment when it became the 1st Cuirassiers 10 October 1801, maréchal des logis 20 June 1802, maréchal des logis-chef 3 April 1803, sub-lieutenant 5 October 1803, lieutenant 24 November 1806, killed at Eylau 8 February 1807.

JEAN (Michel, 1778-?): born in Valauville (Manche) on 13 July 1778. In the Moselle Legion 14 May 1792, in Augereau's Guides 1 August 1797, incorporated into the 11th Hussars 1798 which became the 29th Dragoons 24 September 1803, brigadier 28 June 1799, two shot and sabre wounds at Il Mincio 28 June 1801.

He was maréchal des logis 23 September 1801, in the Company of Finistère Gendarmes 26 November 1803, in the 14th Squadron of the Gendarmerie d'Espagne 1 January 1810, in the 1st Legion à Cheval d'Espagne 16 December 1810, dismissed with the corps 27 February 1813.

He was sub-lieutenant in the 12th Cuirassiers 28 February 1813, wounded at Frankfurt 20 October 1813, no longer appears on the rolls as of 14 July 1814.

JEANNEAU (Jean, 1789-?): born in Jonzac (Charente-Inférieur) on 22 January 1789. In the 11th Cuirassiers 1 June 1808, brigadier 6 February 1812, maréchal des logis 1 February 1813. Sub-lieutenant 3 September 1813, dismissed with the regiment 16 December 1815. LH CH 5 September 1813.

JEANNOT (Aristide Joseph Denis, 1773-1812): born in Besançon (Doubs) on 10 May 1773. Supply store guard in Besançon January 1792, volunteer in the 12th Battalion of the

OSSELIN (Aimé Côme Louis, 1770-?): born in Ham (Somme) on 4 December 1770.

He was n the Chasseurs à Cheval de Normandie 10 November 1788 which became the 11th Chasseurs à Cheval 1 January 1791, fourrier 16 September 1792,.

Maréchal des logis-chef 11 August 1793, shot through his right shoulder at Partenheim 27 September 1796, adjutant sub-officier 22 October 1798, sub-lieutenant 27 February 1800, with 20 Chasseurs captured 2 battalions at Neuburg 27 June 1800.

Acting lieutenant on the battlefield 9 July 1800, confirmed December 1800, lieutenant adjutant-major 10 August 1804, captain adjutant-major 11 August 1805.

He was commanded the Elite Company 2 February 1807, squadron commander in the 2nd Chasseurs à Cheval 14 May 1809, major 17 January 1814 then in the 6th Cuirassiers 3 December 1814.

He was dismissed 21 November 1815. LH CH 5 November 1804, O 17 July 1809.

Shot and wounded in the right arm at the Battle of Jena, Captain Adjutant-Major Josselin nonetheless took part in pursuing the Prussian army in the ranks of the 11th Chasseurs à Cheval.

It was during this mad chase on 4 November 1806, he took five cannon and a howitzer with two men.

Doubs 15 August 1793, sergeant-major 27 September 1793, adjutant-NCO 1 October 1793.

He was lieutenant 19 September 1794, adjutant to the Adjutants-Generals, sabre wound on the left of his head at Wissemburg 1795, aide de camp to General O'Keefe, 5 December 1796, wounded twice in the leg and knee at Mainz 1796, captain 5 October 1796, aide de camp to General Pierre 20 April 1797, commissioned captain 4 October 1797, deputy to Adjutant-General Grillon 22 January 1799, wounded in the elbow by a shell burst at Narkick 5 May 1800, aide de camp to General Grandjean 5 December 1801, battalion commander 3 July 1809.

He was wounded in the right thigh by a bullet at Wagram 6 July 1809, on six months' leave 18 October 1810 and attached temporarily as squadron commander to the 4th Cuirassiers 6 November 1810, took up his appointment in the 5th Cuirassiers 22 January 1811, wounded by a cannonball at the Moskova 7 September 1812 and died of his wounds at Kaluga 4 October 1812.

LH CH 16 November 1808.

Diagram of a squadron in a column.
(Author's collection)

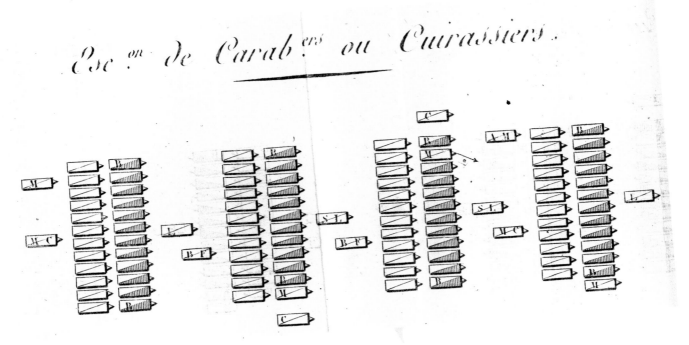

JEANSON (Paul, 1784-1813): born in Castelnaudary (Aude) on 15 March 1785. Win the 6th Cuirassiers 4 September 1805.

He was brigadier 1 October 1806, fourrier 31 July 1807, maréchal des logis 28 June 1809, maréchal des logis-chef 16 September 1809, adjutant-NCO 1 January 1813.

Sub-lieutenant 27 June 1813, killed at Leipzig 18 October 1813. LH CH 11 October 1812.

JOANNES (Louis, baron, 1766-1815): born in Grenoble (Isère) on 9 February 1766. Trooper in the Royal Champagne 27 February 1787 which became the 20th Cavalry 1 January 1791, brigadier 22 September 1792, maréchal des logis 18 May 1793, in the same regiment when it became the 19th Cavalry 4 June 1793,.

He was maréchal des logis-chef 13 March 1794, adjutant 21 March 1797, sub-lieutenant 19 June 1799, lieutenant-quartermaster 22 March 1802, dismissed with the corps 31 December 1802 and incorporated into the suite of the 9th Cavalry 15 February 1803.

He was appointed 8 June 1803 in the same regiment which became the 9th Cuirassiers 24 September 1803, elected captain 15 December 1803, then squadron commander 20 March 1813, took up his appointment in the 1st Carabiniers 24 July, shot and wounded in the right shoulder at Dresden 27 August 1813, wounded by a Biscayan shot in the left shoulder, several lance wounds, left for dead, prisoner at Leipzig 18 October 1813.

Operated on and recovered because he returned to the 1st Carabiniers 15 July 1814, killed at Waterloo 18 June 1815. LH CH 14 April 1807,

Baron of the Empire d. 14 May 1809 and l.p. 3 June 1811.

JOANNET (Philippe, 1776-1809): born in Condom (Gers) on 25 October 1776. With the 3rd Cavalry 1 January 1792, brigadier 28 December 1795,.

He was maréchal des logis 21 March 1798 with the guides of the Army of the Rhine 6 April 1800, sub-lieutenant 25 November 1800, in the 8th Cavalry 24 June 1803, captain 24 February 1807, wounded at Essling 22 May 1809 and died of his wounds in Vienna 8 June 1809. LH CH 18 October 1807.

Epaulettes and counter-epaulettes belonging to junior officers.
(RR)

JOBBE (Charles Joachim, 1788-?): born in Augerville-Lamartelle (Seine-Inférieur) on 20 March 1788. In the 5th Cuirassiers 6 July 1807, brigadier 10 August 1807, maréchal des logis 4 October 1807, maréchal des logis-chef 1 January 1811, four lance wounds near Moscow 18 October 1812, sub-lieutenant 8 July 1913, sub-lieutenant standard-bearer 11 August 1814, dismissed 23 December 1812. LH CH 3 November 1814.

JOHAM (Philippe Charles Chrétien, 1783-1812): born in Strasbourg (Bas-Rhin) on 13 June 1783. Volunteered for the 7th Dragoons 29 December 1803, brigadier 17 March 1804, brigadier-fourrier 6 January 1805, in the Grenadiers à Cheval of the Guard 19 June 1808, brigadier 1 October 1808, fourrier 1 November 1808, sub-lieutenant in the 5th Cuirassiers 1 June 1809, killed at the Moskova 7 September 1812.

JONCKHEER (Gerhardus, 1776-1812): born in Rotterdam (Bouches-de-la-Meuse) on 6 December 1776. Hussar in the King of Holland's Guard 1 March 1807, brigadier 1 April 1807, maréchal des logis in the 2nd Dutch Cuirassiers 1 January 1808, sub-lieutenant in the 3rd Dutch Hussars 29 September 1809, in the 2nd Dutch Cuirassiers 6 October 1809 which had become the 14th French Cuirassiers 18 August 1810, wounded at the Berezina 28 November 1812, disappeared 11 December 1812.

JOUDIOUX (Pierre, 1780-?): born in Belleville (Rhône) on 11 November 1780. In the 3rd Cuirassiers 14 November 1802.

He was brigadier 3 January 1804, two sabre wounds to his left hand at Austerlitz 2 December 1805, maréchal de logis 1 December 1806, sabre wound to the neck at Friedland 14 June 1807, wounded by Biscayan shot in the left leg and his horse killed under him at Essling May 1809, sub-lieutenant 12 August 1812, lieutenant 8 July 1813, shot in his left elbow at Waterloo 18 June 1815, retired 25 November 1815. LH CH 14 May 1813.

JOURNU (Philippe, 1783-?): born in Marseilles (Bouche-du-Rhône) on 17 August 1783. Lieutenant of a wolf-hunting company.

He was volunteer in the 31st Chasseurs à Cheval 1 January 1814, fourrier 12 January 1814, sub-lieutenant in the 14th Cuirassiers 17 January 1814, dismissed with the corps and incorporated into the 12th Cuirassiers 13 July 1814, with the Mousquetaires Noirs 13 December 1814.

JOUSSEAUME (Henri René, 1792-?): born in Charzy (Vendée) on 11 January 1792. A pupil at the school in Saint-Germain 15 April 1810, grenadier 25 January 1812, brigadier 5 July 1812, sub-lieutenant in the 11th Cuirassiers 30 January 1813, intended for the King's Cuirassiers 4 May 1814, but remained in the 11th

Cuirassiers, dismissed 18 December 1815.

JOUVANCOURT (Pierre Charles Etienne de, 1780-1826): born in Ile Bourbon (Reunion Island) on 26 November 1780. Cadet in the Ile-de-France Regiment 22 January 1787, sub-lieutenant 12 February 1796.

He was, in the Horse Artillery 19 March 1797, lieutenant in the Colonial Cavalry 13 March 1799, returned to France on leave 6 May 1801, Gendarme d'Ordonnance 17 September 1806, maréchal des logis 23 December 1806, second-lieutenant 3 April 1807, dismissed with the corps 23 November 1807.

Lieutenant in the 5th Cuirassiers 28 March 1808, took up his appointment 9 April 1809, sabre wound on the left shoulder at Essling 21 May 1809, captain 3 June 1809, wounded while capturing General Likhatchev at the Moskova 7 September 1812.

He was, squadron commander 28 September 1813, in the 4th Cuirassiers 14 March 1814 which had become the Cuirassiers d'Angoulême 6 August 1814, 4th Cuirassiers again April 1815, dismissed with the regiment 21 December 1815. LH CH 11 October 1812, O 9 November 1814 confirmed 11 April 1915.

JOUVENCOURT (de, ?-?): Squadron commander in the suite of the 5th Cuirassiers 28 September 1813, on leave 25 January 1814, took up his post in the 4th Cuirassiers 9 March 1814 in the suite.

JUBERT (Jean Georges, 1774-1813): born in Chatenois (Meurthe) on 25 February 1774. Regimental pupil in the pay of the Royal-Champagne-Cavalerie 9 July 1782, engaged 13 February 1790.

He was in the same regiment when it became the 20th Cavalry 1 January 1791 then 19th Cavalry 4 June 1793, brigadier 1 December 1797, maréchal des logis 23 September 1799, maréchal de logis in the Grenadiers à Cheval of the Guard, maréchal des logis-chef 23 September 1800, sub-lieutenant 1 October 1801, appointed 6 November 1801.

Second-lieutenant 23 September 1804, first-lieutenant 18 December 1805, captain 25 June 1809, squadron commander in the 4th Cuirassiers 23 October 1811, wounded at the Berezina 28 November 1812, prisoner during the retreat 10 December 1812 and died from fever at Vilna Hospital 11 January 1813.

LH CH 14 June 1804.

JUIGNE see **LECLERC de JUIGNE.**

JULIA (Jean Antoine Victor Marcelin, 1783-?): born in Najac (Aveyron) on 14 January 1783. In the 1st Carabiniers 16 March 1804, fourrier 13 October 1805, maréchal des logis 8 Mai 1807.

He was, incorporated into the 1st Provisional Heavy Cavalry Regiment in Spain December 1807 which became the 13th Cuirassiers 21

October 1808, maréchal des logis on the same day 21 October 1808, sub-lieutenant 18 September 1811, wounded in the knee by a lance in Spain 19 September 1812, lieutenant 26 November 1813.

He was confirmed 5 March 1814, two sabre wounds one to his head at Villefranche 18 March 1814, dismissed with the corps and incorporated into the 9th Cuirassiers 9 August 1814, two sabre wounds, one to the head, at Waterloo 18 June 1815, left for the Gendarmerie when the regiment was dismissed 26 November 1815. LH CH 19 March 1815.

JUNCKER (Henry Philippe Charles, 1783-?): born in Obenheim (Bas-Rhin) on 15 December 1786. In the 5th Hussars 20 April 1799, brigadier 30 July 1800.

He was maréchal des logis 16 August 1800, with the 9th Hussars 13 March 1801, acting lieutenant 20 May 1801, not confirmed, sub-lieutenant 30 December 1801, aide de camp to General Walther, retroactively in the Grenadiers à Cheval of the Guard 5 February 1803, received a shot in the leg and had his horse killed under him when charging the enemy artillery at Austerlitz 2 December 1805, in the Grenadiers à Cheval of the Imperial Guard 20 May 1806, detached by ordnance to Bessières, carried the order to charge to the Grenadiers à Cheval, followed one of the squadrons and had his horse killed under him by several blasts of grapeshot at Eylau 8 February 1807.

He was first-lieutenant in the Grenadiers à Cheval 16 February 1807, captain 20 August 1809, squadron commander (Old Guard) 9 February 1813, commanded the squadrons of the Young Guard in Saxony and in France, wounded at Brienne 29 January 1814, non-active 22 July 1814, major in the Dauphin's Cuirassiers 30 November 1814, which became the 3rd Cuirassiers in April 1815, detached to the Compagnies Franches 1 July 1815, dismissed with the 3rd Cuirassiers 25 November 1815. LH CH 26 May 1808, O 14 April 1813.

JUNEMANN (Laurent, 1779-?): born in Boulay (Moselle) on 13 April 1779. In the 8th Cuirassiers 28 May 1802.

He was brigadier 6 August 1802, maréchal des logis 28 December 1803, sub-lieutenant 24 February 1807, lost an arm at Essling 22 May 1809, discharged because of his wound 6 July 1809. LH CH 1809.

JUNG (Jean Thiebault, 1783-?): born in Bitche (Moselle) on 3 February 1783. In the 9th Cavalry 3 July 1800.

He was brigadier 8 October 1801, in the same regiment when it became the 9th Cuirassiers 24 September 1803, maréchal des logis 4 December 1806, adjutant-NCO 16 September 1809, sub-lieutenant 11 March 1812, lieutenant 14 May 1813, left with his retirement pay 26 November 1815. LH CH 14 May 1813.

The 8th Cuirassiers 1810-15

Trumpeter in full dress around 1808 according to L. Rousselot.

Trumpeter wearing full dress around 1813, according to L. Rousselot. As the artist noted, the trumpeter's head dress is curious because this is a carabinier helmet but with a steel crown.

Cantonment dress towards 1810.

Trooper wearing campaign dress according to the 1812 regulations.

Adjudant-Major wearing a frock coat around 1813 according to a card in Commandant Bucquoy's Collection.

Foot drill dress towards 1812.

Trooper wearing foot service dress towards 1813.

Opposite page.
**Two brigadiers from the 1st Cuirassiers
in cantonment dress and campaign dress,
according to the 1812 regulations.**
(Plate by Carle Vernet, private collection, RR)

KALTENBACHER (Dominique, 1776-1860): brother of the following, born in Sélestat (Bas-Rhin) on 11 August 1776.

Child of the regiment in the Royal-Cavalerie, engaged 11 August 1790, in the same regiment when it became the 2nd Cavalry 1 January 1791, brigadier 30 July 1800, lance wound to his side and a shot wound to his left leg at Engen 2 May 1800, maréchal des logis 28 June 1802, in the same regiment when it became the 2nd Cuirassiers 12 October 1802.

He was vaguemestre 1 January 1808, sub-lieutenant 14 May 1809, bruised his right leg with a cannonball at Essling 22 May 1809, lieutenant 15 March 1812, wounded and his horse killed under him at the Moskova 7 September 1812, captain 11 September 1812, shot and wounded in the right leg, several lance wounds to his back and taken prisoner at Orcha 21 November 1812 returned to France and put back in the same regiment which had become the Cuirassiers de la Reine 5 January 1815 and which then became the 2nd Cuirassiers again April 1815. Left with his pension 10 December 1815. LH Ch 14 April 1807.

KALTENBACHER (Louis Bernard, 1787-1813): brother of the above, born in Joigny (Yonne) on 7 November 1797. Child of the regiment in the 12th Cavalry 7 November 1801 which became 12th Cuirassiers 24 September 1803, cuirassier 1804, brigadier 1807.

He was maréchal des logis 29 October 1807, maréchal des logis-chef, sub-lieutenant 12 June 1813, disappeared 1813.

KANGE (?-?): in the 1st Legion of the Gendarmerie à Cheval d'Espagne.

He was sub-lieutenant in the 5th Cuirassiers 1 March 1813, wounded and taken prisoner at Hanau 30 October 1813.

KAUFFER (Jean Alexis Victor, 1783-1812): born in Paris (Seine) on 14 July 1783. In the Gendarmes d'Ordonnance 3 November 1806.

He was sub-lieutenant in the Line 12 July 1807, in the suite of the 8th Cuirassiers 10 September 1807, lieutenant aide de camp to General Espagne 5 May 1809, in the 6th Cuirassiers 22 June 1809, captain 8 October 1811.

Wounded and taken prisoner at Winkovo 18 October 1812 and disappeared.

KEGUELIN de ROSIERES (Honoré de, 1784-?): born in Sarrebourg (Meurthe) on 24 September 1784. In the 3rd Hussars 14 August 1802.

He was maréchal des logis 12 January 1803, in the 9th Cuirassiers 13 March 1805, maréchal des logis-chef 15 December 186, sub-lieutenant in the suite of the 10th Cuirassiers 21 February 1807, in service 31 March 1808, in the 2nd Provisional Cuirassier Regiment in Spain 1808, shot wounded in his left arm at Baylen 16 July 1808 and taken prisoner by capitulation 22 July 1808. Returned 12 July 1814, wounded by a shot to his shoulder at Ligny 16 June 1815, dismissed with the corps 25 December 1815. LH CH 2 November 1814.

KEHL (Philippe Pierre, 1775-?): born in Deux-Ponts (Mont-Tonnerre) on 2 April 1775. In the 1st Hussars 12 September 1792.

He was brigadier-fourrier 5 August 1793, maréchal des logis-chef 16 May 1799, adjutant-NCO 22 December 1800, sub-lieutenant 13 November 1803, lieutenant 5 April 1807, bayonet wound to his right hand in Spain, adjutant-major 9 October 1809, captain 26 March 1811.

He was squadron commander in the 3rd Hussars 14 July 1813, in the 6th Cuirassiers 1 August 1814, wounded at Waterloo 18 June 1815, dismissed as a foreign national on half-pay 21 November 1815. LH CH 18 August 1811, O 28 September 1814.

KNYFF see **LECANDELLE de KNYFF.**

KOEHLER (Joseph Charles, 1785-1815): born in Epinal (Vosges) on 17 May 1785. In the 9th Cavalry 29 December 1802 which became the 9th Cuirassiers 24 September 1803.

He was brigadier, maréchal des logis, in the Grenadiers à Cheval of the Guard 11 July 1807, brigadier 19 May 1808, sub-lieutenant in the 11th Cuirassiers 23 October 1811, lieutenant 16 August 1813, adjutant-major 25 December 1813, died 29 January 1815. LH CH 14 May 1813.

KRAYENHOFF (Cornelius Jean, 1790-?): born in Amsterdam (Zuydersee) on 21 December 1788. Cadet in the service of Holland in the 3rd Artillery Battalion 11 June 1800.

He was Engineer lieutenant 25 April 1808, first-lieutenant in the 3rd Dutch Hussars 31 August 1809, in the 2nd Dutch Cuirassiers 6 October 1809 which became the 14th French Cuirassiers 18 August 1810. He was confirmed lieutenant 5 December 1810, captain 8 October 1811, aide de camp to General Daendels.

KRUYSWYK (Hendrik, 1781-1812): born in Emmenes on 7 August 1791. In the Grenadiers of the King of Holland's Guard 24 March 1806, NCO cadet 2 February 1807, maréchal des logis in the Cuirassiers of the Guard 4 April 1807, maréchal des logis-chef 29 September 1809, in the King of Holland's Horse Guards 26 October 1809.

He was sub-lieutenant in the 2nd Dutch Cuirassiers 12 May 1810 which became the 14th French Cuirassiers 18 August 1810, died at Utrecht Hospital 2 February 1812.

KUHN (Georges, 1770-?): born in Strasbourg (Bas-Rhin) on 20 January 1770. Sub-lieutenant in the 4th Chasseurs à Cheval 15 September 1791, lieutenant 22 July 1792, aide de camp 25 February 1797, captain in the rank of the 4th Chasseurs à Cheval 24 August 1798.

He was commissioned as deputy on the staff of the 7th Military Division 12 December 1800, in the 7th Cuirassiers 8 June 1803, joined his unit 20 July 1803, on six months' leave 22 November 1804, returned 4 February 1805, left with his pension 1 August 1806.

KUPPER (Jean Guillaume, 1789-?): born in Montjoie (Roer) on 22 July 1789. In the 16th Dragoons 24 April 1808, brigadier 24 October 1808, gendarme in the 9th Escadron d'Espagne 20 December 1809 which had formed the 1st Legion of the Gendarmerie à Cheval d'Espagne "Burgos" 1 January 1810, brigadier 16 June 1812, shot and wounded in the left leg at Vollodrigo 23 October 1812, dismissed with the legion 27 February 1813.

He was sub-lieutenant in the 3rd Cuirassiers 28 February 1813, wounded by a bursting shell on his left side at Leipzig 16 October 1813, returned home as a foreign national with 6 months' bonus pay 26 November 1815.

LH CH 4 December 1813.

I.er RÉGIMENT DE CUIRASSIERS.

Brigadier de Cuirassiers en bonnet de police, Veste d'écurie, marques distinctives de veste d'écurie, manteau capotte, pantalon de treillis.

Brigadier, casque à bombe de fer, cuirasse, giberne, banderolle porte mousqueton, chevron d'ancienneté, marques distinctives du grade, sabre, pantalon de cheval.

K ELLERMANN (François Etienne, Count, 1770-1835): son of the Maréchal, born in Metz (Moselle) on 4 August 1770. Replacement sub-lieutenant in the Colonel-Général-Hussards 14 August 1785, accompanied Chevalier de Ternan to the United states 1791, sub-lieutenant 1 May 1791, on stand by in the 2nd Cavalry 15 September 1791.

He was lieutenant 10 May 1792, infantry captain in Kellermann's legion 31 May 1793, supernumerary lieutenant-colonel and aide de camp to his father 29 November 1792, battalion commander in the Hautes-Alpes Chasseurs à Cheval 10 April 1793, returned from America and put at the disposal of the Minister of War 1 May 1793.

He was aide de camp to his father and suspended with him 12 October 1793, accused of corresponding with his father who was being detained at the Abbey, freed, volunteered in the 1 Hussars 8 July 1794, aide de camp to this father 9 March 1795, adjutant-general acting brigade commander in the Army of Italy 25 March 1796, confirmed 8 May 1796, several sabre wounds while crossing the Tagliamento 16 March 1797, ordered by Bonaparte to take the flags captured off the enemy to the Directoire 21 March 1797, brigadier-general 28 May 1797.

He commanded the 3rd Brigade (1st and 7th Hussars) of the 2nd Cavalry Division (Rey), then a brigade of Dragoons in the Army of England 12 January 1798, in the Army of Rome February 1798, commanded the vanguard of the MacDonald Division, in the army of Naples 24 January 1799 then that of Italy 4 August 1799, commanded the Manche Department 29 December 1799, in the Reserve Army 29 March 1800, commanded a brigade of cavalry under Murat 20 April 1800 then a heavy cavalry brigade, Harville's division 14 May 1800, took the initiative and charged at Marengo which decided the outcome 14 June 1800, commanded a brigade of Hussars, Quesnel's division 4 July 1800, major-general 5 July 1800, commanded the Heavy Cavalry Division in the Army of Italy 2 March 1801.

He was nomed inspector of mounted troops in the same army 24 July 1801, commanded the cavalry in the army of Hanover 1 February 1804 then the 3rd light Cavalry Division of the 1st Corps of the Grande Armée 17 September 1805, wounded at Austerlitz 2 December 1805.

He commanded the cavalry in the Reserve Army under his father's orders 5 October 1806, then that of the Gironde Observation Corps then in the Army of Portugal 2 August 1807.

He given the task of negotiating and signing the Cintra Convention 30 August 1808, left for France 30 September 1808, commanded the 8th Corps in Spain 19 October 1808, then the 2nd Dragoon division in the same army 9 January 1909,.

He commanded the Reserve Army in Castile 9 March 1809 then temporarily the 6th Corps 6 November 1809, commanded the 2nd Dragoon division assigned to the 6th Corps 12 February 1810, Governor of the Toro, Palencia and Valladolid Provinces 4 June 1810, commanded the Army of the North in Spain September 1810, recalled to France 20 May 1811, commanded the 3rd Light Cavalry Division 9 January 1812, ill and replaced in the Cavalry Reserve of the Grande Armée, available 26 April 1812.

He given the task of inspecting the 5th Military Division 21 October 1812, retired for health reasons at his own request 18 March 1813, recalled to active duty at his request as commanding the cavalry in the 3rd Corps 8 April 1813, shot and wounded in the chest at Klix 30 May 1813, commanded the 4th (Polish) Cavalry Corps 7 June 1813 then the 6th Cavalry Corps coming from Spain 13 February 1814.

He was member of the War Council for the Royal Guard 6 May 1814, inspector-general of cavalry in Lunéville and Nancy 1 June 1814. He commanded a cavalry division under the Duke of Berry 16 March 1815, Peer of France 2 June 1815.

He commanded the 3rd Cavalry Corps (Cuirassiers) made up of the Lhéritier and Roussel d'Urbal divisions in Belgium 3 June 1815, wounded at Waterloo 18 June 1815, remained with Gérard in Paris to negotiate with the King on behalf of Davout 3 July 1815, available 1 August 1815.

He was non-active 4 September 1815. LH CH 16 October 1803, GC 23 August 1814.

On 16 June 1815, Major-General François Kellermann, the son of the General, commanded the 3rd Cavalry Corps made up of the Roussel d'Urbal and Lhéritier Divisions. His horse was killed under him during a charge near the Quatre-Bras crossroads. He hung onto the stirrups of two cuirassiers from Guiton's brigade and reached the French lines in spite of a sprained ankle.

This incident did not prevent him from charging wholeheartedly during the fatal battle on 18 June on the Mont-Saint-Jean Plateau.

The cuirass could not stand up to everything...
(Collections du Musée de l'Empéri, photo R. Brunon)

LABASSEE (Jean Frédéric de, chevalier, 1761-1832): elder brother of the general and son of Dragoon officer, born in Hesse-Cassel (Prussia) on 15 October 1791. Sub-lieutenant in the Vermandois Regiment 10 May 1778, in the Royal Grenadiers 16 April 1781, in the Chasseurs des Alpes 23 September 1784, second-lieutenant 17 June 1785, lieutenant in post with the Chasseurs de Bretagne 18 June 1788.

He was captain in the 6th Battalion of Chasseurs 1 April 1791, deputy to the adjutant-generals 11 March 1792, resigned 1 December 1793, in the 17th Military Division 6 November 1799, served with zeal on the 18 Brumaire (9 November 1799), deputy on the staff of the same division 8 September 1800, rank of captain in the suite of the 8th Dragoons 8 October 1800, squadron commander in the suite 3 June 1801, in service in he 11th Cavalry 22 December 1801 which became the 11th Cuirassiers 24 September 1803, because of injuries 25 May 1807. Holder of a Sabre of Honour. LH CH 14 June 1804, Chevalier of the Empire l.p. 20 August 1809.

LABADIE (Louis Alexandre, 1788-?): born in Bourg (Gironde) on 27 December 1788. Velite in the Grenadiers à Cheval of the Guard 17 September 1807. He was sub-lieutenant in the 7th Cuirassiers 4 March 1812, returned home and non-active 16 August 1814.

LABARTHE (Jean François, 1785-1812): born in Bruel (Aveyron) on 4 June 1785. Velite in the Grenadiers à Cheval of the Guard 1 September 1806, sub-lieutenant in the 4th Cuirassiers 3 June 1809, lieutenant 19 November 1812, killed at the Berezina 30 November 1812. LH CH 25 September 1812.

AFARGUE (Joseph Marie Alexandre, 1788-?): born in Larroque (Haute-Pyrénées) on 2 May 1788. Boarder in the Ecole Militaire in Fontainebleau.

He was sub-lieutenant in the suite of the 8th Cuirassiers 14 December 1806, in service 10 February 1809, lieutenant 3 June 1809, captain 21 February 1812, lance wound to his chest near Moscow 4 October 1812.

He was dismissed 11 December 1815. LH CH 11 October 1812.

Battle of Leipzig, October 1813: The Saxon troops had just defected and joined the forces of the Coalition. Captain Joseph Lafargue of the 8th Cuirassiers succeeded in recovering Generals Reynier and Durutte from among the enemy together with two battalions and two cannon.

Uniforms of 4th Cuirassier Regiment, circa 1814-1815 by Horace Vernet.
(Musée de l'Armée, © RMN)

LABAT (Louis, 1777-1812): born in Joinville (Haute-Marne) on 15 October 1777. In the 13th Cavalry, in General-in-Chief Moreau's horse guards 25 September 1800, in the 17th Dragoons 20 June 1801, left 3 September 180. He was sub-lieutenant quartermaster in the 14th Cuirassiers 18 December 1810, instated 3 February 1811, shot his brains out 30 June 1812.

LABERTINIERE (de, ?-1807): sub-lieutenant in the 6th Cuirassiers 11 April 1807, wounded at Heilsberg 10 June 1807 and died of his wounds the day after 12 June 1807.

LABIFFE (Pierre Louis Béat Ignace, baron, 1773-1825): born in Strasbourg (Bas-Rhin) on 30 April 1773. In the 4th Hussars 26 May, brigadier-fourrier 26 June 1792, adjutant-NCO 4 October 1793, adjutant sub-lieutenant 3 December 1793, shot and wounded in the left arm at Winterthur 27 May 1799, aide de camp to General Decaen 11 October 1799, lieutenant 23 October 1799, acting captain 9 July 1800, confirmed 7 August 1800, captain adjutant-major of the 7th Hussars 23 March 1802, commanded the 7th Company of the regiment 2 December 1805, ordnance officer to the Emperor 14 February 1807.

He was light cavalry squadron commander 11 July 1807, in the 2nd Provisional Hussar Regiment 19 January 1808, in the 7th Chasseurs à Cheval 4 June 1809, major in the 11th Chasseurs à Cheval 21 September 1809, squadron commander in the Chasseurs à Cheval of the Guard 6 December 1811, at the head of the four service squadrons of the Guard captured a 2000-man strong enemy square at Montmirail 16 February 1814, colonel of the 2nd Cuirassiers 17 March 1814.

He was second-colonel in the suite of the 3rd Cuirassiers 16 November 1814, colonel of the 17th Dragoons 14 April 1815, non-active 14 December 1815. LH CH 14 May 1807, O 17 July 1809, Baron of the Empire d. 16 March 1814 without l.p.

LABORIER (Jean, 1763-1827): born in Lisse (Saône-et-Loire) on 18 February 1763. In the Soissonais-Infanterie 7 April 1780, dismissed 6 April 1788, in the Mestre-de-Camp-Général cavalry regiment 11 December 1788, which became the 24th Cavalry 1 January 1791, dismissed with the regiment 20 February 1791 and re-placed as brigadier in the 24th of the new levy the following day 21 February 1791, maréchal des logis 16 March 1792, maréchal des logis-chef 1 July 1792, adjutant sub-lieutenant 7 August 1792.

He was in the same regiment when it became the 23rd Cavalry 4 June 1793, with 18 troopers surprised an enemy convoy escorted by 20 infantrymen and 30 troopers, put the latter to flight and captured the convoy and the infantry at l'Abbaye de l'Aube 11 May 1794, wounded by a shell burst at Liège 27 July 1794, lieutenant by choice 11 August 1794, unemployed and placed on subsistence in the regiment 20 February 1796, back in post in the regiment shortly afterwards 5 December 1800, confirmed 10 June 181, dismissed with the corps 23 December 1802 and incorporated into the 7th Cuirassiers 15 January 1803, wounded at Essling 21 May 1809.

He was retired and ordered to present himself to

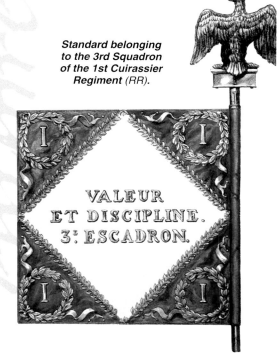

Standard belonging to the 3rd Squadron of the 1st Cuirassier Regiment (RR).

the General Imperial Headquarters 2 June 1809. LH CH 14 June 1804.

LABRETONNIERE EULOGE (Bon Charles Henry, 1788-?): younger brother of the following, born in Cherbourg (Manche) on 21 November 1788. Boarder in the school in Fontainebleau 21 May 1806, sub-lieutenant in the 3rd Cuirassiers 17 February 1807. He was in the 1st Provisional Heavy Cavalry in Spain which became the 13th Cuirassiers 21 October 1808, lieutenant 13 February 1809, captain aide de camp to General Durosnel 28 March 1809, present in Russia.

LABRETONNIERE LACOUDREE (Alexandre Louis Marie David, ? - ?): elder brother of the above, born in Cherbourg (Manche). Pupil in the school in Fontainebleau. He was sub-lieutenant in the 5th of the Line 19 April 1806, in the suite of the 3rd Cuirassiers 5 September 1806, in service 5 January 1807, lieutenant 6 September 1808, aide de camp to General Préval, 27 September 1809.

LABROSSE (Jacques Antoine de, 1793-?): born in Manigues (Puy-de-Dôme) on 6 January 1793. In the 3rd Gardes d'Honneur 2 June 1813, brigadier 21 June 1813, maréchal des logis 29 June 1813, maréchal des logis-chef in the 1st Gardes d'Honneur 13 July 1813, second-lieutenant 2 October 1813, shot and wounded in the left knee at Leipzig 18 October 1813.

A lance wound to his right side at Hanau 28 October 1813, sub-lieutenant in the Line 25 February 1814, in the 6th Cuirassiers 5 March 1814, in the King's Cuirassiers 1 July 1814 which became the 1st Cuirassiers March 1815, in the 1st Cuirassiers of the Royal Guard 1 December 1815.

LABUSSIERE (Gilbert, 1761-1809): born in Chantelle (Allier) on 27 February 1761. In the Roi-Cavalerie 1 July 1781, brigadier 9 October 1786, in the same regiment when it became the 6th Cavalry 1 January 1791.

He was maréchal des logis 1 July 1792, maréchal des logis-chef 1 April 1793, sub-lieutenant 17 July 1799, confirmed 8 February 1801, in the same regiment when it became the 6th Cuirassiers 23 December 1802, lieutenant 30 December 1802, captain wounded at Heilsberg 10 June 1807, killed at Essling 22 May 1809.

LACHAISE see **TERRIER DELACHAISE.**

LACHAPELLE (Charles Hyppolite, 1784-?): born in Versailles (Seine-et-Oise) on 20 October 1784. In the Gendarmes d'Ordonnance 3 November 1806, brigadier 13 July 1807. He was sub-lieutenant in the suite of the 3rd cuirassiers 10 September 1807, retroactively to 16 July 1807, resignation accepted 21 December 1808.

LACHATELAINE de BANANS
see **MARCHANT de la CHATELAINE de BANANS**

LACHERE (Jean Baptiste, 1776-1809): born in Kempten (Bavaria) on 28 November 1776. In the 4th Hussars 27 February 1799, in the 8th Cuirassiers 19 May 1802, fourrier 6 June 1802, maréchal des logis-chef 21 January 1803, adjutant-NCO 30 September 1803.
He was sub-lieutenant 27 January 1807, wounded at Essling and died of his wounds 26 May 1809. LH CH 1 October 1807.

LACOSTE (? - ?): Velite in the Grenadiers à Cheval of the Imperial Guard, sub-lieutenant in the 6th Cuirassiers 16 July 1807, wounded at Essling 22 May 1809, took up his functions again

AMACQ (Guillaume François, 1783-1852) born in Dun (Meuse) on 25 January 1783. In the 8th Hussars 1 May 1803, brigadier 12 July 1803, with his platoon boarded a barge and drove off an English boat with their firepower at Boulogne 1804, maréchal des logis 10 March 1804, joined his unit 17 December 1804, in the 7th Cuirassiers 17 December 1804, instated 24 January 1805, sub-lieutenant 24 January 1805, lieutenant 26 April 1807, in the 1st Provisional Heavy Cavalry in Spain 20 June 1808 which became the 13th Cuirassiers 21 October 1808, several sabre wounds of which one to his left arm.
He was wounded at Sagonte 25 October 1811, first-lieutenant in the Grenadiers à Cheval of the Guard 9 February 1813, wounded at Hanau 30 October 1813, dismissed

23 May 1809, lieutenant 3 June 1809, gendarmerie lieutenant 23 August 1811.

LACOSTE (Pierre Antoine, 1773-?): born in 1773. In the 16th Cavalry 7 July 1799, in the Grenadiers à Cheval of the Guard 12 April 1800, brigadier 1801, in the Dragoons of the Guard 26 July 1806, maréchal des logis 22 September 1808, lieutenant in the 17th Dragoons 19 April 1811, aide de camp 1 August 1813, captain 28 November 1813, attached to the King's Cuirassiers 1814.
He was non-active on half-pay 10 July 1814, left 15 July 1814. LH CH 15 June 1804.

and non-active on half-pay 25 November 1815. LH CH 29 December 1809, O 14 February 1815.

In 1804 a brigadier in the 8th Hussars, Guillaume Lamacq boarded a barge and with its guns drove off an English boat which was approaching Boulogne; he was made Maréchal des Logis on the following 10 March.
In February 1809, having become a lieutenant in the ranks of the 13th Cuirassiers in Spain, he received several sabre wounds, but killed by himself an officer and several Olivenza Chasseurs at Saragossa. His feats of arms in Spain did not stop there since on 17 August 1810, he routed six hundred dragoons at the head of a single cuirassier squadron and took 80 prisoners at Castala on 21 June 1812.

LACOSTE see **DELMAS LACOSTE.**

LACOUDREE
see **LABRETONNIERE LACOUDREE**

LACOUR (Jean Baptiste Alexandre, 1777-?): born in Paris (Seine) on 28 September 1777. In the 7th Artillery 5 March 1792, shot through the body 5 March 1793, 20th Chasseurs à Cheval 17 March 1799, brigadier 22 March 1800, fourrier 21 April 1801, maréchal des logis-chef 9

June 1802, shot and wounded in his right hand at Ulm October 1805, adjutant-NCO 14 January 1807, two sabre wounds 14 January 1807, two sabre wounds to his head.

He was sub-lieutenant 8 August 1808 lieutenant 30 April 1809, shot and wounded in his right arm at Amstetten 6 May 1809, captain 21 September 1809, aide de camp to General Castex, his former colonel 30 September 1809, shot and wounded in his left thigh at Polotsk 11 August 1812,.

Named squadron commander in the 23rd Chasseurs à Cheval 21 November 1812, major in the 4th Chevau-Légers 18 September 1813, in the 14th Cuirassiers 3 January 1814, on 2 months' leave with pay the same day, in the suite of the 12th Cuirassiers 14 July 1814, took up his appointment 5 September 1814. He was confirmed and commissioned 28 September 1814, two month's on half-pay 3 November 1814, in the suite 11 May 1815, on half-pay when the corps was dismissed 1815. LH CH 1807, O 28 September 1813.

LACOUR (Jean, 1785-1812): born in Eymet (Dordogne) in 1785. In the 10th Cuirassiers 20 November 1806, brigadier 9 June 1807, fourrier 22 March 1809, maréchal des logis-chef 16 May 1809, sub-lieutenant 12 August 1809, killed at Winkovo 18 October 1812.

LACROIX (François Théodore, 1783-?): born in Saint-Hyppolite (Gard) on 23 March 1783. In the 12th Cavalry 14 January 1803 which became the 12th Cuirassiers 24 September 1803, in the 2nd Cuirassiers 21 February 1804.

He was maréchal des logis 30 October 1806, maréchal des logis-chef, sub-lieutenant 14 May 1809, wounded at Wagram 6 July 1809, lieutenant 12

March 1812, captain 14 May 1813, non-active on half-pay 10 December 1815. LH CH 14 May 1813.

LACROIX de CHEVRIERES de SAYVE (Auguste de, 1791-1854): Pupil in the Ecole Spéciale Militaire de Saint-Cyr, sub-lieutenant in the suite of the 9th Cuirassiers 14 August 1810, took up his appointment 25 January 1812, lieutenant 21 April 1813, aide de camp.

LACROIX JALLAND (Nicolas François, 1767-?): born in Serrières (Meuse) on 8 February 1767. In the Royal-Cavalerie 5 August 1787, in the same regiment when it became the 2nd Cavalry 1 January 1791, brigadier-fourrier 1 April 1793, maréchal des logis 18 April 1795, maréchal des logis-chef 30 May 1797.

He was adjutant-NCO 21 March 1798, sub-lieutenant in the suite 23 June 1800 for his distinguished conduct at Marengo, in the same regiment when it became the 2nd Cuirassiers 12 October 1802, lieutenant in the 12th cuirassiers 25 August 1806, left or instated 1 October 1806, captain 29 January 1808, wounded at Essling 22 May 1809, retired 14 August 1809.

LAFANGERAYE
see **LECOINTE de LAFANGERAYE**

LAFARGUE (Pierre, 1774-?): born in Tonneins (Lot-et-Garonne) on 13 October 1774. In the Ségur-Dragons 1 July 1787 which became the Hainaut Chasseurs 17 March 1788 then the 5th Chasseurs à Cheval 1 January 1791, sub-lieutenant in the 23rd Chasseurs à Cheval 10 December 1792.

Named lieutenant 25 September 1793, captain 11 October 1793, confirmed 22 April 1795, shot and wounded in the right shoulder in the Army of the Rhine 1 December 1800, commissioned captain 2nd Class 17 May 1803, aide de camp to General Girard aka Vieux 10 July 1804, in the 1st Carabiniers 7 February 1807, joined them 16 March 1807.

He was in the suite of the 2nd cuirassiers 13 April 1807, joined them 5 May 1807, took up his appointment 15 March 1808, in the 13th Cuirassiers 21

October 1808, squadron commander in the suite 11 January 1812, second-major 10 August 1813, acting major deputising for Major Tarbé in the 2nd Carabiniers 9 March 1814, confirmed in the suite of the 2nd Carabiniers 31 May 1814 with the return of Major Tarbé. LH CH 28 May 1811.

LAFERRIERE see **LEGENDRE de LAFERRIERE**

LAFLEUR (Brice Pierre, 1763-?): born in Paris (Seine) on 25 July 1763. In the Aquitaine-Infanterie 30 October 1778, in the Paris National Guard 1 November 1789, in the Volontaires Nationaux à Cheval from the Ecole Militaire 23 August 1792, sub-lieutenant in the same regiment when it formed the 26th Cavalry 21 February 1793 which became the 25th Cavalry 4 June 1793.

He was lieutenant 4 November 1794, dismissed with the corps 12 October 1802 and incorporated into the 2nd Cuirassiers 24 November 1802, captain in the 9th Cuirassiers 1 October 1808, wounded at Wagram 6 July 1809, in the suite of the 6th Provisional Dragoons 13 October 18090, left in order to retire 14 December 1809, pensioned 12 January 1810.

LAFONTAINE (Antoine Joseph, 1765-1807): born in Epinal (Vosges) on 28 June 1765. Trooper in the Mestre-de-Camp-Général Regiment 16 December 1782, brigadier 12 September 1784, fourrier 5 July 1786, maréchal des logis 1 March 1788, discharged 1 May 1788.

He was in the same regiment when it became the 24th Cavalry 1 January 1791, dismissed with the corps 20 February 1791 then put back in the 24th with the new levy when it was formed the following day as maréchal des logis-chef 21 February 1791.

He was sub-lieutenant by choice 17 June 1792, in the same regiment when it became the 23rd Cavalry 4 June 1793, lieutenant by choice 4 January 1794, captain by choice 17 April 1794, squadron commander 26 October 1800, dismissed with the corps 23 December 1802 and put in the suite of the 7th Cuirassiers 21 March 183.

He joined them 21 April 1803, in service 22 December 1803, killed by cannonball at Heilsberg 10 June 1807. LH CH 14 June 1804.

LAFOSSE see **CHATRY DE LAFOSSE**

LAFOUCHARDIÈRE (Jean Alexis de, 1781-after 1868): born in Chatellerault (Vienne) on 21 February 1781. In the 4th Cuirassiers 3 January 1804, fourrier 17 February 1806, maréchal des logis 1 October 1806, sub-lieutenant 17 June 1812,

He was incorporated with his squadron into the 2nd Provisional Heavy Cavalry in Hamburg 11 September 1813, acting lieutenant in post with the 3rd Cuirassiers 20 April 1814, temporary aide de camp to Davout 1814, returned with the garrison 27 May 1814.

He was not confirmed and put back as sub-lieutenant then resigned 18 August 1814, resignation accepted 19 September 1814, left 7 October 1814.

LAFRENAY (Hilaire Noël André de, 1789 -) born in Falaise (Calvados) on 25 September 1789. One of the Emperor's pages 1 September 1806, sub-lieutenant in the 2nd Cuirassiers 17 August 1808, instated 1 September 1808, lieutenant 3 July 1811, captain 11 October 1812, aide de camp to General Hoogendorp 13 March 1813.

He was in the 4th Gardes d'Honneur 3 September 1813, squadron commander in the Line 22 June 1814, in the 5th Cuirassiers 5 July 1814, appointment cancelled and re-placed as captain in the regiment 20 May 1815.

Reinstated as squadron commander 1 August 1815 and dismissed 23 December 1815. LH CH.

LAGARDE see **CARLIER LAGARDE**

LAGARDE see **LANOUGAREDE LAGARDE**

LAGAY (Jérôme François, 1778-?): born in Villefranche (Rhône) on 24 January 1778. In the 12th Cavalry 24 October 1798, fourrier 9 August 1800, maréchal des logis 20 October 1801, maréchal des logis-chef 10 February 1802, in the same regiment when it became the 12th Cuirassiers 24 September 1803, sub-lieutenant 31 October 1806, lieutenant 29 January 1808, adjutant-major 9 August 1809, rank of captain 9 February 1811.

Wounded and taken prisoner at Orcha 21 November 1812, returned to the suite 18 August 1814, four months' leave with pay 8

***7th Cuirassier officer at the Berezina.
Composition by P. Benigni. (RR)***

November 1814, in service by exchanging with captain adjutant-major Mamelet 28 January 1815, captain commanding a company in the regiment 14 June 1815.

He was wounded at Waterloo 18 June 1815, dismissed with the corps 10 December 1815. LH 13 August 1809.

LAGRANGE see **LELIEVRE de LAGRANGE**

LAGRANGE see **REYDY de LAGRANGE**

LAHOUSSAYE
see **LEBRUN de LAHOUSSAYE**

LAHUBERDIERE (Pierre Robert Hubert, baron de, 1771-1859): born in Bernay (Eure) on 11 February 1774. Chasseur à Cheval in the Brittany Regiment 9 February 1789 which became the 10th Chasseurs à Cheval 1 January 1791, brigadier-fourrier 26 May 1793, maréchal des logis 9 November 1793, sub-lieutenant 27 April 1797.

He was in the Grenadiers à Cheval of the Guard 3 January 1800, second-lieutenant 4 May 1800, first-lieutenant 26 October 1800, captain adjutant-major 5 September 1803, commanded the 1st Company of the Squadron of Velites attached to the regiment 18 December 1805, went over to the 2nd Company of the 2nd Squadron 1807, major 26 June 1809.

He was assigned to the Cavalry Depot of the Hanoverian Legion 12 June 1810, major in the 9th Cuirassiers 7 March 1811, joined them 1 April 1811, colonel in the suite 12 May 1812, in service in the 10th Cuirassiers 21 May 1812, confirmed 28 September 1814, on one month's leave 24 January 1815.

He was non-active when the regiment was disbanded 20 November 1815. LH CVH 14 June 1804, O 26 June 1809, Baron of the Empire d. 28 September 1813 and l.p. 24 February 1814.

LAIR (Jean François, 1762-?): born in Sainte-Marie (Calvados) on 9 September 1762. In the Royal-Champagne-Cavalerie 8 December 1788 which became the 20th Cavalry 1 January 1791, fourrier 22 March 1794, in the same regiment when it became the 19th Cavalry 4 June 1793, two sabre wounds to his head at Rousselaer 13 June 1794.

He was maréchal des logis 20 January 1799, maréchal des logis-chef 9 June 1799, sub-lieutenant 19 June 1799, dismissed with the corps 31 December 1802 and incorporated into the 11th Cavalry 5 February 1803 which became the 11th Cuirassiers 24 September 1803. Lieutenant by seniority 25 October 1804, retired and left 13 February 1807.

LAJARTHE DESVERGNES (Jacques, 1785-1813): born in Chasseignac (Dordogne) on 30 July 1785. Health officer under-assistant-major in the 3rd Cuirassiers 22 January 1807, allowed to enlist in the 6th Cuirassiers 5 April 1810, volunteer in the 6th Cuirassiers 11 June 1810, brigadier 25 June 1810, fourrier 15 July 1810.

He was maréchal des logis 17 October 1810, maréchal des logis-chef 10 May 1812, adjutant-NCO 1 September 1813, sub-lieutenant 5 October 1813, wounded, amputated and prisoner at Leipzig 18 October 1813 then disappeared.

LALAING D'AUDE-NAERDE (Charles Eugène de, baron, 1779-1859): born in Paris (Seine) on 13 November 1779. Page at the court in Vienna 1795, sub-lieutenant in the Melas Dragoons 1 April 1799, resigned 15 October 183, commanded the Brussels Guard of Honour during Napoleon's visit 1804, captain in the service of France in the 112th of the Line 28 June 1804, squadron commander of Dragoons 22 July 1805.

He was in the 3rd Cuirassiers 5 September 1805, Ecuyer Cavalcadour of the Empress still keeping his functions 1805, Major 10 September 1807, commanded two marching squadrons 17 July 1808, colonel in the suite of the 3rd Cuirassiers 29 January 1809, commanded the regiment 7 September 1811, brigadier-general 5 December 1812, brigadier in the Escadron Sacré during the retreat, commanded the 1st Brigade (4th, 7th and 14th Cuirassiers) of the 3rd heavy Cavalry Division in the 1st Corps 12 April 1813 which became Doumerc's division 15 August 1813. He was major in the 2nd Chevau-Légers Lancers of the Guard 26 December 1813, commanded the squadrons of the Young Guard, lieutenant in the King's Body Guards 1 June 1814, followed Louis XVIII to Ghent 20 March 1815, ordered by the King to obtain the surrender of Cambrai 25 June 1815, lieutenant commanding the King's Body Guards 1 November 1815. LH CH 1805, O 28 February 1810, C 20 April 1814 confirmed 22 August 1814, Baron of the Empire, l.p. 15 October 1809.

LALIRE (Pierre, chevalier, 1766-?): born in Courgenay (Marne) on 4 November 1766. In the Royal-Navarre-Cavalerie 21 October 1785, brigadier 6 August 1789, in the same regiment when it became the 22nd Cavalry

1 January 1791, maréchal des logis 20 June 1792, adjutant-NCO 1 April 1793, in the same regiment when it became the 21st Cavalry 4 June 1793, adjutant sub-lieutenant 15 June 1793, sub-lieutenant 1 July 1793, lieutenant 3 February 1802, adjutant-major 17 May 1802; dismissed with the corps and incorporated into the suite of the 15th Cavalry 25 January 1803 which became the 24th Dragoons 24 September 1803.

He obtained the rank of captain in the suite 15 October 1803, captain adjutant-major in post in the 8th Cuirassiers 16 March 1804, captain commanding a company 27 January 1807, squadron commander 27 April 1807, shot and wounded in the left leg and three sabre wounds at Heilsberg 10 June 1807, shot and wounded in the left arm at Essling 22 May 1809 and another shot in the left arm at Wagram 6 July 1809, major in the suite 12 September 1809, in service in the 7th Cuirassiers 10 March 1810,.

He joined them the following day 11 March 1810, confirmed 27 September 1814 and 19 May 1815, retired when the corps was disbanded 19 December 1815. LH CH 5 November 1804, Chevalier of the Empire l.p. 2 September 1810.

LALLEMAND (Joseph, 1785-1814): born in Flaigneux (Ardennes) on 3 February 1785. In the 11th Cuirassiers 4 January 1805, brigadier 15 April 1809, gendarme in the Legion à Cheval d'Espagne 25 December 1809, brigadier 25 October 1811, dismissed with the corps 27 February 1813.

He was sub-lieutenant in the 8th Cuirassiers 1 March 1813, shot and wounded twice in the right shoulder at Sézanne 26 March 1814, entered the civilian hospital in Paris 29 March 1814 and died of his wounds 11 April 1814.

LALLEMANT (Albert, 1782-?): born in Lay-Saint-Christophe (Meurthe) on 28 March 1782. Surgeon 3rd Class in the Army of the Côtes de l'Océan 22 April 1803, under-assistant-surgeon in the 11th Chasseurs à Cheval 28 January 1804, assistant-major surgeon in the 16th Chasseurs à Cheval 9 October 1806.

He was surgeon-major in the ambulances of the Grande Armée 9 October 1813, left 4 July 1814, Gendarmerie lieutenant 7 November 1814, lieutenant in the suite of the 11th Cuirassiers 11 May 1815, wounded at Waterloo 18 June 1815, appointment cancelled 1 August 1815, struck off the rolls 19 August 1815.

LALLEMANT (Jean Pierre, 1773-?): born in Void (Meuse) on 2 September 1773. In the 10th Cavalry 12 January 1793, sabre wound to the head near Fleurus 19 June 1794, brigadier 30 April 1801, in the same regiment when it became the 10th Cuirassiers 24 September 1803, maréchal des logis 20 July 1805, sub-lieutenant 21 March 1812, sabre wound to his forehead and lance wound to his neck at Leipzig 18 October 1813, dismissed with the corps 25 December 1815. LH CH 14 March 1806.

LALOMBARDIERE (Louis Claude Juste de, 1785-?): born in Montélimar (Drôme) on 27 March 1785. Volunteer in the 19th Cavalry 25 January 1802, brigadier 27 October 1802, dismissed with the corps 31 December 1802, maréchal des logis 20 January 1803, incorporated into the 9th Cuirassiers 25 January 1803, sabre wound to his face at Austerlitz 2 December 1805.

He was in the 2nd Provisional Heavy Cavalry in Spain which formed the 13th Cuirassiers 21 October 1808, maréchal des logis-chef 1 August 1809, sub-lieutenant 9 February 1814, incorporated into the 9th Cuirassiers 9 August 1814, confirmed in the suite 4 February 1815, non-active on half-pay when the corps was disbanded 26 November 1815.

LALOYERE see **BEUVERAND de LALOYERE**

LAMARCHE see **DUMAS de la MARCHE**

LAMARLIERE (Raymond de, 1788-?): born in Embrun (Hautes-Alpes) on 20 April 1788. In the Gendarmes d'Ordonnance of the Guard 8 April 1807, dismissed with the corps 23 October 1807 and incorporated into the Chasseurs à Cheval of the Guard 24 November 1807.

He was sub-lieutenant in the 7th Cuirassiers 15 January 1810, joined them 22 February 1810, lieutenant 10 April 1813, prisoner 1 January 1814. LH CH 19 November 1812.

LAMARTHE (? - ?): maréchal des logis in the 3rd Cuirassiers, sub-lieutenant 14 May 1809, wounded at Essling 22 May 1809 and Wagram 6 July 1809, retired 1810.

LAMAZELIERE (de, ?-1812): Pupil in the Ecole Impériale de Cavalerie in Saint-Germain, sub-lieutenant in the 2nd Cuirassiers 11 March 1812, remained behind and disappeared presumed prisoner 20 November 1812.

LAMAZELIERE
see **ROUS de LAMAZELIERE**

LAMBERT (Etienne François, 1755-?): born in Gilley (Doubs) on 13 June 1755. Trooper in the King's Regiment 4 February 1777 which became the 6th Cavalry 1 January 1791, brigadier 1 July 1791, maréchal des logis 1 July 1792, maréchal des logis-chef 1 April 1793.

He was sub-lieutenant 11 November 1796, lieutenant 29 March 1802, in the same regiment when it became the 6th Cuirassiers 23 December 1802, on retirement pay 14 January 1806.

LAMBERT de SAINT MARC D'HERBIGNY (César Louis d', 1783-?): brother of the following, born in Rouen (Seine-Inférieure) on 20 December 1783. In the 11th Cuirassiers 29 March 1804, brigadier 13 May 1804, maréchal des logis 5 October 1804, adjutant 3 April 1807, sub-lieutenant 16 May 1809, lieutenant 15 October 1809, adjutant-major 25 September 1811, retroactively to 30 July 1811, rank of captain 30 January 1813, captain in service in a company 25 December 1813, dismissed with the corps 16 December 18151. LH CH 1 October 1807.

LAMBERT de SAINT MARC D'HERBIGNY (François Robert, 1781-?): brother of the above, born in Rouen (Seine-Inférieure) on 29 December 1781. Emigrated 1792, in the 10th Hanoverian Chevau-Légers 5 December 1798, left them to return to France 15 May 1803, volunteer in the 16th Chasseurs à Cheval 29 September 1803, brigadier 21 April 1804, maréchal des logis 18 September 1804, lieutenant in the 20th Wagon Train Battalion 1 April 1812, confirmed 24 August 1812, deputy on the staff of the 34th Military Division 6 August 1813.

He was taken prisoner with the garrison in Danzig and held in Russia January 1814, returned, supernumerary in the suite of the King's Cuirassiers 19 November 1814, remained in Paris at the disposal of the Minister of War 20 January 1815, in service in the Queen's Cuirassiers 18 February 1815, did not join his unit and confirmed in the 1st Cuirassiers 1 April 1815, dismissed and put up for retirement 24 December 1815.

LAMBERTY (Joseph Rey, 1773-?): born in Comberanche (Dordogne) on 15 May 1773. In the King's Guard 30 March 1792, dismissed with the corps and sub-lieutenant in the 2nd Cavalry 24 July 1792, reached the corps 29 September 1792, discharged 27 July 1794, reinstated 18 October 1794, lieutenant 16 March 1795, retroactively to 27 July 1794, captain in the suite on the battlefield of Marengo 14 June 1800, took up his functions 23 October 1800, confirmed 25 May 1801.

He became squadron commander in the 7th Cuirassiers 3 August 1811, joined them 24 October 1811, shot and wounded in the right arm at the Berezina 28 November 1812, second-major 13 August 1813, first major 5 September 1813, non-active and retired 6 November 1814. LH CH 14 June 1804, O 16 May 1813.

LAMBLEZ (Jean François Colin, 1754-?): born in Raon-l'Etape (Vosges) on 3 July 1754. Trooper in the Royal-Etranger 3 January 1787 which became the 7th Cavalry 1 January 1791, brigadier-fourrier the same day, maréchal des logis 1 May 1792.

He was sub-lieutenant 7 May 1793, commissioned 25 August 1793, wounded near Cambrai 26 April 1794, lieutenant 20 January 1799, in the same regiment when it became the 7th Cuirassiers 23 December 1802, captain by choice 25 December 1804, retires 11 March 1807.

LAMIRAL (Claude, ?-1813): born in Membrey (Haute-Saône). Maréchal des logis in the 12th Cuirassiers, sub-lieutenant 9 August 1809, lieutenant 19 March 1812, wounded at the Moskova 7 September 1812, amputated and remained at Elbing 1 January 1813 and disappeared.

LAMOTHE (Etienne, 1759-?): born in Remoncourt (Vosges) on 22 December 1759. Trooper in the Queen's Regiment 14 February 1779, brigadier 9 September 1784, maréchal des logis 1 February 1788, in the same regiment when it became the 4th Cavalry 1 January 1791.

He became maréchal des logis-chef 21 January 1792, adjutant sub-lieutenant 1 April 1793, sub-lieutenant 1 August 1793, lieutenant 27 June 1794, captain 19 February 1799, in the same regiment when it became the 4th Cuirassiers 12 October 1802, wounded at Heilsberg 10 June 1807, retired 20 February 1808. LH CH 1805.

LAMOTHE (Jean, 1778-?): born in Souillac (Lot) on 23 June 1778. In the 5th Cavalry 5 February 1799, brigadier 7 March 1801, in the same regiment when it became the 5th Cuirassiers 24 September 1803, brigadier-fourrier 23 November 1804, maréchal des logis 10 October 1806, wounded by a Biscayan shot to his left knee at Eylau 8 February 1807, maréchal des logis-chef the following day 9 February 1807, sub-lieutenant 15 May 1809.

He was lieutenant 12 March 1812 shot and wounded in the wrist at the Moskova 7 September 1812, captain 18 October 1812, in the suite of the unit with the August 1814 reorganisation, shot and wounded in the right eye at Waterloo 18 June 1815, dismissed with the regiment 23 December 1815. LH CH 14 April 1807.

LAMOTHE see **CRESTAULT de LAMOTHE.**

LAMOTTE (Jacques Louis de, 1757-?): born in Groville (Calvados) on 26 October 1757. In the Orléans-Cavalerie 29 August 1775, brigadier 20 June 1781, maréchal des logis 28 August 1784, maréchal des logis-chef 8 May 1788, in the same regiment when it became the 13th Cavalry 1 January 1791, resigned 2 August 1791, trooper in the 10th Regiment 4 October 1791.

He was brigadier 27 August 1792, brigadier-fourrier 15 September 1793, maréchal des logis 19 December 1795, maréchal des logis-chef 19 June 1798, temporary sub-lieutenant 30 June 1799, confirmed 2 August 1801, lieutenant 18 December 1802, in the same regiment when it became the 10th Cuirassiers 24 September 1803, wounded near Brünn 7 October 1805, retired 24 November 1806, left 1 February 1807.

LAMOTTE GUERY
see **CHRISTOPHE de LAMOTTE GUERY**

LAMOTTE see **PAULTRE de LAMOTTE**

LAMOUREUX (Antoine, 1775-?): born in Rosières (Haute-Marne) on 13 March 1775. In the 24th Cavalry

10 November 1791 which became the 23rd cavalry 4 June 1793, brigadier 30 May 1799, fourrier 16 June 1800, dismissed with the corps 23 December 1802 and incorporated into the 6th Cuirassiers 3 January 1803, maréchal des logis 20 February 1803, maréchal des logis-chef 23 December 1803, several lance wounds to his head and a sabre wound to his chin at Heilsberg 10 June 1807.

He was sub-lieutenant 8 October 1808, lieutenant 3 June 1809, captain 8 October 1811, seven lance wounds to his thighs, back and feet then taken prisoner at Winkovo 18 October 1812, returned 19 March 1815, retired 21 November 1815. LH CH 1 October 1807.

LAMOUSSAYE (Edouard Alexandre de, 1789-1814): born in Lamballe (Côtes-du-Nord) on 4 February 1789. Boarder in the Ecole Impériale Militaire in Fontainebleau 6 August 1805, sub-lieutenant in the suite of the 2nd Cuirassiers 23 September 1806.

He joined them November 1806, took up his appointment October 1807, lieutenant in the 7th Cuirassiers 2 March 1809, instated 1 May 1809, captain 8 October 1811, wounded at the Berezina 28 November 1812, squadron commander 5 September 1813, killed near Brienne 30 January 1814. LH CH 1 October 1807, O 16 May 1813.

LAMPINET (Jacques Louis Auguste de, 1781-?): born in Vesoul (Haute-Saône) on 10 March 1791. Emigrated 1 October 1791, in the Chasseurs Nobles of the Army of Condé 10 November 1791, sub-lieutenant in the Hohenlohe Regiment 19 April 1797, in service of Russia with the corps, left when the Army of Condé was disbanded 16 February 1801.

He returned to France 1 April 1801, in the 23rd Cavalry 20 July 1802, brigadier-fourrier 18 September 1802, dismissed with the corps 23 December 182, maréchal des logis 30 December 1802, incorporated into the 5th Cuirassiers 3 January 1803, maréchal des logis-chef 13 November 1803.

He was adjutant-NCO 3 March 1804, wounded by a Biscayan shot to is head at Austerlitz 2 December 1805, sub-lieutenant 21 December 1805, confirmed 14 January 1806, wounded by a Biscayan shot to his right leg at Eylau 8 February 1807, lieutenant 20 February 1807, adjutant-major 3 April 1807, rank of captain 3 October 1808, went to company 16 May 1809, cannonball wound to his left foot at Wagram 6 July 1809, bayonet wound to his left hand at the Moskova 7 September 1812.

Five lance wounds and sabre wound to his right arm and taken prisoner at Winkovo 18 October 1812, returned 8 June 1814, dismissed 23 December 1815. LH CH 14 April 1807.

LANASCOL see **QUIMPER de LANASCOL**

LANCESSEUR (François Laurent, 1774-?): born in Mainville (Seine-et-Oise) on 8 August 1774. In the

8th Cavalry 23 July 1798 which became the 8th Cuirassiers 10 October 1801, brigadier 31 July 1802, maréchal des logis 1 October 1806, maréchal des logis-chef 27 April 1807, sub-lieutenant 9 August 1809, lance wound to his right side near Moscow 4 October 1812.

He was lieutenant 8 July 1813, lance wound to his right side and sabre wound to his left thigh and his horse killed under him at Hanau 30 October 1813, on the active list when the regiment was disbanded 5 December 1815. LH CH 28 September 1813.

LANG (Jean Georges, 1765-after 1845) born in Seingbouse (Moselle) on 2 January 1765. In the Commissaire-Général-Cavalerie 16 October 1782, brigadier 1 June 1787, in the same regiment when it became the 3rd Cavalry 1 January 1791, maréchal des logis 10 May 1792, saved the regimental standard although unhorsed and wounded at Famars 23 May 1793, maréchal des logis-chef 1 August 1793, adjutant-NCO 13 October 1797, sub-lieutenant 2 March 1798, promoted to lieutenant on the battlefield at la Trebbia 30 June 1799, confirmed 12 December 1800.

He was adjutant-major 13 March 1802, in the same regiment when it became the 3rd Cuirassiers 12 October 1802, rank of captain 9 September 1803, wounded and unhorsed at Austerlitz 2 December 1805, in service 11 December 1805, retired 9 May 1809. Holder of a Sabre of Honour 30 January 1803, LH CH by rights 24 September 1803, O 14 June 1804.

LANGE see **VERGNIAUD de LANGE**

LANGLET (Louis François, 1778-?): born in Prévilliers (Oise) on 24 August 1778. In the 22nd Cavalry 21 December 1798, brigadier 26 January 1802, dismissed with the corps 31 December 1802 and incorporated into the 12th Cuirassiers 25 January 1803.

He became maréchal des logis 28 July 1805, shot and wounded in the left leg at Friedland 14 June 1807, maréchal des logis-chef 14 May 1809, sub-lieutenant 15 March 1812, lieutenant 8 July 1813, in the King's Cuirassiers 1 May 1814, in the 11th Cuirassiers 19 May 1815, forewarned 25 May 1815, rejoined and wounded at les Quatre-Bras 16 June 1815, dismissed with the corps 16 December 1815. LH CH 25 February 1814.

LANGLOIS (François, 1773-?): born in Landouze (Aisne) on 24 March 1773. Requisition officer in the 9th Cavalry 23 August 1793, in the 2nd Carabiniers 16 June 1798, brigadier 8 June 1800, maréchal des logis 20 December 1806, sub-lieutenant in the 13th Cuirassiers 14 July 1813, incorporated into the 4th Cuirassiers 9 August 1814, retired 4 January 1815.

LANOUGAREDE (Etienne Ladislas Honoré de, 1780-?): cousin of the Count of Esterhazy and brother of the following, born in Colmars (Basses-Alpes) on 15 July 1780. In the 3rd Hussars 5 May 1797, brigadier 7 May 1799, maréchal des logis 29 May 1799, acting sub-lieutenant in the Legion des Francs du Nord 25 June 1800, correspondence officer for General Colaud 1801.

He was sub-lieutenant in the 6th Cuirassiers 8 June 1803, detached to the riding school at Versailles, joined them 321 May 1804, returned to his regiment, lieutenant 27 April 1807, captain in the Berg Chevau-Légers 9 July 1807, squadron commander 12 June 1808, confirmed 11 January 1811, sent away and recalled to France for extortion September 1812, served with his brother.

He became squadron commander in French service 29 November 1815. LH CH 13 December 1810.

LANOUGAREDE LAGARDE (Antoine Valentin de, 1767-1853): cousin of the Count of Esterhazy and brother of the above, born in Gannat (Allier) on 14 November 1797. Gentleman cadet in the Esterhazy Hussars 6 February 1780, sub-lieutenant 26 September 1784, second-lieutenant 7 October 1787, supernumerary in the suite of the corps when it was reorganised 17 March 1788, in the same regiment when it became the 3rd Hussars 1 January 1791.

He was lieutenant 25 January 1792, captain end 1792, squadron commander 8 November 1795, in the suite 21 March 1796, took up his appointment 2 August 1799, major of the 2nd Hussars 19 October 1803, commanded the regiment in the Grande Armée 17 October 1806, employed in the Potsdam Central Cavalry Depot in post 16 December 1806, at Bourcier's disposal for harnesses January 1807, commanded the 1st Provisional Hussars 28 October 1807, colonel 15 November 1808, available 11 April 1809, commanded the 3rd Cuirassiers (Marching) 9 June 1809, available 23 November 1809.

He commanded the 3rd Cavalry (Marching) 26 December 1809, in the Orthez Depot 23 February 1810, colonel of the 23rd Chasseurs à Cheval 7 September 1811, allowed to retire 8 August 1812, pensioned 25 March 1813. LH CVH 25 March 1804.

LAPOMMERAIS see **LEGO de LAPOMMERAIS**

LARCHANTEL (André Louis, 1767-?): born in Brest (Finistère) on 15 July 1767. Midshipman 1 June 1782, guard in the Navy 6 June 1783, lieutenant 9 November 1789, left 2 December 1793, in the 8th Hussars 30 December 1793, brigadier-fourrier 6 July 1794.

He was maréchal des logis-chef 29 September 1795, sub-lieutenant 27 May 1800, lieutenant 12 March 1802, took command of the barge which he boarded with 50 Hussars after the losing the commanding officer, took it away from the jetty which was blocking it in front of the English and brought all the men back safe and sound between Calais and Boulogne 25 February 1805, captain 22 November 1806.

He was aide de camp to General Cambacérès 25 March 1807, in the 13th Cuirassiers 4 May 1810, aide de camp to General Cambacérès 24 July 1811, left 1 September 1811. LH CH 26 June 187.

LARCHE (Joseph Vincent, 1787-?): born in Liffol-le-Grand (Visges) on 23 July 1787. Volunteer in the 8th cuirassiers 5 February 1805, brigadier 1 October 1806, fourrier 21 February 1808, concussed by a cannonball on his left thigh and his horse killed under him at Essling 21 May 1809.

Cuirassier General and his staff. Aquarelle by Lucien Rousselot. (RR)

Letterhead of a letter addressed to the Minister of War by the Administration Board of the 13th Cuirassiers.
(Author's collection)

He was maréchal des logis-chef 2 June 1809, sub-lieutenant 12 August 1812, lieutenant 28 September 1813, dismissed with the corps 5 December 1815 and put on the active list 11 December 1815. LH CH 23 September 1814.

LARCHER (Jean Baptiste, 1776-1809): born in Voursach on 28 November 1776. In the 4th Hussars 27 February 1799, in the 8th Cuirassiers 6 May 1802, fourrier 6 June 1802, maréchal des logis-chef 21 January 1803, adjutant-NCO 30 October 1803, sub-lieutenant 27 January 1807, wounded at Essling 22 May 1809 and died of his wounds 26 May 1809.

LAREYNERIE see **GOUJON de LAREYNERIE.**

LARIBIERE see **CHASSAIGNE de LARIBIERE**

LARIVIERE aka **PATUREL** (Jacques, 1769-?): born in Strasbourg (Bas-Rhin) on 21 October 1769. Trooper in the Royal-Etranger 21 October 1785 which became the 7th Cavalry 1 January 1791, trumpeter 7 May 1793, sabre wound to his right hand 26 April 1794 and a sabre wound to his lower lip 10 May 1794, sabre wound to his right arm 3 September 1796, in the same regiment when it became the 7th Cuirassiers 23 December 1802, brigadier 20 July 1805.

He became brigadier-fourrier 1 November 1805, maréchal des logis 18 December 1805, sub-lieutenant 9 August 1809, shot and wounded in the left shoulder at the Berezina 28 November 1812, lieutenant 15 May, retired 19 December 1815. LH CH 19 November 1812.

LAROBERDIERE
see **CHARCELLAY LAROBERDIERE**

LAROCHE (Anne Joseph, 1773-?): born in Epinal (Vosges) on 14 March 1773. In the Angoulême Dragoons 14 October 1790 which became the 11th Dragoons 1 January 1791, fourrier 2 October 1794, maréchal des logis 19 June 1795, maréchal des logis-chef 8 September 1796, adjutant-NCO 21 March 1797, sub-lieutenant 9 July 1799, lieutenant 7 March 1805.

He was adjutant-major 22 November 1806, rank of captain 22 May 1808, commanded a company 23 October 1809, commanded the Elite Company of the 11th Dragoons, shell wound to his left thigh and arm in front of Ciudad Rodrigo 1 April 1812, convalesced at Salamanca 2 April 1812, squadron commander in the suite 14 July 1813, in the 11th Cuirassiers 16 December 1813, joined his unit 25 February 1814.

He was in the suite with the 1 August reorganisation, confirmed 2 June 1815, retired 16 December 1815. LH CH 24 June 1811, O 14 January 1814.

LARONCIERE
see **CLEMENT de LARONCIERE**

LAROULLIERE (de, ? - ?): Boarder in the Ecole Militaire in Fontainebleau, sub-lieutenant in the suite of the 6th Cuirassiers 14 December 1806 and employed as ordnance, took up his appointment as lieutenant 29 April 1809, resignation accepted 8 May 1811.

LARROUX (Joseph, 1788-?): born in Saint-Michel (Gers) on 24 June 1788. Velite in the Grenadiers à cheval of the Imperial Guard 26 February 1806, grenadier 24 August 1810, sub-lieutenant in the 2nd Cuirassiers 13 March 1813, incorporated with his squadron into the 2nd Provisional Heavy Cavalry in Hamburg 11 September 1813, returned with the garrison 27 May 1814, six months' leave 1 March 1815, struck off the rolls as he never reappeared 1815.

LARUELLE (?-1812): maréchal des logis in the 9th Cuirassiers, sub-lieutenant in the 3rd Cuirassiers 12 March 1812, wounded then disappeared at Wilna 6 December 1812.

LASALLE (Louis Adrien, 1782-?): born in Paris (Seine) on 27 April 1782. In the 23rd Cavalry 24 October 1801, brigadier 23 April 1802, dismissed with the corps 23 December 1802 and incorporated into the 7th Cuirassiers 15 January 1803, maréchal des logis 4 May 1805, detached to the riding school in Versailles from 6 July to 25 October 1806, sub-lieutenant 1 November 1806.

He became lieutenant 17 December 1809, instated January 1810, captain in the 6th Cuirassiers 9 February 1813, prisoner near Hamburg 6 September 1813, retur-

ned 27 August 1814, with the veterans 8 November 1815. LH CH 28 September 1814.

LASALLE DUMAIGNEAUX (Bertrand Bernard de, 1786-?): born in Eyzerac (Dordogne) on 1 January 1786. In the 11th Cuirassiers 23 July 1805, brigadier November 1805, in the 10th Cuirassiers 19 April 1807, maréchal des logis 1 May 1807, adjutant 25 May 1807.

He was sub-lieutenant 3 June 1809, two lance wounds to his neck and right thigh and a cannonball wound to his right wrist and his horse killed under him at Winkovo 18 October 1812, incorporated with his squadron into the 3rd Provisional Heavy Cavalry in Hamburg 11 September 1813, returned with the garrison 30 May 1814, dismissed with the regiment 25 December 1815.

LASERRE (?-1812): Pupil at the Ecole Impériale de Cavalerie in Saint-Germain, sub-lieutenant in the 3rd Cuirassiers 11 March 1812, disappeared at the Berezina 28 November 1812.

LAUBUGE (Thomas, 1784-?): born in Périgueux (Dordogne) in 1784. In the 6th Dragoons 18 July 1805, gendarme in the 12th Escadron d'Espagne 16 December 1809, in the 1st Legion of the Gendarmerie à Cheval d'Espagne when it was created 16 December 1810.

He was brigadier 9 June 1812, dismissed with the corps 27 February 1813 and promoted to sub-lieutenant in the 7th Cuirassiers the following day 28 February 1813, joined the unit 6 March 1813, non-active on half-pay 16 August 1814.

He returned as sub-lieutenant in the regiment 9 July 1815, returned home on half-pay 24 August 1815.

LATILLE (- 1810) lieutenant 2 April 1803, in the Dragoons of the Paris Guard, lieutenant in the 3rd Cuirassiers 25 February 1809, died at Mendionde in Spain 10 March 1810.

LAURENCHET (Claude François, 1781-?): born in Maizières (Haute-Saône) on 21 September 1781. In the 3rd Cuirassiers 30 June 1803, brigadier 23 November 1803, fourrier 22 March 1804, maréchal des logis 1 December 1806, maréchal des logis-chef 27 June 1807, sub-lieutenant 14 May 1809, lieutenant 11 March 1812, in the Escadron Sacré during the retreat from Moscow December 1812.

He was detached with his squadron in Hamburg 3 July 1813 and incorporated with his squadron into the 1st Provisional Heavy Cavalry in Hamburg 11 September 1813, returned with the garrison 27 May 1814, placed in the Dauphin's Cuirassiers which became the 3rd Cuirassiers again April 1815. He was dismissed with the regiment 25 November 1815.

LAURENT (Hilaire, 1775-?): born in Nanterre (Seine) in 1775. In the 13th Chasseurs à Cheval 30 March 1794, gendarme in the Seine Department 3 February 1800.

He was sub-lieutenant in the 13th Cuirassiers 21 April 1813, dismissed with the corps July 1814 and retired August 1814.

LAVABRE (Jean Antoine, 1759-?): born in Milhaud (Aveyron) on 27 December 1759. In the Royal-Cavalerie 18 April 1783 which became the 2nd Cavalry 1 January 1791, brigadier 15 September 1791, maréchal des logis 1 April 1793, sub-lieutenant by seniority 23 March 1802, in the same regiment when it became the 2nd Cuirassiers 12 October 1802, confirmed 22 November 1802, lieutenant 30 October 1806, retired 1 May 1808.

LAVILLASSE d'AUDIBERT (Joseph Marie Hyacinthe Siffrin Exupert Eleazard de, 1786-?): born in Carpentras (Vaucluse) on 21 February 1786. Novice helmsman in the Navy 17 October 1798, midshipman 1800, staff sub-lieutenant 1801, in the Gendarmes d'Ordonnance 19 November 1806, brigadier 23 February 1807, dismissed with the corps, lieutenant in the suite of the 7th Cuirassiers 18 February 1808.

He was in service 4 March 1808, joined the unit 14 April 1808, two sabre wounds to his neck and left hand at Essling 21 May 1809, acting captain 3 June 1809, shot and wounded in the right hand at Wagram 6 July 1809, squadron commander 19 November 1812, shot and wounded through his breastplate on the side at the Berezina 28 November 1812, lance wound to his right arm at Könnern 24 May 1813,.

He was in the 1st Eclaireurs of the Guard 4 December 1813, shot and wounded in the forehead at Laon 9 March 1814, on half-pay 1814, in the Chevau-Légers of the Guard 22 May 1815, dismissed 22 December 1815. LH CH 13 August 1809, O 16 May 1813.

LAWOESTINE (Anatole Charles Alexis de, 1786-1870): born in Paris (Seine) on 14 April 1786. Entered for the Ecole Spéciale Militaire in Fontainebleau 15 October 1804, entered 23 December 1804.

He was sub-lieutenant in the 9th Dragoons 19 April 1806, lieutenant in the 2nd Cuirassiers 25 June 1805, aide de camp to Generals Defrance 4 March 1808, Valence 27 September 1808 then Sébastiani September 1809, captain 23 June 1810, squadron commander 8 July 1813, colonel 3 April 1814 for his conduct at Saint-Dizier 26 March 1814.

He commanded the 3rd Chasseurs à Cheval 21 April 1815, general on the battlefield at Waterloo 18 June 1815, non-active as a colonel 12 September 1815. LH CH 1 October 1807, O 28 September 1813.

LEBAS (Pierre, 1783-?): born in Bléville (Seine-Inférieure) on 26 June 1783. In the 5th Cuirassiers 30 January 1804, brigadier 1 January 1806, maréchal des logis 2 November 1806, sub-lieutenant 9 August 1809.

He was wounded at Smolensk 9 March 1812, lieutenant 22 December 1813, wounded at Château-Thierry 14 March 1814, dismissed with the regiment 23 December 1815. Lh CH 1 October 1807.

LEBAULT (Jacques, 1783-?): born in Auxonne (Côte d'Or) on 24 April 1783. In the 27 Dragoons 17 December 1802, gendarme in the 4th Legion 7 August 1808, in the 15th Squadron of the Gendarmerie

ATAYE (Pierre François, Baron, 1755-1827): born in Charny-sur-Meuse (Meuse) on 14 March 1755.

Trooper in the Royal-Cravates 9 March 1773, brigadier 19 October 1778, fourrier 11 July 1781, maréchal des logis-chef 20 June 1784, adjudant-NCO 23 July 1784, standard-bearer 20 August 1789, in the same regiment when it became the 10th Cavalry 1 January 1791, sub-lieutenant 1 March 1791, lieutenant 25 January 1792, captain 26 October 1792, confirmed 10 February 1793.

He was squadron commander 28 June 1795, brigade commander of the regiment 22 April 1797, charged the enemy cavalry which out-numbered him six to one three times and retaking 2 cannon at Erbach 15 May 1768, in the same regiment when it became the 10th Cuirassiers 24 September 1803, invalided out as brigadier-general 5 October 1806, pensioned 20 November 1806, inspector of the National Guards in the Schlestadt Arrondissement 20 March 1815, retired July 1815.

LH CH 12 December 1803, O 14 June 1804, C 25 December 1805, Baron of the Empire d. 19 March 1808 and l.p. 10 February 1809.

Captain Pierre Lataye of the 10th Cavalry with only his squadron routed four hundred Prussian Hussars, taking a number of prisoners at Kirchenpolen on 9 January 1794.

Wounded by a sabre blow to his left cheek after charging three hundred Hussars with only one squadron, taking several prisoners then having had his sword broken in the fray, he was disengaged by Lieutenant Gimet near Nivelles on 4 July 1794.

Gloves and epaulettes having belonged to General Lataye. (RR)

Portrait of sous-lieutenant Legrand de Mercey by Antoine-Jean Gros, circa 1809-1810. *(Photo AKG © Los Angeles County Museum of Art)*

d'Espagne 5 January 1810, in the 1st Legion of Gendarmerie à Cheval d'Espagne "Burgos" 15 December 1810, brigadier 1 March 1812, dismissed with the corps 27 February 1813.

He was promoted to sub-lieutenant in the 5th Cuirassiers 28 February 1813, incorporated with his squadron into the 2nd Provisional Heavy Cavalry in Hamburg 11 September 1813, returned with the garrison 30 May 1814, wounded at Waterloo 18 June 1815 and dismissed with the regiment 23 December 1815.

LEBEL (François, 1772-1809): born in Beauvais (Oise) on 19 May 1772. In the 8th Cavalry 21 November 1793, brigadier 15 July 1799, maréchal des logis 28 November 1800, in the same regiment when it became the 8th Cuirassiers 10 October 1801.

He was maréchal des logis-chef 6 January 1802, adjutant-NCO 212 January 1803, elected sub-lieutenant 28 June 1805, killed near Wagram 5 July 1809. LH CH 5 November 1804.

LEBIS (Joachim Alexandre, 1773-?): born in Vimoutier (Orne) on 19 April 1773. In the 7th Dragoons 25 May 1794, dismissed 6 April 1798, sergeant-major in the 1st Calvados Battalion 8 August 1799, sub-lieutenant in the 19th Chasseurs à Cheval 1 December 1800.

He embarked for Saint Domingo, lieutenant 20 February 1802, gendarmerie lieutenant in Saint Domingo 20 July 1802, returned to France for convalescence leave 31 October 1802, confirmed lieutenant in the Gendarmerie, discharged and struck off the rolls of the 19th Chasseurs à Cheval 31 December 1802.

He was in the 1st Battalion of Dragons à Pied in the Grande Armée 13 November 1806, lieutenant in the 8th Cuirassiers 7 January 1808, wounded at Borghetto July 1809, retired 1 May 1811.

LEBLANC (Jacques Claude, chevalier, 1756-1833): born in Paris (Seine) on 6 August 1756. In the Touraine Regiment 7 July 1777, fourrier-scribe for the chasseurs in the regiment 10 March 1778, training sergeant-major in the Royal Brittany Grenadiers 1 April 1779, adjutant-NCO 1 October 1781, discharged when the corps was disbanded 20 March 1783, captain of the Volunteers of the Saint-Honoré District of Paris 13 July 1789, lieutenant in the 49th Infantry of the Line 15 September 1791.

He was captain 1 June 1792, deputy to the adjutant-generals of the Army of the North 20 August 1792, deputy chief of the general staff 1 October 1792, wounded by shrapnel in the left leg at Neerwinden 18 March 1793, suspended 1793, reinstated on the General Staff of the Army of the Côtes de Brest 13 December 1794, squadron commander in the suite of the 10th Hussars 4 January 1796, deputy chief of staff of the army of the Côtes de l'Océan 21 March 1796, aide de camp to General La Barollière 27 October 1796.

Discharged 2 December 1797, reporter on the review committee of the 6th Military Division 26 November 1798, commanded the general headquarters of the Army of the Rhine 8 January 1800, commandant d'armes at Fort-l'Ecluse 19 August 1801, squadron commander in the 9th Cavalry 30 December 1801 which became the 9th Cuirassiers 24 September 1803, wounded at Austerlitz 21 December 1805, commanded the military district 10 December 1806, on retirement pay because of his disabilities 29 November 1809, available 17 January 1810, commanded the Posen military district 24 August 1812, adjutant-commandant 28 May 1813, chief of staff of the 32nd Military Division of Infantry of the 7th Corps, of the Deux-Ponts remounts depot 22 November 1813 then of the 2nd Reserve Division in Paris 8 March 1814.

He commanded the Pont-Audemer Arrondissement in the 15th Military Division 5 November 1814, retired 24 December 1814, vaguemestre of the general headquarters of the Army of the North 8 June 1815, retired 26 July 1816. LH CH 14 June 1804, O Chevalier of the Empire d., undated and without l.p.

LEBLANC (Nicolas Idatte, 1754-?): born in Laneuveville (Meurthe) on 10 November 1854. In Artois-Cavalerie 15, December 1772, left 15 December 1780, in the suite of the Brigade de Maréchaussée de Nancy 10 April 1781, dragoon in the King's Regiment 1 February 184, maréchal des logis 1 June 1785.

He was in the same regiment when it became the 18th Dragoons 1 January 1791, maréchal des logis-chef 15 July 1791, sub-lieutenant 1 February 1792, lieutenant 10 June 1793, discharged 15 December 1798, lieutenant in the 7th Cuirassiers 16 December 1806, joined up 6 March 1807, left with his retirement pension November 1807.

LEBLANC (Nicolas Maurice, 1758-1819): born in Génicourt (Meuse) on 12 December 1758. In the Artois-Cavalerie 15 March 1779, brigadier 1 October 1786, in the same regiment when it became the 9th Cavalry 1 January 1791, maréchal des logis 1 April 1793, wounded 22 July 1793, sub-lieutenant 11 November 1793, wounded at la Riutte 23 May 1794, lieutenant 21 January 1803.

He was in the same regiment when it became the 9th Cuirassiers 24 September 1803, captain 1808, sabre wound to his left hand 12 May 1809, retired 7 December 1809. LH CH 14 June 1804. LH CH 14 June 1804.

LEBLOND (Julien Vincent, 1786-?): born in Vesoul (Haute-Saône) on 22 January 1786. In the 23rd Cavalry 20 April 1799, dismissed with the corps 23 December 1802 and incorporated into the 6th Cuirassiers 3 January 1803, three sabre wounds to his head, neck and left arm, prisoner 2 May 1809, returned 3 December 1809, brigadier 11 December 1810, lance wound in his back at Winkovo 18 October 1812, maréchal des logis 1 January 1813.

He was sub-lieutenant 22 December 1813, dismissed with the corps 21 November 1815. LH CH 4 December 1813.

LEBOURACHER (Auguste Charles, 1792-1813):

born in Lannay (Seine-Inférieure) on 10 July 1792. Pupil at the Ecole Impériale de Cavalerie in Saint-Germain 22 October 1809, sub-lieutenant in the 8th Cuirassiers 30 January 1813, wounded at Hanau 30 October 1813 and died from his wounds 12 November 1813.

LEBRASSEUR (Louis Michel, 1771-?): born in Audignincourt (Aisne) on 24 October 1771. In the 19th Cavalry 1 July 1799, brigadier 21 April 1802, fourrier 30 May 1802, dismissed with the corps 31 December 1802 and incorporated into the 11th Cuirassiers 5 February 1803, maréchal des logis 21 April 1804, maréchal des logis-chef 1 December 1804.

He was sub-lieutenant 25 May 1807, lieutenant 3 June 1809, wounded and taken prisoner at Toloschinn 21 November 1812, returned 12 October 1814, dismissed with the corps 16 December 1815.

LEBRUN (Alexandre Louis Jules, baron, 1783-1812): second son of the third consul, born in Paris (Seine) on 5 August 1783. Sub-lieutenant in the 5th Dragoons 27 September 1799, deputy on the staff 5 March 1800, aide de camp to General Bessières 8 April 1802, lieutenant 27 November 1802, on the headquarters staff of Gouvion-Saint-Cyr's Observation Corps in Naples 18 May 1803, wounded and crippled two fingers, aide de camp to Bernadotte 1 February 1805, captain 16 November 1806, squadron commander in the 3rd Cuirassiers 5 July 1807.

He was aide de camp to Berthier 15 December 1808, colonel in the 3rd Chevau-Légers 22 June 1811, killed by grapeshot in the head in front of Lepel 26 October 1812. LH CH 14 June 1804, O 24 July 1809, Baron of the Empire d. 15 August 1809 and l.p. 3 May 1810.

LEBRUN DE LAHOUSSAYE (Armand, baron, 1768-1846): born in Paris (Seine) on 20 October 1768. Sub-lieutenant in the 82nd Infantry 15 September 1791, in the 5th Dragoons 10 March 1792, captain in the Moselle Legion and aide de camp to General Beurnonville 6 November 1792, squadron commander 27 February 1793, in the 3rd Hussars 15 March 1793.

He was wounded by a Biscayan shot to his right foot at Froeschwiller 22 December 1793, brigade commander 21 March 1794, under detention for having turned up drunk at the show at the Hague 23 January 1793, commanded provisionally at Utrecht 2 May 1796, returned to the 3rd Hussars before 21 August 1796, shot and wounded in the heel near Frankfurt 5 October 1799, employed in the 1st Military Division 1801.

He became brigade commander of the 16th Chasseurs à Cheval 4 October 1803, CO and Inspector of the Manche and Calvados Department Coasts 5 October 1803, brigadier-general 1 February 1804, president of the commission entrusted with preparing the Light Cavalry manoeuvre regulations, in the Heavy Cavalry Division of the Army of the Côtes

AVAL de CLARY (Jean Pierre, 1786-?) born in Castelnau-de-Montratier (Lot) on 16 June 1786. Velite in the Dragoons of the Imperial Guard 9 June 1809, sub-lieutenant in the 12th Dragoons 19 May 1811. He was at Ebling 10 January 1813, shot and wounded in the left leg while routing 200 Cossacks with only 30 dragoons at Danzig 24 March 1813, shot and wounded in the right foot near Leipzig 16 September 1813, acting lieutenant in the 3rd Cuirassiers during the siege of Danzig 15 October 1813, prisoner 1 January 1814, returned 8 October 1814, two months' leave on half-pay 20 December 1814, re-placed in the 2nd Cuirassiers 1 May 1815, wounded at Waterloo 18 June 1815, dismissed 20 October 1815.

Sous-Lieutenant in the 12th Dragoons, Jean Laval de Clary was wounded by a sabre on his wrist and three times by lances but managed to get through 800 Cossacks with only his platoon after blowing up a bridge near Ebling on 10 January 1813. Two months later on 24 March 1813, he was shot and wounded in the left leg while routing 200 Cossacks with only 30 Dragoons at Danzig.

de l'Océan 14 July 1805, commanded the 1st Brigade (Carabiniers) of the 1st Cuirassier Division of the General Cavalry Reserve of the Grande Armée 29 August 1805, commanding the 2nd Brigade (2nd and 9th Cuirassiers) October 1805, commanded the Light Cavalry in the 1st Corps 21 September 1806, left to join them 16 February 1807.

He was major-general commanding the 4th Dragoon division 14 May 1807, in the 3rd Corps of the Grande Armée 12 July 18707, in the Army of Spain 7 September 1808, in the Cavalry Reserve of the same army 9 November 1808, in the 2nd Corps 1 January 1809, governor of Cuenca April 1811, recalled to France 16 July 1811, commanded the 6th Cavalry Division (Dragons) in the Army of Germany 9 January 1812, in the 3rd Cavalry Reserve Corps 28 January 1812, wounded at the Moskova 7 September 1812, left at Wilna and prisoner 10 December 1812, returned June 1814.

He was non-active 1 September 1814, commanded the 2nd Cavalry Division in the 1st Corps 6 April 1815, at the disposal of the Minister of War for commanding or inspecting the cavalry depots 5 June 1815, non-active 1 August 1815. LH CH 11 December 1803, C 14 June 1814, Baron of the Empire l.p. 22 November 1808.

LECANDELLE de KNYFF (Joseph, 1793-?) boarder in the Ecole Impériale de Cavalerie in Saint-Germain 26 June 1811, grenadier 5 July 1812.

He was sub-lieutenant in the 1st Cuirassiers 30 January 1813, joined a detachment of the regiment 4 March 1813, instated 16 March 1813,

incorporated with his squadron into the 1st Provisional Heavy Cavalry in Hamburg 11 September 1813, returned with the garrison 27 May 1814, then returned home directly as a foreign national 1 July 1814.

LECHARPENTIER (Germain, 1770-1843): born in Saint-Maixent (Deux-Sèvres) on 8 April 1770. Lieutenant in the 2nd Deux-Sèvres Battalion 26 September 1792 which became the 88th Infantry, bayonet wound to his left leg during the crossing of the Rhine 1 July 1796, in the 82nd of the Line 24 June 1799, deputy to the adjutant-generals 18 August 1799, discharged 31 May 18001, in the suite of the 19th Chasseurs à Cheval 13 May 1802, captain 17 May 1803.

He was prisoner of the English 25 June 1803, returned to France as a prisoner on parole 27 January 1804, deputy in the 5th Military Division 21 June 1804, aide de camp to General Defrance 30 January 1806 to General Dumuy 22 January 1807, captain in the 3rd Cuirassiers 26 January 1809, instated 6 February 1809, cannonball wound to his left thigh at Wagram 6 July 1809, squadron commander 12 August 1812, shell burst wound to his chest, arms and right forearm at the Moskova 7 September 1812.

He became major in the 2nd Provisional Heavy Cavalry in Hamburg 11 September 1813, returned with the garrison 30 May 1814, put on the non-active list. LH CH 13 August 1809.

LECHAT (Nicolas François, 1767-1807): born in Saint-Aubin (Mayenne) on 19 March 1767. In the Royal-Cravates 16 January 1786 which became the 10th Cavalry 1 January 1791, brigadier 26 February 1791, maréchal des logis 15 September 1793, maréchal des logis-chef 7 July 1794, several sabre wounds of which one to his head at Guissen 7 September 1796.

He was sub-lieutenant 12 June 1799, confirmed 19 June 1799, lieutenant 22 March 1802, in the same regiment when it became the 10th Cuirassiers 24 September 1803, wounded at Hoff 6 February 1807, captain 14 April 1807, died of his wounds in Poland 4 June 1807. LH CH 14 May 1807.

LECHERPY (? - ?): maréchal des logis in the 9th Cuirassiers, sub-lieutenant 30 October 1806, lieutenant 8 May 1807, adjutant-major 14 May 1809, captain commanding a company 31 August 1810. He was squadron commander in the suite, wounded at Leipzig 16 October 1813, no longer appears on the rolls as of 9 August 1814.

LECHEVALLIER (Pierre Alexandre, 1763-?): born in Honfleur (Calvados) on 28 October 1763. In the Volontaires à cheval de L'Ecole Militaire 25 August 1792, maréchal des logis-chef when the regiment was formed into the 26th cavalry 21 February 1793 which became the 25th cavalry 4 June 1793, adjutant-NCO 19 July 1798, sub-lieutenant 28 August 1799, in the Versailles riding school 5 November 1800, dismissed with

the 25th cavalry 12 October 1802. He was incorporated into the 4th Cuirassiers 23 November 1802, lieutenant by choice of the government 18 December 1802, captain 25 June 1807, wounded at Essling May 1809 and Wagram 6 July 1809, retired 11 April 1811. LH CH.

LECLAIRE (Jacques, 1775-?): born in Sainte-Même (Seine-et-Oise) on 12 March 1775. In the 69th of the Line 19 September 1793, shot and wounded in the right leg 3 March 1795, in the 20th Cavalry 6 August 1798, dismissed with the corps 31 December 1802 and incorporated into the 12th cavalry 25 January 1803, in the 7th Imperial Gendarmerie Legion 4 June 1803, in the 1st Squadron of the Gendarmerie d'Espagne 5 December 1809, brigadier 20 December 1809.

He was in the 1st Legion of the Gendarmerie à Cheval d'Espagne "Burgos" dismissed with the corps 27 February 1813 and promoted lieutenant in the 12th Cuirassiers 28 February 1813, non-active 14 July 1814, returned to his unit April 1815, non-active again 3 August 1815 and returned home 16 August 1815. LH CH 10 February 1813.

LECLERC (Boniface Nicolas, 1791-1812): born in Paris (Seine) on 20 October 1791. In the 7th Cuirassiers 29 December 1810, brigadier-fourrier 16 February 1811.

He became sub-lieutenant 19 November 1812, disappeared at the Berezina 28 November 1812.

LECLERC (Charles Désiré, 1778-1812): born in Rouen (Seine-Inférieure) on 25 July 1778. In the 24th Cavalry 6 October 1797, brigadier 26 April 1801, dismissed with the corps 10 October 1801 and incorporated into the 1st Cuirassiers 1 January 1802, maréchal des logis 7 June 1805.

He was maréchal des logis-chef 16 November 1806, sub-lieutenant 25 May 1807, lieutenant 15 October 1809, captain 8 November 1811, died in the army in Stranz in Prussia 23 May 1812. LH CH 3 April 1807.

LECLERC de JUIGNE (Jacques Gabriel Olivier, 1769-?): born in Paris (Seine) on 19 November 1769. Captain in the King's Cuirassiers in post in 1788, in the same regiment when it became the 8th Cavalry 1 January 1791.

Emigrated then returned, in the Gendarmes d'Ordonnance 15 October 1806, second-lieutenant 4 November 1806, first-lieutenant 1 December 1806, lieutenant in the Line 16 July 1807, in the 9th Cuirassiers 10 September 1807, on a mission in the Army of Portugal by order of the Ministry of War 6 January 1808.

He became captain 12 July 1808, in the 1st Cuirassiers 17 September 1809, resigned 23 October 1810 and accepted 14 November 1810. LH CH 13 August 1809.

LECLERCQ (Antoine Jean, 1775-?): born in Paris (Seine) on 22 June 1775. Volunteered for the 1st Paris

CUIRASSIER OFFICER UNIFORMS, 1804-1815

The Helmet

Initially very much inspired by the dragoons' helmet, the helmet worn by the cuirassier officers had an iron shell with black turban fur. The initial models retained the small palm-leaf at the bottom of the mask and the two volutes above the Gorgon's head at the top of the crest of the dragoons' helmet.

This first model had a mane covering the whole of the top of the crest, the tuft of black horsehair sticking up out of a gold-coloured copper socket. Its round visor was ringed and the fur headband was long. The chin-straps were narrow and had lion-head rosettes.

Very early on, some taller helmets had a little embossed breastplate bearing the regimental number on the front of the crest. There were many variants during the period regarding the height of the crest, the way the tuft was made, or the shape and length of the visor and the thickness of the fur. The more or less well-off cuirassier officers went to reputed Parisian manufacturers who had a lot of models for parts and were ready to supply on demand such and such a style of helmet with particular specifications.

In 1808 another crest, now more curved and inclined further forwards, came into fashion. The numbered silver breastplate was systematically fitted to the front of the crest, itself much more finely worked than on earlier models. All the variants of this model abandoned the wholly horsehair tuft and the braced visor.

In 1810 the "à la Minerve" helmet of the Dragoon Guards seemed to replace the existing models. The shell was higher and inclined further backwards; the visor was covered with skin and the lower part of the crest was further away from the grooved edge. In this form, the helmet seemed to be even taller.

These models were increasingly ornate and silver helmets were seen frequently. The crest was decorated with small palm-leaves on a sanded background on the sides, as on the front face of the crest. Embossed laurel leaves connected by ribbons, leaves and spirals often decorated the overlapping spangle or the top of the crest. The little breastplate was still retained as were the silver lion-head rosettes. The big scarlet plume sported all during the period was slipped into a plume holder affixed to the shell; this was fitted with a tightening screw. The tulip holding the plume had gold trimmings. As with the other French regiments, the senior staff officers wore a white plume whose base was sometimes the distinctive colour.

A ringed nape cover covered with skin is attested sometimes in 1814-1815.

Officer's helmets that are identical are therefore rare. It is better to speak of a type rather than a model.

The breastplate

Three models were worn by officers during the First Empire. The first 1803 model was directly inspired by those made in the 18th century. The 1806 model was longer and offered better protection. The third model appeared after 1809 and was more curved; the cuirass was made up of a breastplate (the front part), a back-plate, two shoulder scales and a belt, the last three elements being used to make the first two fast. A ruff completed the ensemble. The first model evoked the prow of a ship and formed a very marked angle where the belt was situated. The base of the plastron was cut at an obtuse angle. Generally made of laminated or beaten one inch (2.8 cm) - thick iron plate weighing 16 lb (7.5 kg) fully fitted out, it was 15 in (38 cm) wide and 16 in (41 cm) high. They were made in two sizes.

A small protective cloth cushion stuffed with horsehair was fixed to the inside of the plastron.

The base of the breastplate on the heavier and longer second model ended in a point; the busk was less pronounced than earlier. The third type had a more rounded breastplate, a rounded base and was even heavier. The neck line and the armholes were wider.

The cuirass was made of silver metal or steel depending on the officer's means. All the same some breastplates could be richly decorated with leaves or engravings, or with a simple line engraved 1? in (3 cm) from the edge.

The shoulder scales at first were made of leather covered with red cloth and edged with silver embroidery. They were decorated with scalloped gold-coloured copper scales, then small chains. The (fixing) mortise plate with straight edges ended in a red leather heart, decorated with leaves and foliage. The heart was embroidered with silver.

The belt was made of red leather with ornaments embroidered in silver and had a golden buckle.

On the second model of cuirass, these elements did not change. On the other hand, on the third type the shoulder scales had two or three small chains, the mortise plates had straight or wavy edges and the heart was this time edged with embroidered beading. The shoulder scales were fixed to the back-plate - or dossière – with golden straps, decorated with a lion's head.

On the first model, 32 gilt-copper rivets garnished the breastplate with 32 on the back-plate. On the inside the tips of these rivets held the inner padding. The two following models had 34 rivets on each plate.

This number does not include the fixation rivets on the shoulder scales and the belt.

The three models were garnished with a scarlet cloth ruff edged with an embroidered silver stripe. A second, smaller stripe was added towards 1810, on the senior officers' ruff.

Dressed first of all in a long tailed coat with lapels with the distinctive colours, during the period the cuirassiers wore successively a shorter habit-veste without lapels, then in 1809 a long tailed coat with lapels returning in 1812 to the short habit-veste. It goes without saying that the clothing was tailored from finer and much better quality cloth than that used for the troopers. For example caddis was very often used for the facings.

The long-tailed coat

Coming from the Ancien Regime cavalry officer's wardrobe, this item of clothing was worn during the whole of the Empire, as circumstances dictated, most often whatever the weather. The long-tailed coat was made of blue cloth, with square lapels sewn along the whole length. This item of clothing was permitted as social dress.

The "habit-veste" or "habit de cuirasse"

This item of the uniform was mainly worn from 1803 to 1805. This coat with its short tails, with a more or long bust, fastened up the front with a row of 7 to 10 buttons, usually nine, made of white metal. The buttons, embroidered turnback ornaments and epaulette straps were silver.

The grenades on the turnbacks were often embroidered on a piece of blue cloth and sewn onto the turnback. In 1808, fashion oblige, the waistline moved upwards and a band of contrasting coloured cloth prolonged the turnbacks and joined the front piping over the abdomen.

In 1812, a new habit-veste made its appearance. Cuff slashes and false long pockets appeared. The collars, facings and the straps were still edged with the opposite colour (see our tables).

The "habit-surtout" – the overcoat

After 1809 this pocket-less coat with long tails and rounded facings made its appearance.

The "frac" - the tail-coat

This was blue with a collar and bottom facings without visible pockets. The turnbacks were the same colour as the distinctive as were the piping edging the front, the bottom (up to the beginning of the turnback), the collar and the cuffs.

The frock coat described in 1812 fastened with a row of nine white metal buttons. The grenades decorating the facings were silver.

The forage cap

Initially the forage cap had a knot and was blue. The edge of the turban was edged with the distinctive colour and silver embroidery. Senior officers had an extra, smaller stripe on the outside. A coloured grenade was visible on the front of the turban. The tip of the pendant was garnished with a fringed tassel. These fringes were twisted for senior officers. The stitching on the pendant was edged with the distinctive colour.

It is possible that after 1812, some officers might have worn a blue pokalem, with brightly coloured edging, and bearing the regimental number embroidered with silver thread.

The "redingote" – the frock coat

The cuirassier officer was allowed to wear a blue redingote with inverted collar. This fastened up the front with two rows of seven buttons. Traditionally, the redingote was not buttoned at the top and the front, thus unfastened, formed a sort of lapel. The redingote could also be worn over the coat or the overcoat.

The greatcoat

This was tailored in the so-called "trois-quarts" - three-quarter length – fashion; it had a small round cape and was sleeveless. It has been noticed that at the end of the period the coat had sleeves and a longer cape although this tended to be narrower. It was blue (grey for the troopers) and generally had distinctive-coloured facings.

The belt

This was made of stitched buffalo hide. The strap was assembled in three parts linked by two rings and this became subsequently a single piece wrapped round square rings. Just like the belt strap, these were stitched and provided with square buckles for fitting and double copper button

The curved belt plate made of golden copper bore a grenade in its centre denoting what the cuirassiers in fact were: the cavalry's grenadiers. These plates were plain, framed by beading or a golden edge.

The gloves

The gloves were made of leather "*à la Crispin*", i.e. gauntlets, for full dress, mounted

as well as dismounted, or short for town dress or off-duty dress.

The breeches

These were made of sheepskin. Riding breeches were sometimes used when campaigning. In town or social dress, the officers wore breeches made of nankeen or of a thinner cloth than sheepskin.

The boots

The officers wore stiff one-piece jackboots, garnished with a white cloth boot sleeve protecting the base of the breeches. The softer boot with a knee cap was tolerated on campaign or off-duty. The regulation bronze spurs could be golden or silver. They were not fixed permanently but held in place by a leather strap in the shape of a sole; the under-strap was made of leather; sometimes it was a chain.

DRESS

Full dress
Helmet, plume, cuirass, habit-veste or overcoat, sheepskin breeches, or cloth breeches, white cloth knee pads, jackboots, bronze spurs, belt, sabre with white knot.

Marching or campaign dress
Helmet, cuirass, habit-veste or overcoat, sheepskin breeches (or over-breeches) at the end of the period, white cloth knee-pads, stiff jackboots or soft boots with knee-pads, bronze spurs, belt, sabre with white knot.

Social dress
Hat, long-tailed coat with square lapels or overcoat, jacket and cloth or cashmere breeches, white stockings, shoes with buckles, sword with golden knot, narrow belt.

Normal summer town dress
Hat, long-tailed coat or tail-coat after 1812, dimity waistcoat, nankeen breeches, white stockings, narrow belt, sword with service dress knot, buckled shoes, stick.

Normal winter town dress
Hat, long-tailed coat or tail-coat after 1812, cloth or cashmere jacket, breeches, black stockings, narrow belt, sword, service dress knot, shoes with buckles, stick. Officers were permitted to wear blue breeches with white over-sleeves, boots, belts with baldric with the sabre.

Morning dress
Forage cap, redingote, breeches and boots or trousers and buckled shoes.

Mounted service dress
Hat, or helmet, overcoat, cloth or cashmere jacket or dimity waistcoat, simple gloves, skin breeches, boots, spurs, belt with sabre and white leather knot.

Allotment of distinctive colours

1st Regiment   2nd Regiment   3rd Regiment   4th Regiment   5th Regiment

6th Regiment

DISTINCTIVE COLOURS
1800-1810

From 1803 onwards, two distinctive colours were adopted: scarlet and jonquil. The first was attributed to the first six regiments of the arm and the second for the remaining six.

The allocation of the colours was simple and chosen — and one has to bear this in mind — in conjunction with wearing the cuirass.

The first three regiments of each series had slanted pockets, the next three vertical ones.

The distinctive colour was worn on the collar, on the facings (cuffs) and on the flaps for the first regiment of each series; on the facings for the second; on the collar and the facing flaps for the third.

Piping of the opposite colour (blue on the distinctive colour, distinctive colour on blue) garnished the collar, facings, flaps, turnbacks and pockets.

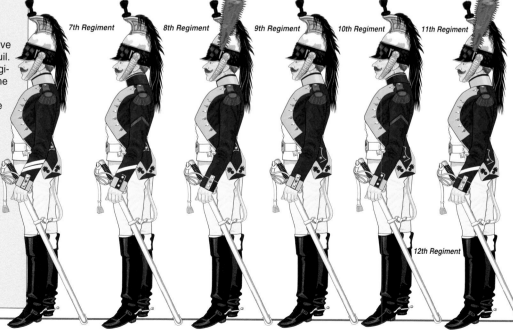

7th Regiment   8th Regiment   9th Regiment   10th Regiment   11th Regiment

12th Regiment

Battalion 19 September 1792, incorporated into the 201st Half-brigade which became the 106th Half-Brigade, left 15 January 1798, in the 8th Cavalry 28 May 1799, fourrier 18 October 1800, in the same regiment when it became the 8th Cuirassiers 10 October 1801.

He was maréchal des logis-chef 12 April 1802, adjutant-NCO 6 June 1802, sub-lieutenant by choice 21 January 1803, lieutenant 27 January 1806, adjutant-major 26 April 1807, wounded at Heilsberg 10 June 1807, rank of captain 26 October 1808, wounded at Essling 21 May 1809, in the 5th Provisional Dragoons 5 October 1809, retired 10 January 1810. LH CH 18 October 1807.

LECLERE (Etienne, 1769-?): born in Hanville (Oise) on 20 April 1769. In the 7th Cavalry 30 November 1793, shot and wounded near Amberg 24 August 1796, brigadier 15 March 1799, brigadier-fourrier 3 September 1799, prisoner 25 May 1800, exchanged at Mannheim 16 July 1800,.

He was in the same regiment when it became the 7th Cuirassiers 23 December 1802, maréchal des logis 6 January 1803, maréchal des logis-chef 12 January 1803, adjutant-NCO 18 December 1805, sub-lieutenant 11 March 1807, lieutenant 7 April 1809, adjutant-major 8 October 1811, captain 19 November 1812, lost the knuckles of six toes and the index of the right hand from frostbite in Russia 1812, retired 19 December 1815. LH CH 8 October 1811.

LECOEUR (Jean Pierre, 1768-?): born in Eschentzweiller (Haut-Rhin) on 11 February 1768. In the Royal-Picardie-Cavalerie 18 November 1785 which became the 21st Cavalry 1 January 1791, brigadier 11 June 1792, maréchal des logis 1 April 1793, in the same regiment when it became the 20th cavalry 4 June 1793, adjutant-NCO 19 July1799.

He was dismissed with the corps 31 December 1802 and put in the suite of the 12th Cavalry 25 January 1803, sub-lieutenant by seniority 4 April 1803, in the same regiment when it became the 12th Cuirassiers 24 September 1803, lieutenant 30 October 1806, wounded at Friedland 14 June 1807, adjutant

1 December 1807, captain of a company 14 May 1809, wounded at Essling 22 May 1809, retired 14 August 1809.

LECOINTE de LANFANGERAYE (Louis Joseph Marc, 1771 - ?) born in Gacé (Orne) on 26 April 1771. In the 7th Cavalry 13 June 1794, brigadier 20 July 1802, in the same regiment when it became the 7th Cuirassiers 23 December 1802.

He was maréchal des logis 16 April 1803, maréchal des logis-chef 20 January 1805, sub-lieutenant 11 March 1807, cannonball wound to the right calf at Essling 22 May 1809, lieutenant 3 June

Officers from the 4th and 5th Cuirassier Regiments in full dress on foot in 1813. Composition by A. Goichon. (RR)

1809, adjutant-major 14 October 1811, captain 6 March 1813, two lance wounds to his left arm and in the back, and by the shaft of a lance to his right shoulder and prisoner at Könnern 24 May 1813, returned to the suite of the 7th Cuirassiers 3 October 1814, took up his appointment 20 January 1815, retired 19 December 1815.

LECOMTE (Jacques Rémy, 1782-?): born in Reims (Marne) on 31 May 1782. In the 17th Cavalry 23 September 1802 which became the

26th Dragoons 24 September 1803, brigadier 5 January 1806, maréchal des logis 16 May 1809.

He was gendarme in the 17th Escadron d'Espagne 16 December 1809, in the 1st Legion of the Gendarmerie à Cheval d'Espagne "Burgos" 11 November 1811, dismissed with the corps 27 February 1813, sub-lieutenant with 14th Cuirassiers 1 March 1813, instated 18 March 1813, in the 10th Cuirassiers 6 August 1814 dismissed with the corps 25 December 1815.

LECOMTE (Victor François, 1779-?): born in Villemomble (Seine) on 16 January 1779. In the 23rd Cavalry 16 May 1794, brigadier 21 May 1797, sub-lieutenant 20 April 1799 23 December 1802

He was incorporated into the 7th Cuirassiers 15 January 1803, in the 1st Cuirassiers 18 August 1804, removed from his command and discharged 14 January 1806, left February 1806.

LECORDIER (Jean Baptiste, chevalier, 1763-1825): born in Cérisy-la-Forêt (Manche) on 4 December 1763.

In the Artois-Cavalerie 15 December 1784 which became the 9th Cavalry 1 January 1791, brigadier 1 December 1791.

He was brigadier-fourrier 1 April 1793, maréchal des logis 11 November 1793, maréchal des logis-chef 21 March 1795, adjutant-NCO 15 May 1797, wounded by a cannonball which took both tips of his shoulder blades off 2 June 1800, elected sub-lieutenant 17 February 1803, in the same regiment when it became the 9th Cuirassiers 24 September 1803, sabre wound to the lower side of his jaw and another sabre wound to the middle and inside of his left thigh at Austerlitz 2 December 1805. He became lieutenant 30 October 1806, captain 3 April 1807, left to retire 30 July 1814, pensioned 4 January 1815. LH CH 14 June 1804, Chevalier of the Empire l.p. 11 September 1813.

LEDROIT (Pierre Jacques, 1763-1805): born in Mayenne (Mayenne) on 25 April 1763. Volunteer in the Commisaire-Général-Cavalerie 12 March 1790

which became the 3rd Cavalry 1 January 1791, brigadier 1 May 1792.

He was wounded by a shell burst in his back and his right foot fractured by his horse falling at Le Quesnoy 7 September 1793, maréchal des logis 25 May 1797, maréchal des logis-chef 15 October 1797, shot and wounded twice 5 April 1799, sub-lieutenant 24 July 1799, lieutenant 13 March 1802, in the same regiment when it became the 3rd Cuirassiers 12 October 1802, killed at Austerlitz 2 December 1805.

LEENDERS (Jean Henri, 1774-?): born in Elslo (Meuse-Inférieure) on 4 September 1774. Trooper in the Hesse-Philipstal Regiment 1790, brigadier 22 March 1793, captured two artillery pieces, one howitzer and 17 horses with one squadron 27 August 1793, sabre wound to the head at Warwick 13 September 1793.

He was dismissed 15 June 1795, hussar in the 2nd Batavian Regiment 12 May 1797, brigadier 17 April 1801, in the Grand Pensioner of Holland's Guard 16 June 1805, in the Dutch Gendarmerie 28 October 1805, sub-lieutenant 18 March 1807, in the 2nd Dutch Cuirassiers 6 October 1809 which became 14th French Cuirassiers 18 August 1810, confirmed 5 December 1810.

He became lieutenant 4 March 1812, wounded at the Berezina 28 November 1812, captain 13 September 1813, dismissed with the corps August 1814.

LEFAIVRE (Louis Jean Claude Clément, baron, 1769-1839): born in Besançon (Doubs) on 28 December 1769. Sub-lieutenant in the 2nd Cavalry 25 January 1792, lieutenant 1 April 1793, shot and wounded in the left leg near Belheim 17 May 1793 and a sabre wound to his right hand 27 July 1793, left for hospital 23 August 1793.

He was aide de camp to General Eickemeyer 10 October 1793, captain 5 October 1796, deputy on the general headquarters staff 13 October 1803, with Lauriston 14 December 1803, at the disposal of the Ministry of War 4 February 1806, on the headquarters staff of the 6th Military Division 10 March 1806 then on that of the Grande Armée 27 October 1806, squadron commander in the 12th Cuirassiers 10 November 1807, second-major 6 April 1811, commanded the light cavalry depot of the Army of Spain in Niort from 24 May 1811 to 1 February 1812, major in the 23rd Dragoons 8 February 1812.

He became colonel of the 8th Cuirassiers 29 March 1813, joined them at the head of a cavalry marching regiment (carabiniers and cuirassiers) June 1813, shot and wounded in the right leg which fractured his tibia in several places at Hanau 30 October 1813 confirmed in his regiment 28 September 1814, on leave with half-pay 7 December 1814 prolonged to 1 May 1815, replaced because of his wounds 19 April 1815, retired 31 May 1815 still wanting to be employed, non-active 11 December 1815. LH CH 14 April 1807 O 28 September 1813, Baron of the Empire d. 13 December 1813 and confirmed by l.p. 2 December 1814.

LEFEBVRE (Antoine, 1769-1808): born in Fismes (Marne) on 13 December 1769. In the 2nd Hussars 1 September 1792, in the Legion de Police Cavalry 23 October 1795 which became the 21st Dragoons 24 December 1796, dismissed with the corps and entered the 11th Dragoons 23 December 1797, wounded at Stockach 25 March 1799, brigadier 2 November 1799, shot and wounded at Salzburg 14 December 1800.

He was maréchal des logis 20 June 1802, maréchal des logis in the Grenadiers à Cheval of the Guard 1 September 1806, sub-lieutenant in the 2nd Provisional Cuirassiers in Spain, took up his post in the 9th Cuirassiers 23 April 1808, shot and wounded twice and a sabre wound at Baylen 16 July 1808, retired 18 June 1809. LH CH 14 June 1804.

LEFEBVRE (Eugène Ernest, 1778-1857): born in Chartret (Sambre-et-Meuse) on 28 August 1778. Conscript in the 5th Cavalry 18 May 1800, brigadier-fourrier 23 October 1800, in the same regiment when it became the 5th Cuirassiers 23 December 1802.

He was maréchal des logis 30 June 1803, adjutant-NCO 20 February 1807, sub-lieutenant 25 May 1807, lieutenant 13 August 1811, captain 9 February 1813, incorporated with his squadron into the 2nd Provisional Heavy Cavalry in Hamburg 11 September 1813, left the town when the siege was lifted and returned with the garrison 30 May 1814, put in the suite 5 July 1814.

He was discharged 29 May 1815, struck of the rolls 1 July 1815 as he had disappeared from the corps. LH CH 1 October 1807.

LEFEBVRE (Jacques François Laurent, 1761-1827): born in Bruxelles (Dyle) on 24 January 1761. In the Mestre-de-Camp-Général Cavalry Regiment 1 April 1789 which became the 24th Cavalry 1 January 1791, dismissed with the corps 20 February 1791 and put as maréchal des logis in the 24th Cavalry of the new levy when it was formed the following day 21 February 1791.

He was sub-lieutenant 1 April 1793, in the same regiment when it became the 23rd Cavalry 4 June 1793, lieutenant 6 January 1794, shot and wounded in the leg at Thuin 16 June 1794, shot and wounded in the head at Fleurus 26 June 1794, captain 20 April 1799, dismissed with the corps 23 December 1802 and incorporated into the 6th Cuirassiers 11 January 1803, aide de camp to Maréchal Jourdan 13 May 1805, shot and wounded in his left foot at Baya 14 May 1807.

He became squadron commander 8 November 1809, on the staff of Maréchal Mortier 5 December 1813, adjutant-commandant 18 February 1814, at the disposal of Mortier 16 August 1814, governor of the 15th Military Division 5 March 1816. LH CH 5 November 1804, O 9 August 1814.

LEFEBVRE (Pierre Antoine, 1773-1812): born in

Cuirassier General.
(Aquarelle by Giuseppe Rava)

G. Rava 07
151

Henin (Somme) on 19 December 1773. Volunteer in the 4th Somme Battalion 21 September 1792, in the 9th Hussars 28 December 1793, in the 11th Cavalry 7 April 1794, brigadier 2 November 1801, brigadier-fourrier 30 January 1802, maréchal des logis-chef 2 March 1802.

He was elected sub-lieutenant 16 April 1804, lieutenant 3 April 1807, captain 16 May 1809 and regimental officier d'état civil, (Civil status officier) lance wound between the shoulder blades and taken prisoner at Toloschinn 21 November 1812, died of his wounds at Vitebsk 17 December 1812. LH CH 13 August 1809.

LEFEBVRE (Vincent, ? - ?): Pupil at the Ecole Impériale de Cavalerie in Saint-Germain, sub-lieutenant 30 March 1814, in the 9th cuirassiers 12 June 1814, not included in the 9 August 1814 re-organisation, in the 78th Cuirassiers 20 June 1815.

LEFELZ (Auguste, 1785-?): born in Arras (Pas-de-Calais) on 10 August 1785. In the 12th Cavalry 16 October 1797, dismissed 21 November 1798, in the 54th Half-Brigade of the Line 25 November 1798, left 5 November 1801, in the 12th Cavalry 25 November 1801.

He was brigadier 21 April 1803, in the same regiment when it became the 12th Cuirassiers 24 September 1803, fourrier 26 December 1803, maréchal des logis 8 September 1804, maréchal des logis-chef 20 December 1807, sub-lieutenant 14 May 1809, sabre wound to his ear at Eckmühl 22 April 1809 and a Biscayan shot to his left foot which killed his horse under him at Wagram 6 July 1809.

He became lieutenant 21 March 1812, several sabre and lance wounds and taken prisoner at Könnern 24 May 1813, returned 17 November 1814, put back in the 12th Cuirassiers 14 June 1815, dismissed 3 August 1815, went home 16 August 1815. LH CH 10 October 1812.

LEFELZ (Louis François Hypolite, 1766-1807): born in Wailly (Pas-de-Calais) on 22 January 1766. In the Royal-Champagne-Cavalerie 6 December 1784 which became the 20th Cavalry 1 January 1791, fourrier 1 November 1792, in the same regiment when it became the 19th Cavalry 4 June 1793?

He was deputy to the adjutant-generals 3 October 1793, lieutenant in the 12th Cavalry 6 April 1795, with his platoon he routed 3 Uhlan platoons and took 3 artillery pieces at Engen 3 May 1800, adjutant-major 13 March 1802, rang of captain 9 September 1803, in the same regiment when it became the 12th Cuirassiers 24 September 1803, in service as captain 21 December 1805.

He was killed at Friedland 14 June 1807. LH CH 14 June 1804.

LEFEVRE (François Nicolas, 1769-1835): born in Toul (Meurthe) on 6 December 1769. Soldier in the Dillon-Infanterie 1 December 1784, left 1 November 1788, adjutant in the 5th Meurthe Battalion 1 October 1791, lieutenant in a company of partisans and deputy to the adjutant-generals 15 August 1792, attached to the 6th Cavalry as a lieutenant

20 October 1797, prisoner at Stockach 25 March 1799, captain attached to the 9th Cavalry during his captivity 18 April 1799, freed on parole 25 July 1799.

He was unhorsed and wounded by a shell burst in both legs and shot and wounded in the stomach, prisoner in the middle of the 27th Half-Brigade with whom he was fighting at Mannheim 18 September 1799, freed when the town was recaptured, not transportable because of his wounds 18 October 1799, exchanged 31 December 1799, deputy squadron commander with the adjutant-generals 6 September 1801, in the suite of 9th Cavalry 20 May 1802 which became the 9th Cuirassiers 24 September 1803, in service 6 April 1804.

He became major in the 11th Cuirassiers 11 April 1807, regimental colonel 3 September 1813, confirmed 28 September 1814, replaced and became adjutant-commandant to serve on the staff 13 April 1815, non-active 1 September 1815. LH CH 14 June 1804. O 24 August 1814.

LEFEVRE (Jacques, ?-?): born in Châtillon (Loiret). Former cavalry sub-lieutenant, in the Gendarmes d'Ordonnance 26 October 1806, brigadier 4 November 1806.

He was dismissed with the corps 23 October 1807, at the disposal of the Minister of War 24 November 1807, sub-lieutenant in the suite of the 4th Cuirassiers 18 February 1808, in post 18 April 1809, retired.

LEFEVRE (Thomas Marcel, 1764-?): born in Gaumont (Ardennes) on 13 December 1794. Trooper in the Commissaire-Général Regiment 19 October 1784 which became the 3rd Cavalry 1 January 1791, maréchal des logis 21 December 1793.

He was maréchal des logis-chef 24 April 1794, shot and wounded in his right side at Mercklsheim 1796, sub-lieutenant 20 May 1798, elected lieutenant 22 December 1811, in the same regiment when it became the 3rd Cuirassiers 12 October 1802, retired 29 November 1806.

LEGENDRE (Etienne, 1780-?): born in Joindre (Seine-et-Oise) on 10 September 1780. In the 5th Cuirassiers 2 February 1803, brigadier 10 October 1806.

He was maréchal des logis 16 May 1809, sub-lieutenant 22 December 1813, dismissed 23 December 1815. LH CH 3 November 1814.

LEGENDRE de LAFERRIERE (Louis Philippe Antoine, 1777-1807): born in Paris (Seine) on 13 February 1776. In the 5th Cavalry 22 March 1802, fourrier 12 April 1802, in the same regiment when it became the 5th Cuirassiers 23 December 1802, maréchal des logis-chef 21 January 1803.

He was elected sub-lieutenant, killed at Eylau 8 February 1807.

LEGO de LAPOMMERAIS (Félix Pierre Prudent, 1786-?): born in Saint-Malo-de-Fity (Ille-et-Vilaine) on 19 July 1786. Velites in the Grenadiers à Cheval of the Guard 12 February 1806, sub-lieutenant in the suite of the 1st Cuirassiers 25 March 1809, in

EBRUN (Jean François, 1772-1815): born in Janville (Calvados 29 April 1772) on 29 April 1772. Volunteer in the Calvados Battalion 10 August 1792, sub-lieutenant 21 February 1793, shell wound near Lille 27 October 1793, resigned 28 March 1793, volunteered as a simple soldier in the 15th Dragoons 27 April 1803, brigadier 29 June 1803.

He was at Austerlitz 2 December 1805, maréchal des logis 1 August 1806, in the Grenadiers à cheval of the Guard 1 October 1807, sub-lieutenant in the 13th Cuirassiers 4 April 1808, lieutenant 18 September 1811, instated 21 October 1811, captain 25 February 1814.

He was incorporated into the 4th Cuirassiers 1814, adjutant-major in the suite 20 January 1815, took up his appointment April 1815, wounded at Waterloo and disappeared 18 June 1815, struck of the rolls 21 December 1815. LH CH 1 May 1808.

On 11 October 1805, Jean-François Lebrun was a brigadier in the 15th Dragoons. He received several sabre wounds while driving off an Austrian squadron at the head of his detachment of thirteen men, near Ulm. At Austerlitz he took two cannon.

service 5 June 1809, lieutenant 31 July 1811. He was aide de camp to General Lefebvre 16 October 1812, returned to the regiment 2 March 1813, arrested 16 May 1815, in the Royal Guard 15 November 1815. LH CH 11 October 1811.

LEGRAND de MERCEY (Charles, 1790-1808): son of the general, born in Metz (Moselle) on 11 December 1790. One of the Emperor's pages 6 March 1805, sub-lieutenant 2 February 1808, in the 9th Cuirassiers 18 February 1808.

He was detached with his squadron to the 2nd Provisional Heavy Cavalry in Spain, murdered in Madrid during the insurrection 2 May 1808.

LEGRET (Joseph Henry, 1789-?): born in La Fère (Aisne) on 14 October 1789. In the 4th Cuirassiers 4 May 1808, brigadier 4 June 1809, maréchal des logis 10 September 1809, maréchal des logis-chef 25 January 1812, sub-lieutenant in the 13th Cuirassiers 21 April 1813, wounded at Neuss 3 December 1813, lieutenant 25 February 1814, in the suite of the Angoulême Cuirassiers 6 August 1814.

He was in service 10 February 1815, in the same regiment when it became the 4th Cuirassiers April 1815, dismissed 21 December 1815. LH CH 27 December 1814 and confirmed 11 April 1815.

LEGROS (Armand Anne Marie, 1788-1809): born in Vannes (Morbihan) on 22 November 1788.

Boarder in the Ecole Militaire in Fontainebleau 23 May 1806, sub-lieutenant in the suite of the 3rd Cuirassiers 14 December 1806, ordnance sub-lieutenant the same day, in service July 1807, lieutenant 14 May 1809, killed at Wagram 6 July 1809.

LEGUAY (Nicolas Elisabeth, chevalier, 1762-?): born in Phalsbourg (Moselle) on 24 January 1762. In the Dauphin-Cavalerie 1 February 1782, brigadier 1 September 1784.

He was in the same regiment when it became the 12th Cavalry 1 January 1791, maréchal des logis 16 January 1792, maréchal des logis-chef 27 June 1792, sub-lieutenant 18 May 1793, lieutenant 4 November 1793, captain 2 September 1794, recaptured 4 cannon and 9 horses off the enemy at the head of his squadron at Hohenlinden 3 December 1800, in the same regiment when it became the 12th Cuirassiers 24 September 1803.

Nomed squadron commander 12 December 1806, wounded at Essling 22 May 1809, retired 2 June 1809. LH CH, Chevalier of the Empire l.p. 29 August 1810.

LEJEUNE (Eustache, 1779-?): born in Œuf (Pas-de-Calais) on 16 March 1779. In the 5th Cavalry 14 August 1801 which became the 5th Cuirassiers 23 December 1802, brigadier 10 October 1807, maréchal des logis 1 February 1808, sub-lieutenant 28 September 1813, dismissed 23 December 1815. LH CH 11 October 1812.

LELIEVRE de LAGRANGE (Armand Charles Louis, comte, 1783-1864): born in Paris (Seine) on 20 March 1783. In the Volunteer Hussars 1800, in the 9th Dragoons 3 May 1800, brigadier 16 May 1800, wounded at Marengo 14 June 1800, maréchal des logis 20 September 1800.

He was sub-lieutenant 23 October 1800, acting aide de camp to Sebastiani, lieutenant 15 July 1803, confirmed 9 February 1804, aide de camp to Berthier 12 September 1805, wounded at Amstetten 6 November 1806, captain in the 23rd Chasseurs à Cheval 20 January 1806, squadron commander in the 9th Hussars 27 January 1807, adjutant-commandant in the 9th Hussars 11 July 1807.

He was employed with the major-general 22 August 1807, in Spain 1808, in Germany 1809, negotiator in Vienna 11 May 1809, wounded by the crowd, equerry to the Emperor 1810 brigadier-general 31 January 1812, acting CO of the 2nd Brigade of the 5th Cuirassier Division 18 February 1812, commanded the Imperial Quarters during the retreat 1812, in the 2nd Cavalry Corps September 1813, in the 7th Division of the Young Guard 12 January 1814 then in the 1st 14 March 1814.

He became lieutenant-general 4 June 1814, in the Musketeers 1 July 1814, non-active 26 March 1815, at the disposal of the Minister of War 3 June 1815. Baron of the Empire 1808, Count l.p. 26 April 1810.

LELOUTRE (Alexandre Auguste, ?-?): Velite in the Dragoons of the Imperial Guard 16 August 1807, maréchal des logis in the 5th Cuirassiers 1 January 1811, maréchal des logis-chef 1812, sub-lieutenant 28 September 1813, standard-bearer in the 1st Cuirassiers 1 May 1814, non-active on half-pay 11 September 1814.

LEMAIRE (Jean François, 1775-?): born in Saint-Martin-aux-Bois (Oise) on 15 February 1775. In the 3rd Cavalry 20 November 1793, disengaged 2 cannon bringing them back to his lines 15 April 1794, brigadier 1800, maréchal des logis 23 September 1800.

He was in the same regiment when it became the 3rd Cuirassiers 12 October 1802, elected sub-lieutenant 21 March 1804, second-lieutenant in the Grenadiers à Cheval of the Guard 1 May 1806, shot and wounded in the arm at Eylau 8 February 1807, first-lieutenant 25 June 1809, captain 6 December 1811, captain adjutant-major in the Royal Corps of Cuirassiers of France 19 November 1814 and confirmed in the same regiment when it became the Grenadiers à Cheval of the Imperial Guard again 14 April 1815.

LEMAIRE (Pierre, 1772-1809): born in Aubrigny (Ardennes) in 1772. In the Volontaires Nationaux à Cheval from the Ecole Militaire 3 September 1792 which formed the 26th Cavalry 7 February 1793, brigadier 21 February 1793, fourrier 1 April 1793, in the same regiment when it became the 25th Cavalry 4 June 1793, maréchal des logis 30 August 1796.

He was maréchal des logis-chef 5 August 1798, took two prisoners and a field gun while in the Army of the Rhine 1800, adjutant-NCO 22 November 1800, dismissed with his corps 12 October 1802 and incorporated into the 2nd Cuirassiers 24 November 1802, sub-lieutenant 8 May 1807.

He was killed at Wagram 6 July 1809. Holder of a Sabre of Honour 30 May 1803, LH CH by rights 24 September 1803.

LEMARCHAND (Gabriel, 1763-?): born in la Ferrière (Calvados) on 12 April 1763. Joined the Navy 1781, left 1782, in the Noailles-Dragons 3 May 1785, deserted 3 March 1789, returned to the regiment which became the 15th Dragoons 1 January 1791.

He was maréchal des logis in the 26th Cavalry 1 September 1792, sub-lieutenant 8 October 1792, lieutenant 6 November 1792, captain 21 February 1793, in the same regiment when it became the 25th Cavalry 4 June 1793, confirmed 22 June 1793; dismissed with the corps 12 October 1802 and incorporated into the 4th cuirassiers 24 November 182, discharged without pay 8 May 1806, reinstated into the 12th Cuirassiers 30 December 1806 and incorporated into the 2nd Provisional Heavy Cavalry in Spain.

He id not reappear, probably prisoner with the capitulation at Baylen 23 July 1808 and disappeared.

LEMARCHANT de CHARMONT (Louis Charles Henry, 1777-?): born in Joinville (Haute-Marne) on 22 September 1777. In the 2nd Cher Battalion 2 March 1793, wounded by a shell burst at Bitche

29 October 1793, corporal in the 132nd Half-Brigade 13 May 1794, gendarme in the 39th Haute-Marne Squadron 22 September 1797, unemployed because under-aged 30 March 1798,?.

He was n the 7th Cavalry 9 April 1798, brigadier 3 December 1799, maréchal des logis 22 March 1801, detached to the headquarters staff of the Cavalry Division of the Army of the Rhine from 23 November 1798 to 7 June 1800, in the same regiment when it became the 7th Cuirassiers 23 December 1802, sub-lieutenant 15 December 1803, lieutenant 11 March 1807, adjutant-major 31 January 1809, wounded at Essling 21 May 1809.

Acting captain 3 June 1809, wounded at Wagram 6 July 1809, retired with pension 22 March 1810. LH CH 1 October 1807.

LEMARCHANT DUMOUTIER (Jean Hégésippe, 1758-1819): born in Cerceaux (Orne) on 12 April 1758. In the Royal-Cavalerie 14 April 1775, cadet 29 March 1780, standard-bearer 1 September 1784, in the same regiment when it became the 2nd Cavalry 1 January 1791, sub-lieutenant 15 April 1791, lieutenant in the 14 Dragoons 15 September 1791, in the 2nd Cavalry 25 January 1792, captain 17 June 1792, saved the regimental standard at Bingen 28 March 1793, commanded a squadron and captured 3 cannon and 5 caissons 17 May 1793, squadron commander 25 June 1793, major in the 4th Cuirassiers 29 October 1803, instated 19 August 1804, colonel of the 6th Gendarmerie Legion in the Army of Spain 7 October 1810, CO of the 23rd Legion 31 May 1812, judge in the special court for the Var Department 30 October 1813, retired 1 October 1814. LH CH 25 March 1804.

LEMIRE (Jean Pierre Antoine, 1773-?): born in Rouppy (Aisne) on 25 May 1773. In the 10th Cavalry 18 March 1793, brigadier 20 January 1799, maré-

EMAIRE (Elie Simon, 1780-?) born in Ecueil (Marne) on 28 October 1780. In the 4th Cuirassiers 6 April 1803, brigadier 1 October 1806, fourrier 25 June 1807, maréchal des logis-chef 22 May 1809, sub-lieutenant 4 March 1812.

He was sub-lieutenant standard-bearer 4 January 1815, dismissed 21 December 1815. LH CH 9 November 1814 confirmed 11 April 1815.

At Fère-Champenoise on 25 March 1814: the army corps under Marshalls Mortier and Marmont had been overwhelmed. Sous-Lieutenant Lemaire of the 4th Cuirassiers gathered together a few troopers, took back a cannon from the enemy which he served together with a second one which did not have enough personnel for half an hour.

During the Battle of Paris on the following 30 March, he freed a colonel and two artillery officers who were about to be taken by the enemy.

*Standard belonging
to the 5th Cuirassiers in 1815. (RR)*

chal des logis 6 May 1802, in the same regiment when it became the 10th Cuirassiers 24 September 1803, sub-lieutenant 12 July 1812, dismissed with the corps 25 December 1815.

LENADIER (Jean Pierre, 1786-?): born in Saint-Pargoire (Hérault) in 1786. In the 10th Cuirassiers 23 December 1806, brigadier 6 July 1807, fourrier 3 June 1809.

He was maréchal des logis 25 January 1811, adjutant 12 August 1812, sub-lieutenant 28 September 1813, in the suite 6 August 1814, took up his appointment 22 December 1814, instated 27 January 1815, shot and wounded in his right foot at Fleurus 16 June 1815, dismissed with the corps 25 December 1815.

LENORMAND de FLAGEAC (Alphonse, ?-1812): sub-lieutenant in the 12th Cuirassiers 7 July 1812, killed in Russia 23 November 1812.

LEONARD see **RAMPAN de LEONARD.**

LEPEIGNEUX (1791-?): born in Paris (Seine) on 13 March 1791. Volunteer in the 6th Cuirassiers 6 February 1809, brigadier 1 May 1809, fourrier 3 June 1809, sub-lieutenant 22 June 1809, lance wound to his right hand at Winkovo 18 October 1812.

He was lieutenant in the 9th Cuirassiers 21 April 1813, incorporated with his squadron into the 3rd Provisional Heavy Cavalry in Hamburg 11 September 1813, returned with the garrison 30 May 1814, obtained one month's leave July 1814, struck off the rolls for overlong absence 25 July 1815 since he never returned to the corps.

LEPETIT de MONTFLEURY (Dominique François, 1763-?): born in Caen (Calvados) on 15 June 1763. Gentleman cadet in the Royal-Cavalerie 12 January 1780, sub-lieutenant 10 April 1785, lieutenant 1 July 1789, in the same regiment when it became the 2nd Cavalry 1 January 1791.

He was sub-lieutenant when it was formed 21 March 1791, lieutenant 15 September 1791, captain 10 May 1792, removed form his post 27 January 1794, reinstated 28 February 1795, in the same regiment when it became the 2nd Cuirassiers 12 October 1802, captain in the Imperial Gendarmerie 8 May 1807.

LEPORCQ d'ANDEVILLE (Anne Charles Vincent Xavier, chevalier, 1789-1817): born in Andeville (Oise) on 23 May 1789. Boarder in the Ecole Militaire 19 July 1806, corporal 22 February 1807, sub-lieutenant in the 2nd Cuirassiers 19 January 1807, joined them 1 April 1807, took up his appointment 23 February 1809.

He became lieutenant aide de camp to General Doumerc 1 June 1809, captain in the 12th Cuirassiers in his post 1812.

LERASLE (Charles Armand, 1795-?): born in Cosne-sur-Loire (Nièvre) on 24 July 1795. Pupil in the Ecole Impériale de Cavalerie in Saint-Germain 15 December 1812, sub-lieutenant 30 March 1814, in the 2nd Cuirassiers 12 June 1814, non-active on half-pay 1814, returned to the regiment April 1815, wounded at Waterloo 18 June 1815 and dismissed 20 October 1815.

LEROUX (Augustin, 1791-?): born in Guise (Aisne) on 17 February 1791. Velite in the 2nd Chevau-

Légers Lancers of the Imperial Guard 9 September 1811, sub-lieutenant in the 16th Chasseurs à Cheval 8 February 18113, in the 12th Chasseurs à Cheval 10 October 1813.

He was lieutenant 4 December 1813, paying officer 3 February 1814, lieutenant in the 1st Cuirassiers 8 May 18115, appointed to the 7th Cuirassiers 19 May 1815, wounded in the ranks of the 1st Cuirassiers at Waterloo 18 June 1815, rejoined the 7th Cuirassiers 1 July 1815, non-active 24 August 1815.

LEROUX (François Nicolas, 1787-?): born in 1787. Conscript in the Grenadiers à Pied of the Guard 1 June 1809, velite in the Grenadiers à Cheval of the Guard 28 April 1810, brigadier 17 September 1811.

He became sub-lieutenant in the 1st Cuirassiers 13 March 1813, wounded at Thionville 27 March 1814, dismissed 24 December 1815, 17 sabre wounds.

LEROUX (Jean Pierre, 1767-?): born in Lisse (Marne) on 27 January 1767. In the 24th Cavalry 28 April 1793 which became the 23rd cavalry 4 June 1793, brigadier 19 October 1802, dismissed with the corps 23 December 1802 and incorporated into the 7th Cuirassiers 14 January 1803, fourrier 23 January 1803, maréchal des logis 23 September 1804.

He became maréchal des logis-chef 11 March 1807, cannonball wound to his right foot at Essling 22 May 1809, sub-lieutenant 4 March 1812, standard-bearer 16 August 1814, retired 19 December 1815. LH CH 8 October 1811.

LEROY (Louis, 1780-1814): born in Courtenay (Loiret) on 24 January 1780. Maréchal des logis in the 1st Legion of the Gendarmerie à Cheval d'Espagne, dismissed with the corps 27 February 1813 and became sub-lieutenant in the 3rd Cuirassiers 28 February 1813.

He was wounded at Leipzig 18 October 1813 and during a reconnaissance 4 March 1814, died of his wounds 22 March 1814.

LEROY (Pierre François Joseph, 1775-?): born in Vieux-Borquin (Nord) on 16 January 1775. In the 19th Cavalry 31 October 1793, with 2 other troopers cut into an enemy column and forced a captain and 91 infantrymen to surrender while also capturing a canon at Lannoy 18 May 1794, dismissed with the corps 31 December 1802 and incorporated into the 10th Cavalry 11 February 1803 which became the 10th Cuirassiers 24 September 1803.

He became brigadier 1 December 1806, maréchal des logis 4 July 1807, wounded by a cannonball in the left thigh at Hoff 6 February 1807, sub-lieutenant 4 September 1812, no longer appears on the rolls as of 6 August 1814. Holder of a Musketoon of Honour with patents 30 May 1803.

LESCAILIER (Adrien Joseph, 1774-?): born in Douai (Nord) on 3 April 1774. In the 2nd Company of Douai Paid Grenadiers 12 October 1792, sabre wound to his nose losing him the use of his left eye at Marchiennes October 1793, in the 21st Chasseurs à Cheval 4 November 1794, brigadier 28 July 1795.

He became maréchal des logis 1 January 1799, invalided out because of his wounds 20 July 1803, Dragoon of the Paris Guard 19 August 1803, brigadier 25 August 1804, maréchal des logis 2 October 1805, adjutant-NCO 1 December 1809, sub-lieutenant 1 July 1812, second-lieutenant in the 2nd Chevau-Légers of the Imperial Guard 27 February 1813.

He was instated 18 March 1813, on half-pay 25 August 1814, retired 10 December 1814, second-lieutenant in the suite of the 4th Cuirassiers April 1815, non-active on half-pay 24 August 1815.

LESPINASSE (? - ?): sub-lieutenant in the suite of the 6th Cuirassiers 14 January 1807, took up his appointment 13 April 1809, wounded at Essling 22 May 1809, lieutenant 3 June 1809, resignation accepted 12 October 1811.

LESPINAY (Louis Armand de, baron, 1789-1869): son of the Deputy, born in the Chateau of Pally at Chantonnay (Vendée) on 19 February 1789. One of the Emperor's pages 19 November 1804, first page 6 February 1806, lieutenant in the 1st Carabiniers 22 March 1807, ordnance officer to the Emperor 21 July 1808.

He became captain 18 August 1809, squadron commander in the 14th Cuirassiers 13 January 1811, two lance wounds to his right shoulder blade and chin after crossing the Berezina 2 December 1812, dismissed with the corps 1814. LH CH 1 October 1807, Baron of the Empire l.p. 31 January 1810 modified 21 February 1814.

LETAVERNIER (Victor, 1792-?): born in Torquesne (Calvados) on 6 January 1792. In the Velites of the Grenadiers à Cheval of the Imperial Guard 11 April 1811, sub-lieutenant in the 12th Cuirassiers 28 November 1813, joined them 1 March 1814, absent and no news of him as of 1 June 1815.

LETELLIER (Henry, 1783-1818): born in Paris (Seine) on 19 February 1783. In the 3rd Cavalry 3 May 1800, brigadier 22 March 1801, maréchal des logis 21 June 1802, in the same regiment when it became the 3rd Cuirassiers 12 October 1802, sub-lieutenant in the 40th of the Line 31 May 1804, lieutenant 8 November 1806, deputy captain on the staff of Maréchal Lannes 24 June 1807 then of Oudinot 1808, aide de camp to Oudinot 2 July 1809, squadron commander 17 July 1809,.

He became adjutant-commandant 25 March 1812, brigadier-general 4 August 1813, commanded the 2nd Brigade of the 44th division of the 14th Corps 6 September 1813, prisoner in Dresden with the capitulation 11 November 1813, prisoner in Hungary,

returned and put on half-pay July 1814, chief of staff of the cavalry under Kellermann 17 March 1815, in the army against the Duke of Angoulême 6 April 1815, available 6 June 1815,.

He commanded the 1st Brigade (8th and 11th Cuirassiers) of the 11th Cavalry Division of the 3rd Corps 30 June 1815, retired to the Loire then expatriated to Germany.

f. Cochi del. Letort

After having commanded a cuirassier brigade in 1813, Letort took over command of the Dragoon Guards. (RR)

LETORT (Louis Michel, comte, 1773-1815): born in Saint-Germain-en-Laye (Seine-et-Oise) on 29 August 1773. In the 1st Eure-et-Loir Battalion 1 November 1791, elected lieutenant 1 December 1791, prisoner 29 August 1792, freed September 1793, lieutenant adjutant-major 15 January 1793, wounded at Neerwinden 18 March 1793, prisoner 8 June 1793, captain 29 July 1793, returned 20 September 1793.

He became aide de camp to General Huet 25 October 1793, sabre wound to his right arm at Landau 26 December 1793, suspended 7 September 1796, sub-lieutenant at his own request in the 9th Dragoons 28 September 1796, lieutenant 13 February 1799, shot and wounded in the left leg 30 March 1799, captain 20 April 1799.

He served during 18 Brumaire, squadron commander 24 August 1801, major in the 14th Dragoons 29 October 1803, commanded the regiment 8 April 1806, major in the Dragoons of the Guard 8 October 1806, sabre wound at Jena 14 October 1806, brigadier-general keeping his command of the Dragoons of the Guard 30 January 1813, commanded the 1st Brigade (2nd, 3rd and 6th Cuirassiers) of the 1st Cuirassiers Division of the 1st Cavalry Corps 19 September1813.

He was wounded at Hanau 30 October 1813, major-general and colonel-major of the

Dragoons of the Guard 13 February 1814, major of the Royal Dragoons of France 19 November 1814, aide de camp to the Emperor keeping his command of the Dragoons of the Imperial Guard 21 April 1815, shot and mortally wounded in the lower abdomen while charging the Prussian squares with the four service squadrons of the Guard at Gilly near Fleurus and Charleroi 15 June 1815. LH CH 25 March 1804, O 16 November 1808, C 23 August 1814, Baron of the Empire d. 19 March and l.p. 9 September 1810, Count 1814.

LEUDET (Pierre Théodore, 1791-1864): born in Pont-Audemer (Eure) on 7 October 1791. Velite in the Grenadiers à Cheval of the Imperial Guard 5 March 1810. He became fourrier 15 January 1813, sub-lieutenant in the 11th Cuirassiers 13 March 1813, dismissed and put on the non-active list 1 August 1814.

LEVILLAIN (Armand Modeste, 1767-1809): born in Canni (Seine-Inférieure) on 18 April 1767. Divisional commander of Artillery Haulage 5 November 1793, resigned 1797, maréchal des logis seconded to General Desfourneaux in Guadeloupe 18 August 1798, deputy to the adjutant-generals until 28 October 1799, wounded aboard la Vengeance, by a shell burst to his left shoulder 20 August then shot and wounded in the neck and taken prisoner by the English 26 August 1800.

Acting second-lieutenant 9 September 1802, acting first-lieutenant in the 4th Gendarmerie Legion 23 September 1802, confirmed sub-lieutenant 14 August 1806, in the 1st Cuirassiers 13 November 1806, joined them 16 December 1806, lieutenant in the 5th Cuirassiers 2 March 1809, went over to the 7th Cuirassiers by changing with Lieutenant Beuverand de la Loyère 21 March 1809, had his horse killed under him and himself killed by a lance at Eckmühl 22 April 1809.

LEYX (Jean Pierre Félix, 1781-1813): born in Lunéville (Meurthe) on 30 May 1781. In the Volunteer Hussars 26 March 1800, brigadier and maréchal des logis the same day 1 March 1801.

He became sub-lieutenant April 1801, put into the 14th Dragoons as maréchal des logis 1 May 1803, acting sub-lieutenant 23 August 1808, in service in the 13th Cuirassiers 17 August 1809, died in Spain 16 February 1813.

LEZERAT (Jean, 1767-1809): born in Verfeuil (Haute-Garonne) on 15 February 1797. In the Ardennes Chasseurs 8 January 1786 which became the Champagne Chasseurs à Cheval 17 March 1788 then 12th Chasseurs à Cheval 1 January 1791, brigadier 21 March 1791, brigadier-fourrier 15 October 1791.

He became maréchal des logis-chef 1 September 1792, sub-lieutenant 1 July 1793, lieutenant 22 September 1793, captain in the 12th Hussars 16 December 1793, resignation accepted 29 March 1796, captain in the 3rd Cuirassiers 12 December 1806, died in the regimental depot 7 September 1809.

LHERITIER (François Samuel, baron, 1772-1829): born in Angles-sur-l'Anglin (Vienne) on 6 August 1772. In the 3rd Indre-et-Loire Battalion 26 September 1792, grenadier corporal 22 December 1792, secretary on the headquarters staff of the Army of the Rhine 18 August 1793, acting deputy to the adjutant-generals with rank of infantry sub-lieutenant 17 May 1794.

He became sub-lieutenant 4 December 1796, aide de camp to Bellavène 2 January 1797 with rank of lieutenant on 3 April 1796, captain 5 October 1797, on General Boudet's staff, wounded in the thigh at Marengo 14 June 1800, seconded to the 6th Dragoons 28 July 1800, took up his appointment 23 October 1800, detached as aide de camp to General Laboissière November 1800, squadron commander whilst keeping his function as and rank in the 11th cavalry 19 September 1801, commissioned as aide de camp 16 December 1801, available 26 August 1803, discharged 13 October 1803, entered the 11th Cuirassiers 15 December 1803, colonel of the 10th Cuirassiers 5 October 1806, wounded his right hand when his horse was killed under him and fell, continued with his charge on a trooper's horse at Eylau 8 February 1807, shot and wounded in the right shoulder and his horse killed under him at Essling 22 May 1809 and wounded by a rifle butt blow to his head at Znaïm 11 July 1809.

He was brigadier-general 21 July 1809, left the regiment the following day 22 July 1809, commanded the 2nd Brigade (7th and 8th Cuirassiers) of the 3rd Heavy Cavalry Division 24 August 1809, available 1 May 1810, inspector of the mounted troop depots in the 1st, 15th, 21st and 22nd Military Divisions 26 March 1811, remount inspector for the 2nd, 3rd, 4th and 5th Military Districts 7 May 1811, commanded the 2nd Brigade (7th Cuirassiers) of the 3rd Heavy Cavalry Division 25 December 1811, major-general 15 March 1813, commanded the 4th Heavy Cavalry Division in the 3rd Cavalry Corps in the Grande Armée 1 July 1813, commanded the Brigades of the 5th bis Cavalry Corps under Milhaud 8 August 1813 then the corps itself in the interim, commanded the 5th division of Heavy Cavalry (Dragoons) 5 October 1813 then the 6th 5 January 1814 (took up his appointment December 1813) and the 4th Dragoon Division end of January 1814, on half-pay 1 June 1814.

He became inspector general of the cavalry for 1,815in the 16th Military Division 30 December 1814, commanded the reserve cavalry in the 4th Army Corps 23 April 1815 then the 11th Cavalry Division (cuirassiers and dragoons) in the Army of Belgium 3 June 1815, shot and wounded in the right shoulder at Waterloo 18 June 1815, non-active 20 September 1815. LH CH 15 June 1804, C 24 August 1814, Baron of the Empire l.p. May 1808.

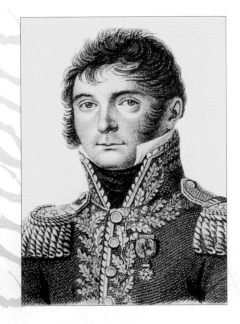

General François Lhéritier. (RR)

LHERITIER DE CHEZELLE (Athanase Lucien, 1787-?): born in Yzeures-sur-Creuse (Indre-et-Loire) on 23 March 1787. Lieutenant in the 44th of the Line, in the 10th Cuirassiers 16 May 1809, aide de camp to General Lheritier 17 February 1810. LH CH 16 June 1809.

LHERMITTE (?-?): lieutenant quartermaster in the 14th Chasseurs à Cheval 15 May 1793, invalided out 24 February 1795, in the Auxiliary Battalions 4 August 1799.

He became deputy on the staff of the Army of Batavia 16 August 1800, left February 1801, on discharge pay 13 March 1802, lieutenant in the 5th Cuirassiers 7 February 1807, retired 14 November 1807.

LHOMME (Claude François, 1753-?): born in Sugey (Doubs) on 19 October 1753. In the Artois-Cavalerie 1 November 1775, brigadier 1 September, in the same regiment when it became the 9th Cavalry 1 January 1791.

He became maréchal des logis 1 April 1793, maréchal des logis-chef 7 September 1793, sub-lieutenant 11 November 1793, lieutenant 21 January 1803, in the same regiment when it became the 9th Cuirassiers 24 September 1803, retired 30 October 1806.

LHOTTE see **LOTHE**.

LIANCOURT (Charles, 1786-?): born in Soissons (Aisne) on 19 August 1786. In the 12th Cuirassiers 29 October 1808, brigadier 13 June 1809, fourrier 7 July 1809, maréchal des logis 1 June 1811, maréchal des logis-chef 4 July 1811, sub-lieutenant 11 September 1812 in he King's Body Guard 11 June 1814.

LIANCOURT see **BERNARD LIANCOURT**

LIETHARD (Henry Séraphin, ?-1809): soldier in the Reniac Regiment (Switzerland) 2 September 1788, left 26 September 1792, brigadier in the Chasseurs à Cheval in the Légion Franche Etrangère 26 September 1792, incorporated into the 13th Chasseurs à Cheval 17 February 1794, in the 21st Chasseurs à Cheval 7 February 1795, maréchal des logis 10 November 1796.

He became brigadier in the Garde du Directoire 21 December 1796, maréchal des logis 20 December 1798, incorporated into the Consular Guard 3 January 1800, sub-lieutenant by choice of the Emperor 30 August 1805, reached the 7th Cuirassiers 14 November 1805, in the 4th Cuirassiers 5 October 1808, warned November 1808, lieutenant 1809, killed at Essling 21 May 1809. LH CH 1 October 1807.

LIEUTAUD (Joseph Louis, 1792-?): born in Brignolles (Var) on 31 July 1792. In Prince Eugène's Gardes d'Honneur 12 July 1809, brigadier 29 July 1811, fourrier 15 April 1812, sub-lieutenant in the 8th Chevau-Légers 15 May 1813.

He was wounded at Dresden 27 August 1813, incorporated with the corps into the 7th Chevau-Légers 1 January 1814, in the 2nd Chevau-Léger Lancers 5 May 1814, in the 8th Cuirassiers 24 August 1814, on six months' leave 1 October 1814, dismissed with the corps 5 December 1815.

LIGNET (Thomas, 1782-1864): born in Duvaumain (Oise) on 19 May 1782. In the 11th Cuirassiers 23 December 1803, brigadier 8 June 1809, maréchal des logis 6 February 1812, sub-lieutenant 3 September 1813, wounded at Leipzig 18 October 1813, dismissed with the corps 16 December 1815. LH CH 5 September 1813.

LIGNOT (Jacques Victor Thérèse, 1780-?): born in Briançon (Hautes-Alpes) on 7 June 1780. In the 1st Hussars 5 September 1801, brigadier-fourrier 5 July 1802, in the Grenadiers à Cheval of the Imperial Guard 19 February 1805 brigadier-fourrier 22 December 1805.

He became maréchal des logis-chef 1 May 1807, second-lieutenant 25 June 1809, captain in the 11th Cuirassiers 28 November 1813, wounded at Waterloo 18 June 1815 and dismissed with the corps 16 December 1815. LH CH 25 November 1807.

LIMAL (Claude, 1786-?): born in Charmontier (Marne) on 7 February 1786. In the 2nd Cuirassiers 19 October 1806, brigadier 1 April 1809, maréchal des logis 21 February 1812, maréchal des logis-chef 20 February 1813, sub-lieutenant in the 2nd Cuirassiers 22 December 1813, incorporated with his squadron into the 1st Provisional Heavy Cavalry in Hamburg 11 September 1813, returned with the garrison 30 May 1814, back in the 2nd Cuirassiers, resignation accepted 18 February 1815 and left 1 Mars 1815.

LIMBURG STIRUM (Govert Fridrik van, 1790-1813): born in Bois-le-Duc (Bouches-du-Rhin) on 30 August 1790. Cadet in the artillery in the service of Holland 2 July 1803, pupil NCO 26 March 1807, maréchal des logis in the Cuirassiers of the Dutch Guard 1807, in the King of Holland's Body Guards 27 September 1809.

Cuirassiers 12 May 1810, in the same regiment when it became the 14th French Cuirassiers 18 August 1810, wounded at Polotsk 18 October 1812, lieutenant 5 September 1813, killed at Leipzig 18 October 1813.

LIMOZIN (André Edouard Louis, 1792-?): born in le Havre (Seine-Inférieure) on 13 March 1792. Pupil in the school in Saint-Germain 11 January 1810, brigadier 8 May 1812, sub-lieutenant in the 1st Cuirassiers 30 January 1813, joined them 14 March 1813.

He was shot and wounded in the neck at Hanau 30 October 1813, two lance wounds to his right side and shot and wounded in the left hand losing two fingers at Sézanne 25 March 1814, in the King's Cuirassiers 1 July 1814, retired with pension 1 November 1814 and put up for the veterans.

LINARD (Ferdinand Joseph, 1780-1862): born in Bruxelles (Dyle) on 23 August 1780. Conscript in the 2nd Carabiniers 22 February 1804, sabre wound to his right arm and his horse killed under him at Austerlitz 2 December 1805, brigadier 20 December 1806, incorporated with his company into the 1st Provisional Heavy Cavalry in Spain December 1807.

He became maréchal des logis 10 January 1808, maréchal des logis-chef when the 13th Cuirassiers were formed from the 1st Provisional 21 October 1808, shot and wounded in the left shoulder while forcing his way into a square of Provincial Grenadiers at the head of his platoon at Lerida 23 October 1810.

He was sub-lieutenant 18 September 1811, retired as a foreign national 9 August 1814, first lieutenant in the Dutch Mounted Police at Nivelles 13 December 1814.

LIONNAIS (François, 1764-?): in service 1 October 1784, captain in the 14th Chasseurs à Cheval 9 May 1793, discharged, in the 8th Cuirassiers 12 December 1806.

He reached the depot 16 January 1807, discharged by the Minister of War 4 March 1808, left 16 April 1808.

LODIN DUMAUVOIR (Joseph Antoine, chevalier, 1781-?): born in Paris (Seine) on 21 October 1781. In the Gendarmes d'Ordonnance 3 November 1806, maréchal des logis 4 November 1806, second-lieutenant 12 April 1807, paying officer 1 May 1807.

He was dismissed with the corps 23 October 1807 and attached to the Imperial Guard until 1 May 1808, lieutenant in the 2nd Cuirassiers 9 June 1808, joined them 6 October 1808; wounded at Wagram 6 July 1809, captain 28 October 1809, confirmed 25 January 1810.

He became squadron commander of a Provisional Heavy Cavalry regiment in Hamburg 13 August 1813, returned to France with the gar-

rison 30 May 1814, in the 8th Cuirassiers 13 December 1813, in the suite following the 25 August re-organisation, on four months' leave on half-pay 11 October 1814. LH CH 11 October 1812, Chevalier of the Empire l.p. 2 October 1813.

LOILIER (Pierre Nicolas, 1774-?): born in Banogne-Recouvrance (Ardennes) on 23 May 1774. In the 11th Cavalry 21 February 1793, brigadier 9 June 1800, brigadier-fourrier 4 July 1800, maréchal des logis 2 November 1801, maréchal des logis-chef 16 January 1802, adjutant 2 Mars 1802, sub-lieutenant 1 September 1802, in the same regiment when it became the 11th Cuirassiers 24 September 1803.

He became lieutenant 2 March 1805, two sabre wounds to his forehead and right hand at Eylau 8 February 1807, adjutant-major 9 May 1807, captain 25 May 1807, squadron commander in the 23rd Dragoons 17 July 1813, instated 28 September 1813, wounded at Leipzig 19 October 1813, incorporated into the Dragoons N°10 1 August 1814 which became the 15th Dragoons April 1815. LH CH 14 April 1807.

LOIR DULUDE (Bonaventure Jean Baptiste Gustave, 1781-1815): born in Saint-Sauveur-sur-Douvres (Manche) on 23 June 1781. Volunteer with Generals Vandamme and Latour-Maubourg 1812, sub-lieutenant in the 10th Cuirassiers 21 April 1813.

He became lieutenant aide de camp to General Lemoine 1 October 1813, returned to the regiment 27 July 1814, aide de camp to General Vandamme 4 May 1815, lance wound in the right thigh and died at Wavres 18 June 1815.

LOMAGNE
see **FLOTARD de MONTAGU LOMAGNE**

LOMBARD (Jean Balthazard, 1786-?): born in Draguignan (Var) on 7 January 1786. Velite in the Grenadiers à Cheval of the Imperial Guard 3 February 1807, incorporated 1 January 1811, supernumerary sub-lieutenant in the 2nd Cuirassiers 17 December 1811, detached with his squadron to Hamburg 3 July 1813 and incorporated with his squadron into the 1st Provisional Heavy Cavalry in Hamburg 11 September 1813, returned with the garrison 30 May 1814, put on half-pay because AWOL 6 August 1814.

LOMBARD (Michel Joseph, 1787-?): born in Mons (Jemmapes) on 15 October 1787. In the Grenadier à Cheval of the Imperial Guard 28 February 1806, sub-lieutenant in the 8th cuirassiers 25 March 1809, lieutenant 12 September 1809, resigned and dismissed from the corps for bad conduct 15 September 1811, struck off the rolls 20 October 1811.

LONCHAMP (Jean François, 1771-?): born in Favernay (Haute-Saône) on 17 August 1771. In the Royal-Cavalerie 1 March 1787 which became the 2nd Cavalry 1 January 1791, sabre wound to his left shoulder at Hedesheim 28 May 1794, in the King's Garde Constitutionnelle 2 August 1795, returned to the 2nd Cavalry 5 December 1798, brigadier 21 December 1798, maréchal des logis 2 November 1801.

He became in the same regiment when it became the 2nd Cuirassiers 12 October 1802, sub-lieutenant 14 May 1809, in the 17th Wagon Train Battalion 26 March 1812, instated 30 April 1812, in his appointment 1814. LH CH 1 October 1807.

LONCLAS (Pierre Etienne, 1774-1814): born in Merlan (Marne) in 1774. In the 23rd Cavalry 14 January 1794, brigadier 23 December 1802, dismissed with the corps the same day and incorporated into the 7th Cuirassiers 15 January 1803, maréchal des logis 15 October 1806, sub-lieutenant 19 November 1812, lieutenant 22 December 1813, wounded and taken prisoner at Fère-Champenoise 25 March 1814, died of his wounds at home. LH CH 14 May 1813.

LONGUET (Louis Hugues, 1779-?): born in Versailles (Seine-et-Oise) on 30 November 1779. Assistant team leader of the Military Wagon Teams 15 August 1793, maréchal des logis-chef in the 34th Artillery Train Battalion 28 June 1800, in the Gendarmerie d'Elite of the Imperial Guard 11 March 1802, brigadier 16 January 1804, sub-lieutenant in the 12th Cuirassiers 30 May 1808, instated 21 August 1808.

He was wounded by a Biscayan shot in his right hip at Wagram 6 July 1809, lieutenant 26 December 1811, wounded by a cannonball in the head at the Moskova 7 September 1812, aide de camp to Maréchal Lefebvre 1 November 1812, returned as captain to the 12th Cuirassiers 15 May 1813.

He was incorporated with his squadron into the 3rd Provisional Heavy Cavalry in Hamburg 11 September 1813, returned with the garrison 30 May 1814, dismissed 22 November 1815. LH CH 13 August 1809.

LOOTZ (Frederik Willem, 1782-?): born in Zeise (Zuydersee) on 17 August 1782. Volunteer in the 1st Batavian Cavalry 27 July 1802, brigadier 4 November 1804, maréchal des logis 1 January 1807, maréchal des logis-chef in the 2nd Dutch Cuirassiers 1 October 1809.

He was in the same regiment when it became the 14th French Cuirassiers 18 August 1810, sub-lieutenant 4 March 1812, wounded at the Berezina 28 November 1812.

EROY (Jacques Marie Joseph Jérôme Laurent, 1762-1842): born in Versailles (Seine-et-Oise) on 1 April 1762. In the La Rochefoucauld Dragoons 28 October 1780, dismissed 21 February 1788, in the National Guard at Pont-à-Mousson 8 January 1790, captain in the 1st Battalion of Meurthe Volunteers 26 June 1791, sub-lieutenant in the 7th Cavalry 25 January 1792, commissioned 10 March 1792, joined his unit 20 May 1792, instated 21 May 1792, lieutenant 17 June 1792, captain 7 December 1793, rallied some fleeing soldiers and held a bridge with them enabling the left wing of the army to retreat at Tournai 10 May 1794, in the inspection under General d'Harville 18 April 1799.

He was squadron commander in the 4th Cavalry 7 December 1799, major of the 6th Cuirassiers 29 October 1803, colonel commandant d'armes, 3rd Class 8 February 1812, at the disposal of the major-general of the Grande Armée 18 August 1812.

He was returned and put on the non-active list 4 September 1814, commanded at Langres 14 May 1815, replaced 4 September 1815, retired 9 December 1815. LH CH 25 March 1804.

Colonel at the disposition of General of the Grande Armée, Jacques Leroy had his hands and feet frozen in Russia. He lost three fingers on his left hand and two on his right and some toes on his right foot, and was taken prisoner on 10 December 1812.

LOTHE or **LHOTTE** (Louis Joseph Nicolas, 1786-?): born in Phalsbourg (Moselle) on 13 April 1786. volunteer in the 2nd Carabiniers 15 March 1804, brigadier 4 December 1806, maréchal des logis 26 May 1807, shot and wounded losing a finger of the left hand at Friedland 14 June 1807, incorporated with his company into the 1st Provisional Heavy Cavalry in Spain December 1807 which became the 13th Cuirassiers 21 October 1808, forced 50 Valencia Chasseurs to lay down their arms after they shot at him at Vimieros 26 November 1810.

He was in the 8th Cuirassiers 6 March 1811, sub-lieutenant 21 February 1812, second-lieutenant (Old Guard) in the Grenadiers à Cheval of the Imperial Guard 9 February 1813, in the Royal Corps of Chevau-Léger Lancers of France 10 August 1814 which became the Chevau-Léger Lancers of the Guard again 14 April 1815, wounded at Waterloo 18 June 1815, dismissed 15 November 1815. LH CH 12 September 1813.

LOTTEAU (Jean Baptiste Joseph, 1786-?): born in Taisinières-sur-Hon (Nord) on 15 November 1786. Velite in the Grenadiers à Cheval of the Imperial Guard 29 March 1806, two sabre wounds to his head at Eylau 8 February 1807.

He became sub-lieutenant in the suite of the 11th Cuirassiers 13 July 1807, in service 16 May 1809,

lieutenant 3 June 1809, retired 5 August 1811. LH CH 13 August 1809.

LOUAPT (Louis Auguste, 1787-?): born in Montsanche (Nièvre) on 4 March 1787. In the 10th Cuirassiers 12 May 1808, brigadier 10 August 1809, fourrier 10 October 1809, maréchal des logis 20 January 1810, maréchal des logis-chef 25 January 1810.

He became adjutant 6 November 1811, sub-lieutenant 12 August 1812, lieutenant 28 September 1813, dismissed with the corps 25 December 1815. LH CH 28 September 1813.

LOUIS (Jean Marie, 1769-?): born in Tilly (Aisne) on 6 April 1769. Trooper in the Royal-Roussillon 11 October 1786 which became the 11th cavalry 1 January 1791, brigadier-fourrier 1 December 1792, maréchal des logis-chef 1 October 1793, adjutant 7 November 1795.

He became sub-lieutenant 19 August 1800, in the same regiment when it became the 11th Cuirassiers 24 September 1803, lieutenant 2 April 1805, captain 25 May 1807, incorporated with his company into the 2nd Provisional Heavy Cavalry in Spain December 1807, prisoner with the capitulation at Baylen 23 July 1808, returned to the 13th Cuirassiers 28 September 1808, retired 20 April 1809. LH CH 14 April 1807.

LOUP (Jean Antoine, 1770-?): born in Carcassonne (Aude) on 19 September 1770. In the 2nd Aude Battalion 12 November 1791, left 26 December 1792, sub-lieutenant in the 14th Cavalry 10 March 1793, sabre wound to his head at Hamburg 4 April 1793, aide de camp to General Joba 9 January 1796, returned to the corps as a supernumerary 30 December 1797.

He was discharged 7 September 1800, recalled and sent to the Versailles riding school 16 December 1801, lieutenant 19 May 1802, captain 16 August 1803, returned to his corps 1803 which became the 23rd Dragoons 24 September 1803, squadron commander 1 July 1812, wounded at Krasnoë 17 November 1812, 8 lance wounds, his horse killed under him and taken prisoner at Yacht 30 December 1812.

He returned to France 21 July 1814, incorporated into the 7th Cuirassiers 7 July 1814, joined them 12 August 1814, shot in the stomach and his horse killed under him at Waterloo 18 June 1815, non-active 19 December 1815. LH CH 28 June 1805.

LOUVEL (François Pierre, 1789-1871): born in Draveille (Seine-et-Oise) on 15 March 1789. In the 11th Cuirassiers 1 November 1808, gendarme in the 3rd Escadron d'Espagne 17 December 1809, in the 1st Legion of the Gendarmerie à Cheval d'Espagne "Burgos" 16 December 1810, dismissed with the corps 27 February 1813.

He became maréchal des logis in the 11th Cuirassiers 14 March 1813, sub-lieutenant 14 May 1813, lance wound to his right thigh at Leipzig 16 October 1813.

He was wounded at Waterloo 18 June 1815 and

dismissed with the corps 16 December 1815. LH CH 4 December 1813.

LOUVENCOURT (Eugène Aimé François de, 1787-?): born in Cléry-le-Chaussoy (Somme) on 20 May 1787. Boarder in the Ecole Spéciale Militaire in Fontainebleau 28 October 1805, sub-lieutenant 8 November 1806, in the suite of the 4th Cuirassiers 14 December 1806, took up his appointment 16 March 1807, lieutenant 5 March 1809, captain 12 September 1809, squadron commander 14 May 1813.

He was wounded at Leipzig 16 October 1813, wounded and prisoner at Meckenheim 1 January 1814, suggested resigning May 1815, offer refused 30 May 1815, sent home to await further orders 14 July 1815, dismissed 21 December 1815. LH CH 1 October 1807, O 27 September 1813.

LUCHAPT (François Malbay, 1790-1815): born in Bellac (Haute-Vienne) on 17 February 1790. Velite in the Grenadiers à Cheval of the Guard 17 February 1808, sub-lieutenant 5th Cuirassiers 30 April 1812.

He became lieutenant adjutant-major 28 September 1813, two months' leave with pay 14 May 1814, wounded at Ligny 16 June 1815 and died at Avesnes 24 June 1815. LH CH 30 September 1814.

LUCOT (Jean Baptiste Pierre, 1787-?): born in Tirlemont (Marne) on 4 June 1787. In the 12th Cuirassiers 6 February 1807, brigadier 14 May 1809, shot and wounded in the right leg and his horse killed under him at Essling 22 May 1809, maréchal des logis 1 June 1809, maréchal des logis-chef 21 April 1812, adjutant-NCO 1 August 1812, sub-lieutenant 8 July 1813.

He was incorporated with his squadron into the 3rd Provisional Heavy Cavalry in Hamburg 11 September 1813, returned with the garrison 30 May 1814, wounded at Waterloo 18 June 1815 and dismissed with the corps 10 December 1815.

LUCOTTE (Dominique, 1784-?): born in Sainte-Sabine (Côte-d'Or) on 25 June 1784. In the 2nd Cuirassiers 9 June 1805, fourrier 20 November 1806, maréchal des logis 1 November 1809, maréchal des logis-chef 1 January 1810.

He became adjutant-NCO 1 February 1813, sub-lieutenant 3 September 1813, wounded at Waterloo 18 June 1815 left on half-pay 10 December 1815.

LURO (Basile, 1790-?): born in Malabat (Gers) on 20 April 1790. Velites in the Dragoons of the Imperial Guard 7 June 1808, sub-lieutenant in the 9th Cuirassiers 13 March 1813, in the 10th Cuirassiers 6 August 1814, dismissed with the corps 25 December 1815.

LUSIGNAN (Armand, 1784-?): born in Toulouse (Haute-Garonne) on 30 August 1784. Sub-lieutenant in the 13th Cuirassiers 17 August 1809, lieutenant aide de camp to Maréchal Suchet, in the suite 16 October 1813.

Cuirassiers charging, officers in the fore! Oil on canvas by J. Rouffet *(© photo Michel Urtado, RMN)*

159

MABILOTTE (Jean Louis, 1767-1813): born in Crécy (Aisne) on 18 March 1767. In the Ségur Dragoons 10 June 1786, left 27 April 1790, in the Paris National Guard 9 August 1790, left 7 November 1791, brigadier in the Volotaires Nationaux à Cheval from the Ecole Militaire 20 December 1792.

He became maréchal des logis 15 January 1793, in the same regiment when it became the 26th Cavalry 21 February 1793 and became the 25th Cavalry 4 June 1793, sub-lieutenant 22 June 1793, lieutenant by choice 5 November 1794, in the General Police Legion 29 October 1795 which became the 21st Dragoons 24 December 1796, in the suite of the 16th Dragoons 24 December 1797, lieutenant in the 2nd Cuirassiers 1 June 1811, remained behind and prisoner in Russia 1 December 1812, died in Vilna 8 January 1813.

MACLER (Charles Christophe, 1766-1809): born in Neuchâtel (Switzerland) on 6 February 1766. Trooper in the Royal-Cravates 16 June 1784 which became the 10th Cavalry 1 January 1791, brigadier-fourrier 15 September 1793, maréchal des logis 20 July 1794, maréchal des logis-chef 6 May 1795.

He became sub-lieutenant 22 March 1800, lieutenant 6 January 1803, in the same regiment when it became the 10th Cuirassiers 24 September 1803, captain 26 June 1807, wounded at Essling 22 May 1809, died of his wounds 24 May 1809. LH CH 5 November 1804.

MAGNIER (Marie Jean Baptiste Balthazard, 1792-?): born in Ribeauvillé (Haut-Rhin) on 7 January 1792. Boarder in the Ecole Spéciale Militaire de Cavalerie 12 October 1809, entered 8 November 1809, grenadier 5 August 1811.

He became brigadier 15 September 1811, sub-lieutenant in the 10th Cuirassiers 19 April 1812, lieutenant 8 July 1813, aide de camp to General Delmas 11 August 1813, wounded in the head at Brunslau 1813, captain 25 November 1813, sabre wound to his head 2 January 1814 and another in the face at Laon 8 March

1814, returned to the 10th Cuirassiers 9 July 1814. He was shot and wounded in the right leg at Waterloo 18 June 1815, retired when the corps was disbanded 25 December 1815. LH CH 5 April 1814.

MAGNON (René, 1758-?): born in Saint-Savin (Vienne) on 22 June 1758. In the Colonel-Général-Cavalerie 8 May 1778, in the same regiment when it became the 1st Cavalry 1 January 1791, brigadier 2 August 1791.

He became brigadier-fourrier 16 April 1792, maréchal des logis 28 August 1792, sabre wound to his head at Neerwinden 18 March 1793, maréchal des logis-chef 10 June 1793, adjutant 24 December 1795, lance wound to his right thigh at the Tagliamento 16 March 1797, sub-lieutenant 21 June 1798, lieutenant 2 May 1799.

He was in the same regiment when it became the 1st Cuirassiers 10 October 1801, captain 7 December 1802, retired 26 December 1806, left with his pension 1 February 1807. LH CH 14 June 1804.

MAHAUT (Nicolas, 1756-?): born in Doutine (Haute-Marne) on 29 July 1756. In the Reine-Cavalerie 8 June 1777, brigadier 18 October 1787, in the same regiment when it became the 4th Cavalry 1 January 1791, maréchal des logis 1 August 1793, maréchal des logis-chef 1 November 1793.

He became sub-lieutenant 19 February 1799, in the same regiment when it became the 4th Cuirassiers 12 October 1802, lieutenant by seniority 27 April 1806, retired 15 November 1806.

MAHIEU (?-?): maréchal des logis-chef in the 9th Cuirassiers, sub-lieutenant in the suite 30 May 1808, in post 31 July 1809, lieutenant 31 August 1810 wounded at the Moskova 7 September 1812, retired April 1813.

MAHIEU (Guillaume, 1766-?): born in Dongen (Belgium) on 8 March 1766. Cadet in the Berwick Cavalry Regiment 25 November 1779, in the Prince of Orange's Body Guards 25 March 1789,

Seal of the 8th Cuirassier Regiment.
(Author's collection)

second-lieutenant in the service of France in the Chasseurs à Cheval of the Legion Franche Etrangère, lieutenant in the 1st Batavian Cavalry 9 July 1795, captain 28 June 1801.

He became lieutenant-colonel in the 3rd Dutch Hussars then of the 2nd Dutch Cuirassiers 10 October 1806, squadron commander in the same regiment which had become the 14th French Cuirassiers 18 August 1810, retired 6 December 1810.

MAILLARD (François Désiré, 1781-?): born in Douai (Nord) on 22 December 1781. In the King of Westphalia's Body Guards 18 February 1809.

He became sub-lieutenant in the 1st Westphalian Cuirassiers 5 May 1809, lieutenant 5 June 1810, captain in the 2nd Westphalian Cuirassiers 9 March 1811, in the suite of the Jérôme-Napoléon Hussars 25 October 1813, took up his appointment 4 November 1813.

He was in the same regiment when it became the 13th French Hussars 1 January 1814, non-active on half-pay 12 August 1814, captain in the 7th Cuirassiers 25 April 1815, joined them 1 May 1815, returned home non-active 24 August 1815.

MAILLIOT (?-?): sub-lieutenant in the 9th Cuirassiers 9 August 1809, lieutenant 9 February 1813, captain 21 April 1813, no longer appears on the rolls as of 9 August 1814.

MAILLOT (Jean Joseph, 1765-?): born in Montaudon (Doubs) on 25 June 1765. In the Reine-Cavalerie 11 April 1781, brigadier 1 November 1786, in the same regiment when it became the 4th Cavalry 1 January 1791, maréchal des logis 1 May 1792,.

He became sub-lieutenant 1 August 1793, lieutenant 6 April 1795, at the Versailles riding school 1797, returned to the corps 1799, captain 9 March 1800, in the same regiment when it became the 4th Cuirassiers 12 October 1802, wounded and his horse killed under him at Essling 21 May 1809, retired 11 May 1812. LH CH 3 May 1807.

MAIRE (Louis Théodore, 1789-?): born in Besançon (Doubs) on 22 February 1789. In the 5th Cuirassiers 4 November 1807, brigadier 6 December 1807, maréchal des logis 1 January 1809, maréchal des logis-chef 20 January 1809. He became adjutant-NCO 6 November 1811, sub-lieutenant 28 September 1813, dismissed 23 December 1815.

MAIRE (Pierre Joseph, 1787-?): born in Pont-à-Mousson (Meurthe) on 9 November 1787. In the Nancy Guard of Honour 1810, in the 2nd Gardes d'Honneur 21 June 1813, brigadier 28 June 1813, maréchal des logis 18 July 1813, second-lieutenant 30 October 1813, lieutenant in the suite of the 6th Cuirassiers 4 August 1814.

He was only considered officially as a sub-lieutenant 20 January 1815, put back as sub-lieutenant in the suite 31 January 1815, confirmed sub-lieutenant in post 4 February 1815, detached to the school in Saumur, dismissed 21 November 1815.

MAJORELLE (Jean Baptiste, 1778-1812): born in Lunéville (Meurthe) on 10 May 1778. Pupil in the Ecole de Mars when it was created 1 June 1794, joined up 23 June 1794, dismissed when the school was disbanded 21 November 1794.

He was, cadet in the Navy 10 April 1795, dismissed when the school was disbanded 26 September 1795, in the 8th Cavalry 15 September 1798, fourrier 26 September 1801, in the same regiment when it became the 8th Cuirassiers 10 October 1801, maréchal des logis-chef 6 January 1802, sub-lieutenant in the suite 26 April 1807, in his post 3 June 1809, lieutenant 9 August 1809, died in Bonn 15 April 1812.

MAJORELLE (Nicolas Henry, 1786-?): born in Lunéville (Meurthe) on 2 February 1786. In the 8th Cuirassiers 15 December 1805, brigadier 1 April 1807, fourrier 16 October 1808, maréchal des logis 1 December 1810.

He became maréchal des logis-chef 11 April 1812, sub-lieutenant 22 December 1813, wounded at les Quatre-Bras 16 June 1815, dismissed with the corps 5 December 1815 and sent home, non-active 11 December 1815.

MALBOISSIERE de PULLY
see **RANDON de MALBOISSIERE de PULLY**

MALHERBE (Adolphe, 1792-1812): born in le Mans (Sarthe) on 9 April 1792. Pupil in the Saint-Germain school 15 October 1809, sub-lieutenant in the 12th Cuirassiers 15 March 1812, killed at Orcha 21 November 1812.

MALLET (Jacques, 1775-1809) : born in Saint-Jacques (Seine-Inférieure) in 1775. In the 4th Cavalry 29 May 1794, brigadier 9 June 1800, brigadier-fourrier 20 June 1800.

MARULAZ (Jacob François, 1769-1842): born in Zeiskam (Prussia) on 6 November 1769.

Child of the regiment in the Esterhazy-Hussars 16 September 1778, hussar 1 November 1784, brigadier-fourrier in the same regiment when it became the 3rd Hussars 1 January 1791, maréchal des logis 23 June 1792, commanded General Valence's escort at Valmy 20 September 1792.

He was lieutenant in the scouts from the Army of the Centre aka the Fabrefonds Scouts 1 October 1792, in the same regiment when it became the 9th Hussars 26 February 1793 then the 8th Hussars 4 June 1793, captain 1 March 1793, aide de camp to General Salomon 1 august 1793.

He was wounded by a Biscayan shot to his left hip at Laval September 1793, got hold of the Vendéens' army cash box after fording the river at Blain December 1793, sabre wound to his right cheek at Menin 30 April 1794, squadron commander 7 May 1794, wounded near Bousbecques 18 May 1794.

He was confirmed in the 8th Hussars 26 February 1795, shot and wounded in the arm at Huningue 25 October 1796, brigade commander of the regiment 23 December 1798, shot and wounded five times of which four to the chest and one which went through his body breaking two ribs 15 June 1799, took a canon and 800 prisoners when crossing the Rhine 1 May 1800, took 100 prisoners after fording Chiemsee Lake 10 December 1800.

He became brigadier-general 6 March 1805, retroactively 1 February 1805, commanded the Haute-Saône Department 12 March 1805 then a cavalry brigade in the 3rd Reserve Corps of the Grande Armée 24 September 1805.

He commanded the Haute-Saône Department 4 June 1806, commanded the 2nd Brigade (10th and 11th Cuirassiers) of the 2nd Heavy Cavalry Division 18 October 1806, went over to the Light Cavalry Brigade (1st, 2nd and 12th Chasseurs à Cheval) of the 3rd Corps 27 November 1806, confirmed 5 December 1806, bayonet wound to his right knee at Golymin 26 December 1806, took 300 prisoners at Dommau 9 February 1807 and 5000 near Labiau 17 June 1807, dismissed for 4 months to enable him to return to France 1 October 1807.

He commanded the Haute-Saône Department 4 February 1808, commanded the Cavalry Marching Regiments in the 5th Military Division in Strasbourg 5 March 1809, commanded the Light Cavalry of the Rhine Observation Corps 4 April 1809.

He was shot and wounded in the thigh at Essling 22 May 1809 and seriously wounded by a shot which shattered his leg, remained stuck under his horse which was killed under him at Wagram 6 July 1809.

He commanded the 1st Light Cavalry Division of the Cavalry Reserve of the Army of Germany 11 July 1809, major-general 12 July 1809, commanded the 6th Military Division 24 September 1809, victor at Baumes-les-Dames 31 December 1813.

He was inspector general of cavalry in the 18th Military Division, in the 15th Military Division 15 January 1815 then the 6th 31 March 1815, commanded the same division 11 April 1815, non-active 21 July 1815, retired 6 December 1815. Holder of a Sabre of Honour 22 March 1801.

LH CH by rights 24 September 1803, C 14 June 1804, Baron of the Empire d.24 June 1808 l.p. 7 December 1808.

Near Boxtel on 15 September 1794 with Captain Becker and thirty Hussars from the 8th Regiment, Squadron Commander Jacob Marulaz took 500 Hessians prisoner.

He became maréchal des logis 15 July 1802, in the same regiment when it became the 4th Cuirassiers 12 October 1802, maréchal des logis-chef 17 May 1803, adjutant-NCO 4 April 1807, sub-lieutenant 25 June 1807, killed at Essling 21 May 1809.

MALTETE (Claude François, 1761-?): born in Antey (Haute-Saône) on 10 October 1761. In the Royal-Cravates 1 March 1779, brigadier 6 September 1784, in the same regiment when it became the 10th Cavalry 1 January 1791, brigadier-fourrier 21 March 1791, maréchal des logis 20 November 1791, maréchal des logis-chef 1 July 1792, confirmed 10 August 1792, sub-lieutenant 15 September 1793.

He became lieutenant 11 August 1794, saved two cannon which were going to fall into enemy hands at Wurtzburg 3 September 1796, captain 5 March 1800, in the same regiment when it became the 10th Cuirassiers 24 September 1803, left to retire 6 June 1810. LH CH 5 November 1804

MALTON (Jean Antoine Honoré, 1761-?): born in Mareuil (Marne) on 16 May 1761. In the Roi-Cavalerie 16 June 1781, brigadier 9 March 1785, in the same regiment when it became the 6th Cavalry 1 January 1791, brigadier-fourrier 17 March 1791, maréchal des logis 10 June 1792, maréchal des logis-chef 22 October 1792.

He became sub-lieutenant 1 April 1793, deputy on the staff of the Cavalry 20 May 1794, aide de camp to General Dubois 15 March 1795, returned to the corps July 1795, detached to the riding school from 1797 to 1799.

He was lieutenant 17 April 1800, confirmed 2 May 1800, in the same regiment when it became the 6th Cuirassiers 23 December 1802, adjutant-major 13 March 1803, captain adjutant-major 12 May 1803, captain in post 9 November 1805, squadron commander 6 October 1808, wounded at Essling and prisoner 21 May 1809, returned 1 August 1809, retired 12 September 1809, pensioned 12 January 1810.

MAMELET (Léopold, 1782-?): born in Conflans (Haute-Saône) on 15 November 1782. In the 12th Cavalry 4 July 1801, fourrier 5 July 1802, in the same regiment when it became the 12th Cuirassiers 24 September 1803, maréchal des logis-chef 17 March 1804, adjutant-NCO 30 October 1806, sub-lieutenant 14 May 1809, wounded at Essling 22 May 1809, lieutenant 9 February 1813.

He became adjutant-major 8 July 1813, instated 21 July 1813, non-active on half-pay by exchanging with Captain Adjutant-Major Lagay 28 January 1815, in service in the 8th cuirassiers 12 May 1815, non-active again because of 1 September 1815 law, dismissed with the corps 5 December 1815 and put in for Gendarmerie 11 December 1815. LH CH 1 October 1807.

Letter addressed and signed by the Quartermaster Mancel de Bouesdenos, 14th Cuirassier Regiment.
(Author's collection)

MANIGUET (François, 1785 -) in the 4th Hussars 31 October 1804, brigadier 1 July 1807, in the 9th Hussars 13 June 1809.

He wasgendarme in the 15th Escadron d'Espagne 1 January 1810, in the 1st Legion of the Gendarmerie à Cheval d'Espagne "Burgos" 1 January 1811, brigadier 25 October 1811, sub-lieutenant in the 1st Cuirassiers 25 February 1813, joined them 12 March 1813, left for Hamburg with his squadron May 1813, incorporated with his squadron into the 1st Provisional Heavy Cavalry in Hamburg 11 September 1813, returned with the garrison 27 May 1814, retired on full pay 1 October 1814, returned to the 1st Cuirassiers April 1815 and put on half-pay 1 September 1815.

MANNECHALLE (Etienne, 1782-?): born in Lyon (Rhône) on 12 August 1782. In the Gendarmes d'Ordonnance 25 October 1806, dismissed with the corps 23 October 1807 and incorporated into the Grenadiers à Cheval of the Guard 24 November 1807.

He became sub-lieutenant in the Line 4 April 1808, in the 2nd Carabiniers 23 April 1808, instated 24 August 1808, in the 13th Cuirassiers 21 October 1808, lieutenant 4 September 1812, instated 5 October 1812, acting captain 21 January 1814, incorporated into the suite of the 9th cuirassiers 9 August 1814, non-active on half-pay 1 October 1814, confirmed captain on the non-active list 4 February 1815, rejoined the war squadrons of the 1st Carabiniers 9 June 1815, wounded at Waterloo 18 June 1815, made non-active again 1 August 1815, returned home 21 August 1815. LH CH October 1814.

MARAIS (Jean Victoire Rodolphe, 1786-?): at the veterinary school in Lyon 5 June 1807, sub-lieutenant in the 30th Dragoons 2 September 18136.

He was non-active 30 September 1814, sub-lieutenant in the 1st Cuirassiers 15 May 1815, put back on half-pay 1 September 1815.

MARAIS (Louis, 1769-?): born in Ambléville (Seine-et-Oise) on 4 October 1769. In the 25th Cavalry 5 September 1792, in the 19th Cavalry 8 June 1796, fourrier 2 June 1797, maréchal des logis 21 November 1798, maréchal des logis-chef 29 June 1799, shot and wounded in the right arm near Munich 7 December 1800.

He was incorporated into the 1st Carabiniers 6 February 1803, in the 1st Cuirassiers 23 March 1803,

MANCEL de BOUESDENOS (Jean Louis César, 1792-?): born in Caen (Calvados) on 25 January 1792. Sub-lieutenant quartermaster-treasurer of the Battalion of French Chasseurs 8 February 1811, quartermaster-treasurer of the 14th Cuirassiers 22 July 1812, instated 1 August 1812.

He became lieutenant quartermaster-treasurer 3 January 1814, prisoner, returned to the suite of the King's Cuirassiers 1 August 1814 which became the 1st Cuirassiers April 1815, in the Rhône Dragoons 1 December 1815. LH CH 17 March 1815.

MANGEOT (Jean Nicolas, 1778-?): born in Pont-sur-Meuse (Meuse) on 5 December 1778. In the 25th Cavalry 21 November 1798, brigadier 12 December 1801, fourrier 1 August 1802.

He was dismissed with the corps 12 October 1802 and incorporated into the 4th Cuirassiers 24 November 1802, maréchal des logis 1 October 1806, maréchal des logis-chef 1 April 1808, sub-lieutenant 3 July 1809, wound by a Biscayan shot at Wagram 6 July 1809, had his right leg shattered by a cannonball at Czaszniki 31 October 1812, lieutenant 19 November 1812.

He was wounded at the Berezina 28 November 1812, non-active on half-pay 6 August 1814, back as lieutenant in post 4 January 1815 in the same regiment when it became the Angoulême Cuirassiers and 4th Cuirassiers again April 1815, retired 21 December 1815. LH CH 5 September 1813.

sub-lieutenant 24 November 1806, shot and wounded in the head at Hoff 6 February 1807, lieutenant 25 May 1807, captain 31 July 1811, left with his squadron for Hamburg May 1813, incorporated with his squadron into the 1st Provisional Heavy Cavalry in Hamburg 11 September 1813, returned with the garrison 27 May 1814, kept in the King's Cuirassiers 1 July 1814, remained in Paris at the disposal of the Minister of War 20 January 1815.

He returned 1 April 1815 to the same regiment when it became the 1st Cuirassiers again, dismissed and put up for retirement 24 December 1815. LH CH 14 April 1807.

MARCHAND (Jean, 1773 -) born in Angers (Maine-et-Loire) on 10 July 1773. In the 10th Cavalry 10 July 1791, sabre wound to his left hand at Wurtzburg 3 September 1795, sabre wound to his head at Brackenheim 3 November 1799, in the same regiment when it became the 10th Cuirassiers 24 September 1803, bayonet wound to his right arm at Eylau 8 February 1807, brigadier 9 February 1807, maréchal des logis 22 March 1809, sub-lieutenant 8 July 1813, shot in the right arm in front of Paris 30 March 1814, dismissed with the corps 25 December 1815. LH CH 16 June 1809.

MARCHAND (Simon, 1780 - 1815) born in Voisigny (Ardennes) in 1780. In the 4th Cavalry 29 March 1800 which became the 4th Cuirassiers 12 October 1802, brigadier 21 December 1805, fourrier 1 October 1806, maréchal des logis 25 June 1807, maréchal des logis-chef 4 June 1809.

He became adjutant-NCO 4 July 1809, sub-lieutenant 17 June 1812, lieutenant adjutant-major 17 July 1813, in the same regiment when it became the Angoulême Cuirassiers 6 August 1814, rank of captain 17 January 1815, went to command a company 22 February 1815.

He was in the same regiment when it became the 4th Cuirassiers April 1815, killed at Waterloo 18 June 1815. LH CH 1 October 1807, O 27 December 1814.

MARCHANT de la CHATELAINE de BANANS (Charles Philippe Joseph, chevalier, 1782-1858): brother of the following, born in Salins-les-Bains (Jura) on 1 May 1782.

In the 93rd Half-Brigade 11 September 1799, in the 3rd cavalry 21 September 1801, brigadier 24 September 1801, in the same regiment when it became the 3rd Cuirassiers 12 October 1802, maréchal des logis 2 June 1803, sub-lieutenant 1 March 1804, lieutenant 3 April 1807, wounded at Friedland 14 June 1807, retired 28 February 1811. LH CH, Chevalier of the Empire l.p. 18 March 1809.

MARCHANT de la CHATELAINE de BANANS (Ferdinand Henri Marie, 1786-?): younger brother of the above, born in Salins-les-Bains (Jura) on 28 September 1786. In the 3rd Cavalry 20 June 1802 which became the 3rd Cuirassiers 12 October 1802, fourrier 20 July 1803.

He became maréchal des logis 22 March 1804, maréchal des logis-chef 16 December 1806, wounded at Friedland 14 June 1807, sub-lieutenant 25 June 1807,

Cuirassier general and his staff.
(Composition by Lucien Rousselot. RR)

lieutenant 14 May 1809, adjutant-major 2 June 1809, wounded and his horse killed under him at Wagram 6 July 1809, rank of captain 2 December 1810.

He was wounded and his horse killed under him at Leipzig 18 October 1813, captain in the 1st Cuirassiers 1 July 1814, in the 2nd Cuirassiers 9 June 1815, instated 18 June 1815, in the Cuirassiers of the Royal Guard 10 October 1815. LH CH 1 October 1807.

MARCHE see
DUMAS de la MARCHE

MARCOTTE de FORCE-VILLE (Alexandre Julien, 1769-?): born in Paris (Seine) on 25 January 1769. Sub-lieutenant in the 6th Cavalry in post end 1792, in the 22nd Dragoons.

He became squadron commander in the 12th Cuirassiers 15 December 1803, under-inspector of parades 30 October 1806.

MARCOUX (?-?): Sub-lieutenant in the suite of the 6th Cuirassiers 12 September 1809, in his post 1810, lost an arm at the Moskova 7 September 1812, no longer appears on the rolls in 1813.

MARCREZ (?-1815): lieutenant in the 4th Cuirassiers wounded at Waterloo 18 June 1815 and died of his wounds 23 June 1815.

MARECHAUX (André, 1779-1815): born in Fontainebleau (Seine-et-Oise) on 7 October 1779. In the 10th Dragoons 1 February 1802, brigadier 25 February 1806, discharged 25 May 1808.

He became maréchal des logis in the Gardes d'Honneur 21 May 1813, sub-lieutenant in the 14th Cuirassiers 19 March 1814, dismissed with the corps and put in the suite of the 12th Cuirassiers 13 July 1814, presumed killed at Waterloo 18 June 1815.

MARGARON (Pierre, baron, 1765-1824): born in Lyon (Rhône) on 1 May 1765. Sub-lieutenant in the suite March 1788.

He became , deputy lieutenant on the general staff of the Army of the North 29 April 1792, captain in the 1st Compagnie Franche 1 July 1792, incorporated into the Ardennes Legion 15 August 1792, CO of the Ardennes Legion and rank of infantry lieutenant-colonel 15 October 1792, battalion commander second in command of the 1st Battalion of the same legion 10 December 1792, first battalion commander 10 April 1793, adjutant-general and acting brigade

**Colonel of the 6th Cuirassier Regiment
in full dress, mounted in 1813.
after Carle Vernet.**
(RR)

commander of the Ardennes Legion 14 April 1793, suspended 30 July 1793, in the Army of the North temporarily 4 October 1794, commanded the escort for the arrested deputies during Prairial (21 May 1795).

He was confirmed on the active list 7 June 1795, confirmed adjutant-general brigade commander 13 June 1795, at general headquarters 23 August 1795, in the Army of the Sambre-et-Meuse 20 September 1796 then in that of Italy 1798, brigade commander of the 1st Cavalry 23 December 1798, shot and wounded at Novi 15 August 1799 and a broken leg at Fossano, in the same regiment when it became the 1st Cuirassiers 10 October 1801, brigadier-general 29 August 1803, left the 1st Cuirassiers 21 September 1803, commanded the Cavalry Division (8th Hussars, 11th Chasseurs à Cheval and Gendarmerie à Cheval) at Saint-Omer Camp 20 September 1803, d° under d'Hautpoul 17 November 1803, commanded the Chasseurs à Cheval 3 August 1805.

He commanded a light cavalry brigade in the 4th Corps of the Grande Armée 11 September 1805, shot and wounded twice at Austerlitz 2 December 1805, returned to France 28 February 1806, available 11 April 1806, at the general headquarters of the Grande Armée 28 July 1806, commanded the Light Cavalry Brigade (11th and 16th Chasseurs à Cheval) of the 4th Corps 20 September 1806 then the 1st Brigade (17th and 18th Dragoons) of the 4th Dragoon Division 7 November 1806, in the Gironde Observation Corps 28 August 1807, commanded the cavalry depots in the Deux-Sèvres and the Charente-Inférieure Departments 10 December 1808, in the 2nd Corps of the Army of Spain 4 January 1809, in Strasbourg 24 March 1809, Valence's division in Spain 12 July 1809, returned end 1809, commanded the Haute-Loire 6 September 1810, in the suite of the general staff 22 July 1812.

He became major-general 16 August 1813, commanded the cavalry division organised in Leipzig and governor of the town 20 September 1813, inspector general of the Gendarmerie 18 July 1814, available 3 April 1815, inspector of cavalry depots in the 12th and 13th Military Divisions 29 May 1815, non-active 22 October 1815. LH CH December 1803, C 14 June 1804, Baron of the Empire l.p. 29 January 1809.

MARILLAC (Jacques Victor Hyppolite de, 1773-1812): born in le Puy (Haute-Loire) on 29 December 1773. In the Picardy Chasseurs à Cheval 10 December 1788 which became the 7th Chasseurs à Cheval 1 January 1791, lieutenant in the 57th Infantry 1 June 1792, gave up 23 May 1793, commanded a group of partisans in the Vendée 1795.

He was incorporated into the Guides of the Army of the Rhine 21 December 1797, brigadier 14 February 1799, maréchal des logis 21 March 1799, in the Guides à Cheval of the Army of Helvetia 19 May 1799, sub-lieutenant in the Guard of the General in Chief 9 May 1800, lieutenant 23 September 1800, in the 8th Cavalry 5 May 1801, confirmed 10 July 1801?.

He became lieutenant in the Elite Company when the 8th Cuirassiers was formed 10 October 1801, adjutant-major 27 January 1807, captain 17 April 1807, killed at the Moskova 7 September 1812. LH CH 1 October 1807.

MARIN see **CAYEN** aka **MARIN**

MARLIER (Claude Joseph, 1760-?): born in Dommartemont (Meurthe) on 15 March 1760. In the Reine-Cavalerie 2 March 1779, brigadier 2 April 1786, in the same regiment when it became the 4th Cavalry 1 January 1791.

He became maréchal des logis 21 January 1792, maréchal des logis-chef 12 May 1792, sub-lieutenant 6 April 1795, in the same regiment when it became the 4th Cuirassiers 12 October 1802, retired 25 March 1805.

MARQUIS (Louis Anselme, 1787-1813): born in Bourgueil (Indre-et-Loire) on 24 July 1787. In the Gendarmes d'Ordonnance 16 January 1807, dismissed with the corps 23 October 1807 and incorporated into the Dragoons of the Imperial Guard 24 November 1807, confirmed 8 January 1808, sub-lieutenant in the 8th Cuirassiers 3 June 1809.

He became lieutenant 6 November 1811, killed during one of the Danzig garrison sorties 28 August 1813. LH CH 11 October 1812.

MARS see **SAINT-MARS**

MARSAN voir **ASINARI de SAINT MARSAN**.

MARTENS (Jean Henri, 1768-?): born on 5 April 1768. In the Dutch Cavalry 1 February 1785, brigadier 4 October 1789, maréchal des logis 31 March 1791, maréchal des logis-chef in the 2nd Batavian Cavalry 1 August 1795.

He became lieutenant quartermaster 25 April 1797, captain quartermaster of the 2nd Dutch Cuirassiers 21 October 1806 which became the 14th French Cuirassiers 18 August 1810, put in command of a company 1 September 1810, retired 26 December 1810 not having ever joined his corps following its reorganisation.

Senior officers

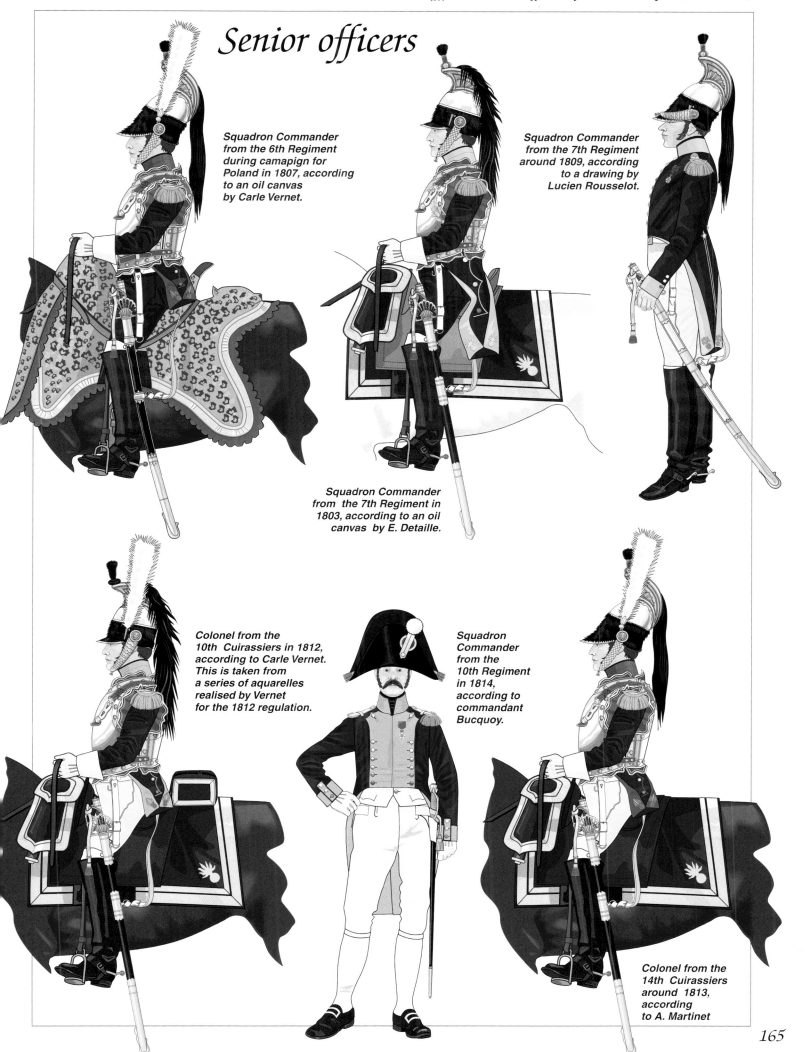

Squadron Commander from the 6th Regiment during camapign for Poland in 1807, according to an oil canvas by Carle Vernet.

Squadron Commander from the 7th Regiment around 1809, according to a drawing by Lucien Rousselot.

Squadron Commander from the 7th Regiment in 1803, according to an oil canvas by E. Detaille.

Colonel from the 10th Cuirassiers in 1812, according to Carle Vernet. This is taken from a series of aquarelles realised by Vernet for the 1812 regulation.

Squadron Commander from the 10th Regiment in 1814, according to commandant Bucquoy.

Colonel from the 14th Cuirassiers around 1813, according to A. Martinet

MARTHE (Pierre Laurent Cyprien, 1777-1812): born in Estages (Pyrénées-Orientales) on 16 September 1777. Fourrier in the Corbières Chasseurs Legion from the Aude Department 21 March 1793, incorporated into the 20th Half-Brigade of Light Infantry 2 April 1794, in the 11th cavalry 6 November 1799, brigadier 9 October 1800.

He became fourrier 2 November 1801, maréchal des logis-chef 12 October 1802, in the same regiment when it became the 11th Cuirassiers 24 September 1803, sub-lieutenant 16 May 1809, lieutenant 6 November 1811, disappeared with 3 other officers during fighting beyond the River Niemen 31 December 1812.

MARTIGNON (Jean Etienne, 1774-?): born in Dommartin (Marne) on 27 March 1774. In the 7th Cavalry 17 October 1793, shot and wounded in the left shoulder near Guisen 19 September 1796, brigadier 2 March 1801.

He was in the same regiment when it became the 7th Cuirassiers 23 December 1802, brigadier-fourrier 5 January 1804, maréchal des logis 28 February 1805, adjutant-NCO 24 November 1807, sub-lieutenant 7 April 1809, temporary lieutenant 3 June 1809, cannonball wound to his left hand at Wagram 6 July 1809, captain 9 February 1813, returned home on half-pay 16 August 1814. LH CH 5 September 1813.

MARTIN (François Xavier, 1778-?): born in Scherviller (Haut-Rhin) on 26 October 1778. In the 6th Cavalry 26 February 1794 which became the 6th Cuirassiers 23 December 1802, brigadier 9 October 1803, maréchal des logis 1 October 1806, sub-lieutenant 15 March 1812, wounded at Waterloo 18 June 1815, dismissed 21 November 1815.

MARTIN (Jean Baptiste Isidore, baron, 1772-1853): born in Saint-Dizier (Haute-Marne) on 6 August 1772. In the Dauphin-Dragons 9 May 1789, left 29 January 1793, in the 24th Cavalry of the so-called new levy when it was formed 21 February 1791, brigadier-fourrier 12 July 1792.

He became maréchal des logis 7 August 1792, maréchal des logis-chef 1 April 1793, in the same regiment when it became the 23rd Cavalry 4 June 1793, several sabre wounds and shot several times during a reconnaissance mission near Florenville and Villiers 24 February 1794, adjutant-NCO 25 August 1796, sub-lieutenant 1 August 1798, lieutenant 22 December 1799, confirmed 19 February 1800, two sabre wounds at Salzburg 14 December 1800.

He was adjutant-major 13 March 1802, first-lieutenant in the Chasseurs à Cheval of the Guard 13 October 1802, captain adjutant-major 3 February 1804, squadron commander 16 February 1807, colonel of the 6th Cuirassiers 6 August 1811, joined them

Brevet for promotion to the Order of the Légion d'Honneur.
(Author's collection)

1 October 1811, in the Escadron Sacré during the retreat from Moscow November 1812, two months' leave with pay 30 April 1814, confirmed as Colonel of the 6th Cuirassiers 28 September 1814, on six months' leave on half-pay 3 November 1814, wounded by a Biscayan shot and amputated at Waterloo 18 June 1815.

He was retired because of his wounds 21 November 1815. LH CH 14 June 1804, O 17 November 1808, Chevalier of the Empire d. 10 September 1808 and l.p. 15 March 1810, Baron d. 3 September 1813.

MARTIN (Jean Baptiste, 1782-?): born in Dannemois (Seine-et-Oise) on 28 October 1782. In the Seine-et-Oise Reserve Company 30 November 1805, in the 8th Cuirassiers 1808, brigadier 10 April 1809, maréchal des logis 22 June 1809, maréchal des logis-chef 1 August 1811.

He became adjutant-NCO 15 August 1812, sub-lieutenant 19 October 1813, prisoner at Danzig 2 January 1813, returned to the suite 16 October 1814, in his post 4 February 1815, dismissed with the corps 5 December 1815 and put on the non-active list, returned home 11 December 1815.

MARTIN (Jean Louis, 1767-?): born in Paris (Seine) on 23 April 1767. In the Condé-Dragons 16 July 1784, left September 1785, in the Ségur-Dragons 3 January 1786 which became the Hainaut Chasseurs à Cheval 17 March 1788 the 5th Chasseurs à Cheval on 1 January 1791.

He became maréchal des logis-chef in the Gendarmerie d'Elite of the Consular Guard 3 March 1802, left 24 April 1804, volunteer in the 11th Cuirassiers 6 March 1805, brigadier 7 March 1805, maréchal des logis 1 December 1806, maréchal des logis-chef 15 December 1806, adjutant 3 April 1807, sub-lieutenant 16 May 1809, lieutenant in the 6th Wagon Train Battalion

23 January 1812, left to join them 11 February 1812, prisoner at Torgau 9 January 1814

He returned 15 August 1814, non-active on half-pay 20 November 1814, retired with discharge pay 1815. LH CH 1 October 1807.

MARTIN (Jean, 1779-?): born in Petites-Armoises (Ardennes) on 25 December 1779. In the 4th Cavalry 5 June 1799, brigadier 4 August 1802, in the same regiment when it became the 4th Cuirassiers 12 October 1802, fourrier 7 December 1802, maréchal des logis 15 May 1807, maréchal des logis-chef 4 June 1809, adjutant-NCO 8 October 1811, sub-lieutenant 17 June 1812, resigned 1815.

MARTIN (Louis, 1772-?): born in Coutance (Manche) on 25 January 1772. In the Angoulême-Infanterie 25 January 1788, in the 7th bis Hussars 1792, in the General Police Legion 1796.

He was incorporated into the 1st Dragoons December 1797, retired with pension 1801, in the Gendarmes d'Elite of the Guard 18 April 1803, in the Léman Gendarmerie 19 December 1803, brigadier 5 September 1808, maréchal des logis 21 April 1812, sub-lieutenant in the 14th Cuirassiers 3 January 1814, dismissed with the corps and put in the 12th Cuirassiers 13 July 1814, non-active 1814, returned to the 12th Cuirassiers 7 April 1815, put back on the non-active list 3 August 1815 and returned home 16 August 1815.

MARTIN (Pierre, 1789-1812): born in Saint-Symphorien (Gironde) on 22 April 1789. Velite in the Grenadiers à Cheval of the Imperial Guard 26 February 1807.

He became Grenadier à Cheval 1 January 1812, sub-lieutenant in the Line 17 December 1811, in the 8th Cuirassiers 25 January 1812, instated 11 February 1812, in his post 25 February 1812, wounded and taken prisoner leading a detachment at the Berezina 28 November 1812, died at Borisov 24 December 1812.

MARTIN (Rémi Armand, 1773-?): born in Tilleux (Haute-Marne) on 4 March 1773. In the 1st Dragoons 23 January 1794, in the Grenadiers à Cheval of the Guard 14 March 1799.

He became brigadier 25 November 1802, maréchal des logis 1 August 1806, lieutenant in the suite of the 11th Cuirassiers 23 October 1811, in his post 25 February 1812, wounded at Toloschinn 21 November 1812, prisoner 31 December 1812. LH CH 14 March 1806.

MARTIN DUMEGNOT (Joseph, 1788-?): born in 1788. Velite in the Grenadiers à Cheval of the Guard 29 June 1806, sub-lieutenant in the suite of the 1st Cuirassiers 8 May 1813.

He joined them 25 May 1813, non-active on full pay 1 October 1814, returned to the regiment 1815, put on half-pay 1 September 1815.

MARTINE (Jean Louis, 1787-1812): born in 1787. In the 1st Cuirassiers 18 March 1807, brigadier 1 October 1808, maréchal des logis-chef 16 May 1809.

He became adjutant-NCO 7 September 1811, sub-lieutenant 25 September 1812, prisoner then disappeared in Russia 29 November 1812.

MARULAZ (Jacques Christophe, 1773-?): born in Belfort (Haut-Rhin) on 3 August 1774. In the 6th Cavalry 15 March 1792, fourrier 21 April 1800, maréchal des logis-chef 27 May 1802, in the same regiment when it became the 6th Cuirassiers 23 December 1802, adjutant-NCO 1 July 1807, sub-lieutenant 3 June 1809.

He was lieutenant 12 September 1809, captain 8 October 1811, in the Escadron Sacré during the retreat from Russia November 1812, incorporated with his squadron into the 2nd Provisional Heavy Cavalry in Hamburg 11 September 1813, returned with the garrison 30 May 1814, shot and wounded, his left arm broken and his horse killed under him at Waterloo 18 June 1815.

He retired because of his wounds 21 November 1815. LH CH 6 October 1808.

MARULAZ (Nicolas, 1769-?): born in Belfort (Haut-Rhin) on 14 November 1769. In the Roi-Cavalerie 1 February 1788 which became the 6th Cavalry 1 January 1791, brigadier-fourrier 29 November 1792, maréchal des logis 1 April 1793, maréchal des logis-chef 9 January 1794.

He became adjutant 11 March 1797, sub-lieutenant 17 April 1800, confirmed 2 May 1800, in the same regiment when it became the 6th Cuirassiers 23 December 1802, elected lieutenant 2 October 1804, captain 4 March 1808, confirmed in his post 6 June 1810, gendarmerie captain 8 October 1811.

MARULAZ (Philippe Joseph, 1767-?): born in Belfort (Haut-Rhin) on 11 August 1767. In the 6th Cavalry 15 March 1792, brigadier-fourrier 19 May 1794, maréchal des logis 2 April 1799, maréchal des logis-chef 11 April 1799, in the same regiment when it became the 6th Cuirassiers 23 December 1802, adjutant-NCO 24 September 1803. He was sub-lieutenant by seniority 14 June 1805, saved his colonel by giving him his horse and himself wounded at Heilsberg 10 June 1807, lieutenant 30 September 1807, captain 3 June 1809, retired 12 September 1809.

MASCHEK (Antoine Joseph, 1787-?): born in Valkenburg (Bouches-de-la-Meuse) on 5 August 1787. Cadet in the Batavian Light Dragoons 19 October 1804.

He became sub-lieutenant in the Dutch Cuirassiers 25 February 1807 which became the 14th French Cuirassiers 18 August 1810, lieutenant 5 December 1810, wounded and taken prisoner at Polotsk 18 October 1812, returned to Holland and resignation accepted 5 February 1816.

MASSARTS (Nicolas Joseph, 1785-?): born in Liège (Ourthe) on 20 November 1785. In the 2nd Gardes d'Honneur 5 July 1813, maréchal des logis-chef 21 August 1813, sub-lieutenant in the 1st Chasseurs à Cheval 28 November 1813.

He became second-lieutenant in the 2nd Gardes d'Honneur 21 January 1814, incorporated as lieutenant into the 8th Cuirassiers 24 August 1814, assigned to the Saumur school February 1815, resignation accepted 2 November 1815.

MASSET (Pierre Rémy, 1778-?): born in Magne (Ardennes) on 21 January 1778. In the 22nd Cavalry 21 November 1798, dismissed with the corps 31 December 1802 and incorporated into the 5th Cuirassiers 3 January 1803.

He became brigadier 9 November 1803, maréchal des logis 10 October 1806, shot and wounded in the left shoulder at Eylau 8 February 1807, shot and wounded in the left thigh at Essling 22 May 1809, sub-lieutenant 3 June 1809, lieutenant 9 February 1813, dismissed 23 October 1815. LH CH 1 October 1807.

MASSON (Louis, 1772-?): born in Châtillon-l'Abbaye (Meuse) on 16 September 1772. In the 10th Cavalry 3 September 1793, 4 sabre wounds to his head, shoulder and chest at Wislock 9 November 1799, brigadier 14 March 1800, in the same regiment when it became the 10th Cuirassiers 24 September 1803, wounded by a Biscayan shot to his right chest at Austerlitz 2 December 1805, maréchal des logis 3 December 1805, sub-lieutenant 16 May 1809, wounded at Essling 21 May 1809, lieutenant 19 June 1813, dismissed with the corps 25 December 1815. LH CH 28 September 1813.

MASSON see **HAZOTTE** aka **MASSON**.

MATHE (Jean Baptiste, 1773-?): born in Poitiers (Vienne) on 17 December 1773. In the 54th Infantry 6 January 1791, in the 5th Dragoons 14 April 1793, in the 24th Chasseurs à Cheval 8 April 1796, brigadier 22 March 1800, in the Chasseurs à Cheval of the Guard 10 December 1801, brigadier 15 October 1802, lance wound to his left cheek while he was on guard near the Emperor at Ulm 22 October 1805, maréchal des logis 1 April 1806, in the Dragoons of the Imperial Guard 26 July 1806, lieutenant in the 10th Cuirassiers 8 February 1813, dismissed with the corps 25 December 1805. LH CH 17 May 1811.

MATHEVON de CURNIEU (Jean Louis, baron, 1776-1813): born in Lisbon (Portugal) on 29 July 1776. Volunteer in the 9th Dragoons 10 September 1799, brigadier-fourrier 17 January 1800, maréchal des logis 31 March 1800, sub-lieutenant 23 October 1800, wounded during the crossing of the Mincio 26 December 1800, lieutenant 18 December 1801, aide de camp to General Sebastiani 9 February 1804, had a horse killed under him and two others wounded during the 1805 campaign, aide de camp to Berthier 2 November 1806, captain in the 21st Chasseurs à Cheval 31 December 1806, aide de camp to Berthier 21 February 1807, squadron commander 11 July 1807, in the 1st Dragoons 22 August 1807, aide de camp to Berthier 9 June 1808, adjutant-commandant 30 May 1809, on the staff of the 2nd Cuirassiers Division, colonel of the 12th Cuirassiers 3 August 1809, seriously wounded and taken prisoner at

MENOU DUJONC (Michel, Baron, 1774-1841) a relation of General Menou, born in Loudun (Vienne) on 20 July 1774. Sub-lieutenant in the 11th Cavalry 3 October 1792, lieutenant 4 February 1799.

He entered eleventh into the enemy camp killing the guards and most part of the gunners in the enemy artillery 26 June 1799, with 9 Troopers and his trumpeters captured 3 artillery pieces near Marengo 14 June 1800, second-lieutenant in the Grenadiers à Cheval of the Consular Guard 2 December 1800

He was commissioned 1 October 1801, first-lieutenant 13 December 1801, captain 5 September 1803, wounded by a Biscayan shot to his right thigh at Eylau 8 February 1807, squadron commander 14 February 1807, colonel in the suite of the 4th Cuirassiers 7 September 1811, in service commanding the regiment 28 January 1812, in the same regiment when it became the Angoulême Cuirassiers N°4 21 September 1814, confirmed 28 September 1814, dismissed for a month on half-pay 3 November 1814, retired 22 April 1815 and pensioned 9 May 1815, left 11 May 1815,.

He becamemaréchal de camp colonel of the 2nd Cuirassiers of the Royal Guard 8 September 1815. Holder of a Sabre of Honour 20 October 1802, LH CH by rights 24 September 1803, O 14 June 1804, C 9 November 1814, Chevalier of the Empire l.p. 18 March 1809, Baron d. 15 March 1810 and l.p. 3 May 1810.

Forgotten with a detachment of 13 troopers and a few infantry during Macdonald's retreat from Pullia, Lieutenant Michel Menou Dujonc wandered for a month in the Apennines escaping from the rebellious peasants; surprised by a considerable party of men who had captured his two vanguards near Naples, he serried his ranks and forced a way through the attackers.

He entered the stronghold and then came out again with a Neapolitan guard unit to recover his two men from the hands of the brigands before throwing himself into Capua. He withstood the siege in which, during a sally, he saw his brother captured and killed.

He distinguished himself again at Marengo on 14 June 1800 where he took three cannon with only his trumpeter and nine troopers.

Lackzyn near Orcha 21 November 1812, died from his wounds at Vitebsk during the night of 2 to 3 February 1813. LH CH 14 March 1806, Baron of the Empire d. 15 August 1809 and l.p. 15 June 1810.

MATHIEU (Hyacinthe, 1788-?): born in Guéret (Creuse) on 23 December 1788. Velite in the Grenadiers à cheval of the Imperial Guard 7 August 1807, sub-lieutenant in the 9th Cuirassiers 22 March 1812, lost two toes on his right foot from frostbite 1812.

He became lieutenant 21 April 1813, incorporated with his squadron into the 3rd Provisional Heavy Cavalry in Hamburg 11 September 1813, returned with the garrison 30 May 1814, dismissed with the corps and non-active at the disposal of the government 26 November 1815.

MATHIS (Marc, 1775-?): born in Boucknom (Bas-Rhin) on 20 May 1775. In the 19th Cavalry 30 March 1793 which became the 18th Cavalry 4 June 1793, in the 12th Cavalry 5 March 1797, fourrier 5 March 1799.

He became maréchal des logis-chef 10 May 1799, sub-lieutenant 24 February 1800, confirmed 28 March 1800, lieutenant by seniority 18 March 1803, in the same regiment when it became the 12th Cuirassiers 24 September 1803, lieutenant adjutant-major 12 December 1806, instated 23 December 1806, captain 7 February 1808, retroactively to 29 June 1808 by decision dated 9 May 1808, squadron commander 14 May 1813.

He took command of the regiment during Colonel Daudiès' absence, commanded the brigade in May and until 27 June 1813, sabre wound to his head and wounded by a pole to his left side at Jauer 28 May 1813, shot in the chest and broken shoulder bone at Dresden 7 August 1813, prisoner 20 October 1813, returned 4 May 1814. LH CH 1 October 1807, O 27 September 1813.

MATTHES (Nicolas Charles, 1786-?): born in Amsterdam (Zuydersee) on 5 October 1786. Pupil NCO in the king of Holland's Guard 10 January 1807, maréchal des logis in the Cuirassiers of the Dutch Guard 6 April 1807.

He became sub-lieutenant in the 2nd Dutch Cuirassiers 25 August 1809, in the same regiment when it became the 14th French Cuirassiers 18 August 1810, lieutenant adjutant-major 13 September 1813, incorporated into the 12th Cuirassiers 13 July 1814, captain adjutant-major 13 March 1815, resigned 20 April 1815.

MAUBERT (Jean, 1767-?): born in Houdelaincourt (Meuse) on 23 March 1767. Trooper In the Colonel-Général Regiment 15 January 1785 which became the 1st Cavalry 1791.

He became brigadier-fourrier 1 June 1793, maréchal des logis-chef 16 September 1793, adjutant-NCO 10 July 1797, sub-lieutenant 15 January 1799, lieutenant 23 February 1800, in the same regiment when it became the 1st Cuirassiers 10 October 1801, adjutant-major 13 October 1803, rank of captain 10 April 1805, captain commanding a company 24 December 1805, instated

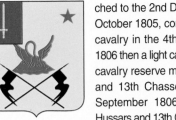

MILHAUD (Edouard Jean Baptiste, Count, 1766-1833) born in Arpajon (Cantal) on 10 July 1766. Pupil in the Navy Engineers 1788, infantry sub-lieutenant in the colonies 1790, commanded the Arpajon National Guard, Legion commanded in that of Aurillac 1791, deputy for the Cantal in the Convention 3 September 1792, member of the military committee 17 September 1792, voted for the death of Louis XVI, on a mission in the Army of the Ardennes 30 April 1793, commissioned as captain in the 14th Chasseurs à Cheval 9 May 1793.

He was recalled to the Convention 17 June 1793, on a mission with the Army of the Rhine 19 July 1793, squadron commander in the 20th Chasseurs à Cheval 22 July 1793, returned to the Convention 26 August 1794, freed when the Convention was dissolved 26 October 1795, brigade commander of the 5th Dragoons 28 January 1796, wounded in the head at Saint-Michel, commanded the Palais du Luxembourg on 18 Brumaire and chief of staff under Murat the following day 10 November 1799.

He became brigadier-general 5 January 1800, in the 14th Military Division 9 January 1800, commanded the Vaucluse Department 2 March 1800, in the Reserve Army 23 May 1800, in that of Italy 5 July 1800 then of the Midi 25 April 1801, commanded at Mantua 1801. He was employed in the Italian Republic 23 September 1802, commanded Liguria 7 July 1803, in the Army of the Côtes de l'Océan 18 July 1805, in the camp at Boulogne 3 August 1805, commanded the Light Cavalry Brigade (16th and 22nd Chasseurs à Cheval) atta-

ched to the 2nd Dragoon division 20 October 1805, commanded the light cavalry in the 4th Corps 1 January 1806 then a light cavalry brigade in the cavalry reserve made up of the 11th and 13th Chasseurs à Cheval 20 September 1806 then of the 1st Hussars and 13th Chasseurs à Cheval 7 October, got 6 000 Prussians to capitulate at Pasewalk 29 October 1806, major-general commanding the 3rd Dragoon Division in the general cavalry reserve of the Grande Armée 30 December 1806, with his division went over to the 4th Corps of the Army of Spain 7 September 1808, allowed to return to France 12 July 1811, commanded the 25th Military Division 20 June 1812.

He was in the suite of the general headquarters staff of the Grande Armée 13 July 1812, commanded a cavalry corps being formed in Mainz 15 February 1813 then the 1st Marching Division of the 1st Cavalry Corps 5 April 1813, commanded the cavalry in the Bavaria Observation Corps 18 June 1813 then the 5th bis Cavalry Corps and the 6th Dragoon Division 9 August 1813, commanded the Cavalry Corps 11 November 1813, inspector general of cavalry in the 14th Military Division 1 June 1814, retired 4 February 1815, commanded the Cuirassiers Division 30 March 1815 the 1st Reserve Cavalry Division 6 April 1815, CiC of the 4th Cavalry Corps (Cuirassiers) May 1815.

Acting inspector general of cavalry 6 August 1815, non-active 9 September 1815, retired 18 October 1815.

LH CH 11 December 1803, C 14 June 1804, GO 23 June 1810, Count of the Empire d. 10 March 1808 and l.p. 10 September 1808.

(Musée d'Aurillac, RR)

1 January 1806. He was squadron commander 16 May 1809, shot and wounded in the right thigh at Essling May 1809, wounded by a cannonball in the right leg at Wagram 6 July 1809 and shot and wounded in the left arm at Hanau 30 October 1813, retired 16 August 1814. LH CH 15 June 1804.

MAUBLANC (Léonard Martial, 1786-?): born in Saint-Junien (Haute-Vienne) on 17 May 1786. Boarder at the Ecole Spéciale Militaire in Fontainebleau 16 September 1805.

He became supernumerary sub-lieutenant in the suite of the 1st Cuirassiers 14 December 1806, shot and wounded in the neck at Eylau 8 February 1807, in service 20 February 1807, lieutenant 29 April 1809, shot and wounded at Hollabrünn 9 July 1809, adjutant-major 15 October 1809, rank of captain 29 October 1810, in post as captain 5 November 1811, dismissed with the corps and put up for retirement 24 December 1815. LH CH 16 June 1809.

MAUGER (Pierre Michel Thomas, 1770-?): born in Dieppe (Seine-Inférieure) on 29 September 1770. In the 1st Dieppe Battalion 16 November 1793, incorporated into the 4th Cavalry Regiment 2 July 1794, brigadier 11 December 1798.

He became maréchal des logis 15 March 1800, adjutant-NCO 13 July 1800, in the same regiment when it became the 4th Cuirassiers 11 January 1803, elected sub-lieutenant 21 October 1806, instated 19 December 1806 and confirmed 9 January 1807, lieutenant 25 June 1807, captain adjutant-major 5 March 1809, sabre wound to his head and his horse killed under him at Essling 21 May 1809, in post as captain 3 June 1809.

He was shot and wounded in his right arm at the Drissa 11 August 1812, in the 1st Cuirassiers 30 April 1814, confirmed in the King's Cuirassiers when they were formed 1 July 1814 which then became the 1st Cuirassiers again April 1815, wounded at Waterloo 18 June 1815, retired 24 December 1815. LH CH 1 October 1807, O 4 December 1813.

MAUGERY (Claude, 1768-1818): born in Wassy (Haute-Marne) on 16 December 1768. In the 7th Chasseurs à Cheval 24 August 1793, brigadier-fourrier 2 March 1774, maréchal des logis 2 October 1794, sub-lieutenant 15 December 1794, lieutenant 19 February 1798.

He became adjutant-major 12 February 1802, rank of captain 10 August 1803, shot and wounded in the head and a sabre wound to his right arm and his horse killed under him, taken prisoner at Jena 14 October 1806, sabre wound to his head and his horse killed under him at Guttstadt 5 June 1807, two lance wounds, his horse killed under him and taken prisoner 1 May 1809.

He was squadron commander in the 9th Cuirassiers 11 May 1809, in the 12th Cuirassiers 1 July 1811, commanded the regiment temporarily 1 February 1813, major in the 9th Cuirassiers 3 September 1813, in General Grouvel's Light Brigade 16 March 1814, in the King's Cuirassiers 11 May 1814, in the suite of the same regiment when it became the 1st Cuirassiers again 11 May 1815, dismissed 24 December 1815. LH CH 5 November 1804.

MAULEON see **DUPAS de BELLEGARDE et de MAULEON**

MAUPERCHE (Auguste Jean, chevalier, -?): born in Launoy (Ardennes). Maréchal des logis in the Cuirassiers, lieutenant 25 November 1811.

He became adjutant-major in the 3rd Cuirassiers 10 September 1812, captain 14 May 1813, aide de camp to General Audenarde 15 May 1813. LH CH, Cheval de L'Empire l.p. May 1808.

MAUPRIVEZ (Jean Baptiste, 1770-1815): born in Renay (Seine-et-Marne) in 1770. Soldier in the Pondichéry Regiment 16 January 1786, left 14 August 1792, in the 26th Cavalry 20 February 1793 which became the 25th Cavalry 4 June 1793, brigadier 21 September 1798, maréchal des logis 4 August 1802,.

He was dismissed with the corps 12 October 1802, incorporated into the 4th Cuirassiers 24 November 1802, sub-lieutenant 3 June 1809, lieutenant 9 February 1813, wounded at Dresden 27 August 1813 and Waterloo 18 June 1815, died as a result of his wounds in Brussels Hospital 23 June 1815. LH CH 1 July 1804.

MAUR de PRUDHOMME see **SAINT MAUR de PRUDHOMME**

MAURIN (Pierre, 1753-?): born in Joyeuse (Ardèche) on 3 September 1753. Enrolled in the Royal-Cavalerie 4 July 1776, instated 19 July 1776, brigadier 11 August 1784, maréchal des logis 11 September 1786.

He was in the same regiment when it became the 2nd Cavalry 1 January 1791, sub-lieutenant 25 June 1793, lieutenant by seniority 22 March 1802, in the same regiment when it became the 2nd Cuirassiers 12 October 1802, retired 30 October 1806, left 1 May 1807.

MAUROY (Nicolas de, 1784-1870): born in Troyes (Aube) in 1774. In the Gendarmes d'Ordonnance, sub-lieutenant in the suite of the 5th Cuirassiers 16 July 1807.

He was confirmed 10 September 1807, in post 23 March 1809, wounded at Eckmühl 22 April 1809, retired 20 November 1809.

MAZEAT (Claude, 1768-1809): born in Cébazat (Puy-de-Dôme) on 11 July 1768. In the Reine-Cavalerie 24 April 1784 which became the 4th Cavalry 1 January 1791, brigadier-fourrier 13 May 1792, maréchal des logis 1 August 1793, maréchal des logis-chef 29 July 1794, two sabre wounds to his head and shoulder at Wurtzburg 3 September 1796, sub-lieutenant 20 February 1799, lieutenant 9 March 1800.

He was in the same regiment when it became the 4th Cuirassiers 12 October 1802, captain in the 6th Cuirassiers 19 April 1806, wounded at Essling 22 May 1809, died of his wounds 31 May 1809.

MAZOYER (?-?): Velite in the 2nd Chevau-Légers Lancers of the Imperial Guard, sub-lieutenant in the suite of the 62nd of the Line 4 September 1814, non-active 1814, took up his appointment in the 12th Cuirassiers 13 May 1815, put back on the non-active list 3 August 1815 and returned home 16 august 1815.

MEGUET (Jean Baptiste, 1760-?): born in Sarrelibre (Moselle) on 26 June 1760. Provincial soldier in the sub-delegation from Sarrelibre 15 March 1778, in the Dauphin-Cavalerie 6 April 1784 which became the 12th Cavalry 1 January 1791.

He became fourrier 20 October 1792, maréchal des logis 1 April 1793, wounded in the arm at Guetresheim 15 November 1793, maréchal des logis-chef 5 May 1795, captured a seven-man enemy post at Haguenau, adjutant 5 July 1795, sub-lieutenant 30 December 1801.

He was elected lieutenant 4 April 1803, in the same regiment when it became the 12th Cuirassiers 24 September 1803, retired 31 October 1806.

MELINE (Joseph Charles de, 1776-?): born in Lay-Saint-Christophe (Meurthe) on 30 October 1776. In the 6th Meurthe Battalion 3 August 1792, in the 11th Cavalry 14 January 1794, in Bonaparte's Guides à Cheval 17 April 1797, brigadier 20 May 1797, in the Grenadiers à cheval of the Consular Guard 3 January 1800.

He became brigadier-fourrier 22 December 1800, maréchal des logis-chef 22 December 1801, sub-lieutenant 13 October 1802, second-lieutenant 23 September 1804, first lieutenant in the Squadron of Velites 18 December 1805, captain 16 February 1807, squadron commander in the 10th Cuirassiers 1 June 1809.

He was supernumerary major 6 November 1811, in the 3rd Cuirassiers 1 February 1814, took up his appointment 26 February 1814, confirmed 28 September 1814, dismissed 25 November 1815. LH CH 14 June 1804, O 28 September 1814.

MENARD (Jacques, 1779-?): born in Aujac (Charente-Inférieure) on 17 November 1779. In the 19th Cavalry 22 July 1799, brigadier 19 April 1802, dismissed with the corps 31 December 1802 and incorporated into the 11th Cuirassiers 5 February 1803.

He became maréchal des logis 7 October 1803, sub-lieutenant 16 May 1809, lieutenant 15 March 1812, captain 3 September 1813, wounded at Leipzig 18 October 1813, retired 1 August 1814. LH CH 14 May 1813.

MENISSIER (Jean Germain, 1780-1813): born in Versailles (Seine-et-Oise) in 1780. In the 6th Cavalry 21 June 1799, brigadier 24 June 1802, in the same regiment when it became the 6th Cuirassiers 23 December 1802, maréchal des logis 7 August 1805, adjutant-NCO 12 October 1811, sub-lieutenant 12 September 1812, killed at Leipzig 18 October 1813.

MENNERET (Pierre, 1765-1815): born in Estinac (Aube) on 5 April 1765. In the Dauphin-Cavalerie 7 October 1787 which became the 12th Cavalry 1 January 1791, sabre wound to his head 17 May 1793, brigadier 2 December 1795, maréchal des logis 8 August 1800, supernumerary maréchal des logis-chef 21 April 1803, in the same regiment when it became the 12th Cuirassiers 24 September 1803.

He became sub-lieutenant 29 January 1808, lieutenant 3 June 1809, captain 9 February 1813, killed at Waterloo 18 June 1815 with his leg blown off by a cannonball. LH CH 14 April 1807.

MENY (Jean Baptiste, 1774-?): born in Saint-Denis (Seine) on 4 April 1774. In the 7th Hussars 9 February 1794, in the Grenadiers à Cheval of the Garde du Directoire 1 August 1799, brigadier when they were incorporated into the Grenadiers à Cheval of the Consular Guard 3 January 1800.

He became maréchal des logis 12 March 1801, maréchal des logis-chef 13 October 1801, sub-lieutenant 13 October 1802, second-lieutenant in the Grenadiers à Cheval of the Imperial Guard 23 September 1804, first-lieutenant 1 May 1806, wounded at Eylau 8 February 1807, captain 16 February 1807.

He was squadron commander in the 3rd Cuirassiers 1 June 1809, second-major in the suite of the regiment 19 April 1812, major in the 2nd Dragoons.

MERCEY see **LEGRAND de MERCEY**

MERCHER (Jacques Antoine Marc, 1791-?): born in Caudemuche (Calvados) on 29 April 1791. In the Ecole Impériale de Cavalerie in Saint-Germain 4 November 1810.

He became sub-lieutenant in the 7th Cuirassiers 30 January 18113, left 19 February 1813 and joined them 1 March 1813, prisoner near Lutzen 7 May 1813 and escaped the following day, prisoner at Meaux 2 March 1814, adjutant-major 16 March 1814, returned 31 March 1814, non-active on half-pay 16 August 1814. LH CH 25 February 1814.

MERCIER (François, 1755-?): born in Troussey (Meuse) on 19 March 1755. Soldier in the Orléans-Infanterie from 29 October 1773 to 5 January 1782, in the Reine-Cavalerie 16 September 1782 which became the 4th Cavalry 1 January 1791, brigadier 16 May 1791, maréchal des logis 19 May 1792.

He became maréchal des logis-chef 20 May 1792, sub-lieutenant 29 July 1793.

He was wounded and taken prisoner then escaped at Kreutznach 28 December 1793, commissioner at the general depot of the Army of the Moselle at Pont-à-Mousson with the rank of cavalry captain 9 April 1794, put as supernumerary captain in the suite of the 4th Cavalry 5 January 1795, joined them 8 May 1795, in service in the 2nd Cavalry 12 March 1800, joined 17 March 1800.

He was in the same regiment when it became the 2nd Cuirassiers 12 October 1802, shot and wounded at Tholey 21 December 1805, retired 30 October 1806 and left 1 December 1806. LH CH.

MERCIER (Jacques Laurent, 1776-?): Pierre Joseph's brother (see below), born in Donnemarie (Seine-et-Marne) on 14 April 1776. In the 2nd Seine-et-Marne Battalion 23 August 1793, fourrier in the 2nd Deux-Sèvres

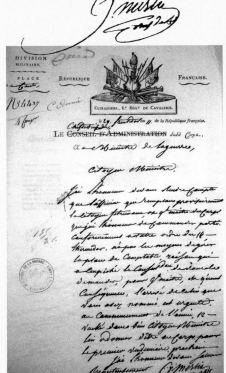

MERLI aka **MERLIN de THIONVILLE** (Jean Baptiste Gabriel, Baron, 1768-1842): brother of the Convention Member and of the two generals, born in Thionville (Moselle) on 17 April 1768. In the Royal-Cravates 13 August 1787 which became the 10th cavalry 1 January 1791.

He became sub-lieutenant in the 7th Dragoons 10 March 1792, aide de camp to General Charbonnier May 1794, captain in the 7th Dragoons 5 July 1794, commanded the Versailles riding school end 1794, squadron commander in the cavalry of the General Police Legion 27 June 1795.

He was in the same regiment when it formed the 21st Dragoons 29 October 1795, commissioned 6 February 1797, in the Garde du Directoire Exécutif 29 July 1797, brigade commander of the 8th Cavalry 20 November 1799, joined 9 December 1799, in the same regiment when it became the 8th Cuirassiers 10 October 1801, commissioned 10 June 1806, slightly wounded June 1807, returned to the regiment 15 July 1807, wounded by a shell burst in his right thigh at Essling 21 May 1809.

He was brigadier-general 5 June 1809, commanded the Departments of the Yonne 24 December 1810, then the Orne 9 June 1812, non-active 21 July 1815. LH CH 11 December 1803, C 14 June 1804, Baron of the Empire l.p. 28 January 1809.

Top.
Merlin as Colonel of the 8th Cuirassier Regiment.
(Musée des Arts Lorrains de Nancy. M. Ring, RR)

The same portrait seen by H. Feisz. *(RR)*

Battalion 20 January 1794, in the 19th cavalry 22 October 1798. He became fourrier 20 January 1799, maréchal des logis 19 February 1799, sub-lieutenant 5 June 1800, confirmed 12 December 1800, dismissed with his regiment 31 December 1802 and incorporated into the 10th Cavalry 21 January 1803 which became the 10th Cuirassiers 24 September 1803, lieutenant by seniority 18 December 1805, retroactively to 8 October 1805, wounded at Hoff 6 February 1807.

He was deputy on the staff of the Cavalry reserve 26 March 1807, left to join them 1 April 1807, captain 25 June 1807, on the staff of the 3rd Cuirassier Division 15 November 1808 then the Caffarelli Division in Spain 4 December 1810, squadron commander of a provisional heavy cavalry regiment in Hamburg 13 August 1813, squadron commander in post in the 7th Cuirassiers 16 December 1813, joined them 22 January 1814, one year's leave 1 September 1814, non-active 19 December 1815. LH CH 18 August 1814.

MERCIER (Louis, 1769-?): born in Saint-Laurent (Gard) on 5 September 1769. In the 9th Dragoons 2 February 1791, brigadier 8 March 1794, maréchal des logis 27 September 1796, in the Grenadiers à Cheval of the Guard 23 January 1802, brigadier 19 March 1802, maréchal des logis 27 April 1803.

He became lieutenant in the 5th Cuirassiers 8 February 1813, wounded at Waterloo 18 June 1815, retired 23 December 1815. Sabre of Honour 15 September 1802, LH CH by rights 24 September 1803.

MERCIER (Pierre Joseph, 1774-?): elder brother of Jacques Laurent, born in Donnemarie (Seine-et-Marne), on 12 March 1774. In the National Guard, sub-lieutenant in the 20th Cavalry 24 July 1792 which became the 19th cavalry 4 June 1793, lieutenant 16 November 1793, adjutant to Adjutant-General Brayer 27 August 1796, returned to the 19th Cavalry 20 May 1797, supernumerary 21 March 1798, in service 19 June 1799.

He was assigned to the Versailles riding school 21 April 1800, returned 27 April 1802, dismissed with the corps 31 December 1802 and incorporated into the suite of the 1st Carabiniers 6 February 1803, in post in the 10th Cavalry 8 June 1803 which became the 10th Cuirassiers 24 September 1803, captain 8 October 1805, confirmed 18 December 1805, slightly wounded by a shot to his leg and his horse killed under him at Hoff 6 February 1807, squadron commander in the 4th Cuirassiers 13 July 1808, instated 4 September 1808, major at the disposition of the Minister of War 8 October 1811. LH CH 1 October 1807.

MERGEZ (Georges Nicolas, baron, 1772-1846): born in Arcis-sur-Aube (Aube) on 10 November 1772. Lieutenant in the 9th Hussars 1 March 1793, deputy to the adjutant-generals in the Army of the North 12 April 1793, taken prisoner by the Austrians with Ambassador Sémonville, aide de camp to Beurnonville 17 March 1796, captain in the 9th Hussars 13 September 1797.

He became aide de camp to Bernadotte 8 July 1799, acting squadron commander 21 September 1799, confirmed in the 9th Hussars 11 April 1800, deputy to the staff of the Army of the Côtes de l'Océan 4 February 1804, in

the Grande Armée 1805, in the general war depot 1 July 1806, on the general staff of the Army of Spain 28 February 1808, on that of the Army of Germany 11 March 1809, adjutant-commandant 30 May 1809, chief of staff of the Light Cavalry Brigade of the 2nd Corps of the Army of Germany, available 19 July 1810, chief of staff of a cavalry corps in Holland 11 September 1810.

He was on the staff of the Army of Germany 25 December 1810, in the suite 24 July 1811, chief of staff of the 5th Infantry Division, of the assembled cavalry division at Cologne 19 October 1811, of the 4th Cuirassier Division of the 2nd Cavalry Corps January 1812, several lance wounds and taken prisoner at Winkovo 18 October 1812, returned August 1814, non-active 1 September 1814, on the staff of the 2nd Military Division 22 December 1814, chief of staff of the 5th Division of the Cavalry Reserve 26 April 1815, of the mass levies in the 3rd and 4th Military Divisions 12 June 1815 then of the Paris Military Area 31 July 1815, non-active 28 March 1816.

LH CH 14 June 1804, O 11 October 1812, Baron of the Empire d. 15 August 1809 and l.p. 19 September 1810.

MERLANI see CASTELLANI de MERLANI

MERLET (Camille, 1796-?): born in Soulangé (Maine-et-Loire) on 25 November 1796. Pupil at the Ecole Impériale de Cavalerie in Saint-Germain 1 May 1813, sub-lieutenant 30 March 1814, in the 6th Cuirassiers 12 June 1814, dismissed 21 November 1815.

MESLE (Alphonse Joseph Désiré de, 1790-?): born in Voilly (Aisne) on 1 August 1790. Velite in the Chasseurs à Cheval of the Imperial Guard 28 May 1808, chasseur à cheval 28 May 1812.

He became sub-lieutenant in the 11th Hussars 12 July 1812, lieutenant 12 March 1814, in the suite of the 8th Cuirassiers 24 August 1814, in post April 1815, wounded at les Quatre-Bras 16 June 1815, dismissed with the corps and sent home, non-active 11 December 1815.

MESTRE (Simon Mathias, 1778-1807): born in Sainte-Foix (Gironde) on 3 February 1778. In the 12th Chasseurs à Cheval 20 May 1799, in the 20th Cavalry 4 October 1799, brigadier 21 May 1800, maréchal des logis 31 May 1800.

He became maréchal des logis-chef 14 June 1800, sub-lieutenant 22 November 1800, confirmed 10 July 1801, dismissed with the corps 31 December 1802 and incorporated into the 12th Cavalry 25 January 1803 which became the 12th Cuirassiers 24 September 1803, lieutenant 4 October 1804, killed at Friedland 14 June 1807.

METZ (?-?): sub-lieutenant in the 6th Cuirassiers 27 April 1807, lieutenant in the suite from 6 October 1808, in post in the 2nd Cuirassiers 8 November 1808 but remained in the 6th Cuirassiers, wounded at Essling 21 May 1809, captain in the 6th Cuirassiers 3 June 1809, retired 8 October 1811.

METZ (Jean Antoine, 1777-?): born in Epsigue (Bas-Rhin) on 19 February 1777. In the 12th Cavalry 29 April 1802, brigadier 4 July 1803, in the same regiment when it became the 12th Cuirassiers 24 September 1803.

He became maréchal des logis 20 December 1806, sub-lieutenant 15 March 1812, lieutenant 22 December 18113, in the suite of the corps 14 July 1814, dismissed with the corps 10 December 1815. LH CH 5 September 1813.

MEUNIER (?-?): Pupil in the Navy, sub-lieutenant I the 14th Cuirassiers 17 January 1814, dismissed with the corps.

MEUNIER (Charles Laurent, 1777-?): born in Pinchard (Seine-et-Marne) on 1 October 1777. In the 6th Cavalry 19 June 1799, brigadier 19 August 1802, in the same regiment when it became the 6th Cuirassiers 23 December 1802, maréchal des logis 1 January 1807.

He became maréchal des logis-chef 16 March 1809, sabre wound to his left hand and shot in the right arm at Essling 21 May 1809, adjutant-NCO 3 June 1809, sub-lieutenant 12 September 1809, in the King's Cuirassiers 1 July 1814 which became the 1st Cuirassiers April 1815.

He was wounded at Waterloo 18 June 1815, dismissed and put up for service 24 December 1815. LH CH 14 May 1813.

MEURET (?-?): maréchal des logis-chef in the 11th Cuirassiers, sub-lieutenant 16 May 1809, wounded at Essling 22 May 1809, retired 12 April 1810.

MEYER (Pierre, 1786-?): born in Saint-Louis (Moselle) on 18 March 1786. Pupil in the Ecole Polytechnique 20 November 1804, sub-lieutenant in the 8th of the Line 10 October 1806, lieutenant 13 April 1807, captain 31 May 1809, shot and wounded and a cannonball wound to his right leg at Essling 22 May 1809.

He was in the 3rd Provisional Heavy Cavalry 11 October 1810, in the 7th Cuirassiers 9 March 1811, joined 2 April 1811, wounded by a shell burst to his neck at Polotsk 26 October 1812 and shot in the right foot at the Berezina 28 November 1812, detached with his squadron and incorporated into the 2nd Provisional Heavy Cavalry in Hamburg 11 September 1813, acting squadron commander 20 April 1814.

He returned with the garrison 30 May 1814, placed as captain 27 August 1814, two months' leave 1 September 1814, confirmed squadron commander 14 January 1815, non-active on half-pay 26 January 1815 but remained in the corps, in post 10 March 1815, retired to his property and put back on the non-active list on half-pay 16 July 1815, left 24 August 1815. LH CH 19 November 1812, O 18 August 1814.

MICHEL (?-?): maréchal des logis in the 9th Cuirassiers, sub-lieutenant 30 October 1806, lieutenant 2 March 1809, discharged without pay 15 May 1810.

MICHEL (Georges, 1777-1812): born in 1777. In the Chasseurs à cheval 20 November 1796, in the Grenadiers à cheval of the Guard 11 June 1801.

He became brigadier 11 October 1802, sub-lieutenant in the 1st Cuirassiers 23 October 1811, joined them 27 October 1811, died in Russia 25 November 1812. LH CH 14 April 1807.

MICHEL (Nicolas, 1759-?): born in Audecourt (Meuse) on 18 December 1759. In the Royal-Guyenne-Cavalerie

10 February, brigadier 12 October 1786, in the same regiment when it became the 23rd Cavalry 1 January 1791 then 22nd Cavalry 4 June 1793, maréchal des logis 27 July 1793, sub-lieutenant by seniority 20 February 1801.

He was , dismissed with the corps 31 December 1802 and incorporated as a supernumerary in the 2nd Carabiniers 10 February 1803, in the 4th Cuirassiers 6 April 1803, lieutenant in the 12th Cuirassiers 25 August 1806 and allowed to go over to the 2nd Carabiniers as the post had been filled 26 August 1806, sabre wound to his right hand at Friedland 14 June 1807, in the 13th Cuirassiers 21 October 1808, captain 13 February 1809, retired 17 August 1811. LH CH 1 October 1807.

MICHELHOFF (Dirk, 1778-?): born in Loene on 11 January 1778. In the Batavian Dragoons 17 July 1794, brigadier 6 April 1804, in the same regiment when it became the 2nd Dutch Cavalry 14 July 1806.

He became , maréchal des logis 1 January 1807, in the same regiment when it became the 2nd Dutch Cuirassiers then 14th French Cuirassiers 18 August 1810, maréchal des logis-chef 1 February 1811, shot and wounded in the head at Smolensk 18 August 1815, shot and wounded in the right leg at the Berezina 28 November 1812, sub-lieutenant 13 September 1813, dismissed with the corps 12 July 1814.

MIES (Johan Henri, 1775-?): born in Hatzfelden on 4 January 1775. In the 1st Batavian Cavalry, brigadier 26 March 1796, in the Batavian Dragoons 28 June 1805 which became the 2nd Dutch Cavalry 14 July 1806, maréchal des logis 11 February 1807.

He was in the same regiment when it became the 2nd Dutch Cuirassiers then 14th French Cuirassiers 18 August 1810, sub-lieutenant in the suite 8 April 1811, in post 8 April 1812, dismissed with the corps 12 July 1814.

MIGNOT (Simon, 1791-?): born in Annonay (Loire) on 3 April 1791. Brigadier in the 4th Gardes d'Honneur 30 May 1813.

He became sub-lieutenant in the King's Cuirassiers 1 May 1814, in Paris at the disposal of the Minister of War 20 January 1815, returned to the corps 1 April 1815 which had become the 1st Cuirassiers again, dismissed 24 December 1815. LH CH 25 November 1813.

MILGIN (Vincent, 1780-?): born in Revel (Somme) on 24 April 1780. In the 11th Cavalry 4 March 1803 which became the 11th Cuirassiers 24 September 1803, brigadier 1 December 1806.

He became maréchal des logis 3 April 1807, adjutant 16 May 1809, sub-lieutenant 3 June 1809, resigned 14 July 1810. LH CH 16 June 1809.

MILLOT (Jean, 1776-?): born in Paris (Seine) on 25 September 1776. In the Volontaires Nationaux à Cheval from the Ecole Militaire 28 August 1792 having formed the 25th Cavalry 7 February 1793 which became the 24th Cavalry 4 June 1793, brigadier 20 June 1798.

He became fourrier 11 January 1800, in the Grenadiers à Cheval of the Guard 7 September 1801, brigadier 22 December 1801, maréchal des logis 11 October 1802, maréchal des logis-chef 24 September 1803, sub-lieutenant in the 2nd Cuirassiers 30 August 1805, confirmed

29 September 1805, joined them 11 November 1805.

He was supernumerary and placed in the suite 30 October 1806, adjutant-major 23 March 1809, rank of captain 23 September 1808, wounded in the left shoulder at the Moskova 7 September 1812, squadron commander 19 February 1814, dismissed with the corps and put on the non-active list 10 December 1815. LH CH 13 August 1809, O 5 September 1813.

MILLOT (Raphaël, ?-?): in the Gendarmes d'Ordonnance 11 March 1807. Maréchal des logis 20 June 1807, instated 2 July 1807, dismissed with the corps and sent home 23 October 1807.

He became lieutenant in the suite of the 12th Cuirassiers 12 February 1808, in the suite of the 9th Cuirassiers 29 March 1808, took up his appointment 31 May 1808, wounded at Wagram 6 July 189, Gendarmerie lieutenant in Avesne 17 September 1810.

MINE (?-1812): maréchal des logis in the 9th Cuirassiers, sub-lieutenant 14 May 1809, lieutenant 1 April 1812, killed at the Moskova 7 September 1812.

MIRAMONT (J P V de, ?-?): maréchal des logis in the 5th Cuirassiers, sub-lieutenant 16 May 1809, wounded and prisoner at Essling 2 May 1809. He returned to France and put in the suite then in the 2nd Carabiniers 5 September 1809 and finally kept in the 5th Cuirassiers 8 February 1810, resignation accepted 4 June 1811.

MOIGNET (?-?): maréchal des logis in the 11th Cuirassiers, sub-lieutenant 14 May 1809, wounded at Essling 22 May 1809, retired 28 February 1810.

MOISSON (Charles Antoine, 1756-?): born in Hesdin (Pas-de-Calais) on 5 April 1756. In the Royal-Champgne-Cavalerie 20 January 1774, brigadier 1 March 1780, fourrier 23 January 1782, maréchal des logis-chef 11 September 1784, standard-bearer 8 April 1785, in the same regiment when it became the 20th Cavalry 1 January 1791.

He became sub-lieutenant 1 April 1791, lieutenant 25 January 1792, captain 22 September 1792, in the same regiment when it became the 19th Cavalry 4 June 1793, deputy captain, in service in the 2nd Cavalry 24 August 1795,

confirmed 21 October 1795, left 22 May 1796, discharged 4 April 1805, grenadier captain in the 2nd Cohort of the 2nd Legion from 23 November 1805 to 21 January 1806.

He returned as captain to the 2nd Cuirassiers 29 October 1806, joined 22 November 1806, detached to the 1st Provisional Heavy Cavalry December 1807 which formed the 13th cuirassiers 21 October 1808, retired 7 July 1810.

MOISSONNIER (Georges Christophe, 1777-?): born in Oberbruck (Haut-Rhin) on 5 November 1777. In the 1st Cavalry 3 July 1798, sabre wound to his right hand at la Trebbia 17 June 1799, in the same regiment when it became the 1st Cuirassiers 10 October 1801, brigadier 1 June 1802.

He became fourrier 2 January 1804, sabre wound to his right cheek at Jena 14 October 1806, maréchal des logis-chef on the same day 14 October 1809, sub-lieutenant 16 May 1808, lieutenant in the 6th Wagon Train Battalion 23 January 1812, instated 12 February 1812, prisoner with the capitulation at Torgau 10 January 1814, freed 15 August 1814 and returned to the 2nd Battalion 27 August 1814.

He was non-active 10 November 1814, put back in the 2nd Battalion of the Train 28 April 1815 and put on half-pay 15 September 1815. LH CH 3 April 1807.

MOITHE (Pierre Jean, 1780-?): born in Guillencourt (Oise) on 12 February 1780. In the 1st Cuirassiers 16 July 1803, brigadier at Eylau 8 February 1807, maréchal des logis 12 April 1808, seconded to the 1st Provisional Heavy Cavalry December 1807 which formed the 13th Cuirassiers 21 October 1808, adjutant NCO 1 September 1813, sub-lieutenant 26 February 1814.

He was dismissed with the corps and incorporated into the 9th Cuirassiers 9 August 1814, confirmed in the suite 4 February 1815, left with his pension 26 November 1815. LH CH 29 May 1810.

MOLARD (Claude, 1760-?): born in Cordier (Ain) on 5 March 1760. In the Cuirassiers du Roy 30 May 1783 which became the 8th Cavalry 1 January 1791, brigadier 1792.

He became maréchal des logis 12 September 1792, maréchal des logis-chef 28 August 1793, wounded at Altendorf 6 August 1796, sub-lieutenant by seniority 3 August 1797, lieutenant by seniority 19 August 1800.

He was in the same regiment when it became the 8th Cuirassiers 10 October 1801, captain 12 April 1808, retired 21 November 1811. LH CH June 1805.

MONAL de SCARAMPI (Antoine Raymond, 1779-1814): born in Asti (Marengo) on 13 January 1779. Page to the Prince de Carignan 21 March 1789, sub-lieutenant of the Guards 30 May 1794.

He became lieutenant in the 1st Piedmont Half-Brigade 26 January 1799, prisoner at Verderio 25 April 1800 returned home on parole when the regiment was disbanded 17 June 1800, lieutenant in the suite of the 1st Carabiniers 4 May 1805, shot and wounded in the left arm at Eschenau near Nuremberg 20 October 1805, in service with the 2nd Carabiniers 12 April 1806, captain in the 1st Carabiniers 12 February 1807.

He was detached to the 1st Provisional Heavy Cavalry in Spain December 1807 which became the 13th Cuirassiers 21 October 1808, squadron commander 29 February 1810, killed at Mâcon 19 February 1814.

MONCHARD (Jean Claude Didier, 1784-?): born in Monceux (Vosges) on 25 October 1784. In the 24th Dragoons 27 October 1805, brigadier 21 June 1808, maréchal des logis 1 May 1811.

He became gendarme in the 1st Legion of the Gendarmerie à Cheval d'Espagne 5 December 1811, sub-lieutenant in the 10th Cuirassiers 1 March 1813, dismissed with the corps 25 December 1815.

MONGOBERT (Frédéric, 1780-?): born in Grenoble (Isère) on 3 December 1780. In the 4th Light Infantry 29 January 1799, gendarme à cheval (Finistere Company) 21 October 1806.

He was in the 14th Squadron of the Gendarmerie d'Espagne 16 December 1809, in the 1st Legion of the Gendarmerie à Cheval d'Espagne "Burgos" 5 February 1811, dismissed with the corps 27 February 1813, sub-lieutenant in the 8th Cuirassiers 1 March 1813, non-active and put up for retirement 1814.

MONNET (?-1808): boarder in the Ecole Militaire in Fontainebleau or Polytechnique, sub-lieutenant in the suite of the 9th Cuirassiers 14 December 1806, took up his post 16 February 1808, died in Prussia 2 July 1808.

MONSCH (Joseph, 1780-1815): born in Rocroi (Ardennes) on 3 May 1780. In the 3rd Hussars 9 June 1798, fourrier 13 June 1799, gendarme in the Bas-Rhin Company 31 January 1803, brigadier 24 August 1804.

He became maréchal des logis in the 20th Escadron à Cheval d'Espagne 20 February 1810, maréchal des logis-chef in the Legion of the Gendarmerie à Cheval d'Espagne "Burgos" 1 January 1811.

He became sub-lieutenant 11 April 1812, dismissed with the corps 27 February 1813, captain in the 14th Cuirassiers 28 February 1813, dismissed with the corps and incorporated into the 12th Cuirassiers 13 July 1814, wounded and presumed prisoner at Waterloo 18 June 1815, disappeared without trace. LH CH 1 March 1813.

MONTAGU LOMAGNE s
ee **FLOTARD de MONTAGU LOMAGNE**

MONTALAN (Jean Baptiste, 1773-?): born in Lyon (Rhône) in 1773. In the 1st Basses Alpes Battalion 27 March 1795, caporal-fourrier 28 May 1795, sergeant 23 September 1795, sergeant-major 1796, chief driver with the Artillery Trains 20 July 1796, bureau chief on the staff of the Lombardy Division 21 August 1797, lieutenant in the Artillery Train 20 April 1798, discharged 2 April 1801.

He became secretary of a military district 21 May 1801, left 21 January 1803, maréchal des logis-chef of the 1st Neapolitan Artillery Battalion 24 June 1807, in the Chevau-Légers of the Neapolitan Guard 21 September 1808, adjutant-NCO 4 November 1808, sub-lieutenant payments officer for the Gardes d'Honneur 9 May 1809, lieutenant 26 September 1809, lance wound to his right hand in Russia 8 December 1812, in the Cuirassiers of the Neapolitan Guard 12 April 1813.

He was captain 16 November 1813, resigned 24 January 1814, returned to French service as lieutenant in the 19th Chasseurs à Cheval 23 March 1814, on the non-active list on half-pay 1 September 1814, captain in the 4th Cuirassiers 3 May 1815, dismissed 21 December 1815.

MONTAULIEU (Paul Maurice Julien, 1782-?): born in Valréas (Vaucluse) on 22 September 1782. In the 93rd Half-Brigade 11 December 1800, in the 3rd Cuirassiers 1 February 1803, brigadier 19 May 1803, maréchal des logis 31 July 1803.

He became, sub-lieutenant 12 March 1804, lieutenant 1 May 1807, adjutant-major 14 May 1809, captain 3 June 1809, wounded by a shell burst at Leipzig 16 October 1813 and shot through the thigh at Champaubert 10 February 1814, dismissed with the corps 25 November 1815. LH CH 14 April 1807, O 7 June 1814.

MONTCHOISY (Abel Jean Louis de, 1790-?): born in Moras (Drôme) on 12 September 1790. One of the Emperor's pages, sub-lieutenant in the 12th Cuirassiers 2 February 1808.

He was detached to the 2nd Provisional Heavy Cavalry in Spain, prisoner with the capitulation at Baylen 22 July 1808, wounded in the right knee while escaping from the hulk, l'Argonaute off Cadiz 26 May 1810 and returned to the 12th Cuirassier.

He became, lieutenant 12 March 1812, instated 1 July 1812, captain 14 May 1813, captain in the Deux-Sèvres Gendarmerie Legion 21 May 1817. LH CH 4 December 1813.

Montchoisy [signature]

MONTEIL (Etienne, 1792-1812): born in 1792. In the 1st Cuirassiers 1 December 1809, brigadier 1 January 1810.

He became maréchal des logis 10 January 1810, sub-lieutenant in the suite 28 May 1812, in his post 24 June 1812, disappeared in Russia 30 November 1812.

MONTEIL (Joseph, chevalier de, 1760-1826): born in Saint-Chély (Lozère) on 7 May 1760. Midshipman 1 January 1774, Navy Guard 18 February 1775, ensign 2 March 1777, wounded in the right arm on the Cérès 3 June 1779, wounded in the chest aboard the Epervier 10 August 1779.

He shattered his leg on the Petit Annibal 12 April 1782, in the service of the United States 17 October 1784, returned 7 October 1790, sergeant-major in the Saint-Denis Volunteers 6 September 1792, wounded by grapeshot in his right leg near Valenciennes 8 May 1793, deputy to the Commissioners for War 14 May 1794, lieutenant in the 1st Cavalry 22 October 1794, captain 17 July 1799, in the same when it became the 1st Cuirassiers 10 October 1801, shot and wounded in the head at Austerlitz 2 December 1805, two pistol shots, seven sabre wounds to his head, arms, losing his right thumb at Jena 14 October 1806.

He became squadron commander 9 May 1807, sabre wound to his left hand at Eckmühl 22 April 1809, major 16 May 1809, colonel-major of the 4th Gardes d'Honneur 21 April 1813, left to join them 1 June 1813,

(Composition by L. Rousselot, private collection, RR)

maréchal de camp 23 August 1814, non-active 20 March 1815, commanded the Cantal Department 17 August 1815. LH CH 14 June 1804, Chevalier of the Empire l.p. 6 October 1810.

MONTENDRE (Jean Charles Guillaume, ?-?): in the Gendarmes d'Ordonnance 26 December 1806, brigadier 13 January 1807, maréchal des logis 1 July 1807, dismissed with the corps 23 October 1807, lieutenant in the 2nd Cuirassiers 18 February 1808, instated 1 March 1808, resignation accepted 11 April 1811.

MONTESQUIOU FEZEN-SAC (Ambroise Anatole Augustin de, baron, 1788-1878): grandson of the general, son of the Count Grand Chamberlain, born in Paris (Seine) on 8 August 1788. Sub-lieutenant in the 8th Cuirassiers, ordnance to Maréchal Davout 19 May 1807, lieutenant aide de camp to Davout 12 October 1809, ordnance officer to the Emperor 28 March 1809, captain 19 January 1810, chamberlain 13 January 1811, squadron commander and aide de camp to Berthier 14 March 1812, colonel 5 November 1813.

He became aide de camp to the Emperor 18 January 1814, adjutant-commandant on the staff of the 1st Military Division 7 August 1814, in Austria with his mother who was the governess of the King of Rome February 1815, accused of wanting to kidnap King Rome in Vienna to bring him back to France.

He was authorised to return to France after Waterloo, non-active 1 September 1815. LH CH 1 August 1809, O 23 March 1814, Baron of the Empire d. 15 August 1809 and l.p. 20 April 1810.

MONTEYNAUD (Claude Auguste Antoine, 1784-?): born in Vernoux (Ardèche) on 4 June 1784. In the 4th Cuirassiers 10 October 1805, brigadier 1 September 1810.

He became maréchal des logis 1 January 1811, maréchal des logis-chef 14 March 1812, incorporated with his squadron into the 1st Provisional Heavy Cavalry in Hamburg 11 September 1813, sub-lieutenant 19 September 1813, returned with the garrison 27 May 1814, non-active on half-pay 6 August 1814, returned to the corps May 1815, on-active again 1 September 1815.

MONTFLEURY see **LEPETIT de MONTFLEURY**

MONTFORT (Louis, 1788-?): born in Valenciennes (Nord) on 7 October 1788. Velite in the Grenadiers à Cheval of the Guard 20 December 1806?

He was shot and wounded in the left shoulder in Spain 151 June 1811, sub-lieutenant in the 4th Cuirassiers 13 March 1813, shot and wounded in the right arm at Fère-Champenoise 25 March 1814, non-active on half-pay 6 August 1814, left 28 August 1814, in the suite of the 4th Cuirassiers and went over to the

7th Cuirassiers the same day 9 June 1815, non-active and went home 24 August 1815.

MONTHIERES see **GODDE de MONTHIERES**

MONTIGNY (Charles dè, 1789-?): born in Metz (Moselle) on 8 October 1789. In the Gendarmes d'Ordonnance 20 January 1807, sub-lieutenant in the 26th Chasseurs à Cheval 16 July 1807, wounded in the right leg at the Duero 10 March 1813, lieutenant 12 May 1813.

He became lieutenant adjutant-major 16 may 1813, in the suite of the 8th Cuirassiers 24 August 1814, three months' leave on half-pay 7 December 1814, left February 1815, retired 31 May 1815.

MONTLUZIN (?-1808): Velite in the Grenadiers à cheval of the Imperial Guard, sub-lieutenant in the suite of the 9th Cuirassiers 13 July 1807, took up his post 19 January 1808.

He was incorporated into the 2nd Provisional Heavy Cavalry in Spain, killed at Baylen 16 July 1808.

MONTMOLIN see **BRADICOURT MONTMOLIN**

MONTRICHARD (Arsène, 1792-?): In the Ecole Spéciale Impériale de Cavalerie in Saint-Germain, sub-lieutenant in the 6th Cuirassiers 30 January 1813, incorporated with his squadron into the 2nd Provisional Heavy Cavalry in Hamburg 11 September 1813, returned with the garrison 30 May 1814, but was ill en route, in the King's Musketeers end 1814.

MONTROMANT (François Alexandre de, 1782-?): born in Gible (Saône-et-Loire) on 14 June 1782. In the Gendarmes d'Ordonnance 29 October 1806, brigadier 6 August 1807, dismissed with the corps 23 October 1807.

He became sub-lieutenant quartermaster in the 2nd Cuirassiers 18 February 1808, joined 14 April 1808, instated 1 June 1808, rank of lieutenant 17 September 1810, captain 16 October 1813, dismissed and went home 10 December 1815.

MORAINE aka **MOREL** (Jean Baptiste, 1775-?): born in Soindres (Seine-et-Oise) on 5 March 1775. In the 3rd Cavalry 10 December 17493, brigadier 19 June 1797, fourrier 21 March 1798, maréchal des logis-chef 23 May 1798.

He became , adjutant-NCO 22 December 1801, in the same regiment when it became the 3rd Cuirassiers 12 October 1802, sub-lieutenant 27 May 1803, lieutenant 30 October 1806, wounded at Essling 21 May 1809, captain 29 April 1809, wounded at Waterloo 18 June 1815, retired 15 November 1815. LH CH 14 April 1807.

MORAND (François, 1773-1812): born in Lisieux (Calvados) on 22 August 1773. Grenadiers in the 1st Calvados Battalion 22 September 1791, in the 2nd Carabiniers 24 April 1794, in the 21st Dragoons 22 December 1795, brigadier 20 April 1797, fourrier 26 October 1797, incorporated into the 2nd Dragoons 21 December 1797, maréchal des logis 4 June 1799, maréchal des logis-chef 22 November 1799, adjutant

8 October 1801. He became sub-lieutenant 15 January 1804, in the Elite Company, wounded by a shot in the right arm and his horse killed under him at Jena 14 October 1806, supernumerary lieutenant 7 November 1806, in service 1 May 1807,n lieutenant adjutant-major in the 11th Cuirassiers 28 August 1807, rank of captain 28 February 1809, shot and wounded in the left side at Regensburg 23 April 1809.

He was captain in service 16 May 1809, wounded at the Moskova 7 September 1812 and killed at Wiasma 4 November 1812. LH CH 1 October 1807.

MORAND (Gustave Philippe de, 1792-?): born in Saint-Girod (Mont-Blanc) on 16 September 1792. In the Ecole Spéciale Impériale de Cavalerie in Saint-Germain 21 July 1810, brigadier 8 May 1812.

He became sub-lieutenant in the 7th Cuirassiers 30 January 1813, joined 14 March 1813, in the 1st Cuirassiers 1 May 1814, in the King's Cuirassiers when they were formed 1 July 1814, in the 2nd Cuirassiers of the Royal Guard 23 October 1815.

MORANDO (François, ?-?): born in Genoa. Supernumerary sub-lieutenant in the 7th Cuirassiers 15 February 1810, joined 28 April 1810, in service 4 March 1812.

He was shot and wounded in the right shoulder at the Berezina 28 November 1812, lieutenant in the 13th Hussars 16 August 1813, aide de camp in place 1 September 1813, had not joined the 13th Hussars by 1 December 1813. LH CH 16 May 1813.

MORANGE see **ROUOT de MORANGE**

MOREAU (Louis Joseph Jacques René, 1786-?): born in La Châtaigneraie (Vendée) on 28 November 1786. Velite in the Grenadiers à Cheval of the Imperial Guard 27 February 1806, sub-lieutenant in the 10th Cuirassiers 25 March 1809, lieutenant 6 November 1811.

He was incorporated with his squadron into the 3rd Provisional Heavy Cavalry in Hamburg 11 September 1813, returned with the garrison 30 May 1814, no longer appears on the rolls as of 6 August 1814. LH CH 11 October 1812.

MOREL (?-?): Velite in the Grenadiers à Cheval of the Guard 13 July 1807, sub-lieutenant 28 February 1809, instated into the 3rd Cuirassiers 14 May 1809, lieutenant 3 June 1809, retired 8 February 1810, pensioned 28 February 1810.

MOREL see **MORAIN** aka **MOREL.**

MORELLE (François, 1774-?): born in Paris (Seine) on 8 July 1774. In the 48th Infantry 8 July 1791, in the 9th Cavalry 14 June 1792, brigadier 24 May 1801, in the same regiment when it became the 9th Cuirassiers 24 September 1803, maréchal des logis 4 December 18063.

He became adjutant-NCO 24 September 1807, sub-lieutenant 14 May 1809, lieutenant 21 March 1812, shot and wounded in the right leg at Ostrovno 9 July 1812; lieutenant adjudant-major 15 March 1813 shot and wounded in the head near Brienne

2 February 1814, rank of captain 5 September 1814.

He was confirmed captain adjutant-major 3 November 1814, non-active at the disposal of the government 26 November 1815. LH CH 14 March 1806.

MORETON de CHABRILLAN (Jules Edouard, 1784-1812): born in Felines (Ardèche) on 29 April 1784. In the 10th Cuirassiers 12 September 1804, brigadier 23 June 1806, maréchal des logis 24 November 1806.

He became adjutant 26 November 1806, shot and wounded twice in the leg at Eylau 8 February 1807, sub-lieutenant 25 May 1807, lieutenant 16 May 1809, wounded by a Biscayan shot in the left thigh and his horse killed under him at Essling 22 May 1809, killed near Moscow 4 October 1812. LH CVH 14 April 1807.

MORICEAU (Valentin Mérault, 1772-?): born in Cées (Maine-et-Loire) on 15 July 1772. In the 10th Cavalry 23 March 1791.

He became brigadier-fourrier 15 September 1793, maréchal des logis 20 January 1799, maréchal des logis-chef 20 July 1799, two lance wounds to his right thigh and two sabre wounds to his head and taken prisoner at Erbach near Ulm 16 May 1800, returned to the regiment 30 April 1801, adjutant 3 June 1801, in the same when it became the 10th Cuirassiers 24 September 1803.

He was sub-lieutenant 8 October 1806, lieutenant 26 June 1807, adjutant-major 16 May 1809, lost 2 horses killed under him at Essling 21 May 1809, rank of captain 16 November 1810, captain in service 14 May 1811, dismissed with the corps 25 December 1815. LH CH 5 November 1804.

MORIN (Denis Charles, 1773-?): born in Plessis (Seine-et-Oise) on 28 November 1773. In the 24th Cavalry 6 September 1792, brigadier 4 August 1796, fourrier 6 July 1797.

He was dismissed with the corps 10 October 1801, incorporated into the 8th Cuirassiers 6 January 1802, maréchal des logis-chef 9 February 1802, adjutant-NCO 5 June 1806, sub-lieutenant 17 April 1807, sabre wound to his left cheek at Heilsberg 10 June 1807, detached to the 3rd Provisional Heavy Cavalry in Spain 1808, lieutenant 3 June 1809.

He became captain 12 September 1809, returned to the 8th Cuirassiers February 1811, sabre wound to his face at the Moskova 7 September 1812, remained ill in the hospitals and taken prisoner near Danzig January 1813. LH CH 1 October 1807.

MORIN (François, ?-?): in the 22nd Cavalry 10 December 1793, brigadier 3 October 1799, fourrier 20 February 1802.

He was dismissed with the corps 31 December 1802 and incorporated into the 12th Cavalry 25 January 1803 which became the 12th Cuirassiers 24 September 1803, maréchal des logis-chef 20 July 1804, sub-lieutenant 3 June 1809, lieutenant 9 February 1813, wounded in the head at Waterloo 18 June 1815, dismissed with the corps 10 December 1815. LH CH 1 October 1807.

MORIN (Léonard, baron, 1774-1814): born in Saint-Léonard-de-Noblet (Haute-Vienne) on 4 November 1774. In the 2nd Haute-Vienne Battalion 21 October 1791. He became corporal 29 January 1793, sergeant-major 11 April 1793, sub-lieutenant in the 5th Cavalry 28 May 1793, aide de camp to General Pellapra, lieutenant in the depots at Vienna and remained aide de camp 25 October 1794, lieutenant in the Hussar companies of the same depot 21 November 1794 which had formed the Hussars of the Alps 31 January 1795, in the 11th Chasseurs à Cheval, refused, lieutenant in the suite of the Hussars of the Alps 14 April 1795 without joining them and having already been replaced, in the same regiment when it became the 13th Hussars 1 September 1795.

He was incorporated into the suite of the 1st Hussars when the 13th was disbanded 18 May 1796, instated 20 may 1796, wounded by a shot when crossing the Piave, deputy to the adjutant-Generals of the Army of Italy 20 March 1797, captain 23 October 1798, in the Armies of England 1798, of the Danube the Helvetia 1799, aide de camp to General Walther 7 December 1800.

He was wounded at Austerlitz 2 December 1805, in the Grenadiers à Cheval of the Guard 16 February 1807, squadron commander 17 February 1811, lance wound in the shoulder at Malojarolavete 24 October 1812, colonel in the Line 13 August 1813, commanded the 2nd Cuirassiers 5 November 1813, took up his command 14 November 1813, commanded the 3rd Provisional Heavy Cavalry in which his regiment was incorporated 1814, wounded at Vauchamps while taking 2 500 prisoners 14 February 1814 and died in Paris of his wounds 20 February 1814. LH CH 14 March 1806, O 26 June 1809, C 25 February 1814, Baron of the Empire d.14 September 1813 without l.p.

MOSNERON (Auguste, 1788-?): born in Nantes (Loire-Inférieure) on 5 September 1788.

In the Ecole Militaire in Fontainebleau 23 May 1806, sergeant 6 December 1806, sub-lieutenant in the 5th Infantry 9 January 1807, in the 10th Cuirassiers 2 February 1807.

He became lieutenant 6 November 1811, captain 19 June 1813, no longer appears on the rolls as of 6 August 1814. LH CH 11 October 1812.

MOTET (Charles Antoine, 1782-?): born in Amagney (Doubs) on 17 January 1782. In the 6th Light Infantry 19 March 1802, in the 82nd of the Line and returned to the 6th Light Infantry, left 27 June 1808, in the 3rd Guards of Honour 20 July 1813.

He became brigadier 16 September 1813, fourrier 17 September 1813, maréchal des logis and vaguemestre 24 November 1813, dismissed with the corps 20 July 1814, sub-lieutenant in the 11th Cuirassiers 12 May 1815, wounded at Waterloo 18 June 1815, appointment

cancelled 1 August 1815, returned home 25 August 1815. LH CH.

MOUFFET (Paul, 1787-?): born in Port-sur-Saône (Haute-Saône) on 12 September 1787. In the 5th Cuirassiers 22 October 1805, brigadier-fourrier 22 October 1805, maréchal des logis 13 April 1807.

He became maréchal des logis-chef 20 November 1810, several sabre wounds to his head and several bayonet gashes on the regimental standard when taken prisoner at the Moskova 7 September 1815, returned to the regiment 8 January 1815, sub-lieutenant 2 February 1815.

He was confirmed in the 5th Cuirassiers 10 February 1815, dismissed 23 December 1815. LH CH 1815.

MOUGEOT (Jean François, 1768-?): born in Corre (Haute-Saône) on 4 April 1768. In the Royal-Navarre-Cavalerie 18 March 1788 which became the 22nd Cavalry 1 January 1791, then 21st Cavalry 4 June 1793, brigadier 1 August 1793.

He was wounded in the arm at the siege of Furne 1795, maréchal des logis 29 January 1796, wounded in the left leg at Ypres 1793, maréchal des logis-chef 18 December 1796, sub-lieutenant in the 18th Cavalry 26 April 1799, in the 5th Cavalry 21 October 1800, lieutenant 23 July 1801, in the same regiment when it became the 5th Cuirassiers 23 December 1802, in the 2nd Provisional Heavy Cavalry in Spain.

He was wounded 17 times of which four were serious during the Madrid insurrection 2 May 1808, captain of the 10th Cuirassiers 6 September 1808, retired 1 October 1811.

MOUGEOT (Joseph, 1779-?): born in 1779. Trooper in the 1st Regiment 22 December 1800 which became the 1st Cuirassiers 10 October 1801.

He became brigadier 11 May 1803, maréchal des logis 16 October 1806, shot and wounded twice in the head and the back at Essling 22 May 1809, sub-lieutenant 5 November 1811, lance wound to his

8th Cuirassier Regiment in 1804 by Marbot. *(RR)*

right arm and taken prisoner at Krasnoë 15 November 1812, returned 13 September 1814 and incorporated into the King's Cuirassiers the same day, retired with his pension 1 November 1814.

MOULBLAIX
see **DUCHASTELER de MOULBAIX**

MOULIN (Jean Pierre, 1781-?): born in Versailles (Seine-et-Oise) on 29 December 1781. In the 25th Dragoons 20 September 1799, shot and wounded in his left leg at Lübeck November 1806, and two bayonet wounds in the stomach at la Corona January 1809, brigadier 20 September 1809, in the Gendarmerie d'Espagne 20 December 1809.

He became maréchal des logis in the 1st Legion of the Gendarmerie à Cheval d'Espagne "Burgos" 16 December 1810, dismissed with the corps 27 February 1813, sub-lieutenant in the 3rd Cuirassiers 1 March 1813, incorporated with his squadron into the 1st Provisional Heavy Cavalry in Hamburg 11 September 1813.

He returned with the garrison 27 May 1814, shot and wounded in the left shoulder at Waterloo 18 June 1815, dismissed 25 November 1815.

MOURER (François, 1763-1809): born in Hambach (Moselle) on 5 September 1763. Trooper in the Colonel-Général Regiment 22 April 1786 which became the 1st Cavalry 1 January 1791, brigadier 1 June 1793.

He became maréchal des logis 11 July 1796, in the same regiment when it became the 1st Cuirassiers 10 October 1801, sub-lieutenant by seniority 23 February 1805, lieutenant 24 November 1806.

He was captain in the 11th Cuirassiers 29 April 1809, killed at Essling 21 May 1809. LH CH 1 October 1807.

MOURGUES (François Louis Maxime, 1784-?): born in Saint-Hyppolite (Gard) on 23 December 1784. In the 19th Cavalry 11 October 1800, brigadier 6 November 1802, dismissed with the corps 31 December 1802.

He became maréchal des logis 20 January 1803, incorporated into the 11th Cuirassiers 5 February 1803, in the 2nd Cuirassiers 20 July 1804, sub-lieutenant in the suite 30 October 1806, in service 1 November 1806, supernumerary lieutenant in the 3rd Cuirassiers 27 March 1809, left to join them 21 May 1809, in the 5th Provisional Dragoons 24 October 1809.

He returned to the 3rd Cuirassiers 26 May 1810, in service 13 May 1811, captain 13 February 1812, in the Cuirassiers of the Royal Guard 1 November 1815. LH CH 28 September 1814.

MOUSSON (Pierre, 1769-?): born in Salmaize (Côtes-d'Or) in 1769. Fusilier in the Colonel-Général-Infanterie 4 December 1790 which became the 1st infantry 1 January 1791.

He was in the 4th Cavalry 22 December 1793, insta-ted 2 February 1794, shot and wounded on the chin at Fleurus 26 June 1794, in the same regiment when it became the 4th cuirassiers 12 October 1802, briga-dier 25 June 1807, maréchal des logis 4 June 1809, shot and wounded in the right wrist at Wagram 6 July 1809, sub-lieutenant 14 May 1813.

He was non-active on half-pay 6 August 1814, retur-ned as sub-lieutenant to the 4th Cuirassiers April 1815, put back on the non-active list 1 September 1815. LH CH 25 September 1812.

MOZER (Joseph, 1778-?): born in Burfeld (Bas-Rhin) on 19 September 1778. In the 12th Cavalry 14 November 1798.

He became brigadier 16 April 1803, in the same regi-ment when it became the 12th Cuirassiers 24 September 1803, maréchal des logis 1 December 1806, sub-lieute-nant 22 December 1813, not kept on with the 14 July 1814 re-organisation. LH CH 14 March 1806.

MUFFAT (Charles François, 1786-?): born in Grange-le-Bourg (Haute-Saône) on 27 January 1786. In the 3rd Cuirassiers 6 October 1806.

He became four sabre wounds to his head at Friedland 14 June 1807, brigadier in the 13th Cuirassiers 21 October 1808, maréchal des logis 14 July 1813, adjutant-NCO 15 August 1813, sub-lieute-nant 25 February 1814.

He was incorporated into the Angoulême Cuirassiers 6 August 1814 which became the 4th Cuirassiers again April 1815, dismissed 221 December 1815.

MUIRON (Pierre, 1775-?): born in Reims (Marne) on 18 November 1775. In the 1st Marne Battalion 4 September 1791, in the 24th Cavalry 23 March 1793 which became the 23rd Cavalry 4 June 1793, dismis-sed with the corps 23 December 1802 and incorpo-rated into the 5th Cuirassiers 3 January 1803.

He became brigadier-fourrier 9 February 1807, maré-chal des logis 6 February 1808, sub-lieutenant 3 June 1809, lieutenant 28 September 1813, on retirement pay 23 December 18151. LH CH 16 June 1809.

MULLER (Pierre, 1784-1856): born in Frommesen (Röer) on 4 November 1784. In the 11th Cuirassiers 4 February 1807.

He was wounded by a shell burst on his left leg at Essling 21 May 1809 and a lance wound at Wagram 6 July 1809, brigadier 8 September 1810, maréchal des logis 1 October 1810, sub-lieutenant 16 August 1813, lance wound at Leipzig 16 August 1813, shell burst wound at Waterloo 18 June 1815, dismissed with the corps 16 December 1815. LH CH 5 September 1813.

MULLOT (Pierre, 1770-?): born in Francastel (Oise) on 28 October 1770. In the 10th Cavalry 10 January 1794, brigadier 22 March 1802, in the same regiment when it became the 10th Cuirassiers 24 September 1803.

He became maréchal des logis 11 December 1806, cannonball wound to his left knee at Essling 22 May 1809, sub-lieutenant 3 June 1809, resignation accepted 14 November 1810, struck off the rolls 21 November 1810.

MUNIER (Jean François, 1772 - 1812) born in Aquers (Haute-Saône) on 19 January 1773. In the 82nd Infantry 1 September 1793, in the 8th Light Artillery 13 August 1794, in the 8th Cavalry 7 December 1798, fourrier 4 March 1799, maréchal des logis-chef 26 August 1800, in the same regiment when it became the 8th Cuirassiers 10 October 1801.

He became sub-lieutenant 28 June 1805, lieutenant 24 February 1807, two sabre wounds to his right arm and head at Essling 21 May 1809, lieutenant adjutant-major 9 August 1809, rank of captain 9 February 1811, wounded and taken prisoner at Krasnoë 16 December 1812, taken to Siberia and disappeared. LH CH 5 November 1804

MURAT SISTRIERES (Michel François, Baron de, 1765 - 1825) born in Vic-sur-Cèze (Cantal) on 3 July 1765. Artillery Pupil 1 August 1778, sub-lieute-nant in the suite of the infantry 5 April 1780, lieutenant in the Maillebois Legion 21 October 1785, left 1786, Major in the Vic-sur-Cèze National Guard 3 August 1789, lieu-tenant in the 12th Infantry 15 September 1791.

He became adjutant-major in the 3rd Battalion of the Reserve at the Menin Camp in the Army of the North 20 January 1792, captain in the Legion of the centre 1792, infantry lieutenant-colo-nel in the same legion 31 May 1792, in the 20th Chasseurs à Cheval formed from the cavalry in the Legion 6 June 1793, brigade commander of the regiment 22 June 1793, shot and wounded in the right leg at Jamognes 25 September 1793.

He was brigadier-general in the Army of the Ardennes, reduced in rank because he was a noble the same day and warned 5 October 1793, kept in his post by the representatives of the peo-ple, acting major-general, commanded at Givet 2 November 1793, acting commander in chief of the 2nd Ardennes Division 26 November 1793.

He was replaced 3 February 1794, left his post 6 February 1794, retired because he was not reinstated 15 February 1793, allowed to retire as brigade commander 23 June 1797, simple trooper in the Gendarmes d'Ordonnance 1 December 1806, maréchal des logis 2 December 1806, first-lieutenant 11 January 1807.

He was dismissed with the corps 23 October 1807, squadron commander in the 4th Cuirassiers 10 November 1807, interim regimental comman-ding officer and several sabre wounds to his right arm at Essling 22 May 1809 and shot twice and wounded in his right thigh and head at Wagram 6 July 1809, colonel in the suite of the 4th Cuirassiers 8 August 1809, commanded the 9th Cuirassiers 7 September 1811, wounded by a Biscayan shot to his left hip at the Moskova 7 September 1812.

He lost his right leg and his horse killed under him at Dresden 27 August 1813, amputated, bri-gadier-general and allowed to retire 2 September 1813. LH CH 13 August 1809, O 10 October 1812, Baron of the empire d.3 September 1813.

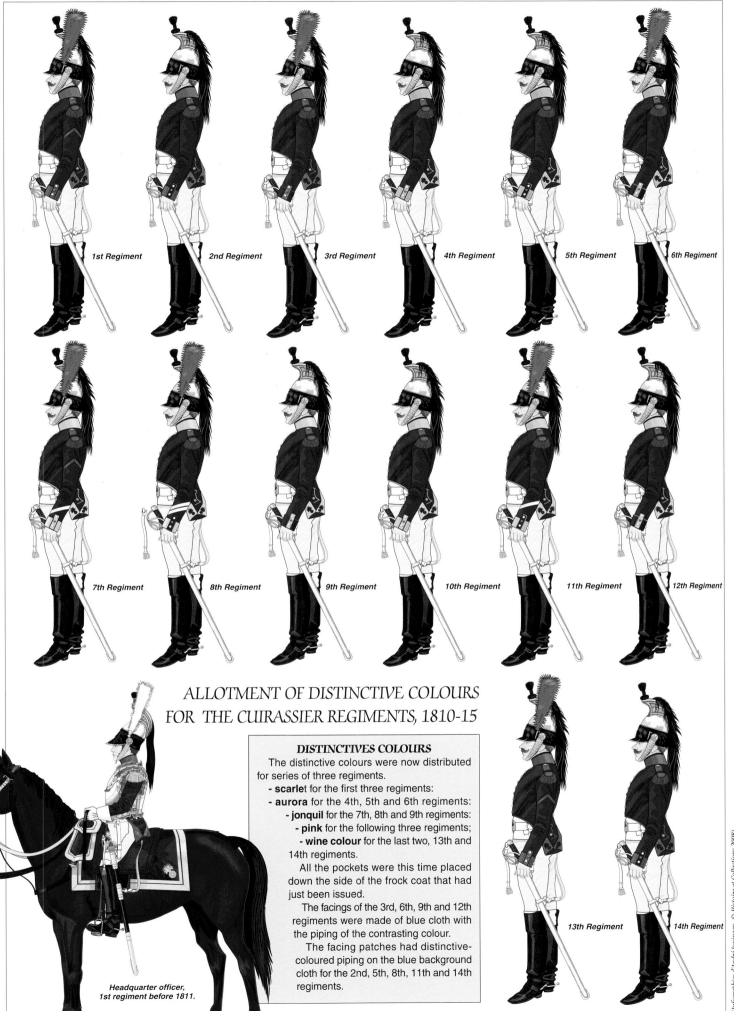

1st Regiment

2nd Regiment

3rd Regiment

4th Regiment

5th Regiment

6th Regiment

7th Regiment

8th Regiment

9th Regiment

10th Regiment

11th Regiment

12th Regiment

13th Regiment

14th Regiment

ALLOTMENT OF DISTINCTIVE COLOURS FOR THE CUIRASSIER REGIMENTS, 1810-15

DISTINCTIVES COLOURS

The distinctive colours were now distributed for series of three regiments.

- **scarlet** for the first three regiments:
- **aurora** for the 4th, 5th and 6th regiments:
- **jonquil** for the 7th, 8th and 9th regiments:
- **pink** for the following three regiments;
- **wine colour** for the last two, 13th and 14th regiments.

All the pockets were this time placed down the side of the frock coat that had just been issued.

The facings of the 3rd, 6th, 9th and 12th regiments were made of blue cloth with the piping of the contrasting colour.

The facing patches had distinctive-coloured piping on the blue background cloth for the 2nd, 5th, 8th, 11th and 14th regiments.

Headquarter officer,
1st regiment before 1811.

(Infographies d'André Jouineau, © Histoire et Collections 2008)

He was lieutenant 1792, captain in the 9th Dragoons September 1796, joined the Gendarmerie 22 December 1801, captain adjutant-major in the 5th Cuirassiers but employed in a company 23 November 1806, two sabre and one lance wounds, leaving the battlefield only when repeatedly ordered to do so at Eylau 8 February 1807, squadron commander 20 February 1807, in the 3rd Cuirassiers 13 February 1809 but retired meanwhile 19 November 1808, put back in service on the staff of the Army of Spain 28 December 1809 then that of Portugal and in the Grande Armée 25 May 1813.

He was non-active on half-pay 1 April 1814, on the staff of the Jura Observation Corps 10 May 1815, dismissed and non-active 1 August 1815.

NICEVILLE (François Théophile Hippolyte, 1780-?): born in Fresnes (Nord) on 2 March 1780. In the 16th Cavalry 20 March 1798, brigadier-fourrier 27 July 1800

He was maréchal des logis 23 October 1802, in the same regiment when it became the 25th Dragoons 24 September 1803, sub-lieutenant 8 December 1803, lieutenant 10 September 1807, captain 11 September 1809, in the 6th Cuirassiers 21 November 1811, in command of the regiment during the retreat from Moscow and took part in the Escadron Sacré November 1812, prisoner by capitulation at Danzig 2 January 1814, returned to France 2 July 1814.

He became squadron commander 24 December 1814, non-active on captain's half-pay then squadron commander 24 February 1815. LH CH 14 March 1806.

NICOD (Edouard, 1788-?): born in Luynes (Indre-et-Loire) on 18 February 1788. Pupil at the Ecole Spéciale Militaire at Fontainebleau 30 September 1806, passed out 1 December 1806.

He was caporal-fourrier 28 January 1807, sub-lieutenant 27 February 1807, in the 26 Chasseurs à Cheval 11 April 1807, lance wound at the Passarge 8 June 1807, lieutenant 30 June 1809, captain in the Chasseurs à Cheval 9 February 1813.

He was shot in the right side near Bautzen 23 September 1813, captain adjutant-major in the 2nd Gardes d'Honneur 6 October 1813, wounded at the Mainz blockade 4 February 1814, in the 2nd cuirassiers 18 August 1814, wounded at Waterloo 18 June 1815.

Dismissed with the regiment and put on half-pay 10 December 1815. LH CH 5 October 1813.

NICOLAY (Alexandre Ignace Guillaume de, 1780-?): born in Arles (Bouches-du-Rhône) on 26 September 1780. Velite in the Grenadiers à Cheval of the Imperial Guard 18 November 1808, grenadier 1 January 1812. He was sub-lieutenant in the 4th Cuirassiers 8 February 1813, incorporated into the 1st Provisional Heavy Cavalry with

NADAL (François, 1782-1814): born in Banne (Ardèche) on 24 June 1782. In the 1st Cavalry 10 October 1799.

He was brigadier 1 June 1801, in the same regiment when it became the 1st Cuirassiers 10 October 1801, maréchal des logis 20 June 1802, shot in the left hand at Jena 14 October 1814, sub-lieutenant 16 May 1809.

He became lieutenant 31 July 1811, wounded in front of Paris 30 March 1814, died from his wounds at the hospital of the Paris Medical School 4 May 1814. LH CH 11 October 1812.

NANCRE see **DREUX NANCRE.**

NANSOUTY see **CHAMPION de NANSOUTY.**

NAVETIER (?-1808): maréchal des logis in the 12th Cuirassiers.

He was sub-lieutenant 10 January 1807, seconded with his company to the 2nd Provisional Heavy Cavalry in Spain, included with most of the regiment in the capitulation at Baylen 23 July 1808 and disappeared.

He was probably died in the hulks or in Cabrera.

NENOT (Jacques, 1771-?): born in 1771. In the 9th Cavalry 19 December 1798 which became the 9th Cuirassiers 24 September 1803, brigadier 14 May 1809.

He was maréchal des logis 1 May 1812, in the King's Cuirassiers 1 July 1804, sub-lieutenant 25 March 1815, in the same regiment when it became the 1st Cuirassiers again April 1815, wounded and taken prisoner at Waterloo 18 June 1815, struck of the rolls

because still a prisoner 24 December 1815 with the rank of maréchal des logis. LH CH 4 December 1813.

NEROUX see **BOUILLARD** aka **NEROUX**

NEVEUX (Alexis Pierre, 1760-?): born in Paris (Seine) on 10 February 1760.

In the Dauphin-Infanterie 21 May 1777, left 23 May 1779, in the Volontaires Nationaux à Cheval of the Ecole Militaire 12 September 1792, maréchal des logis 1 February 1793, in the same regiment when it became the 26th Cavalry 7 February 1793 which became the 25th Cavalry 4 June 1793, sabre wound to his head at Landrecies 29 March 1794.

He was incorporated into the 2nd cuirassiers 24 November 1802, sub-lieutenant 30 October 1806, lieutenant 1 April 1809, wounded at Wagram 6 July 1809, captain 9 February 1813, incorporated with his squadron into the 1st Provisional Heavy Cavalry in Hamburg 11 September 1813, returned with the garrison 27 May 1814, retired 6 September 1814. LH CH 12 July 1804.

NEYROUD SAINT ALBIN (Pierre, 1771-1820): born in Saint-Cassieu (Isère) on 31 January 1771. In the Brie-Infanterie 1778, left 1790, sub-lieutenant in the 10th Infantry 1792.

6th Cuirassier Regiment officer.
(Photo © Figurines Magazine)

OIROT (Jean Baptiste, baron, 1768-1826), born in Port-sur-Saône (Haute-Saône) on 26 December 1768. Supernumerary bodyguard for the Comte d'Artois 19 October 1788, discharged when the corps was disbanded 12 September 1791 sub-lieutenant in the 19th Cavalry 25 January 1792, instated 15 March 1792, acting aide de camp to his father-in-law General Duteil 15 March 1793, confirmed 23 March 1793, rang in the same regiment when it became the 18th Cavalry 1793.

He was captain 30 December 1793, acting aide de camp to General Schérer in the Army of Italy, squadron commander 10 January 1796, gave up his functions as aide de camp 27 March 1796, in the Inspection Générale of Cavalry 28 December 1796, in the 13th Dragoons 18 April 1797, second in command of the school for mounted troops at Versailles 12 May 1798, brigade commander of the 23rd Cavalry 12 August 1799.

He was dismissed with the corps 23 December 1802 and appointed colonel of the 5th Cuirassiers 30 December 1802, instated 3 January 1803, brigadier-general in the 1st Dragoon Division 31 December 1806, wounded at Hoff 6 February 1807 and sent away to recover in France, in Mainz to inspect and organise the Provisional Cavalry Regiments 15 March 1807, in the Reserve Army 8 July 1807, in the 25th Military Division 2 March 1808. He commanded the Meuse-Inférieure Department 12 April 1808 then the Burgos Cavalry Depot 12 December 1808, at the disposition of Jourdan in the Army of Spain 7 April 1809, governor of Santander 24 April 1809, commanded a brigade of Dragoons in the Milhaud Division in the 4th Corps in the same army September 1809, authorised to return to France 10 September 1811, commanded the Seine-et-Oise Department 13 February 1812.

He commanded the 2nd Brigade of the 2nd Cavalry Division of the 1st Cavalry Division in Germany 4 April 1812, commanded the Erfurt Depot 9 May 1812, in the 1st Cavalry Reserve Corps 16 June 1812, ordered to bring back the Grande Armée's Cavalry Depot from Leipzig to Mainz 18 September 1812, allowed himself to be surprised.

He was imprisoned for incompetence and negligence 30 September 1813, destitute 28 December 1813, reinstated with his rank 4 July 1814, Inspector-General of the Gendarmerie 10 July 1814, unemployed 8 April 1815, non-active 1 January 1816.

LH CH 11 December 1803, O 14 June 18004, C 25 December 1805, Baron of the Empire l.p. 22 March 1813.

Brigade commander of the 23rd Cavalry, Jean-Baptiste Noirot with his two squadrons stopped 1 500 enemy cavalry advancing, taking fifty prisoners and two cannon at Valtz, near Salzburg on 14 December 1800.

his squadron in Hamburg 11 September 1814, kept in the Angoulême Cuirassiers 6 August 1814 which became the 4th Cuirassiers again April 1815, in the Gardes du Corps du Roi 24 August 1815. LH CH.

NICOLLE (François Godefroy, 1764-?): born in Douvres (Calvados) on 18 January 1764. In the Artois-Cavalerie 1 March 1780, fourrier 1 September 1784, maréchal des logis 1 October 1786, in the same regiment when it became the 9th Cavalry 1 January 1791.

He was maréchal des logis-chef 1 April 1792, adjutant sub-lieutenant 29 April 1792, sub-lieutenant 29 October 1792, aide de camp to General Loubat 1 May 1793, returned to the 9th Cavalry 13 October 1793, lieutenant 11 November 1793, captain 14 November 1794, adjutant-major 13 March 1802, in the same regiment when it became the 9th Cuirassiers 24 September 1803.

He went over to a company by seniority 16 September 1806, squadron commander in the 3rd Cuirassiers 22 March 1809, in the 12th Cuirassiers 12 June 1809, retired 19 September 1811, Mayor of Turckheim 1813.

NOEL (François, 1781-?): born in Caen (Calvados) on 13 July 1781. In the 18th Dragoons 7 June 1802, brigadier 7 March 1803, fourrier 5 October 1804, lance wound at Austerlitz 2 December 1805, in the Berg chevau-Légers 18 February 1807, in the Chasseurs à Cheval of the Imperial Guard 10 January 1809, brigadier 17 April 1811, maréchal des logis-chef 27 February 1813.

He was lieutenant (Young Guard) 21 December 1813, lieutenant quartermaster-treasurer in the suite of the 8th Cuirassiers 25 August 1814, instated 11 September 1814, dismissed with the corps 5 December 1815 and put up for the Gendarmerie 11 December 1815. LH CH 27 August 1813.

NOEL (Nicolas, 1772-?): born in Laneuville (Ardennes) on 21 April 1772.

In the Condé-Infanterie 1 April 1790 which became the 55th Infantry 12 January 1791, left 1 April 1793, in the 24th Cavalry 27 May 1793 which became the 23rd Cavalry 4 June 1793, sabre wound to his left hand at Fleurus 26 June 1794. He was brigadier-fourrier, maréchal des logis 20 April 1799, maréchal des logis-chef 21 April 1799, took 50 prisoners with only 15 troopers at Philisbourg November 1799, incorporated into the 7th Cuirassiers 15 January 1803, sub-lieutenant by choice of the corps 25 December 1804, lieutenant quartermaster 31 December 1804, captain quartermaster 17 September 1810, instated October 1810, judge for the special court in Seine-Inférieure keeping his functions in the regiment 26 December 1812.

He was deputy judge 30 October 1813, retired 19 December 1815. LH CH 4 December 1813

NOIREY (Noël Etienne, 1793-?): born in Charolles (Saône-et-Loire) on 23 December 1793. Pupil at the Ecole Impériale de Cavalerie at Saint-Germain, sub-lieutenant 30 March 1814, in the 8th Cuirassiers 12 June 1814.

He was non-active when the regiment was disbanded 11 December 1815.

NOIROT (Claude François, 1786-?): born in Venisey (Haute-Saône) on 8 May 1786. In the 5th Cuirassiers 14 September 1806, brigadier 16 May 1809, brigadier-fourrier 1 December 1810, maréchal des logis 1 February 1812, maréchal des logis-chef 12 August 1812.

He was sub-lieutenant 28 September 1813, wounded at Waterloo 18 June 1815, dismissed 23 December 1815.

NOORDMANN (David, 1772-?): born in Schiedam (Bouches-de-la-Meuse) on 10 April 1772. Trooper in the Van den Duin Regiment 2 January 1794, fourrier in the 1st Batavian Cavalry 6 March 1798, maréchal des logis in the 1st Light Dragoons 7 January 1800.

He became sub-lieutenant in the 2nd Dutch Cuirassiers 21 October 1806 which became the 14th French Cuirassiers 18 August 1810, lieutenant 5 December 1810, captain 22 December 1813, dismissed with the corps 13 July 1814.

NORAS (Henry, 1788-?): born in Collioures (Basses-Pyrénées) on 26 June 1788. In the 2nd Gardes d'Honneur 23 June 1813.

He was maréchal des logis-chef 30 June 1813, dismissed 1814, sub-lieutenant in the 5th Cuirassiers 3 May 1815, absent from the regiment on 11 August 1815.

NORMAND (Jean Dominique, 1769-?): born in Margny-aux-Cerises (Somme) on 18 April 1769. Trooper in the King's Regiment 19 April 1787 which became the 6th Cavalry 1 January 1791.

He was brigadier-fourrier 1 April 1792, maréchal des logis 1 July 1792, maréchal des logis-chef 1 April 1793, sub-lieutenant 3 June 1799, lieutenant by seniority 11 August 1802.

He was in the same regiment when it became the 6th Cuirassiers 23 December 1802, captain 27 April 1807 and sent back to the depot 22 April 1807.

NORMAND de FLAGEAC
see **LENORMAND de FLAGEAC**

NORMANDIE see **DENORMANDIE.**

NOUSSE (Jean, 1788-?): born in Keglin (Mont-Tonnerre) on 8 October 1788. In the 21st Dragoons 15 October 1808.

He was in the 12th Squadron of the Gendarmerie d'Espagne 16 May 1810, in the 1st Legion of the Gendarmerie à Cheval 'Burgos' 15 March 1813.

He became sub-lieutenant in the 2nd Cuirassiers 22 December 1813, struck of the rolls and left as a foreign national 6 August 1814.

NOVILLARD see **GIROD de NOVILLARD**

Friedland, 14th of june 1807, cuirassiers of the 12th Regiment cheer the Emperor before charging. (Oil canvas, by Meissonnier, © Metropolitan Museum of Art New York)

OURIET (?-?): maréchal des logis in the 5th Cuirassiers, maréchal des logis-chef after the battle of Austerlitz.

He was sub-lieutenant by seniority 21 December 1805, lieutenant 25 May 1807, wounded at Essling 22 May 1809, captain 3 June 1809,.

He was retired 15 November 1810 .

Austerlitz, 2 December 1805: Maréchal des logis Ouriet from the 5th Cuirassiers was unhorsed, his helmet broken on his head by several bullets.

He ran towards the artillery pieces which the enemy abandoned, cut the ropes of one of the horses, rode bareback and went back into the charge.

OFFENSTEIN (François Joseph, baron, 1760-1837): born in Erstein (Bas-Rhin) on 27 July 1760.

In the Deux-Ponts-Dragons 10 March 1777, dismissed 23 December 1786, grenadier in the Alsace-Infanterie 1 January 1787, dismissed 5 May 1789, major in the Erstein National Guard 14 June 1789, lieutenant-colonel commanding the 1st Bas-Rhin Battalion 2 October 1791.

He was brigadier-general 30 July 1793, major-general 25 September 1793, commanded at Neuf-Brisach 4 October 1793, discharged 24 July 1794, taken back as adjutant-general brigade commander in the Army of the Rhine 27 August 1794, in the suite of the 10th Half-Brigade of the Line 28 June 1796,.

He commanded the 77th of the Line 24 June 1797 then the 44th of the Line 28 April 1799, brigade comman-

der in the suite of the 12th Chasseurs à Cheval 31 July 1799, commanded the 7th Cavalry 30 May 1800, confirmed 212 October 1800, in the same regiment when it became the 7th Cuirassiers 23 December 1802, commanded the brigade formed by his regiment and the 8th Cuirassiers 23 September 1805, a shell burst broke his left arm at Heilsberg 10 June 1807.

He was brigadier-general 25 June 1807, on Brune's staff 1 August 1807, commanded the Haute-Marne Department 12 September 18098, appointed to Dordogne but did not take up his position, assigned to Imperial Headquarters 2 March 1814, non-active 17 April 1814, retired 24 December 1814, commanded two lancer regiments of the Haut and Bas-Rhin national Guard 1 May 1815.

He was relieved of his command 9 May 1815, entrusted with the mass levy in Sélestat 11 May 1815, stopped his functions 10 June 1815, at the disposition of Molitor but remained unemployed 18 June 1815. LH CH 11 December 1803, O 14 June 1804, Baron of the Empire l.p. 28 May 1809.

OLIER (?-?): lieutenant in the Gendarmerie d'Espagne, captain in the 9th Cuirassiers 28 February 1813, incorporated with his squadron in to the 3rd Provisional Heavy Cavalry in Hamburg 11 September 1813, returned with the garrison May 1814.

OLIVIER (Gabriel, ?-?): born in Longwy (Moselle), pupil at the school in Saint-Germain on 13 December 1813.

He was cavalry sub-lieutenant 9 November 1814, in the 7th Cuirassiers 6 February 1815, rejoined his regiment 28 February 1815, non-active when the corps was dismissed 19 December 1815.

OMORE (Jean Baptiste Emmanuel, 1781-?): born in Boulay-sur-Moselle (Moselle) on 24 February 1781. In the 8th Cuirassiers 30 April 1802, brigadier 1 October 1806, maréchal des logis 7 April 1807, in the 1st cuirassiers 25 January 1808.

He was sub-lieutenant 2 March 1809, dismissed and put on the active list 24 December 11815. LH CH 28 February 1813.

ORDENER (Antoine, 1793-1815): son of the following, born in Huningue (Haut-Rhin) on 21 January 1793. Page to the Emperor 16 September 1807, supernumerary sub-lieutenant in the 7th Cuirassiers 20 July 1810, rejoined 1 September 1810, took up his appointment 8 October 1813, wounded at Polotsk 18 October 1812.

He was lieutenant in the Gardes d'Honneur 12 April 1813 then lieutenant in the 30th Dragoons 17 July 1813, wounded and taken prisoner at Leipzig 18 October 1813, returned to France 5 September 1814, in service as lieutenant in the 7th Cuirassiers 23 January 1815, seriously wounded at Waterloo 18 June 1815 and died of his wounds 10 July 1815.

ORDENER (Michel, comte, 1787-1862): eldest son of the general commanding the Grenadiers à cheval of the Guard, born in Huningue (Haut-Rhin) on 3 April 1787.

Volunteer in the 11th Chasseurs à Cheval 23 September 1802, at the Fontainebleau military school 10 May 1803, sub-lieutenant in the 24th Dragoons 8 December 1803, lieutenant aide de camp to his father 6 September 1805, aide de camp to Duroc 23 September 1806, captain 7 April 1807.

He was squadron commander in the 1st Provisional Chasseurs à Cheval Regiment 30 March 1809, in the 7th Cuirassiers 3 June 1809, lance wound to his head at Polotsk 18 October 1812, colonel 19 November 1812, lance wound to his left thigh at Borisov 20 November 1812, and shot in the right thigh at the Berezina 28 November 1812 colonel in the 30th Dragoons 11 March 1813, left thigh woun-

***Appointment of
Antoine Ordener to
the rank of lieutenant.**
(Author's Collection)*

ded while he was freeing a battery served by the pupils of the Ecole Polytechnique near Paris 30 March 1814, in the suite of the 15th Dragoons 20 November 1814, colonel of the 1st Cuirassiers 25 March 1815, interim CO of the brigade after General Dubois was wounded and wounded himself by a shot in the neck at Waterloo 18 June 1815, non-active on half pay 17 October 1815.

He left 21 October 1815. LH CH 14 March 1806, O 5 September 1813, Chevalier of the Empire d. 15 August 1809, inherited his father's title of Count.

ORIOT (Claude, 1773-?): born in Colombey-les-Deux-Eglises (Haute-Marne) on 21 November 1773. Hussar in the 10th Regiment 19 October 1796, brigadier 10 November 1799.

He was maréchal des logis 5 August 1801, maréchal des logis-chef 27 April 1803, sub-lieutenant 29 August 1803, lieutenant in the 9th Cuirassiers 25 February 1809, adjutant-major 1 September 1811, commissioned adjutant-major 1 February 1812, captain commanding a company 21 March 1812, lance wound to his head and another through his thigh at Winkovo 18 October 1812.

He was in the King's Cuirassiers 1 July 1814 which became the 1st Cuirassiers again March 1815, dismissed and put on the active list 24 December 1815. LH CH 11 October 1812.

ORMANCEY (François Léon, baron d', 1754-1824): born in Saint-Jean (Côte-d'Or) on 3 August 1754.

In the Grenadiers de France 25 August 1768, in the Condé Legion 29 August 1772, incorporated into the Penthièvres-Dragons as a chasseur 6 January 1776, went over to the Chasseurs à Cheval N° 4 when they were formed 8 April 1779 which became the Cévennes Chasseurs 8 August 1784, maréchal des logis 24 September 1784.

He was maréchal des logis-fourrier 1 September 1785, maréchal des logis-chef 23 May 1787, in the same regiment when it became the Chasseurs à Cheval de Bretagne 17 March 1788 which became the 10th Chasseurs à Cheval 1 January 1791, adjutant 1 September 1791.

He became lieutenant 1 September 1792, aide de camp to General de Chastellet 1 April 1793, captain 15 May 1793, deputy to the adjutant-generals of the Army of the North 1 September 1793, adjutant-general, acting brigade commander 29 September 1793, chief of staff of the Fromentin Division 19 April 1794

then of the Kléber Division 3 June 1794, in the Army of the Sambre-et-Meuse 2 July 1794, i/c of remounts in the same army at the Verdun Depot 28 October 1794, confirmed 13 June 1795, employed in the Line in the same army 28 July 1795, resigned for health reasons 4 October 1796, remained in the army carrying on with his functions temporarily, kept on the active list at the disposition of the Inspector General of Cavalry of the Army of the Sambre-et-Meuse 24 March 1797.

He was in the Army of Germany 20 October 1797, chief of staff of the Cavalry Division of the Army of Mainz 16 December 1797, in the Army of the Danube 7 March 1799, suspended by Jourdan for disobedience 28 April 1799, put back in service by him in the Army of the Rhine 3 September 1799, in the reserve 11 May 1800, then in Army of Italy 4 July 1800, employed in the Cisalpine Republic 2 July 1801, adjutant-commandant chief of the staff of the Pully Cuirassier Division 2 December 1805, then of the 3rd Dragoon Division 31 December 1806, in the Army of Spain 7 September 1808, in the 4th Corps of the Army of the Midi in Spain May 1810.

He became brigadier-general 30 December 1810, commanded the brigade of Light Cavalry of the 4th Corps 1 September 1811, governor of Jaen and CO of the 2nd Brigade of the 3rd Division on the same day 7 February 1812, commanded the 2nd Brigade of the 2nd Cavalry Division of the Army of the Pyrenees 16 July 1813, left for champagne with his division 16 January 1814, wounded by Biscayan shot at Bar-sur-Aube 27 February 1814, on half-pay 15 June 1814, at the Remount Depot of the Army of the Rhine and the Moselle 18 May 1815, non-active 30 August 1815, retired 18 October 1815.

LH CH 18 September 1808, Baron of the Empire d. 28 October 1808 and l.p. 25 May 1811.

ORMANCEY (François Louis Bernard, 1789-?): son of the general, born in Colmar (Haut-Rhin) on 20 April 1789.

Volunteer in the 4th Cuirassiers 1 October 1806, brigadier-fourrier 15 October 1806, maréchal des logis 1 November 1806, sabre wound to his face at Heilsberg 10 June 1807.

He was sub-lieutenant 25 June 1807, lieutenant 3

July 1809, wounded and his horse killed under him at Wagram 6 July 1809, captain 5 September 1813, dismissed 21 December 1815. LH CH 27 December 1814, confirmed 11 April 1815.

OS (van, ?-?): sub-lieutenant 4 April 1807, in the suite of the 14th Cuirassiers 1 November 1810, appointed 26 December 1811. He was lieutenant 19 November 1812, in the 4th Hussars 25 November 1813, left and went home 15 December 1813.

OSSONCE (Jean Baptiste, 1771-?): born in Vitry-sur-Marne (Marne) on 21 July 1771. In the 20th Cavalry 21 July 1793, in the Gardes à Cheval of the Directoire 21 December 1796, incorporated into the Grenadiers à Cheval of the Consular Guard 3 January 1800, brigadier same day, maréchal des logis 22 December 1805, lieutenant in the 8th Cuirassiers 17 February 1811, bayonet wound to his right thigh in front of Moscow 4 October 1812.

He was captain 5 June 1813, detached with his squadron to the 2nd Provisional Heavy cavalry in Hamburg 11 September 1813, returned with the garrison May 1814, dismissed with the corps 5 December 1815 and put up for retirement 11 December 1815. LH CH 14 March 1806.

OUDIOT (Edme Michel, 1750-1807): born in Passy (Aube) on 12 January 1750. Fusilier in the Roi-Infanterie 15 September 1770, left 25 September 1778, in the Colonel-General-Cavalerie 7 November 1778, brigadier 1 September 1784, maréchal des logis 1 March 1787, He was in the same regiment when it became the 1st Cavalry 1 January 1791, adjutant sub-lieutenant 25 January 1792.

He was sub-lieutenant 17 April 1792, lieutenant 1 June 1793, shot and wounded near Maubeuge 15 June 1793, relieved of his command and accused of being an enemy of the Republic 16 September 1793, still detained 23 March 1794, reinstated in the suite of the corps 22 August 1796, appointed lieutenant 27 May 1797.

He became captain by seniority 29 April 1799, in the same regiment when it became the 1st Cuirassiers 10 October 1801, killed at Hoff 6 February 1807. LH CH 15 June 1804.

OUDRY (François, 1785-?): born in Villersexel (Eure) on 14 January 1785. In the 9th Cuirassiers December 1805, brigadier 1 January 1810, maréchal des logis 1812, sub-lieutenant 21 April 1813. He was in the King's Cuirassiers 1 July 1814 which became the 1st Cuirassiers again April 1815, captain by mistake 25 March 1815, rectified lieutenant 30 March 1815, in the 6th cuirassiers 23 May 1815, arrived 1 June 1815, admitted 65 June 1815, returned sub-lieutenant in the 1st Cuirassiers 24 September 1815 and arrived 27 September 1815. He was dismissed and put on half-pay 24 December 1815. LH CH 25 February 1814.

OULLEMBOURG see **DOULLEMBOURG**

PAER see **GROUT de SAINT PAER**

PAGANY (Antoine, 1791-?): born in Tortone (Genoa) on 11 June 1791. In the Gardes d'Honneur of Prince Borghese 6 June 1810, sub-lieutenant in the 7th Cuirassiers 15 March 1812.

He joined the war squadrons 12 June 1812, lieutenant 5 September 1813, captain 16 March 1814, returned home as a foreign national when the corps was disbanded 19 December 1815. LH CH 16 May 1813.

PAGE (Pierre, 1774-?): born in Goizan (Haute-Garonne) on 17 September 1774. In the Tarn Dragons 1 April 1794, incorporated with the corps into the 15th Dragoons 31 May 1794, brigadier 21 January 1800, maréchal des logis 24 September 1803, in the Dragoons of the Imperial Guard 25 June 1806, brigadier 13 July 1807, sub-lieutenant in the 8th Cuirassiers 15 February 1813.

He was incorporated with his squadron into the 2nd Provisional Heavy Cavalry in Hamburg 11 September 1813, lance wound to his head at Hamburg 14 March 1814, returned to France with the garrison 30 May 1814, wounded at Les Quatre-Bras 16 June 1815, dismissed with the corps 5 December 1815 and put up for retirement 11 December 1815.

PAGES (Jean Baptiste Adrien, 1789-1813): born in Riom (Puy-de-Dôme) on 11 June 1789. In the Gendarmes d'Ordonnance of the Guard 4 January 1807, prisoner at Colberg 20 March 1807, returned 18 September 1807.

He was dismissed with the corps 23 October 1807 and incorporated into the Dragoons of the Guard 24 November 1807, sub-lieutenant in the 7th Cuirassiers 3 June 1809, joined them 17 June 1809, lieutenant 12 July 1812, killed at Leipzig 16 October 1813. LH CH 14 May 1813.

PAGNY (Charles de, 1795-?): born in Ploppécourt (Moselle) on 30 January 1795. In the 2nd Gardes d'Honneur 2 June 1813, brigadier 15 January 1814, sub-lieutenant in the 6th Cuirassiers 1 August 1814, dismissed 21 November 1815.

PAIX see **COEUR DEPAIX de COEUR**

PALAMEDE de FORBIN de la BARBEN (?-?): maréchal des logis-chef in the Gendarmes d'Ordonnance 1 February 1807, first-lieutenant 22 March 1807, captain 1 April 1807, captain in the 26th Dragoons 16 July 1807, staff officer.

He became captain in the 4th Cuirassiers 10 February 1813, captain in the 4th Gardes d'Honneur 6 September 1813.

PAPERE (Nicolas, 1784-?): born in Nancy (Meurthe) on 12 April 1784. In the 23rd Cavalry 21 March 1799, dismissed with the corps 23 December 1802 and incorporated into the 5th Cuirassiers 3 January 1803.

He was brigadier-fourrier 22 March 1807, maréchal des logis-chef 16 May 1809, adjutant-NCO 18 April 1812, sub-lieutenant 8 July 1813, non-active on half-pay 23 December 1815.

PAPILIER (Alexis, 1769-?): born in Belleville (Meurthe) on 19 January 1769. In the 11th Cavalry 1 January 1794, brigadier 3 January 1798, in the same regiment when it became the 11th Cuirassiers 24 September 1803, maréchal des logis 1 December 1806.

He was wounded by a Biscayan shot in the neck at Eylau 8 February 1807, sub-lieutenant 16 May 1809, retired 1 December 1811. LH CH 14 April 1807.

PAQUE (Joseph Anne, 1752-?): born in Gacilly (Morbihan) on 5 April 1752. In the Artois-Cavalerie 2 January 1771, brigadier 16 December 1778, maréchal des logis 1 September 1784, in the same regiment when it became the 9th Cavalry 1 January 1791, maréchal des logis-chef 1 May 1791, adjutant 29 April 1792, lieutenant 1 April 1793, captain 11 November 1793.

He was wounded in the right leg and taken pri-

soner 8 August 1796, returned 1798, in the same regiment when it became the 9th Cuirassiers 24 September 1803, on retirement pay 2 July 1806.

PAQUELIN (Jean Baptiste, 1776-?): born in Beaune (Côte-d'Or) on 2 August 1776. In the 2nd Cuirassiers 29 April 1803, brigadier 4 August 1804, fourrier 1 January 1806, maréchal des logis 30 October 1806, maréchal des logis-chef 16 May 1807.

He became sub-lieutenant 14 May 1809, lieutenant 8 July 1813, lance wound to his right hand 9 February 1814, resignation accepted 17 January 1815, left 1 February 1815. LH CH 4 December 1813.

PAQUIN (Esprit Jacques Louis, 1779-?): born in Goupillière (Seine-Inférieure) on 19 May 1779. In the 19th Dragoons 14 September 1800, brigadier 31 December 1800, fourrier 31 August 1802, maréchal des logis 3 May 1803, maréchal des logis-chef 7 February 1805, in the Eure-et-Loire Gendarmerie 5 February 1811, in the 4th Cuirassiers 4 April 1813.

He was maréchal des logis-chef 16 May 1813, sub-lieutenant in the 12th Cuirassiers 22 May 1813, does not appear on the rolls as of 14 July 1814.

PARENT (Alexis, 1777-?): born in Lyon (Rhône) on 20 November 1777. In the 254th Chasseurs à cheval 20 November 1793, in the Chasseurs à Cheval of the Guard 9 November 1799, dismissed 7 September 1802, in the 8th Cuirassiers 14 November 1803, brigadier 15 October 1806, brigadier-fourrier 12 July 1807, maréchal des logis 21 February 1808, maréchal des logis-chef 9 August 1809, adjutant-NCO 12 September 1809, sub-lieutenant 1 June 1812.

He was lieutenant adjutant-major 8 July 1813, wounded by a Biscayan shot to his left side at Hanau 30 October 1813 and shot in the left leg at Paris 31 March 1814, rank of captain 8 January 1815, shot thought the body at Ligny 16 June 1815, dismissed with the corps 5 December 1815 and put up for retirement 11 December 1815. LH CH 28 September 1813

PARES (Philippe, 1780-?): born in 1780. In the 1st Cavalry 1797 which became the 1st Cuirassiers 10 October 1801, brigadier 19 August 1802, three bayonet wounds to his left fore-arm and right hip at Austerlitz 2 December 1803, maréchal des logis 18 January 1806, maréchal des logis-chef 1 October 1808.

He was sub-lieutenant 5 November 1811, had his left thigh torn off by a cannonball at Leipzig 18 October 1813, taken prisoner the following day 19 October 1813, returned 30 May 1814, retired on his pension 16 August 1814. LH CH 29 July 1814.

PARISET (Charles Joseph Augustin, 1794-?):

born in Saint-Dié (Vosges) on 18 June 1794. In the Ecole Spéciale Impériale de Cavalerie in Saint-Germain 7 December 1812, sub-lieutenant 30 March 1814, in the 11th Cuirassiers 12 June 1814, wounded at Waterloo 18 June 1815, resigned and struck off the rolls 11 October 1815.

PARMENTIER (Auguste Léonard, 1794-?): born in Phalsbourg (Moselle) on 28 March 1794. Pupil at the Ecole Spéciale Impériale de Cavalerie in Saint-Germain 14 November 1810, passed out 27 November 1810, sub-lieutenant in the 8th Cuirassiers 30 January 1813, in the 2nd Cuirassiers 16 August 1813, prisoner 20 November 1813.

he returned 1814, dismissed with the corps and put on the non-active list on half-pay 10 December 1815.

PARMENTIER (Hippolyte Hyacinthe, 1774-?): born in Bapeaume (Pas-de-Calais) on 27 September 1774. In the 24th Infantry 12 May 1791, in the 3rd Artillery 6 August 1793, in the 10th Chasseurs à Cheval 1799, in the Grenadiers à Cheval of the Guard 23 April 1802, brigadier 16 February 1807, maréchal des logis 20 November 1811, in the Grenadiers à cheval of the King's Household 7 August 1814, sous-brigadier and rank of sub-lieutenant 12 November 1814, returned to the Grenadiers à Cheval of the Imperial Guard 1 April 1815, confirmed sub-lieutenant in the cavalry 22 April 1815, in the suite of the 4th Cuirassiers 54 May 1815, non-active on half-pay 24 August 1815. LH CH 14 March 1806.

PARQUIN (Denis Charles, 1786-1845): the famous memoirist, born in Paris (Seine) on 20 December 1786. Volunteer in the 20th Chasseurs à cheval 1 January 1803, brigadier 25 October 1803, instated 2 May 1804, temporary brigadier-fourrier December 1805, confirmed in the Elite Company 1 May 1806, wounded and stuck under

Parquin at the time he was an officer in the Chasseurs à cheval of the Guard. *(RR)*

his horse which had been shot under him and five lance wounds of which one to his hip, taken prisoner near Königsberg 16 February 1807, left for France 15 September 1807.

He returned to the regiment 15 October 1807, instated 8 November 1807, maréchal des logis 2 February 1809, instated 29 February 1809, sub-lieutenant 30 April 1809, shot and wounded in the left arm at Amstetten 6 May 1809, commanded the stronghold of Oldenburg from 7 to 28 June 1809, sub-adjutant-major July 1810, shot in the face (which cost him six teeth) at Fuentes d'Oñoro 5 May 1811, ordnance on Marmont's staff July 1811, incorporated with two squadrons of his regiment into the 13th Chasseurs à Cheval 5 December 1811.

He was captured a Portuguese flag at Mondego 12 April 1812, sabre wound to his wrist at Los Arapiles 22 July 1812, lieutenant 27 February 1813, second-lieutenant in the chasseurs à cheval of the Guard (Old Guard) 10 March 1813, bayonet wound to his right eyebrow at Hanau 30 October 1813, captain (Young Guard) 21 December 1813, lance wound to his left arm at Oulchy-le-Château near Soissons 2 March 1814, captain in the 5th Cuirassiers 4 June 1814, in the 11 Cuirassiers 18 June 1814.

He was commissioned 19 June 1814, in the 2nd Chasseurs à Cheval of the Guard 25 May 1815, instated 13 June 1815, dismissed and non-active 3 November 1815, left 8 November 1815. LH CH 6 April 1813.

PASCAL (Louis, 1772-1812): born in Versailles (Seine-et-Oise) on 29 June 1772. In the 8 Cuirassiers 1 April 1803, brigadier 13 May 1813, maréchal des logis 1 June 1806, maréchal des logis-chef 25 March 1807, adjutant-NCO 3 June 1809. He was sub-lieutenant 9 August 1809, remained behind and presumed dead at the Berezina 28 November 1812.

PASCARD (Jean Baptiste, ?-?): born in Achomply (Haute-Saône). In the 9th Pyrenees Chasseurs à Pied 29 April 1792, in the 13th Hussars 5 January 1796, dismissed with the corps and incorporated into the 7th bis Hussars 18 May 1796, in the Grenadiers à Cheval of the Guard 18 June 1802, brigadier 1 January 1810.

He was maréchal des logis 27 November 1811, in the Grenadiers à Cheval of the King's Household 7 August 1814, sous-brigadier with rank of sub-lieutenant 12 November 1814, entered on the rolls of the Grenadiers à Cheval of the Imperial Guard 1 April 1815, confirmed as sub-lieutenant 22 April 1815, in the 3rd Cuirassiers 5 May 1815, instated 21 May 1815, left 1 September 1815. LH CH 1 August 1805.

PATIGNIEZ (Jean, 1770-after 1828): born in Jambles (Saône-et-Loire) on 17 September 1770. In the 20th Cavalry 17 November 1798, captured the correspondence of the Vendéens together with an officer at the Chateau of La-

ATZIUS (Jean Charles, 1766-1834): born in Vauvilliers (Haute-Saône) on 11 October 1766. Adjutant in the 3rd Haute-Saône Battalion 22 October 1791, sub-lieutenant in the 20th Cavalry 17 June 1792, quartermaster treasurer 1 May 1793.

He was in the same regiment when it became the 19th Cavalry 4 June 1793, lieutenant in a company 16 November 1793, left to carry orders to General Duvignau.

He was elected captain 19 June 1799.

He was dismissed with the regiment 31 December 1802 and incorporated into the 9th cavalry 15 February 1803 which then became the 9th Cuirassiers 24 September 1803, squadron commander on the battlefield 14 May 1809, captured 13 carriages, 53 horses and a few prisoners with his squadron near Regensburg 23 May 18109, deputy 1st Class to the Inspectors of Parades in Hamburg 22 June 1811.

He was in the Army of the Midi in Spain 1 September 1809, Sub-Inspector of Parades 3rd Class 7 February 1812, prisoner when Badajoz was captured 7 April 1812, returned from English prisons 29 May 1814, active again to organise the 4 Royal Regiments of French Cavalry 26 June 1814, in the 6th Military Division 2 September 1814, in the 12th Military Division 30 August 1815 then the 21st 22 September 1815.

Holder of a Sabre of Honour 15 September 1802, LH CH by rights 24 September 1803, O 14 June 1804.

Having gone off to carry orders to General Duvignau, Lieutenant Patzius managed to escape with his ordnance from Waldeck's Hussars and the peasants who were chasing him by swimming across the Mein, joining his division which had withdrawn to Russelsheim on 8 September 1796.

On 3 December 1799, at Wisloch, having been made a captain, he was shot and wounded in the right hip and his horse killed under him. He continued to fight in foot, containing and stopping twenty troopers, saving Decaen's division.

Chaud 4 and 5 February 1800, captured a canon at Marengo 14 June 1800, dismissed with the corps and incorporated into the Grenadiers à Cheval of the Guard 12 February 1803, brigadier 1 August 1806, maréchal des logis 1 December 1808, lieutenant in the 12th Cuirassiers 28 November 18113, dismissed and non-active on half-pay 212 November 1815. Holder of a Musket of Honour 8 February 1800, commissioned 30 May 1803, LH CH by rights 24 September 1803.

PATUREL see **LARIVIERE** aka **PATUREL**

PATZIUS (Stéphanus, 1779-?): born in 1779. In the 19th Cavalry 21 August 1799, brigadier 22 November 1800, maréchal des logis 13 April 1802, assigned to the riding school in Versailles from 14 August 1803, incorporated into the 9th Cuirassiers but kept in Versailles 24 September 1803, returned 12 August 1805, maréchal des logis-chef 1 November 1806, adjutant- NCO 4 April 1807, sub-lieutenant 14 May 1809, lieutenant 11 March 1812.

He became captain 14 May 1813, shell burst wound to his left cheek at Leipzig 18 October 1813, captain adjutant-major of the Cuirassiers du Roi when they were formed 1 July 1814, squadron commander 25 March 1815.

He was in the same regiment when it became the 1st Cuirassiers again April 1815, wounded at Waterloo 18 June 1815, retired because of his wounds 24 December 1815. LH CH 1 October 1807.

PAULTRE de LAMOTTE (Pierre Louis François, baron, 1774-1840): born in Saint-Sauveur (Yonne) on 3 February 1774.

Sub-lieutenant in the 24th Infantry 12 January 1792, lieutenant 1 October 1792, aide de camp to General Hédouville 22 March 1793, returned to his regiment September 1793, captain 25 May 1794, in the same regiment when it became the 47th Half-Brigade 21 June 1795, aide de camp to Hédouville 13 December 1795, in the Army of the West and then of the Côtes de l'Océan, on Hoche's expedition to Ireland December 1796, acting battalion commander 19 February 1798, in Saint Domingo 1798, confirmed 19 October 1799, squadron commander 17 February 1800.

He was in the suite of the 7th Dragoons but still keeping his functions as aide de camp 23 February 1800, entrusted with several diplomatic missions with Hédouville, major in the 12th Chasseurs à Cheval 15 December 1803, colonel of the 9th Cuirassiers 31 December 1806, shell burst wound to his left leg at Wagram 6 July 1809, brigadier-general 6 August 1811, in Cologne 19 October 1811, commanded the 2nd Brigade of the 4th Cuirassier Division 25 December 1811, then in the brigade formed by the 1st Cuirassiers in the same division in the 2nd Reserve Cavalry Corps of the Grande Armée 15 February 1812, dismissed and returned to France for health reasons January 1813, commanded a brigade of the 2nd Marching Division of the 1st Cavalry Corps 8 May 1813, commanded the mass levy in the Marne Department 15 January 1814, available 9 March 1814.

He was lieutenant in the Gardes du Corps du Roi 1 June 1814, followed Louis XVIII to the frontier in 1815 and did not serve during the Hundred Days, commanded a company of the Gardes du Corps 1 November 1815. LH CH 25 March 1804, O 11 July 1807, C 17 August 1814, GO 31

October 1815, Baron of the Empire d. 17 March 1808 and l.p. 15 October 1809.

PAYARD (François Eugène, 1785-?): born in Saint-Dizier (Haute-Marne) on 10 July 1785. In the 26th Dragoons 11 August 1802, in the Dragoons of the Imperial Guard 20 June 1808, fourrier 9 December 1810, sub-lieutenant in the 6th Cuirassiers 15 March 1812, lieutenant 6 October 1813, shot and wounded in the shoulder and his horse killed under him at Leipzig 18 October 1813

He became adjutant-major 21 December 1813, two sabre and two lance wounds and his horse killed under him at Ligny 16 June 1815, rank of captain 21 June 1815, dismissed 21 November 1815. LH CH 4 December 1813.

PEDEZERT (Jean, 1773-?): born in Mauléon (Basses-Pyrénées) on 11 June 1773. In the 3rd Basses-Pyrénées Battalion 17 October 1791, in the 12th Hussars 5 December 1793, brigadier 3 June 1796, maréchal des logis 21 May 1800, gendarme à cheval in the 9th Gendarmerie Legion 27 August 1800, brigadier in the 1st Squadron of the Gendarmerie d'Espagne 1 March 1810, maréchal des logis in the 1st Legion of the Gendarmerie à Cheval d'Espagne "Burgos" 20 November 1811.

He was dismissed with the legion 27 February, promoted to lieutenant in the 10th Cuirassiers the following day 28 February 1813, non-active and not included in the new organisation of 6 August 1814.

PELLAPRA (Louis Joseph, 1785-?): born in Montélimar (Drôme) on 24 June 1785. In the 11th Cuirassiers 19 April 1805, brigadier 14 May 1805, maréchal des logis 20 May 1805, sub-lieutenant in the 10th Cuirassiers 12 September 1806, wounded at Hoff 6 February 1807, lieutenant 25 May 1807, shot and wounded in his left hand and a bayonet wound in his right leg at Essling 21 May 1809, captain 6 November 1811, discharged without pay 29 May 1813, left 25 June 18113. LH CH 1 October 1807.

PELLECHET (Alexandre Pierre, 1778-1814): born in Versailles (Seine-et-Oise) on 30 May 1778. In Bonaparte's Guides 15 April 1798, brigadier-fourrier 28 June 1799, in the Grenadiers à Cheval of the Consular Guard 3 January 1800, maréchal des logis-chef 15 October 1802, sub-lieutenant in the 4th Cuirassiers 3 August 1805, lieutenant 21 April 1807, captain 3 June 1809, wounded in Russia 18121, killed during the second attack on Compiègne during the defence of Paris 1 April 1814. LH CH 8 October 1811, O 5 September 1813.

ETIT (Louis Victor, 1775-?): born in Quintray (Haute-Saône) on 8 April 1775. In the gendarmerie corps organised in Tours 10 July 1793,.

He was a gendarme in Gray's brigade 19 July 1794, in the 1st Cavalry 20 December 1798, rejoined his unit 7 March 1799, sabre wound to his neck at la Trebbia 20 June 1799, brigadier 9 April 1800, fourrier 14 April 1800, in the same regiment when it became the 1st Cuirassiers 10 October 1801.

He was maréchal des logis 20 June 1802, maréchal des logis-chef 3 April 1804, captured a howitzer single-handed after killing or wounding several servers at Austerlitz, elected sub-lieutenant 31 December 1805, confirmed 6 January 1806, lieutenant 20 February 1807, instated 23 February 1807, adjutant-major 25 May 1807.

He obtained the rank of captain 25 November 1808, captured a standard at Eckmühl 22 April 1809, captain 16 May 1809, shot and wounded in the left shoulder at Essling 22 May 1809, wounded at Winkovo 18 October 1812, retired 21 October 1813. LH CH 1 October 1807.

Maréchal des logis chef Louis Petit of the 1st Cuirassiers distinguished himself at Austerlitz on 2 December 1805. Alone he took a howitzer after killing or wounding several gunners. Four years later, with the rank of captain, he captured an Austrian standard at Eckmühl on 22 April 1809. He was shot and wounded in the left shoulder at Essling on the following 22 May.

PERRAUD (Jean Pierre Marie de, 1786-?): in 1st Cuirassiers 31 October 1803, brigadier 16 December 1805, maréchal des logis 16 November 1806, adjudant- NCO 3 June 1809, sub-lieutenant 5 November 1811.

He became lieutenant 14 November 1813, non-active on half-pay 1 October 1814, returned to the regiment 1 April 1815, on half-pay again 1 September 1815. LH CH 16 June 1809.

PERRIER (Auguste Louis Henry, 1789-?): born in Valence (Drôme) on 13 June 1789. Maréchal des logis in the Drôme Gardes d'Honneur à Cheval 15 June 1806, sub-lieutenant 2 January 1807, eagle-bearer 2 March 1808, sub-lieutenant in the team assembly park in Danzig 17 December 1811, quartermaster 8 August 1813, lieutenant commanding a company attached to the same park 6 September 1813, acting lieutenant for a provisional cavalry regiment, took up his post in the 6th Cuirassiers 26 December 1813.

He was prisoner with the garrison 1 January 1814, returned 3 September 1814, confirmed in the suite of the 6th Cuirassiers and commissioned 6 December 1814, took up his appointment 19 May 1815, dismissed 21 November 1815.

PERRIN (Jacques, 1775-1809): born in Saint-Marcel (Isère) on 3 January 1775. In the 5th Cavalry 9 May 1793, fourrier 18 August 1798, maréchal des logis 22 March 1800, maréchal des logis-chef 21 April 1800, in the same regiment when it became the 5th Cuirassiers 23 December 1802.

He was sub-lieutenant 30 December 1802, lieutenant by seniority 2 December 1805, captain 23 February 1807, killed at Essling 22 May 1809.

PERRIN DESISLES (?-1812): Velite in the Grenadiers à Cheval of the Imperial Guard, sub-lieutenant in the suite of the 5th Cuirassiers 13 July 1807, took up his appointment 24 April 1808, lieutenant in the suite 6 November 1811, in post 21 February 1812, killed at Winkovo 18 October 1812.

PERRON (?-1809): maréchal des logis in the 8th Cuirassiers, sub-lieutenant in the 6th Cuirassiers 22 June 1809, wounded at Wagram 6 July 1809 and died of his wounds 11 July 1809.

PERROTET (Jean Baptiste, 1783-?): born in Sercey-le-Grand (Haute-Saône) on 10 April 1783. In the 12th Cavalry 28 April 1802 which became the 12th Cuirassiers 24 September 1803, brigadier 1 July 1806, maréchal des logis 1 December 1806, shot and wounded in his leg at Wagram 6 July 1809.

He was adjutant-NCO 21 April 1812, lance wound to his side at Toloschinn 21 November 1812, sub-lieutenant 8 July 1813, struck of the rolls 1 April 1815 because AWOL.

PERROTET (Joseph, 1772-1808): born in Sercey-le-Grand (Haute-Saône) on 7 September 1772. In the Dauphin-Cavalerie 1 May 1790 which became the 12th Cavalry 1 January 1791, wounded after having two horses killed under him 17 May 1793, fourrier 1 October 1793, maréchal des logis 14 September 1795, maréchal des logis-chef 16 April 1798, adjutant-NCO 30 December 1801, in the same regiment when it became the 12th Cuirassiers 24 September 1803, sub-lieutenant 1 March 1804, lieutenant 31 October 1806, died 10 February 1808.

PERTHUIS (Alphonse Hippolyte de, 1793-?): born in Nandy (Seine-et-Marne) on 3 March 1793. One of the Emperor's pages 24 August 1808, sub-lieutenant in the suite of the 1st Cuirassiers 14 January 1811, in service 31 July 1811.

He was shot twice and wounded with a broken right arm at Hanau 30 October 1813, supernumerary lieutenant 5 February 1814, on 2 months' leave with pay 24 May 1814, remained in Paris at the disposal of the Minister of War 20 January 1815, returned to the corps 1 April 1815, first-lieutenant in the 1st Cuirassiers of the Garde Royale 1 December 1815. LH CH 28 Septmeber 1813.

PERTUS (Jean Baptiste, 1772-1812): born in Aurillac (Cantal) on 10 January 1772.

In the Beaujolais-Infanterie 21 May 1789 which became the 74th infantry 1 January 1791, in the Fabrefonds Eclaireurs 14 November 1792 which

became the 9th Hussars 26 February 1793 then the 8th Hussars 4 June 1793, maréchal des logis 7 May 1794, in the Cavalry of the Légion de Police 23 October 1795 which formed the 21st Dragoons.

He was elected maréchal des logis-chef 7 June 1797, dismissed with the corps and incorporated into the 2nd Dragoons 18 December 1797, in the Grenadiers à cheval of the Guard 24 April 1800, adjutant sub-lieutenant 17 June 1801, sub-lieutenant 13 December 1801.

He was second-lieutenant 23 September 1804, lieutenant in the Line 18 December 1805, in the suite of the 11th Cuirassiers 1 January 1806, in service in the 6th Cuirassiers 11 April 1806, captain in the 11th Cuirassiers 24 November 1806, disappeared during the rearguard fighting near the River Niemen 31 December 1812. LH CH 14 June 1804.

PETIT (Claude, 1764-?): born in Neuray (Haute-Saône) on 23 March 1794. In the Royal-Cavalerie 29 June 1783 when it became the 2nd Cavalry 1 January 1791, brigadier 11 January 1802.

He was in the same regiment when it became the 2nd Cuirassiers 12 October 1802, maréchal des logis April 1806, sub-lieutenant 14 May 1809, lieutenant 9 February 1813, retired 6 August 1814. LH CH 1 October 1807.

PETIT (Claude, 1784-?): born in Brabant (Meuse) on 24 September 1784. In the 5th Cavalry 16 April 1800 which became the 5th Cuirassiers 23 December 1802, brigadier 21 December 1802, maréchal des logis 7 February 1807, sub-lieutenant 13 August 1809, wounded at the Moskova 7 September 1812, Kaluga 4 October 1812 and Château-Thierry 14 March 1814, lieutenant 27 January 1815, dismissed 23 December 1815. LH CH 3 November 1814.

PETIT (François, 1764-1805): born in Saint-Sauveur (Haute-Saône) on 3 December 1764. In the Royal-Pologne-Cavalerie 29 January 1785 which became the 5th Cavalry 1 January 1791, fourrier 1 April 1793, maréchal des logis 9 May 1795, maréchal des logis-chef 24 January 1796, adjutant-NCO 22 March 1800, sub-lieutenant 11 February 1802, in the same regiment when it became the 5th Cuirassiers 23 December 1802, killed at Austerlitz 2 December 1805.

PETIT (Jean Marie Ambroise, 1787-?): born in 1787. In the 3rd Cuirassiers 29 January 1807, brigadier 25 June 1807, maréchal des logis 1 September 1808, maréchal des logis-chef 5 June 1809.

He was adjutant-NCO 1812, sub-lieutenant 8 July 1813, wounded at Leipzig 18 October 18113, in the Cuirassiers du Roi when they were set up 1 July 1814, obtained two months' leave 28 January 1815, arrested 16 May 1815, in the 1st Cuirassiers of the Garde Royale 1 December 1815. LH CH 4 December 1813.

ETITPAS (Joseph, 1770-1807): born in Conantre (Marne) on 12 October 1770. In the Volontaires Nationaux à Cheval from the Ecole Militaire 3 September 1792.

He was fourrier 1 February 1793, in the same regiment when it became the 26th Cavalry 21 February 1793, maréchal des logis 1 April 1793, in the same regiment when it became the 25th Cavalry 4 June 1793, maréchal des logis-chef 8 January 1794, adjutant sub-lieutenant 9 February 1794.

He was assigned to the Versailles Riding School 1799, returned 1800, sub-lieutenant 22 November 1800, lieutenant 7 April 1802.

He was dismissed with the corps 12 October 1802 and incorporated into the 4th Cuirassiers 24 November 1802, lieutenant adjutant-major 8 April 1807, killed at Heilsberg 10 June 1807. LH CH 1805.

Near Marseilles on 27 March 1794, Adjutant Sous-Lieutenant Joseph Petipas of the 26th Cavalry was wounded by a shell burst.

He continued his fight however and defended himself against four enemy soldiers, wounding two of them and taking the other two prisoner.

PETIT (Louis Marie, 1786-?): born in Paris (Seine) on 30 August 1786. In the 12th Dragoons 1 November 1806, brigadier 20 April 1810, in the Dragoons of the Imperial Guard 2 July 1812, sub-lieutenant in the 11th Cuirassiers 8 February 18113, dismissed with the corps 16 December 1815.

PETIT de MONTFLEURY
see **LEPETIT de MONTFLEURY**

PETITFILS (Nicolas François, 1780-?): born in Reims (Marne) on 2 July 1780. In the 8th Cavalry 27 July 1799 which became the 8th Cuirassiers 10 October 1801, brigadier-fourrier 12 April 1802, maréchal des logis 15 October 1806, maréchal des logis-chef 9 August 1809, sub-lieutenant 12 September 1809.

He was incorporated with his squadron into the 2nd Provisional Heavy Cavalry in Hamburg 11 September 1813, returned with the garrison 30 May 1814, wounded at les Quatre-Bras 16 June 1815, dismissed with the corps 5 December 1815 and non-active on half-pay 11 December 1815.

PETITJEAN (Jean, 1774-?): born in Dieppe (Meuse) on 17 February 1774. In the 43rd Half-Brigade 12 March 1792, in the 4th Cavalry 2 February 1794, brigadier 19 February 1799, fourrier on the following day 20 February 1799, maréchal des logis 15 July 1800, in the same regiment when it became the 4th Cuirassiers 12

October 1802, maréchal des logis-chef 27 December 1802, adjudant-NCO 1 December 1806 and instated 9 January 1807.

He was sub-lieutenant 21 April 1807, wounded at Heilsberg 10 June 1807, supernumerary lieutenant 7 April 1809, took up his appointment 22 May 1809, adjudant-major 12 September 1809, rank of captain 12 March 1811, went over to a company by exchanging with Captain Beauchamp 25 May 1812, retired 21 December 1815. LH CH 1 October 1807.

PETITJEAN (Nicolas, 1768-1808): born in Pont-Saint-Vincent (Meurthe) on 6 January 1768. Trooper in the Artois Regiment 18 December 1785 which became the 9th Cavalry 1 January 1791, brigadier 29 April 1792, maréchal des logis 12 December 1795, sub-lieutenant 8 June 1803.

He was in the same regiment when it became the 9th Cuirassiers 24 September 1803, lieutenant 3 April 1807, seconded to the 2nd Provisional Heavy Cavalry in Spain December 1807, wounded at Baylen 16 July 1808 and died of his wounds 3 November 1808.

PETITOT (Germain François, 1767-1815): born in Magny-les-Jussey (Haute-Saône) on 21 August 1767. In the Royal-Cavalerie 15 March 1786 which became the 2nd Cavalry 1 January 1791, brigadier 9 July 1791, maréchal des logis 1 April 1793, maréchal des logis-chef 11 September 1793, sub-lieutenant 18 August 1799.

He was elected lieutenant in the suite 23 June 1800, in post 25 May 1801, in the same regiment when it became the 2nd Cuirassiers 12 October 1802, two sabre wounds to his face, one on the hand and two on his neck at Edisheim 14 July 1804, captain 30 October 1806.

He was squadron commander 1 April 1813, intended to be incorporated with his squadron in the 1st Provisional Heavy Cavalry in Hamburg June 1813, in the 2nd Provisional Heavy Cavalry in Hamburg 3 July 1813, returned with the garrison 30 May 1814, put in the 2nd Cuirassiers, wounded at Waterloo 18 June 1815 and died of his wounds 29 August 1815. LH CH 1 October 1807, O 29 September 1814.

PEUMARTIN (Barthélémy, 1791-?): born in Saint-Etienne (Loire) on 1 November 1791. Volunteer in the Dragoons of the Imperial Guard 1 June 1811, shot and wounded in his leg and sabre wound in Russia 1812, sub-lieutenant in the 3rd Cuirassiers 13 March 1813, went and joined irregular forces 1815, dismissed with the 3rd Cuirassiers 25 November 1815.

PETOT (Clément, 1758-) born in Nicey (Côte-d'Or) on 9 April 1758. In the Royal-Etranger-Cavalerie 1 March 1777, brigadier 6 September

1784, brigadier-fourrier in the same regiment when it became the 7th Cuirassiers on the same day 1 January 1791, maréchal des logis 1 April 1792.

He was maréchal des logis-chef 10 May 1792, wounded and prisoner at Neerwinden 18 March 1793, returned 23 November 1795, sub-lieutenant 7 May 1793, lieutenant by seniority 20 January 1799, instated the day after (22 January 1799), commissioned 11 March 1799, three lance wounds and taken prisoner 29 November 1800, returned 14 February 1801, in the same regiment when it became the 7th Cuirassiers 23 December 1802, captain by seniority 1 August 1806, retired 11 March 1807, left 12 April 1807. LH CH 22 June 1805.

PFISTER (François Joseph, 1769-?): born in Dannemarie (Haut-Rhin) on 26 November 1769. In the 12th Cavalry 3 September 1792, brigadier-fourrier 11 August 1798, maréchal des logis 17 December 1798, maréchal des logis-chef 14 January 1799, sub-lieutenant 30 June 1804.

He was lieutenant 30 October 1806, wounded by a Biscayan shot to his foot and leg at Friedland 14 June 1807, captain 11 November 1811, wounded in the head at Waterloo 18 June 1815, dismissed with the corps 10 December 1815.

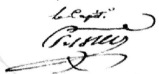

PICARD (Adrien, 1768-1809): born in Saint-Valuval (Seine) in 1768. In the 25th Cavalry 24 May 1799, brigadier 25 August 1802, dismissed

with the corps 12 October 1802 and incorporated into the 2nd Cuirassiers 24 November 1802, fourrier 23 September 1804.

He was maréchal des logis 20 November 1806, sub-lieutenant 14 May 1809, wounded at Essling 22 May 1809 and at Wagram 6 July 1809, died of his wounds 24 July 1809.

PICARD (Charles Auguste, 1776-?): born in Villevinar (Marne) on 6 January 1776. In the 6th Cavalry 19 June 1799 which became the 6th Cuirassiers 23 December 1802, brigadier 1 October 1806.

He was maréchal des logis 16 September 1809, sub-lieutenant 3 September 1813, standard-bearer 1 August 1814, dismissed 21 November 1815. LH CH 5 September 1813.

PICARD (Nicolas Marie Hilaire, 1780-1862): born in Paris (Seine) on 10 December 1780. In the 1st Cavalry 23 August 1801 which became the 1st Cuirassiers 10 October 1801, fourrier 20 June 1802, maréchal des logis-chef 21 January 1804.

He was sub-lieutenant 25 May 1807, lieutenant 16 May 1809, wounded at Essling 22 May 1809, aide de camp to General Berckheim his former colonel 19 July 1809, captain 14 May 1813, non-active on half-pay 31 December 1815. LH CH 1 October 1807, O.

PICOT (Pierre Jean François, 1772-?): born in Falaise (Calvados) on 28 July 1772.

He was in the Commissaire-Général-Cavalerie 15 September 1790 which became the 3rd Cavalry 1 January 1791, right foot hurt when

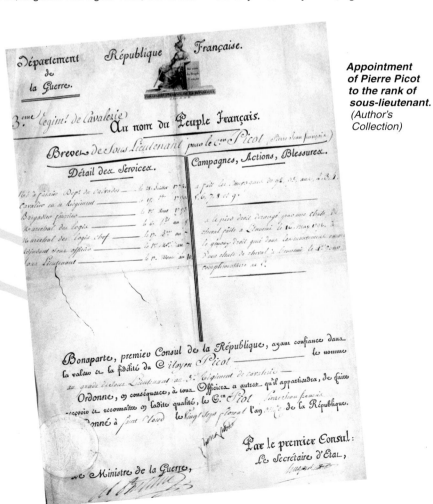

Appointment of Pierre Picot to the rank of sous-lieutenant.
(Author's Collection)

LANÇON (François, 1764 -after 1840): born in Nancray (Doubs) on 16 January 1764.

In the Carabiniers de Monsieur 19 December 1788, sabre wound to his right wrist at Lunéville during the Nancy Affair 15 August 1790, in the same regiment when it formed the 2nd Carabiniers 1 January 1791, two sabre wounds to his head and one to his right hand at Moesskirch 14 September 1792, brigadier 9 January 1794, maréchal des logis 2 September 1794, with his platoon captured a canon and two caissons at Boxtel 14 September 1794, brought his seriously wounded sub-lieutenant back on his horse to safety at Petersheim 10 November 1795, with 6 Carabiniers disengaged forty volunteers who were about to be captured at Ulm 18 September 1796.

He was sub-lieutenant by choice 16 September 1799, after crossing the Danube the first to enter Lanningen taking a great number of prisoners he himself having been shot and wounded in the left arm near Hochstaedt 19 June 1800, elected lieutenant 9 May 1800, wounded and his horse killed under him at Austerlitz 2 December 1805, captain in the 4th Cuirassiers 10 July 1806, unhorsed and three lance wounds to his head, his right side and left arm and taken prisoner after having captured three cannon at the head of his squadron at Heilsberg 10 June 1807, returned 1807, cannonball wound to his left heel, his horse also killed under him at Essling 21 May 1809.

He was wounded by a Biscayan shot to his left arm at Wagram 6 July 1809, squadron commander 12 September 1809, put to flight a column of 2 000 men with two squadrons near the Drissa 11 August 1812, with his squadron recaptured 14 cannon from the Russian Imperial Guard and had his horse killed under him at Polotsk 18 August 1812.

He became major in the suite 21 August 1812, in service 19 November 1812, one of the first soldiers in the division to break through the Russian ranks by charging at them and his horse killed under him at the Berezina 29 November 1812, confirmed as major of the Cuirassiers d'Angoulême 28 September 1814 which became the 4th Cuirassiers again in April 1815, retired 21 December 1815. LH CVH 18 December 1803, O 17 June

François Plançon's service record is a long list of brilliant military feats. On 14 September 1794 at Boxtel, Maréchal des Logis in the 2nd Carabiniers, he took a canon and two caissons with his platoon. On 10 November 1795 at Petersheim, he brought back his seriously wounded Sous-Lieutenant. At Ulm, on 18 September 1796 with six carabiniers he disengaged forty volunteers who were about to be captured. On 19 June 1800, near Hochstaedt, he crossed the Danube and was the first to enter Lanningen taking a large number of prisoners although he himself was shot and wounded in his left arm. He was a lieutenant at that moment.

At Austerlitz he was wounded and his horse killed under him. Promoted to captain in the 4th Cuirassiers, he was unhorsed and wounded by three lance wounds to his head, his right side and left arm, and was taken prisoner after having taken three cannon at the head of his squadron at Heilsberg on 10 June 1807. As Squadron Commander he put to flight a column of 2 000 men with two squadrons at Drissa on 11 August 1812, then recaptured fourteen guns with his squadron off the Russian Imperial Guard, had his horse killed under him at Polotsk on 18 August 1812.

He was promoted to Major three days later. At the Berezina on 29 November 1812, he was one of the first in his division to enter the Russian ranks charging. His horse was killed under him.

his horse fell in front of the enemy 16 May 1792, brigadier-fourrier 1 August 1793, maréchal des logis 25 May 1797, knee hurt when he fell from his horse again in front of the enemy 20 September 1797, maréchal des logis-chef 7 November 1798, adjutant-NCO 19 June 1799.

He was sub-lieutenant 7 January 1802, in the same regiment when it became the 3rd Cuirassiers 12 October 1802, commissioned sub-lieutenant 17 May 1803, elected lieutenant 9 November 1803, commissioned 6 February 1804, captain 30 October 1806, retired 11 July 1811 and left 10 August 1811.

PICQUANT (Jean Baptiste Alexis Charles Hubert, 1785-?): born in Thiaucourt (Meurthe) on 29 October 1785. In the 11th Cuirassiers 21 April 1805, brigadier 26 July 1806, fourrier 1 December 1806, maréchal des logis-chef 16 May 1809, adjutant-NCO 8 June 1809.

He was sub-lieutenant 25 September 1812, incorporated with his squadron into the 3rd Provisional Heavy Cavalry in Hamburg 11 September 1813, returned with the garrison May 1814, resignation accepted 25 February 1815. LH CH 16 June 1809.

PIEFFORT (Florimond Jules Hippolyte, 1785-1813): born in Paris (Seine) on 29 April 1785. In the Ecole Spéciale Impériale Militaire in Fontainebleau October 1803, sub-lieutenant in the 11th Cuirassiers 1805, instated 22 January 1805, bayonet wound to his left hand at Austerlitz 2 December 1805.

He was lieutenant 24 November 1806, sabre wound to his left shoulder at Eylau 8 February 1807, captain in the 1st Cuirassiers 27 March 1809, died at Kustrin 22 January 1813, admitted into the Imperial Guard 18 February 1813.

PIERRE (François Claude, 1775-?): born in Fuland (Haut-Rhin) in 1775. In the 2nd Cavalry 28 December 1793, brigadier 15 June 1800, fourrier 21 April 1802, in the same regiment when it became the 2nd Cuirassiers 12 October 1802.

He was maréchal des logis-chef 20 November 1806, adjutant-NCO 14 May 1809, sub-lieutenant 12 March 1812, dismissed with the regiment and left with his pension 10 December 1815.

PIERRE (Jean, baron, 1773-1825): born in Lunéville (Meurthe) on 20 January 1773. In the Volontaires Nationaux à Cheval from the Ecole Militaire 11 September 1792 which formed the 26th Cavalry 21 February 1793 which became the 25th cavalry 4 June 1793, unhorsed at Tournai he continued the fight on foot killing two opponents 16 April 1794, three sabre wounds and his horse killed under him the follo-

wing day 17 April 1794, brigadier 8 July 1798, fourrier 10 October 1800, maréchal des logis 2 March 1802, maréchal des logis-chef 7 March 1802, dismissed with the corps 12 October 1802 and incorporated into the 3rd Cuirassiers 22 December 1802, adjutant-NCO 28 December 1803, elected sub-lieutenant 25 June 1806, lieutenant 25 June 1807, captain 14 May 1809, shot and wounded twice at the Moskova 7 September 1812, in the Escadron Sacré during the retreat December 1812, retired 25 November 1815. LH CH 6 February 1804, Baron of the Empire l.p. 14 May 1809.

PIERRE (Pierre, 1789-?): born in Fontenay (Calvados) on 11 July 1789. In the 5th Cuirassiers 21 May 1808, brigadier 11 September 1810, brigadier-fourrier 1 December 1810.

He was maréchal des logis 11 February 1812, maréchal des logis-chef 10 July 1813, adjutant-NCO 1 October 1813, sub-lieutenant in the suite 20 January 1815, commissioned 2 February 1815, dismissed 23 December 1815. LH CH 30 September 1814.

PIERREDON (Jean Pierre, 1775-?): born in Monaco (Alpes-Maritimes) on 17 November 1775. Child of the regiment in the Colonel-Général-Cavalerie 25 February 1787, enrolled in the same regiment 21 December 1790 which became the 1st Cavalry 1 January 1791.

He was shot and wounded in the right arm near Maubeuge 23 October 1793, brigadier 2 August 1799, fourrier 7 September 1799, maréchal des logis 14 April 1800, in the same regiment when it became the 1st Cuirassiers 10 October 1801, maréchal des logis-chef 22 November 1802, adjutant-NCO 25 April 1804.

A cannonball wound to his left thigh at Austerlitz 2 December 1805, sub-lieutenant 14 January 1806, lieutenant 3 April 1807, captain 25 May 1807, shot and wounded in the right knee at Essling 22 May 1809 and shot through his right arm at Leipzig 18 October 1813, in the Cuirassiers du Roi 1 July 1814 which became the 1st Cuirassiers again March 1815, dismissed and put up for retirement 24 December 1815. LH CH 14 April 1807.

PIERROT (?-?): brigadier in the Grenadiers à Cheval of the Imperial Guard, sub-lieutenant in the Line 23 October 1811

He was in the suite of the 3rd Cuirassiers 19 November 1811, in service 25 January 1812, dismissed and no longer appears on the rolls as of 20 August 1814.

Seal belonging to the 11th Cuirassier Regiment.
(Author's collection)

**Nicolas Pierrot, officer
in the 11th Cuirassier Regiment.**
(© Photo Jean-Louis Viau)

PIERROT aka **SARREBOURG** (Jean Nicolas Gabriel, 1759-?): born in Sarrebourg (Meurthe) on 13 September 1759. Trooper in the Royal-Cravates 9 August 1778, fourrier 6 September 1784, maréchal des logis-chef 30 October 1789, in the same regiment when it became the 10th Cavalry 1 January 1791. He was adjutant 15 September 1792, lieutenant 6 May 1795.

He was captain 21 April 1797, squadron commander 7 September 1799, surrounded by four Austrian cuirassiers but managed to break through after killing two of them by himself at Brackenheim 3 November 1799, in the same regiment when it became the 10th Cuirassiers 24 September 1803.

He was wounded at Hoff 6 February 1807, major in the suite 25 May 1807, took up his appointment 9 February

1808, left with his pension 6 November 1811. LH CH 15 June 1804.

On 3 September 1796, Jean Pierrot, called Sarrebourg, was a Lieutenant in the 10th Cavalry. At Wurtzburg, his horse was killed under him by a cannonball. The officer mounted the horse belonging to a dead trooper and returned to the fray.

Three years later, having become Squadron Commander, he was surrounded by four Austrian cuirassiers in the fighting around Brackenheim on 3 November 1799. He managed to get through them by killing two of them himself.

PIERROT (Nicolas, 1765-?): born in Pariede (Meuse) on 19 February 1765. In the Deux-Ponts-Dragons 19 July 1787 which became the Flanders Chasseurs à Cheval 17 March 1788 then the 3rd Chasseurs à Cheval 1 January 1791, left 30 November 1791.

He was in the Volontaires Nationaux à Cheval from the Ecole Militaire 4 September 1792, brigadier

January 1793, maréchal des logis when the 26th Cavalry was formed 21 February 1793, maréchal des logis-chef 5 September 1797, sub-lieutenant by seniority 12 August 1799, sabre wound to his left arm at Vieux-Brisach 5 January 1800, incorporated into the 3rd Cuirassiers 22 December 1802, lieutenant by seniority 28 January 1803, lieutenant of the veterans 23 January 1804.

PIERROT (Nicolas, 1784-?): born in Fressigny (Haute-Marne) on 8 March 1784. Velite in the Grenadiers à Cheval of the Guard 20 February 1806, sub-lieutenant in the 11th Cuirassiers 3 June 1809.

He was lieutenant 14 May 1813, wounded at Dresden 27 August 1813, captain 19 February 1814, in the suite 1 August 1814, dismissed with the corps 16 December 1815. LH CH 14 May 1813.

PIET (Bartholomus, 1770 - ?) born in Veelen (Meuse-Inférieure) on 25 August 1770. In the 1st Batavian Cavalry 15 August 1789, brigadier 4 November 1792, right hand wounded at Verwick near Lille, maréchal des logis in the 2nd Dutch Cuirassiers 28 February 1807 which became the 14th French Cuirassiers 18 August 1810.

He was sub-lieutenant 5 September 1813, dismissed with the corps and put in the 12th Cuirassiers 13 July 1814, returned home as a foreign national 23 September 1815.

PILLERAULT (Armand Louis, 1789-?): born in 1789. Brigadier 25 May 1809, fourrier 25 June 1809, maréchal des logis in the 13th Cuirassiers 5 September 1809, maréchal des logis-chef 1 July 1811, sub-lieutenant in the 1st Cuirassiers 12 June 1813, rejoined his unit 7 August 1813, non-active on half-pay 6 July 1814.

PINEAU (?-?): maréchal des logis in the Grenadiers à Cheval of the Guard, lieutenant in the Line 23 October 1811, in the suite of the 3rd Cuirassiers 19 November 1811, in service 21 February, wounded at Wurschen 21 May 1813, captain in the 13th Cuirassiers 21 April 1813.

He was remained in the 3rd Cuirassiers and promoted to captain 28 July 1813, incorporated with his squadron into the 1st Provisional Heavy Cavalry in Hamburg 11 September 1813, returned to France with the garrison 27 May 1814 and non-active, in service with the Cuirassiers du Dauphin 20 January 1815 which became the 3rd Cuirassiers again in April 1815 and dismissed with the corps 25 November 1815.

PIRONNEAU (François, 1774-?): born in Saumur (Maine-et-Loire) on 30 March 1774. In the 22nd Light Infantry 6 March 1793, in the 19th Dragoons 18 March 1794, brigadier 2 August 1795, maréchal des logis 19 July 1797, maréchal des logis-chef in the Imperial Gendarmerie 10 April 1798, lieutenant 12 July 1812.

He was captain in the 3rd Cuirassiers 21 February 1813, incorporated with his squadron into the 1st Provisional Heavy Cavalry Regiment in Hamburg 11 September 1813, returned with the garrison 27 May 1814 and put back in the 3rd Cuirassiers, dismissed with the regiment 25 November 1815.

PLIQUE (Claude Alexandre, 1773-?): born in Montier-en-Der (Haute-Marne) on 25 September 1773. In the 9th Cavalry 5 May 1793, fourrier 20 February 1802, in the same regiment when it became the 9th Cuirassiers 24 September 1803, sabre wound to his head at

Austerlitz 2 December 1805, maréchal des logis 13 December 1805, maréchal des logis-chef 1 November 1806, sub-lieutenant 14 May 1806, lieutenant 1 August 1812, dismissed with the corps 25 November 1815 and left with his pension 26 November 1815. LH CH 14 April 1807

PLIQUE (Louis Jean Baptiste, 1763-?): born in Vassy (Haute-Marne) on 7 November 1763. In the Colonel-Générale-Cavalerie 1 January 1781, brigadier 16 June 1785, maréchal des logis 8 September 1786, maréchal des logis-chef 1 June 1789, in the same regiment when it became the 1st Cavalry 1 January 1791, adjutant-NCO 25 January 1792, sub-lieutenant 17 April 1792.

He was lieutenant 1 June 1793, instated 4 June 1793, captain quartermaster-treasurer 16 September 1793, rank of squadron commander 17 July 1799, in the same regiment when it became the 1st Cuirassiers 10 October 1801, then the Cuirassiers du Roi 1 July 1814, then 1st Cuirassiers again April 1815, retired 24 December 1815. LH CH 15 June 1804.

PLUMEREL (Alexandre Charles, 1784-?): born in Neufchâteau (Vosges) on 9 August 1784. In the 8th Cuirassiers 11 December 1804, brigadier-fourrier 19 June 1806, maréchal des logis-chef 16 October 1808, adjutant-NCO 9 July 1809, sub-lieutenant 12 September 1809.

He was lieutenant 12 August 1812, instated 24 September 1812, dismissed with the corps 5 December 1815 and put up for the active list 11 December 1815. LH CH 23 September 1814.

POIGNANT (Jean Louis Honoré, 1783-?): born in Pennesières (Haute-Saône) on 24 June 1783. In the 5th Cuirassiers 5 December 1805, brigadier 8 October 1806, brigadier-fourrier 24 December 1806, maréchal des logis 20 February 1807.

He was maréchal des logis-chef 15 May 1809, sub-lieutenant 13 August 1809, wounded at the Moskova 7 September 1812, lieutenant 22 December 18131, dismissed 23 December 1815. LH CH 28 September 1813.

POINSIGNON (?-1812): maréchal des logis in the 9th Cuirassiers, sub-lieutenant 21 March 1812, killed near Smolensk 10 November 1812.

POINSOT (Pierre Hippolyte, 1792-1815): born in Paris (Seine) on 1 March 1792. One of the Emperor's pages 18 October 1807, sub-lieutenant in the 2nd Cuirassiers 27 July 1810, shot and wounded at the Moskova 7 September 1812, lieutenant 29 September 1812, adju-

tant-major 8 July 1813, captain 22 December 1813, shot and wounded in the left knee at La Rothière 1 February 1814, in the 1st Cuirassiers 30 April 1814, captain adjutant-major in the suite of the Cuirassiers du Roi when they were established 1 July 1814, which then became the 1st Cuirassiers again April 1815, disappeared at Waterloo in the ranks of the 6th Hussars 18 June 1815. LH CH 5 September 1811.

POINSOT (Pierre, baron of Chansac, 1764-1833): born in Chalons-sur-Saône (Saône-et-Loire) on 7 February 1794. In the Beauvoisis-Infanterie 1 April 1779, shot and wounded in the leg in Corsica 1779, dismissed and replaced 31 July 1784, in the La Rochefoucauld-Dragons 20 October 1787, brigadier, fourrier, in the same regiment when it became the 11th Dragoons 1 January 1791, dismissed 21 May 1791, garde à cheval in the Garde Constitutionnelle du Roi 23 March to 20 May 1792, captain in the Chasseurs à Cheval of the Légion du Nord 31 May 1792, sabre wound to his right arm at Breda 23 February 1793, adjutant-general battalion commander 25 February 1793, in the Army of the Pyrénées Orientales 7 June 1793, shot and wounded in the chin at Le Mas d'Eu 18 July 1793, acting brigadier-general 7 August 1793.

He commanded the Dagobert vanguard 28 August 1793, acting major-general 24 September 1793, suspended for having served in the Garde Constitutionnelle and for lack of tact and integrity 27 November 1793, reinstated as a brigadier-general 18 July 1796, in the Army of the Rhin-et-Moselle 15 September 1796 then in that of Mainz December 1797, discharged 21 August 1798, active 21 July 1799, in the Victor division September 1799 then Gazan's March 1800, commanded a brigade of heavy cavalry in Rivaud's division, allowed to return home on full-pay 1 July 1801, ceased to be employed 23 September 1801, in the 18th Military Division 2 November 1801, Army of Saint Domingo 21 February 1803.

He returned to service in Brunet's division 11 May 1803, returned to France 1 August 1803, sent to the Island of Walcheren, discharged 20 August 1805, in the 18th Military Division 24 May 1806, commanded a brigade in Malher's division 11 November 1807, commanded the 1st Brigade of Vedel's division in the 2nd Gironde Observation Corps 15 December 1807, escaped with Vedel's division but recalled by Dupont and taken at Baylen 22 July 1808, landed at Marseilles 12

November 1808, in the 2nd Dragoons Division in the Army of Italy 28 November 1808, shot twice in the lower abdomen and back at Piave 8 May 1809, returned to Paris 13 November 1809, attached to the cavalry of the Army of Spain 19 December 1809, commanded the 2nd Brigade, 2nd Division of the 2nd Corps of the Army of Portugal 20 June 1810, in the Army of the North in April 15 September 1810, available 2 July 1811, organised four squadrons in the 6th Military Division 2 January 1812, in the 11th Corps of the Grande Armée 11 August 1812.

He commanded the cavalry of the same corps, won at Strausberg 17 February 1813, in the 31st military Division 11 March 1813 then in the 2nd Cuirassier Division of the 2nd Cavalry Corps of the Grande Armée 12 April 1813, two lance wounds and taken prisoner at Könnern 24 May 1813, returned 6 May 1814. He was non-active 1 September 1814, retired 24 December 1814, in the Amiens Cavalry Depot under Margaron 28 May 1815, allowed to retire 1 October 1815. LH CH 11 December 1803, C 14 June 1804, Baron of Chansac d. 14 February 1810 and l.p. 14 September 1810.

POIROT (Joseph, 1757-?): born in Barisey-au-Plain (Meurthe) on 30 July 1757. In the

Captain wearing social dress.
(Aquarelle by Michel Pétard, RR)

PREVAL (Claude Antoine Hippolyte de, baron, 1776-1853): eldest son of the general, born in Salins (Jura) on 6 November 1776. Volunteer in the Enghien Regiment 24 August 1782 where his father was first-lieutenant by substituting his brother's birth certificate (he was born in 1772), sub-lieutenant 2 September 1789 in the same regiment when it became the 93rd Infantry 1 January 1791.

He was in the 21st infantry 5 March 1791, lieutenant 26 August or April 1792, captain commanding the artillery in the 42nd Half-Brigade 23 June 1794, unemployed 7 May 1795, deputy to Adjutant-General Ducomet in the Army of the Rhin-et-Moselle 22 December 1795 then to Adjutant-General Grandjean 13 April 1796, adjutant-general battalion commander 5 February 1799, in the Army of Italy in Delmas' division.

He was adjutant brigade commander 23 April 1799 in Laboissière's division, deputy chief of staff of the Army of Italy 12 August 1799, Suchet's chief of staff in the same army 20 February 1800, colonel of the 3rd Cavalry 5 March 1801 which became the 3rd Cuirassiers 12 October 1802, refused to be a reporter on the commission charged with investigating and judging the Duke of Enghien March 1804, entrusted with the negotiation of the Erfurt Convention 15 October 1806, brigadier-general in Klein's Dragoon Division 31 December 1806, in Pontivy Camp 20 January 1807, commanded a cavalry brigade 25 March 1807, commanded the Manche Department 24 August 1807, in the 5th Military Division 8 May 1809, employed in training and inspection of the provisional cavalry regiments in the same division 30 May 1809, available 1 August 1809.

Inspector-General of the Cavalry Depots in the 5th military Division 12 September 1809, Master of Requests in the Conseil d'Etat 8 February 1810, Inspector-General of Cavalry 16 January 1811, chief of staff to Maréchal Kellermann 1813, commanded the cavalry depot at Hanau.

He was in charge of the mass levy in the Jura Department 4 January 1814, commanded the Versailles Cavalry Depots 1 February 1814, member of the war council 6 May 1814, lieutenant-general 10 May 1814, Chief of Staff and Inspector-General of the Gendarmerie 16 May 1814, war committee member 18 May 1814, accepted the post of chief of staff to Suchet proposed by the latter 5 April.

He waiting for the Emperor to approve this post, commanded the Beauvais Cavalry Depot 12 May 1815, commanded the Cavalry Division of the Ministry of War from 213 May to 6 September 1815, available 1 October 1815. LH CH December 1803, O 14 June 1804, Baron of the empire l.p. 7 June 1808.

Top.
Colonel Préval
of the 3rd Cuirassier
Regiment mounted
wearing full dress
in 1804-1805.
(RR)

Reine-Cavalerie 1 April 1778, brigadier 8 July 1784, in the same regiment when it became the 4th Cavalry 1 January 1791, maréchal des logis 1 June 1792, maréchal des logis-chef 1 August 1793, recaptured a canon and 11 horses from the enemy at Charleroi 16 June 1794.

He disengaged General Lérivint and a trooper who were on the point of being captured at Fleurus 26 June 1794, sub-lieutenant 29 July 1794, lieutenant 13 March 1802, in the same regiment when it became the 4th Cuirassiers 12 October 1802, retired 15 November 1806.

POMMEROUX de **BORDESOULLE** see **TARDIF de POMMEROUX de BORDESOULLE**

PONCET (Jean Jacques Eugène, 1783-?): born in Chalons-sur-Saône (Saône-et-Loire) on 23 June 1783. Carabinier in the 1st Consular Battalion of the Reserve Army 18 May 1800, left 20 May 1801, in the 19th Dragoons 12 March 1802, brigadier-fourrier 27 March 1802, maréchal des logis 5 April 1802, sub-lieutenant 5 October 1803, lieutenant in the 2nd Cuirassiers 24 December 1805.

He was aide de camp to General Roussel 12 February 1807, second-lieutenant in the Grenadiers à Cheval of the Imperial Guard 10 September 1808, first-lieutenant 20 August 1809, squadron commander in the Line 9 February 1813, in the 12th Cuirassiers 17 February 1813, aide de camp to General Dumas 20 March 1813.

PORTIER (Louis Philibert Marie, 1780-?): born in Bourgoing (Rhône) on 9 November 1780. In the 3rd Cuirassiers 20 August 1803, brigadier 2 January 1804, fourrier 23 September 1804, maréchal des logis-chef 3 December 1805, sub-lieutenant 14 May 1809, wounded in the thorax by two horses that were killed under him and by a shot to the left hand at Essling 21 and 22 May 1809, lieutenant 3 June 1809, captain 11 March 1812.

A cannonball wound to his left thigh at Leipzig 16 October 1813 and by a Biscayan shot at Waterloo 18 June 1815, recovered at home July 1815, dismissed with the regiment 25 November 1815. LH CH 1 October 1807.

POSTEL (Thomas, 1773-?): born in Conches (Eure) on 2 February 1773. In the 4th Cavalry 16 August 1794, brigadier 21 September 1798, fourrier 11 December 1798, maréchal des logis 13 March 1800, maréchal des logis-chef 26 April 1800, in the same regiment when it became the 4th Cuirassiers 12 October 1802.

He was adjutant-NCO 9 September 1803, sub-lieutenant by seniority 16 March 1807, lieutenant 25 June 1807, supernumerary captain 7 April 1809, captain quartermaster 2 June 1809, retired 21 December 1815. LH CH 1 October 1807.

POTTIER (Charles Sigisbert, 1790-?): born in Fléville (Meurthe) on 20 June 1790. In the 1st Chasseurs à Cheval 24 April 1808, lance wound to his right side at Landshut 23 April 1809 and shot and wounded in the left leg at Raab 4 June 1809, sabre wound to his right hand, a bayonet through the body and a lance wound to his right thumb at Wagram 6 July 1809, brigadier 8 September 1809, maréchal des logis 1 February 1811, in the 28th Chasseurs à Cheval 6 August 1813, adjutant 25 August 1813, sub-lieutenant 7 February 1814, non-active 1814. He was in the

Le Colonel Préval, Commandant le 3me Régiment de Cuirassiers

11th Chasseurs à Cheval 4 January 1815, allowed to go over to the 11th Cuirassiers 2 June 1815, instated 3 June 1815, wounded at les Quatre-Bras 16 June 1815 and dismissed with the corps 16 December 1815.

POTTY (Joseph Louis, 1792-?): born in Strasbourg (Bas-Rhin) on 19 August 1792. In the 2nd Gardes d'Honneur 12 May 1813, sub-lieutenant in the 19th Dragoons during the Strasbourg blockade 13 February 1814, incorporated into the Cuirassiers du Dauphin 20 September 1814 which became the 3rd Cuirassiers again in April 1815, dismissed 25 November 1815.

POUILLY (de, ? - ?): lieutenant wounded at Essling 21 May 1809, lieutenant in the suite of the 6th Cuirassiers 29 April 1810, captain 29 June 1810, employed as deputy on the staff of the Army of Holland 31 June.

POUILLY (Louis François Albert de, 1787-?): born in Nîmes (Gard) on 4 October 1787. In the Ecole Imperiale in Fontainebleau 8 November 1806, sub-lieutenant in the 8th Cuirassiers 14 January 1807, attached to the 3rd Provisional Heavy Cavalry in Spain 1808.

He was wounded because he was the first in the assault on Gerona 20 June 1808, shot and wounded above the left knee at Saint-André near Barcelona 8 November 1808, lieutenant in the 21st Infantry 17 October 1811. LH CH 13 January 1809.

POULAIN (Michel Désiré, 1782-?): born in Saint-Pierre (Seine-Inférieure) on 16 August 1782. In the 5th Cuirassiers 21 January 1804, brigadier 1 January 1807, maréchal des logis 9 February 1807.

He was maréchal des logis-chef 16 May 1809, sub-lieutenant 22 December 1813, wounded at Waterloo 18 June 1815, dismissed with the corps 23 December 1815.

POUPIER (Joseph, ?-?): born in Landrecies (Nord).
In the Lorraine-Dragons 15 January 1783 which became the 9th Dragoons 1 January 1791, left 15 January 1791, in the 10th Hussars 25 January 1793, brigadier, maréchal des logis, maréchal des logis-chef, sub-lieutenant 10 July 1793.

He was discharged, in the 2nd Carabiniers 12 December 1806, in the 1st Provisional Heavy Cavalry December 1807 which became the 13th Cuirassiers 21 October 1808, retired 11 June 1810.

POUVERNEL (Nicolas Victor, 1778-?): born in Charmes (Vosges) on 6 May 1778. In the 24th Cavalry 1798, brigadier 5 November 1799, maréchal des logis 23 September 1800, adjutant-NCO, incorporated into the 8th Cuirassiers 7 January 1802.

He was sub-lieutenant by governmental choice 5 October 1803, resignation accepted by the Emperor 6 March 1806, retired 1 June 1806.

POYART (?-?): adjutant-NCO in the 3rd Cuirassiers, sub-lieutenant 13 February 1812, prisoner in Russia 1812.

PRADELET see **TEYNIER DUPRADELET**

PREPONIER (Pierre Sauveur, 1777-?): born in Cadix

(Spain) on 6 August 1777. Maréchal des logis in the 1st Italian Hussars 21 November 1797, in the Légion Italique, wounded at the Lecho Bridge, in the service of France as acting sub-lieutenant in the 25th Cavalry 21 April 1802.

He was dismissed with the corps 12 October 18702 and incorporated with his squadron into the suite of the 3rd Cuirassiers 22 December 1802, in service 3 October 1803, retired and pensioned off 6 March 1806.

PREVENIER (Jean Henri Chrétien, 1787-?): born in Lochem (Yssel-Supérieur) on 22 April 1787. Cadet in the 2nd Batavian Cavalry 22 June 1801, sub-lieutenant in the new unit in the 2nd Dutch Cavalry 28 June 1805 which became the Dutch cuirassiers then the 14th French Cuirassiers 18 August 1810, lieutenant 2 December 1810, dismissed with the corps 13 July 1814.

PREVOST (?-?): In the 12th Cavalry 2 August 1798, fourrier June 1799, maréchal des logis-chef 9 August 1800, in the same regiment when it became the 12th Cuirassiers 24 September 183, sub-lieutenant 15 December 1805.

He was wounded at Friedland 14 June 1807, lieutenant 29 January 1808, adjutant-major 14 May 1809, became captain in a company 9 August 1809, retired 13 October 1809.

PREVOST DU BORD (Antoine Henri Honoré, chevalier, 1766-?): born in Paris (Seine) on 8 November 1766, grenadier in the 1st Puy-de-Dôme Battalion 18 September 1791, in the Garde Constitutionnelle du Roi when it was created 20 January 1792, dismissed with the corps and left 1 June 1791, in the Volontaires Nationaux à Cheval from the Ecole Militaire 1 September 1792., brigadier 8 October 1792, maréchal des logis 20 December 1792, maréchal des logis-chef when they were formed up into the 26th cavalry 21 February 1793 then when they became the 25th Cavalry 4 June 1793, sub-lieutenant 27 August 1796, lieutenant quartermaster 8 December 1797, dismissed with the corps 12 October 1802, incorporated with his squadron as supernumeraries into the 3rd Cuirassiers 14 April 183.

He was in the 8th Cuirassiers 1803, rank of captain 4 May 1805, commanded a company 14 April 1813, non-active 25 August 1814.

He returned to suite of the corps, non-active again 1 September 1815. LH CH 5 November 1804, Chevalier of the Empire l.p. 4 April 1809.

PREVOT de SAINT HILAIRE (Amable Henry, 1787-?) born in Hesdin (Pas-de-Calais) on 17 January 1787. In the 11th Cuirassiers December 1803, brigadier-fourrier 221 April 1804.

He was maréchal des logis 15 December 1806, maréchal des logis-chef 3 April 1807, sub-lieutenant 16 May 1809, wounded in the arm and to his left side by a cannonball at Znaïm 11 July 1809, lieutenant 6 November 1811, adjutant-major 25 September 1812, rank of captain 25 March 1814, dismissed with the corps 16 December 1815. LH CH 1 October 1807.

PRIMAUX (?-?): sub-lieutenant in the 3rd Cuirassiers 3 June 1809, prisoner 1812.

PROVOST (Pierre Jean, 1787-?): born in Paris (Seine) on 24 November 1787. In the Gendarmes d'Ordonnance 7 December 1806, dismissed with the corps 23 November 1807, incorporated into the Dragoons of the Imperial Guard 24 November 1807.

He was sub-lieutenant in the 7th Cuirassiers 3 June 1809, rejoined his unit 17 June 1809, lieutenant 17 June 1812, adjutant-major 26 April 1813, captain 16 March 1814, wounded at Waterloo 18 June 1815, dismissed with the corps 19 December 1815. LH CH 16 May 1813.

PRUDHOMME (?-1809): sub-lieutenant in the 6th Cuirassiers killed at Essling 22 May 1809.

PRUDHOMME see **SAINT MAUR de PRUDHOMME**

PUISSANT aka **VIGUES** (Dieudonné Claude, 1780-?): born in Nancy (Meurthe) on 21 May 1780. Child of the regiment on the payroll of the Royal-Cravates 1 June 1788 which became the 10th Cavalry 1 January 1791, trumpeter 23 September 1795, trooper 22 September 1794, brigadier 11 April 1802, maréchal des logis 23 September 1802, in the same regiment when it became the 10 Cuirassiers 24 September 1803, sub-lieutenant 16 May 1809.

He was lieutenant 21 March 1812, sabre wound to his head and two lance wounds to his right leg and a shot wound in his right arm and taken prisoner near Moscow 4 October 1812 returned to the suite of the regiment 7 November 1814, took up his appointment 20 January 1815, dismissed 25 December 1815. LH CH 1 September 1807.

PULLY see **RANDON de MALBOISSIERE de PULLY**

QUIMPER de LANASCOL (Frédéric de, 1792-?): born in Mainz (Mont-Tonnerre) on 2 July 1792. One of the Emperor's pages, sub-lieutenant in the 4th Cuirassiers 14 January 1811, prisoner in Koblenz 1 January 1814, returned and put back in the same regiment when it became the Angoulême Cuirassiers 6 August 1814. Non-active on lieutenant's half-pay 4 February 1815, three months' leave with pay 28 March 1815, returned as a lieutenant in the suite and dismissed with the corps 21 November 1815.

QUIMPER de LANASCOL (Georges Marie Charles Yvan, 1795-?): born in 1795. In the 1st Gardes d'Honneur 21 June 1813, fourrier 23 June 1813, sub-lieutenant 1st Cuirassiers 23 November 1813, joined his unit 4 February 1814, arrested 16 May 1815, in the 1st Cuirassiers of the Royal Guard 1 December 1815.

QUINETTE de CERNAY (Jean Charles, baron, 1776-1822): born in Paris (Seine) on 25 July 1776. Second-lieutenant in the 9th Light Artillery Company 1 August 1792 assigned to the 2nd Horse Artillery, shot and wounded in the left leg at Spire 30 September 1792, first-lieutenant 9 November 1793, captain 31 August 1794, aide de camp to General Hoche 20 April 1795, supernumerary squadron commander in the 12th Chasseurs à Cheval 6 July 1797, took up his appointment 10 May 1799, discharged 23 September 1800, in service in the same regiment 24 June 1801, major of the 2nd Chasseurs à Cheval 29 March 1805, colonel in the 5th Cuirassiers 31 December 1806, briga-

QUAINE (Claude, 1760-?): born in Clermont-Ferrand (Puy-de-Dôme) on 11 August 1760. In the Reine-Cavalerie 18 April 1779, brigadier 9 September 1784, maréchal des logis 21 December 1786, maréchal des logis-chef 6 September 1789, in the same regiment when it became the 4th Cavalry 1 January 1791, adjutant sub-lieutenant 26 January 1793.

He was elected lieutenant 29 July 1793, captain 22 July 1794, clothing captain 1800 and 1801, in the same regiment when it became the 4th Cuirassiers 12 October 1802, allowed to retire 29 May 1809. LH CH 1805.

QUAITA (Reinhartz Joseph, 1784-?): born in Strasbourg (Bas-Rhin) on 20 February 1784. Cadet

in the 2nd Dutch Hussars 1 March 1798, sub-lieutenant 21 October 1803, lieutenant in the Cavalry of the King of Holland's Guard 1 June 1806. He was captain in the 2nd Dutch Cuirassiers 9 July 1811 which became the 14th French cuirassiers 18 August 1810, wounded and taken prisoner at Vilna 11 December 1812, returned and non-active 22 December 1814.

QUETEL (Jean, 1772-?): born in Pennedepie (Calvados) on 6 February 1772. In the 11th Cavalry 28 May 1794, brigadier 9 February 1799, maréchal des logis 19 October 1802, in the same regiment when it became the 11th cuirassiers 24 September 1803, sub-lieutenant 27 May 1808, in the 13th Cuirassiers 1 October 1808, lieutenant 27 November 1813, captain 26 February 1814, dismissed with the corps 9 August 1814, captain adjutant-major in the 11th Cuirassiers 1 September 1814, wounded at Waterloo 18 June 18115, dismissed with the corps 16 December 1815. LH CH 11 January 1812.

7th Cuirassiers Colonel probably in 1813, by A. de Marbot. (RR)

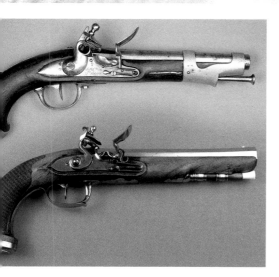

Top. **An IX-model cavalry pistol.**
Bottom. **General officer's pistol with a butt in the form of a Medusa.**
(© Photo Jean-Louis Viau)

Troopers' models of helmet and cuirass.
(Collections Musée de l'Empéri, photo RR)

dier-general 6 August 1811, commanded the 2nd Brigade of the 5th Cuirassiers Division in the Elbe Observation Corps 25 December 1811; put on availability 18 February 1812 for having borrowed money as the colonel from the regimental cash box to pay for clothing extras and pay off some of his debts, commanded the 2nd Brigade of the 1st Cuirassier Division in the Grande Armée 14 February 1813.

He commanded the Leipzig Cavalry Depot 16 June 1813, CO of the 2nd Heavy Cavalry Brigade of the 4th Division (Defrance) in the 3rd Cavalry Corps 15 July 1813, then the 2nd Brigade, Jacquinot's division 20 December 1813, commanded the 2nd Brigade of the 5th Dragoon Division in the 6th Corps of the Grande Armée March 1814, non-active 1 September 1814, deputy to the Inspector-General of Cavalry Defrance in the 12th military Division 30 December 1814, in the 8th Cavalry Division of the Army of the Rhine 15 May 1815, non-active 5 September 1815. LH CH 14 July 1804, Baron of the Empire d. 17 March 1808 and l.p. 5 October 1808.

QUINTIN (Charles, 1780-?): born in Donzère (Drôme) on 3 August 1780. In the 2nd Cuirassiers 20 October 1802, brigadier 4 December 1802, maréchal des logis August 1806, maréchal des logis-chef 20 November 1806, adjutant-NCO 1 October 1807, sub-lieutenant 14 May 1809, wounded at Wagram 6 July 1809, lieutenant quartermaster in the 3rd Provisional Cuirassiers 1 January 1811, entered as a lieutenant in the suite of the 2nd Cuirassiers 23 July 1811, joined them 5 September 1811, in service 28 March 1812, captain 14 May 1813, wounded at Waterloo 18 June 1815, non-active on half-pay 10 December 1815. LH CH 1 October 1807.

QUINTO see
AVOGARDO de QUINTO

UEUNOT (Mathieu, Baron, 1766-1845): born in Gray (Haute-Saône) on 27 March 1766. In the colonel-Général-Cavalerie 8 January 1783, dismissed with permission 26 August 1790, lieutenant in the Hussars of the Ardennes Legion 1 October 1791, captain 1 May 1793.

He was in the same regiment when it became the 23rd chasseurs à cheval 10 September 1793, deputy to the adjutant-generals 23 June 1794, shot and wounded in the back at Le Quesnoy 15 August 1794, shot in his right leg 27 August 1794 and shot in the left foot at Sulzbach 17 August 1796, deputy to Adjutant-General Delotz 1 August 1799,.

He was elected squadron commander in the suite of the 23rd Chasseurs à Cheval 23 June 1800, deputy on the general staff of the Army of the Rhine 20 February 1801 then in that of the Expeditionary Army of Brest 28 July 1801 in service in the 4th cavalry 14 December 1801 which became the 4th cuirassiers 12 October 1802, major of the 1st Dragoons 29 October 1803, colonel of the 9th Dragoons 31 December 1806, brigadier-general 6 August 1811, commanded the 3rd Brigade of the 1st Cuirassiers Division in the Army of Germany 25 December 1811.

His left leg fractured when he fell off his horse near Golymin 6 January 1812 and cannonball wound to his right thigh at the Moskova 7 September 1812, in the 2nd Division of the 1st Corps of the Grande Armée 5 May 1813, sent to the waters to get over his wounds 1 June 1813, commanded the 2nd Brigade of the 5th Heavy Cavalry Division (Lhéritier) in the Bavaria Observation Corps 13 July 1813 then the 1st Brigade in the same division in the Grande Armée 3 August 1803, in the 5th Cavalry Corps under Milhaud then Pajol, retired 19 September 1813.

LH CH 25 March 1804, O 6 June 1811, Baron of the Empire.

At Dillingen on 19 May 1800, Captain Queunot was wounded by a shot to his right foot while swimming across the Danube, his sabre between his teeth, bring back a barge under enemy fire.

RACT aka **RACTMADOUX** (Joseph, 1767-1807): born in Chevron (Mont-Blanc) on 19 November 1767.

In the Mestre-de-Camp-Général-Cavalerie 19 November 1786, dismissed with the corps 20 February 1791 and put as brigadier into the 24th of the new troops levied from the corps 21 February 1791, fourrier 24 March 1792, maréchal des logis 1 April 1793, in the same regiment when it became the 23rd Cavalry 4 June 1793.

He became lieutenant in the 19th Chasseurs à Cheval 10 August 1793, seven sabre wounds at Kreuznach 30 November 1794, retired and pensioned-off because of his wounds 15 January 1795, captain in the suite of the 23rd Cavalry 14 June 1796, wounded at Philisbourg September 1799, deputy to the adjutant-generals 28 September 1799, sabre wound when crossing the Danube 19 June 1800, shot and wounded in his thigh while crossing the Inn 9 December, in service in the 12th Cavalry 20 February 1801. He was in the same regiment when it became the 12th cuirassiers 24 September 1803, killed at Friedland 14 June 1807.

RADET (Louis, 1784-?): born in Stenay (Meuse) on 18 June 1784. In the 4th Cavalry 21 May 1802 which became the 4th cuirassiers 12 October 1802, brigadier 17 April 1806, maréchal des logis 1 November 1806.

He was sub-lieutenant 11 September 1809, lieutenant 5 September 1813, aide de camp to General Radet, Grand Provost of the Grande Armée 10 November 1813. LH CH 14 May 1813.

RAFELIS de SAINT SAUVEUR (Aldonce Charles Joseph François Paule Samaritain de, baron, 1772-1849): son of a Maréchal de Camp Inspector of Cavalry, born in Tulles (Corrèze) on 30 March 1772.

He was second supernumerary unpaid sub-lieutenant in the Roi-Infanterie 24 April 1785, in service as sub-lieutenant 27 October 1789, several sabre wounds to his head, arms and hands during the Nancy Mutiny 30 August 1790, discharged when the regiment was dismissed 12 December 1790, in the 102nd infantry 27 February 1791 which became the 105th Infantry 28 August 1791.

He became adjutant-major 15 September 1791, emigrated 26 March 1792, in the company of the Cavalry Officers of the Duke of Lorges in the Army of the Princes 26 April 1792, dismissed 1 July 1793, cadet in the Austrian Carabiniers 1 August 1793, sub-lieutenant in the Rohan Hussars in the service of England 1 July 1794, shot and wounded in the left leg at Nienhuss (Holland) March 1795, cadet in the Imperial Austrian Zetschwitz Cuirassiers 1 November 1795, NCO 10 December 1795, sub-lieutenant 30 May 1796, lieutenant 4 April 1799, resigned 1 February 1801, cavalry captain in the ser-

vice of France 21 March 1806, in the 6th Cuirassiers 10 April 1806, squadron commander in the 4th Cuirassiers 22 March 1807, put in the 6th Cuirassiers 14 July 1807, major in the suite 6 October 1808, took up his post in the 8th Cuirassiers 13 February 1809, colonel of the 13th Hussars 8 February 1813, joined them before 20 April 1813.

He commanded the 1st Provisional Heavy Cavalry in Hamburg 22 July 1813, left to join his command 9 September 1813, instated November 1813, returned with the garrison after the capitulation 27 May 1814, sub-lieutenant in the King's Body Guard 1 June 1814.

He was maréchal de camp 10 November 1814, in employment when the cavalry regiments were disbanded 11 September 1815. LH CH 11 July 1807, O 18 July 1814, C 24 August 1814, Baron of the Empire d.15 January 1810 and l.p. 25 March 1810.

RAIMBOUVILLE (Alexandre Eugène Grandin, 1791-?): born in 1791.

Pupil in the Ecole Spéciale Impériale de Cavalerie in Saint-Germain 4 March 1811, sub-lieutenant in the 5th Cuirassiers 30 January 1813, in the King's Cuirassiers when they were formed 1 May 1814 which became the 1st Cuirassiers April 1815, under arrest 16 May 1815, in the 1st Cuirassiers of the royal Guard 1 December 1815.

RAINAL (Pascal, 1793-?): born in 1793. In the 4th Cuirassiers 20 September 1810,.

He was brigadier 21 February 1812, maréchal des

ACLOT (Pierre, 1774-?): born in Joigny (Yonne) on 2 October 1774. In the 3rd Paris Battalion 24 January 1792, five sabre wounds to his head, two to his side and right hip and shot and wounded in the right thigh at Aldanoven 1 March 1793.

He was incorporated into the 7th of the Line 22 September 1796, left with permission of the Minister 19 February 1798, gendarme à cheval in the 25th Legion Roer Company 8 July 1798.

He was maréchal des logis 23 February 1799, lieutenant 22 April 1802, lieutenant aide de camp to General Wirion, the Inspector-General of the Gendarmerie, 12 September 1808; captain in the 9th Cuirassiers 16 March 1810.

He was dismissed with the corps and non-active at the disposal of the government 26 November 1815. LH CH 24 April 1813.

A captain in the 9th Cuirassiers he was wounded by sabres four times and twice by lances at Leipzig where, as CO of the regiment, he decided to sacrifice himself to stop the enemy and save the cavalry division on 18 October 1813.

He was made prisoner by the Russians in the ambulance the following day.

French eagle.
(© Photo Jean-Louis Viau)

(RR)

RANDON de MAL-BOISSIERE de PULLY (Charles Joseph, Count, 1751-1832): born in Paris (Seine) on 18 August 1751. In the Bercheny Hussars 22 April 1768, lieutenant in the 1st Company of Musketeers 14 January 1769, captain 11 April 1770 in the La Rochefoucauld-Dragons which became the Angoulême-Dragons.

He was second-captain 8 June 1776, captain commanding 8 June 1780, squadron commander 1 May 1788, lieutenant-colonel in the Royal-Cravates 17 May 1789 which became the 10th Cavalry 1 January 1791, colonel of the 8th cavalry 5 February 1792, joined them 25 February 1792, maréchal de camp 19 September 1792, major-general commanding the Vosges Corps in the Army of the Moselle 8 March 1793.

He was suspended 5 September 1793, imprisoned then freed 16 November 1794, retired 14 April 1795, commanded the 3rd Division of the Army of the North 13 June 1795, then the 2nd Division 22 August 1795, invited to give up his functions 27 September 1795, Inspector-General of Cavalry in the Army of the Rhin-et-Moselle 12 May 1796, did not take up his post and remained unemployed, Inspector-General of Cavalry in the Army of Italy 22 April 1797.

He commanded a division in the same army 11 November 1799, commanded the 15th Military Division 9 January 1800, in the Army of the Rhine 24 March 1800, commanded the 2nd Division of the Army of the Grisons 17 November 1800, acting CO of the same army from 15 April to 20 May 1801, commanded a cavalry corps (right wing) in the Cisalpine Republic 11 September 1801 then the 3rd Cuirassier Division in the Army of Italy 6 September 1805.

He commanded a division of heavy cavalry (dragoons and cuirassiers) in the same army 23 September 1805 then the 3rd Cuirassier Division which was reconstituted November 1805, responsible for inspecting the cavalry depots of the Armies of Italy and Naples 30 September 1806, commanded the 2nd Dragoon Division 1 April 1809, commanded the 3rd Division on the right wing 1 June 1809.

He was responsible for inspecting and training the cavalry corps in the Army of the North 4 September 18090, then for training 12 temporary dragoon regiments as well as their depots 20 November 1809.

Inspector of mounted troops posted in Italy 1810 then inspector of the Remount Depots of the 6th and 8th Military Divisions 7 May 1811.

He became governor of the Imperial Palace at Meudon 5 January 1812.

He was colonel of the 1st Gardes d'Honneur 8 April 1813, put back in 1814, at the disposal of the Minister of War for commanding the depots and inspecting 3 June 1815, responsible for the defence of Paris 13 June 1815, commanded at Boulogne and Saint-Cloud 29 June 1815, retired 4 September 1815. LH CH 11 December 1803 14 June 1804, GO 23 August 1814.

He was Count of the Empire d. 15 August 1809 and l.p. 12 November 1809.

Letter addressed by General Charles Randon de Pully to the Minister of War on 29 Vendémiaire Year 14. (Author's collection)

logis 13 September 1813, in the King's Cuirassiers 1 July 1814 which became the 1st Cuirassiers April 1815, sub-lieutenant 2 March 1815, struck off the rolls and his appointment cancelled 1 September 1815.

RAMPAN de LEONARD (Edouard Charles François de, 1790-?): born in Colomby (Manche) on 7 July 1790.
Velite in the Dragoons of the Imperial Guard 10 June 1808, sub-lieutenant in the 8th Cuirassiers 13 March 1813, on two months' leave with half-pay 18 December 1814.

RANC (Auguste Stanislas Saint Ange, 1788-?): born in Vernoux (Ardèche) on 7 May 1788.
Velite in the Grenadiers à Cheval of the Imperial Guard 16 July 1807, sub-lieutenant in the 7th Cuirassiers 13 March 1813, joined them 9 May 1813, wounded at Neustadt 1 January 1814, six months' leave 1 September 1814.
He returned April 1815 and wounded at Waterloo 18 June 1815, dismissed with the corps 19 December 1815.

RATIEZ (Etienne Jacques, 1764-1829): born in Ile Bourbon (Reunion Island) on 8 June 1764. Sub-lieutenant in the 12th Cavalry 20 April 1792, deputy on the staff of the Army of the Rhine 21 May 1793, lieutenant 4 November 1793,
He was captain 13 November 1794, aide de camp to General Beaupuy 17 December 1795 until the death of his general, then to Brunneteau de Sainte-Suzanne 19 October 1796, squadron commander in the 19th cavalry 12 December 1800, dismissed with the corps 31 December 1802 and incorporated into the suite of the 10th cavalry 21 January 1803, commissioned 26 February 1803, in the 3rd Cuirassiers 21 April 183, major of the 5th Cuirassiers 29 October 1803, second-colonel 14 October 1811, sent to Berlin to take delivery of 15000 horses from Prussia 30 March 1812.
He commanded the remount depots in Glogau and Hanover March 1813, Hanau June 1813 then Deux-Ponts November 1813, non-active 1814. LH CH 25 March 1804.

RAYNAL (Joseph Marie, 1783-?): born in Béziers (Hérault) on 30 December 1783. In the 4th Cuirassiers 20 June 1805.
He was brigadier-fourrier 1 August 1806, maréchal des logis-chef 25 June 1807, sabre wound to his right arm at Essling 21 May 1809, adjutant-NCO 22 May 1809, sub-lieutenant 3 July 1809, wounded and his horse killed under him at Wagram 6 July 1809, lieutenant 17 June 1812, wounded at the Drissa 11 August 1812 and at the Berezina 28 November 1812, aide de camp to General de Narbonne 21 August 1813, returned to the corps which had become the Angoulême Cuirassiers 6 August 1814, captain 4 January 1815, instated 10 February 1815, in the same regiment when it became the 4th cuirassiers again April 1815, dismissed 21 December 1815. LH CH September 1813.

REBILLOT (Chéri, 1794-?): born in Vitry-le-François (Marne) on 31 March 1794. In the 16th

Chasseurs à Cheval 1 July 1810, fourrier 14 October 1810, maréchal des logis 1 January 1811.

He was maréchal des logis-chef 1 February 1813, sub-lieutenant in the 4th Cuirassiers 22 July 1813, lance wound to his neck and a sabre wound which cost him his right eye, his horse killed under him and taken prisoner at Epinal 11 January 1814, returned 26 April 1814 and put in the same regiment when it became the Angoulême Cuirassiers 6 August 1814 which became the 4th Cuirassiers again April 1815, dismissed 21 December 1815. LH CH 9 November 1814, confirmed 11 April 1815.

REDER (Jean, 1771-?): born in Puttelange (Moselle) on 18 December 1771. In the 1st Cavalry 6 July 1791, sabre wound to his head at Neerwinden 18 March 1793, brigadier 23 October 1799, maréchal des logis 20 June 1802, maréchal des logis-chef 1 January 1806, adjudant-NCO 18 January 1806, sub-lieutenant 25 May 1807.

He was shot and wounded in the leg at Koenigsberg June 1807, lieutenant 16 May 1809, in the King's cuirassiers 1 July 1814 which became the 1st Cuirassiers again April 18115, dismissed and put up for retirement 24 December 1815. LH CH 1 October 1807.

REGEON (Pierre, 1782-1824): born in Paris (Seine) on 11 October 1782. In the 14th chasseurs à Cheval 29 September 1796, shot and wounded in the left leg and a sabre wound to his head at Fossano 4 November 1798, brigadier 14 June 1801, maréchal des logis 7 November 1804.

He was in the dragoons of the Imperial Guard 13 June 1808, brigadier 22 September 1808, sub-lieutenant in the 7th Cuirassiers 8 February 1813, joined them 6 March 1813, wounded and prisoner at Neustadt 1 January 1814, returned 9 July 1814,.

He was non-active 16 August 1814, put back in the regiment 6 April 1815 and returned home 24 August 1813.

REGNAULT de CHATILLON (Charles François, 1778-?): born in Rosières

(Meurthe) on 13 february 1778. In the 2nd Carabiniers, elected lieutenant 2 September 1802, aide de camp to General Grandjean 19 November 1804.

He was captain courier taken with Chouard, the squadron commander, by Prussian soldiers after being stripped and robbed but managing to escape after seeing Chouard shot near Anklam end of March beginning of April 1807, managed to reach the French positions, captain in the 2nd Cuirassiers 25 June 1807, wounded at Wagram 6 July 1809, left to retire 5 October 1809.

REGNONVAL (Nicolas, 1791-?): born in Beauvais (Oise) on 26 October 1791. Velite in the Dragoons of the Imperial Guard 8 June 1808. He became sub-lieutenant in the 14th Cuirassiers 8 February 1813, dismissed with the corps and incorporated into the 12th Cuirassiers 13 July 1814, wounded at Waterloo 18 June 1815, dismissed with corps 10 December 1815.

RELINGUE see **FOULER RELINGUE**

REMACLE see **CONROT REMACLE**

REMOND (François, 1776-?): born in Conche (Ain) on 16 January 1776. In the 4th battalion of Volontaires Nationaux 24 June 1793, sabre wound to his right arm at Dunkirk 1793, incorporated into the 60th Half-Brigade 1796, bayonet wound to his head while crossing the Mincio 1800, in the 3rd Cavalry 10 July 1801.

He was brigadier 5 November 1801, maréchal des logis 15 June 1802 in the same regiment when it became the 3rd Cuirassiers 12 October 1802, sub-lieutenant 8 May 1807.

He became lieutenant 14 May 1809, captain 12 March 1812, eleven lance wounds and taken pri-

REMY (Claude Charles, Baron, 1769-1836) born in Seant-Jean-devant-Possesse (Marne) on 5 February 1769.

In the 23rd Cavalry 11 November 1793, brigadier 21 December 1798.

He was maréchal des logis 15 November 1802, dismissed with the corps 23 December 1802 and incorporated with his company into the 5th Cuirassiers 3 January 1803, maréchal des logis-chef 21 December 1805, adjutant-NCO 24 November 1806, two horses killed under him at Eylau 8 February 1807.

He became sub-lieutenant 20 February 1807, lieutenant 2 February 1808, captain 1 June 1812, incorporated into the 2nd Provisional Heavy Cavalry in Hamburg 11 September 1813, returned with the garrison 30 May 1814.

He was retired 23 December 1815. Holder of a Sabre of Honour 15 September 1802,.

LH CH by rights 24 September 1803, Chevalier of the Empire d. 1809 and l.p. 26 April 1811, Baron d. 1811 and l.p. 1813

Brigadier in the 23rd Cavalry, Claude Remy at the head of five troopers dispatched a detachment of pandours and routed a squadron of the Kayser's Hussars, taking several prisoners and then disengaging a canon near Offenburg on 26 June 1799.

soner at Winkovo 18 October 1812, returned to his regiment 1814, retired 25 November 1815.

REMY (Dominique, 1777-?): born in Rambercourt (Meurthe) on 6 August 1777. In the 11th Cavalry 1 April 1794, brigadier 24 June 1799, maréchal des logis 30 January 1802, in the same regiment when it became the 11th Cuirassiers 24 September 1803, had his horse killed under him and captured an artillery piece at Austerlitz 2 December 1805.

He was sub-lieutenant in the suite 24 November 1806, took up his post 3 April 1807, lieutenant 25 May 1807, bruised his right shoulder with a cannonball and his horse killed under him at Essling 22 May 1809, captain 3 June 1809, two lance wounds to his left elbow and under his armpit and two more in the back as he had had his horse killed under him, taken prisoner at Toloschinn 21 November 1812, returned 12 October 1814 and sent home non-active. Holder of a sabre of Honour 15 September 1802, LH CH by rights 24 September 1803, O 6 November 1811.

REMY (Jean Baptiste, 1777-1812): born in Saint-Jean-devant-Possesse (Marne) on 8 September 1777. In the 7th Cavalry 22 June 1799, brigadier 23 October 1802.

Officer from the 3rd Regiment in mounted service dress.
(P. Begnini, RR)

RENARD (Alexandre, 1766-?): born in Roville (Meurthe) on 31 January 1766.

In the Royal-Champagne-Cava-lerie 31 December 1785 which became the 20th Cavalry 1 January 1791, brigadier 18 May 1793, in the same regiment when it became the 19th cavalry 4 June 1793.

He was maréchal des logis 18 June 1793, maréchal des logis-chef 21 March 1797, sub-lieutenant 18 May 1802, dismissed with the corps 31 December 1802 and incorporated into the 10th Cavalry 11 February 1803 which became the 10th Cuirassiers 24 September 1803, shot and wounded in the arm and his horse killed under him at Jena 14 October 1806.

He was lieutenant 24 November 1806, reti-red 21 April 1809. LH CH 1 October 1807.

Maréchal des logis in the 19th Cavalry, Alexandre Renard brought back his company to French lines after all the officers had been killed or put out of action at Rousselaer, on 13 June 1794.

He was in the same regiment when it became the 7th Cuirassiers 23 December 1802, maréchal des logis 1 October 1806, marechal des logis-chef 16 October 1811, sub-lieutenant 17 June 1812, disappeared at the Berezina 28 November 1812.

RENAUDIN (Jean Eloi, 1789-?): born in Paris (Seine) on 28 January 1789. In the 88th of the Line 27 June 1808, prisoner at Badajoz 7 April 1808, returned, fourrier 13 December 1808.
He saved his regiment's eagle at Albuhera 16 May 1811, in the King's Body Guards 26 June 1814, cavalry sub-lieutenant 4 October 1814, non-active on half-pay 17 February 1815, in the 3rd Cuirassiers 26 April 1815, instated 13 May 1815, returned to being non-active 1 September 1815.

RENNO (Jean Louis, 1771-?): born in Laasphe (Duchy of Wittgenstein) on 15 November 1771. Hussar in the Count of Tulm's corps 2 May 1778, brigadier 2 February 1793, sabre wound to his head and prisoner at Rysbergen, fourrier 1 August 1795, maréchal des logis 1 September 1795, maréchal des logis-chef 3 January 1797.

He was deputy sub-lieutenant 3 March 1802, first deputy sub-lieutenant 1 October 1802, with-drawn from service on two-thirds pay 1 June 1805, Gendarmerie first-lieutenant 1 October 1802, captain in the Royal Dutch Gendarmerie 18 March 1807, in the 2nd Dutch Cuirassiers 6 October 1809 which became the 14th French Cuirassiers 18 August 1810, wounded and his horse killed under him at the Berezina 28 November 1812,.
He was wounded at Leipzig 18 October 1813, prisoner at Langres 28 January 1814, returned and resignation accepted 19 November 1814. LH CH 8 October 1811.

REVEILLON (Etienne, 1771-?): born in Davaye (Saône-et-Loire) on 28 February 1771. In the 44th of the Line 4 May 1793, shot and wounded in the right leg at Pirmasens 14 September 1793 and three shots to his thigh and head at Kaiserlautern 29 November 1793, in the 4th Cavalry 2 February 1794 which became the 4th Cuirassiers 12 October 1802, brigadier 28 December 1803.

He was maréchal des logis 1 October 1806, shot and wounded in the neck at Heilsberg 10 June 1807, sub-lieutenant 5 September 1813, reti-red 21 December 1815. LH CH 8 October 1811.

REVERCHON (?-?): maréchal des logis in the 9th Cuirassiers, sub-lieutenant 8 May 1807, lieute-nant 14 May 1809, wounded at Wagram 6 July 1809, retired 14 December 1809.

REYDY de LAGRANGE (?-?): maréchal des logis in the 8th Cuirassiers, sub-lieutenant in the 3rd Cuirassiers 26 December 1814, commissioned the same day, resignation accepted 7 June 1815.

REYNAUD (Balthazard, 1777-?): the general's bro-ther, born in le Puy (Haute-Loire) on 6 January 1777. In the Chasseurs à Cheval of the Légion des Pyrénées 13 April 1793, brigadier 16 May 1793, maréchal des logis-chef 7 July 1793, incorporated

RENNEBERG (Frédéric Pierre Félicité Zéphirin de, 1781-?): born in Paris (Seine) in 1781.
Cadet in the 1st Dutch Dragoons 1 May 1796, deputy on the staff of General Augereau 1800.

He was sub-lieutenant in the 1st Dutch Dragoons 3 April 1802, lieutenant July 1802, aide de camp to General Daendels 9 February 1807.

He was prisoner of the English by going to India and held in England 1807, exchanged 1808, captain in the 2nd Dutch Cuirassiers 6 October 1809 which became the 14th French Cuirassiers 5 December 1810, aide de camp to Daendels 1 February 1812, kept in the regiment 20 May 1812, squadron commander 19 November 1812, wounded at the Berezina 28 November 1812.

He was incorporated into the King's Cuirassiers when they were formed 1 July 1814 and which became the 1st Cuirassiers again March 1815.

He was wounded and prisoner at Waterloo 18 June 1815, struck of the rolls because still pri-soner when the corps was dismissed 24 December 1815.
LH CH, O.

While aide de camp to General Daendels on 9 February 1807, Captain Rennenberg charged at the head of 12 of the General's Escort Dragoons against a group of forty enemy dra-goons, freeing a canon and taking 17 prisoners among whom an officer wounded in the hand.

RICHARD (Louis Maurice, 1772-1805): born in Verdun (Meuse) on 3 May 1772. Child of the regiment in the Royal-Cravates, paid from 23 August 1786, trooper 1 May 1788, in the same regiment when it became the 10th Cavalry 1 January 1791. He was brigadier 16 October 1792, brigadier-fourrier 1 October 1793.

He became maréchal des logis 19 June 1794, maréchal des logis-chef 8 December 1795

He was sub-lieutenant 6 January 1803, in the same regiment when it became the 10th Cuirassiers 24 September 1803, wounded in the shoulder by a cannonball at Austerlitz 2 December 1808.

he died form his wounds at Brünn 6 December 1805. Holder of a sabre of Honour 30 May 1803,
LH CH by rights 24 September 1803.

On 7 November 1799, Maréchal des logis chef Richard, at the head of a platoon of the 10th Cavalry, forced an enemy detachment which out-numbered him to go back over the Eisenbach Bridge. A year later near Schwonstadt, he charged alone against eight enemy troopers, killed one, wounding two and capturing them and finally putting the others to flight so as to be able to free two French pri-soners.

with the corps into the 22 Chasseurs à Cheval 6 September 1793, lieutenant 18 February 1795, adjutant-major in the 20th Dragoons 25 June 1802, captain 28 December 183, aide de camp to General Reynaud 1809.he was promoted squa-dron commander in the 8th Cuirassiers 18 August 1813, wounded before Paris 23 March 1814, took up his appointment in the 2nd Carabiniers 4 October 1814, wounded at Waterloo 18 June 1815. LH CH 14 April 1807.

REYNAUD (Nicolas, baron, 1771-1828): born in le Puy (Haute-Loire) on 29 September 1771. Sub-lieute-nant in the 34th Infantry 1 February 1791, infantry cap-tain in the Légion des Pyrénées 10 September 1792, with his uncle in the Chasseurs à Cheval in the same region 1 November 1792, incorporated with it into the 22nd Chasseurs à Cheval 6 September 1793, sabre wound to his head and shot in his thigh and appointed squadron com-mander on the Salahieh battlefield 11 August 1798, brigade-commander of the 20th Dragoons 23 September 1800, wounded by a bayonet in his hand at Canope 21 March 1801, returned to France end of 1801, brigadier-general commanding the 1st Brigade (4th and 6th Cuirassiers) of the 3rd Cuirassier Division.

He joined them 1 February 1807, interim CO of the division after General Espagne was wounded at Heilsberg 10 June 1807 until July 1807, same division in the Army of Germany, shot through his right arm at Wagram 6 July 1809, commanded the cavalry depot at Penzing 21 July 1809, returned to France 3 November 1809, commanded the Libourne depot 9 November 1809, available September 1810, commanded the 3rd Mobile Column searching for draft dodgers and deserters in the 21st Military Division 18 March 1811. He commanded the Lippe Department 30 November 1811, then the 1st Brigade in the 5th Cuirassier Division 25 December 1811, available 1 April 1813, responsible for inspecting cavalry depots in the 9th, 10th, 11th and 20th Military Divisions 10 May 1813, commanded a mobile column looking for deserters and draft dodgers 21 August 1813, non-active 28 April 1814.

He became cavalry inspector in the 9th to 11th and 20th Military divisions 30 December 1814, non-active 20 March 1815, at the Troyes cavalry depot 12 May 1815, did not reach them. LH CH 11 December 1803, O 14 June 1804, C 25 December 1805, Baron of the Empire l.p. 10 February 1809.

RHEEDEN (Charles Podolphe Friso de, 1788-?): born in Seer (Ems-Oriental) on 4 May 1788.

He was Cadet in the cuirassiers in the service of Prussia 2 November 1800, sub-lieutenant 2 December 1803, lieutenant in the 14th French Cuirassiers 3 July 1811, captain 9 February 1813, wounded and prisoner at Leipzig 18 October 1813.

RICARD (Pierre Antoine, 1776-?): born in l'Etre (Hautes-Alpes) on 2 July 1776. In the 77th of the Line 16 October 1798, in the 3rd Cavalry 23 October 1800 which became the 3rd Cuirassiers 12 October 1802.

He was brigadier 3 April 1803, maréchal des logis 1 December 1806, shot and wounded in his left hand at Essling May 1809, sub-lieutenant 16 August 1813, dismissed with the corps 25 November 1815.

RICARDI (Antoine, 1790-?): born in Oneille (Montenotte) on 24 August 1790. In the 4th Reserve Legion 10 September 1806.

He was incorporated into the 10th Hussars

Model 1814 standard belonging to the 12th Cuirassiers, First Restoration. (RR)

The Cuirassiers played an important role in capturing the Great Redoubt at the Battle of the Moskova. Among the many dead was General Caulaincourt. (RR)

1 February 1809, brigadier then maréchal des logis, in the Grenadiers à cheval of the Guard 16 December 1812, brigadier 21 January 1813, sub-lieutenant in the 2nd Cuirassiers 8 February 1813, incorporated into the 2nd Provisional Heavy Cavalry in Hamburg 11 September 1813.

Returned with the garrison 27 May 1814, then returned home as a foreign national 1 July 1815.

RICHARD (Jean Baptiste, 1766-?): born in Vesoul (Haute-Saône) on 6 November 1766. Child of the regiment on the payroll of the Royal-Cravates 2 September 1780, enrolled as a trooper 1 August 1784, in the same regiment when it became the 10th cavalry 1 January 1791, brigadier 20 November 1791, maréchal des logis 15 September 1793, sabre wound between the shoulders at Kreuznach December 1793, adjutant 21 December 1798, sub-lieutenant 3 June 1801 in the same regiment when it became the 10th Cuirassiers 24 September 1803, second-lieutenant in the Grenadiers à Cheval of the Imperial Guard 18 December 1805, joined them 1 January 1806, first-lieutenant 11 April 1809, non-active when the corps was formed into the Royal Cuirassiers de France 22 July 1814.

RICHARD (Joseph, 1778-?): born in Saint Mihiel (Meuse) on 29 December 1778. Child of the regiment on the payroll of the Royal-Cravates which became the 10th Cavalry 1 January 1791, trooper 1 December 1793.

He was brigadier 22 March 1800, maréchal des logis on the battlefield 16 May 1800, in the same regiment when it became the 10th Cuirassiers 24 September 1803, sub-lieutenant 26 June 1807, wounded by a shell burst in the left thigh and his horse killed under him at Essling 22 May 1809. He became lieutenant 3 June 1809, captain 10 April 1813, retired when the corps was disbanded 25 December 1815. LH CH 16 June 1809.

RICHARDOT (Claude François, 1776-1821): born in Pont-de-Vaux (Ain) on 9 July 1776. In the 75th Infantry 26 April 1792, corporal in the 1st Ain Battalion 10 August 1792. Acting lieutenant in a requisition battalion 5 November 1793, trooper in the chasseurs à cheval 14 March 1794, sub-lieutenant 16 January 1798, aide de camp to Joubert 5 April 1798, then to Championnet 16 September 1799, acting lieutenant 20 October 1799, acting captain on the Mondovi battlefield 13 November 1799, confirmed 30 December 1801.

He became aide de camp to Generals Marchand 12 January 1802, then Pannetier 7 October 1803, in the 25th Chasseurs à Cheval 29 July 1805, aide de camp to General Marchand 17 March 1807, squadron commander 14 November 1808, colonel 1812, commanded the 7th Cuirassiers 2 July 1813, joined them 24 July 1813, confirmed colonel in the 7th Cuirassiers 28 September 1814.

He retired when the corps was disbanded 19 December 1815. LH CH 18 February 1808, O 5 September 1813, C 25 February 1814.

RICHE (Nicolas, 1755-1805): born in Saint-Albin (Isère) on 8 February 1755. Volunteer in the Royal-Pologne 9 April 1777 which became the 5th Cavalry 1 January 1791.

He was brigadier 25 January 1792, maréchal des logis 1 April 1793, maréchal des logis-chef 15 July 1794, sub-lieutenant 21 April 1800, in the same regiment when it became the 5th Cuirassiers 23 December 1802, lieutenant by seniority 23 November 1804, killed at Austerlitz 2 December 1805. LH CH 5 November 1804.

RICHELET (Jacques, 1778-?): born in Sugny (Ardennes) on 17 May 1778. In the 23rd Cavalry 20 November 1798.

He was brigadier 2 January 1803, dismissed with the corps 23 December 1802 and incorporated into the 6th Cuirassiers 3 January 1803, maréchal des logis 1 October 1806, maréchal des logis-chef 6 October 1808, two sabre wounds to his head at Essling 22 May 1809, sub-lieutenant 12 September 1809, lieutenant 9 February 1813, wounded at Leipzig 16 October 1813 and Champaubert 10 February 1814, in the King's Cuirassiers 1 May 1814.

Confirmed 1 July 1814, in the same regiment when it became the 1st Cuirassiers March 1815, dismissed and put up for retirement 24 December 1815. LH CH 25 February 1814.

RICHOUX (Urbain, 1771-1813): born in Chaumont (Haute-Marne) on 10 March 1771. Trooper in the Royal-Etranger 3 April 1788 which became the 7th Cavalry 1 January 1791, sabre wound to his head at Neerwinden 18 March 1793, brigadier 7 May 1793.

He was shot and wounded in the head near Combourg 26 April 1794, maréchal des logis the following day 27 April 1794, several sabre wounds near Cambrai 10 May 1794, maréchal des logis-chef 10 June 1794, adjutant-NCO 20 January 1799, lance wound to his right arm and a sabre wound to his side at Blinfeld 29 November 1800, in the same regiment when it became the 7th Cuirassiers 23 December 1802, sub-lieutenant by seniority 31 December 1804.

He became lieutenant adjutant-major 8 March 1807, rank of captain 8 September 1808, captain in the suite 7 April 1809, sabre wound to his left arm and concussed by a cannonball at Essling 21 May 1809, took up his position 12 December 1810, died at Joinville while returning to the depot 21 March 1813. LH CH 22 June 1804, O 17 June 1812.

RICHTER (?-1812): adjutant-NCO in the 3rd Cuirassiers, sub-lieutenant 12 August 1812, killed at the Moskova 7 September 1812.

RICHTER (Jean Louis, 1783-1815): born in Geneva (Léman) on 26 July 1783.
In the 15th Dragoons 11 February 1803, brigadier 12 May 1803, maréchal des logis 20 July 1803, in the 3rd Cuirassiers 21 April 1808, adjutant-NCO 22 April 1808, sub-lieutenant 14 May 1809, lieutenant 3 June 1809.

He was captain 11 September 1811, killed at Waterloo 18 June 1815. LH CH 14 April 1807.

RICHTER (Jean Louis, baron, 1769-1840): born in Geneva (Léman) on 24 October 1769. Captain in the Light Dragoons of the Allobroges Legion 13 August 1792 incorporated into the 15th Dragoons 5 February 1794, shot and wounded in the head at

Pavia 25 May 1796. He was squadron commander 11 September 1798, returned from Egypt end 1801, major in the 22nd Dragoons 29 October 183, commanded the 1st Provisional Dragoons at Austerlitz 2 December 1805, colonel of the 3rd Cuirassiers 31 December 1806, wounded at Essling 22 May 1809, brigadier-general 6 August 1811.

He commanded the 2nd Brigade of the 2nd Cuirassier Division 25 December 1811 then the 3rd Brigade of the same division May 1812, allowed to returned to France 26 January 1813, in the 2nd Division of the 1st Cavalry Corps of the Grande Armée 1 March 1813.

He was commanded the Moselle Department 9 June 1813 then the military post at Metz temporarily 14 January 1814, senior commander at Longwy during the Hundred Days, commanded the Moselle Department 12 June 1815, kept 11 October 1815.
LH CH 25 March 1804, O 11 July 1807, Baron of the Empire d.19 March 1808, l.p. 25 March 1809.

RIDRAY (Joseph, 1773-?): born in Saint-Calais (Sarthe) on 7 January 1777. In the Lorraine-Infanterie 19 October 1789 which became the 47th Infantry 1 January 1791, in the 6th Dragoons 1794, admitted to the Invalides because of his wounds from three shots 1797, in the Grenadiers of the Corps Législatif 1798, in the Grenadiers à Cheval of the Consular Guard 3 January 1800, brigadier 22 December 1801, in the Dragoons of the Guard 26 July 1806, maréchal des logis 13 July 1807.

He was lieutenant in the 4th Cuirassiers 13 March 1813, incorporated into the 2nd Provisional Heavy Cavalry in Hamburg 11 September 1813, returned with the garrison 27 May 1814, kept in the regiment which became the Angoulême Cuirassiers 6 August 1814 and became the 4th Cuirassiers again April 1815, retired 21 December 1815.
LH CH 14 June 1804.

RILLIET (Alfred Philippe de, 1791-1853): cousin of the following, born in Paris (Seine) on 13 June 1791.
Pupil at the school in Saint-Germain 13 October 1810, sub-lieutenant in the 3rd Cuirassiers 24 April 1812, instated 5 March 1812, lance wound to his left thigh at the Berezina 28 November 1812, sabre wound to his right arm at Reims March 1814, shot and wounded in the right arm at Fére-Champenoise 25 March 1814, aide de camp to General Dupont 29 July 1814, aide de camp to the same man now Minister of War 1 September 1814, aide de camp to Maréchal Soult 14 December 1814.

He was on the staff of the Duke of Feltre 13 March 1815, first-lieutenant in the Hussars of Royal Guard 12 October 1815.

OBICHON (Louis, 1765-?): born in Orléans (Loiret) on 20 July 1765. Sub-lieutenant in the 1st Loiret Battalion 6 October 1791.

He was shot and wounded twice in the left hand and the corner of the right eye at Maubeuge 1792, captain adjutant-major 23 April 1793, aide de camp to General Teza 21 November 1793.

He returned to the corps 17 January 1795 which became the 36th Half-Brigade of the Line, commanded a company and aide de camp to General Poncet the same day 8 February 1795, shot and wounded in the leg at Charleroi 2 June 1795, staff officer 18 August 1795, deputy to the Adjutant-General Grosjean 4 December 1795, aide de camp to General Ambert 12 February 1797.

He was attached to the 13th Chasseurs à Cheval 21 March 1800, captain in the suite of the 3rd cavalry 21 January 1801.

He was in service 2 August 1801 in the same regiment when it became the 3rd Cuirassiers 12 October 1802, in the 13th Cuirassiers 221 October 1808, squadron commander then cavalry major 1 February 1812.
LH CH 15 June 1804, O 19 May 1810.

Oldeconna, Spain, 12 April 1811: Squadron Commander Louis Robichon charged at the head of 57 cuirassiers against 5 Spanish squadrons putting forty men out of action and taking a hundred prisoners and four hundred weapons. His own troop only had seventeen light casualties.

RILLIET de CONSTANT (Frédéric Jacques Louis, 1794-1856): cousin of the above, born in Mont-le-Grand (Léman) on 17 January 1794.
Pupil in the Saint-Germain School 7 August 1810, passed out 8 September 1810, grenadier 15 September 1811, brigadier, maréchal des logis fourrier 23 November 1812.

He was maréchal des logis-chef 24 November 1812, left on leave for Geneva 26 November 1812, sub-lieutenant in the 1st Cuirassiers 28 January 1813, left to rejoin his unit 22 February 1813, joined up 25 February 1813, ordnance officer, returned to the corps October 1813, allowed to go to Paris 7 April 1814, two months' leave with pay 17 May 1814, in the Gendarmes of the King's Household with rank of lieutenant 6 July 1814.

resigned because a foreign national, returned voluntarily to the corps 16 March 1815, followed Louis XVIII to Belgium, dismissed 11 August 1815, returned to Switzerland 12 August 1815. LH.

Alfred de Rilliet. (RR)

RIOULT de VILLAUNAY D'AVENAY (Archange Louis, baron, 1768-1809): born in Caen (Calvados) on 21 November 1768. Replacement sub-lieutenant in the Royal-Normandie-Cavalerie 1 February 1785, took up his post 21 June 1787, in the same regiment when it became the 19th Cavalry 1 January 1791, commissioned Lieutenant 15 September 1791, captain 14 November 1792.

He was in the same regiment when it became the 18th Cavalry 4 June 1793, squadron commander 16 September 1793, commanded the regiment took up his post 3 November 1793, brigade commander 10 November 1793, suspended July 1794, brigade commander again 15 April 1795, reinstated 20 July 1795, brigade commander of the 16th cavalry 10 June 1796, suspended 28 August 1797, discharged with pay 12 September 1797, colonel of the 6th Cuirassiers 24 February 1805, interim CO of the 2nd Brigade (4th and 6th Cuirassiers) of the 3rd Cuirassier division 3 September 1805, same brigade Pully's division 23 September 1805 and the 2nd Brigade of the reconstituted 3rd Cuirassier Division November 1805, two sabre wounds to his left arm at Heilsberg 10 June 1807. He became brigadier-general 25 June 1807, commanded the 2nd Brigade (18th and 19th Dragoons) of the 4th Dragoon Division in the Army of Spain 7 September 1808, commanded a provisional brigade in Madrid made up of the 3rd Dutch Hussars and various dragoon squadrons 22 December 1808, recalled to Paris 5 January 1809, temporarily commanded the 3rd Brigade (3rd and 12th Cuirassiers) of the 1st Heavy Cavalry Division 30 March 1809, in the Army of Italy end April 1809.

He commanded a brigade of Light Cavalry (8th and 25th Chasseurs à cheval) Sahuc's division 6 May 1809, cannonball took off his thigh while crossing the Piave 8 May 1809, amputated and died of his wounds 27 May 1809. LH O 4 October 1808, Baron of the Empire d. 1807 and l.p. 15 January 1809.

RIPERT (Charles Antoine Calixte, baron, 1769-1832): born in Mazan (Vaucluse) on 17 September 1769.
Deputy on the staff of the Army of Helvetia 28 February 1798 shot and wounded in the right arm at Berne 5 March 1798.

He was captain in the suite of the 18th Cavalry 14 January 1800, deputy to Adjutant-General Hervo 19 August 1800, acting squadron commander 23 November 1802, confirmed 12 March 1804, in the camp of General Montreuil 2 April 1804, attached to the 3rd Cuirassiers 28 April 1804, on the staff of the 6th Corps of the Grande Armée 1805, adjutant-commandant 22 March 1807, shot and wounded in his left foot at Mondenedo 11 March 1809, concussed by a cannonball neat Krasnoë 17 November 1812, taken prisoner near Vilna 17 December 1812, returned August

1814, chief of staff in the 13th Military Division then in the 10th Cavalry Division in the 2nd Corps in the Army of the North May 1815, non-active August 1815.

LH CH 14 June 1804, O February 1808, Baron of the Empire l.p. 28 January 1809, confirmed as a hereditary peer 27 January 1815.

RISSE (Jacques, 1780-?): born in Verdun (Meuse) in 1790. In the 7th Cuirassiers 16 July 1803, brigadier 31 January 1811.

He was maréchal des logis 15 February 1812, maréchal des logis-chef 3 June 1813, sub-lieutenant 22 December 1813, non-active on half-pay 16 August 1814, reigned 15 January 1815.

RISTELHUEBERT (Louis Joseph, 1780-1813): born in Hagenau (Bas-Rhin) on 22 August 1780. In the 8th Hussars 19 June 1797, in the 12th Cavalry 23 September 1799, brigadier 13 January 1800, in the 3rd Hussars 24 February 1800, maréchal des logis 20 April 1800,.

Acting sub-lieutenant on the battlefield 12 July 1800, confirmed 28 August 1800, commissioned 7 June 1803, in the 8th Cuirassiers 26 January 1804, instated 2 February 1804, lieutenant by seniority 22 December 1804, adjutant-major 17 May 1805, rank of captain 17 November 1806,.

He was captain commanding a company 9 August 1809, wounded at Wiasma 3 November 1812, died of his wounds in Smolensk Hospital 18 February 1813. LH CH 5 November 1804.

RIVAT (Jean Baptiste, 1759-1807): born in Herpemont (Vosges) on 9 May 1759. In the Royal-Guyenne-Cavalerie 11 November 1784 which became the 23rd Cavalry 1 January 179.

He was brigadier 1 February 1792, maréchal des logis 17 May 1793, in the same regiment

ROMAGNY (Pierre, 1762-1805) born in Gomont (Ardennes) on 5 September 1761.
He was trooper in the Commissaire-Général Regiment 19 October 1784 which became the 3rd cavalry 1 January 1791, brigadier 1 October 1791.
He became maréchal des logis 1 June 1792, sub-lieutenant 1 August 1793.
He was lieutenant 16 April 1797, commissioned captain 20 May 1798, in the same regiment when it became the 3rd Cuirassiers 12 October 1802.
He was killed at Austerlitz 2 December 1805.
Holder of a Sabre of Honour 15 September 1802, LH CH by rights 1803, O 14 June 1804.

Sous-Lieutenant in the 3rd Cavalry, Pierre Romagny distinguished himself at Landshut on 13 November 1794. With twenty troopers he took 120 enemy infantrymen. He handed them over to several of his troopers for guarding and went off again to charge a detachment of 500 men which he put to flight.

ONDOT (Philibert Xavier, 1782-?) born in Montigny-les-Dames (Haute-Saône) on 22 July 1792. In the 23rd Cavalry 17 December 1802, dismissed with the corps 23 December 1802 and incorporated into the 5th Cuirassiers, brigadier 2 March 1803, fourrier 24 April 1803, maréchal des logis-chef 24 October 1803.

He was sub-lieutenant 30 July 1804, captain 24 November 1806, wounded at Essling 22 May 1809, squadron commander wounded at Winkovo 18 October 1812, major in the 5th Cuirassiers

He commanded the provisional regiment made up of the remnants from the regiments of the 2nd Heavy Cavalry Division beginning of February 1814.

He was wounded at Sézanne 4 March 1814, confirmed as supernumerary major in the suite of the Berri Cuirassiers 8 November 1814 which became the 5th Cuirassiers again April 1815.

He was dismissed 23 December 1815. LH O 1814.

Austerlitz, 2 December 1805: unhorsed in the middle of an enemy battalion formed into a square, Sous-Lieutenant Rondot managed to force his way out with his sabre before being dragged from the fray hanging on to the tail of one of his cuirassiers, then seeing a horse whose cuirassier had been killed, he mounted it and rejoined his platoon in combat. He was made a Lieutenant on 31 December 1805.

when it became the 22nd Cavalry 4 June 1793, maréchal des logis-chef 27 July 1793, sub-lieutenant 23 October 1795, lieutenant 15 September 1802, dismissed with the corps 31 December 1802 and incorporated into the 9th Cavalry 15 February 1803 which became the 9th Cuirassiers 24 September 1803, elected captain 16 September 1806.

He was killed at Friedland 14 June 1807.

RIVET d'ALBIGNAC (Philippe François Maurice, 1775-1824): son of the general, born in Millau (Aveyron) on 25 July 1775. One of the King's pages, emigrated 1791, lieutenant aide de camp to his great-uncle, de Montboissier, in the Army of the Princes 1792.

He was in the service of Austria then of England in the Choiseul and Salm Regiments, left 1795, returned to France 1800, in the service of France in the Gendarmes d'Ordonnance 29 October 1806, brigadier 4 November 1806, maréchal des logis 11 November 1806, maréchal des logis-chef 1 January 1807, second-lieutenant 16 July 1807,.

He became lieutenant in the suite of the 5th Cuirassiers 10 September 1807, allowed to go into service with Westphalia 8 November 1807, lieutenant-colonel aide de camp to King Jérôme 20 November 1807, counsellor of state for War 9 January 1808, colonel 9 February 1808, Grand Equerry to the Crown 1 July 1808, brigadier-general 28 July 1808.

He was inspector-general of cavalry 17 November 1808, commanded the vanguard of the 10th Corps in the Army of Germany 1 April 1809, minister of war in Westphalia 29 January 1810, disgraced for having slandered King Jérôme, resigned 23 September 1810, struck off the list of Westphalian army officers 11 November 1810, adjutant-commandant in the service of France 24 January 1812, chief of staff of the 6th (Bavarian) 6 March 1812, left Vilna with a detachment to join up with Napoleon end November 1812, allowed to go to France on leave February 1813, commanded the Gard Department 2 November 1813, available 30 June 1814, on half-pay 1 September 1814, maréchal de camp 29 November 1814.

He became chief of staff to Gouvion-Saint-Cyr 20 March 1815, under the Duke of Angoulême April 1815 then joined Louis XVIII in Ghent, secretary-general of the Ministry of War under Gouvion-Ssaint-Cyr 10 July 1815, commanded the Ecole Spéciale Militaire at Saint-Cyr 14 September 1815. LH CH 25 September 1812.

RIVIERE (Pierre, 1789-1815): born in Montmerle (Ain) on 8 May 1789. Boarder in the Ecole Spéciale Militaire de Cavalerie 12 October 1809, passed out 4 November 1809.

He was grenadier 18 May 1810, brigadier 15 September 1811, sub-lieutenant in the 10th Cuirassiers 24 April 1812, killed at Ligny 16 June 1815.

ROBAS (Didier Alexis, 1769-?): born in Pazoches (Meuse) on 24 February 1769. In the 16th Cavalry 6 August 1792 which became the 15th Cavalry 4 June 1793.

He was brigadier 8 October 1799, in the Grenadiers à Cheval of the Guard 21 March 1802, brigadier 26 February 1806, maréchal des logis 1 October 1808, lieutenant in the 8th Cuirassiers 1 April 1813, incorporated with his squadron into the 2nd Provisional Heavy Cavalry in Hamburg 11 September 1813.

Returned with the garrison 30 May 1814, wounded at Waterloo 18 June 1815, dismissed with the corps 5 December 1815 and put up for retirement 11 December 1815.

ROBERT (?-?): maréchal des logis-chef in the 13th Cuirassiers, sub-lieutenant 25 February 1814, confirmed 26 February 1814.

ROBERT (Bernard, 1772-1812): born in Verneuil (Marne) in December 1772. In the 7th Cavalry 29 May 1792 which became the 7th Cuirassiers 23 December 1802, brigadier 11 October 1803, maréchal des logis 12 February 1806.

He was sub-lieutenant 4 March 1812, killed at Polotsk 31 October 1812.

ROBERT (Paul Frédéric, 1785-?): born in Charny (Meuse) on 19 June 1785. In the 10th Cavalry 23 October 1801, brigadier 23 September 1802.

He was fourrier 25 June 1803, in the same regiment when it became the 10th Cuirassiers 24 September 1803, maréchal des logis and maréchal des logis-chef the same day 20 December 1805, adjutant 25 May 1807, sub-lieutenant 16 May 1809, shot and wounded shattering his jaw and his horse killed under him at Essling 22 May 1809, lieutenant 12 August 1812.

He became captain 19 June 1813, shot and wounded in the left leg at Ligny 16 June 1815, dismissed with the corps 25 December 1815. LH CH 16 June 1809.

ROBIDET (Amable, 1770-?): born in Gouanternois (Pas-de-Calais) on 23 April 1770. In the 8th Cavalry 8 October 1792, sabre wound to his right arm at Fleurus 26 June 1794.

He was in the same regiment when it became the 8th Cuirassiers 10 October 1801, brigadier 18 March 1802, maréchal des logis 17 January 1807, in the 7th Squadron of the Gendarmerie d'Espagne 1 February 1810, in the 1st Legion of the Gendarmerie à Cheval d'Espagne "Burgos" 16 December 1810, sabre wound to his head at Burgos November 1810, dismissed with the legion 27 February 1813, sub-lieutenant in the 4th Cuirassiers 1 March 1813, two lance wounds in his thigh and a sabre wound to his head and his horse killed under him at Epinal 11 January 1814, sabre wound to his wrist and shot in the leg at Waterloo 18 June 1815.

He was retired with the disbanding of the corps 21 December 1815. LH CH 27 December 1814, confirmed 11 April 1815.

ROBIEN de TREULAN (Paul Julien Malo de, 1766-?): born on 25 July 1766, in the Gendarmes du Dauphin 17 June 1783, sub-lieutenant in the Mestre-de-Camp-Général-Cavalerie 12 July 1786, lieutenant 1 June 1789, in the same regiment when it became the 24th Cavalry 1 January 1791, dismissed with the corps 20 February 1791.

He was re-placed as sub-lieutenant in the 24th of the so-called new levy when it was formed the following day 21 February 1791, lieutenant 1792, in the same regiment when it became the 23rd Cavalry 4 June 1793, left 6 December 1793, re-placed in the suite of the same regiment 18 September 1796, captain-adjutant of the military position 6 December 1796, aide de camp to General Lestranges, retroactively in the suite of the 23rd Cavalry 17 June 1799.

He became captain adjutant-major in the 6th Cuirassiers 13 March 1802, in the 5th Cuirassiers 22 January 185, struck off the rolls 24 November 1806.

ROCHAT (Claude Jean Baptiste, 1776-1810): born in Metz (Moselle) on 9 April 1776. In the health service 31 July 1794.

He was commissioned as surgeon, 3rd Class in the 10th Cavalry 18 July 1797, brigadier 27 March 1802, fourrier 15 April 1802, in the same regiment when it became the 10th Cuirassiers 24 September 1803, maréchal des logis 22 November 1804, maréchal des logis-chef 14 February 1805, adjutant-NCO 8 October 1806, sub-lieutenant 24 November 1806.

ROUSSELOT (Maurice, 1773-?): born in Brabant (Meuse) on 5 December 1773. In the 24th Cavalry 30 March 1793 which became the 23rd Cavalry 4 June 1793,.

He was brigadier 19 April 1800.

He was dismissed with the corps 23 December 1802 and incorporated into the 5th Cuirassiers 3 January 1803, maréchal des logis 23 September 1804

He became sub-lieutenant 25 May 1807, lieutenant 17 May 1811, retired 27 July 1811.

Holder of a Rifle of Honour 29 May 1802, LH CH by rights 24 September 1803.

At Offemburg in June 1799, Maurice Rousselot charged an enemy platoon alone killing several troopers to disengage one of his officers who was too seriously wounded, but unfortunately he was only able to bring back his horse.

He was wounded twice by Biscayan shots to his shoulder and left heel at Hoff 6 February 1807, lieutenant 25 May 1807, adjutant-major 6 June 1807, in service as captain 16 May 1809, died in Metz 30 June 1810. LH CH 14 May 1807.

ROCHAT (Pierre Eugène Dieudonné, 1786-?): born in Saint-Privat (Moselle) on 8 May 1786. In the 10th Cuirassiers 20 June 1803, brigadier 1 December 1806, fourrier 23 April 1809,.

He was maréchal des logis 16 May 1809, sub-lieutenant 12 August 1812, lieutenant 28 September 1813, dismissed with corps 25 December 1815. LH CH 28 September 1813.

ROCHE (François, 1777-?): born in Champagne-sur-Vingeanne (Côte-d'Or) on 13 December 1777. In the 3rd Cavalry 5 September 1799 which became the 3rd Cuirassiers 12 October 1802, brigadier 2 December 1803, maréchal des logis 25 June 1809, adjutant-NCO 1 April 1813, sub-lieutenant 4 December 1813, in the King's Cuirassiers 1 May 1814 which became the 1st Cuirassiers again April 1815. He was wounded at Waterloo 18 June 1815, dismissed 24 December 1815. LH CH 4 December 1813.

ROCHE (Jean, 1765-1807): born in Qunitenas (Ardèche) on 7 May 1795. In the Reine-Cavalerie 12 April 1785.

He was brigadier-fourrier in the same regiment when it became the 4th Cavalry on the same day 1 January 1791, maréchal des logis 27 February 1792, maréchal des logis-chef 1 August 1793, sub-lieutenant 2 October 1794, lieutenant 201 February 1799.

He became lieutenant-adjutant-major 21 February 1802, in the same regiment when it became the 4th Cuirassiers 12 October 1802, captain adjutant-major 9 September 1803, captain commanding a company 8 April 1807, killed at Heilsberg 10 June 1807.

ROCHEBRUNE (Charles Sébastien de, 1784-?): born in Trogon (Meuse) on 23 March 1784. In the 4th Cavalry 20 May 1799 which became the 4th cuirassiers 12 October 1802, brigadier 1 October 1804, maréchal des logis 1 October 1806, shot and wounded in the right arm at Heilsberg 10 June 1807, maréchal des logis-chef 1 May 1809, wounded by a Biscayan shot to his right leg at Essling 22 May 1809, sub-lieutenant 3 June 1809.

He was ieutenant 17 June 1812, Captain 19 November 1812, incorporated with his squadron into the 2nd Provisional Heavy Cavalry in Hamburg 11 September 1813, returned with the garrison 30 May 1814 and to the regiment, dismissed 21 December 1815. LH CH 1 August 1809.

ROCHEMORE (Maurice, 1788-?): born in chateau d'Aigremont (Tarn) on 2 September 1788.
Sub-lieutenant in the 13th Cuirassiers 17 August 1809, lieutenant 3 November 1812, adjutant-major 18 April 1813, incorporated into the 9th Cuirassiers 9 August 1814.
He became captain adjutant-major 26 December 1814, retroactively to 25 November 1814, left the corps 1 April 1815. LH CH 19 March 1815.

ROCHON (Léonard, 1763-1809): born in Vénissieux (Rhône) on 5 January 1763. In the Cuirassiers du Roy 10 June 1784 which became the 8th Cavalry on 1 January 1791.
He was brigadier and maréchal des logis the same day 28 August 1793, maréchal des logis-chef 3 September 1794, elected sub-lieutenant 23 October 1798, lieutenant by seniority 3 June 1801, in the same regiment when it became the 8th cuirassiers 10 October 1801, captain 21 January 1803, wounded at Heilsberg 10 June 1807 and Essling 22 May 1809, died of his wounds 5 July 1809. LH CH June 1805.

RODENBACH (Pierre Charles, 1794-1848): born in Roulers (Lys) on 18 June 1794. Velite in the Grenadiers à Cheval of the Imperial Guard 6 February 1811, sub-lieutenant in the 14th Cuirassiers 13 March 1813, returned home as a foreign national 22 June 1814.

ROESINGHE see **THIBAULT ROESINGHE**

ROGER (?-?): maréchal des logis in the 3rd Cuirassiers. He was sub-lieutenant 22 December 1813, no longer on the rolls as of 20 August 1814.

ROGER (Jacques, 1766-?): born in Revel (Haute-Garonne) on 30 September 1766. In the Guyenne-Infanterie 27 December 1783, corporal 21 March 1788, in the same regiment when it became the 21st Infantry 1 January 1791.
He was sergeant 15 November 1791, resigned 14 March 1792, in the 12th Hussars 23 November 1803, brigadier 24 March 1794, maréchal des logis 12 July 1795, acting sub-lieutenant 13 August 1798 and embarked on the Irish Expedition on the same day, taken prisoner with the other troops on the expedition, returned to the 8th Cuirassiers 12 December 1806,.

He was incorporated into the 3rd provisional Heavy Cavalry in Spain 1808, retired 1 May 1811.

ROGET de BELLOQUET (Louis Dominique François, 1796-?): born in Bergheim (Haut-Rhin) on 8 January 1796.
Pupil at the Ecole Spéciale Impériale de Cavalerie in Saint-Germain 28 June 1812, sub-lieutenant in the cavalry 25 December 1813, sub-lieutenant (Young Guard) in the Grenadiers à Cheval of the Imperial Guard 19 February 1814, non-active 22 July 1814, in the Berri Cuirassiers 2 February 1815, acting aide de camp 11 May 1815.
He became aide de camp to General Jacquinot 1 June 1815, returned to the regiment 1 August 1815 which had become eh 5th Cuirassiers again, dismissed with the corps 23 December 1815. LH CH 14 February 1815.

ROHAN CHABOT (Anne Louis Fernand de, 1789-?): born in Paris (Seine) on 14 October 1789. Sub-lieutenant in the 4th Cuirassiers 25 May 1809.
He was lieutenant aide de camp to General de Narbonne 18 March 1812.

ROICOMTE (Joseph Xavier, 1774-?): born in Domprichard (Doubs) in 1774. In the 9th Cavalry 18 January 1794, brigadier 9 July 1800.
He was in the same regiment when it became the 9th Cuirassiers 24 September 1803, maréchal des logis 1 November 1806, maréchal des logis-chef 1 August 1807, in the 13th Cuirassiers 21 October 1808, adjutant-NCO 25 February 1810, sub-lieutenant 18 September 1811. He became lieutenant 6 November 1813, confirmed 5 March 1814, wounded at Sézanne 25 March 1814, retired 6 August 1814, pensioned 29 October 1814.

ROIZE (Louis Félix, 1772-?): born in Toulon (Var) on 14 January 1772. Volunteer in the 1st Hussars 6 October 1793,.
He was deputy on the general staff of the cavalry 10 February 1796, sub-lieutenant in the 20th Dragoons 22 September 1797, deputy to the adjutant-generals in th Army of the Orient 21 June 1799, lieutenant 22 June 1800, captain aide de camp to General Davout 23 October 1800, taken prisoner by the English 17 February 1801, returned 20 July 1801, captain in the Gendarmerie d'Elite of the Guard 31 October 1801, squadron commander in the 1st Cuirassiers 16 May 1806
He joined them 21 September 1806, wounded at Jena 14 October 1806 and Hoff 6 February 1807, major in the 14th Dragoons 9 May 1807, left 25 June 1807. LH O 10 April 1815.

ROLLAND (Pierre, baron, 1772-1848): born in Montpellier (Hérault) on 8 June 1772.
He was in the Battalion des Braconniers Montagnards (the "Mountain Poachers' Battalion") from the Aude Department aka Chasseurs de l'Aude 10 January 1791

which formed the guides for the Army of the Pyrénées Orientales 7 September 1793.

He was deputy sub-lieutenant to the Adjutant-General Desroches 15 September 1794, captain in the suite of the 1st Police Legion whilst maintaining his functions 28 September 1794, available when Desroches was suspended 18 October 1795, active again 8 January 1799, deputy to the adjutant-generals in the Army of Naples 21 February 1799, on the staff of the Reserve Army May 1800 then that of Italy 5 July 1800, captain in the suite of 14th Cavalry 11 July 1800, deputy on the staff of the Army of the Grisons 5 October 1800, squadron commander in the suite of the 14th Cavalry 17 April 1801, in service in the 19th cavalry 20 November 1801, dismissed with the corps 31 December 1802 and incorporated into the suite of the 11th Cavalry 21 January 1803, in the 12th Cavalry 26 February 1803 which became the 12th Cuirassiers 24 September 1803, major in the 2nd Cuirassiers 15 December 1803, joined them 15 February 1804 and placed as commandant of the depot in Caen 1804 then Sarre-Libre,.

He was employed in a provisional cuirassiers regiment sent to Spain 15 January 1808, allowed to return to the depot 18 June 1808, commanded a heavy cavalry regiment sent to Germany 18 February 1809.

He was shot and wounded in the right arm at Regensburg 23 April 1809, second-colonel in the war squadrons in the 2nd Cuirassiers 31 March 1809, sent home at the disposal of the minister of War, commanded the 3rd Provisional Cuirassiers 1 April 1810, in the 2nd Mobile Column searching for deserters and draft dodgers in the 9th and 10th Military Divisions 18 March 1811, colonel of the 2nd Cuirassiers 7 September 1811, lost a leg blown off by a cannonball at Leipzig 16 October 1813

He became brigadier-general 28 October 1813, withdrew to Paris to look after his wound, commanded the Avignon Branch of the Invalides 28 May 1814, replaced and gave up his post 9 December 1815. LH CH 25 March 1804, O 11 October 1812, C 5 September 1813, Chevalier of the Empire l.p. 28 January 1809, Baron d. 15 August 1809 and l.p. 23 July 1810.

RONCIERE see **CLEMENT de la RONCIERE**

ROSIERES see **KEGUELIN de ROSIERES**

ROSSIGNOL (Jacques Henri Louis, chevalier, 1769-1827): born in Coucy-le-Château (Aisne) on 26 August 1769.
In Colonel d'Urre's Legion 25 September 1792, fourrier 10 December 1792, maréchal des logis 13 January 1793, incorporated into the 12th Chasseurs à Cheval 2 April 1793.

He was sub-lieutenant in the 21st Chasseurs à Cheval 14 August 1793, lieutenant 16 August 1794 (24 August 1795), discharged 29 August 1796, back in activity 2 March 1797, in the Grenadiers

10.ᵉᵐᵉ REGIMENT DE CUIRASSIERS.

Colonel from the 10th Cuirassier Regiment.
(Reprint by R. and J. Brunon, Musée de l'Empéri, private collection)

(Chasseurs) à Cheval of the Consular Guard 3 January 180, captain 26 October (5 November) 1800.

He was squadron commander in the Grenadiers à cheval 5 September 1805, in the Dragoons of the Guard 13 September 1806, adjutant-commandant 23 October 1811, chief of the staff of the 5th Cuirassiers Division in the 1st Cavalry Reserve Corps 11 January 1812, wounded in his right thigh at Wiasma 3 November 1812, several sabre wounds to his chest.

He lost a finger and taken prisoner in Russia 6 December 1812, returned and non-active 1 August 1814. LH CH 14 June 1804, O 14 March 1806, Chevalier of the Empire l.p. 5 October 1808.

ROSSIGNOL (Pierre Jean Henri, 1782-1815): born in Bouzy (Oise) on 19 January 1782. In the 11th Cuirassiers 2 January 1804, brigadier 1 December 1806.

He was maréchal des logis 16 April 1809, maréchal des logis-chef 1 December 1809, sub-lieutenant 14 May 1813, killed at Les Quatre-Bras 16 June 1815. LH CH 14 May 1813.

ROSTAING (Charles Antoine, 1790-?): born in Giarsieux (Isère) on 11 June 1790. Velite in the Grenadiers à Cheval of the Imperial Guard 1 June 1808.

He became sub-lieutenant in the 9th Cuirassiers 13 March 1813, incorporated with his squadron into the 3rd Provisional Heavy Cavalry in Hamburg 11 September 1813, returned with the garrison 30 May 1814, struck off the rolls because he was absent for too long 25 July 1815.

ROUBIN (Jean Baptiste Louis Marie Jacques, 1792-?): born in Villeneuve-les-Avignon (Gard) on 24 June 1792. At the Ecole Spéciale Impériale de Cavalerie in Saint-Germain 1 July 1811, grenadier 8 May 1812, brigadier 2 August 1812, fourrier 17 January 1813.

He was sub-lieutenant in the 3rd Cuirassiers 30 January 1813, lance wound in the shoulder at Fère-Champenoise 25 March 1814, aide de camp 14 March 1815.

ROUDIER (?-?): maréchal des logis in the Dragoons of the Imperial Guard, lieutenant in the 9th Cuirassiers 8 February 1813, wounded at Leipzig 18 October 1813, no longer appears on the rolls as of 9 August 1814.

ROUGET (Jean, 1777-1812): born in Reims (Marne) on 28 April 1777. In the 3rd Cavalry 4 July 1799, brigadier-fourrier 30 June 1801.

He was maréchal des logis-chef 27 December 1801, in the same regiment when it became the 3rd Cuirassiers 12 October 1802, adjutant-NCO 3 December 1805, sub-lieutenant 1 May 1807, Regimental officier d'Etat Civil (civil status officer).

He became lieutenant 3 June 1809, adjutant-major 29 October 1811, died 1812.

ROUGET (Pierre Nicolas, 1776-?): born in Courcey (Marne) on 23 March 1776. In the 6th Cavalry 19 June 1799.

He was brigadier 24 May 1801, in the same regiment when it became the 6th Cuirassiers 23 December 1802, maréchal des logis 25 February 1803, maré-

chal des logis-chef 13 March 1810, sub-lieutenant 12 October 1811.

He became lieutenant 6 August 1813, prisoner with the capitulation at Danzig 1 January 1814, returned October 1814, dismissed 21 November 1815. LH CH 10 June 1807.

ROULIER (Julien Marie, 1772-?): born in Saint-James (Manche) on 7 January 1772. Volunteer in the 1st Manche Battalion and elected lieutenant the same day 28 October 1791.

He was sub-lieutenant in the 4th Hussars 22 December 1792 two sabre wounds to his head and to his wrist and his horse killed under him near Maubeuge June 1794, aide de camp to General Roulland 4 January 1796, lieutenant 3 January 1797.

He became captain 2 July 1798, in the 9th Cavalry 3 November 1801 which became the 9th Cuirassiers 24 September 1803, bayonet wound to his right foot at Regensburg 23 April 1809, in the 7th Chasseurs à Cheval 9 September 1809, retired 1 December 1911. LH CH 14 April 1807.

ROULLOY (Théodore Michel, 1778-?): born in Nancy (Meurthe) on 18 May 1778. In the 10th Cavalry 22 December 1795, brigadier 11 April 1802.

He was maréchal des logis 25 February 1803, in the same regiment when it became the 10th Cuirassiers 24 September 1803, maréchal des logis-chef 24 November 1806, sub-lieutenant 16 May 1809, concussed by a cannonball on his chest at Essling 22 May 1809.

He was lieutenant 12 August 1812, prisoner 26 January 1813. LH CH 1 October 1807.

ROULX (Edme François, 1764-?): born in Chateaurenard (Loiret) on 13 September 1764. In the Royal-Cravates which became the 10th cavalry 1 January 1791, brigadier 10 August 1792, fourrier 15 September 1793.

He was maréchal des logis 1 October 1793, maréchal des logis-chef 17 June 1794, sub-lieutenant 11 December 1801, in the same regiment when it became the 10th Cuirassiers 24 September 1803, lieutenant 10 July 1806, wounded on his left side and stomach by his horse falling after it was killed at Hoff 6 February 1807.

He was captain 3 June 1809, retired 25 September 1811. IH CH 1 October 1807.

ROUMET (Louis, 1775-?): born in 1775. In the 12th Cavalry 13 December 1793, gendarme in the 6th Legion, Indre Company 20 July 1802, in the Legion of the Gendarmerie d'Elite of the Imperial Guard 23 October 1804, brigadier in the Indre Company 1 March 1806, in the 4th Squadron of the Gendarmerie d'Espagne 25 December 1809, fourrier 17 January 1810, maréchal des logis 1 January 1811, maréchal des logis-chef 4 September 1811.

He was lieutenant in the 1st Cuirassiers 28 February 1813, joined them 12 May 1813, in the King's Cuirassiers 1 July 1814, remained in Paris at the disposal of the Minister of War 20 January 1815, returned to the corps 1 April 1815 which had become the 1st Cuirassiers again, dismissed 24 December 1815.

ROUOT (Antoine Philippe de, 1782-?): born in Saint-Dié (Vosges) on 25 September 1782. In the 12th Cavalry 16 September 1801, fourrier 3 February 1802.

He was in the same regiment when it became the 12th Cuirassiers 24 September 1803, maréchal des logis 21 February 1804, sabre wound to his right hand and his horse killed under him at Friedland 14 June 1807, shot and wounded in the right thigh at Regensburg 23 April 1809, sub-lieutenant 14 May 1809, wounded at Essling 22 May 1809, lieutenant 21 March 1812, wounded in the right leg by a cannonball which also killed his horse under him at the Moskova 7 September 1812, unhorsed and his horse killed under him then wounded himself by a lance and taken prisoner at Krasnoë 21 November 1812, returned and put on the non-active list 1814.

He put back in the 12th Cuirassiers 14 June 1815, lieutenant adjutant-major 25 July 1815, non-active 3 August 1815, left 11 September 1815. LH CH 11 October 1812.

ROUOT DE MORANGE (?-1812): maréchal des logis-chef in the 12th Cuirassiers, sub-lieutenant 3 June 189, died 23 March 1812.

ROUS de LAMAZELIERE (?-?): sub-lieutenant in the cavalry 16 April 1809, in the suite of the 7th Cuirassiers 26 December 1809, in the 3rd Provisional Heavy Cavalry in Spain, took up his appointment 25 January 1812, wounded at the Berezina 28 November 1812.

He was lieutenant wounded at Neustadt 1 January 1814, no longer appears on the rolls as of 16 August 1814.

ROUSSEAU (Charles François Marie, 1761-?): born in Montigny-sur-Crécy (Aisne) on 29 January 1761. In the Royal-Etranger-Cavalerie 1 January 1781.

He was brigadier 1 January 1787, brigadier-fourrier in the same regiment when it became the 7th Cavalry on the same day 1 January 1791, maréchal des logis 1 may 1792, maréchal des logis-chef 19 March 1793, sub-lieutenant 16 November 1793, lieutenant 13 January 1794, captain 11 May 1794, re-placed as a lieutenant 6 August 1795.

Standard belonging to the 12th Cuirassiers in 1815. (RR)

ULM
JENA
EYLAU
FRIEDLAND
ECKMÜHL
ESSLING
WAGRAM

He became captain 20 January 1799, on six months' leave 23 September 1801 then returned to the corps, in the same regiment when it became the 7th Cuirassiers 23 December 1802, wounded at Essling 21 May 1809, on the retirement payroll 9 August 1809. LH CH 1 October 1807.

ROUSSEAU (François Maurice, 1788-?): born in Noisy-le-Grand (Seine-et-Oise) on 10 April 1788. Velite in the Grenadiers à cheval of the Imperial Guard 20 March 1809.

He was sub-lieutenant in the 10th Cuirassiers 13 March 1813, incorporated with his squadron into the 3rd Provisional Heavy Cavalry in Hamburg 11 September 1813.

He returned with the garrison May 1814, shot and wounded at Waterloo 18 June 1815, dismissed with the corps 25 December 1815.

ROUSSEAU de CHAMOY (?-?): pupil in the Ecole Spéciale Militaire de Cavalerie in Saint-Germain.

He was sub-lieutenant in the suite of the 3rd Cuirassiers 19 April 1812, taken prisoner by the Russians near Ormiana 5 December 1812.

ROUSSEL d'HURBAL (Nicolas François, baron, 1763-1849): born in Neufchâteau (Vosges) on 7 September 1763.

In the service of Austria as a cadet in the Kaunitz Infantry Regiment 1 January 1782, sub-lieutenant in the Chevau-Légers under Vincent 8 February 1785, first-lieutenant in Latour's dragoons 13 October 1789, shot and wounded through the body at Aldednhoven against the French 2 March 1793, second-captain 20 April 1793, first captain 1 March 1797, major 1 March 1802.

He was lieutenant-colonel of Latour's Chevau-Légers 2 September 1804, colonel of the Maurice de Lichtenstein's Cuirassiers 1 January 1807, sabre wound through his helmet at Essling 22 May 1809, general-major 23 May 1809, resigned October 1810, retired 1 April 1811, brigadier-general in the service of France 31 July 1811, inspector and CO of the 9th Chevau-Légers 3 August 1811.

He commanded the 8th (Polish) Lancers 1 May 1812, in the suite of the staff of the 1st Corps of the Grande Armée assigned to Bruyère's Light Cavalry Division from the 1st Reserve Corps 1 June 1812, in the 4th Foreign Cavalry Brigade, bruised on his left leg by a cannonball at the Moskova 7 September 1812, major-general 4 December 1812.

He commanded the cavalry regiment made up with the remnants of the 2nd Cavalry Corps under Sebastiani in the army of the Elbe 15 February 1813, commanded the 2nd Light Cavalry Division 19 April 1813, sabre wound to his skull at the Katzbach 26 August 1813, on leave in Paris November 1813, inspector-general of the Central Cavalry Depot in Versailles 17 January 1814, commanded the Fontainebleau Arrondissement 11 February 1814, commanded the 6th Cavalry Division (Dragoons) of the 6th Cavalry Corps 19 February 1814.

He was detached to the 2nd Corps 23 February

1814, took part in the defection of Marmont's corps and led his division to Evreux 5 April 1814, inspector-general in charge of organising the cavalry in the 3rd and 19th Military Divisions 1 June 1814, inspector-general of the cavalry for 1815 30 December 1814, ordered to go to Lyon to be with the Count of Artois 11 March 1815.

He commanded the 2nd Cavalry Reserve Division at Metz 8 April 1815, commanded the 12th Heavy Cavalry Division of the 3rd Cavalry Corps 3 June 1815.

He was wounded at Waterloo 18 June 1815, interim CO of the same corps 29 June 1815, non-active 1 August 1815, retired 9 September 1815. LH, Baron of the Empire d. 28 September 1813 and l.p. 26 February 1814.

ROUSTANT (André Balthazard, 1762-?): born in Nîmes (Gard) on 4 July 1792. In the Gardes Françaises 3 February 1779, left 15 May 1779, in the Queen's Gendarmes 8 October 1780, discharged and pensioned 1 April 1788, gendarme national of the Gard Department 6 January 1792.

He was sub-lieutenant in the 9th Dragoons 10 May 1792, lieutenant 1 April 1793, aide de camp to General Vaubois 6 August 1793, captain 25 November 1796, deputy on the staff of the 8th Military Division 12 December 1800, squadron commander 2 January 1801, in the suite of the 9th Dragoons 20 January 1802.

He was in service of the 10th Chasseurs à cheval 3 October 1803, in the 5th Cuirassiers 15 December 1803, shot and wounded in the arm at Austerlitz 2 December 1805, retired 30 April 1807.

ROUVEROY see **BOUSIES de ROUVEROY**

ROUX (Joseph Julien, 1784-?): born in Tournon (Ardèche) on 29 March 1784. In the 4th Cuirassiers 4 October 1805, wounded at Marienwerder 11 February 1807.

He was brigadier 1 May 1808, fourrier 4 June 1809, maréchal des logis 16 October 1810, maréchal des logis-chef 16 April 1812, wounded at the Berezina 28 November 1812, sub-lieutenant 14 May 1813.

He was wounded by several lances at Meckenheim 1 January 1814, shot and wounded in his right arm at Waterloo 18 June 1815, retired 21 December 1815.

ROUYER (Christophe, 1759-?): born in Aunoy (Meuse) on 19 June 1759. In the Royal-Guyenne-Cavalerie 2 September 1781 which became the 23rd Cavalry 1 January 1791 then the 22nd Cavalry 4 June 1793.

He was brigadier-fourrier 27 July 1793, maréchal des logis 3 November 1794, maréchal des logis-chef 25 July 1795, adjudant-NCO 21 May 1801, sub-lieutenant 22 December 1801, dismissed with the corps and incorporated into the 9th Cavalry 15 February 1803 which then became the 9th Cuirassiers 24 September 1803.

He was elected lieutenant 18 June 1806, captain 29 April 1809, retired as a lieutenant 15 May 1809.

ROVERETTO (Jean François, 1790-?): born in Tortona (Genoa) on 30 March 1790. In the Italian Guards of Honour 1 July 1810, maréchal des logis the same day 1 July 1810, maréchal des logis-chef 29 July 1811.

He was sub-lieutenant in the 4th French Cuirassiers 15 March 1812, wounded at Polotsk 24 October 1812 and at the Berezina 28 November 1812, not included in the reorganisation of the Angoulême Cuirassiers as he was a foreigner 6 August 1814.

ROYER (François, 1788-?): born in Mardet (Indre-et-Loire) on 25 January 1788. In the 4th Drôme Battalion 25 March 1803, in the Gendarmerie d'Espagne 16 December 1810.

He was shot and wounded in the leg at Corunna January 1809 and two sabre wounds to his head at Burgos November 1809, maréchal des logis 1 September 18121, shot and wounded in the shoulder at Vittoria.

He became sub-lieutenant in the 3rd Cuirassiers 28 February 1813, wounded at Fère-Champenoise 25 March 1814, shot and wounded in the right hand at Waterloo 18 June 1815, dismissed with the corps 25 November 1815. LH CH 10 February 1813.

RUAULT (François Auguste, 1781-?): born in Bons (Calvados) on 28 July 1781. in the 1st Cuirassiers 29 August 1803, fourrier 14 June 1805.

He was maréchal des logis 16 November 1806, maréchal des logis-chef 18 November 1806, adjudant-NCO 25 May 1808, sub-lieutenant 31 July 1811, quartermaster treasurer of the 11th Cuirassiers 28 January 1814.

He joined them 27 February 1814, dismissed with the corps 16 December 1815. LH CH 17 March 1815.

RUBENS (Guillaume, 1755-?): born in Repan (Dyle) on 24 June 1755. In the Latour dragoons in the service of Austria 1771.

He was brigadier 1778, maréchal des logis 1783, maréchal des logis-chef in the Flanders Dragoons in the Army of the Brabant Patriots 20 December 1787, lieutenant 5 September 1791, captain commanding a squadron of the Belgian Legion in the service of France 15 January 1793.

He was captain in the suite of the French hussars 24 January 1795, discharged 21 November 1800, in the Chasseurs à cheval of the Legion des Francs du Nord 4 February 1801, discharged 31 July 1801, in the 10th Cuirassiers 30 November 1806, retired 1 June 1810.

RUDOLPH (Johan Frantz David, 1784-?): born in Cleves (Grand-Duchy of Berg) on 15 April 1784. In the 2nd Dutch Cuirassiers 5 December 1805, sabre and lance wounds at Eylau 8 February 1807.

He was brigadier 11 February 1807, maréchal des logis 10 September 1807, incorporated with his squadron into the 2nd Provisional Heavy Cavalry in Hamburg 11 September 1813, returned with the garrison 30 May 1814, 14th French Cuirassiers 18 August 1810, adjudant-NCO 11 September 1810.

He became sub-lieutenant 13 September 1813, dismissed with the corps 13 July 1814.

SOME ELEMENTARY ORGANISATIONAL PRINCIPALS

These organisation diagrams for the platoons, companies and squadrons have been drawn up based on the 1804 Cavalry ordnance. The tactical dispositions and the indications come from the same source. The tables concerning the total strength have been reconstructed from the archives of the Armée de Terre, and the work

COMPANY IN DEPLOYED FORMATION

carried out by Rigo, Lucien Rousselot together with research carried out by the author.

The silhouettes and the profiles have been made by André Jouineau and the topside views by Christophe Camilotte.

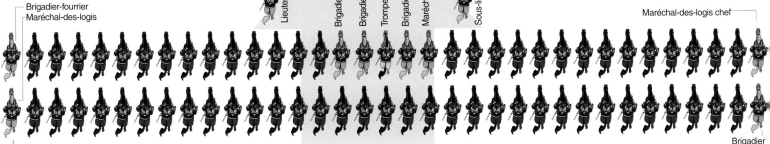

---

18 January 1810: the fifth squadron was suppressed and the company had a strength of 120 troopers.

Beginning of 1812: the regiments were asked to form a fifth squadron, the four which had originated with the 1810 reforms becoming war squadrons for the Russian Campaign.
At the end of that campaign, most of the regiments could no longer put anything more than a company's strength into the line.

Spring 1813: the regiments at the beginning of the campaign aligned two or three companies, rarely at full strength.

1815, during the Hundred Days: after the First Restoration the regiment returned to five two-company squadrons, of which four war squadrons.

THE COMPANY IN A COLUMN, BY PLATOONS, TO THE RIGHT

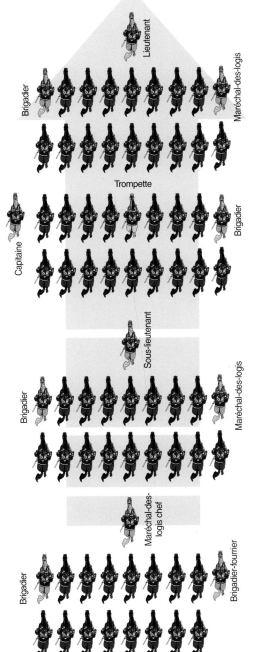

THE CUIRASSIER REGIMENT, OCTOBER 1803

THEORETICAL HQ STAFF

1 colonel
1 majors
2 squadrons commanders
2 adjudants majors
1 quartermaster
1 surgeon-major
1 surgeon-major 2nd class
2 under surgeon-major
2 adjudants NCOs
1 veterinaire
5 master craftsmen
tailor
saddlemakerculottier
bootmaker
tailor (pants)
armourer
1 brigadier trumpeter

THE THEORETICAL COMPANY

1 captain
1 lieutenant
1 second-lieutenant
1 maréchal-des-logis-chef
2 maréchaux-des-logis
1 brigadier-fourrier
4 brigadiers (corporals)
63 cuirassiers
1 trumpeter
75 troopers

HOW THE COMPOSITION OF THE CUIRASSIER REGIMENT EVOLVED

24 September 1803: the cuirassier regiment was formed with four two-company squadrons (three war squadrons and one depot squadron) and a regimental HQ.

August 1805: four war squadrons and an HQ. A fifth depot squadron was created.

30 October 1806: return to four two-company squadrons (of which one depot).

10 March 1807: back to five two-company squadrons.

THE CUIRASSIER REGIMENT, JULY 1809

THEORETICAL HQ STAFF

1 colonel
1 majors
2 squadrons commanders
2 adjudants majors
1 quartermaster
1 surgeon-major
1 surgeon-major 2nd class
2 under surgeon-major
2 adjudants NCOs
1 veterinaire
5 master craftsmen
tailor
saddlemakerculottier
bootmaker
tailor (pants)
armourer
1 brigadier trumpeter

THE THEORETICAL COMPANY

1 captain
1 lieutenant
1 second-lieutenant
1 maréchal-des-logis-chef
2 maréchaux-des-logis
1 brigadier-fourrier
4 brigadiers (corporals)
63 cuirassiers
2 trompeters
76 troopers

THE FIRST SQUADRON OF THE 1ST CUIRASSIER REGIMENT
in deployed formation according 1804 regulations

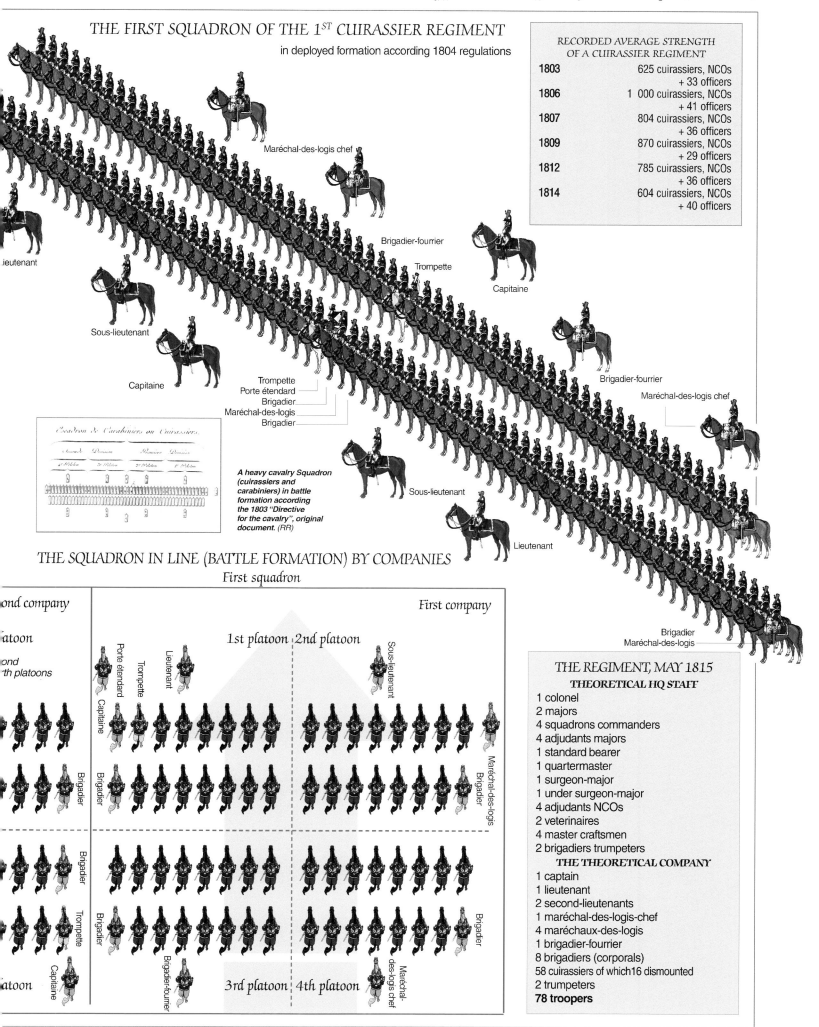

RECORDED AVERAGE STRENGTH OF A CUIRASSIER REGIMENT	
1803	625 cuirassiers, NCOs + 33 officers
1806	1 000 cuirassiers, NCOs + 41 officers
1807	804 cuirassiers, NCOs + 36 officers
1809	870 cuirassiers, NCOs + 29 officers
1812	785 cuirassiers, NCOs + 36 officers
1814	604 cuirassiers, NCOs + 40 officers

Maréchal-des-logis chef

Brigadier-fourrier

Trompette

Capitaine

Sous-lieutenant

Capitaine

Trompette
Porte étendard
Brigadier
Maréchal-des-logis
Brigadier

A heavy cavalry Squadron (cuirassiers and carabiniers) in battle formation according the 1803 "Directive for the cavalry", original document. (RR)

Brigadier-fourrier

Maréchal-des-logis chef

Sous-lieutenant

Lieutenant

Brigadier
Maréchal-des-logis

THE SQUADRON IN LINE (BATTLE FORMATION) BY COMPANIES
First squadron

ond company

First company

atoon

1st platoon 2nd platoon

ond
th platoons

Porte étendard
Trompette
Lieutenant
Capitaine

Sous-lieutenant

Brigadier
Brigadier

Maréchal-des-logis

Brigadier

Brigadier
Trompette
Brigadier

Brigadier

atoon
Capitaine

Brigadier-fourrier

3rd platoon 4th platoon

Maréchal-des-logis chef

THE REGIMENT, MAY 1815
THEORETICAL HQ STAFF
1 colonel
2 majors
4 squadrons commanders
4 adjudants majors
1 standard bearer
1 quartermaster
1 surgeon-major
1 under surgeon-major
4 adjudants NCOs
2 veterinaires
4 master craftsmen
2 brigadiers trumpeters
THE THEORETICAL COMPANY
1 captain
1 lieutenant
2 second-lieutenants
1 maréchal-des-logis-chef
4 maréchaux-des-logis
1 brigadier-fourrier
8 brigadiers (corporals)
58 cuirassiers of which16 dismounted
2 trumpeters
78 troopers

GRava 07

SAART (François Xavier, 1768 -after 1819): born in Belfort (Haut-Rhin) on 25 January 1768. In the Royal-Etranger-Cavalerie 1 September 1787 which became the 7th Cavalry 1 January 1791, brigadier-fourrier 27 April 1794, maréchal des logis 3 January 1802, maréchal des logis-chef 8 January 1802, in the same regiment when it became the 7th Cuirassiers 23 December 1802, adjutant-NCO 13 June 1805, sub-lieutenant 29 December 1806, lieutenant 7 January 1807, adjutant-major 7 April 1809, rank of captain 7 October 1810, retired and left the same day 8 October 1811, adjutant of a 2nd Class military area in Metz 7 October 1813, adjutant of a 1st Class military area at Landskron 27 October 1813, taken prisoner by capitulation of the fort after 4 days' bombardment 25 December 1813, returned 24 June 1814, adjutant 1st class of a military area at Longwy 31 May 1815, dismissed on half-pay after the surrender in 1815. LH CH 1 October 1807.

SAILLET (Charles Jean Baptiste, 1782-1809): born in Bar-le-Duc (Meuse) on 19 September 1782. Ordnance attached to the Army of the Danube and of Helvetia 20 January 1799, maréchal des logis in the 13th Chasseurs à Cheval 11 November 1800, in the 11th Cavalry 3 March 1802, sub-lieutenant 5 March 1803, in the same regiment when it became the 11th Cuirassiers 24 September 1803, lieutenant 21 December 1805, aide de camp to General Fouler his former colonel 30 April 1807, captain in the 13th Chasseurs à Cheval 1 March 1808, died 4 March 1809.

SAINT see ALBIN NEYROUD SAINT ALBAIN

SAINT ALPHONSE
see WATIER SAINT ALPHONSE.

SAINT CHERON (Alexandre, 1768-?): born in Saulay (Indre) on 2 October 1768. In the Royal-Cravates 22 September 1788 which became the 10th Cavalry 1 January 1791, sub-lieutenant in the 41st Light 15 September 1795, sub-lieutenant in the Lamoureux Chasseurs à Cheval when they were formed 7 October 1796, admitted into the organisation of the corps 2 November 1796, taken prisoner during the second Irish Expedition 30 September 1798, returned to France on parole April 1979 and employed in the 22nd Military Division 1800, deputy on the staff of Saint Domingo 1802, lieutenant 20 July 1804, returned to France because of the capitulation 30 November 1809, lieutenant in the 14th Cuirassiers 27 March 1812, captain 13 September 1813, dismissed with the corps and incorporated into the suite of the 12th Cuirassiers 13 July 1814, dismissed with the corps 10 December 1815.

SAINT GEORGES (Charles, ?-1809): maréchal des logis in the 2nd Carabiniers, sub-lieutenant in the 2nd Cuirassiers 3 April 1807, joined his unit the same day, wounded at Friedland 14 June 1807, lieutenant 28 May 1809, killed at Wagram 6 July 1809.

SAINT GEORGES (Louis Marie, 1782-?): born in 1782. In the 23rd Cavalry 7 December 1800, in the 5th Cavalry 2 November 1801, brigadier 29 January 1802, in the same regiment when it became the 5th Cuirassiers 23 December 1802, bayonet wound to his left thigh at Austerlitz 2 December 1805, maréchal des logis 17 October 1806, shot and wounded in the left arm at Eylau 8 February 1807, sub-lieutenant 16 May 1809, shot and wounded in his leg and three sabre wounds to his head and taken prisoner at Essling 22 May 1809, returned and put in the suite 8 August 1809, in the 1st Cuirassiers 22 October 1809, detached to the dismount company of the division October 1812, prisoner 2 December 1812. LH CH 14 April 1807.

SAINT GERMAIN see DECREST de ST GERMAIN

SAINT GILLES (Marie Joseph Auguste de, 1791-?): born in Saint-Méloir (Ille-et-Vilaine) on 14 September 1791. Pupil at the Ecole Impériale de Cavalerie in Saint Germain 1 May 1811, sub-lieutenant in the 12th Cuirassiers 30 January 1813, incorporated with his squadron into the 3rd Provisional Heavy Cavalry in Hamburg 11 September 1813, returned with the garrison May 1814, wounded at Waterloo 18 June 1815, dismissed and returned home 22 November 1815.

SAINT HILAIRE see PREVOT de SAINT HILAIRE

SAINT LOUIS see GREZES SAINT LOUIS

SAINT MARC d'HERBIGNY
see LAMBERT SAINT MARC d'HERBIGNY

SAINT MARS (?-?): In the 7th Infantry Half-Brigade 25 August 1797, in the 8th Cavalry 1 May 1799, fourrier 26 August 1800, in the Grenadiers à Cheval of the Consular Guard 4 October 1801, brigadier 22 December 1801, maréchal des logis 24 September 1803.
He was sub-lieutenant in the 12th Cuirassiers 2 May 1805, lieutenant 12 December 1806, adjutant-major 1 December 1807, captain 9 August 1809, adjutant on the general staff 27 April 1813.

SAINT MARSAN see ASINARI de SAINT MARSAN

SAINT MAUR de PRUDHOMME (François Frédéric Ladislas Angélique de, 1787-1810) born in Castres (Tarn) on 9 January 1787. Boarder in the Ecole Spéciale Militaire in Fontainebleau 24 June 1806, sub-lieutenant in the 4th Cuirassiers 19 February 1807.
He was incorporated into the 3rd Provisional Heavy Cavalry in Spain 1808, killed in the Mollit Gorges in Catalonia 21 January 1810.

SAINT MAURICE see BARBEYRAC de SAINT MAURICE

SAINT PAER see GROUT de SAINT PAER

SAINT SAUVEUR see RAFELIS de SAINT SAUVEUR

SAINT SULPICE see BONARDI de SAINT SULPICE

SAINT THIBAULT see CHANOINE de SAINT THIBAULT

SAINT VICTOR see DUPORT de SAINT VICTOR

SAINTE MESME (Louis Camille, 1763-?): born in Granfontaine (Doubs) on 20 September 1793. In the Royal-Cavalerie 4 January 1785, maréchal des logis 13 April 1787, in the same regiment when it became the 2nd Cavalry 1 January 1791, adjutant 15 September 1791, lieutenant 29 November 1792, confirmed 8 February 1793.
He was captain 14 March 1795, retroactively to 27 July 1794, in the same regiment when it

became the 2nd Cuirassiers 12 October 1802, squadron commander in the 3rd Cuirassiers 10 November 1807, instated 1 March 1808, commanded district at Valence in the 27th Military Division 28 October 1808.

SAINT ROSE see **DURAND** aka **SAINT ROSE**

SALLE (?-?): in the Reine-Cavalerie 23 February 1787 which became the 4th cavalry 1 January 1791, brigadier 19 July 1794, maréchal des logis 17 March 1800, maréchal des logis-chef 15 July 1800.

He was in the same regiment when it became the 4th Cuirassiers 12 October 1802, sub-lieutenant by seniority 16 March 1807, lieutenant 3 July 1809, left in order to retire 23 March 1810.

SALLMARD (Aimé de, 1786-1809): younger brother of the two men following. In the 2nd Cuirassiers and secretary to the colonel beginning October 1802, sub-lieutenant 1 March 1809, shot twice and wounded once in his arm and once in the weak spot of the breastplate penetrating his body, died from his wounds at Regensburg 23 April 1809.

SALLMARD (Jean François Louis Auguste de, 1784 - 1850) brother of the two above, born in Vienne (Isère) on 24 August 1784. In the 3rd Cavalry 24 May 1802, in the 2nd Cavalry 28 September 1802 which became the 2nd Cuirassiers 12 October 1802, brigadier 22 November 1802, brigadier-fourrier 19 August 1803, maréchal des logis 30 April 1804, maréchal des logis-chef 30 October 1806, sub-lieute-

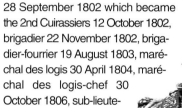

Cuirassier Colonel.
(© Photo J.-L. Viau)

nant 14 May 1809, sabre wound which cut half his nose off at the Moskova 7 September 1812.

He returned with frozen feet 1812, on convalescence leave, returned to the 22nd Dragoons August 1813, lieutenant in the 22nd Dragoons 16 October 1813

He was wounded twice defending Colmar Bridge with only his grand-garde of 25 Dragoons against a column of 6000 troopers giving the brigade enough time to come up in reinforcement 24 December 18413, wounded at Epinal 12 January 1814.

He was incorporated into the Dragoons N°13 1 August 1814 which became the 18th Dragoons again April 1815, dismissed 13 December 1815. LH CH 8 January 1814.

SALMON (René Guillaume Marin, 1773-?): born in Dinan (Côtes-du-Nord) on 18 June 1773. In the Forez-Infanterie 6 January 1790 which became the 14th Infantry 1 January 1791, prisoner of the Guadeloupe insurrectionists September 1792, caporal-fourrier 1793, sergeant-major 11 October 1794, shot and wounded in the right leg 1795, gendarme à cheval in the Côtes-du-Nord Department 21 December 1798.

He was maréchal des logis and maréchal des logis-chef in the 15th Squadron of the Gendarmerie d'Espagne 1 February 1810, sub-lieutenant in the 1st Legion of the Gendarmerie à Cheval "Burgos" 20 July 1811.

He was dismissed with the corps and promoted captain in the 11th Cuirassiers 28 February 1813, dismissed with the corps 16 December 1815. LH CH 27 September 1814.

SALOMON (François, 1762-?): born in Breda (Deux-Nèthes) on 11 February 1762. Trooper in the Stavenisfon Regiment 26 December 1782, brigadier 18 October 1790, maréchal des logis in the Thuil Regiment 1 January 1792, maréchal des logis-chef 1 August 1795. He was elected sub-lieutenant in the 2nd Dutch Cuirassiers 1 May 1807 which became the 14th French Cuirassiers 18 August 1810, left on retirement leave 18 March 1813.

SALOMON (Johan Theodor, 1791-1812): born in Zwoll (Yssel) on 12 December 1791. In the 2nd Dutch Cuirassiers 25 July 1807, brigadier 1 January 1808, maréchal des logis 1 November 1809, in the same regiment when it became the 14th French Cuirassiers 18 August 1810, sub-lieutenant 4 March 1812, killed at the Berezina 28 November 1812.

SALVAING (François Elysée, 1781-1815): born in Revel (Haute-Garonne) on 2 November 1781. In the 12th Hussars 31 October 17989, trooper in the 11th

SALLMARD (Charles Gabriel de, 1783-1858): elder brother of above and below, born in Vienne (Isère) on 11 May 1783. Engaged in the 3rd Cavalry 24 May 1802, fourrier in the 2nd Cavalry 28 September 1802 which became the 2nd Cuirassiers 12 October 1802, maréchal des logis 3 August 1804, in the 22nd Dragoons 22 September 1805, intended for the 2nd Dragons à Pied 1805.

He was at the 1st Provisional Dragoons end of May 1808, prisoner at Baylen 23 July 1808, held captive on the hulk "Vieille Castille", sub-lieutenant in the suite during his captivity 2 March 1809, escaped after taking part in the beaching of the hulk 16 May 1812, sub-lieutenant commanding the 60 Dragoons of the Governor (General Darricau) of Seville's Guard which he organised June 1810, returned to the 22nd Dragoons with his detachment 19 March 1811.

He was lieutenant by seniority 1 June 1812, in the Elite Company August 1813, captain 16 October 1813, non-active on half-pay 1 August 1814, rejoined the Duke of Angoulême 2 April 1815 then Louis XVIII at Ghent 4 May 1815, captain in the Chasseurs Royaux à Cheval 15 June 1815.

He returned to France with the King 8 July 1815, second captain in the Chasseurs à Cheval of the Royal Guard with the rank of Squadron Commander 10 October 1815.

LH CH 25 February 1814.

On 25 December 1806, Maréchal des Logis Charles Sallmard of the 2nd Cuirassiers had his horse killed under him and remained stuck under it during a reconnaissance mission at Pultusk. Wounded several times by lances, he was taken prisoner. He escaped on the following 15 January and reached his lines on 22 January 1807 travelling more than fifty leagues.

He joined the dragoons in Spain, was taken prisoner at Baylen on 23 July 1808, and escaped after he had taken part in the beaching of the hulk on 16 May 1810.

Regiment 25 April 1800, instated 2 May 1800, brigadier 18 January 1802, maréchal des logis 12 October 1802 retroactively to 23 May 1802, in the same regiment when it became the 11th Cuirassiers 24 September 1803, in the Grenadiers à Cheval of the Guard 15 August 1805, instated 14 September 1805, brigadier 1 April 1806, with his squadron he charged through 3 successive enemy lines at Eylau 8 February 1807, sub-lieutenant in the 2nd Carabiniers 4 April 1808, with his company went over to the 1st Provisional Heavy Cavalry in Spain which became the 13th Cuirassiers 21 October 1808, wounded by Biscayan shot on his left side at Tudela 23 November 1808, lieutenant 17 August 18090, incorporated into the 9th Cuirassiers 9 August 1814, captain 24 December 1814, shot in the head and killed at Waterloo 18 June 1815. LH CH 1 May 1808.

SAMBUY (de, ?-?): lieutenant in the suite of the 5th Cuirassiers 20 July 1811, took up his appointment 1 February 1812, captain in the 14th Hussars 13 March 1813.

SANDIFORT van den STRUITE (Willem Hendrikus, 1774-?): born in Brille (Bouches-de-la-Meuse) on 16 July 1774. Cadet in the Weserloo Marine Regiment 6 January 1789, sub-lieutenant in the 1st French Half-Brigade 14 July 1795, resigned 17 April 1797, sub-lieutenant in the National Guard 13 October 1799, dismissed 26 November 1799, cadet in the Batavian Sailors 6 August 1802, dismissed 4 September 1804, lieutenant in the 2nd Chasseurs à Cheval 2 March 1807, in the 2nd of the Line 1 April 1807, pensioned 9 January 1808, lieutenant in the 14th Cuirassiers 4 March 1812, wounded three times at Polotsk 18 October 1812, dismissed with the corps 13 July 1814.

SANTO DOMINGO (Joseph, 1787-?): born in Nantes (Loire-Inférieure) on 21 July 1787. In the Gendarmes d'Ordonnance 30 January 1807, dismissed with the corps 23 October 1807 and incorporated into the Grenadiers à Cheval of the Guard 24 November 1807, sub-lieutenant in the 3rd Cuirassiers 3 June 1809, lieutenant in the 12th Cuirassiers 14 May 1813.

He was in the King's Cuirassiers 1 May 1814, allowed to return to the 9th Cuirassiers 9 June 1815, instated 18 June 1815, dismissed with the corps 26 November 1815. LH CH 4 December 1813.

SANTON (François Louis, 1784-?): born in Forges (Doubs) on 28 May 1784. In the 2nd Cuirassiers 18 May 1805, brigadier 14 May 1809, in the 4th Squadron of the Gendarmerie d'Espagne 16 December 1809, sub-lieutenant in the 2nd Cuirassiers 28 February 1813, shot and wounded in the lower abdomen at Waterloo 18 June 1815 and admitted to hospital, came out after the regiment was disbanded and returned home.

SARREBOURG see **PIERROT** aka **SARREBOURG**

SAUBAIGNE (François, 1794-?): born in Saint-Esprit (Landes) on 18 October 1794. Pupil at the Ecole Spéciale Militaire 31 October 1811, sub-lieutenant in the 11th Cuirassiers 10 January 1813, instated 30 January 1813.

He was incorporated with his squadron into the 3rd Provisional Cavalry in Hamburg 11 September

Cuirassier Squadrons in marching column. (Author's collection)

1813, returned with the garrison May 1814, resignation accepted 10 December 1814, left 28 December.

SAULNIER (Pierre, 1778-?): born in 1778. In the 12th Dragoons 27 November 1798, in the Grenadiers à cheval of the Guard 28 November 1800, brigadier 23 October 1805, fourrier 22 December 1805, instated 6 January 1806, in the Dragoons of the Imperial Guard 14 January 1806, maréchal des logis 1 July 1807.

He was lieutenant in the 3rd Cuirassiers 13 March 1813, in the King's Cuirassiers when they were formed 1 July 1814 and which became the 1st Cuirassiers again March 1815, dismissed and put up for the active list 24 December 1815.

SAVELKOUL (Guillaume, 1767-?): born in Ywol (Yssel) on 13 May 1767. Trooper in the Stakum Regiment 6 December 1787, brigadier in the van den Duin Regiment 6 June 1789, fourrier 20 April 1793, maréchal des logis in the 1st Batavian Cavalry 1 August 1795, maréchal des logis-chef in the 1st Light Dragoons 11 January 1803, sub-lieutenant in the 2nd Dutch Cuirassiers 21 October 1806 which became the 14th French Cuirassiers 5 December 1810, lieutenant 4 March 1812, wounded at Polotsk 18 October 1812, prisoner near Kovno 25 December 1812.

SAVIOT (Jean Baptiste Alexandre, 1770-1830): born in Charleville (Ardennes) on 22 December 1770. In the Royal-Vaisseaux 1 January 1788 which became the 43rd Infantry 1 January 1791, sergeant-major in the 2nd Ardennes Battalion 11 August 1791, grenadier lieutenant 12 August 1791, captain 19 November 1791, sub-lieutenant in the 1st Hussars 12 March 1792, 13 sabre wounds and taken prisoner at Jemmapes 6 November 1792 returned 1 April 1793, aide de camp to General Walther 22 September 1793, lieutenant 23 December 1794, captain 27 September 1796, shell burst wound at la Piave 12 March 1797, while out reconnoitring captured small enemy posts and 20 chariots and 200 prisoner of which 17 officers with his detachment losing only two men at Klagefurth, acting squadron commander on the battlefield, deputy to the adjutant-generals 21 November 1798.

He was named aide de camp to General Grandjean 26 March 1799, acting squadron commander again 4 November 1799, cannonball wound at Hohenlinden 3 December 1800, in the 23rd Cavalry 30 December 1801, dismissed with the corps 23 December 1802 and incorporated

into the suite of the 6th Cuirassiers 3 January 1803, squadron commander in the 2nd Division of the Army of Italy 12 September 1805, returned to the suite of the 6th Cuirassiers 9 February 1806, in service as squadron commander in the 7th Cuirassiers 7 January 1807.

He was wounded at Heilsberg 10 June 1807, major in the 5th Dragoons 25 June 1807, chief of staff of the 1st Division of the North 25 August 1809, in the 5th Dragoons 25 January 1810, colonel of the 21st Dragoons 29 March 1813, non-active when the corps was dismissed 25 August 1814, colonel of the 8th Dragoons 18 April 1815 which became the 13th Dragoons 25 April 1815, maréchal de camp 3 July 1815, non-active as a colonel 20 February 1816. LH CH 19 June 1805.

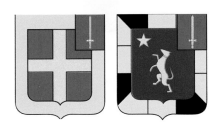

SAVOIE CARIGNAN (Joseph Marie de, baron, 1783-1825): born in Paris (Seine) on 30 October 1783. In the 2nd Carabiniers 21 January 1803, brigadier 23 October 1803, maréchal des logis 7 November 1803, sub-lieutenant in the 23rd Dragoons 8 December 1803, in the Gendarmes d'Ordonnance 25 January 1807, first-lieutenant 1 February 1807, instated 4 February 1807, captain 22 March 1807, captain in the suite of the Line 16 July 1807, in the suite of the 3rd Cuirassiers 10 September 1807, took up his appointment 10 May 1808, aide de camp to General Mermet 20 July 1808 and ordnance officer to the Emperor the following day 21 July 1808, squadron commander in the 8th Hussars 18 August 1809

He was colonel of the 6th Hussars 18 October 1812, confirmed in the same regiment when it became the Berri Hussars 20 August 1814 which became the 6th Hussars again in April 1815, colonel of the Meurthe Hussars N°2 27 September 1815. LH CH 1 August 1809, O 10 October 1813, C 28 September 1814, Baron of the Empire d. 15 August 1809 and l.p. 25 March 1810 with entailed estate and new arms l.p. 27 September 1810.

SAYVE see **LACROIX de CHEVRIERES de SAYVE**

SCARAMPI see **MONAL de SCARAMPI.**

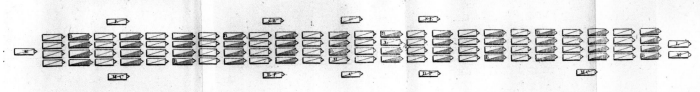

Milhaud

la Haye
Sainte

Mont St Jean

la Belle
Alliance

Kellermann

Guyot

Hougoumont

THE CHARGES OF
THE CUIRASSIERS
AT WATERLOO

18 June 1815

N

(Illustration © Gregory Proch, 2007)

213

Horace Sébastiani de la Porta. (RR)

SCHAEFFER (François Joseph, 1771-?): born in Strasbourg (Bas-Rhin) on 31 May 1771. In the 1st Carabiniers 16 August 1791, brigadier 11 October 1798, maréchal des logis 24 October 1807, sub-lieutenant in the 13th Cuirassiers 27 March 1814.

He was dismissed with the corps and incorporated into the suite of the 9th Cuirassiers 9 August 1814, sub-lieutenant standard-bearer 22 December 1814, in service 27 January 1815, left with pension 26 November 1815.

SCHALLER (François Joseph, 1763-?): born in Rischeim (Haut-Rhin) on 22 July 1763. In the Royal-Etranger-Cavalerie 1 November 1783 which became the 7th Cavalry 1 January 1791, brigadier 1 April 1792.

He was maréchal des logis 7 May 1793, maréchal des logis-chef 20 March 1802, in the same regiment when it became the 7th Cuirassiers 23 December 1802, sub-lieutenant by seniority 18 July 1803, lieutenant 10 January

General Sébastiani was sent by the Emperor to Turkey where he successfully organised the defence of Constantinople against the English. (RR)

205ᵉ Série — Tome IV — Chap. XIV

LES UNIFORMES DU Iᵉʳ EMPIRE
Les Cuirassiers
93 — Chef d'Escadron I. Scherb du IIᵉ Régiment à Wagram — 1809
et son frère A. Scherb sous-lieutenant au 10ᵉ Régiment
D'après un tableau de famille

Horace François de la Porta Graf Sebastiani, Marschall von Frankreich.
Nach Gemälde von Gerard, gestochen von W. Dickensen.

1807, on the retirement payroll 2 June 1809 and ordered to report to the Imperial Headquarters. LH CH 1 October 1807.

SCHERB (Armand Antoine, 1783-?): elder brother of the following and the general's nephew, born in Werthoffen (Bas-Rhin) on 30 November 1793. In the 10th Cuirassiers 28 February 1804, cannonball wound to his right hip and forearm at Austerlitz 2 December 1805, brigadier 16 June 1806, maréchal des logis 1 December 1806, sub-lieutenant 16 May 1809, shot and wounded at Winkovo 18 October 1812, lieutenant 8 July 1813, shot and wounded twice in the shoulder and chest at Waterloo 18 June 1815, dismissed with the

corps 25 December 1815 and retired 10 February 1816. LH CH 28 September 1813.

SCHERB (Ignace Léopold Elysée, chevalier, 1776-1842): brother of the above and below, the general's nephew and son-in-law of General Dorsner, born in Werthoffen (Bas-Rhin) on 9 March 1776. in the 62nd Infantry 1 March 1792. He was sub-lieutenant 10 June 1792, deputy to the adjutant-generals 8 February 1794, first-lieutenant 2 May 1794, aide de camp to his uncle 6 December 1794, captain 5 October 1796, bayonet wound to his left hand, captured for a short while but managed to escape and recaptured the fort at Kehl with a platoon 18 September 1797, deputy to Adjutant-General Saligny 20 January 1799 then to Adjutant-General Garabuau 18 March 1800, in service in the 10th Cavalry 20 February 1801 which became the 10th Cuirassiers 24 September 1803, captain and ordnance officer to the Emperor 20 September 1806, squadron commander in the 11th Cuirassiers 5 October 1806, instated 11 October 1806.

He was wounded by Biscayan shot to his left thigh and his horse killed under him at Eylau 8 February 1807, retired 1 September 1811. LH CH 14 March 1806, Chevalier of the Empire l.p.2 September 1810.

SCHERB (Joseph Romain, 1789-1815): brother of the two above and the general's nephew, born in Werthoffen (Bas-Rhin) on 27 September 1789. In the 2nd Battalion of Pontoneers 20 June 1808, in the 11th Cuirassiers 29 August 1809.

He wasbrigadier-fourrier 1 December 1809, maréchal des logis-chef 16 January 1811, sub-lieutenant 25 September 1812, lieutenant in the 11th Cuirassiers 2 September 1813, killed at les Quatre-Bras 16 June 1815. LH CH 5 September 1813.

SCHLESSER (Jean Georges, 1768-1807): born in Grussenem (Haut-Rhin) on 17 August 1768. In the Colonel-Général-Cavalerie 24 June 1786 which became the 1st Cavalry 1 January 1791, brigadier-fourrier 28 August 1794, maréchal des logis 21 June 1798, maréchal des logis-chef 19 January 1799, adjutant 29 May 1799, in the same regiment when it became the 1st Cuirassiers 10 October 1801. He was elected sub-lieutenant 7 December 1802, elected lieutenant 24 December 1805, confirmed 1 January 1806, lieutenant adjutant-major 15 September 1806, killed at Eylau 8 February 1807. LH CH 14 March 1806.

SCHLINCKER (Joseph, 1768-?): born in Stuckange (Moselle) on 11 August 1768. Child of the regiment on the payroll of the Royal-Cravates 17 September 1776, trooper 1 September 1786, in the same regiment when it became the 10th Cavalry 1 January 1791, brigadier 10 August 1792, brigadier-fourrier 15 September 1793, maréchal des logis 1 October 1793, maréchal des logis-chef 19 June 1798, sub-lieutenant 28 June 1802 in the same regiment when it became the 10th Cuirassiers 24 September 1803 , lieutenant 8 October 1806, adjutant-major 24 November 1806, wounded by a shell burst to his right arm and his horse killed beneath him at Eylau 8 February 1807, rank of captain 24 May 1808, in service in a company 16 May 1809, shell burst wound to his right arm and his horse killed under him at Essling 22 May 1809, wounded by a Biscayan shot to his right hip and his horse killed under him at the Moskova 7 September 1812, not included in the 6 August 1814 reorganisation. LH CH 14 April 1807.

SCHMID (Auguste Philippe, 1786-1813): born in Halchter on 19 March 1786. In the 2nd Dutch Cuirassiers 20 December 1806, brigadier 20 February 1807, fourrier 6 October 1809, in the same regiment when it became the 14th French Cuirassiers 18 August 1810, mdl/-chef 11 September 1810, adjutant-NCO, sub-lieutenant 13 September 1813, killed at Leipzig 18 October 1813.

SCHOVEL (Cornelius Baas, 1784-?): born in Appel (Escaut) on 7 June 1784. Volunteer cadet in the Hussars of the King of Holland's Guard 6 April 1806, maréchal des logis in the Cuirassiers of the Guard 17 July 1807. He was sub-lieutenant in the 3rd Dutch Hussars 29 September 1809, in the 2nd Dutch Cuirassiers 6 October 1809 which became the 14th French Cuirassiers 18 August 1810, dismissed with the corps 13 July 1814.

SEBASTIANI (Horace François Bastien, comte de la Porta, 1772-1851): born in la Porta (Golo) on 17 November 1772. Sub-lieutenant in the Vintimille-Infanterie 27 August 1789, lieutenant in the 15th Light Infantry Battalion 15 April 1793, aide de camp to General Rochon 9 December 1793 then to General Casablanca 30 June 1794, acting captain 19 March 1795.

He was in the 9th Dragoons 20 June 1795, confirmed 29 June 1795, shot and wounded in the right wrist at Dego 15 April 1796, acting squadron commander 19 February 1798, confirmed 24 January 1799, acting brigade commander of the regiment 20 April 1799, prisoner at Verderio 28 April 1799, freed, confirmed as brigade commander in the 9th Dragoons 13 August 1799, sent on a mission to Turkey 11 October 1801, in Egypt 29 August 1802.

He was brigadier-general 28 August 1803, commanded the coast between Brest and the mouth of the Vilaine 4 October 1803, in the 2nd dragoon division 27 December 1803, in Utrecht Camp 15 January 1805, commanded the cavalry in Holland 2 March 1805, in the 4th Corps 11 September 1805, commanded the 1st Brigade in Walther's dragoon division 22 September 1805, shot through his body at Austerlitz 2 December 1805, major-general 21 December 1805, commanded the 2nd Division of the 2nd Corps of the Grande Armée 23 April 1806, joined his unit 27 April 1806, replaced 16 July 1806, ambassador to Turkey end of 1806, organised the defence of Constantinople and repulsed an English attack February 1807, in Spain 22 August 1808, commanded the 1st Division of the 4th Corps 7 September 1808, commanded the 4th Corps of the Army of Spain 21 February 1809, replaced 10 May 1811.

He commanded the Boulogne Camp 9 January 1812, commanded the 21st Cuirassier Division in the 2nd Cavalry Corps of the Grande Armée 22 January 1812 then the 2nd Light Cavalry Division in the same corps by exchange May 18121, replaced 9 August 1812. He commanded the 2nd Cavalry Corps 8 September 1812, the 2nd and 4th Corps 12 November 1812, captain commanding the 2nd Company of the Escadron Sacré 1812, commander in chief of all the remnants of the cavalry of the Grande Armée 8 December 1812, having reformed the 2nd Cavalry Corps of the Army of the Elbe under Eugène 15 February 1813, slight lance wound to his chest at Leipzig 18 October 1813.He commanded the remains of the 5th Infantry Corps 18 November 1813, evacuated Cologne 14 January 1814, commanded a cavalry corps in Champagne 4 February 1814, commanded at Troyes 23 February 1814, evacuated the town 4 March 1814.

He commanded the 3 divisions of the Guard (Exelmans, Colbert and Letort) 17 March 1814, available from 1 September 1814, responsible for the levy of National Guards in the 16th Military Division and the Somme and Aisne Departments 10 April 1815.

He was elected to the Chamber of the Hundred Days 7 May 1815, responsible for the defence of the right bank of the Seine 13 June 1815, went to England August 1815, non-active 1 September 1815. LH CH 11 December 1803, C 14 June 1807, GA 7 April 1807, Comte de la Porta l.p. 31 December 1809.

SEBILLOTTE (Etienne, 1777-?): born in Fresne (Côte-d'Or) on 3 November 1777. In the 1st

Document proposing that Sous-Lieutenant Servas be retired for reasons of ill-health.
(Author's collection)

DÉPARTEMENT DE LA GUERRE.

BUREAU des RÉCOMPENSES MILITAIRES. 3me. DIVISION MILITAIRE.

Iᵉʳ. REGIMENT DE CUIRASSIERS.

MÉMOIRE de Proposition pour *la Sœur de Retraite* en faveur *de M Servas (Joseph)* Fils de *Jean Servas* et de *marie catherine Thiblert*, né le *16 8 1783* à *Pocourt* Canton de *Varenne*, Département de *la meuse* *Sous-lieutenant* à la *1e* Compagnie du *1er* Escadron

MOTIFS SUR LESQUELS CETTE DEMANDE EST FONDÉE.

Mauvaise Santé

Cuirassiers 30 December 1802, brigadier 1 December 1807, maréchal des logis 1 March 1809, in the 13th Cuirassiers 1 January 1810, sub-lieutenant 20 February 1814, confirmed 5 March 1814, incorporated into the 9th Cuirassiers 9 August 1814, dismissed with the corps and put on the non-active list 26 November 1815. LH CH 11 January 1812.

SECRETANT (?-?): maréchal des logis in the 9th Cuirassiers, sub-lieutenant 14 May 1809, lieutenant 9 March 18121, wounded and lost a leg at the Moskova 7 September 1812.

SEEROOSKERKEN see **THUIL van SEEROOSKERKEN**

SEGUIN (Auguste, 1790-?): born in Besançon (Doubs) on 10 May 1790. In the 4th Gardes d'Honneur 6 July 1813, fourrier 11 July 1813. He was elected sub-lieutenant in the suite of the 11th Hussars 5 February 1814, in the suite of the 10th Cuirassiers 22 March 1814.

He was shot and wounded in his right foot at Waterloo 18 June 1815, dismissed with the regiment 25 December 1815.

SELLIER (Nicolas, ?-1812): maréchal des logis in the 12th Cuirassiers, sub-lieutenant 30 October 1806, lieutenant 29 January 1808, wounded at Essling 22 May 1809.

He was captain 9 August 1809, wounded at the Moskova 7 September 1812 and killed at Orcha 21 November 1812.

SELLIER (Nicolas, 1761-1807): born in Neufchâteau (Vosges) on 17 November 1791. Provincial soldier in the Sarrelibre delegation 1 April 1782, in the Dauphin-Cavalerie 1 April 1785, fourrier 1 January 1791, in the same regiment when it became the 12th cavalry the same day, maréchal des logis 20 October 1792, maréchal des logis-chef 26 October 1792.

He was adjutant sub-lieutenant 1 April 1793, sub-lieutenant 18 May 1793, wounded at Schweigenheim 28 May 1794, lieutenant 2 September 1794, captain 30 December 1801, in the same regiment when it became the 12th Cuirassiers 24 September 1803, squadron commander 30 October 1806, wounded at Friedland 14 June 1807 and died of his wounds 6 August 1807. LH CH 14 June 1804.

SENILHAC (Jacques Jean Louis, chevalier, 1764-1841): born in Béziers (Hérault) on 24 July 1764. Enrolled in the Languedoc Dragons 10 February 1781, dismissed 10 November 1784, sub-lieutenant in the 38th Infantry 20 January 1792.

He was lieutenant 12 November 1792, deputy on the staff of the army of the Alps 3 December 1793, in the 25th Chasseurs à Cheval, shot and wounded in his left side 1794, squadron commander 14 November 1794, regimental brigade commander 10 March 1795, put up for retirement 11 October 1796. He put back in service and taken prisoner during the Irish Expedition 12 October 1798, exchanged August 1799, on the staff of the Army of Italy 1800, in the suite of the 5th Cavalry 22 January 1802 which became the 5th Cuirassiers 23 December 1802, colonel of the 12th Chasseurs à Cheval 1 February 1805, decision cancelled 22 February 1805, remained in the suite of the 5th Cuirassiers, with the squadron commander, Jacquemin, captured a standard at Austerlitz 2 December 1805, adjutant-commandant 3 October 1806, in the 1st Corps of the Grande Armée 1806, in the Army of the North 1 August 1809, then of the Midi in Spain 30 March 1811, allowed to retire 9 October 1811, pensioned off 13 December 1811. LH CH 14 June 1804, O 12 May 1810, Chevalier of the Empire d.16 September 1806 .

SENTUARY (Louis Joseph Paulin, baron, 1752-1827): born in Ile Bourbon (Reunion Island) on 9 November 1752. Sub-lieutenant in the Corsican Legion Dragoons 10 October 1773, in the Schomberg-Dragons 23 November 1776, acting lieutenant-colonel of the 2nd Light Dragoons in the United States, wounded in the heel at Germantown 4 October 177, returned to the Chasseurs à Cheval N° 6 from 1783 to 1785, reemployed as lieutenant-colonel in the United States 1785 to 1789, volunteered in cavalry company levied in Bordeaux to fight the Vendéens 1793, simple Hussar in the 12th Regiment 1794, wounded in the left hand 25 November 1794. Captain 27 March 1795, in the 11th Hussars 13 October 1797, squadron commander in the 3rd Cavalry 22 December 1800 which became the 3rd Cuirassiers 3 October 1802, allowed to retire 11 May 1806, pensioned off 30 October 1806, aide de camp to General Valence 16 May 1807, commandant d'armes 3rd Class 6 February 1812, at San Sebastian, wounded defending the town 31 August 1813.

He was retired 17 February 1815, commandant d'armes at la Rochelle 15 June 1815, retired and pensioned off 6 July 1816. LH CH 14 June 1804, Chevalier of the Empire l.p. 23 July 1810.

SERREVILLE (Marie Dominique Charles de, ?-?): born in Guile-Longrois (Eure-et-Loir). In the Gendarmes d'Ordonnance 26 October 1806, brigadier, sub-lieutenant in the Line 16 July 1807, in the suite of the 2nd Cuirassiers 10 September 1807. He took up his function 11 April 1809, wounded at Wagram 6 July 1809, lieutenant 9 August 1809, resignation accepted 7 February 1811.

SERVAS (Joseph, 1783 -after 1832): born in Vocourt (Meuse) on 26 October 1783. In the 1st Cuirassiers 27 August 1805, fourrier 20 December 1806, maréchal des logis 1 October 1808, adjutant-NCO 16 may 1809.

He was elected sub-lieutenant 3 June 1809, three months' leave July 1810 and a month August 1811, resigned 12 September 1811, resignation accepted 23 November 1811 but retired meanwhile 5 November 1811, pensioned off 26 February 1812. LH CH.

SESTIER (Joseph, 1770-?): born in Metz (Moselle) on 29 September 1770. Child of the regiment on the payroll of the Royal-Pologne-Cavalerie 24 September 177 which became the 5th Cavalry 1 January 1791, brigadier 25 December 1798, brigadier-fourrier 17 April 1799, sabre wound at la Trebbia 18 June 1799, maréchal des logis 22 March 1802.
He was in the same regiment when it became the 5th Cuirassiers 23 December 1802, sub-lieutenant 23 February 1807, lieutenant 25 May 1807, captain 6 November 1811, retired 23 December 1815. LH CH 1807.

SEVIN (Joseph Antoine, 1784-1812): born in Simandre (Ain) on 12 October 1784. In the Velites of the Imperial Guard 22 February 1806, acting sub-lieutenant in the 7th Cuirassiers 25 March 1809, joined the war squadrons 26 May 1809.

He was in service 5 June 1809, lieutenant 4 March 1812, instated 11 April 1812, disappeared at the Berezina 28 November 1812.

SIBER aka **DAVID** (David Antoine, 1782-1812): born in Bille (Meurthe) on 27 December 1782. In the 8th Cavalry 21 April 1800, fourrier 10 October 1801, in the same regiment when it became the 8th Cuirassiers the same day, maréchal des logis 6 August 1802, maréchal des logis-chef 1 June 1806.

He was elected sub-lieutenant 24 February 1807, lance wound through his left thigh at Heilsberg 10 June 1807, lieutenant 3 June 1809.

He was shot and wounded in his left arm at Wagram 6 July 1809, shot and wounded twice in the right leg at the Moskova 7 September 1812, seriously wounded and remained behind at the Berezina 28 November 1812, presumed dead. LH CH 13 August 1809.

SIBLAS see **BEYLIE de DOUMET de SIBLAS.**

SIGRE (?-1812): maréchal des logis in the 9th Cuirassiers, sub-lieutenant 14 May 1809, killed at the Moskova 7 September 1812.

SIGRE (Charles, 1763-?): born in Tinay (Meurthe) on 24 January 1763. In the Artois-Cavalerie 11 November 1784, brigadier 1 January 1791, in the same regiment when it became the 9th Cavalry the same day, maréchal des logis 2 April 1793, sub-lieutenant 19 November 1793, several sabre wounds to his right arm and his horse killed under him 11 December 1795, sabre wound to his head while crossing the Danube 19 June 1800.

He was elected lieutenant 14 September 1803, in the same regiment when it became the 9th Cuirassiers 24 September 1803, retired 8 May 1807.

SIMEON (François, 1778-?): born in Blondy (Seine-et-Marne) on 20 October 1778. In the Artillery Teams 24 August 1799, in the team trains 22 March 1800, in the 12th Cavalry 14 June 1801 which became the 12th Cuirassiers 24 September 1803, brigadier 1 October 1806, maréchal des logis 1 March 1807, maréchal des logis-chef 16 August 1809.

He was shot and wounded in the right leg at Leipzig 16 October 1813, sub-lieutenant 22 December 1813, non-active August 1814, returned to the regiment 14 June 1815, non-active again 5 August 1815 and returned home 16 August 1815.

SIMIANE see **TOURNON SIMIANE.**

SIMON (Hubert Augustin, 1781-?): born in Perthe (Ardennes) on 6 August 1781. In the 4th Cuirassiers 15 February 1803, fourrier 28 December 1803, maréchal des logis 1 October 1806, adjutant-NCO 25 June 1807.

He was elected sub-lieutenant 5 March 1809, lieutenant 3 July 1809, lieutenant adjutant-major 4 March 1812, lance wound to his head at Uczacz near Polotsk 24 October 1812, captain adjutant-major 4 September 1813, wounded by a bursting shell to his left thigh at Leipzig 16 October 1813, dismissed 21 December 1815. LH CH 8 October 1811, O 27 December 1814.

 SIMONET (Pierre François, 1767-?): born in Soulanges (Marne) on 15 October 1767. In the King's Cuirassiers 14 February which became the 8th Cavalry 1 January 1791, in the 1st Carabiniers 4 April 1792, fourrier 2 January 1797, maréchal des logis-chef 6 May 1800.

He was incorporated with his company into the 1st Provisional Heavy Cavalry December 1807 which became the 13th Cuirassiers 21 October 1808, adjutant-NCO, sub-lieutenant 11 November 1810, retired 6 August 1814.

SIMONOT (Louis Alexis, 1783-?): born in Blussans (Doubs) on 28 March 1783. In the 7th Hussars 11 October 1801, in the Grenadiers à Cheval of the Guard 9 July 1807, brigadier 15

November 1809, maréchal des logis 27 November 1811, in the same regiment when it became the Royal Corps of the Cuirassiers de France 7 August 1814, which became the Grenadiers à Cheval of the Guard again 1 April 1815.

He was elected sub-lieutenant in the 1st Cuirassiers 22 April 1815, instated 5 May 1815, dismissed with the corps and non-active 24 December 1815. LH CH 14 April 1807.

SISTRIERES see **MURAT SISTRIERES**

SOHIER (Etienne, 1757-?): born in Clessis (Calvados) on 20 November 1757. In the Royal-Pologne-Cavalerie 2 February 1782 which became the 5th Cavalry 1 January 1791, brigadier 25 January 1792, maréchal des logis 20 August 1792, maréchal des logis-chef 16 July 1793, shot and wounded in the leg at la Chataigneraie 2 May 1794, adjutant-NCO 17 April 1798.

He was elected sub-lieutenant 20 April 1799, lieutenant 21 April 1800, in the same regiment when it became the 5th Cuirassiers 23 December 1802, captain by seniority 28 January 1804, retired 24 November 1806.

SOLMON (Alexis Bernard Clément, 1769-?): born in Vieulaine (Somme) on 23 November 1769. A requisitioned conscript in the 16th of the Line 23 August 1793, caporal-fourrier 26 December 1793, in the same regiment when it formed the 31st Half-Brigade, assistant-controller at the Remount Depot at Alfort 28 October 1794, left to join his unit 31 October 1794, instated 16 December 1794. Dismissed when the depot was shut down 9 April 1798, in the 16th Cavalry 21 November 1798, in the Grenadiers à Cheval of the Guard 22 March 1800, instated 16 April 1800, fourrier 23 September 1800, maréchal des logis-chef 15 October 1802, sub-lieutenant in the suite of the 3rd Cuirassiers 30 August 1805, in service 4 April 1806, lieutenant 21 June 1807, instated 5 July 1807, quartermaster-treasurer 21 October 1808.

He was captain quartermaster-treasurer of the 13th Cuirassiers 13 February 1809, incorporated into the Angoulême Cuirassiers 6 August 1814 which became the 4th Cuirassiers again April 1815, dismissed with the corps 21 December 1815. LH CH 14 March 1806.

SOMMAN (Pierre, 1758-1808): born in Ewendorff on 29 December 1758. In the Dauphin-Cavalerie 14 March 1780, brigadier 22 July 1786, in the same regiment when it became the 12th Cavalry 1 January 1791, maréchal des logis 27 June 1792, maréchal des logis-chef 1 April 1793, sub-lieutenant 4 November 1793, lieutenant 11 September 1795.

He was elected captain 3 May 1803, in the same regiment when it became the 12th Cuirassiers 24 September 1803, died 4 January 1808.

 **SOPRANSI** (Louis Charles Barthélémy, baron, 1783-1814): son of Mme de Visconti, born in Milan (Italy) on 23 December 1783. Volunteered for the 12th Hussars November 1798, shot and wounded and promoted sub-lieutenant at Marengo 14 June 1800, lieutenant in the 1st Dragoons 1 October 1800.

Named lieutenant adjutant-major 1 May 1805, captured General de Wimpffen, aide de camp to Emperor Alexander at Austerlitz 2 December 1805, captain 6 February 1806, wounded by a shell burst to his right thigh at Jena 14 October 1806, aide de camp to Berthier 1 April 1807, in post in the 4th Cuirassiers and kept on as aide de camp to Berthier 22 August 1807. He was squadron commander in the 1st Dragoons 2 August 1808, captured 7 flags and 6 cannon at Uclès with his squadron 13 January 1809, aide de camp to Berthier in Austria 14 August 1809, colonel 29 January 1811, commanded the 21st Chasseurs à Cheval 17 February 1812 then the 7th Dragoons 13 June 1812, re-joined his unit 14 July 1812, cannon-ball wound at the Moskova 7 September 1812, in the 2nd Brigade of the 3rd Heavy Cavalry Division 15 August 1813, brigadier-general 13 October 1813, wounded at Leipzig 18 October 1813, commanded the 1st Brigade of the 1st Cuirassier Division of the 1st Cavalry Reserve 15 November 1813, in the Cavalry Depot in Versailles 5 February 1814.

He commanded the 4th Cuirassiers Brigade in the 2nd Cavalry Corps 1814, died in Paris 27 May 1814. LH CH, O, Baron of the Empire l.p. 6 October 1810.

SORNIN (Martial, 1779-?): born in Bessine (Haute-Vienne) on 1 October 1779. In the 1st Carabiniers 22 March 1803, brigadier 1 January 1807, sabre wound to his right hand at Villemberck, maréchal des logis 1 January 1808, assigned to the 1st Provisional Heavy Cavalry in Spain December 1807 which formed the 13th Cuirassiers 21 October 1808, adjutant-NCO 27 August 1813.

He was elected sub-lieutenant 26 November 1813, confirmed 5 March 1814, dismissed with the corps and incorporated into the 9th Cuirassiers 9 August 1814, shot and wounded in the knee at Waterloo 18 June 1815, entered the Philippeville Hospital 20 June 1815, struck off the regimental rolls 26 November 1815.

SORREL (Jean, 1778-?): born in Crautance (Meurthe) on 9 February 1778. In the 84th of the Line 10 October 1798, gendarme à pied in the Finistère Department 19 December 1803, in the 15th Squadron of the Gendarmerie à Cheval d'Espagne 16 December 1809, in the 1st Legion of Gendarmerie à Cheval "Burgos" 16 December 1810. He dismissed with the corps 27 February 1813 and promoted to sub-

lieutenant in the 4th Cuirassiers 28 February 1813, incorporated with his squadron into the 1st Provisional Cuirassiers in Hamburg 11 September 1813, returned with the garrison 27 May 1814, put on half-pay 6 August 1814.

 **SOUBDES** (Jean Marie, chevalier, 1787-?): born in Saint-Puy (Gers) on 19 July 1787. Boarder in the Ecole Spéciale Militaire in Fontainebleau 24 December 1806, sergeant-major 22 February 1807, wounded at Essling 22 May 1809, lieutenant 3 June 1809, captain 8 July 1813, on leave 6 January 1814, on two months' leave with pay 24 June 1814, non-active 1814. LH 1809, Chevalier of the Empire.

SOULET (Nicolas, 1784-1845): born in Metz (Moselle) on 8 March 1784. Velite in the Grenadiers à Cheval of the Imperial Guard 3 March 1806, grenadier à cheval 15 September 1806, sub-lieutenant in the 12th Cuirassiers 13 July 1807. He joined his unit 1 October 1807, lieutenant 14 May 1809, captain 21 March 1812, wounded at Waterloo 18 June 1815, dismissed with the corps 10 December 1815. LH CH 13 August 1809.

[signature]

SOULIE (Jean, 1761-?): born in Mirbelle (Lot) on 17 June 1761. In the Royal-Pologne-Cavalerie 11 March 1778, brigadier 1 July 1784, maréchal des logis 2 September 1784, in the same regiment when it became the 5th Cavalry 1 January 1791.

He was elected adjutant sub-lieutenant 20 August 1792, lieutenant 1 April 1793, shot and wounded in the thigh and his horse killed under him at la Chataigneraie 2 May 1794, captain 20 April 1799, bayonet wound on his right thigh at la Trebbia 18 June 1799, in the same regiment when it became the 5th Cuirassiers 23 December 1802, retired 25 May 1807.

SPENNEL (François Joseph Balthazard, 1769-?): born in Nitterothe (Bas-Rhin) on 5 January 1769. In the Royal-Cravates 27 October 1787 which became the 10th Cavalry 1 January 1791, brigadier 30 September 1797, brigadier-fourrier 7 November 1797, maréchal des logis and adjutant the same day 20 January 1799, in the same regiment when it became the 10th Cuirassiers 24 September 1803, elected sub-lieutenant 21 January 1805, second-lieutenant in the Grenadiers à Cheval of the Imperial Guard 1 May 1806.

He was elected second-lieutenant under-adjutant-major 10 September 1808, first-lieu-

tenant adjutant-major 25 April 1809, captain adjutant-major 6 December 1811, captain in a company 9 February 1813, wounded at Hanau 30 October 1813, major in the Line 28 November 1813, in the suite of the 2nd Cuirassiers 18 November 1814, wounded at Waterloo 18 June 1815.

He left for retirement when the regiment was disbanded 10 December 1815. LH CH 5 November 1804, O 6 August 1813.

STAPPERS (Alexandre Guillaume André de, 1780-?): born in Saint-Trond (Meuse-Inférieure) on 17 October 1780. In the Gendarmes d'Ordonnance December 1806, wounded near Colberg 3 March 1807.

He was wounded at Stettin May 1807, returned to convalesce in the Potsdam Depot June 1807, sub-lieutenant in the suite of the 4th Cuirassiers 16 July 1807, instated 10 September 1807, retired 18 August 1808.

STIRUM see **LIMBURG STIRUM.**

STRUITE see **SANDIFORT van den STRUITE**

SUREAU (Bon Joseph Auguste, 1792-?): born in Bayeux (Calvados) on 3 September 1792. In the Ecole Impériale Militaire de Cavalerie in Saint-Germain, sub-lieutenant in the 4th Cuirassiers 30 January 1813, in the Gardes du Corps 1814.

Squadron commander Scherb, from the 11th Cuiras in full town dress, 1806-1810, by P. Benigni. (RR)

Officer's Cuirass breastplate. *(RR)*

the same regiment when it became the 2nd Cuirassiers 12 October 1802, joined his unit 16 May 1802, died in the war squadrons at Bischofwerda 14 March 1807.

TALHOUET (Victor de, 1777-?): born in La Boussaine (Ille-et-Vilaine) on 30 January 1777. Sub-lieutenant in the Chasseurs de Côtes 27 May 1793 which entered into the formation of the 15th Chasseurs à Cheval 4 June 1793, resigned for reasons of infirmity 20 May 1796, returned as a sub-lieutenant in service 23 March 1800.

He was lieutenant aide de camp to General Espagne 11 January 1807, in the 6th Cuirassiers 10 October 1809, captain 8 October 1811, squadron commander in the suite on full pay 7 August 1814, dismissed 21 November 1815. LH CH 28 September 1814.

TANDEAU de CHABANNE (Henry, 1788-?): born in Saint-Léonard (Haute-Vienne) on 26 July 1788. Boarder in the Ecole Spéciale Militaire in Fontainbleau 198 January 1806, sergeant 1 November 1806, sub-lieutenant in the 11th Cuirassiers 14 December 1806, ordnance officer to the Grand Duke of Berg 15 December 1806, returned to his regiment 15 March 1807, detached with his company to the 2nd Provisional Heavy Cavalry in Spain December 1807, prisoner with the capitulation at Baylen 22 July 1808, lieutenant during his captivity 29 April 1809, escaped from the hulks off Cadiz and returned to the corps 17 November 1810 which had become the 13th

TABOUROT (Hubert, 1769-?): born in Lavoncourt (Haute-Saône) on 1 July 1769. In the Volontaires Nationaux à Cheval from the Ecole Militaire 8 September 1792 which became the 25th Cavalry 7 February 1793 which in turn became the 24th cavalry 4 June 1793, brigadier 16 November 1797, dismissed with the corps and incorporated into the 1st Cuirassiers 6 January 1802, resigned 21 May 1803.

He returned as a brigadier in the 8th Cuirassiers 6 January 1806, maréchal des logis 15 October 1806, sabre wound to his face while saving the regimental eagle at Heilsberg 10 June 1807, sub-lieutenant 29 May 1815, replaced as Maréchal des logis 1 September 1815. LH CH 13 August 1809.

camp to General Goguet, captain in the 3rd Dragoons 20 April 1794, aide de camp to General Junot in Egypt 13 January 1799.

He was elected deputy on the general headquarters staff of the Army of the Orient 28 September 1799, aide de camp to General Damas and rank of squadron commander in the suite of the 3rd Dragoons 13 March 1800, in service with the 2nd Cavalry 8 February 1802, in

TABUR (Nicolas Christophe, 1776-?): born in Hara (Orne) on 23 August 1773. In the 11th Cavalry 5 April 1800, brigadier 31 May 1802, maréchal des logis 8 January 1803, in the same regiment when it became the 11th Cuirassiers 24 September 1803, sub-lieutenant 16 May 1809.

He was elected lieutenant 6 November 1811, wounded and prisoner at Toloschinn 21 November 1812. LH CH 11 October 1812.

TAINTURIER (Prosper Claude, 1759-1807): born in Beaune (Côte-d'Or) on 31 August 1759. Volunteer in the 1st Côte-d'Or Battalion 1 January 1792, sub-lieutenant in the 5th Hussars 20 August 1792, lieutenant in the 17th Chasseurs à Cheval 18 October 1792, captain 1793, aide de

General d'Hautpoul leading his division during the famous charge at Eylau. Composition by Patrice Courcelle.
(Private collection)

ARDIF de POMMEROUX de BOR-DESSOULLE (Etienne, Count, 1771-1837): born in Luzeret (Indre) on 4 April 1771.

In the Chasseurs des Evéchés 27 July 1789 which became the 2nd Chasseurs à Cheval 21 January 1791, bayonet wound to his thigh while cutting up an enemy column at Spire 30 September 1792, brigadier 1 December 1792.

Held fast with twenty or so chasseurs against the enemy for an hour, rallied the infantry and saved the guns near Landau March 1793, maréchal des logis 24 May 1793, taken prisoner after being ordered by his colonel to go through enemy lines to get help in front of the Wantzenau October 1793, freed.

He was elected sub-lieutenant 3 August 1794, with his platoon took the Prussian forward positions in front of Turckheim 25 August 1794. Acting aide de camp to General Garnier de Laboissière his former colonel 19 July 1795, lieutenant 19 July 1796,

Two sabre wounds one of which to his right wrist at Emmendingen 19 October 1796, confirmed as aide de camp 27 August 1797, captain 20 January 1798, acting squadron commander in the 6th Hussars 14 May 1799.

He was in the 7th Gendarme Legion 18 September 1800, in the 2nd Chasseurs à Cheval 24 May 1802, confirmed 19 October 1812, major in the 1st Chasseurs à Cheval 29 October 1803, colonel of the 22nd Chasseurs à Cheval 27 December 1805, wounded at Waren 1 November 1806 and two bayonet wounds to his right forearm and chest at Güttstadt 9 June 1807, brigadier-general 25 June 1807, commanded a light cavalry brigade (9th Hussars, 7th and 20th Chasseurs à Cheval) December 1807, at Bayonne 21 September 1808

He commanded the 2nd Brigade of Chasseurs à Cheval of the Cavalry Reserve of the Army of Spain 15 November 1808, recalled to Paris 15 January 1809, returned and commanded a cavalry brigade of the 4th Corps April 1809 then the 2nd Brigade of the 3rd Cuirassiers Division 24 May 1809, wounded in the arm at Wagram 6 July 1809, commanded the 1st Light Cavalry Brigade in the 4th Corps then the 1st Brigade of the Marulaz Division 10 August 1809.

Sent to the Hanseatic towns in February 1810 to the Holland Observation Corps 17 March 1810, commanded the 3rd Light Cavalry Brigade in the Army of Germany 2 December 1810, joined his unit January 1811.

He commanded the 4th Light Cavalry Brigade of the Elbe Observation Corps 19 April 1811, in the 1st Light Cavalry Division 15 September 1811, commanded the 2nd Brigade (1st and 3rd Chasseurs à Cheval) 25 December 1811, in the Elbe Observation Corps 15 February 1812 which became the 1st Corps of the Grande Armée 1 April 1812, victor at Soleschnisky 30 June 1812, took Mohilev 23 July 1812, had his jaw shattered by Biscayan shot at the Moskova 7 September 1812, major-general 4 December 1812.

He commanded the 1st Cuirassier Division of the 1st Cavalry Corps 15 February 1813, commanded the 2nd Cavalry Corps 18 November 1813, commanded the 2 divisions organised in Versailles 3 January 1814, the cavalry reserve in Paris 7 February 1814 then the Heavy Cavalry Division of the 1st Cavalry Corps 19 February 1814, Inspector-General of Cavalry May 1814.

He commanded the cavalry of the 2nd Military division 12 March 1815, followed Louis XVIII to Ghent 20 March 1815, chief of staff to the Duke of Berry 25 June 1815.

He was returned with him to France July 1815, commanded the 1st Cavalry Division of the Royal Guard 8 September 1815.

Holder of a Sabre of Honour 15 September 1802, LH CH by rights 24 September 1803, O 14 June 1804, C 14 May 1813, GC 15 August 1815, Baron of the Empire l.p. 17 May 1810 then Count d. 19 September 1813.

Maréchal des Logis in the 2nd chasseurs, Etienne Bourdesoulle was wounded by a sabre to his left arm having charged a dozen Prussian Hussars to disengage his unhorsed colonel at Erixheim, near Landau on 28 June 1794. Six months later, promoted to Lieutenant, he received two sabre wounds to his head during a charge in which he cut down five or six troopers and himself killed the enemy commanding officer at Saltzbach near Mainz.

At Neuburg on 27 June 1800, he was acting Squadron Commander in the 6th Hussars. He charged 500 enemy cuirassiers who had just routed two of the regiment's squadrons. The charge enabled them to put almost 200 cuirassiers out of action, Bourdesoulle himself taking the Austrian commanding officer in the middle of the fray and freeing the Hussars who had been taken during the previous charge including his unhorsed brigade commander.

Cuirassiers, second-lieutenant (Old Guard) in the Grenadiers à Cheval of the Imperial Guard 9 February 1813, wounded at Craonne 7 March 1814 and at Waterloo 18 June 1815.

TARTARIN (Nicolas François, 1773-?): born in Bussières (Haute-Marne) on 2 March 1773. In the 4th Seine-et-Oise Battalion 2 November 1791, fourrier 3 May 1792, shot and wounded at Mons 1792, sergeant-major 8 October 1793, wounded by a Biscayan shot at Kaiserlautern November 1793, simple trooper in the 4th Dragoons 1 October 1795, sabre wound at Fribourg 1796, fourrier 11 April 1799, in the Grenadiers à Cheval of the Guard 3 April 1800, brigadier 3 October 1802.

He was maréchal des logis 1 October 1805, maréchal des logis-chef 27 March 1807, lieutenant in the suite of the 3rd Cuirassiers 17 February 1811, took up his appointment 11 June 1811, lieutenant in the Gendarmerie Départementale, Basse-Pyrénées Company 22 June 1811, Creuse Company 27 July 1811, Jura Company 1814, retired 16 April 1816. LH CH 14 March 1806.

TAUPIN (Pierre François, 1758-?): born in Creil (Oise) on 3 October 1758. In the Royal-Roussillon-Infanterie 1781, set off on the frigate la Diane, left 1785, wounded at Paris 10 August 1792.

He was captain in the Volontaires Nationaux à Cheval from the Ecole Militaire 24 August 1792 which became the 25th Cavalry 7 February 1793 in turn becoming the 24th Cavalry 4 June 1793, dismissed with the corps 10 October 1801 and incorporated into the 8th Cuirassiers 6 January 1802, retired 24 February 1807. LH CH June 1805.

TAUREL (Jean, 1777-?): born in Damvilliers (Meuse) on 1 March 1777. In the 10th Cavalry 16 March 1800 which became the 10th Cuirassiers 24 September 1803, brigadier 1 December 1806, maréchal des logis 9 June 1807, maréchal des logis-chef 16 May 1809, sub-lieutenant 3 June 1809, in the 6th Battalion of the Engineer Wagon Trains 17 April 1812.

TEILLARD BEYNAC (1791-?): born in Murat (Cantal) on 25 November 1791. Vélite in the Grenadiers à Cheval of the Imperial Guard 10 August 1810, sub-lieutenant in the 12th Cuirassiers 13 March 18131, dismissed with the corps 10 December 1815.

TELINGE (Louis, 1780-1807): born in Nouveau-Forvillier (Moselle) on 23 November 1780. In the 6th Dragoons 10 November 1798, ordnance to General Muller in the Army of Italy 27 September 1800, acting sub-lieutenant in the Legion des Francs du Nord 17 December 1800,

Colonel in the 1st régiment of Cuirassiers. *(Aquarelle by Michel Pétard, RR)*

took up his post in the 4th Cuirassiers 6 April 1804 and retrospectively to that date only, lieutenant 8 January 1807.

He was killed at Heilsberg 10 June 1807.

TERHOVE see **TIECKEN de TERHOVE**

TERRASSE (Louis Alexandre Guy, 1779-?): born in Rambouillet (Seine-et-Oise) on 29 October 1799. Conscripted into the 1st Cuirassiers 29 March 1802, sub-lieutenant 15 September 1802, intended for the Louisiana Expedition keeping his post in the regiment 16 November 1802, left 22 November 1802, lieutenant by seniority 2 July 1804.

Captain 25 May 1807, he retired with his pension 22 May 1810. LH CH 1 October 1807.

TERRIER DELACHAISE (Jacques Jean Gaston, 1792-?): born in Loiret on 10 May 1792. Pupil in the Ecole Impériale Militaire de Cavalerie in Saint-Germain 30 June 1810, grenadier 25 January 1812, sub-lieutenant in the 3rd Cuirassiers 30 January 1813, incorporated with his squadron into the 1st Provisional Heavy Cavalry in Hamburg 11 September 1813. He returned with the garrison 27 May 1814, standard-bearer of the 3rd Cuirassiers 16 August 1814, dismissed while still fetching remounts 25 November 1815.

TETTIER (Louis Joseph, 1764-1811): born in Léquelle (Aisne) on 9 February 1764. In the Royal-Etranger-Cavalerie 2 April 1782, brigadier 6 May 1785, in the same regiment when it became the 7th Cavalry 1 January 1791, maréchal des logis 7 May 1793, sublieutenant 20 May 1794, supernumerary 20 February 1796, took up his appointment 20 February 1800, in the same regiment when it became the 7th Cuirassiers 23 December 1802, lieutenant by seniority 12 December 1804, cap-

Disposition of a squadron in battle formation. (Author's collection).

tain 11 March 1807, died in the barracks in Rouen 5 January 1811. LH CH 1 October 1807.

TEYNIER DUPRADELET (Alexandre Jean Louis, 1775-1805): born in Paris (Seine) on 26 September 1775. In the Rohan-Soubise-Infanterie 14 November 1789 which became the 84th Infantry 1 January 1791, left 20 July 1792, conscripted into the 5th Hussars 28 September 1799, fourrier 1 June 1800, in the 12th Cavalry 10 September 1801.

He was maréchal des logis March 1803, in the same regiment when it became the 12th Cuirassiers 24 September 1803, sub-lieutenant 5 October 1803, died in the Grande Armée as a result of the exhaustion of war 16 November 1805.

THERVAIS (Pierre Joseph Stanislas, 1778-1815): born in Arras (Pas-de-Calais) on 13 March 1778. In the 7th Cavalry 26 November 1798 which became the 7th cuirassiers 23 December 1802, brigadier 6 January 1807, maréchal des logis 25 December 1807.

He was maréchal des logis-chef 3 June 1809, sub-lieutenant 6 March 1813, seriously wounded and disappeared at Waterloo 18 June 1815. LH CH 4 December 1813.

THEVENARD (1788-?): born in Amboise (Loire) on 7 June 1788. Vélite in the Dragoons of the Guard 7 June 1806, sub-lieutenant in the 30th Dragoons 9 June 1809, lance wound to his right arm when disengaging 115 soldiers and three officers of the 57th Of the Line near Kaluga 4 November 1812.

He was elected lieutenant 21 April 1813[1], adjutant-major 17 March 1814, in the suite of the 7th Cuirassiers 20 January 1815, non-active 19 December 1815.

THIBAULT de ROESINGHE (Louis Marie Joseph, 1788-1813): born in Bruges (Lys) on 1 May 1788.

In the 7th Hussars 2 May 1805, brigadier 15 September 1806, in the 11th Cuirassiers 20 Mars 1809, maréchal des logis 1 April 1809, maréchal des logis-chef 8 June 1809, sub-lieutenant 31 May 1810, lieutenant 19 June 1813, wounded at Dresden 27 August 1813 and died of his wounds at Frankfurt Hospital 7 September 1813.

THIBAULT see **CHANOINE de SAINT THIBAULT**

THIEBAUT (Pierre, 1765-?): born in Mantes (Isère) on 17 November 1765. In the Royal-Cavalerie 7 January 1787 which became the 2nd Cavalry 1 January 1791, brigadier 1 April 1793, maréchal des logis 20 January 1799, in the same regiment when it became the 2nd Cuirassiers 12 October 1802, sub-lieutenant 14 May 1809. He was elected sub-lieutenant standard-bearer in the same regiment when it formed the Queen's Cuirassiers 6 August 1814, lieutenant standard-bearer 4 February 1815, in the same regiment when it became the 2nd Cuirassiers again April 1815, retired 10 December 1815. LH CH 4 December 1813.

THIELMAN (François Xavier, 1776-?): born in Reims (Marne) on 20 December 1776. Secretary of the Under-Inspector of Parades Barthe, in the 3rd Hussars 25 July 1799, fourrier 25 April 1801.

He employed in the Inspection of Parades 18 September 1806, sub-lieutenant quartermaster in the 13th Wagon Train Battalion 26 March 1812, confirmed 30 April 1812, incorporated into the 3rd Wagon Team Battalion 1 October 1813, in the 7th Wagon Train Battalion 6 November 1813.

He joined his unit 22 November 1813, dismissed with the Wagon Trains and put into the 3rd Chasseurs à Cheval 14 March 1814, put back in the suite as the incumbent had refused a transfer, went into the suite of the 12th Cuirassiers 14 July 1814, dismissed with the corps 10 December 1815.

THIEMBRONNE de VALENCE see **TIBRUNE de THIEMBRONNE de VALENCE**

THIESSE (Jean Jacques Antoine, 1782-?): born in Caen (Calvados) on 1 September 1782. In the 11th Chasseurs à Cheval 21 January 1803, in the Legion of the Gendarmerie à Cheval d'Espagne "Burgos" 11 December 1809, brigadier 5 February 1813, dismissed with the corps 27 February 1813 and promoted to sub-lieutenant in the 8th Cuirassiers 28 February 1813, non-active 25 August 1814.

THIONVILLE (Pierre Joseph, 1784-?): born in Bar-le-Duc (Meuse) on 11 February 1784.

AVERNIER (François Joseph Antoine, Baron, 1769-1844): born in Colmar (Haut-Rhin) on 19 March 1769. In the Alsace Chasseurs à Cheval 1 September 1788, brigadier in the same regiment when it became the 1st Chasseurs à Cheval 1 January 1791.

He was maréchal des logis 1 May 1792, sub-lieutenant 10 July 1793, aide de camp to General Paillard 12 October 1793, bayonet wound in his chest near Worms 3 November 1795, lieutenant 3 April 1796, shot and wounded twice in his right side and elbow at Stockach 16 August 1796, acting captain 5 October 1797, captain in the suite of the guides of the Army of Helvetia while still being prisoner 19 May 1799, deputy to the Adjutant-General Ormancey 23 September 1799.

Named captain in service 3 May 1800, in the 1st Chasseurs à Cheval 12 October 1800, shot and wounded near Schwanstadt, wounded twice at Matiesk 24 December 1805, gathered together a contribution from the town of Spire illegally on his colonel's (Exelmans) orders 15 January 1806, for this he was condemned to three months' prison and for not wanting to denounce his colonel, dismissed 2 February 1806, freed and withdrew to Colmar 25 February 1806, reinstated at the request of the regiment's officers, its colonel and Maréchal Davout 29 October 1806.

He was wounded by two grapeshot blasts at Nazielsk 24 December 1806.

He was quadron commander 25 February 1807, in the 12th chasseurs à Cheval took up his functions 28 February 1807, adjutant-commandant 16 May 1809, squadron commander of the Montbrun division (Walther) then the 1st Light Cavalry division in the 1st Reserve Cavalry Corps 1812.

He was shot and wounded at Ostrovno 25 July 1812, commanded a platoon in the Escadron Sacré during the retreat, in Pajol's Light Cavalry Division 6 April 1813, taken prisoner when Dresden capitulated 11 November 1813, returned 14 June 1814, non-active on half-pay 1 August 1814, Inspector of the National Guard at Colmar from 17 to 23 March 1815.

He was rallied to napoleon 27 March 1815, chief of staff of Strasbourg 31 March 1815, chief of staff of the 3rd Cuirassier Division 23 April 1815, had not yet taken up his appointment as chief of staff of the 11th Cavalry Division of the Observation Corps of the Pyrenees 26 April 1815, reached it May 1815, assistant chief of staff under General Rapp in the Army of the Rhine 18 June 1815.

He was non-active 15 September 1815. LH CH 14 June 1804, O 7 July 1809, Baron of the Empire d. 15 August 1809 and l.p. 3 May 1810.

On 15 November 1806, Captain François Tavernier halted the advance of one thousand five hundred Cossacks during a period of eight hours with only one hundred men, stopping them from entering Nieborow.

Supernumerary deputy in the Engineers 16 August 1800, discharged June 1801, maréchal des logis in the 1st Cuirassiers 32 April 1802, lieutenant aide de camp to General Campredon 17 May 1805, in the King of Naples' Chevau-Légers 12 March 1807, taken prisoner by the English in Spain 25 March 18709, returned 18 June 1814, cavalry captain in the service of France and put on the non-active list 4 January 1815, recalled to the 1st Cuirassiers 10 July 1815, put back of half-pay 1 September 1815.

THIONVILLE see **MERLIN** aka **MERLIN de THIONVILLE.**

THIRION (Auguste Jean Michel Isidore, 1787-1869): born in Morhange (Moselle) on 11 December 17887. Volunteer in the 22 Dragoons 30 May 1805, brigadier 20 August 1806, brigadier 3 August 1806, lance wound to his right flank at Ostrolenka 3 February 1807, brigadier-fourrier 20 October 1807, maréchal des logis 10 April 1809, in the 2nd Cuirassiers 6 May 1810, joined his unit 13 September 1810, shot and wounded in his right foot at Porto 1810, maréchal des logis-chef 26 July 1812, shot and wounded in

his left arm at the Moskova 7 September 1812, sub-lieutenant in service April 1813, in the 9th Cuirassiers 13 May 1813, shot and wounded in the right knee his horse killed under him at Leipzig 16 October 1813, in the King's Cuirassiers 1 July 1814 which became the 1st Cuirassiers again April 1815, dismissed with the corps and intended for the active list 24 December 1815. LH CH 5 September 1813.

THIRION (Jean, 1778-?): born in Nancy (Meurthe) in 1778. In the 2nd Cavalry 11 October 1797 which became the 2nd Cuirassiers 12 October 1802, brigadier 9 October 1803, fourrier 30 October 1806, maréchal des logis 20 November 1806, sub-lieutenant 14 May 1809, lieutenant 9 February 1813, incorporated with his squadron into the 1st Provisional Heavy Cavalry in Hamburg 11 September 1816, returned with the garrison 27 May 1814, non-active on half-pay 10 December 1815.

THOMASSIN (Louis Colomban, ?-?): In the 2nd Gardes d'Honneur 21 June 1813, brigadier 20 July 1813, maréchal des logis-chef 12 August 1813, second-lieutenant

ESTOT FERRY (Claude, Baron, 1773-1856) born in Arnay-le-Duc (Côte-d'Or) on 20 May 1773. In the Brittany Chasseurs à Cheval 25 December 1789 which became the 10th Chasseurs à Cheval 1 January 1791, brigadier-fourrier 16 May 1793, maréchal des logis-chef 19 July 1794, adjutant-NCO 16 May 1795.

Acting sub-lieutenant 20 May 1796, confirmed 4 January 1797, crossed through the Russian army alone to rejoin his regiment after having being cut off from it by the Cossacks June 1799, acting lieutenant 30 June 1799, took 50 prisoners at Landshut 7 July 1800, confirmed 20 July 1800.

He was elected lieutenant adjutant-major 11 February 1802, captain 10 August 1803, accompanied August de Colbert, his colonel, on a diplomatic mission to Russia 1803, returned to the 10th Chasseurs à Cheval 1804, aide de camp to General Marmont 9 February 1804.

He was squadron commander at the disposal of the Minister of War 3 March 1808, in the 2nd Provisional Heavy Cavalry in Spain 10 May 1808 which the became the 13th Cuirassiers 21 October 1808, major of the regiment 7 June 1809.

He returned to France to command the regimental depot August 1809, squadron commander in the Dragoons of the Guard 23 October 1811, instated 1 January 1812.

He was promoted to colonel in the Line on 28 November 1813, in the 7th dragoons 16 December 1813, colonel-major of the 1st Eclaireurs of the Imperial Guard 21 December 1813, prisoner of the Cossacks but escaped almost immediately 20 March 1804, dismissed with the regiment 12 May 1814, retroactively to the Grenadiers à Cheval of the Imperial Guard which formed the Corps Royal des Cuirassiers de France, non-active 22 July 1814, first aide de camp to Maréchal Marmont 27 September 1814, accompanied Louis XVII to the border 20 March 1815, returned home refusing to serve during the Hundred Days.

LH CH 14 March 1806, O 14 April 1813, C 22 December 1814, Baron of the Empire d. 16 March 1814 and confirmed l.p. 27 January 1815.

A captain in the 10th Chasseurs, Claude Testot Ferry, with 125 troopers took a battalion of 450 Austrian soldiers and 19 officers at Reiffling in 1805. At Hanau on 30 October 1813, having become Squadron Commander in the Dragoons of the Guard, he had his horse killed from under him and received 22 sabre wounds.

28 November 1813, dismissed with the corps 31 July 1814.

He was sub-lieutenant in the 6th Cuirassiers 4 August 1814, resigned 15 December 1814.

THORRE (François Julien, 1792-?): born in 1792. In the 1st Cuirassiers 21 May 1808, brigadier 11 May 1811, maréchal des logis 28 January

1813, in the same regiment when it became the King's Cuirassiers 1 July 1814 then 1st Cuirassiers again April 1815, sub-lieutenant 25 March 1815.

He was wounded at Waterloo 18 June 1815, struckoff the rolls, his sub-lieutenant's appointment cancelled 1 September 1815.

THOUVENIN (Pierre, 1765-?): born in Armoncourt (Vosges) on 9 April 1765. In the Royal-Cavalerie 30 November 1785 which became the 2nd Cavalry

1 January 1791, brigadier-fourrier 6 November 1792, maréchal des logis 17 June 1793.

He was maréchal des logis-chef 18 August 1799, in the same regiment when it became the 2nd Cuirassiers 12 October 1802, sub-lieutenant 14 May 1809, lieutenant 14 May 1813, retired 10 December 1815. LH CH 14 April 1807.

THUEUX (Félix Alexandre, 1788-?): born in Montreuil-sur-Mer (Pas-de-Calais) on 19 June

1788. Vélite in the Grenadiers à Cheval of the Imperial Guard 31 August 1806, grenadier à cheval 1 October 1810, sub-lieutenant in the 14th Cuirassiers 17 December 1811, took up his appointment 25 February 1812, wounded et the Berezina 28 November 1812, dismissed with the corps 13 July 1814.

THUIL van SEEROOSKERKEN (Vincent Jean Rainier, 1792-?): born in Utrecht (Zuydersee)

on 4 November 1792. Page to the King of Holland 10 February 1808, lieutenant in the 2nd Dutch Cuirassiers 25 October 1809 which became the 14th French Cuirassiers 18 August 1810, captain 19 November 1812, dismissed with the corps 13 July 1814.

At Eylau, the Cuirassiers, here led by Murat and d'Hautpoul, paid a heavy tribute or their victory. No rank of officers was spared. Composition by Patrick Courcelle. (Private Collection)

P. Courcelle

Belt buckle and chinstrap rosette. (RR)

THUMANN (Florent, 1778-?): born in Estens (Bas-Rhin) in 1778. In the 2nd Cavalry 7 May 1798 which became the 2nd Cuirassiers 12 October 1802, brigadier 20 November 1806, maréchal des logis 14 May 1809, sub-lieutenant 8 July 1813, prisoner 10 October 1813, returned 1814, dismissed with the corps and put on half-pay 10 December 1814.

THUON (Nicolas, 1769-1805): born in Moronvilliers (Haute-Marne) on 17 February 1769. In the Armagnac-Infanterie 17 February 1783, left 16 October 1789, in the 10th Battalion of Gévaudan Chasseurs 17 October 1789 which became the 13th Light Infantry Battalion 1 April 1791, corporal 1 January 1792, maréchal des logis in the 32nd Gendarmerie Division 12 January 1793, shot and wounded in the left shoulder 11 April 1793 and wounded again in the thigh 21 November 1793, adjutant-NCO in the Legion de Police Générale 23 May 1795.

He was elected lieutenant 23 February 1796, adjutant-major 11 March 1793, discharged 18 January 1798, pensioned 19 March 1798, maréchal des logis in the 1st Cavalry 22 September 1798, sub-lieutenant by choice of the government 29 May 1799, confirmed 2 June 1799 and 25 May 1801.

He was in the same regiment when it became the 1st Cuirassiers 10 October 1801, lieutenant by governmental choice, 5 March 1803, commissioned 11 April 1803, wounded at Austerlitz 2 December 1805 and died of his wounds at Brünn 9 December 1805.

TILLY see **DELAISTRE de TILLY**

TIMBRUNE de THIEM-BRONNE de VALENCE (Jean Baptiste Cyrus Adélaïde Marie de, comte, 1757-1822): born in Agen (Lot-et-Garonne) on 22 September 1757. In the artillery school in Strasbourg 23 September 1772. He was elected second-lieutenant in the Besançon Regiment 23 September 1773, discharged captain in the Royal-Cavalerie 28 February 1778, aide de camp to Maréchal de Vaux 1,779 in the Army of England, assistant maréchal des logis in the same army 1780, second-captain in the Royal-Cavalerie 3 December 1781, second mestre-de-camp in the Bretagne-Infanterie 1 June 1784 then of the Chartres-Infanterie 24 November 1784, attached to the Dutch Embassy and commanded the detachment sent from the various channel ports to Amsterdam 1787, First Equerry to the Duke of Orléans.

Colonel attached to the Chartres-Infanterie 17 March 1788, colonel of the Chartres-Dragons 21 December 1788, elected to the Estates-General but did not sit 24 May 1789, commanded the 1st Carabiniers 24 July 1791, special maréchal de camp commanding the Carabiniers and Corps Inspector 13 December 1791, commanded at Strasbourg and Inspector-General for mounted troops in the Haut and Bas-Rhin Departments and of the Carabiniers, lieutenant-general in the Kellermann's Army 5 September 1792, retroactively to 20 August 1792.

He commanded the Army of the Ardennes 12 October 1792, under Dumouriez 25 October 1792, interim C-i-C of the Armies of the North and Ardennes from 30 December 1792 to January 1793 and from 23 February 1793 to 11 March 1793, wounded at Neerwinden 18 March 1793, went over to the enemy with Dumouriez 5 April 1793, in exile in England, in America the Hamburg, returned to France 1799, on discharge pay 23 October 1800, senator 1 February 1805.

He commanded inspector of the 5th Reserve Legion in Grenoble 20 March 1807, returned to the Senate 31 December 1807, commanded the 3rd Division of the 4th Corps 7 September 1808, commanded the 5th Cuirassiers Division in Germany 25 December 1811, in the same division in the 1st Corps of the Cavalry Reserve of the Grande Armée 10 January 1812, commissioner-extraordinary for the Emperor in Besançon December 1813, secretary of the Senate 1814, Peer of France 4 June 1814 and 2 June 1815, responsible for defending the left bank of the Seine in Paris 13 June 1815, struck off the payroll 24 July 1815, retired 4 September 1815. Count of Valence l.p. 1 June 1808

RIP van ZOUTLANDT (Albert Dominicus, 1776-1835): born in Groningen (Ems-Occidental) on 13 August 1776. Cadet in the Wilke Regiment 1 July 1791.

He was elected ensign 5 September 1792, first-lieutenant in the 2nd Batavian Cavalry 5 July 1795.

He was ordnance officer to General van Zuylen van Nyevelt 1799, captain in the 2nd Batavian Cavalry 28 July 1805 and aide de camp to General Dumonceau, lieutenant-colonel of the 2nd Batavian Cavalry 1 October 1806.

He was in the Grenadiers à Cheval of the Royal Guard 23 October 1806, colonel of the 2nd Dutch Cuirassiers 3 August 1808, first captain in the King of Holland's Body Guards 25 September 1809, dismissed with the corps 12 May 1810.

Albert Trip van Zoutland was the Colonel of the 2nd Dutch Cuirassiers which became the 14th French cuirassiers when Holland was united to France on 18 August 1810.

He was shot and wounded in the head during the Battle of the Berezina on 28 November 1812.

When he left French service on 18 April 1814, he became a cavalry colonel and aide de camp to the King of Holland on 7 June 1814 then General-Major on 21 April 1815.

He commanded the cavalry brigade of the Prince of Orange at Waterloo on 18 June 1815.

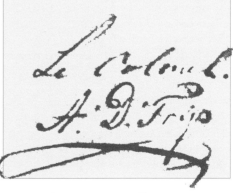

TITARD (Jacques, 1765-?): born in Auxey (Côte-d'Or) on 8 May 1765. In the Royal-Picardie-Cavalerie 27 July 1785, brigadier 1 November 1789, in the same regiment when it became the 21st Cavalry 1 January 1791, maréchal des logis 7 May 1792, maréchal des logis-chef 16 March 1793.

He recaptured two caissons at Bousbruck 24 March 1793, sub-lieutenant 1 April 1793, in the same regiment when it became the 20th Cavalry 4 June 1793.

He was lieutenant 19 February 1794, shot and wounded in his left leg at Tournai 8 May 1794, cap-

UROT (Charles Nicolas, Baron, 1773-1835): born in Bressolles (Allier) on 29 March 1776. Cadet in the Angoulême Regiment 9 March 1790, volunteer in the 34th Infantry 3 March 1791.

He was grenadier 16 April 1792, shot and wounded in the thigh at Grisuelle 11 June 1792, shot and wounded in his right leg at Valmy 20 September 1792, in the 6th Hussars 20 March 1793, maréchal des logis 15 April 1793, shot and wounded in his left thigh and taken prisoner at Marchiennes 31 October 1793, escaped 8 February 1794, wounded by Biscayan shot to his left thigh at Nijmegen 8 November 1794, shot in the left shoulder on the Island of Bommel 12 December 1794 and two sabre wounds to his head at Grave 28 December 1794, maréchal des logis-chef in the Legion des Francs 31 May 1796.

He received two sabre wounds and a bayonet wound at Kempten 11 August 1796, shot and wounded in his left foot at München 1 September 1796, cavalry sub-lieutenant in the Legion des Francs 22 September 1796, in the guides of the Army of Germany 26 October 1797, in the 8th Hussars 11 September 1798, with two men took twenty prisoners, two wagons and six caissons, shot and wounded in the chest at Zürich 25 September 1799.

He was elected lieutenant 20 February 1800, captain 19 August 1802, wounded by a Biscayan shot in the right thigh at Austerlitz 2 December 1805, three sabre wounds at Jena 14 October 1806, shot and wounded in the head at Eylau 7 February 1807.

He was shot and wounded in his left leg and his horse killed under him at Heilsberg 10 June 1807, two sabre wounds to his forehead and left hand at Koenigsberg 15 June 1807, supernumerary squadron commander 22 October 1808, took up his appointment in the 1st Hussars 15 February 1809, wounded at Sabugal 3 April 1811.

He was wounded by a shot to his right leg at Santurem 1812, in the 2nd Chevau-Légers Lancers

of the Guard 29 December 1812, reached the depot 1 April 1813 and the war squadrons 1 July 1813.

He was colonel of the 8th Hussars 18 October 1813, wounded in the ranks of the 2nd Chevau-Légers of the Guard at Leipzig by a cannonball to his right thigh 16 October 1813, confirmed 28 November 1813, commanded a provisional brigade made up of the 8th Hussars, 7th Chasseurs à Cheval and 17th Light February 1814, acting brigadier-general 5 March 1814, non-active and not confirmed in his post 1 August 1814, in the suite of the Dragons N° 14 18 October 1814 which became the 19th Dragoons again April 1815.

Colonel in the 12th Cuirassiers 19 April 1815, joined them 22 April 1815, acting CO of the brigade after General Travers was wounded, having four horses killed under him of which one was killed by three bayonet blows, confirmed general at Waterloo 18 June 1815, non-active as a colonel 18 January 1816. LH CH 14 June 1804, 25 August 1811, Chevalier of the Empire d. 2 May 1808, Baron.

Sous-Lieutenant in the 8th Hussars, with two men he took twenty prisoners, two wagon and six caissons was shot and wounded in the chest at Zurich on 25 September 1799.

He was wounded three times during the Polish Campaign in 1807, shot and wounded in the head at Eylau on 7 February, shot in the left leg and his horse killed under him at Heilsberg on 10 June 1807, and received two sabre wounds on his forehead and left hand at Koenigsberg on 15 June 1807.

16 May 1809, shot and wounded in his foot at Essling 22 May 1809, lieutenant adjutant-major 16 November 1810.

He was captain commanding a company 25 September 1812, three lance wounds of which two to his left side at Winkovo 18 October 1812, lance wound to his back and taken prisoner at Kovno 12 December 1812, stripped of his clothes except for his boots, lost consciousness then caught up with the army with two comrades at Koenigsberg January 1813.

He was shot and wounded in the left side of his chest at Hanau 30 October 1813, dismissed with the corps and put up for retirement 24 December 1814. LH CH 16 June 1809.

TOURNEBUS (Louis François Michel, 1785-?): born in Caen (Calvados) on 15 December 1785. In the 2nd Cuirassiers 5 August 1804, brigadier 14 April 1805, maréchal des logis 20 November 1806, sub-lieutenant 14 May 1809.

He was wounded at Wagram 6 July 1809, lieutenant 11 October 18121, captain 22 December 1813, non-active on half-pay 10 December 1815. LH CH 4 December 1813.

TOURNON SIMIANE (Victor Alexandre Maurice de, 1790-1812): born in 1790. In the Ecole Spéciale Militaire in Fontainebleau 1 March 1808, corporal 16 April 1809, fourrier 9 May 1809, sergeant 8 October 1809, sergeant-major 15 August 1810.

He was elected sub-lieutenant in the suite of the 1st Cuirassiers 14 August 1810, joined hi unit 17 September 1810, in service 31 July 1811, prisoner in Russia 16 December 1812 and disappeared.

TOURNY (Joseph, ?-?): born in Paris (Seine). In the Volontaires Nationaux à Cheval from the Ecole Militaire aka Dragons de la République 22 September 1792 which formed the 26th Cavalry XX February 1793 which became the 25th Cavalry 4 June 1793, brigadier 3 October 1800, dismissed with the corps 12 October 1802 and incorporated into the 2nd Cuirassiers 24 November 1802, fourrier 1 August 1806, maréchal des logis-chef 20 December 1806, adjutant-NCO 23 April 1808, in the 13th Cuirassiers when they were formed 21 October 1808.

He was elected sub-lieutenant 18 September 1811, lieutenant 22 November 1813, incorporated into the 9th Cuirassiers 9 August 1814, dismissed with the corps and put up for the gendarmerie 26 November 1815, retired 21 September 1816. LH CH 29 May 1810.

tain 19 July 1799, charged the Hungarian troops at the head of his company taking a huge number of prisoners at Marengo 14 June 1800, adjutant-major 13 March 1802.

He dismissed with the corps 31 December 1802 and incorporated as captain in the suite of the 12th Cavalry 25 January 1803 which then became the 12th Cuirassiers 24 September 1803, adjutant-major in service in the 5th Cuirassiers 16 March 1804, captain commanding a company 11 February 1805, squadron commander 5 May 1807, retired 25 July 1811.

Holder of a Sabre of Honour 3 July 1800, LH CH by rights 24 September 1803, O 14 June 1804.

TONNELIER (?-?): Pupil in the Ecole Spéciale Militaire in Saint-Cyr, sub-lieutenant in the 3rd Cuirassiers 24 July 1809, lieutenant aide de camp to General Richter 25 November 1811.

TONNERRE see **CLERMONT TONNERRE**

TORRINI (Etienne, 1789-?): born in Nice (Alpes-Maritime) on 26 December 1789. In the 21st Dragoons 20 August 1806, fourrier 9 July 1807, in the Dragoons of the Imperial Guard 24 June 1808, brigadier 11 March 1811, fourrier 1 October 1811. He was sub-lieutenant in the 6th Cuirassiers 8 February 1813, resignation accepted 6 August 1814, left for home as a foreign national 6 November 1814.

TOURETTE (Henry Ernest, 1790-?): born in Versailles (Seine-et-Oise) on 14 June 1790. Boarder in the Ecole Spéciale Militaire in Fontainebleau 7 June 1806, supernumerary sub-lieutenant in the suite of the 1st Cuirassiers 14 December 1806, took up his appointment 20 February 1807, lieutenant

TOURTEBATTE (Nicolas, 1773-?): born in Reims (Marne) on 14 August 1773. In the 24th Cavalry 23 March 1793 which became the 23rd 4 June

1793, brigadier 26 May 1799, shot and wounded in his left thigh in Salzburg 4 December 1800, dismissed with the corps 23 December 1802 and incorporated into the 7th Cuirassiers 15 January 1803, maréchal des logis 28 February 1805, sabre wound to his right arm at Essling 21 May 1809, sub-lieutenant 9 August 1809.

He was lieutenant 9 February 1813, left with his squadron for Hamburg 21 July 1813, incorporated into the 2nd Provisional Heavy Cavalry in Hamburg 11 September 1813, returned with the garrison 30 May 1814, on six months' leave from 1 September 1814 to 1 March 1815, retired 19 December 1815.

TOUSSAINT (Jean René, 1789-?): born in Saint-Dizier (Haute-Marne) on 7 August 1789. In the 1st Cuirassiers 22 April 1806, brigadier 1 April 1807, fourrier 28 July 1807, incorporated into the 13th Cuirassiers 21 October 1808, maréchal des logis-chef 1 January 1812, sub-lieutenant 12 June 1813, sabre wound to his chin near Lyons 20 March 1814. He dismissed with the corps and incorporated into the 11th Cuirassiers 9 August 1814, instated 1 September 1814, wounded at Waterloo 18 June 1815, resignation accepted 20 November 1815.

TOUTAIN (?-1812): maréchal des logis-chef in the 5th Cuirassiers, sub-lieutenant 3 June 1809, prisoner 1812 and disappeared.

TRAVERS (Etienne Jacques, baron de Jever, 1765-1827): born in Néhou (Manche) on 22 October 1765. In the Colonel-Général-Dragons 11 May 1790 which became the 5th Dragoons 1 January 1791, shot and wounded near Le Quesnoy 1793, brigadier-fourrier 1 May 1792, maréchal des logis 20 April 1796, maréchal des logis-chef 22 April 1796, elected sub-lieutenant 6 January 1797 then lieutenant 12 January 1799, captain 2 February 1800, squadron commander 22 June 1804, in the 3rd Dragons à Pied, 2nd Brigade (Boussart), Baraguey d'Hilliers' division 26 August 1805, allowed to go over to the service of the King of Holland 7 June 1806, colonel of the Cuirassiers of the Royal Dutch Guard 4 July 1806.

He was major-general aide de camp to King Louis 5 March 1808, colonel of the Gendarmerie and mounted troops 6 August 1808, first aide de camp to the King 10 August 1808, captain of the Guards 27 March 1809, first captain of the Gardes à cheval 18 September 1809, brigadier-general in the service of France 11 November 1810, commanded the Dyle Department 24 December 1810, acting remounts inspector in the 16th, 24th and 25th Military Divisions 7 May 1811, commanded the National Guard Cohorts from the first mobilisation 6 April 1812, commanded the Dyle Department 15 June 1812, commanded the

9th brigade of the National Guards from the first mobilisation 21 August 1812, commanded the Lancer Brigade from the Grand Duchy of Berg 10 February 1813, shot and wounded in the chest at Leipzig 16 October 1813, senior in command to Condé 5 February 1814, non-active 20 June 1812, deputy in the General Inspection of the Cavalry in the 18th and 21st military Divisions 30 December 1814, commanded the 2nd Cavalry Brigade (7th and 12th Cuirassiers) of the 3rd cavalry Division in the Army of the North 12 May 1815 which became the 13th Cavalry Division in the 4th Reserve Cavalry Corps 3 June 1815, wounded at Waterloo 18 June 1815, non-active 6 August 1815, resigned 5 April 1816.

Baron of Jever by the King of Holland 1808, recognised Baron of the Empire by Imperial l.p. 3 January 1813.

TRECA (Ildephonse Nicolas Joseph, 1785-?): born in Escaudain (Nord) on 9 October 1785. In the Velites of the Grenadiers à cheval of the Imperial Guard 12 October 1806, sub-lieutenant in the 7th Cuirassiers 4 April 1808, joined them in the 1st Provisional Heavy Cavalry in Spain 12 May 1808, wounded at Barcelona 24 July 1808, in the same regiment when it became the 13th Cuirassiers 21 October 1809, shot and wounded in the left foot at Barcelona 12 July 1809, lieutenant in the suite of the 7th Cuirassiers 8 October 1811, took up his appointment 4 March 1812, wounded at the Berezina 28 November 1812, captain 15 May 1813, left for Hamburg 16 July 1813, incorporated with his squadron into the 2nd Provisional Heavy Cavalry in Hamburg 11 September 1813, returned with the garrison 30 May 1814, wounded at Waterloo 18 June 1815, absent from 19 June to the disbanding of the corps 19 December 1815. LH CH 13 January 1813, O 16 May 1813.

TREUILLE de BEAULIEU (Jean Baptiste Pierre, baron, 1768-1861): born in Saint-Secondin (Vienne) on 5 August 1768. Lieutenant in the 1st Vienne Battalion 21 November 1791, sub-lieutenant in the 4th Dragoons 1 November 1792, lieutenant 16 November 1796, deputy to Adjutant-General Rheinwald 16 December 1796, captain 15 May 1799, aide de camp to the same man 19 June 1799, acting squadron commander in the suite of the 4th Dragoons 2 October 1799, confirmed in the 10th Cavalry and put in the suite 14 December 1801, discharged 12 January 1804, put back in the 1st cuirassiers 15 December 1803.

He joined them 27 January 1804, in the Grenadiers à Cheval of the Imperial Guard 5 September 1805, left to join them 26 September 1805, put on the Army's roll of

honour for his conduct at Eylau 8 February 1807, colonel 14 February 1807, in the 15th Dragoons 5 April 1807, returned home 5 June 1809, retired because of his disabilities 1 July 1809.

He was elected Mayor of Selestat 28 April 1811, commanded the Bouches-du-Rhône Department 8 September 1812, non-active 21 December 1813. LH CH 14 June 1804, O 14 March 1806, Baron de Beaulieu l.p. 2 July 1808.

TREULAN see **ROBIEN de TREULAN**

TRIBOUT (Louis François Cyprien, 1769-?): born in Lihus-le-Grand (Oise) on 31 January 1769. Trooper in the Royal-Pologne 16 April 1787 which became the 5th Cavalry 1 January 1791, brigadier-fourrier 16 July 1793, maréchal des logis 18 August 1798, adjutant-NCO 20 April 1799, sub-lieutenant 21 October 1800, in the same regiment when it became the 5th Cuirassiers 23 December 1802, elected lieutenant 6 April 1805. He was adjutant-major 24 November 1806, captain in the suite 20 February 1807, in service 3 April 1807, retired 1 January 1810. LH CH.

TRONCHON (?-1807): Pupil in the Ecole Spéciale Militaire in Fontainebleau, sub-lieutenant in the suite of the 9th cuirassiers 23 September 1806, took up his appointment 17 May 1807, died 30 July 1807.

TRONVILLE (Louis, 1776-?): born in Verdun (Meuse) in 1776. In the 25th cavalry 4 July 1799, dismissed with the corps 13 October 1802 and incorporated into the 2nd Cuirassiers 24 November 1802, brigadier 30 October 1806, maréchal des logis 16 May 1807, sub-lieutenant 22 December 1813, non-active on half-pay 10 December 1815.

TROOYEN (Jean Frédéric van, 1763-?): born in Groningen (Ems-Occidental) on 5 January 1763. Cadet in the General-Major's Dutch Cavalry Regiment 10 October 1777, cornet, lieutenant, retired and pensioned off 1 August 1795, captain in the 2nd Dutch Cuirassiers 26 February 1807 which became the 14th French Cuirassiers after the annexation 18 August 1810, left with his pension 6 December 1810.

TURPIN (Adam, 1755-?): born in Reidsheim (Moselle) on 1 January 1755. In the Royal-Cravates 1 April 1775, brigadier 18 July 1790, in the same regiment when it became the 10th Cavalry 1 January 1791, maréchal des logis 15 September 1793, maréchal des logis-chef 11 August 1794, confirmed 3 October 1794, sub-lieutenant 25 August 1795, discharged with the reorganisation then took up his appointment 20 January 1799, lieutenant 11 December 1801, in the same regiment when it became the 10th Cuirassiers 24 September 1803, retired 24 November 1806, left 26 December 1806 LH CH 5 November 1804.

VACOSSIN (François, 1772-?): born in Bacoville (Oise) on 7 December 1772. In the 1st Cavalry 7 February 1794, shot and wounded in the left thigh at Tournai 17 May 1794, brigadier 7 September 1799, in the same regiment when it became the 1st Cuirassiers 10 October 1801, fourrier 20 June 1802, maréchal des logis 3 October 1805, shot and wounded in his right knee at Austerlitz 2 December 1805, maréchal des logis-chef 8 January 1806, shot and wounded, three bayonet wounds, eleven sabre wounds and two lance wounds to his head, right arm and left side at Hoff 6 February 1807, sub-lieutenant 3 April 1807, lieutenant 20 June 1809, prisoner in Russia 10 December 1812. LH CH 14 April 1807.

VACQUIER (Pierre, 1771-1820): born in Canet (Hautes-Pyrénées) on 9 February 1771. Grenadier in the 44th Infantry 1 May 1791, shot and wounded twice in the left thigh bone and left tibia at Kaiserlautern 27 November 1793, 3rd class health officer in the army hospitals 5 December 1793, under-assistant-surgeon in the 3rd Cavalry 19 July 1796, discharged but remained in the corps, maréchal des logis in the 3rd Cavalry 24 March 1802 which became the 3rd Cuirassiers 12 October 1802, maréchal des logis-chef 6 July 1803, sub-lieutenant by seniority 18 February 1804, sabre wound to his left arm and his horse killed under him at Austerlitz 2 December 1805, elected lieutenant 11 December 1805, unhorsed at Friedland 14 June 1807 he picked up a rifle and fought in a battalion of infantry grenadiers and shot down an enemy officer, taking his horse to rejoin his regiment and resume his charge.

He was retired complaining too frequently about his lack of promotion 28 July 1808. LH CH 5 February 1804.

VADUREL (Philippe, 1762-?): born in Marcelcave (Somme) on 18 February 1762. In the Roi-Cavalerie 10 February 1788 which became the 6th Cavalry 1 January 1791, brigadier-fourrier 1 April 1793,

wounded by a Biscayan shot to the stomach at Fleurus 26 June 1794, maréchal des logis 21 December 1794, maréchal des logis-chef 3 June 1799, in the same regiment when it became the 6th Cuirassiers 23 December 1802

He was sub-lieutenant by seniority 18 April 1803, lieutenant 19 June 1807, seconded to the 3rd Provisional Heavy Cavalry in Spain, returned to the regiment when the 3rd Provisional was disbanded 27 December 1810, retired 16 May 1811.

VALENCE see
TIMBRUNE de THIEMBRONNE de VALENCE

VALET (Jean Baptiste, 1778-?): born in Guignicourt (Ardennes) in 1778. In the 4th Cavalry 1 December 1798, brigadier 4 August 1802, in the same regiment when it became the 4th Cuirassiers 12 October 1802, maréchal des logis 1 October 1806, shot and wounded at Essling 21 May 1809, maréchal des logis-chef 1 January 1811, sub-lieutenant 4 March 1811, non-active on half-pay 6 August 1814, recalled to the same regiment 4 January 1815, retired 21 December 1815.

VALLABREGUE see **VIDAL de VILLABREGUE**

VALLET (Charles, 1773-?): born in Boncham (Jura) on 23 September 1773. Volunteer in the 8th Jura Battalion 25 August 1792, corporal 6 April 1793, sergeant in the 74th Half-Brigade of the Line 8 January 1796, gendarme in the Forêts Department in the 18th Legion 4 April 1802, brigadier in the 1st Legion of the Gendarmerie d'Espagne "Burgos" 1 March 1812, dismissed with the corps 27 February 1813 and out in the 10th Cuirassiers with the rank of sub-lieutenant 28 February 1813, not kept on 6 August 1814.

VALLET (Claude Simon, 1761-?): born in Salins (Jura) on 8 March 1791. Provincial soldier 7 February 1791, corporal 1 January 1782, sergeant

5 November 1782, trooper in the Royal-Roussillon-Cavalerie 3 January 1786, brigadier 8 June 1790, in the same regiment when it became the 11th Cavalry 1 January 1791, maréchal des logis 30 June 1792, maréchal des logis-chef 14 July 1792, quarter-master-treasurer 1 January 1793, lieutenant 3 April 1795, captain 30 July 1802, in the same regiment when it became the 11 Cuirassiers 24 September 1803, prisoner at Capua 29 July 1799, wounded at Eylau 8 February 1807, retired 25 May 1807.

VALLET (Jean Baptiste, ?-?): maréchal des logis in the 4th Cuirassiers, sub-lieutenant 4 March 1812, wounded at the Berezina 28 November 1812, incorporated with his squadron into the 1st Provisional Heavy Cavalry in Hamburg 11 September 1813, returned with the garrison 27 May 1814 and non-active 6 August 1814. He was in the suite of the Angoulême Cuirassiers 4 January 1815 which became the 4th Cuirassiers again in April 1815, dismissed with the corps 21 December 1815.

VALLOT (Louis, 1775-1812): born in Courcelle-Valdemon (Haute-Marne) on 15 March 1775. In the 11th Cavalry 14 February 1794, brigadier 1 May 1800, fourrier 27 May 1800, maréchal des logis-chef 12 October 1802, in the same regiment when it became the 11th Cuirassiers 24 September 1803, maréchal des logis-chef 1 October 1803, sub-lieutenant 25 May 1807, lieutenant 3 June 1809, captain 19 June 1812, wounded at the Moskova 7 September 1812, disappeared during fighting beyond the Niemen 31 December 1812. LH CH 22 June 1804.

VALTER (Jean Pierre, 1769-?): born in Epinal (Vosges) on 25 October 1769. In the Noailles-Dragons 16 January 1785 which became the 15th Dragoons 1 January 1791, left 28 January 1791, in the 7th Chasseurs à Cheval 2 August 1791, brigadier-fourrier 12 September 1792, maréchal des logis 1 May 1793, sub-lieutenant 15 August 1793, shot and wounded in the left leg at Frankfurt 1793, lieutenant 15 April 1800, adjutant-major 11 February 1802, rank of captain 10 August 1803, bayonet wound to his left arm at Jena 14 October 1806, squadron commander 27 July 1810, in the 4th Cuirassiers 13 February 1813. Wounded in the forward positions and taken prisoner 24 May 1813. LH CH 5 November 1804.

VAMBRE (Jean Baptiste, 1767-?): born in the Nord in 1767. In the Forêt-Infanterie 28 August 1785 which became the 14th Infantry 1 April 1791, in the 1st Cavalry 11 July 1791 shot and wounded in the right foot at Neerwinden 18 March 1793 and a sabre wound at Moucron near Lille 1794, recaptured several wagons from the enemy at Saint-Maxime 2 January 1801. He was in the same regiment when it became the 1st Cuirassiers 10 October 1804, brigadier 4 November 1803, maréchal des logis 23 February 1805, sub-lieutenant 3 June 1809, retired with pension 16 August 1814.

Holder of a Rifle of Honour 13 August 1801, commissioned 30 May 1803, LH CH by rights 24 September 1803.

General Valence, wearing Republican general officer's campaign dress, during Revolution period.
(© Musée des Beaux-Arts, Agen)

VANDENBERGH (Charles Joseph, 1785-?): born in 1785. Sub-lieutenant in the suite of the 1st Cuirassiers 21 January 1810, took up his functions 31 July 1811, incorporated with his squadron into the 1st Provisional Heavy Cavalry in Hamburg 11 September 1813, acting lieutenant adjutant-major during the siege, confirmed adjutant-major 20 April 1814, returned with the garrison 27 May 1814 and put back in the 1st Cuirassiers, resigned from French service and left the corps 1 October 1814. LH CH 29 July 1814.

VANDENDRIES (Henry, 1784-?): born in Soissons (Aisne) on 11 June 1784. Volunteer in the 16th Dragoons 1804, instated 1 July 1804, brigadier 20 July 1805, invalided out because of his wounds 15 December 1806, left 31 December 1806, enrolled as a volunteer in the war squadrons of the 2nd Cuirassiers 1 November 1809, maréchal des logis 1 January 1810, honorary adjutant 1 May 1810, adjutant-NCO in post 21 April 1812, instated 12 May 1812, sub-lieutenant 12 August 1812, lieutenant 3 September 1813, lieutenant 3 September 18113, lieutenant adjutant-major 27 September 1813, in the suite of the Queen's Cuirassiers 20 January 1815, non-active on half-pay 10 December 1815. LH CH 5 March 1814.

VANDENSTRUITE
see **SANDIFORT van den STRUITE**

VANDERKELEND (Jacques, 1785-?): born in Brussels (Dyle) on 17 December 1785. In the 2nd Cuirassiers 24 April 1808, brigadier 1 September 1809, maréchal des logis 16 January 1813, sub-lieutenant 29 September 1813, resigned from French service and left 5 August 1814.

VANGOCH (Jean François, 1787-?): born in Bois-le-Duc (Bouches-du-Rhin) on 8 July 1787. Maréchal des logis in the 2nd Gardes d'Honneur, sub-lieutenant in the suite of the 13th Cuirassiers 19 March 1814, placed in the suite of the 12th Cuirassiers 23 May 1814, not included in the 14 July 1814 reorganisation because he was a foreign national.

VANHEULLE (Auguste Joseph, 1778-?): born in Roncq (Nord) on 1 October 1778. In the 3rd Chasseurs 24 September 1793, in the Legion of Police Générale 12 August 1795 which became the 21st Dragoons 24 December 1796, dismissed with the corps and incorporated into the 16th Dragoons 24 December 1797, in the 1st Carabiniers 26 June 1798, shot and wounded in his right leg when crossing the Danube near Dillingen 18 June 1800, wound by a shot to his stomach near Bruchsal 28 September 1800.

He was in the chasseurs à Cheval of the Imperial Guard 7 July 1806, brigadier 16 February 1807, sabre wound to his left arm at Benavente 29 December 1808, maréchal des logis 15 September 1809, maréchal des logis-chef 26 December 1811, second-lieutenant (Old Guard) 27 February 1813, in the Royal Corps of the Chasseurs à Cheval de France 30 July 1814 which became the Chasseurs à cheval (Old Guard) 8 April 1815. He was elected lieutenant in the Line at the disposal of the Minister of War 14 April 1815, in the 5th Cuirassiers 1 May 1815, wounded at Waterloo 18 June 1815 and retired 23 December 1815. LH CH 29 November 1813.

VANOS see **OS**.

VARANCEAU (?-1809): adjutant-NCO in the 1st Cuirassiers, sub-lieutenant 25 May 1807, killed by a cannonball at Essling 22 May 1809.

VAST VIMEUX (Charles Louis, 1787-?): born in Paris (Seine) on 26 October 1787. In the 10th Hussars 1 October 1805, brigadier 1 October 1806, maréchal des logis 3 May 1808, infantry sub-lieutenant in the 69th Infantry 21 November 1808, shot and wounded in the left leg at Saragossa February 1809, lieutenant in the 59th Of the Line 11 July 1810.

He was aide de camp to General Roget 22 January 1811, captain aide de camp to General Dornès and retroactively in the 5th Cuirassiers 30 August 1812, returned to the regiment, dismissed 23 December 1815. LH CH 28 September 1813.

VATTIER (André Hilaire, 1786-1809): born in Antony (Seine) on 7 January 1786. In the gendarmes d'Ordonnance, 25 October 1806, shot and wounded in the right arm and two sabre wounds to his head and taken prisoner at Colberg 20 March 1807, returned to the regiment 18 September 1807, dismissed with the corps 23 October 1807 and incorporated into the Grenadiers à Cheval of the Imperial Guard 24 November 1807.

He was sub-lieutenant in the 1st Carabiniers 19 May 1808, in the 13th Cuirassiers 21 October 1808, died at Tarbes 11 May 1809.

VAUCONSENT (Jean Mathias, 1758-1812): born in Sannois (Seine-et-Oise) on 19 October 1758. In the Volontaires Nationaux from the Ecole Militaire 4 September 1792, maréchal des logis 6 April 1793, maréchal des logis-chef 25 October 1793, adjutant-NCO in the 1st Hussars 9 February 1793, sub-lieutenant in the new unit 1796.

He was discharged because of officers being dismissed from the suite 23 October 1803, back in service with the 8th Cuirassiers 27 November 1806, detached to the 3rd Provisional Heavy Cavalry in Spain 1808, returned to his corps 1809, lieutenant 6 November 1811, right thigh blown off by a cannonball at the Moskova 7 September 1812 and died of his wounds.

VAUDORE (Jacques Marin, 1782-?): born in Joué-de-Plain (Orne) on 212 June 1782. In the 10th Cuirassiers 14 June 1804, brigadier 1 December 1806, shot and wounded in his left leg, fourrier 16 May 1809, maréchal des logis 25 January 1811, adjutant 12 August 1812, sub-lieutenant 28 September 1813, wounded by a Biscayan shot to his left side at Hanau 29 October 1813, standard-bearer 6 August 1814, dismissed with the corps 25 December 1815.

VAUFRELAND (Alphonse Etienne Georges, 1798-?): born in Embrun (Hautes-Alpes) on 10 July 1798. In the Prytaneum 15 December 1806, sub-lieutenant in the suite of the Berri Chevau-Légers 5 July 1814, in the Berri Cuirassiers 16 October 1814, confirmed 20 February 1815, in the same regiment when it became the 5th Cuirassiers April 1815, dismissed 23 December 1815.

Senior officer. His jonquil collar shows us that he belongs to the 7th, 9th, 10th or 12th Cuirassier Regiment. Composition by Maurice Toussaint.
(Collection Lefevre-Vakana, RR)

VAUTRIN (Augustin, 1773-1807): born in Beauzée (Meuse) on 28 March 1773. In the 24th Cavalry 4 September 1791, brigadier 1 April 1793, in the same regiment when it became the 23rd Cavalry 4 June 1793, fourrier 5 February 1795. He was maréchal des logis 1 August 1798, maréchal des logis-chef 20 April 1799, adjutant-NCO 15 December 1800, dismissed with the corps 23 December 1802 and incorporated into the 5th Cuirassiers 3 January 1803, sub-lieutenant 1 March 1804, killed at Eylau 8 February 1807.

VEIRAT (Jean François, 1757-?): born in Nîmes (Gard) on 22 August 1757. Trooper in the Royal-Cravates 19 May 1777, brigadier 8 June 1787, in the same regiment when it became the 10th Cavalry 1 January 1981, brigadier-fourrier 21 March 1791, maréchal des logis, 4 October 1791, maréchal des logis-chef 15 September 1793, adjutant-NCO 14 November 1793, adjutant sub-lieutenant 14 November 1793, sabre wound to his head at Wurtzburg 3 September 1793, lieutenant 21 March 1797. He was elected adjutant-major 13 March 1802, in the same regiment when it became the 10th Cuirassiers 24 September 1803, rank of captain 9 September 1803, retired 17 August 1807. LH CH 5 November 1804.

VENDEUR (Jean Baptiste, 1774-?): born in Champvaut (Haute-Saône) on 4 March 1774. Grenadier in the 10th Haute-Saône Battalion 5 August 1792, corporal 14 July 1794, fourrier in the Carabiniers in the 23rd Light Infantry 15 February 1796, gendarme in the 20th Legion 28 March 1802, saved the Archbishop of Besançon and his two vicars' lives by jumping into the River Doubs three times to save them 23 June 1808, brigadier in the 12th Squadron of the Gendarmerie d'Espagne 20 December 1809, fourrier 15 January 1810. He was maréchal des logis in the 1st Legion of the Gendarmerie à Cheval "Burgos" 16 December 1810, maréchal des logis-chef 1 November 1811, dismissed with the corps 27 February 1813 and put in the 5th Cuirassiers as a lieutenant 28 February 1813, retired 23 December 1815. LH CH 28 February 1813.

VENDOME (Jean Joseph, 1782-?): born in Ressones (Oise) on 22 May 1782. In the 11th Cuirassiers 27 December 1803, brigadier-fourrier 21 February 1806.

He was maréchal des logis-chef 16 May 1809, sub-lieutenant 15 March 1812, 7 sabre wounds to his neck, left side, face, right shoulder and back at Leipzig 16 October 1813, dismissed with the corps 16 December 1815. LH CH 13 August 1809.

VERAN (Barthélémy, 1785-?): born in Fontvieille (Bouches-du-Rhône) on 15 November 1785. Velite in the Grenadiers à Cheval of the Imperial Guard 25 March 1806, sub-lieutenant in the 7th Dragons 7 January 1808, lieutenant 1 June 1812, lieutenant adjutant-major in the 13th Cuirassiers 23 October 1813, captain adjutant-major 5 March 1814, dismissed with the regiment and incorpora-

ted into the 9th Cuirassiers 9 August 1814, dismissed with the corps 25 November 1815 and non-active at the disposal of the Minister of War 26 November 1815. LH CH 19 March 1815.

VERDIERE see **COLLIN VERDIERE**

VERGE (François, 1753-?): born in Laval (Mayenne) on 16 April 1753. In the Royal-Cavalerie 8 June 1774, brigadier 13 September 1784, in the same regiment when it became the 2nd Cavalry 1 January 1791, maréchal des logis 22 December 1791, maréchal des logis-chef 1 April 1793. He was elected sub-lieutenant 28 November 1793, lieutenant 17 March 1795, wounded at Neresheim 11 August 1796, captain by seniority 12 November 1800, confirmed 22 March 1801, in the same regiment when it became the 2nd Cuirassiers 12 October 1802, retired 21 August 1806, left 15 September 1806.

VERGEZ (Jean Baptiste Louis de, 1784-1839): born in Préchac (Hautes-Pyrénées) on 1 November 1784. Boarder in the Ecole Spéciale Militaire in Fontainebleau, sub-lieutenant in the suite of the 5th Cuirassiers 14 December 1806 and employed as ordnance officer, took up his appointment in the regiment 19 March 1807, lieutenant 16 May 1809, wounded at Essling 22 May 1809, adjutant-major 6 November 1811, captain adjutant-major 6 May 18131, captain in the 1st Gardes d'Honneur 3 September 18113, in the suite of Monsieur's Dragoons N° 4 1814, non-active 20 January 1815, returned as squadron commander in the suite of the 5th cuirassiers 3 June 1815, put back on the non-active list 1 September 1815. LH CH 16 June 1809.

VERGNETTE d'ALBAN (Victor Constantin de, 1745-?): born in Evreux (Eure) on 212 May 1745. One of the King's pages in the Grande Ecurie from 27 May 1762 to 4 September 1766, sub-lieutenant In the Colonel-Général-Cavalerie 14 July 1767, lieutenant 1 June 1772, second-lieutenant 1776, captain discharged 28 February 1778, second-captain in the Chevau-Légers N°1 8 May 1779, which became the Orléans-Cavalerie 25 July 1784, major of the Colonel-Général-Cavalerie 5 March 1786, lieutenant-colonel 13 September 1789, instated 16 December 1789.

He was in the same regiment when it became the 1st Cavalry 1791, gave up his post 6 October 1791, left 12 October 1791, colonel in the suite of the King's Cuirassiers 13 September 1814, joined his unit 16 September 1814, dismissed for 2 months 31 January, allowed to withdraw to his property 13 March 1815, left the regiment 29 March 1815, retired 24 December 1815.

VERGNIAUD de LANGE (Bernard, 1787-?): born in Petit-Magniac (Haute-Vienne) on 21 September 1787. Boarder in the Ecole Spéciale Militaire in Fontainebleau 23 September 1805, at the Grande Armée's General Headquarters 9 October 1809, sub-lieutenant in the suite of the 5th Cuirassiers

Belt plate belonging to an officer from the 7th Cuirassiers. (RR)

14 December 1806, detached to the 2nd Provisional Heavy Cavalry in Spain December 1807, wounded at Baylen 19 July 1808 and prisoner by capitulation 22 July 1808, detained in England, lieutenant in the 7th Cuirassiers during his captivity 29 April 1809, returned to France 11 July 1814, returned to the 7th Cuirassiers 10 August 1814 and put on the non-active list 16 August 1814.

VERHOEFF (Antoine Rainier, ?-?): Sub-lieutenant in the Dutch Cuirassiers 26 October 1806 which became the 14th French Cuirassiers 18 August 1810, wounded and prisoner at the Berezina 28 November 1812, disappeared.

VERNEREY (Jean Antoine, 1774-?): born in Baume (Doubs) on 212 September 1774. Fusilier in the 2nd Doubs Battalion 20 March 1792, sub-lieutenant in the 55th of the Line 221 February 1794, sabre wound to his head during the blockade of Breda 1794, sub-lieutenant in the 1st Chasseurs à Cheval 31 October 1795, lieutenant aide de camp to General Blondeau and retroactively in the 114th Of the Line 21 March 1796, returned to the corps 4 March 1797, aide de camp to General Muller 22 January 1799, shot and wounded in the left leg at Fossano, in the 1st Chasseurs à Cheval 11 June 1811, discharged 21 May 1801, captain in the 5th Cuirassiers 30 March 1807, shot and wounded in the leg at Baylen 19 July 1808 and prisoner with the capitulation 22 July 1808, escaped from the hulk Vieille Castille 16 August 1810 and put back in the 5th Cuirassiers 28 August 1810, left arm wounded at the Moskova 7 September 1812 and at Winkovo 4 October 1812, squadron commander in the 12th Cuirassiers 28 June 1813, wounded at waterloo 18 June 1815, dismissed with the corps 10 December 1815. LH CH 11 October 1812.

VERNET (Nicolas Geoffroy, 1787-?): born in Bitche (Moselle) on 4 April 1787. Velite in the Grenadiers à cheval of the Imperial Guard 3 March 1806, sub-lieutenant in the 6th Cuirassiers 25 March 1809, lieutenant 8 October 1811, wounded at the Moskova 7 September 1812 and prisoner at Osmiana 6 December 1812, returned to France 3 October 1814, wounded at Waterloo 18 June 1815, dismissed with the corps 21 November 1815.

VERNET (Pierre, 1778-?): born in Vernot (Puy-de-Dôme) in July 1778. In the 2nd Cavalry 22 June

1794, brigadier 31 January 1802, in the same regiment when it became the 2nd Cuirassiers 12 October 1802, maréchal des logis 1 January 1807, maréchal des logis-chef 1 January 1808. He was electedsublieutenant 11 March 1812, lieutenant 14 May 1813, left with his pension on the disbanding of the corps 10 December 1815. LH CH 29 September 1814.

VERPILLAT (Marie Philippe Etienne, 1779-?): born in Ruffey (Jura) on 28 November 1779. In the 4th Chasseurs à Cheval 3 April 1800, taken prisoner in front of Ferrara 27 November 1800, returned 1 April 1801, in the Grenadiers à cheval of the Guard 6 May 1802, brigadier 15 October 1802, brigadier-fourrier 29 September 1805, maréchal des logis-chef 16 February 1807.

He wassecond lieutenant 25 June 1809, supernumerary in the 12th Cuirassiers 28 November 1813, joined his regiment 15 January 1814, aide de camp to General Dériot 31 May 1815, left to take up his post 16 June 1815. LH CH 14 March 1806.

VERRIER see **BORE VERRIER**

VERSIGNY (Ambroise Ferdinand, 1786 -after 1838): born in Gray (Haute-Saône) on 4 april 1786. Velite in the Grenadiers à cheval of the Imperial Guard 31 March 1806, sub-lieutenant in the suite of the 4th Cuirassiers 13 July 1807, supernumerary lieutenant 7 April 1809, took up his appointment 6 June 1809, captain 9 June 1812, lance wound to his shoulder at Uczacz near Polotsk 24 October 1812, wounded at the Berezina 28 November 1812, commanded the regimental detachment in Hamburg 3 July 1813, incorporated with it into the 1st Provisional Heavy Cavalry in Hamburg 11 September 1813, left for France with the garrison after the surrender of the city 27 May 1814 and returned to the 4th Cuirassiers which became the Angoulême Cuirassiers 6 August 1814 then the 4th Cuirassiers again April 1815, two sabre wounds to his head and left arm at Waterloo 18 June 1815, dismissed 21 December 1815. LH CH 9 November 1814, confirmed 11 April 1815.

VERTHE (Martin, 1754-?): born in Erstein (Bas-Rhin) on 14 June 1754. In the Chartres-Infanterie 25 August 1773, left 25 August 1781, in the Reine-Cavalerie 19 January 1782, brigadier 19 November 1786, in the same regiment when it became the 4th cavalry 1 January 1791, maréchal des logis 26 December 1791, sub-lieutenant 1 August 1792, lieutenant 20 April 1794, shot and wounded at Charleroi 6 June 17494, supernumerary 1796, took up his post 1797, in the same regiment when it became the 4th Cuirassiers 12 October 1802, retired 25 June 1806. LH CH 1805.

VESPA (Joseph, 1783-?): born in Naples (Mont-Blanc) in 1783. In the 2nd Cuirassiers 28 February 1803, brigadier 20 November 1806, maréchal des logis 1 September 1809, sub-lieutenant 14 May 1813, left as a foreign national.

VETTER (Ignace Hubert, 1777-1809): born in Portenruy (Haut-Rhin) on 6 November 1777. In the 3rd Cavalry 27 June 1799, maréchal des logis 4 February 1800, sub-lieutenant 23 October 1800, confirmed 24 June 1801, in the same regiment when it became the 3rd Cuirassiers 12 October 1802, lieutenant by seniority 18 February 1804, wounded at Austerlitz 2 December 1805, elected captain 11 December 1805, squadron commander 14 May 1809, killed at Essling 21 May 1809.

VETTER (Jean François, 1776-?): born in 1776. In the 7th Dragoons 28 April 1799, brigadier 30 January 1801, gendarme in the 13th Legion 9 May 1805, in the 8th Squadron of the Gendarmerie d'Espagne 2 December 1809, in the 1st Legion of the Gendarmerie à cheval d'Espagne "Burgos" 16 December 1810, brigadier 9 June 1812, dismissed with the corps 27 February 1813 and placed as sub-lieutenant again in the 1st Cuirassiers 28 February March 1813, joined them 1 April 1813. He stayed in the same regiment when it became the King's Cuirassiers 1 July 1814, discharged 1 August 1814.

VEYGOUX see **DESAIX de VEYGOUX**

VEYSSET (?-?): In the Berri-Cavalerie 17 September 1779, brigadier 15 June 1787, in the same regiment when it became the 18th Cavalry 1 January 1791, fourrier 16 March 1791, maréchal des logis 1 November 1791, maréchal des logis-chef 21 June 1792, in the same regiment when it became the 17th Cavalry 4 June 1793, sub-lieutenant 16 June 1793, lieutenant and captain the same day 12 November 1793, aide de camp to General Micas October 1796, returned to the corps 14 January 1800, captain in the 5th cuirassiers 30 December 1802, bayonet wound to his hip at Austerlitz 2 December 1805, wounded at Eylau 8 February 1807, retired 25 May 1807.

VEZIN (Pierre, 1779-1805): born in Gaillac (Aveyron) on 29 November 1779. Coastguard gunner in the 2nd Company of the Antibes Arrondissement 13 October 1799, sub-lieutenant in the 10th Cavalry 7 August 1800, discharged 2 August 1801, sub-lieutenant in the 22nd Cavalry 22 December 1801, dismissed with the corps 31 December 1802 and incorporated into the 15th Cavalry 25 January 1803, lieutenant in the

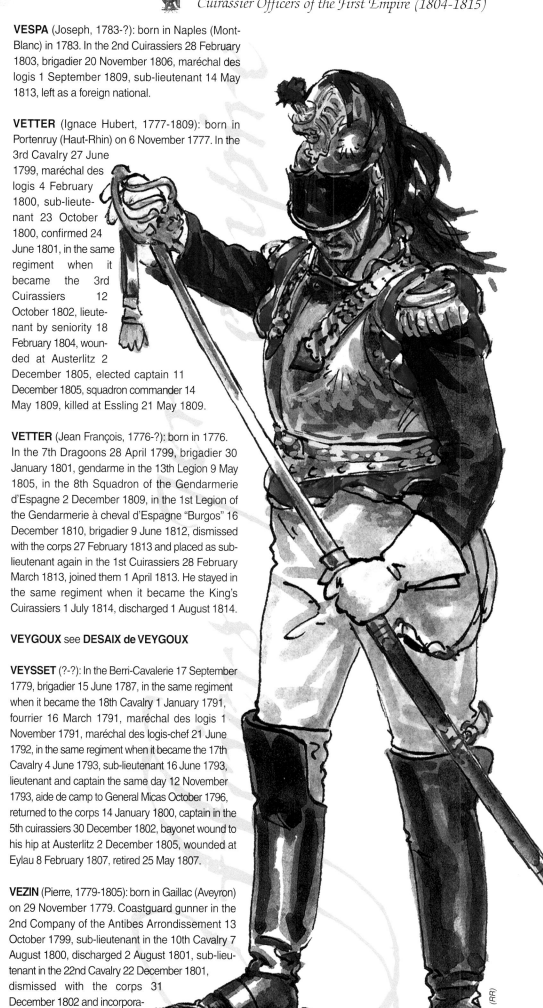

(RR)

G. Rava 07

12th Cuirassiers 5th October 1803, wounded at Austerlitz 2 December and died of his wounds at Brünn 12 December 1805.

VIAL (Jacques Laurent Louis Augustin, baron, 1774-1855): brother of General Honoré Vial, born in Antibes (Var) on 9 August 1774. Sub-lieutenant in the 26th Infantry 27 October 1792, shot and wounded four times and taken prisoner near Saint-Florent in Corsica 17 February 1794, taken to Gibraltar then freed, returned 25 December 1795, deputy to Adjutant-General Vial his brother end of March 1796, adjutant of the Paris military district 20 July 1797, acting lieutenant in the suite of the 11th Cavalry 9 August 1797, deputy on the staff of the Army or the Orient 27 April 1798, shot and wounded in the right arm at Alexandria 2 July 1798, acting captain 12 August 1798, acting aide de camp to General Lagrange 1 August 1798, confirmed in his post 15 October 1798.

He was squadron commander 6 March 1801, in the 17th Cavalry 14 December 1803, colonel of the 26th Chasseurs à cheval 4 April 1807, brigadier-general commanding the 2nd Brigade of the 9th Light Cavalry Division in the 5th Cavalry Corps under Pajol 22 July 1813, commanded the 2nd Light Cavalry Brigade (5th, 10th, 15th and 22nd Chasseurs à Cheval) of the 1st Cavalry Division (Soult) of the Army of the Pyrenees 27 December 1813.

He was non-active 1 September 1814, commanded the 2nd Brigade (6th and 9th Cuirassiers) of the 14th Division of the Cavalry Reserve in the 4th Corps in the Army of the North 31 March 1815, non-active 22 October 1815. Baron of the Empire d. 21 December 1808 and l.p. 28 June 1809.

VIALLET (?-1809): maréchal des logis in the 12th Cuirassiers, sub-lieutenant in the suite 2 March 1809, wounded at Essling 22 May 1809, took up his post 23 May 1809, died of his wounds 3 June 1809.

VIARD (Pierre François, 1785-?): born in Saint-Mihiel (Meuse) on 15 June 1795.

In the Gendarmes d'Ordonnance 12 October 1806, dismissed with the corps 23 October 1807 and incorporated into the Grenadiers à Cheval of the Guard 24 November 1807, sub-lieutenant in the Line 4 April 1808, in the 2nd Cuirassiers 23 April 1808, in the 13th cuirassiers 21 October 1808, shot and wounded in the left knee at Tudela 23 November 1808 and shot and wounded in the chest at Sagonte 25 October 1811, lieutenant in the 4th cuirassiers 21 April 1813

He was captain 14 July 1813, nine sabre and lance wounds ay Neuss 3 December 1813, in the suite of the same regiment when it became the Angoulême Cuirassiers 6 August 1814, in service 4 January 1815, in the same regiment when it became the 4th Cuirassiers again, shot and wounded in the stomach at Waterloo 18 June 1815, dismissed 21 December 1815. LH CH 16 March 1812.

Seal belonging to the 12th Cuirassier Regiment.
(Author's collection)

VICAT (Joseph, 1790-?): born in Nevers (Nièvre) on 23 July 1790. Pupil in the Ecole Spéciale Militaire in Fontainebleau 12 September 1807, corporal 26 July 1808, sergeant 27 July 1808, sub-lieutenant in the 4th Cuirassiers 24 July 1809, lieutenant 22 December 1813, in the suite of the same regiment when it became the Angoulême Cuirassiers 6 August 1814; in service 4 January 18151.

He obtained 2 months' leave 12 May 1815, wounded at Waterloo 18 June 1815 without going on leave, dismissed with the corps 21 December 1815. LH CH 27 December 1814, confirmed 11 April 1815.

VICHARD (Jean Baptiste, 1773-1813): born in Aisey (Haute-Saône) on 11 March 1773. Waggoner in the military transport 13 March 1793, adjutant-NCO 1 July 1794, simple chasseur in the 12th Chasseurs à Cheval 24 November 1798, brigadier 4 October 1803, in the Grenadiers à Cheval of the Imperial Guard 30 June 1803, sabre wound to his right hand and shot in the right thigh at Eylau 8 February 1807, sub-lieutenant in the 13th Cuirassiers 23 April 1808, wounded at Maria 15 June 1809 and Lerida 23 April 1810.

He was lieutenant 18 September 1811, insta-ted 21 October 1811, died in Barcelona Hospital 11 November 1813. LH CH 1 May 1808.

VIDAL de VALLABRE-GUE (David Elzéar, cheva-lier, 1776-?): born in Paris (Seine) on 8 August 1776. In the 14th chasseurs à Cheval 30 March 1794, maréchal des logis-chef 24 October 1795, sub-lieutenant 21 December 1797, deputy on the staff 19 June 1799, lieute-nant 20 June 1800, captain reporter on the military commission in Turin and attached to the 3rd Light 20 November 1800, shot and wounded in the left thigh at Adige and shot in the arm in Italy, captain commanding Rimini 27 July 1801, aide de camp to General Debelle 20 April 1802 then to Generals Lacroix 1803, Quentin 1804 and Boussard 1805, captain adjutant-major in the Isembourg Regiment 1806.

He was elected deputy on the general staff of the Grande Armée 1 October 1806; aide de camp to Prince Isembourg 10 February 1807,

deputy on the general staff of the Army of Portugal 2 October 1807, sabre wound to his right hand, aide de camp to General Thiébaut 15 January 1809, battalion commander 26 November 1810, retired 14 May 1811, return-ned as squadron commander in the 2nd Cuirassiers 8 May 1815, returned home and put back on the non-active list 20 October 1815.

LH CH 15 July 1809, O 17 January 1815, Chevalier of the Empire l.p. 12 November 1809.

VIDAME (Jean Baptiste, 1770-?): born in Houdelaincourt (Meuse) on 2 January 1770. In the Colonel-Général-Cavalerie 13 October 1789 which became the 1st Cavalry 1 January 1791, brigadier 12 February 1796, fourrier 31 May 1796, maréchal des logis 14 May 1799, maréchal des logis-chef 10 August 1799, in the same regiment when it became the 1st Cuirassiers 10 October 1801, elec-ted sub-lieutenant 28 September 1806, wounded at Eylau 8 February 1807, in the 13th Cuirassiers 21 October 1808, lieutenant 13 February 1809, reti-red 5 September 1810. LH CH 14 March 1806.

VIEL (Antoine, 1771-1855): born in Létanville (Calvados) on 28 October 1771. Volunteer in the Bayeux Cavalry 6 November 1793, shot and woun-ded in the left thigh while escorting a stagecoach near Vitry 7 January 1794, left 28 July 1794, in the 19th Cavalry 6 September 1794, fourrier 4 September 1797, maréchal des logis-chef 12 May 1799, adjutant-NCO 19 June 1799, shot and woun-ded in the back while taking several prisoners near Acho 28 June 1800, dismissed with the corps 31 December 1802 and incorporated into the 9th Cavalry 25 January 1803 which became the 9th Cuirassiers 24 September 1803, elected sub-lieu-tenant 21 January 1805, confirmed 5 February 1805.

He was lieutenant 30 October 1806, adjutant-major 25 June 1807, rank of captain 25 December 1808, captain commanding a company 14 May 1809, shell burst wound to his left foot at Wagram 6 July 1809, three sabre wounds of which one to his cheek and acting CO of the regiment after the colonel and the two squadron commanders were wounded at Leipzig 16 October 1813, squadron commander 19 February 1814, in the 10th cui-rassiers 6 August 1814, dismissed and retired to his property 25 December 1815. Holder of a Sabre of Honour 16 September 1802, commis-sioned 30 May 1803. LH CH by rights 24 September 1803, O 5 September 1813.

VIEUX (?-1809): pupil, sub-lieutenant in the suite of the 12th Cuirassiers 16 May 1807, took up his post 29 January 1808 and assigned to the 2nd Provisional Heavy Cavalry in Spain, prisoner by capitulation at Baylen 22 July 1808 and held on the prison hulks off Cadiz, escaped by swimming 28 November 1809, murdered on the Moroccan coast the following day 29 November 1809.

VIGUES see **PUISSANT** aka **VIGUES**.

VILLATE (Etienne, 1765-?): born in Terrasson (Dordogne) on 22 November 1795. In the Dauphin-Cavalerie 25 April 1785 which became the 12th Cavalry 1 January 1791, fourrier 1 April 1793, maréchal des logis 18 May 1793, maréchal des logis-chef 17 September 1797, adjutant 10 May 1799.

He was elected sub-lieutenant 26 December 1802, in the same regiment when it became the 12th Cuirassiers 24 September 1803, lieutenant by seniority 12 August 1806, captain 29 January 1808 and retired 25 July 1810.

VILLAUNAY d'AVENAY
see **RIOULT de VILLAUNAY d'AVENAY**

VILLEMAIN (Louis, 1775-?): born in Harloy (Meurthe) on 25 September 1775. In the 9th Meurthe Battalion 1 May 1793, sergeant in the 58th Infantry which became the 55th Half-Brigade of the Line 1 December 1793, gendarme in the 21st Haute-Marne Company 20 February 1803, brigadier 21 April 1805. Named brigadier en chef in the 11th Squadron of the Gendarmerie d'Espagne 20 February 1810.

He was maréchal des logis in the 2nd Legion of the Gendarmerie à cheval d'Espagne 1 January 1811, maréchal des logis-chef 1 September 1811, freed a wounded officer of the 25th Chasseurs à Cheval from 8 English Dragoons by killing two of them himself and recapturing the officer's mount with a second charge 23 October 1812, lieutenant in the 2nd Cuirassiers 28 February 1813.

He was incorporated into the 1st Provisional Heavy Cavalry with his squadron in Hamburg 11 September 1813, returned with the garrison 27 May 1813, dismissed with the corps and put on the non-active list with half-pay 10 December 1815. LH CH 10 February 1813.

VILLEMAIN (Sébastien, 1761-?): born in Epinal (Vosges) on 20 January 1761. In the Artois-Dragons 6 August 1777, dismissed 1 August 1786, in the Volontaires Nationaux à Cheval from the Ecole Militaire 3 September 1792.

He was lieutenant in the same regiment when it formed the 26th Cavalry 7 February 1793 which then became the 25th Cavalry December 1793, commissioned 22 June 1793, captain 4 November 1794, discharged and remained in the suite 87 January 1796, took up his appointment 13 July 1797.

He commanded the Elite Company 22 March 1802, dismissed with the regiment 12 October 1802 and incorporated into the 2nd Cuirassiers 24 November 1802, wounded at Essling 22 May 1809 and Wagram 6 July 1809, left to retire 5 October 1809.

VILLEMINOT (Jean Baptiste, 1771-?): born in Tornay (Haute-Marne) on 8 December 1771. In the Volontaires Nationaux à Cheval from the Ecole Militaire 24 August 1792 which formed the 26th Cavalry 7 February 1793 which then became the

25th Cavalry 4 June 1793, brigadier 3 October 1799, fourrier 22 November 1800, maréchal des logis 22 July 1802.

He dismissed with the corps 13 October 1802 and incorporated into the 2nd Cuirassiers 24 November 1802, maréchal des logis-chef 30 October 1806, sub-lieutenant 14 May 1809, detached with his squadron to the 1st Provisional Heavy Cavalry in Hamburg 11 September 1813, returned with the garrison 27 May 1814, retired 10 December 1815. LH CH 1 October 1807.

VILLEMONTES
see **GRAMONT de VILLEMONTES**

VILLIET (François Louis Eloy, 1778-?): born in Chenoy-Rivière (Ardennes) on 1 December 1778. In the 7th Cavalry 26 November 1798 which became the 7th Cuirassiers 23 December 1802, brigadier 12 February 1806, maréchal des logis 15 October 1806, maréchal des logis-chef 26 January 1813, sub-lieutenant 6 March 1813, non-active and returned home 26 August 1814.

VILLIEZ (Jean Baptiste, 1778-?): born in Nancy (Meurthe) on 2 November 1778. In the 8th Hussars 6 February 1794, brigadier 19 June 1795, sub-lieutenant 9 November 1798, in the 12th Cavalry 23 October 1800, in service 25 May 1801, lieutenant 30 December 1801, adjutant-major 27 February 1806, rank of captain 27 August 1807, captain commanding a company 1 December 1807, squadron commander in the suite 25 November 1811, in the 9th Cuirassiers 16 February 1812, took up his post 3 March 1812, wounded in the thigh at Leipzig 16 October 1813, amputated and prisoner in the hospital of the town.

VILQUIN (?-1812): maréchal des logis in the 6th Cuirassiers, sub-lieutenant 3 June 1809, lieutenant 8 October 1811. Killed at Winkovo 18 October 1812.

VIMEUX see **VAST VIMEUX**.

VINCQ (Alexandre, 1786-?): born in Valet-au-Tertre (Nord) on 11 May 1786. In the 25 Dragoons 23 February 1806, brigadier 1 December 1811, in the 1st Legion of the Gendarmerie à cheval d'Espagne 3 December 1811, two sabre wounds to his head, one shot in his right leg, one lance wound to his side at Rodrigo, two sabre wounds to his right arm at Villarodrigo 23 October 1812, dismissed with the corps 27 February 1813, maréchal des logis in the 3rd Cuirassiers 16 March 1813, maréchal des logis-chef 14 May 1813.

He was elected sub-lieutenant 22 December 1813, shot twice through his body and hip on Rosnay Bridge 2 February 1814, shot and wounded at Waterloo 18 June 1815, retired to his property to convalesce and then dismissed with the regiment 25 November 1815.

VINDROIS (?-1809): adjutant-NCO in the 12th Cuirassiers, sub-lieutenant 14 May 1809, killed at Essling 22 May 1809.

VINET see **BONNET** aka **VINET**

VINOT (Jean, 1755-?): born in Chaumont (Haute-Marne) on 6 October 1755. In the Commissaire-Général-Cavalerie 9 May 1774, brigadier in the Chevau-Légers N°1 27 March 1784 which became the Orléanais-Cavalerie 15 July 1784, maréchal des logis 1 September 1784, in the same regiment when it became the Royal-Guyenne-Cavalerie 17 March 1788, then the 23rd Cavalry 1 January 1791, maréchal des logis-chef 20 March 1792, sub-lieutenant 19 March 1793, lieutenant 1 April 1793, in the same regiment when it became the 22nd Cavalry 4 June 1793, captain 18 August 1795, dismissed with the corps 31 December 1802 and incorporated in the 9th Cavalry 15 February 1803 which became the 9th Cuirassiers 24 September 1803, on retirement pay 2 July 1806.

VION (Louis François, 1779-1812): born in 1779. In the 2nd Cavalry 9 September 1798 which became the 2nd Cuirassiers 12 October 1802, brigadier 23 September 1804, fourrier 30 October 1806, maréchal des logis 20 November 1806, maréchal des logis-chef, adjutant-NCO 1 September 1809, sub-lieutenant 21 March 1812, wounded at the Moskova 7 September 1812, died in Moscow Hospital 21 October 1812.

VIRIAC aka **VITRY** (Nicolas, 1767-?): born in Vitry-le-François (Marne) on 19 May 1767. In the Septimanie-Cavalerie 2 July 1784, discharged with the corps 17 March 1788 and went over to the Chamborant Hussars, in the Royal-Etranger-Cavalerie 29 May 1789 which became the 7th Cavalry 1 January 1791, brigadier 7 May 1793, maréchal des logis 27 April 1794, maréchal des logis-chef 2 April 1802, in the same regiment when it became the 7th Cuirassiers 23 December 1802, sub-lieutenant 26 April 1807, wounded at Essling 21 May 1809, retired 9 September 1811 and left the war squadrons 8 October 1811.

VITRY see **VIRIAC** aka **VITRY**

VOILLEMIER (Joseph, 1765-?): born in Poisson (Haute-Marne) on 1 September 1765. In the Royal-Roussillon-Cavalerie 15 May 1782, brigadier 1 February 1787, in the same regiment when it became the 11th Cavalry 1 January 1791, maréchal des logis 19 October 1792, maréchal des logis-chef 3 December 1793, sub-lieutenant 9 June 1800, in the same regiment when it became the 11th Cuirassiers 24 September 1803, lieutenant by seniority 6 September 1805, wounded by a Biscayan shot to his left thigh and a bayonet wound in his stomach at Austerlitz 2 December 1805, captain 27 March 1809, retired 6 November 1811. LH CH 1 October 1807.

VOLUSPERT (Pierre, 1775-1813): born in Broussey (Meuse) on 28 March 1775. In the 7th Cavalry 26 August 1792, brigadier 22 March 1802, in the same regiment when it became the 7th Cuirassiers 23 December 1802, maréchal des logis 16 June 1804, maréchal des logis-chef 4 May 1805, sub-lieutenant 9 August 1809, died in Glogau Hospital 18 January 1813. LH CH 19 November 1812.

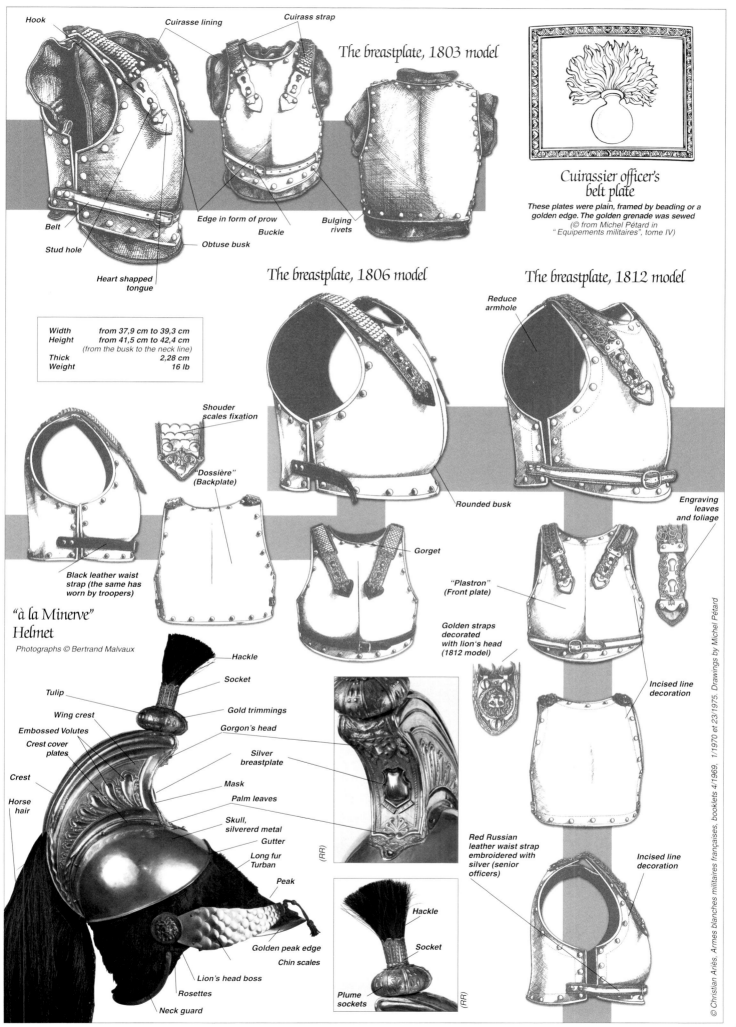

Hook
Cuirasse lining
Cuirass strap
Belt
Stud hole
Heart shaped tongue
Edge in form of prow
Buckle
Obtuse busk
Bulging rivets

The breastplate, 1803 model

Cuirassier officer's belt plate

These plates were plain, framed by beading or a golden edge. The golden grenade was sewed
(© from Michel Pétard in "Equipements militaires", tome IV)

Width	from 37,9 cm to 39,3 cm
Height	from 41,5 cm to 42,4 cm
	(from the busk to the neck line)
Thick	2,28 cm
Weight	16 lb

The breastplate, 1806 model

The breastplate, 1812 model

Reduce armhole

Shouder scales fixation

"Dossière" (Backplate)

Black leather waist strap (the same has worn by troopers)

Rounded busk

Gorget

Engraving leaves and foliage

"Plastron" (Front plate)

Golden straps decorated with lion's head (1812 model)

Incised line decoration

"à la Minerve" Helmet

Photographs © Bertrand Malvaux

Tulip
Wing crest
Embossed Volutes
Crest cover plates
Crest
Horse hair

Hackle
Socket
Gold trimmings
Gorgon's head
Silver breastplate
Mask
Palm leaves
Skull, silvererd metal
Gutter
Long fur Turban
Peak
Golden peak edge
Chin scales
Lion's head boss
Rosettes
Neck guard

(RR)

Hackle
Socket
Plume sockets

(RR)

Red Russian leather waist strap embroidered with silver (senior officers)

Incised line decoration

© Christian Ariès, Armes blanches militaires françaises, booklets 4/1969, 1/1970 et 23/1975. Drawings by Michel Pétard

1805, general 24 December 1805, commanded the depots of the five dragoon regiments in Versailles and Saint-Germain 17 June 1806, commanded the 2nd Light Cavalry Brigade (2nd and 4th Hussars, 5th Chasseurs à Cheval) Tilly's division in the 1st Corps of the Grande Armée 11 July 1806 then the recently created 3rd Light Cavalry Brigade (11th Chasseurs à Cheval and Bavarian Chevau-Légers) in the Cavalry Reserve of the Grande Armée 1 December 1806, commanded the 2nd Brigaded of the Lasalle's division 30 December 1806 then a light cavalry brigade under Davout 12 July 1807 and a hussar brigade under Grouchy in the Côtes-de l'Océan Observation Corps 14 November 1807, under Moncey during the Valencia expedition June 1808, commanded a light cavalry brigade in the 3rd Corps of the Army of Spain 7 September 1808, commanded the cavalry if the same corps at Saragossa December 1808, called to the Army

WALDNER de FREUNDSTEIN (Edouard de, 1789-?): born in Mulhausen (Haut-Rhin) on 29 May 1789. Sub-lieutenant in the 11th Chasseurs à Cheval 23 March 1805, six sabre wounds to his head, right wrist and left hand at Heilsberg 10 June 1807, ordnance to general Montbrun 217 May 1809, aide de camp to General Rapp 15 October 1809, captain 15 April 1812, in the 10th Cuirassiers 29 September 18121, shot and wounded in his right arm at Waterloo 18 June 1815, dismissed with the corps 25 December 1815. LH CH 25 July 1809.

WATHIEZ (François Isidore, baron, 1777-1856): born in Versailles (Seine-et-Oise) on 1 September 1777. Acting sub-lieutenant in the 25th Chasseurs à Cheval 3 November 1793, shot and wounded above the left knee near Cairo 21 September 1794, resigned 2 March 1796, at the Remount Depot in Versailles 4 May 1799, deputy captain on the staff of the Reserve Army 28 March 1800, discharged 24 September 1800, deputy on the staff of the 1st Military Division 13 March 1801 then on that of the Cavalry Reserve of the Grande Armée 20 September 1805, squadron commander first aide de camp to General Lasalle 7 January 1807, lance wound to his neck at Heilsberg 10 June 1807 and a bayonet wound at Medina-del-Rio-Seco 14 July 1808, adjutant-commandant 28 August 1808.

He was chief of staff of the Lasalle Division in the Pyrénées-Occidentales Army Corps September 1808, shot and wounded between the eyes at Burgos 10 November 1808, in the 9th Corps in the Army of Germany 19 June 1809, chief of staff of the Light Cavalry Division (Marulaz) 31 July 1809, chief of staff of the 3rd Cuirassiers Division in the Army of

Germany 13 October 1811, chief of staff of the 2nd Cavalry Corps 18 January 1812, brigadier-general in the 2nd Cavalry Division of the 2nd Cavalry Corps 4 June 1813. He commanded the 2nd Brigade of the 4th Light Cavalry Division assembled at Versailles 6 January 1814, commanded the 1st Brigade (6th, 7th and 8th Hussars and 1st, 3rd, 5th and 8th Lancers) Roussel d'Hurbal Cavalry Division 26 February 1814, suspended for disobedience 4 March 1814. He was non-active 1 September 1814, in the 2nd Corps of the Army of the North 31 March 1815, commanded the 2nd Brigade (Lancers) of the 2nd Cavalry Division of the 2nd Corps in the Army of Belgium June 1815, wounded at Waterloo 18 June 1815, non-active 30 October 1815. LH, Chevalier of the Empire l.p. 6 October 1810, Baron d. November 1813.

WATIER SAINT ALPHONSE (Pierre, comte, 1770-1846): born in Laon (Aisne) on 4 September 1770. Sub-lieutenant in the cavalry of the Legion of the Centre 3 September 1792, sub-lieutenant in the Escadron Franc constituted at Arras and serving in the suite of the 12th Chasseurs à Cheval 31 October 1792, incorporated into the 12th Chasseurs à Cheval 2 April 1793, lieutenant in the 16th Chasseurs à Cheval 26 May 1793, captain 14 August 1793, squadron commander 18 November 1793, brigade commander of the 4th Dragoons 4 October 1799, Ecuyer Cavalcadour to Napoleon keeping his command 2 August 1804, taken prisoner at Dürrenstein while trying to escape by boat with General Graindorge 11 November 1805, exchanged 13 November

Seal belonging to the 4th Cuirassiers Regiment. (Author's collection)

of Germany 16 June 1809, commanded the 2nd Brigade of the 2nd Cuirassiers Division 26 August 1809, commanded the cavalry of the Caffarelli Reserve Division in Spain 4 October 1810, in the Army of the North in Spain March 1811, commanded a cavalry brigade in the Army of Portugal 1 June 1811. He was major-general 31 July 1811, in the Army of the North in Spain September 1811, commanded the 2nd Light Cavalry Division at Mainz 9 January 1812, in the 2nd Reserve Cavalry Corps 15 February 1812, commanded the 2nd Cuirassiers Division of the same corps May 1812, same division same corps in the Army of Germany 15 February 1813, commanded the Cavalry Division of the 13th Corps under Davout in Hamburg 3 September 1813, two months' leave, returned to France after Hamburg capitulated 9 May 1814, non-active June 1814, commanded the 3rd Cavalry division of the 2nd Corps 31 March 1815 which became the 13th Cavalry Division of the 4th Cavalry Corps of the Army of Belgium 3 June 1815, non-active 1 August 1815. LH CH 11 December 1803, O 14 June, C 14 May 1809, Count of Saint-Alphonse d. 26 October 1808, l.p. 12 November 1809.

WENDLING (Michaël, 1770-1822): born in Wahlenheim (Bas-Rhin) on 7 April 1770. Trumpeter-pupil in the school at Strasbourg 3 March 1785, trumpeter in the Royal-Etranger-Cavalerie 20 June 1787 which became the 7th Cavalry 1 January 1791, sabre wound to his right knee at Cambrai 26 April 1794 and shot and wounded in the right leg near Lille 10 May 1794, brigadier-trompette 10 April 1795, in the same regiment when it became the 7th Cuirassiers 23 December 1802, maréchal des logis 11 March 1807, sabre wound to his head 1810, sub-lieutenant in the 14th Cuirassiers 17 June 1812, lieutenant 22 December 1813, dismissed with the corps and replaced in the 12th Cuirassiers 14 July 1814, lieutenant 1 June 1815, adjutant-major 14 June 1815, sabre wound to his head at Waterloo 18 June 1815, captain 28 July 1815, re-placed as lieutenant 3 August 1815, dismissed November 1815, retired 7 April 1816. LH CH 1 October 1807.

WILHELM (Georges, 1775-?): born in Blentsveiller (Bas-Rhin) on 7 September 1775. In the 12th Chasseurs à Cheval 11 October 1797, sabre wound to his head near Pfuffendorf March 1799, in the 7th Cavalry 11 June 1800 which became the 7th Cuirassiers 23 December 1802, brigadier-fourrier 13 June 1805, maréchal des logis 21 January 1807, maréchal des logis-chef 25 January 1807, sabre wound to his right hand at Essling 21 May 1809, adjutant-NCO 18 August 1809, sub-lieutenant 8 October 1811, shot and wounded in the left buttock at Polotsk 18 August 1812, aide de camp to general Dubois 16 June 1813. LH CH 1 October 1807.

G.Rava cP

YUNG (Léopold, 1778-?): born in Forbach (Moselle) on 12 January 1778. In the 1st Chasseurs à Cheval 28 September 1796, in the Grenadiers à Cheval of the Guard 13 October

1801, brigadier 27 April 1803, maréchal des logis 22 December 1805, second-lieutenant 25 June 1809, captain in the 6th Cuirassiers 9 February 1813, incorporated with his squadron into the 2nd Provisional Heavy Cavalry in Hamburg 11 September 1813. He returned with the garrison 30 May 1814, wounded and his horse killed under him at Waterloo 18 June 1815, dismissed 21 November 1815. LH CH 24 March 1806.

YVE de BAVAY see **DYVE de BAVAY**

YVENDORFF (Johann Friedrich, baron, 1751-1816): born in Hamburg (Bouches-de-l'Elbe) on 19 October 1751. Carabinier à Cheval in the Saint Domingo Militia 10 January 1770, sub-lieutenant in the Southern Battalion of the Colonial Militia 15 March 1778.

He was elected lieutenant in the infantry 1 February 1780, left 4 November 1790, boarded for France, in the Volontaires Nationaux à Cheval from the Ecole Militaire 7 September 1792, captain 213 October 1792, confirmed when the 25th cavalry was formed 7 February 1793, in the same regiment when it became the 24th Cavalry 4 June 1793, squadron commander 21 March 1794.

He was brigade commander in the 2nd Cavalry 3 September 1799, joined them 25 October 1799, shot and wounded in the fort at Plaisance 9 June 1800, in the same regiment when it became the 2nd Cuirassiers 12 October 1802, brigadier-general employed as commandant d'armes 1st Class 24 December 1805, confirmed 23 January 18706, allowed to return to France 19 April 1806, in the general cavalry depot in Potsdam, took up his appointment 16 December 1806.

He commanded at Spandau 26 December 1806, in Mainz 14 October 1808, in the 8th Military Division 14 November 1808, commanded the Vaucluse Department 21 November 1808, retired 6 August 1811, commandant d'armes in his native city Hamburg 19 December 1811.

He was retired 25 April 1813, with the inspection of cavalry 14 June 1815, deputy to the Imp sector of Cavalry Frégeville 6 August 1815, put back in retirement October 1815. LH CH

Seal belonging to the 12t h Cuirassiers Regiment.
(Author 's collection)

P.Hénique

11 December 1803, O 14 June 1804, Baron of the Empire l.p. 29 June 1808.

ZEPPENFELD (Eugène Hugues François, 1786-?): born in Castelnovo (Piedmont) on 7 December 1784. Volunteer in the 1st Piedmont Hussars 7 November 1800, in the same regiment when it became the 26th Chasseurs à Cheval 26 October 1801, brigadier 23 February 1806, maréchal des logis 4 April 1807, two sabre wounds to his right hand at Landsberg and two lance wounds to his lower abdomen and shot in the back at Koenigsberg 13 June 1807, adjutant-NCO 1 January 1813, three lance wounds and taken prisoner at Leipzig October 1813, sub-lieutenant 29 January 1814, returned and incorporated in the suite of the Angoulême Cuirassiers 9 August 1814, in service 5 January 1815, in the same regiment when it became the 4th Cuirassiers again April 1815, shot and wounded in the right leg at Waterloo 18 June 1815, retired 21 December 1815.

ZOEPFFEL (François Antoine, 1753-?): born in Dambach (Bas-Rhin) on 13 April 1753. In the Roi-Cavalerie 10 August 1774, brigadier 30 November 1789, in the same regiment when it became the 6th Cuirassiers 1 January 1791, maréchal des logis 1 January 1793, maréchal des logis-chef 1 April 1793, sub-lieutenant 15 October 1793, prisoner at Cambrai 21 January 1794, returned 1 February 1796, lieutenant 12 March 1802, in the same regiment when it became the 6th Cuirassiers 23 December 1802, allowed to retire 7 December 1805.

ZOUTLANDT see **TRIP van ZOUTLANDT**

FROM THE "CAVALERIE DU ROY" TO THE CUIRASSIERS

January 1791: the *"cy-devant"* regiments of the royal cavalry* took their place in the new French cavalry.
- **Colonel-General** became the 1st Cavalry Regiment then the 1st Cuirassiers.
- **Royal Cavalerie** became the 2nd Cavalry Regiment then the 2nd Cuirassiers.

- **Commissaire-Général** became the 3rd Cavalry regiment then the 3rd Cuirassiers.
- **The Reine cavalry** became the 4th Cavalry Regiment then the 4th Cuirassiers.
- **Royal Pologne** became the 5th Cavalry Regiment then the 5th Cuirassiers.
- **the Régiment du Roi** became the 6th

Cavalry Regiment then the 6th Cuirassiers.
- **Royal Etranger** became the 7th Cavalry Regiment then the 7th Cuirassiers.
- **the Cuirassiers du Roi** became the 8th Cavalry Regiment then the 8th Cuirassiers.
- **the Artois Cavalerie** became the 9th Cavalry Regiment then the 9th

- **the Royal Cravates** became the 10th Cavalry Regiment then the 10th Cuirassiers.
- **the Montclar Catalan** became the 11th Cavalry Regiment then the 11th Cuirassiers.
- **the Dauphin Cavalerie** became the 12th Cavalry Regiment then the 12th Cuirassiers.
(* Only those that became cuirassier regiments are mentioned here.)

Acknowledgements

The author and the Publisher are keen to thank François-Guy Hourtoulle, Michel Pétard, Patrice Courcelle for their kindly contribution, Jean-Louis Viau, Laurent Mirouze, Stephan Ciejka and all photographers who took part in this book.

Bibliography

"Les cuirassiers des consuls" by Rigo in *Uniformes* n° 44.
"Les cuirassiers". Cards from Cdt. Bucquoy. J. Grancher éditeur.

"Les cuirassiers, 1801-15". Rigo, M. Pétard, A. Pigeard, B. Malvaux. Special issue in *Tradition magazine* n° 62.
"Les uniformes de l'Armée française". Lucien Rousselot. Colour plates n° 37, 46, 91 and 102.

Colour plates by Giuseppe RAVA - www.militaryart.it
Computer drawings by André JOUINEAU and Jean-Marie MONGIN
Design and lay out by Magali MASSELIN, Denis GANDILHON.
© Histoire & Collections 2008

A book published by
HISTOIRE & COLLECTIONS
"SA au capital de 182 938, 82 €"
5, avenue de la République F-75541 Paris Cedex 11
Fax 01 47 00 51 11
www.histoireetcollections.fr

This book has been designed, typed, laid-out and processed by *Histoire & Collections* fully on integrated computer equipment.
Pictures integrated by *Studio A&C*
Printed by *Elkar*,
Spain, European Union
May 2008